Founders of Modern Political and Social Thought

FOUNDERS OF
MODERN POLITICAL AND
SOCIAL THOUGHT

SERIES EDITOR
Mark Philp
Oriel College, University of Oxford

Founders of Modern Political and Social Thought present critical examinations of the work of major political philosophers and social theorists, assessing both their initial contribution and continuing relevance to politics and society. Each volume provides a clear, accessible, historically-informed account of each thinker's work, focusing on a reassessment of their central ideas and arguments. *Founders* encourage scholars and students to link their study of classic texts to current debates in political philosophy and social theory.

Also available:

JOHN FINNIS: *Aquinas*
GIANFRANCO POGGI: *Durkheim*
MAURIZIO VIROLI: *Machiavelli*
CHERYL WELCH: *De Tocqueville*

ARISTOTLE
Political Philosophy

Richard Kraut

UNIVERSITY PRESS

OXFORD
UNIVERSITY PRESS

Great Clarendon Street, Oxford OX2 6DP
Oxford University Press is a department of the University of Oxford.
It furthers the University's objective of excellence in research, scholarship,
and education by publishing worldwide in
Oxford New York
Auckland Bangkok Buenos Aires Cape Town Chennai
Dar es Salaam Delhi Hong Kong Istanbul Karachi Kolkata
Kuala Lumpur Madrid Melbourne Mexico City Mumbai Nairobi
São Paulo Shanghai Singapore Taipei Tokyo Toronto
and an associated company in Berlin

Oxford is a registered trade mark of Oxford University Press
in the UK and in certain other countries

Published in the United States
by Oxford University Press Inc., New York

© Richard Kraut 2002

The moral rights of the author have been asserted
Database right Oxford University Press (maker)

First published 2002

All rights reserved. No part of this publication may be reproduced,
stored in a retrieval system, or transmitted, in any form or by any means,
without the prior permission in writing of Oxford University Press,
or as expressly permitted by law, or under terms agreed with the appropriate
reprographics rights organizations. Enquiries concerning reproduction
outside the scope of the above should be sent to the Rights Department,
Oxford University Press, at the address above

You must not circulate this book in any other binding or cover
and you must impose this same condition on any acquirer

British Library Cataloguing in Publication Data
Data available

Library of Congress Cataloging in Publication Data
Data available

ISBN 0-19-878200-4

Typeset in Trump Mediaeval
by RefineCatch Limited, Bungay, Suffolk
Printed in Great Britain
on acid-free paper by
T.J. International Ltd., Padstow, Cornwall

for S., A., N., J.

Now it appears to me that almost any Man may like the Spider spin from his own inwards his own airy Citadel—the points of leaves and twigs on which the Spider begins her work are few, and she fills the Air with a beautiful circuiting: man should be content with as few points to tip with the fine Web of his Soul, and weave a tapestry empyrean full of Symbols for his spiritual eye, of softness for his spiritual touch, of space for his wandering, of distinctness for his Luxury. But the Minds of Mortals are so different and bent on such diverse Journeys that it may at first appear impossible for any common taste and fellowship to exist between two or three under these suppositions. It is however quite the contrary. Minds would leave each other in contrary directions, traverse each other in Numberless points, and at last greet each other at the Journey's end. An old Man and a child would talk together and the old Man be led on his Path and the child left thinking. Man should not dispute or assert but whisper results to his neighbour and thus by every germ of Spirit sucking the Sap from mould ethereal every human might become great, and Humanity instead of being a wide heath of Furs and Briars with here and there a remote Oak or Pine, would become a grand democracy of Forest Trees.

> Letter from John Keats to John Hamilton Reynolds,
> 19 February 1818

Preface

Anyone who undertakes an investigation of Aristotle's political philosophy must admit from the start that he accepted and even defended doctrines that no longer have credibility—if they ever had any. In the *Politics*, he argues that some human beings are naturally inferior to others and therefore deserve to be enslaved; he thinks the proper place of women is in the home and assigns them no role in public life; he holds that manual labor is degrading and bars farmers and workers from citizenship in his ideal city; he claims that democracy—one of the greatest achievements of the ancient Greek world—is inherently corrupt; his ideal community, composed of a few thousand men who share a single moral perspective and have enough wealth to live at leisure and hold political office without pay, is no longer achievable and, to many, not particularly attractive.

Furthermore, his political thought depends crucially on his ethical theory, which is in turn embedded in a metaphysical framework some take to be incompatible with modern science, because it assumes that every living thing has an eternal essence that is the principal cause and natural goal of its development. Admittedly, many of Aristotle's contemporary readers believe that his ethical theory contains insights that can be detached from his framework of essences. His discussion in the *Nicomachean Ethics* of such topics as moral character, practical reason, pleasure, and the interpenetration of thought and emotion are still widely admired and carefully studied. But many who esteem these components of his moral philosophy have little interest in him as a political thinker, because they assume that his hostility to democracy, freedom, and equality make him useless to an age in which these have become core values.

I believe, on the contrary, that there are riches in Aristotle's political thought that are unrecognized or undervalued, and that his perspective deserves to be included in contemporary debates about social issues. Although there is much about which he was dead wrong, most elements of his political philosophy—his ideas about a good society, justice, citizenship, equality, democracy, community, property, family, class conflict, and the corrosive effect of poverty and wealth—are still worth taking seriously, and can contribute to intelligent reflection about our own problems. I will not try to show that our only reasonable option in politics is to become

Aristotelians; my more modest ambition is to present him in a way that shows how he speaks to the politics of our own time. Even if we decide in the end to reject his theory, we will understand ourselves better if we examine ourselves through his eyes.

Although the text that I will most fully examine is the *Politics*, I begin with the theory of human well-being and excellent activity that Aristotle puts forward in the *Nicomachean Ethics*, for I believe that his most fundamental contribution to political philosophy lies in his conception of what it is for a human being to do well, and for a human life to go well. He believes that the political community must aim, above all, at the good of its members—more specifically, at the realization of their powers as thinking, feeling, and social beings. If we do not take that conception of the human good seriously, we will have little to learn from him as a political thinker.

I have written this book primarily for newcomers to Aristotle's social thought, people who are looking for an introductory overview that will make him come alive as a political philosopher. But throughout this work I make claims, both about what Aristotle had in mind and about the viability of his practical thought, that are bound to be controversial. I therefore hope that seasoned readers of Aristotle and political theorists will also find something worthwhile in what follows.

I am grateful to Northwestern University for the sabbatical leaves without which I could not have begun or completed this book. I am also indebted to many members of the academic community for their comments, criticism, and encouragement. An early and much shorter draft of this work was presented to a seminar at the University of Chicago in 1997, and the penultimate draft was aired at a seminar at Northwestern University three years later. I am grateful to members of these audiences for the opportunity to try out my ideas on them, and particularly to Paul Bullen and Ian Mueller, for their criticism and suggestions. Martha Nussbaum and two referees for Oxford University Press (one was Malcolm Schofield, the other continued to be anonymous) provided me with valuable critiques of an intermediate draft. Several chapters were transformed into lectures, and the criticism I received on these occasions allowed me to see errors and weaknesses that I would not have been able to detect on my own. In particular, I would like to single out Terence Irwin, Scott MacDonald, and Jennifer Whiting for the help they have given me with some of the material that appears in Chapters 2 and 3; Fred Miller and Jean Roberts for their comments on some of the ideas in Chapter 4; and Danielle Allen, Charles Brittain, Robert Gooding-Williams, Terence Irwin, Rachana Kamtekar, Thomas McCarthy, Robert Wallace, and Julie Ward for their help with earlier drafts of Chapter 8. Audiences at Princeton, Stanford, the University of Colorado, Cornell, Johns Hopkins, Northern Illinois University, and the University of North Carolina at Chapel Hill helped me to rethink my ideas. An invitation to give the Carlyle Classes in Political Thought at Oxford University in Trinity Term 2001 gave me a final opportunity to try out my interpretation. I am grateful to Mark Philp not only for hosting my stay at Oxford, but for the guidance he gave me throughout my work on this project. To all of the many generous people who encouraged me and stimulated my thinking as I wrote this book, I give my heartfelt thanks.

Contents

Abbreviations   xiii

PART I

1. Aristotle's Political World and Writings   3
2. Prolegomenon to Aristotle's Ethics: Against Subjectivism   20
3. Well-Being and Virtue   50
4. Justice in the *Nicomachean Ethics*   98

PART II

5. Introduction to the *Politics*   181
6. *Politics* VII and VIII: The Ideal Polis   192
7. *Politics* I: Nature, Political Animals, and Civic Priority   240
8. *Politics* I: Slavery   277
9. *Politics* II: Family, Property, and Civic Unity   306
10. *Politics* III: Citizenship, Stability, and Obedience   357
11. *Politics* III: Correct Constitutions and the Common Good   385
12. *Politics* IV–VI: Non-Ideal Constitutions   427
13. Final Thoughts   471

References	483
Index Locorum	497
General Index	505

Abbreviations

Ath. Pol.	*Constitution of the Athenians*
Cat.	*Categories*
De An.	*De Anima*
EE	*Eudemian Ethics*
Gen. An.	*Generation of Animals*
Hist. An.	*History of Animals*
Mem.	*De Memoria*
Met.	*Metaphysics*
Meteor.	*Meteorologica*
NE	*Nicomachean Ethics*
Part. An.	*Parts of Animals*
Pol.	*Politics*
Rhet.	*Rhetoric*

PART I

I

Aristotle's Political World and Writings

1.1. The Political Nature of the Nicomachean Ethics

To understand and assess Aristotle's contributions to political thought, we must come to terms not only with the treatise whose political content is advertised by its title—the *Politics* (in Greek: *Politikōn*)—but also with the work that bears the peculiar name, *Nicomachean Ethics* (*Ēthikōn Nikomacheiōn*).[1] For Aristotle announces, at a very early point in that ethical treatise, that the subject he has chosen to examine—the good of human beings—is one that belongs to the science of politics (I.2 1094a27–8).[2] He holds that understanding where our good lies is of central importance to the way we conduct our lives (a18–26); and that since politics is the science that controls all other practical disciplines, its proper business is to undertake an investigation of the human good, and to regulate human affairs in the light of what it discovers (1094a26–b7). As Aristotle continues his discussion in the *Ethics*, he frequently

---

[1] See 1.5 for an explanation of the title, *Nicomachean Ethics*. Aristotle wrote two ethical works; the other is the *Eudemian Ethics* (more fully discussed in 1.5). For the sake of brevity, I will often use the simple title *Ethics* to designate the *Nicomachean Ethics*. Throughout this study, I use arabic numerals (e.g. 1.5) to refer to chapters and sections of this study. References to footnotes are indicated by e.g. 1.n.1 (Ch. 1, footnote 1). A roman numeral followed by an arabic numeral (e.g. I.2) refers to a book and chapter of Aristotle's work.

[2] See 3.15 for a fuller discussion of the conception of politics put forward in *NE* I.2.

reminds his audience of the political nature of his material.³ Finally, when he comes to the concluding chapter of this treatise, he dwells at length on the importance of turning next to a detailed examination of laws and the proper arrangement of the political community. For those who have studied his treatment of virtue, friendship, and pleasure (the topics to which he has been led, in his examination of the human good) will not be able to put what they have learned into practice, and will therefore not have profited from their study, unless they complete their investigation by moving on to the questions examined in the *Politics*: what preserves and destroys cities, what makes them well or poorly governed, what laws and customs would exist in the best kind of political system?⁴

Since Aristotle conceives of the *Ethics* and the *Politics* as following a logical progression—the former establishing the foundation of politics, the latter providing the further detail that allows his examination of human well-being to be put into practice—we ought to carry out our investigation of his political philosophy in the order that he recommends. We begin with the *Ethics* and move on to the *Politics*. But not every subject Aristotle discusses in the *Ethics* will receive our careful attention, for that would make an already long book far too long. We will focus instead on one of the leading ideas of the *Ethics*, namely that human well-being consists in excellent activity; and on justice, the central virtue of political life. The *Ethics*

---

³ See I.3 1095a2–3, I.4 1095a14–17, I.4 1095b4–6, I.9 1099b29–32, I.13 1102a7–9, I.13 1102a18–21, II.3 1105a10–12, VII.11 1152b1–2. Although I sometimes speak of Aristotle's 'audience', I do not mean, by my use of this word, to commit myself to the thesis that such treatises as the *Nicomachean Ethics* and the *Politics* were read aloud by him to his students. They may instead have been intended as works to be read by his students, not spoken aloud by their author. (Even so, we can call the intended readership of a work its audience.) The relation between Aristotle's written works and his oral teaching is difficult to determine, for there is little basis for forming a hypothesis. For brief treatments of the issue, see Ross, *Aristotle*, p. 17; and Burnyeat, *A Map of Metaphysics Zeta*, p. 115, n. 60. Ross reasonably questions the idea that the works we possess are mere lecture notes (whether of Aristotle or a student). But he thinks that most treatises were polished elaborations of Aristotle's oral presentations, and his translation of the *Nicomachean Ethics* reflects his belief that Aristotle sometimes addressed his audience as a group of listeners. Thus he translates: 'a young man is not a proper hearer of lectures on political science' (I.3 1095a2–3). But there is nothing in the Greek that corresponds to 'lectures'. The term that Ross translates 'hearer' is *akroatēs*, which can mean 'listener', but also 'pupil'. An alternative reading is provided by Irwin: '. . . a youth is not a suitable student of political science.' Aristotle uses *akroatēs* to mean 'pupil' (not 'listener') at *Pol.* II.12 1274a25. (Ross himself uses 'student' for *akroatēs* at X.9 1179b25.) In any case, it is difficult to believe that works as dense and complex as the logical and scientific treatises were delivered orally; I believe the same can be said of Aristotle's ethical and political writings.

⁴ The whole of X.9, starting with its opening sentence, is an argument for the fruitlessness of studying ethics in isolation from politics. See X.9 1181b15–23 for Aristotle's preview of the topics to be covered in the *Politics*.

1.1. THE POLITICAL NATURE OF THE *NICOMACHEAN ETHICS*

devotes more attention to justice than to any other virtue (as befits a political treatise); it is the sole subject of one of its ten books. Students of Aristotle's political philosophy who do not come to terms with his examination of justice in the *Ethics*, or who fail to understand the theory of well-being and excellent activity in which his conception of justice is embedded, will be missing one of his most important contributions to their subject, and will be impeded in their understanding of the *Politics*.

It should be evident that any philosophical study of politics must ask what prospects there are for human beings to live together peaceably and fruitfully in large communities. We must ask whether the good of one human being inevitably comes into conflict with the good of others—or, at any rate, with those others who do not belong to one's family or circle of friends. Are conflicting interests between fellow citizens a permanent feature of the human situation, and therefore an unavoidable feature of political life? Any attempt to answer that question presupposes a conception of what is good for human beings. We cannot say how often your good and mine come into competition, how deep and troubling those conflicts are, or how they are best resolved, unless we possess some understanding of what is good for you and what is good for me. Aristotle proposes an answer to these questions that no student of political theory can afford to ignore. His conception of well-being holds out to us the possibility that political life can be, to a large extent, nonconflictual—or far less conflictual than it typically is. He has a sharp eye for and keen understanding of the many social and psychological factors that create conflicts between human beings—in fact, that is the main theme of the central books of the *Politics* (IV–VI). But he regards political communities rent by faction as sites of human pathology. They are unhealthy cities, and do not provide evidence that deep-seated conflict is an inevitable part of the human condition, properly understood. The foundation of this optimistic component of Aristotle's political philosophy (which must not be studied in isolation from his deep pessimism) lies in his theory of the human good.[5]

---

[5] See 6.8 and 13.1 on Aristotle's pessimism regarding our prospects for making great improvements in the human condition. In 3.15 I explain how conflicts can occur, in Aristotle's system, between the good of individuals. Civic friendship will be discussed in 6.9 and Chs. 9 and 12. Aristotle's analogy between bodies and cities (to be explored in Ch. 7) expresses his idea that each individual's well-being is, in a certain sense, integrated with the good of others. Even so, as we will see in 6.11, he realizes that disagreement is part of the human condition, even in the best of circumstances.

1.2. Aristotle in His Time and Place: Macedon

Before we explore Aristotle's two principal political works, something must be said about the political circumstances of his life. Political thinkers are often shaped by historical events or persons, and our understanding of their ideas is often enriched when set in a biographical context. For example, we cannot fully understand Hegel's political thought or that of his contemporaries unless we know something about the course of the French Revolution and how they perceived that event. The political philosophies of Hobbes and Locke were developed against the background of English politics; similarly, to understand Machiavelli we must know something about Cesare Borgia, Pope Julius II, the Medicis, and Florentine politics. In the ancient world too, political thought is shaped by political happenstance. The death of Socrates, for example, forms the backdrop to the *Gorgias* and the *Republic*. So we must ask: what do we need to know about Aristotle's life and his historical circumstances in order to understand his political thought?[6]

Of course, we know that he was wealthy enough to be able to devote himself to study and writing, without having to work for a living. That is true of nearly every philosopher, poet, scientist, and historian of the ancient world. And we know that in that world prejudice against manual labor was widespread, especially among the rich, and that Aristotle shared this prejudice. These points are familiar, and will be addressed later, when we ask whether there is any principled basis for Aristotle's treatment of class conflict, or whether he ought to be read as an apologist for the wealthy elite (12.4).[7] Setting this issue aside, what we must ask now is whether there are other facts about his life, not apparent from his own writings, that help us better understand his political orientation. Did certain powerful persons, dramatic events, or historical tendencies play a crucial role in shaping his thought?

To examine this issue, let us review the basic biographical facts:[8]

---

[6] For a brief account of the major political developments of the fourth century, see Hornblower, *The Greek World 479–323 BC*, pp. 181–293. For a more detailed account, see Sealey, *Demosthenes and his Time*.

[7] For the latter point of view, see Wood and Wood, *Class Ideology and Ancient Political Theory*, ch. 5.

[8] For more information, see Chroust, *Aristotle*, pp. 117–76. A full treatment of the ancient testimony about Aristotle is presented in Düring, *Aristotle in the Ancient Biographical Tradition*. A brief account can be found in the introduction to Lord's translation of the *Politics*, pp. 2–8.

I.2. ARISTOTLE IN HIS TIME AND PLACE: MACEDON

Born in 384 BC in Stagira, a town near the Aegean Sea in the north of Greece, and raised in Pella, the royal residence of the kingship of Macedon, Aristotle moved to Athens at the age of 17 to pursue his education at Plato's Academy. Athenian citizenship was no more available to him than it was to any other resident alien, and so he observed the political scene not as a participant but as an outsider. He remained a resident for some nineteen years, departed after the death of Plato in 348/7, and took up residence again from 335/4 to 323, when he departed once again. The causes of these comings and goings are a matter of conjecture, but it is well known that during this period Macedonian power over the rest of Greece increased, and there was significant hostility towards Macedon in Athens. Aristotle was connected with this kingdom in several ways. He had lived there as a boy because his father, Nicomachus, was the physician of the king of Macedon, Amyntas III. After Amyntas died in 370/69, a long power struggle ensued, and in 359 he was succeeded by Philip, who ruled for twenty-three years until his assassination in 336. Five years after his departure from Athens, Aristotle returned to Macedon and remained for eight years (343–335), and there are indications that he had close personal ties to Philip, although the story that he served as tutor to Philip's son, Alexander (familiar to all as 'Alexander the Great'), has meager historical support. Near the end of his reign, in 338, Philip defeated Athens and Corinth in the battle of Chaeronea, and held power over the whole of Greece. After he was assassinated in 336, Alexander succeeded to the throne, and in 335/4 Aristotle returned to Athens and established his own center of research and teaching in the Lyceum.[9] He departed once again in 323 when Alexander died and several cities, including Athens, unsuccessfully tried to escape from the control of Macedon. There is little doubt that this second departure from Athens (one year before his death in 322) was motivated by the Athenian revolt against Macedon. It is plausible to believe that his first departure from Athens and his return were also connected to the ebb and flow of Athenian–Macedonian relations.

Aristotle's life was therefore intimately connected with one of the most significant historical events of the fourth century—the rise of Macedonian power and its eventual hegemony. But does this information bear on a proper understanding of his political thought? There are no references in his writings to Alexander, or to

---

[9] See Lynch, *Aristotle's School*.

Demosthenes, the leader of the anti-Macedonian faction in Athens. He does not discuss the rise of Macedonian power and the threat this posed to the autonomy of Greek cities. Philip is mentioned just once (*Pol.* V.10 1311b1–2), but there is no discussion here or elsewhere of his policies or method of rule, merely a sentence on his assassination. There is one other passage that some scholars take as an allusion to Philip: at IV.11 1296a38–40 Aristotle says that there is only one man who has been persuaded to establish the sort of mixed constitution he favors. But even if this is an allusion to Philip, it must be taken to mean not that Philip's policies influenced Aristotle, but that Aristotle influenced Philip: it was the philosopher who arrived at the conclusion that a regime dominated by the middle class is best, and the king who put that theory into action. If Philip is really the person to whom Aristotle is referring, this passage provides a nice example of the way philosophy can make a practical difference. But it does not provide an example of what we are looking for, namely an event or person that shaped Aristotle's thought.

There is one other passage that might be taken to reflect the rise of Macedon. At one point Aristotle remarks that 'the race of the Greeks ... is capable of ruling all of the others, if it acquires a single political system' (*Politics* VII.7 1327b29–33). This can plausibly be read as an expression of the hope that control over Persia (a traditional rival of Greek cities) will be the result of Macedonian hegemony. Aristotle does not elaborate on this remark, but as any reader of the rest of Book VII (or the entirety of the *Politics*) can easily see, his whole way of thinking opposes the development of some single superstate that would destroy the plurality of cities and absorb all Greeks into a single set of political institutions. Different political systems are suitable for different cities, he says throughout Book IV of the *Politics*; the destruction of local institutions and absorption of all Greeks into a single empire would not allow such diversity. And the creation of a single and immense polis would also fly in the face of his thesis that ideally a city should be quite small—small enough to allow all the citizens to know each other (VII.4 1326b2–24). What Aristotle must have in mind, then, when he proposes that the Greeks be united into a single political system, is a federation that would allow each city to govern itself in ways suitable to its own circumstances.

So even where Aristotle briefly alludes to the rise of Macedonian power, his remarks are not shaped in any important way by that political development. What he hopes can be achieved by the hegemony of Macedon is an end to the threat of Persian influence over the internal affairs of Greek cities, not the elimination of separate political institutions. The political phenomenon that cast the largest shadow over Aristotle's life—the tension between Athens and Macedon—does not play a significant role in his thought. He is concerned not with the shifting alliances and struggles between different cities, but with the internal merits and deficiencies of political systems, the various ways of preserving and improving them, and the depiction of an ideal society.

However, there is one other way, not yet mentioned, in which Macedonian power may have figured in Aristotle's thinking. It is possible that his conception of the ideal constitution changed over time—we will discuss that possibility in 10.1 and 11.13—and, if it did, then political or personal circumstances might help explain this shift. In Books VII and VIII of the *Politics* he proposes a constitution for a perfect city, one that is to be established by colonists in a new location well suited to civic life. It will be ruled equally by all citizens: no adult male will have more power than any other, because all will have the same qualifications for citizenship and higher office. So the ideal polis will not be a kingship. By contrast, in the last few chapters of Book III, he holds that the best kind of political system is a kingship—if a king with the requisite abilities is available.[10] Is there a contradiction here? And if there is, might Aristotle at different times of his life have thought differently about the merits of the Macedonian political system—not because of shifting philosophical ideas, but because of a change in historical or personal circumstances? Might he have wished to flatter or appease the Macedonian court when he wrote Book III, but not when he wrote Book VII?[11] Alternatively, might the rise of Macedonian power and its conquest of western Asia in the 330s have created new

---

[10] More precisely, he holds at the end of Book III that either kingship or aristocracy would be ideal. But as we will see (10.1, esp. 10.nn.5 and 6), what he means here by an aristocracy is something quite different from the *politeia* described in VII and VIII.

[11] The explanatory value of this hypothesis is discussed by Kahn, 'The Normative Structure of Aristotle's "Politics",' pp. 373–5, 379–80. See too Kelsen, 'The Philosophy of Aristotle and the Hellenic-Macedonian Policy'; for effective criticism of Kelsen, see Brunt, 'Plato's Academy and Politics', app. B: 'Aristotle and the Macedonian People and Monarchy', pp. 335–6. My own view accords with that of Düring: 'The influence of Macedonian politics on his political thinking was faint': *Aristotle in the Ancient Biographical Tradition*, pp. 289–90. Newman writes: 'The object of the Politics is to carry on and complete the work that Plato had begun . . . Aristotle's relation to Plato was the critical fact of his life, not his relation to Philip or Alexander' (*The Politics of Aristotle*, i. 478). I accept Newman's second point, but for significant differences between the political orientation of Plato and Aristotle, see Ch. 4.

possibilities—possibilities that did not exist when he wrote Book III—for the establishment of an ideal city in a new part of the world by colonists eager to be guided by Aristotle's political ideas? In that case, Books VII and VIII of the *Politics* were composed as a blueprint for the creation of a society that had not yet become a practical possibility when other parts of this treatise were composed.[12]

These speculative hypotheses are difficult to prove or refute. And they all presuppose that there is a contradiction between Aristotle's conception of the ideal constitution in Books III and in Books VII and VIII of the *Politics*. I will argue, however, that there is really no conflict here. Once again, we will find that there is no need to look outside the *Politics* to explain what we find within it.

1.3. Sparta, Athens

There was one other notable major shift in the fortunes of cities in the fourth century: Sparta, whose formidable power and successful war against Athens are the principal subject of Thucydides' *Histories*, suffered a disastrous military defeat at Leuctra in 371, and lost its ability to influence other cities. Aristotle alludes to this decline several times, but it is apparent from his many remarks about Sparta that he regards its military defeat as confirmation of a conclusion he had already drawn on theoretical grounds. Although in some respects he admires the Spartan constitution, he regards their political institutions as flawed, and he frequently criticizes their devotion to physical strength and military might as ends in themselves. His thought is not: Sparta has declined; this must reflect a serious deficiency; and we must discover what this is. Rather, he moves in the opposite direction: Our political theory shows what the weaknesses of the Spartan constitution are; these weaknesses threaten its viability; and its defeat gives us further confirmation that our criticism is on the mark.[13] So the decline of Sparta is no more a turning point in Aristotle's thinking than is the

---

[12] This is the suggestion made by Ober in *Political Dissent in Democratic Athens*, ch. 6, e.g. pp. 339–40.

[13] Aristotle alludes to Leuctra at II.9 1270a29–34, VII.11 1330b32–5, and VII.14 1333b5–16. He admires Sparta because it pays attention to education; see *NE* I.13 1102a10–11; cf. *NE* X.9 1180a24–6; *Pol.* VIII.1 1337a29–32. For his critique of its militarism, see *Pol.* VII.2 1324b5–9, VII.14 1333b5–35, VII.15 1334a40-b5, VIII.4 1338b9–17.

rise of Macedon. In both cases, major historical events are integrated into his political theory, but the theory is not supported solely or primarily by an appeal to those events.

Although Athens was defeated by Sparta in the Peloponnesian War, its democracy was restored at the end of the fifth century, and remained intact throughout much of the fourth century, until it came under the rule of Macedon. There were no oligarchic coups in Athens during the fourth century, as there had been at the end of the fifth; its constitution was stable and, judged by the standards of the time, long-lasting. Aristotle's residence there, as well as its great size, power, and influence, insured that the problems of running a democracy—or what he perceived to be its problems—would play an important role in his thinking. The evidence for this is in Aristotle's own writing, for Books III–VI of the *Politics* are filled with reflections on the varieties and deficiencies of democracy. Although he holds that the defects of democracy and oligarchy mirror each other —one is wrongful rule by the poor, the other wrongful rule by the rich—it is democracy that has a greater hold on his thinking, and receives far more of his attention.[14] That is because of the continuing power of Athens in the fourth century, and Aristotle's long-term residence there.

But Athens is certainly not his sole preoccupation. His political writing is filled with observations about the way institutions work in many actual cities.[15] These empirical data were more fully and systematically presented in the series of constitutional studies undertaken by Aristotle's school, the only one of which has survived is the *Constitution of Athens*.[16] So even though there is no pivotal event that decisively shaped his thinking, his political philosophy is thoroughly integrated with the observations he makes about political life in a variety of cities, among which Athens was of

---

[14] See Keyt, *Aristotle: Politics Books V and VI*, p. 193: in Book VI, Aristotle 'spends four times as many words' on democracy as on oligarchy.

[15] As Hansen notes (in a personal communication to Ober), 'of some 270 historical examples in the *Politics*, some thirty concern Athens' (Ober, *Political Dissent in Democratic Athens*, p. 291 n. 4).

[16] Scholars disagree about whether this work (lost until the late nineteenth century) was composed by Aristotle himself or one of his students. Ancient lists of Aristotle's works attribute to him a collection of 158 constitutions (see *NE* X.9 1181b17), but it is unlikely that he wrote every one of them. Would he have assigned himself the task of writing this one in particular? For a brief account of the arguments on both sides, see the introduction of Rhodes to the Penguin edition, pp. 11–13; and the same author's commentary, pp. 61–3. There is no doubt that the general political orientations of the *Politics* and the *Constitution of Athens* are similar. Rhodes himself believes that the latter was the work of a member of Aristotle's school, not Aristotle himself.

considerable importance. Perhaps, in some cases, noted at the end of the preceding section, we might be tempted to go outside of his writings to seek a biographical explanation of his political thought. But, for the most part, what shaped his thinking is presented to us on the written page.

1.4. City, Citizen, Government, Constitution

It is possible to grasp some of the essential elements of Aristotle's conception of well-being, and other components of his ethical theory, even if we have little or no acquaintance with the institutions or culture of the fourth-century Greek world. But after Chapters 2 and 3, we will move away from Aristotle's most general thoughts about human happiness in order to consider his more specific notions about the qualities we need in order to fare well, and the civic institutions that foster those qualities. In Chapter 4, we will take up his conception of justice; and after that, we will examine some of the leading themes of his *Politics*. To prepare the way for our discussion of this material, it will be helpful to make some observations about the vocabulary in which his political theory is expressed, and the civic institutions he took for granted. Aristotle's thoughts about justice, citizenship, equality, democracy, community,[17] property, and family are worth taking seriously, and can contribute to intelligent reflection about our own problems. But in order to understand what he has to say, and assess his contemporary significance, we must know something about the political vocabulary and the civic institutions of his time.

Aristotle philosophizes about the polis—the 'city-state' or 'city' as it is sometimes translated. There were in ancient Greece more than 1,000 poleis (plural of *polis*), most of them small societies of some 1,000 citizens who had some degree of personal familiarity with each other. (The Greek term for citizen, *politēs*, is cognate to *polis*.) A few were much larger. Athens, the largest, had about 60,000 male citizens in the age of Pericles and about half that number in the fourth century; its total population, including women, children,

---

[17] I use the word 'community' to translate Aristotle's *koinōnia*, because he is conscious of the connection between it and *koinon* ('common'). The members of every community, he thinks, must have something in common. Others prefer 'association' as a translation of *koinōnia*, because that is a word that lacks the warmth of 'community', and Aristotle's term lacks this tone. For discussion of these issues, see 9.22.

1.4. CITY, CITIZEN, GOVERNMENT, CONSTITUTION

slaves, and resident aliens, was several hundred thousand.[18] Typically, poleis had a single urban center surrounded by an expanse of terrain used principally for farming. The term *polis* could be applied both to this physical object (one could speak of the distance between two poleis) and also to the whole collection of people who had citizen rights and a single set of decision-making institutions. It is principally in the latter sense that Aristotle uses the term; as he says, 'the polis is a certain number of citizens' (*Pol.* III.1 1274b41). The study of the different ways in which citizens are organized, and of how they should be organized—who is to have power over whom, and what ends are to be served by this power—is the principal focus of his political writings. The different ways of configuring citizens—into democracies, oligarchies, and the like—are called 'constitutions'.[19]

These remarks about the term *polis* lead to an intriguing question. Do poleis still exist, or is this an institution that is no longer found in the modern period? No one would call Ireland or Germany or China a 'city-state'—the term often used as a translation of *polis*.[20] We use the word 'state' for the major units of modern politics, whereas 'city' is often used to translate *polis*. Great differences between modern nation-states (as they are sometimes called) and Greek city-states can be found; the most striking is that their populations are of a different order of magnitude. But differences in size do not by themselves constitute differences in kind.[21] Furthermore, it is obvious that *citizens* still exist; and if a polis is a certain number of citizens arranged in a certain way, then how can it be denied that modern nation-states are poleis? Many of the terms Aristotle uses to describe different kinds of political system—*dēmokratia, tyrannis,*

---

[18] See Hansen, *The Athenian Democracy*, pp. 53–5, 93.

[19] The Greek term here is *politeia*. I will use 'political system' and 'regime' to translate it, as well as 'constitution'. It should always be kept in mind that 'constitution', when used as a translation of *politeia*, does not refer to a document.

[20] The term 'city-state' is sometimes used to refer to very small states in the modern world—e.g. Singapore. But apart from these few cases, the phrase is reserved for political units of such earlier times and places as ancient Greece and early modern Italy. On some differences between modern states and Greek poleis, see Hansen, *The Athenian Democracy in the Age of Demosthenes*, pp. 57–64.

[21] The proper size of contemporary political units is a matter that is open to investigation and debate. It is sometimes said, for example, that the nation-states of our world are both too large (to solve local problems) and too small (to solve global problems). We therefore should not assume in advance that nothing can be learnt from a study of the smaller political units of an earlier age. For the view that 'polis' should be translated 'city' rather than 'state', in part because of the size of modern states, see Simpson's translation of the *Politics*, pp. xxiv–xxvi.

monarchia—have English counterparts that are familiar in contemporary political discourse. If some of these systems of allocating power still exist, how can there not be poleis?

The underlying issue is whether the political problems of the ancient world are sufficiently similar to our own to warrant the use of a common vocabulary. If Greek civic life has nothing to teach us, or if the institutions presupposed by ancient political thinkers make their ideas irrelevant to contemporary politics, then we will want to highlight our distance from the past by employing different terms: 'nation-state' for modern political units, 'city-states' or 'cities' for ancient polities. On the other hand, we might choose to call them both 'states', if we become convinced that many of the issues facing the polis, as Aristotle portrays them, are our issues as well.

I hope to show that we should not make a sharp division between, on the one hand, the problems that afflicted the ancient polis and set the agenda for Aristotle's political reflections and, on the other hand, the issues that confront modern politics and political theory. The polis and the modern state are kindred institutions, because they must confront kindred predicaments, having to do with the distribution of power and wealth and the proper ends to which these resources should be put.[22] Nonetheless, throughout this study I will use 'city' rather than 'state' to render *polis*, simply because the close verbal relationships that exist within our own political vocabulary—'city', 'citizen', 'civic'—parallel the equally close relationships among the terms that are omnipresent in Aristotle's political writings: *politikē*, *politeia*, *politikos*, *politēs*, *polis*. Some of the conventional equations we use—'constitution' for *politeia*, 'statesman' for *politikos*, 'state' for *polis*—mask the way in which his political vocabulary so often moves back and forth between words that employ a single root. Using 'city' rather than 'state' therefore has at least this much to be said in its favor: it helps us mirror in English the single-rootedness of a great deal of Aristotle's political vocabulary.

We should bear in mind throughout this study that *polis* is not used by Aristotle and his fellow Greeks as we often use the word 'government'. The government of the United States is located

---

[22] See Holmes, 'Aristippus in and out of Athens' for a defense of the opposite thesis: that Greek political thought rests on a conception of society that has become obsolete in the modern world, and that the study of Plato and Aristotle therefore has little bearing on the problems of our time. (Those whom Holmes takes to task for thinking otherwise are Hannah Arendt, Karl Popper, and Leo Strauss.) See 13.n.10.

principally in Washington, DC, far removed from most of its citizens. But the polis is not the sort of thing that can be far from the citizens, for they collectively are the polis. When we choose our political leaders, we are choosing our government; but when Greek citizens selected their rulers, they were not choosing their polis; rather it was they, the polis, who were selecting their leaders. Aristotle is not proposing a theory about what the government should do, but about what the whole body of citizens should do, and how they should be organized.

In the same spirit, we should be careful to avoid too narrow a conception of what a *politeia* is. One common translation of this term, 'constitution', brings to mind a set of rules that grants powers and places restrictions on governmental offices. This captures some of what Aristotle means by a *politeia*, for the different kinds of *politeia* differ from each other by giving control over a city's collective decisions to different groups: democracy, for example, empowers ordinary people; oligarchy restricts power to the wealthy. But we also think of a constitution as something that is addressed especially or exclusively to the government rather than the citizen. The First Amendment of the US Constitution says that '*Congress* shall make no law respecting an establishment of religion, or prohibiting the free exercise thereof' (my emphasis). But it does not address the conduct of individuals when they are not acting in a governmental capacity. By contrast, Aristotle takes a constitution—a *politeia*—as a way of organizing all of the citizens, not merely those who have special powers of political office. It is, as he says at one point, the way of life (*bios*) of a polis (IV.11 1295a40–b1).[23] That is why he thinks it appropriate for the *Politics* to discuss not only ways of distributing offices and power but also the household, property, education, religion, and the like. These all have to do with the *politeia*—the way we live together—even though they may not be 'constitutional' matters in our sense. For Aristotle, the question, 'how should we organize our offices?' cannot be answered in isolation from a discussion of the more basic question, 'how is it best to live?' The latter is not merely an issue for individuals to ponder and resolve in their private lives. It is an issue deeply implicated in the way we make our collective decisions as citizens.

---

[23] See 10.4 and 10.n.12 on the various goals of political systems.

1.5. Ethics and Politics: The Compositional Order of Aristotle's Political Works

I pointed out earlier (1.1) that Aristotle takes political science to be the discipline whose proper business it is to carry out an investigation of human well-being. That is what he says in I.2 of the *Ethics*. And we might infer from this that the proper name for the treatise that goes under the name *Nicomachean Ethics* really ought to be *Politics*, and that Aristotle himself had no notion that these are two distinct subjects, one of which can be called 'politics' and the other 'ethics'. But the truth is somewhat more complicated than this. Aristotle himself makes a distinction between politics and ethics— although he never doubts that the subjects they investigate must be studied together. (In fact, he is the *first* to think of these two fields as distinct subjects of investigation. Plato does not conceive of ethics as a separate branch of philosophy, and does not distinguish ethics from politics.) The best way to describe Aristotle's use of the word 'politics' (*politikē*) is to say that he *sometimes* uses it in a general sense, in which it designates the study of human well-being and character; but *often* he uses it in a narrow sense, in which it refers to the study of constitutions and cities. In I.2 of the *Ethics*, he uses 'politics' in the broad sense. But he frequently refers to certain of his writings as *ta ēthika* or *ēthikoi logoi*—his 'ethical discourses'. He uses these expressions six times in the *Politics*, in order to refer his audience to something he has said in another work.[24] *Ēthica* means 'having to do with character' (*ēthos*), and so Aristotle's way of referring to some of his discourses indicates that he takes character to be their principal theme. So the title of the *Nicomachean Ethics* accords with Aristotle's own way of referring to his works in the *Politics*. It is a treatise on character, and does not address constitutional or legal questions—the topics of politics in the narrow

---

[24] These occur at II.2 1261a31, III.9 1280a18, III.12 1282b20, IV.11 1295a36, VII.13 1332a8, VII.13 1332a22. Note also that in one passage Aristotle distinguishes between the subject investigated in his ethical works and the subject treated in the *Politics*: see *Pol.* VII.2 1324a13–23. Ethics is a study of the most choice-worthy life; 'political thought or theory' (a19–20) a study of constitutions and cities. See too *Rhet.* I.8 1366a21–2: here he refers his audience to his 'political [discourses]' (*en tois politikois*)—meaning by this not his ethical works but the *Politics*. He blurs that distinction, and suggests that the works he calls ethical can reasonably be called political, at both *NE* I.2 1094a26–8 and *Rhet.* I.2 1356a26–7. To avoid the confusion that Aristotle creates with his shifting vocabulary, it is best to say that for him there is politics in the general sense (human well-being and character) and politics in the narrow sense (constitutions and cities).

sense. It might be called a political treatise—but only in the broader sense of politics.

I also pointed out (1.1) that the *Nicomachean Ethics* and the *Politics* have a logical order: the former provides the foundations for the latter, but it is only through the latter that the former can achieve its practical purpose. But the logical order between the two works should be distinguished from their order of composition. The closing sentences of the *Ethics* suggest that some parts of the *Politics* had already been drafted. Aristotle tells his audience that they will examine 'what sorts of things preserve and destroy cities'—the topic of Books V and VI of the *Politics*; and then, having done so, they will be better able to see 'what sort of political system is best'— the question examined in Books II, VII, and VIII (as well as in portions of III). Not every topic we find in our copies of the *Politics* is mentioned in these closing lines of the *Ethics*, and so it is possible that some parts of the *Politics* were composed after the *Ethics* was completed. But in any case, at least those portions of the *Politics* to which the *Ethics* alludes can be safely assumed to have been written at an earlier time. The *Politics* (or much of it) was written first, even though it is to be studied second.

I said (two paragraphs above) that there are six passages in the *Politics* in which Aristotle refers to points that he has made in a work that he calls *ta ēthika* or *ēthikoi logoi*—his 'ethical discourses'. Does that not create an obvious difficulty for my thesis that the *Politics* was written before the *Nicomachean Ethics*? Aristotle could not refer, in the *Politics*, to points already made in his ethical writings, if they had not yet been composed. The way out of this difficulty is to recognize that there is another work besides the *Nicomachean Ethics* to which the *Politics* may be alluding: the *Eudemian Ethics*. The Greek words corresponding to 'Eudemian' and 'Nicomachean' were added to the titles of these treatises after Aristotle completed them, perhaps because the former was edited by his friend Eudemus and the latter by his son, Nicomachus. Since Aristotle did not himself assign different names to these two works, it is possible that when the *Politics* refers to *ta ēthika*, it is alluding to points made in the *Eudemian Ethics*.

There are subtle and important differences between Aristotle's two ethical treatises, but since they cover many of the same topics— happiness, virtue, practical reasoning, friendship, pleasure, and so on —one of them is evidently a partial revision of the other, rather than an entirely new book. The revision is only partial, for some material is simply repeated in both works: *EE* IV = *NE* V, *EE* V = *NE* VI, *EE* VI = *NE* VII. Which of the two ethical works was composed first is a matter of controversy, but for many centuries philosophers and scholars have assumed that the *Nicomachean Ethics* represents Aristotle's last and best thoughts about the topics it treats. This is still the orthodox position, and it is the one I will adopt here.[25] It is also widely assumed that the books common to both works were originally written as parts of the *Eudemian Ethics*, and then incorporated into the *Nicomachean Ethics*. (Note that Aristotle's essay on justice, which we will discuss in Chapter 4, is one of the books found in both works.)

An examination of the passages in which the *Politics* refers to 'the ethical discourses' shows that some allude to material contained only in the *Eudemian Ethics*, and others allude to points made in books that that the two ethical treatises share in common.[26] That is a telling fact. Even though the *Nicomachean Ethics* is later than the *Eudemian Ethics*, Aristotle never uses a Nicomachean rather than a Eudemian formulation, when he refers, in the *Politics*, to a point he has made in the 'ethical discourses'. Presumably that is because when he was working on the *Politics* (or, at any rate, those portions of it that refer to *ta ēthika*), he had not yet composed the *Nicomachean Ethics*. There can be only one reason why the *Politics* does not use the terminology of Aristotle's new and improved ethical treatise: it (or, at any rate, the relevant portions of it) had not yet been written.

It is reasonable to assume, therefore, that the order in which Aristotle composed these three works (or large portions of them) is: (A) *Eudemian Ethics*, (B) *Politics*, (C) *Nicomachean Ethics*. Once we put these works in this order, we cannot help noticing a striking difference between the first and second versions of his ethical treatise: the *Nicomachean Ethics* opens and closes with statements affirming its political nature, whereas the *Eudemian Ethics* has nothing corresponding to these passages. The *Nicomachean Ethics* begins by asking what the highest good is (I.1), and argues that it is political science that studies this issue (I.2). By introducing his work

---

[25] For an important challenge to this tradition, see Kenny, *The Aristotelian Ethics*; and for later thoughts, *Aristotle on the Perfect Life*.

[26] For explicit references in the *Politics* to 'the ethical writings', see 1.n.24. At *Pol.* VII.8 1328a38 and VII.13 1332a8–9 Aristotle defines happiness in terms that correspond more closely to Eudemian than to Nicomachean formulations (see esp. *EE* II.1 1219a38–9, 1219b1–2). Similarly, at IV.11 1295a36–7, he characterizes happiness in terms reminiscent of *NE* VII.13 1153b9–21.

1.5. ETHICS AND POLITICS

in this way, Aristotle calls attention to the importance of his treatise to the organization of civic life. And he re-emphasizes the political nature of his work in the final chapter of Book X, when he points out that his 'philosophy of human affairs' (as he calls his project: 1181b15) has not yet been completed, because it has not yet examined the best way to put the goals of ethical life into practice by means of laws and political systems. The *Eudemian Ethics* provides a striking contrast: it is not framed in a way that highlights the political implications of its theories.

This should not be taken to mean that when Aristotle wrote the former work, he doubted or had no inkling of its political importance. A more reasonable hypothesis is that since much of the *Politics* had not yet been composed, when Aristotle was working on the *Eudemian Ethics*, he had no particular reason to construct that ethical treatise in a way that would call the reader's attention to its being the first of two related works on the 'philosophy of human affairs'.[27] It is prudent not to advertise one's composition as Part I of a two-volume treatment, before Part II is in hand. By contrast, the *Nicomachean Ethics* can bill itself as a political work and a prelude to the study of constitutional systems, because Part II of this two-volume study—or large portions of it—had already been completed.

Knowing the chronological relationship between the *Politics* and the *Nicomachean Ethics* can contribute to our efforts to understand and assess Aristotle's political theory. As we are about to see, one of the questions that must be asked about the *Politics* is whether some portions of it abandon doctrines or lines of thought that are present elsewhere within its covers. When we ponder that question of internal consistency, it will be of some help to know that all or much of the *Politics* precedes the *Nicomachean Ethics*. For if we find Aristotle endorsing a certain doctrine in the *Nicomachean Ethics*, that gives us an excellent reason to reject the hypothesis that this same doctrine is affirmed by one book of the *Politics* but then contradicted or silently abandoned in another. Aristotle may have changed his mind about certain matters; that is a possibility we must always be willing to consider. But it is hard to believe that he would have changed his mind *twice*—dropping one of the ideas explored in the *Politics* as he continued to work on it, but then affirming it once again in the *Nicomachean Ethics*.

---

[27] Book IV of the *EE* (which is also *NE* V) does allude at several points to themes that are fully developed in the *Politics*. See 4.n.1.

2

Prolegomenon to Aristotle's Ethics: Against Subjectivism

2.1. *Doubts about Aristotle's Universalism*

Aristotle's aim in the first book of the *Nicomachean Ethics* is to present an account of what is good for all human beings. His goal is to help his students improve their beliefs about what is good, and in this way to change their lives and the lives of others with whom they come into contact.[1] He therefore avoids debates that are of merely theoretical interest. When he disputes the ideas of other philosophers, he does so because he fears that their theories will lead many others (and not merely philosophers) astray in the conduct of their lives. What he offers to his audience is a substantive and

---

[1] Aristotle emphasizes his practical orientation at I.2 1094a22–4, II.2 1103b26–9, X.9 1179a35-b4. That 'pragmatic' approach to ethics is characteristic of Greek and Roman philosophy in general, and is not peculiar to Aristotle. All of the philosophers of this period —including Plato and the Hellenistic schools (Stoics, Epicureans, and Skeptics)—assume in their ethical writings that the members of their audience are deficient, to some degree, in the conduct of their lives, and their writings aim to remedy this deficiency. It is only later that moral philosophers understand their primary task to be theoretical. Thus Rawls, *Lectures on the History of Moral Philosophy*, pp. 10–11, says of the schools of modern moral philosophy that they 'more or less agree on what is in fact right and wrong, good and bad. They do not differ about the content of morality, about what its first principles of rights, duties and obligations, and the rest, really are. . . . The problem for them was not the content of morality but its basis: How we could know it and be moved to act from it.'

2.1. DOUBTS ABOUT ARISTOTLE'S UNIVERSALISM

systematic account of the highest goods of human life, an account that he hopes will enable them to achieve those goods more fully and successfully. The conception of human well-being that he develops and defends in Book I is then presupposed in nearly every other part of his ethical treatise, and as we shall see, it plays a large role in much of the *Politics* as well. The ideal city he describes in Books VII and VIII of the *Politics* shows how rich and enjoyable human lives can be, when social institutions reflect and encourage a proper understanding of happiness. In fact, political power in *all* cities ought to be used impartially for the good of every member of the community, and so any critique of existing political systems (all of which are deformed), and their amelioration, must be guided by a conception of the good of citizens. The theory of well-being that guides Aristotle's practical philosophy must therefore be our first subject of investigation.

We will find—if the argument of this book is correct—that the conception of human flourishing that guides Aristotle's political thought is enormously attractive, because it rests on deep insights and plausible assumptions about human nature, and provides a fruitful framework that can guide our own practical reflections about ethics and politics. That does not mean that we ought to retain every component of his theory, or defend everything he says in support of it. It is his general approach to well-being, suitably modified, that provides a powerful tool for thinking about moral and political issues.

Aristotle's conception of happiness will be presented and defended in the next chapter. The purpose of the present chapter is to prepare the way for that discussion, by undermining some common assumptions about well-being that stand in the way of a proper appreciation of Aristotle's approach to the subject. For it must be admitted that the very generality of his theory invites suspicion. He offers an account of the good that holds true of all human beings at all times and places, and it is reasonable to entertain doubts about whether a program of such scope and ambition can succeed. Our awareness of the diversity of cultures, and of the variety of human beings within each culture, may make us wary of accepting any broad generalizations about human well-being.[2] If we immerse ourselves in the

---

[2] But see Sober and Wilson, *Unto Others*, pp. 159–94, for a careful attempt to base some broad generalizations about human cultures on a large random sample drawn from hundreds of ethnographic studies. They use multi-level selection theory to cast doubt on egoistic hedonism, and emphasize instead our susceptibility to altruism and the influence of

details of his theory, without first addressing our doubts about any general conception of the human good, we may not give his ideas the hearing they deserve. Our own political predilections (which favor diversity, individualism, freedom, and creativity) may make us leery of any theory of the good that seems to impose a stifling uniformity on human life.

In fact, we can take our skepticism about any universal theory of the good a step farther: doubts can be raised as to whether philosophical reflection can arrive at substantive results about what is good even for a single human being. Suppose, for example, that I merely want to know what is good for *me*; I leave aside what is good for you or anyone else. Is this a matter about which I should turn to others for advice? Is my question something to which there already exists an answer? Are there facts about me and my circumstances that make it true that certain kinds of life are good for me, or that one way of living is best for me? When I choose to lead a certain kind of life, is it possible for me to be mistaken in thinking that it is good for me to live that way?

Aristotle simply assumes that the answers to these questions are yes. But we may wonder whether his affirmative answers can be defended. We might think that what makes something good for me is the favorable attitude I have towards it—my desire for it, or my belief that it is good, or my intention to pursue it. According to this way of thinking, objects come to be valuable for me because I *place* value on them. To put the point more generally: we human beings are creators of value. We confer goodness on our goals and activities by adopting or pursuing them. We are attracted to them, and so they become good for us; it is not as though they are already good for us, whether we realize this or not. To use philosophical jargon, we might say: what is good for someone is a subjective, not an objective, matter.

A defender of subjectivism must concede that what is good for oneself as a means towards one's ends is not a product of one's

---

social norms. Human groups are 'potentially adaptive units that are comparable to bee hives, coral colonies, and single individuals in their functional organization' (p. 159). Such studies as these cannot by themselves validate a substantive theory of well-being, but they cast doubt on the idea that there are no true and important generalizations about all human cultures. Furthermore, to the extent that they undermine theories that posit simple psychological mechanisms like egoism and hedonism, they leave the door open to reflection about which general goals we should pursue. Aristotle's political philosophy places great emphasis on the importance of social groups larger than the family, and psychological theories of the sort proposed by Sober and Wilson are congenial to his approach.

2.1. DOUBTS ABOUT ARISTOTLE'S UNIVERSALISM

psychological attitudes. Instrumental effectiveness is not conferred on a plan of action by the agent's thought that it is the best strategy, or by his desire to pursue it. But as for what is good for oneself, not as a means to some further goal, but as an end: here, it might be said, it is one's own desires, plans, or intentions that confer value.[3]

It should be noticed that subjectivism about the good is universal in scope. It applies to all members of our species at all times: it says that each and every human being confers goodness on things by taking up certain attitudes towards them. Even so, this subjective form of universalism does not raise the suspicion that Aristotle's approach encounters, because it does not seek to give practical guidance to all human beings—or, for that matter, *any* human beings—as Aristotle's theory does. The subjectivist says that we make things good for us through our attitudes, and since there is no such thing as a bad choice of one's ultimate ends, there is no justification for advising someone to adopt certain ends rather than others. Aristotle's theory offers practical guidance to all human beings about how to live, but in giving such advice he presupposes that it is possible to go astray in these matters, and this is precisely what the subjectivist denies.

The allure of subjectivism is something we must come to terms with. Because it is a component of the intellectual atmosphere in which we live (2.6), it stands in the way of a serious engagement with Aristotle's ideas about well-being. It is therefore worthwhile to examine subjectivism at some length, before we consider the details

---

[3] The philosophical idea that I here call 'subjectivism about the good' ('subjectivism', for short) has antecedents in such diverse authors as Hume, Kant, Nietzsche, and Sartre. It replaces the late medieval notion that God's will creates value with a form of humanism: value is created by human or rational will. The root idea has been developed in sophisticated ways by several contemporary philosophers. For example, the theory of the good advanced by Rawls in ch. 7 of *A Theory of Justice* contains a significant subjectivist component: one's plan of life creates one's good, provided that it meets certain tests of rationality. See too Gauthier, *Morals by Agreement*, ch. 2, for an avowedly subjectivist approach to all value (not merely the good). It would take me too far afield to discuss any particular version of subjectivism that has been defended by this or that author. I hope instead to show that we should resist the root idea. For a recent overview of subjective and objective theories of well-being, and a defense of subjectivism, see Sumner, *Welfare, Happiness, and Ethics*. Objective approaches are defended by Adams, *Finite and Infinite Goods*, pp. 83–101; Arneson, 'Human Flourishing versus Desire Satisfaction'; Hurka, *Perfectionism*; Nussbaum, *Women and Human Development*; and Sher, *Beyond Neutrality*, pp. 199–244. For other important contributions to the contemporary literature on well-being, see: Brandt, *A Theory of the Good and the Right*, pp. 1–162; Dworkin, *Sovereign Virtue*, pp. 237–84; Gewirth, *Self-Fulfillment*; Griffin, *Well-Being*, pp. 7–124; Griffin, *Value Judgement*, pp. 19–26; Parfit, *Reasons and Persons*, pp. 493–502; Raz, *The Morality of Freedom*, pp. 288–320; Scanlon, *What We Owe to Each Other*, pp. 108–43. The approach to well-being I criticize here is similar to the kind that Parfit calls a 'Desire-Fulfillment Theory'.

of Aristotle's theory. As we are about to see, it is a theory that faces insuperable difficulties. But recognizing where its defects lie will not be a merely negative exercise; working our way through subjectivism and rejecting it will lead us to appreciate the great plausibility of Aristotle's conception of well-being.

2.2. Which Attitude Makes Things Good?

Subjectivism about the good holds that something is made good for oneself—good as an end—by one's favorable attitude towards it. But what sort of favorable attitude makes something good for its own sake? Believing it to be good? Desiring it? Aiming at it? Intending it?

Often these attitudes are found together. For example: I intend to marry; I believe that it will be good for me to do so; and it is something I desire. The subjectivist might say that each of these attitudes makes marriage good for me—good not as a means, but as a component of living well.

But there is a serious problem here, for people[4] sometimes pursue goals without believing that it does them the least bit of good to do so. For example, suppose someone develops a deep hatred of a rival and devotes a large part of his life to humiliating and harming him. He might not care whether this project depletes his resources and undermines his own well-being. In fact, he may firmly believe that he is destroying himself as well as his enemy. Self-interest is not what motivates him; rather, he is consumed by hatred. By hypothesis, he is carrying out his plan, and doing what he desires. But he does not adopt or pursue his goal because he believes that his

---

[4] Here and throughout, I use 'people' and 'person' as a way of speaking about human beings or a particular human being. Aristotle's ethical and political theory is about *anthropoi*, and because he always uses that term to refer to one of the many species of living things, it is most accurately translated 'human beings' (not 'people'). But in practice it would be awkward always to avoid the terms 'people' or 'person' in discussing his theory, or even in translating him. (See e.g. *NE* V.5 1132b34–1133a1, X.9 1180a22–3; *Pol.* IV.4 1295b24–5; and my translations at 9.n.22, 9.n.39, 12.n.34.) His term *dēmos*, which is appropriately translated 'people', has a political connotation: it refers to the citizens of a democracy, and especially to those among them who are not members of any elite. Our use of the term 'people' often lacks this political connotation. An exception: when democracy is treated as a system of government that gives power to the people, the word 'people' is colored by the contrast it provides with 'elite'. Another term I find it impossible to avoid in my discussion of Aristotle is 'individual', even though nothing in his vocabulary corresponds to it. He says, for example, that the city is prior to each of us (*Pol.* I.2 1253a19–29), not that it is prior to the individual. But it would be cumbersome for a study of Aristotle's politics never to use the word 'individual'.

2.2. WHICH ATTITUDE MAKES THINGS GOOD?

well-being consists in carrying out this plan. On the contrary, he may believe that seeking his own well-being would require him to lead a very different kind of life.[5]

If one's aims determine where one's good lies, then our rancorous man is seeking his own good, despite his belief to the contrary. But surely it is more plausible to say that by dedicating himself to the destruction of his enemy, he reveals his indifference to his own good. After all, he himself describes his situation in that way. So the subjectivist would be well advised to hold that the attitude that makes something good for oneself as an end is one's belief: what one believes to be in itself good or bad for oneself really is such.

A different sort of example supports the same conclusion. The rancorous man just described aims at the destruction of his enemy, and accepts his own ruin as the price he must pay to achieve his goal. But it is possible to aim *directly* at what one knows to be contrary to one's own good. Suppose a man feels guilty for having committed a crime and therefore wants to punish himself. He seeks to atone for some great ill-gotten gain by doing an equally great amount of harm to himself. He intends, plans, and desires to do what he takes to be bad for himself. But if intending, planning, and wanting to do something make it good to do, then the subjectivist will be forced to accept the conclusion that the punishment this man assigns himself is good for him. That contradicts the self-punisher's conception of his plan of action. He believes that the painful experiences he imposes on himself are bad for him. He plans to punish himself precisely because he believes that he deserves to fare badly.[6]

If the subjectivist says that *believing* something to be bad makes it bad, then he can easily account for the badness of self-punishment, because the self-punisher takes the process he puts himself through to be bad for himself. On the other hand, if the subjectivist holds that *planning* to do something makes it *good* to do, then he must describe the self-punisher as someone who is doing himself some good, even though he, the self-punisher, mistakenly believes it to be bad.

The right move for the subjectivist to make at this point is to hold that our beliefs about what is good for us determine where our good

---

[5] The moral psychology I presuppose in this section conflicts with Aristotle's, for he assumes that no one can choose to harm himself (*NE* V.6 1134b9–12, V.9 1136b7–8). But there is nothing amiss in using non-Aristotelian materials to reach an Aristotelian conclusion.

[6] I use this example in 'Desire and the Human Good'.

lies. That is the form of subjectivism that will be examined here. But we will also see that many of the weaknesses in subjectivism remain, even if it holds that it is not beliefs but rather intentions, plans, or desires that create what is good for us.

2.3. *Does Thinking Make It So?*

The word 'good' is a member of a group of interconnected terms: 'bad', 'better than', 'worse than', 'equal to', 'best', 'worst', and the like. What subjectivism says about good applies to all of the other concepts in this family. It holds that if I believe something is bad for me, then it is bad for me; if I believe that one thing is (all things considered) better for me than another, then it is (all things considered) better for me than another. And of course, subjectivism also holds that if I do not believe that something is good (bad) for me, then it is not good (bad) for me.

Let us now subject this theory to criticism. The first point to notice is that people sometimes change their minds about what is good for themselves, and the subjectivist must therefore accept contradictory statements. Suppose that in January I come to believe that it will be better for me (all things considered) to get married and remain so for the rest of my adult life. But in February I change my mind and arrive at the opposite conclusion, namely that it would be best for me (all things considered) to remain single for the rest of my life. These two beliefs are about the same period of time: one favors and the other opposes my being in a state of matrimony for the rest of my life. So it cannot be the case that both beliefs are correct. But which should the subjectivist choose: January's belief or February's? Obviously, there is nothing to be said for picking one over the other. (A later decision is not better simply because it is later.) The subjectivist might try to evade this difficulty by saying that when one changes one's mind, neither the earlier nor the later belief can be correct. But why should this be accepted? It would be far more reasonable to allow for the possibility that when we change our minds, the opinion that is based on a more careful process of reflection is more likely to be correct.

(This difficulty will remain even if we reformulate subjectivism. Suppose the subjectivist holds that it is not my belief about what is good for me that makes things such, but rather my planning or deciding to do things. That alteration will not alleviate the difficulty at all. In January, I make plans to become and remain married for the rest of my life; in February, I plan to call the whole thing off, and to remain single forever. Is it on balance good for me or bad for me to get married? Both, if my plans and intentions create what is good for me. Once again, subjectivism leads to a contradiction.)

The underlying problem for subjectivism is that it is too lenient: it allows all beliefs of a certain kind—namely, beliefs about one's own good—to be correct; or it allows all intentions, plans, and decisions to be such that their fulfillment is good. But one's beliefs, plans, intentions, and the like can come into direct conflict with each other. They cannot all be creators of what is good.

Here is another way of seeing that something must be wrong with subjectivism: suppose I spend January and February trying to decide whether it will be good for me to marry, but throughout this period I remain uncertain, and in the end find myself unable to come to any resolution. I never form the belief that it will be better for me to marry; nor do I believe that it will be worse; nor do I believe that these are equally good alternatives. Since I lack these convictions, subjectivism holds that it is not true that it is good for me to marry (since I don't believe this), nor is it true that it is good for me to remain single (since I don't believe that), nor is it true that these alternatives are equal in value (since I don't hold that belief either).

But if this is a correct characterization of my situation, then why should I profess ignorance about the value of my options? I know that I lack both the belief that marriage is good for me and the belief that it is bad for me. So I can use the truth of subjectivism to infer that marriage is neither good nor bad for me. After all, I have not yet conferred positive or negative value on it by forming a belief about its goodness or badness. (Once again, a reformulation of subjectivism will not help. Suppose a subjectivist holds that it is our intentions or plans that create what is good for us, rather than our beliefs. That form of subjectivism will also reach the conclusion that, since I am unable to decide one way or the other, marriage is neither good nor bad for me. And my uncertainty about what to do should therefore be relieved.)

We should now be able to see that subjectivism is deeply at odds with the way we normally think about the major decisions we make about our future. When we take time to deliberate carefully about where our good lies, we go through a process of reflection that presupposes that if we are not careful, we might make a poor choice. Even when we think that all of our alternatives are good ones, we try to make the best decision we can, within the time we allot ourselves. When the stakes are large, we try to achieve some insight into the kind of person we are or hope to become, the kinds of relationship we seek with others, and the sorts of ambition it is reasonable for us to pursue. We are concerned not to overlook some important factor that should be given weight in our deliberations. We ask those who know us and our situation to advise us, and hope to learn from their experience. This entire process is guided by the thought that there are better and worse solutions to our problem, that we are not necessarily aware of them from the start, but that with enough care we can learn something about which the better solutions are.

The goal of deliberation is not merely the formation of some belief or other about what we should do, regardless of the content of that belief. We want our beliefs about our future good to be correct, and we think they are more likely to be correct if we look for reasons for and against alternative lines of action. If we entertain fresh doubts about a decision that we have already made, we do not suppose that in doing so we have changed the value of the alternatives between which we are choosing. There would be no point in changing our minds if we thought that our earlier decision could not have been mistaken. Rather, when we change our minds, we do so because we think that our having made a decision is by itself no assurance that we did so correctly. If we remain uncertain about what to do, and withhold judgment, that is because we think that the competing value of the alternatives is difficult for us to discern. But we think that considerations for and against these alternatives exist, waiting for our recognition, and are not the creations of our own thought.

All of these commonplace thoughts would be a delusion if subjectivism, as we have formulated it, were correct. Our ordinary methods of making decisions, and our attitudes towards vacillation and uncertainty, are based on the assumption that we can make mistakes about what is good for us, and that we need to be careful to avoid them. If subjectivism can offer us no reason to suppose that these ordinary deliberative practices are incorrect, then it has nothing to recommend it.[7]

---

[7] There is a form of subjectivism that escapes the objections put forward in this section. I turn to it ('ideal subjectivism') in 2.10.

2.4. Learning about Goods

Let us ask whether subjectivism is compatible with another simple truth about the human situation: we need help from each other in learning about what is good for us. The point is most easily recognized when we consider young children. Infants enter the world with no beliefs about what is or will be good for them, for they have no concept of goodness. If what is good for them were simply a matter of what they take to be good, nothing would be in their interest. At a later stage, children do begin to develop beliefs about what is good for them, but there are many important truths about their present and future well-being that remain beyond their grasp. To have a happy childhood, they must be introduced to activities that they would not know about without guidance from adults. And of course children will not do well as adults unless they begin to acquire the cognitive and social skills that are the stuff of later life. Left entirely to their own devices, children fail to recognize what is good for them during their childhood, and what will be good for them when they become adults. If parents are good caretakers, they know better than their children where their children's good lies, because they have learnt at least something from their own experience about what is good and what is bad.

Can subjectivism accommodate these commonplace ideas? Because it holds that my belief that something is good for me (alternatively: my plan, intention, or desire) is precisely what makes it good for me, it must say that whatever lies beyond my awareness— anything about which I have no beliefs (plans, intentions, desires)— is not yet something that has been made good for me. But this line of thought is at odds with the way parents reason about the good of their children. They want their children to develop certain skills and engage in various activities because they think this will be good for them, even though their children do not yet realize this. They think that if their children fail to learn these skills, and fail to believe that such skills are good for them, then that constitutes a great misfortune for their children. But according to subjectivism, if children fail to confer value on the social and cognitive skills that parents normally try to inculcate, then those aptitudes are not good for them, and they are none the worse for their failure. Subjectivism cannot agree that there are truths about one's well-being that one is unaware of, though they are known to others. For that would conflict with the thesis that one's own attitudes create what is good for oneself. This thesis evidently cannot accommodate the way we think about the well-being of children.

A further point can be made here: it is implausible to suppose that whatever children believe is good for them as an end really is good. (Similarly, it is doubtful that whatever they intend or desire is good for them.) Regarding their own good, children not only make errors of omission—that is, errors that consist in their failure to be aware of what is good for them—they also make errors of commission, in that they acquire mistaken beliefs about what is good for them. (And similarly, they form harmful desires and intentions.) Their cognitive skills are limited. There is therefore no reason to suppose that their intentions or judgments about what is good are constitutive of where their good lies.

The limitations of childhood persist, to some degree, throughout our lives. Our need to rely on others for ideas about what is good is part of being human. Consider a simple case. Suppose someone spends an hour walking to work every day, and finds nothing intrinsically desirable about doing so. He does not enjoy walking or the environment in which he walks; this is merely a way for him to stay in shape and get to his destination. But then a friend suggests to him that he would enjoy his walk, if he developed an interest in his environment. There are in fact many beautiful and unusual plants and birds along his way, and with no loss to himself he can find much enjoyment in recognizing and observing them. His friend offers to accompany him for several weeks, so that he can learn what to look for. All goes well, and, some time later, our walker fully enjoys his walks. By relying on the experience and advice of a friend, he has learned about a type of good that he was not aware of before. But someone who thinks that his beliefs about good things make them good for him has no reason to look for advice about what he may be missing. If he thinks he is missing nothing, if he has all that he desires, then, according to subjectivism, his life could not be better. Subjectivism thus falls into complacency: it blocks the thought that our conception of what is good might be too narrow, and that we have something to learn from others about our own well-being.[8]

---

[8] It is perhaps in order to avoid this narrowness that Rawls proposes what he calls a 'principle of inclusiveness' as a test for the rationality of a plan of life. He holds that one long-term plan is better than another 'if it allows for the encouragement and satisfaction of all the aims and interests of the other plan and for the encouragement and satisfaction of some further aim or interest in addition' (*A Theory of Justice*, p. 363). Rationality, so understood, requires us to develop an interest in goals, merely so that, having adopted them, we are then in a position to fulfill them. But we do not (and should not) make

We have been considering an example in which someone who lives in a world like ours learns about a new type of good. But in parts of the world where conditions of extreme deprivation prevail, there is widespread ignorance about many of the basic elements of a good life. Those who must concern themselves throughout their lives with bare survival may be so isolated from more fortunate people and so lacking in information about alternatives to their own way of life that they fail to realize how badly off they are. If they do have some idea of what they are missing, they may try to dismiss such thoughts, in order not to fall into greater despair. Habit might even lead them to be content with the little they have. According to subjectivism, if they do not believe that there are any goods that they lack, if their desires are as limited as their resources, then in fact there *is* nothing they are missing. But surely this cannot be right.[9] We should not shrink from saying that we who are more fortunate have a better idea of what a good life is. We have the good luck to have become familiar with many components of human well-being, and possess the resources needed to achieve them. What makes others worse off than us is that they cannot share fully enough in these goods. Whether they realize it or not, they are missing a great deal.

2.5. *Passion and Pleasure*

An inquiry into human well-being should not leave common sense behind. There is no reason for us to begin our investigation by abandoning all of our beliefs about what is good or bad, or at least the ones about which we have considerable confidence. In ordinary life,

---

long-term plans in this way. We do not abstract from their content and enlarge them merely in order to take on additional desires that can be fulfilled. When we ask whether we would like to have and achieve goals A, B, and C—or merely A and B, caring nothing for C—we cannot decide, unless we know something about what these letters designate. If we are assured that C is a good thing for us to have, then the larger plan is superior; but that is because more goods are better than fewer, not because it is a good thing to have and achieve a goal, regardless of what it is. It is only when we are fighting boredom or listlessness that we work up an interest in something, merely in order to increase our level of activity. (I take Scanlon, *What We Owe to Each Other*, pp. 119, 121, to be making a similar point, though he does not direct it against Rawls's principle of inclusiveness.)

[9] This objection to subjectivism is advanced by Sen in *On Ethics and Economics*, pp. 45–6. Sunstein, *The Partial Constitution*, pp. 162–94, uses this same phenomenon—adaptive preferences—to attack the thesis that, in democracies, governmental decisions must reflect existing preferences.

we act on the assumption that such things as misery, physical incapacitation, humiliation, pain, hunger, and loneliness are in themselves bad for people. Other things we implicitly treat as intrinsically good: friendship, pleasure, understanding, health, humor, and so on. And we take it for granted there are a great many things that are in themselves neither good nor bad: picking up sticks, blinking one's eyes, and the like.

Of course, these assumptions are not sacrosanct. Perhaps we will discover, as we carry out our investigation, that our list of goods and evils needs to be revised. In any case, it would be complacent to assume that we possess a *complete* list of the things that are good and bad. Nonetheless, there is no reason—as yet—for us to put on hold our belief that such things as friendship and pleasure are good, loneliness and poor health bad. Should we run into difficulties that can be traced back to these assumptions, we can always revise them. Until we do so, we should acknowledge their plausibility.[10]

If we are asked *why* we find it so plausible that pleasure and friendship are good, or pain and ill health bad, we can reply that we and nearly all other human beings have some experience of these things. It is unlikely that all of us have misinterpreted our experience—that, unbeknownst to us, pain is really good and pleasure really bad. Just as we become more confident in our perceptual judgments when they are confirmed by many other observers, each looking at the same phenomena from different positions in space, so we reasonably become more confident in our beliefs about what is good and bad when the experience of many different human beings regarding pleasure, friendship, health, and so on conforms with our own.

These commonplace assumptions about goods and evils lie behind a point made earlier (2.2): people sometimes carry out plans that they know will be ruinous to their well-being, because they care

---

[10] The methodology I adopt owes much to Aristotle (whose ideas about method will be discussed more fully at 3.1–5). Contrast the one proposed by Sumner in *Welfare, Happiness, and Ethics*, pp. 18–19. He argues that a theory of well-being must set aside all assumptions about how life should be lived, because they merely express personal preferences and are likely to be biased. An Aristotelian methodology is defended by McDowell throughout many of the essays of *Mind, Value, and Reality*. See e.g. 'Some Issues in Aristotle's Moral Psychology', p. 36, where he applauds Aristotle for standing 'in a line of descent from Socrates' commendation of the examined life' without 'stepping outside the standpoint constituted by an inherited mode of thought, so as to supply it (if all goes well) with an external validation'. An 'external validation' of a theory of well-being is one that begins by putting in doubt all assumptions about goodness and what is good—precisely what Sumner thinks we must do.

little about themselves. Someone driven by hatred may devote a large part of his life to the destruction of his enemy, even though he believes that the cost to himself will be great, and that he would have a far better life were he to let bygones be bygones. We recognize this to be a plausible example, because we can easily imagine how the single-minded pursuit of the destruction of others can undermine one's physical well-being, destroy one's family and friends, and cut short one's life. These things we reasonably assume to be evils. And yet people are willing to accept them as the necessary cost of destroying their enemies. That shows that fulfilling our desires and successfully executing our plans is not what constitutes our well-being.

But suppose we were to come across someone who leads a life devoted to the destruction of his enemies, but insists that he is not in fact sacrificing his well-being at all. He claims that it is not good for him to have friends or a family; he regards physical injuries as a matter of indifference; and he does not consider the fear and anxiety he experiences on a regular basis to be bad things. Furthermore, he holds that persecuting his enemies is in itself a good thing for him. So, he judges his life to be a good one: it contains the one thing that is good for him, and it involves no sacrifice.

Subjectivism says that this man's belief must be true: persecuting his enemies is by itself good for him, because he believes it to be so. But surely it is reasonable to ask whether he is in a favorable position to make this judgment. He is a man in the grip of hatred. Such a person does not arrive at his plan to persecute his enemies by first asking himself what sort of life he thinks will be in his best interest, and then, after carefully considering a wide range of options, deciding that his best option will be to forego all of the things that others consider good, in order to destroy his enemies. He is driven by a passion for revenge, and we know that people in this condition do not think clearly, if they think at all, about their future well-being. (They may of course be thinking extremely well about how to destroy their enemies.) If someone bent on a life of vengeance denies that he is making any sacrifices, because he does not believe that ill health and social isolation would be good things for him to have, we need not take his belief to be true, because we can plausibly claim that he is in a poor position to make that judgment. When certain psychological forces—hatred, anger, spite, and the like—become too intense, they deflect people from making sound judgments about what is good or bad for themselves. If such people believe that nothing is good for them except the destruction of their enemies, we can regard this belief as a device by means of which they keep themselves single-mindedly devoted to their destructive tasks. They refuse to give serious consideration to the possibility that they are doing themselves great harm, because such a thought might diminish their resolve to harm others. So the subjectivist thesis that we must accept whatever people believe about their well-being is far too crude. It overlooks our normal standards for distinguishing between cases in which people are well positioned to judge what is good for them and cases in which they are not.

Of course, someone bent on revenge can take considerable pleasure from seeing his enemies humiliated. He knows what this experience is like, and his characterization of it as extremely pleasant seems plausible to the rest of us. Who has not sometimes been pleased to hear of the troubles of people he dislikes? We do not have to devote ourselves to the destruction of others in order to have reason to believe that those who achieve this goal can derive considerable pleasure from doing so.

But that point does not by itself prove that pleasure taken in the destruction of others is a good thing. To reach that conclusion we would have to ask whether pleasure is to some extent good regardless of the circumstances in which it occurs, and regardless of the kind of pleasure it is. Can pleasure lose the goodness it ordinarily has, when it is directed at certain objects? Suppose, for the sake of argument, that a full discussion of that question came to the conclusion that pleasure is always good, regardless of what one is pleased by. That conclusion would provide no support for subjectivism; on the contrary, it would give us one additional reason for rejecting it. For, if reflection on the nature of pleasure leads us to agree that it is always good, then we have, by means of such reflection, rejected the thesis that what makes something good for someone is his belief that it is good (or his desire for it, or any other favorable attitude or pursuit of it). Rather, our position would be: someone who denies that pleasure is good, or who has lost all desire for it, is making a mistake.

Alternatively, reflection on the nature and value of pleasure might lead to the conclusion that enjoying the destruction of others is not even slightly good. That result should also lead us to reject the claim that whatever someone takes to be good really is such. (After all, many people do suppose that it is good for them to enjoy the misfortunes of others.) So, in either case—whether all pleasures are good

2.5. PASSION AND PLEASURE

or only some are good—we arrive at the conclusion that it is not a person's belief that something is good for him that makes it so.

Pleasure is often used as a guide to what is good for us, and there is sound reason for this. It is difficult to sustain our confidence that something is good—in itself, and not merely as a means—if it gives us no enjoyment at all. At any rate, much that is widely thought to be good (for example, friendship, understanding, health) offers considerable pleasure. But it does not follow that pleasure alone is good. Other things may lose their goodness when unaccompanied by pleasure, but that would hardly show that what pleasure accompanies is not also good. In fact, reflection might lead us to conclude that pleasure diminishes in goodness, when what we take pleasure in is not also good for us. We should not assume that pleasure always has the same amount of value, regardless of its object, and regardless of the circumstances in which it is felt. And if it does vary in its degree of goodness, depending on what its object is, then why can its value not sometimes sink to zero?

Pleasure is not our principal topic, and so we must leave these questions aside. What must be emphasized is that subjectivism derives no support from the central role that pleasure plays in a good life—assuming, until we have reason to think otherwise, that it does play such a role. According to the subjectivist, we must say about someone who convinces himself that pleasure is not worth pursuing and should not be welcomed (either because he has been ruined by the lure of pleasure at an earlier point in his life, or because he has read philosophical attacks on pleasure): he is not missing anything that would make his life better. If we think that a person who has these attitudes towards pleasure is making a mistake, and is living less well than he might, then we have rejected subjectivism. And surely we should reject it, because it is plausible to think that our lives are enhanced to some degree by pleasure. We know what it is like to enjoy things, and there is no reason to suspect that so many of our fellow human beings are completely wrong about the value of such experiences. We are therefore in a good position to reject the idea that nothing would be missed by someone who regarded pleasure as a matter of indifference.

Having reached this conclusion about pleasure, there is no reason not to extend it to other things that are widely thought to be good by those who have experienced them: such things as friendship, health, and understanding. We should not think of these states as mere means to pleasure, devoid of intrinsic goodness. Friendship, for example, would lose much of its value if it were thought of as a mere means to something else. It is good for its own sake, and when it is valued in this way, it brings its own peculiar kind of pleasure. The good is multiform; there is not just one kind of thing that is good for its own sake, whether that one thing is pleasure or anything else. Someone who fails to recognize this diversity, and who places value on only one type of good, is missing a great deal. That is one more commonplace that subjectivism cannot accommodate.

Taking our argument one step further, we are now ready to see in another way that what is good for someone need not be something he plans, intends, desires, or thinks good. Pleasures and some other goods sometimes come to us unbidden, without our going after them—in fact, even when we have tried to avoid them. For example: a man's wife plans a party for him, against his objections. (He doesn't want to burden her or the people she invites.) She carries out her plans, and as the party gets under way, he realizes that, though this is something he does not want, he is thoroughly enjoying himself. No plan of his has been executed; he preferred that the party not take place. He might even be one of those people who don't think that such frivolous pleasures as these are good. But that would not prevent them from being so. Our beliefs about what is good, our desires, and our plans often move us towards what is good; but at times what is good is moved towards us, without our going after it. Subjectivism goes wrong not only in its thesis that the psychological forces that impel us towards things make them good, but also in its thesis that only such forces can make something good.

2.6. *The Politics of Subjectivism*

Despite its many defects, subjectivism is an alluring doctrine, because it accords with the culture of our times—or so it seems. The liberal political tradition grants to each citizen a zone of privacy and freedom, within which he is allowed to devise a life according to his own lights, unhindered by social pressure or criticism. If someone does no harm to others, the rest of us should mind our own business, and not make negative judgments about the way he conducts his private life. Subjectivism therefore seems to have a salutary effect: it deprives us of any basis for criticizing others, so long as they restrict themselves to making judgments about themselves.

Furthermore, our culture of autonomy encourages the thought

that in designing our lives there is no mold, no obligatory pattern, to which we ought to conform. Since we are autonomous, nothing beyond our will should dictate to us the terms in which we ought to fashion a good life for ourselves. One is free to create one's good from one's imagination, like an artist faced with an empty canvas. Human beings are different from the rest of nature in that we are choosers of our own ends: what is good for us is something we must invent, and we misconceive our situation if we suppose that there are facts about what our final ends should be, facts that exist independently of our decisions about how to lead our lives.

In any case, it might be said that if there were such facts, we would expect a consensus to have emerged by now about what they are, and there would be a field of study that would lead to a scientific understanding of what is good or bad for human beings. But obviously no such area of expertise has been established. Philosophers do not know any better than others what our final ends should be, and it would be arrogant for them to claim such expertise. Nothing entitles them or anyone else to adopt such a position of superiority. Each of us knows best what his own final ends should be—and the best explanation for this point is that adopting something as a final end is precisely what makes it worthwhile.

Finally, subjectivism may derive some of its appeal from the appearance that its widespread acceptance would give our social world a pleasing diversity. The subjectivist might say, in defense of this doctrine, that a community that adheres to a single conception of a well-lived life is one of oppressive uniformity. We should be glad that there are many different styles of life, and many different ideas about what is good and bad. So long as each of us pursues the good as he conceives it without interfering with the like pursuit of others, our lives are enriched by the multiplicity of our many different conceptions of well-being. Subjectivism seems to underwrite a diverse society; its rejection might be thought to open the door to stifling uniformity.

2.7. *Endless Controversies*

How should we respond to these points? Consider, to begin with, the claim that no universal agreement about final ends has emerged. That is a point that can be used against subjectivism itself, and against nearly every philosophical theory—including theories about the nature of justice and other aspects of political and ethical life. We should not excuse ourselves from pursuing difficult questions in areas of controversy simply because they are difficult and controversial. After all, subjectivism itself does not shy away from such matters. It is a doctrine that seeks to solve, once and for all, the question of what is good; it does so not by telling us specifically what we are to pursue (pleasure, friendship, and the like) but by assuring us that, once we have formed our beliefs about where our own good lies, or have developed our plans, whatever we have selected must be good for us. Subjectivism does not withdraw from the philosophical arena, but is one of the contenders among competing doctrines. It must therefore be evaluated on its merits, like any other philosophical doctrine.

Furthermore, we should reject the claim that there is no consensus at all about what is good or bad for human beings. Pleasure, for example, is sought and considered good by nearly every human being. At any rate, there is little disagreement about the point that certain kinds of pleasure (for example, the pleasure of listening to music) are desirable for their own sake. Although some philosophers have held that pleasure is never good, that gives us no good reason to suspend judgment about its value.[11] If we find the arguments proposed by these philosophers to be unpersuasive, then we are justified in continuing to believe that pleasures, or at least some of them, are good things. And that is not the only item that nearly all human beings place in the category of goods.

Can philosophical reflection lead to the conclusion that other things are good in themselves, besides the small number that are already widely acknowledged to be such? That is a question that can be answered only through a process of trial and error. But it would certainly be premature, at this early stage in our discussion, to agree that philosophers do not know any better than others what our final ends should be, for we are about to investigate whether that statement applies to one philosopher in particular—Aristotle. The issue before us is not whether philosophers as a group have a special kind of wisdom as regards human well-being, but whether we have something to learn in this domain from some of them. Our goal need not be described as 'scientific understanding' or 'expertise' about what is good or bad. It would be better to say that we are engaged in the more modest task of making at least some improvements in our

---

[11] Aristotle confronts this thesis at *NE* VII.11–13, X.2–3.

beliefs about these matters, and therefore in the conduct of our lives. We should not shrink from this reasonable goal simply because it would be presumptuous to suppose that we will achieve something grander—something we could call 'expertise' about the good, or 'scientific understanding' of it.

2.8. Freedom

Let us turn to another idea that lies behind the appeal of subjectivism in our political culture: Unlike other animals, we are free to lead a life of our own devising. They are confined by their nature to certain patterns of behavior, but for us there is no pre-established mold that dictates to us how we should live. It would be a misinterpretation of our situation and a denial of our freedom if we were to suppose that there are facts about our good to which we must conform.[12] Therefore, what is good for oneself is one's own creation or invention. There is no body of truths about one's well-being that exists independently of one's will.

But is it true to say that human beings in all conditions and circumstances are free to lead lives of their own devising? We would not make that statement about people who live under a tyrannical regime—a regime that gives them no say about who their friends are to be, what kind of work they will do, where they may travel, and the like. Nor would we say that an abandoned infant is free to live as he chooses. Similarly, those whose lives are used up in a relentless and anxious struggle to find nourishment are not free to lead lives of their own choosing. It is only in special circumstances that we have the kind of freedom that has significant value. What is good for us is to have attractive options, to be aware of what those options are, and

---

[12] Something like this idea is endorsed by Putnam in *The Many Faces of Realism*, pp. 46–51, although he does not accept subjectivism as I define it. He claims that our autonomy depends on the unknowability of our good, an insight he attributes to Rawls and Kant. 'Kant's ideal community is a community of beings who think for themselves without knowing what the "human essence" is, without knowing what "Eudaemonia" is, and who respect one another for doing that' (p. 51). In 'Kantian Constructivism in Moral Theory', Rawls holds that the rational intuitionism that 'dominated moral philosophy from Plato and Aristotle onward until it was challenged by Hobbes and Hume' (and is still found in Sidgwick, Moore, and Ross) is incompatible with autonomy, and credits Kant with this insight (p. 343). It is not clear that Aristotle (or, for that matter, Plato) is a rational intuitionist in Rawls's sense, since this doctrine holds that the first principles of morality are self-evident and that there is a 'moral order that is prior to and independent of our conception of the person and the social role of morality' (p. 344). Neither thesis can be found in Aristotle (though the second might plausibly be attributed to Plato).

to have the mental and external resources needed to pursue them. If we live in unfortunate circumstances, and the only choices we are free to make are between alternatives that are equally bad for us, then the kind of freedom we have is of no value.

What makes unfortunate circumstances unfortunate? By what standard are we to determine whether the choices one faces are good or bad? The subjectivist makes each individual the arbiter of these matters. If, for example, a prisoner is free to choose whether he should spend his days picking up sticks or picking up stones, we should not, according to subjectivism, impose on him our own ideas about whether he has a worthwhile kind of freedom. *We* think that these two activities are in themselves neither good nor bad, and that his freedom to choose among them is therefore worthless; but the prisoner may think otherwise, and subjectivism holds that it is the prisoner's judgment that determines the value of his alternatives. Similarly, the subjectivist would be forced to admit that if someone prefers to live under a tyrannical regime rather than under conditions of freedom, because he likes austerity and authority, then that is the better alternative for him. When freedom is construed as a politically meaningful concept—that is, when it is the sort of thing that is diminished or obliterated by tyrants and poverty—then it is, according to the subjectivist, good only for those who judge it to be good. That subjectivist judgment does not accord with the way we normally think about the value of freedom.

The kind of freedom the subjectivist thinks human beings have is not the sort that is created by some political systems and destroyed by others. Rather, it is the freedom one has if there are no facts about what is good for oneself, apart from what one believes good, or desires or plans to do. The subjectivist would feel oppressed living in a world in which human beings can be mistaken about where their good lies, for in such a world the way we ought to live is 'dictated' to us by facts about which things are good and bad for us. Only a world in which whatever we choose to do is good will satisfy him as one that offers us a genuine choice about how to lead our lives. In such a world, there would be a zone in which we need feel no sense of accountability or responsibility for the choices we make; in the realm of our own ultimate good, mistakes and criticism have no place. The responsibility we normally have to get things right would be suspended. And the subjectivist might argue that our liberal political culture is founded on the recognition that human beings possess this zone of freedom. We do not criticize people for pursuing the

2.8. FREEDOM

good according to their own lights, so long as they harm no one else; for there can be no basis for such criticism.

What should we make of this? Notice, first, that the subjectivist cannot be understood to be making a recommendation. He cannot be taken to be saying that it would be good for all of us to allow each other an area of activity and thought in which we do not hold each other accountable. The subjectivist cannot present the kind of freedom that comes with the absence of facts about well-being as a good thing, for he insists that whether or not such freedom is good for someone depends on that individual's judgment. What the subjectivist must be taken to mean is that this sort of freedom is something we have, regardless of whether we want it to exist or think it a good thing. And it is something that young children have no less than adults. It would make no sense to suppose that there are facts about what is good for children—facts that are independent of their desires and beliefs—but that as they develop into adults, these facts mysteriously fade away.

But we realized long ago (2.4) that children can acquire final ends that are bad for them to fulfill, as well as mistaken beliefs about what is good for them to pursue. We try to have some influence over our children's conception of well-being, and we assume that if we leave them entirely without guidance in the formation of their goals, they will fare badly. It is only adults who are allowed, in liberal societies, to pursue their good as they see fit, so long as they do not harm others. And therefore our basis for this policy of toleration cannot be that there are no facts about what a human being's final ends should be. On the contrary, those who favor such toleration might believe that the final ends of their fellow citizens are a waste of time or even self-destructive. They refrain from interfering because they believe they owe it to others to allow them to go their own way, even to their ruin. Toleration does not presuppose that the behavior tolerated is good. On the contrary, it is precisely when one thinks that others are mistaken about their well-being that one needs to call upon oneself to be tolerant of them.

It is when human beings become adults, and live in communities that make available to them abundant resources and opportunities, that they become free to live lives of their own devising, and to call upon their imagination and inventiveness as they choose and pursue their ends. If we believe (quite plausibly) that one of the things that makes a way of life appealing is the scope it gives to such qualities as creativity, ingenuity, and resourcefulness, then we should acknowledge that we are advancing a claim about what is good for human beings—a claim that is incompatible with subjectivism. These qualities of mind do not require, for their development and exercise, a sphere in which our normal responsibility to respond to the criticism of others is suspended. Think of how much ingenuity and imagination is needed for the invention of new devices and strategies for achieving our ends. A clever new tool is something that must pass muster: it must provide a better way to get the job done. Its designer's belief that it is good does not make it so. Similarly, it is no easy matter, but takes unusual qualities of mind, to expand or refine our received stock of ideas about what is good in itself. But new ideas about the components of well-being are not made true by virtue of someone's thinking them so: they too must be subjected to criticism, and to the tests of experience and reflection. It would be wrong to assume, then, that if we reject subjectivism, we leave no room for creativity in the conduct of our lives, and are restricted to living unreflectively and unimaginatively in conformity with a pre-established pattern.

In any case, there is no reason to suppose that if we do live in accordance with certain well-established ideas about which ultimate ends are good—if, for example, we take friendship, pleasure, understanding, health, and the like to be our goals—then we are not living well. It would be absurd to hold that the *only* genuine goods are those one has discovered on one's own. It is only a more modest claim that has been put forward here: that although many genuine goods have long been familiar to human beings, we are not entitled to assume that they are the only ones there are. Nor should we complacently take it for granted that we already have an adequate understanding of what is involved in friendship, pleasure, health, and other widely recognized goods, and how they are best achieved. These points entitle us to reject the idea that if we do not embrace subjectivism, we must live in conformity with accepted ideas about what is good.

2.9. *Diversity*

Let us now take up the suggestion (made in 2.6) that subjectivism is appealing because, if it were generally accepted, many different ways of life would flourish, and our social world would contain a pleasing diversity. The thought is as follows. If, as subjectivism maintains, I confer goodness on things through my beliefs or plans, then there is no reason for me to look outside myself for a model of how to live. Nor is there reason for others to criticize or interfere with my pursuit of my good, provided I am harming no one else. When each person views himself as having limitless options in his choice of what is good, and sees no reason to criticize or interfere with others in their pursuit of their good, the result will be a society that contains a great variety of ways of life. Those who are attracted by this vision of society may find subjectivism alluring because they think it provides the philosophical foundation for such a society. Conversely, it might be thought that the rejection of subjectivism must be motivated by an oppressive vision of social life. The subjectivist asks: do we really want to live in a world in which everyone has the same conception of what is good and bad? Surely that would be dull and stifling. Since subjectivism does not endorse any one way of life as being superior to any other—since, in fact, it regards all such endorsements as wrongheaded—it can present itself as a doctrine that is favorable to the formation of a diverse society.

How should we respond to this? We can begin with the point that a community in which subjectivism is widely accepted might itself contain a stifling uniformity. Of course, by hypothesis, its members would be alike in their acceptance of subjectivism. But that need not be the only point on which they agree. They might also pursue the same ends and have the same beliefs about what is good. Even though each regards himself as having the power to confer goodness through his beliefs and plans, all might confer goodness on the same things. In fact, many of them might simply imitate the choices made by a handful of others. The acceptance of subjectivism is compatible with mindless conformism in the shaping of desires, plans, and beliefs about what is good. A society in which subjectivism is the reigning philosophical thesis about well-being can be one in which most people lack independence of mind and fall in with the pattern set by a few others.

Furthermore, significant differences of opinion and an agreeable diversity in ways of life can exist in a society in which subjectivism is not the reigning philosophical thesis about well-being, and in which there is no disagreement about which final ends are good. To see this, we need only notice that certain worthwhile activities are enhanced when there is considerable variation in people's tastes, abilities, and ideas. Music provides a common example: it is enriched by the complexity and variety that occurs when different styles and traditions develop, and many instruments, each with its distinctive emotional appeal, are played. Furthermore, in many areas of life, diversity of opinion has great instrumental value. Philosophy and science thrive and sometimes progress through controversy. An exchange of views between opposing doctrines sometimes leads all parties to modify their first thoughts and make improvements in their theories. Similarly, political life can be enhanced by the existence of organized parties devoted to criticizing governmental policies. Even relaxation can be enhanced by opposition. In competitive games we artificially create rivalry, because the pursuit of incompatible goals creates a drama that takes us away from our ordinary lives.

Notice that in each of these cases, variety and opposition exist within a broader context of uniformity and agreement. The members of an ensemble must be united by a common interest in the music they are playing, or else they will not play well. Scientific and philosophical disagreements can exist only among those who share a common interest in these pursuits. If opposed political parties are not unified by an acceptance of at least some common goals, there will be nothing for them to discuss. What these examples indicate is that there is considerable room for variation and disagreement, even when people are unified by their pursuit of common ultimate ends. In fact, shared ideas about ends and common tastes make fruitful variation and disagreement possible. When people have nothing in common, when their conceptions of what is worthwhile, right, and pleasant do not overlap, they have little reason to interact with each other, and will not easily form a stable community. In a society divided into sub-communities each of which regards the ends of other groups as self-destructive, there would be no enthusiasm for cooperation between groups. Why provide resources to those whose conception of the good is leading them to their ruin—except perhaps to hasten their destruction? A well-functioning society needs some common understanding about what is good and what is right.[13] And there may be some goods that cannot be fully achieved unless nearly every member of the

---

[13] Rawls holds, by contrast, that there is 'no urgency to reach a publicly accepted judgment as to what is the good of particular individuals' (*A Theory of Justice*, p. 393). I take him to mean not merely that *different* conceptions of well-being are welcome, but also that *disagreements* are not matters of social concern. (A mere difference occurs when A's good consists in X-ing, but B's does not. A disagreement occurs when A takes his good to consist in X-ing, but B thinks X-ing is bad for A.)

community recognizes them as valuable and cooperates in pursuing them. Suppose, for example, that active democratic citizenship is a good, and not merely a means to a further end. Obviously, it is a good that cannot be acquired in a community that contains only a few members who recognize its value.

Disagreement is not in itself a good thing. When it serves no useful purpose, it can be quite bad. It would not, for example, add to the attractiveness of our society if it contained a thousand conflicting ideas about which foods are safe to eat. It is best if certain matters are taken to be settled and widely acknowledged. Controversy is to be welcomed only when an issue is not yet well understood and profits from being examined from several different points of view. And this applies to ends no less than means. It would surely serve no useful purpose if there were disagreement about whether health or loving relations among people are good, or whether humiliation and pain are bad for them.

Of course, we are glad that not everyone plays the same instrument, and that not everyone wants to pursue the same career. But these examples of fruitful variety do not show that it is good for people to disagree in their conceptions of which final ends are worth pursuing. People pursue different lines of work because they have different opportunities, talents, and interests—not because they have conflicting beliefs about what is good. Those who enter public service, for example, are not making a choice that commits them to disagreeing with those who pursue a career in the arts about what is the best kind of life for a human being to lead. The variation in ways of life that makes for a flourishing and rich society is not an opposition in conceptions of the good. Not all differences are disagreements.

A community of people who reject subjectivism and agree with each other about which things are ultimately good and bad can exhibit great variety. Universal agreement that the development of talent is a great good does not necessarily lead to uniformity; on the contrary, so long as a wide variety of talents are appreciated, such agreement would foster a society of considerable variety. And we should keep in mind the point made in the previous section: universal agreement about which things are good would not prevent us from acknowledging that our inventory of goods may be incomplete, and that future generations may come to recognize goods that have escaped our notice. The rejection of subjectivism is entirely compatible with an eagerness to conduct 'experiments of living' that promise to lead to the invention of new final ends.[14] It is a mistake to suppose that subjectivism provides the philosophical foundation of a diverse society, or that its rejection must lead to rigid uniformity.

2.10. *Ideal Subjectivism*

There is a form of subjectivism that concedes that one's actual beliefs, desires, or plans do not necessarily create one's good. Ideal subjectivism, as we might call it, holds that the self that is the creator of one's good is the person who would emerge when everything that impedes one's ability to think clearly about one's well-being has been stripped away, and everything that enhances that ability is added.[15]

What would be involved in such a process of cognitive improvement? An idealized version of oneself should have more information about the future than most of us normally have. It would be free of any forms of irrationality that interfere with one's ability to make practical decisions. Presumably an ideal self will also have the creativity needed to imagine options that do not occur to one's real self. If the points we have made against subjectivism are correct, then the metamorphosis advocated by ideal subjectivism must be rather extensive. The new self must not simply be that version of the old self that is best able to make decisions about how to accomplish the goals of the old self. For our critique of subjectivism argued that one's ends, and not merely one's means, can lead to one's ruin, and that one's beliefs about what is in itself good for oneself can be mistaken. So the process that takes me to my ideal self must be one that guarantees that this new self is beyond criticism in its selection of ends, and not merely in the means it proposes to achieve them.

But if the transformative process is this extensive, then it would be an illusion to think that we already know everything that needs to be included in it, or when it should come to an end, or what conclusions it would reach. For consider: in order to enhance someone's cognitive skills so that he is better able to think about what ends he should have, should we not require him to read some

---

[14] John Stuart Mill's term. See *On Liberty*, Chapter 3, paragraph 1.
[15] A view of this sort is advanced by Brandt, *A Theory of the Good and the Right*, pp. 1–162. For criticism, see Velleman, 'Brandt's Definition of Good'; and for a sympathetic overview, Rosati, 'Brandt's Notion of Therapeutic Agency'. The process of idealization Brandt proposes is far more limited than the one I suggest in this section. There is also some degree of idealization in Rawls's complex version of subjectivism. See *A Theory of Justice*, p. 366.

philosophical works? Presumably we should, for there is a considerable philosophical literature devoted to the question of how one should lead one's life, filled with arguments about which final ends we should adopt for our own good. How much of this literature should one read? Surely all of it; after all, an ideal self is not pressed for time. But philosophical works are not the only items that should be put on the ideal self's reading list. Novelists, poets, and all sorts of imaginative writer have ideas about what is good and how one should live one's life. The list of works that must be considered is endless.

But the fatal objection that should be made against ideal subjectivism is not that the process of producing a perfect self is indeterminate in length, or that we have no clear sense of what would bring it to a conclusion. Rather, it is this: once we see all that is involved in the production of a perfect self, we should realize that psychological attitudes—even the beliefs, desires, or plans of an ideal self—do not make things good for someone. If we suppose, for example, that an ideal self would come to the conclusion that pleasure is always good to some extent, regardless of its object, then our supposition must rest on our conviction that this is the right conclusion for anyone to reach—not on the hypothesis that this thesis is made so by someone's thinking it. If the transformation of the real self into the ideal self includes the assessment of philosophical ideas and theories, then the conclusions at which the ideal self arrives are not made true by their being thought true. If the desires and plans formed by a philosophically enriched self are good to satisfy, that is because the thinking that leads to those desires and plans stands up to criticism. The idea that psychological attitudes create one's good is entirely out of place here.

2.11. *Aristotle's Universalism Restored*

Now that we have seen how many difficulties beset subjectivism, we should be ready to return to Aristotle's project with renewed interest.[16] Certain generalizations about human good and bad seem far more plausible than subjectivism about the good. Physical incapacitation, humiliation, pain, and loneliness are in

---

[16] Some further differences between subjectivism and Aristotle's theory of the good are discussed in 3.n.8 and 3.13.

themselves bad for people; friendship, pleasure, understanding, and health are intrinsically good. Further reflection can only strengthen this conviction: Is there any human being for whom it is good to be filled with anxiety, boredom, or self-doubt over the course of a lifetime? Anyone for whom the absence of zest, enthusiasm, and joy would not make his life less worth leading? Anyone for whom it would not be a loss to be indifferent to beauty, or unable to associate with others on friendly terms, or incapable of taking pleasure in the use of the senses, or totally lacking in humor?

These thoughts can be given further support if we remind ourselves of some highly general features of human life, and some assumptions we make about our proper development. When we are young, we need care and supervision. Unless we are extremely unfortunate, we enter into social relations with each other, express (and sometimes suppress) certain emotions, seek pleasure and avoid pain, learn to speak and understand a language, go through a period of sexual maturation, acquire greater self-command, intelligence, and understanding. Not all members of our species experience all of these things; disease or mishap sometimes prevents them from doing so. But we confidently take these human beings to be unfortunate, and do all we can to foster normal development. In doing so, we presuppose that certain things are good for all members of our species.

These reflections suggest that in seeking a conception of well-being that holds true for all human beings, Aristotle is working at the right level of generality. But it might be objected that he should have been more general still. Perhaps he should have asked, not merely what is good for human beings, but what is good for all primates? Or perhaps: all living things? We can reply, on his behalf, that there is nothing arbitrary about choosing human beings as the unit of investigation, because some of the points just made about normal human development do not apply at all, or at least not in the same way, to other species. Our social relations, linguistic skills, and emotions seem sufficiently different from those of other species to make a special investigation of the human good a reasonable undertaking. Even if certain things are good or bad for human beings and other primates alike (pleasure and pain, for example), they are transformed by our attitudes towards them, and take on a peculiarly human shape. And other goods—for example, music, beauty, understanding, humor, games—seem to be available to our species alone, even when they arise out of the rudimentary traces of these goods in certain primates.

The conclusion at which we have arrived is a modest one: there is reason to have confidence in some broad generalizations about the well-being of all human beings, at all times and places. Subjectivism (in both its simple and its ideal forms) does not deny this; it too offers a universal account of the human good, but it refuses to direct us towards certain goals rather than others, and its weakness lies precisely there. What we must explore, in the next chapter, is whether we can go beyond the secure but unexciting truths on which our critique of subjectivism depended: namely, that we can list some things that are good and others that are bad for all human beings. Aristotle offers us a theory of the good that has considerably more structure and detail than a mere list of goods and evils. And he uses his conception of human well-being to construct a critique of existing political communities, and a vision of an ideal society. Now that the ground has been cleared, and we see that the type of theory he offers cannot plausibly be dismissed from the start, we can turn to the rich details of his political philosophy.

3
Well-Being and Virtue

3.1. Beyond a List of Goods

This much has emerged from our rejection of subjectivism in Chapter 2: if our aim is to improve our beliefs about well-being, and thereby to improve our lives, a reasonable first step is to begin with what we know—or, at any rate, with what we think we know. As a working hypothesis, we can say that misery, physical incapacitation, humiliation, pain, hunger, and loneliness are in themselves bad; and that friendship, pleasure, understanding, health, and humor are good.[1] Those who have experienced these things so regard them, and their opinion should not be lightly dismissed.

But this does not take us very far. Questions quickly arise. Are there more good things than one person can possibly possess? If so, how is one to decide which of them to pursue? Is that an arbitrary matter? Are all goods equally good, all evils equally bad? That would be incredible. We often need to decide which of two evils is the lesser; and we forego certain small pleasures to preserve a friendship or maintain our health. But how should we go about making these comparisons? Is there a way to determine which goods and evils are the most important to pursue or avoid? Can reflection help us guard against overvaluing and undervaluing things?

---

[1] The Aristotelian theory of well-being we are exploring might therefore be called an 'Objective List Theory', to use Parfit's terminology (*Reasons and Persons*, app. I). But although Aristotle's theory is objective in some sense (it does not embrace the kind of subjectivism discussed in Ch. 2), it has far more structure and theoretical backing than the term 'list' implies.

Our ability to list things that are good or bad is not necessarily accompanied by a deep understanding of the items on these lists. Consider friendship. Surely some people know better than others what it is and how it is sustained. And it ought to be possible, through experience and reflection, to come to a better understanding of what it is, and why it is valuable. Among the questions we might ask ourselves about it are these: Is it worth pursuing in part because it normally leads to other valuable things? Would it be worth having, even if it led to nothing else? Is it good in all circumstances—regardless of the sort of people our friends are? Does its value depend on how it is combined with other goods? Is it always better, all other things being equal, to have more friends? Are there some things that we cannot have too much of? Others that we should have only a certain amount of? Into which category does friendship fall?

These are precisely the sorts of question Aristotle thinks we should be asking. Like us, he believes that the right place to start an inquiry into well-being is to take note of the multiplicity of good things, and then to move beyond a mere listing of them. By pursuing these sorts of questions, he arrives at a systematic account of how human beings should live their lives, an account that he thinks will be of considerable practical value to his audience. Therefore, when we read him, we should ask whether his theory accomplishes what it sets out to do. Does he have something of practical value to say, not only to his contemporaries, but to us as well? Does he offer us persuasive considerations for accepting his conception of well-being —if not entirely, then at least in part?

I said earlier (2.1) that we should regard Aristotle's conception of the human good as an attractive framework for thinking about our lives. It contains deep insights, even though it also needs modification and development. In this chapter I will explain why we should hold his conception of well-being in such high regard, and why it remains an unfinished project.

3.2. *The Organization of Goods*

The *Nicomachean Ethics* starts with what *seems* good to us: 'Every craft and every inquiry, and similarly every action and choice, seems to aim at some good' (I.1 1094a1–2).[2] Eventually, we want to know

---

[2] Here and throughout, translations are my own, unless otherwise indicated.

what *is* good—not just what seems so; and, to the extent that we can, we want to be able to explain why the things that seem good to us really are good. But, Aristotle assumes, when we first start reflecting on what is good, we do not have this kind of understanding.

To acquire such knowledge, we must organize our initial beliefs about what is good, so that they are no longer a mere hodgepodge of isolated opinions.³ The first step we take is to notice that apparent goods are extremely heterogeneous: to take the examples Aristotle uses in the first chapter of the *Ethics*, they include artifacts, health, victory, wealth, and much else that we or others aim at. The second step is to notice interdependencies among some of these apparent goods, and differences in their importance. He thinks his readers will agree with him that the goods just mentioned are not the highest goods there are. And he proposes an explanation for their lowly status: we aim at each of them because we assume that they will be put to further use. If we accept that explanation, we are led immediately to further questions: what are artifacts, health, victory, and wealth for? When we find our answers, we will have moved from a list of apparent goods of lowly status to a list of apparent goods of greater value. But if those higher goods are in turn sought because they lead to still others, we will continue to pursue our investigation by asking which further goods those are. Victory in battle is desirable for the sake of peace, but to what further purposes do we wish to use peace?

This process of investigation cannot continue indefinitely (I.2 1094a18–22). At some point, Aristotle thinks, we will discover a good that we take to be of the highest importance. It need not be a goal that can be achieved only in some distant future; rather, it might be something that we are already attaining with some degree of success. That good, Aristotle says, will not simply be one among many; because of its unique status, it should be called *the* good—not simply *a* good. It will be something we seek for itself rather than for the sake of something further, and everything else will be desired for its sake. Even if we already possess it to some degree, we might be able to achieve it more fully if we can identify it and more fully understand what it is (a22–6).

---

³ For a brief account of Aristotle's methodology for the study of ethics, see Irwin's glossary to his translation of the *Ethics*, s.v. 'ethics'; also the same author's 'Aristotle's Method of Ethics'; Barnes, 'Aristotle and the Methods of Ethics'; Reeve, *Practices of Reason*, pp. 7–66. On Aristotle's conception of ethical learning, see Burnyeat, 'Aristotle on Learning to be Good'.

3.2. THE ORGANIZATION OF GOODS

Aristotle is inclined to think that our plans and the tasks undertaken within our community contain this hierarchical structure, because he believes that, when asked, many people will in fact say that they pursue a single ultimate end. Their ultimate goal, they will say, is to be *eudaimōn* ('happy', I.4 1095a14–20).[4] They seek this for itself, and not for the sake of some further end; and everything else is sought because it leads to or is a part of happiness. Furthermore, Aristotle believes that many people have a definite idea of what it is to be happy: they take some concrete goal, like pleasure, or health, or virtue, to be the highest good there is, and pursue everything else for the sake of this ultimate end (a20–5).

We can justifiably object that many people are far less single-minded than this. They think that a wide variety of things are good for their own sake, and they do not take any one of them to be *the* good for the sake of which they pursue all others.

But Aristotle can afford to grant our point. His goal is to lead us to the conclusion that we *should* have one highest end—provided we know which good deserves to be placed in that supreme position. His project in the remainder of the first book of the *Ethics* is to lead his readers to identify that highest goal, in a preliminary way. He hopes that they will not object, from the very start, to the idea that we should pursue a single ultimate end in all that we do—and he expects that few, if any, will demur. But if they do, then he believes that their doubts will be assuaged when they arrive at a full understanding of the good that he proposes as our ultimate end.[5]

---

[4] Although 'happiness' is often used as the conventional equivalent for Aristotle's term *eudaimonia*, it must be kept in mind that his term does not designate a mood or feeling, as 'happiness' often does. 'Well-being' or 'flourishing' have therefore been proposed as less misleading translations. The Greek term *eudaimon* is composed of two parts: *eu* means well and *daimon* means 'divinity' or 'spirit'. To be *eudaimon* is therefore to be living in a way that is well favored by a god. Aristotle calls attention to this etymology at *Topics* II.6 112a36–8, where he is discussing argumentative techniques, but it seems to have little influence on his thinking. In his practical works, he regards *eudaimon* as a mere substitute for *eu zēn* ('living well'). These terms play an evaluative role, and are not simply descriptions of someone's state of mind. It would be a great mistake to assume without argument that one's good consists in experiencing a certain pleasant state of mind called 'happiness', and to view all other goals as means to that end. Aristotle avoids that mistake, and we should not be misled by the translation of *eudaimonia* as 'happiness' into supposing that he erred in this way. For further discussion of this issue, see Kraut, 'Two Conceptions of Happiness'.

[5] For an alternative way of reading Book I of the *Ethics*, see Ackrill, 'Aristotle on *Eudaimonia*'. He holds that *eudaimonia* is a composite of all intrinsic goods; from this, it follows that everything that is not a component of happiness is desirable for the sake of happiness. My reasons for rejecting this interpretation are presented in *Aristotle on the Human Good*. For a brief presentation of my position, see Kraut, 'Aristotle on the Human Good: An Overview'.

Book I of the *Ethics* does not by itself attempt to give its readers a full picture of what the ultimate end of human life is. Its more modest goal is to provide a sketch of what that good is (I.7 1098a20–1), and to propose an explanation of its supreme value. That highest good, Aristotle claims, is virtuous activity of the parts of the soul that have reason (a3–17). Although he briefly defends this idea in I.7, we should postpone making a final assessment of his conception of the good until we have understood what he means by virtue—and that is something that unfolds gradually over the course of his treatise.

Aristotle believes that when the members of his audience have finished their course of study, and have rehearsed all of the issues addressed in the *Ethics*, they will have achieved a far better understanding of why the things that seemed good to them at the beginning of their inquiry really are good. Subordinate goods will have been shown to be good, because at least part of their goodness derives from the way in which they sustain higher ends. Having started with a disorderly list of what seems good, they will end by knowing full well what is good, because they will have systematically investigated the relationships that hold among them, and will recognize the proper place each has in a well-lived life. Goods form a structure. We therefore need to know not only that friendship, pleasure, health, and understanding are good, but also how they fit together. By investigating the proper organization of goods, we develop a better sense of what each of them is, and as a result, we should be better prepared to achieve them.

3.3. *Is Aristotle Too Conservative?*

It might be objected that there is an unacceptable conservatism in Aristotle's method: his investigation of well-being appears to be excessively narrow, because it is confined to a consideration of those things that already seem good to us at the beginning of our inquiry— such things as health, pleasure, and friendship. The objection that can be made against this procedure is that it overlooks the possibility that there are good things—perhaps very important good things— that we are unaware of. We will never find them (so the accusation runs) if we confine our examination to what we already take to be good. Admittedly, Aristotle's method might allow us to improve our understanding of the goals we already pursue. But why not search for

3.3. IS ARISTOTLE TOO CONSERVATIVE?

new goals, instead of merely reflecting on the ones we already have? Why assume that the best thing for us to pursue is something we are already familiar with?

In fact, Aristotle's method is not conservative in this way.[6] On the contrary, he introduces students of well-being to conceptions of the good with which they (or some of them, at any rate) are probably quite unfamiliar. In I.6 of the *Ethics*, he considers the proposal that the highest end of human life is the universal and eternal good posited by Platonists: the good, they say, is not health, or pleasure, or understanding, but something that all of these familiar goods have in common. We need not consider the arguments Aristotle gives against the Platonists. What is important for our purposes is that he does not confine his inquiry about well-being to a consideration of those goods that are already widely recognized. Aristotle's social universe contained just a handful of Platonists, and yet he devotes more space to a consideration of their conception of well-being than to any other. So it is no part of his method to limit his inquiry to goods that his audience is already pursuing, or goods that are universally acknowledged. On the contrary, the student of well-being must examine any conception of goodness that seems to have some merit, even if it is one that has only recently been introduced by a small band of philosophers. There is no reason why some of these new ideas about what is good might not be correct. Aristotle's objection to the Platonists is not that they introduce an unfamiliar conception of the good, but that the arguments they give for their new conception are deficient.

Aristotle's method requires the student of well-being to examine not only what seems good to himself, but also what seems good to anyone who has given serious thought to this subject. It takes the student outside of himself, and requires him to consider the possibility that until now he has been ignorant of goods far better than the ones he has so far been pursuing. That hypothesis may lead nowhere, but the only way to test it is to consider the arguments of the philosophers.

In fact, it turns out that Aristotle himself proposes to his readers a conception of well-being that will strike them, or at least some of them, as novel and bizarre. He eventually arrives at the conclusion, in X.7–8, that the best activity for a human being is to contemplate

---

[6] In a different sense, I believe that Aristotle's political thought can reasonably be called 'conservative'. See 9.21.

the truths that have been learned from an investigation of the highest causes of the cosmos.[7] That is certainly not an idea that students of well-being are likely to have at the beginning of his investigation. Aristotle's students are taken through a course of reasoning that begins with a list of goods made familiar to them by their own experience, but it eventually leads them to the conclusion that the good is something they may not yet have begun to acquire. The *Ethics* is in part a defense of the philosophical life, but it is addressed to anyone who has been brought up well (more on this in 3.5) and is willing to give serious thought to questions about what is good. By the time the treatise draws to a close, those who were not philosophers when they began their study of ethics will have been introduced to a good that is new to them. Whether they decide to pursue that good or not, they will have enlarged their conception of well-being.[8]

3.4. *Experience, Passion, and Reason*

Although Aristotle's method requires the student of well-being to reflect on the way other people live their lives, and the conception of happiness they have proposed, he also insists that this is a subject in which one can progress only if one makes use of one's own experience of life (I.7 1098b3–4).[9] He assumes that, just as someone investigating the causal order of the visible universe must employ his own faculty of perception, and cannot rely entirely on what others report to him, so the student of the human good must make use of what has become familiar to him through his own encounters with his social world. He should know what it is like to receive the goodwill of others; to be ashamed or proud; to help a friend; to forego

---

[7] The material in X.7–8 is sometimes taken to be inconsistent with the main tenets of Aristotle's ethical theory. See e.g. Ackrill, 'Aristotle on *Eudaimonia*'; and Nussbaum, *The Fragility of Goodness*, pp. 273–7. I address this issue, and argue that there is no such inconsistency, in *Aristotle on the Human Good*.

[8] Note how different this approach to well-being is from the subjectivism examined in Ch. 2. Because the subjectivist holds that each of us confers goodness on things, he cannot find any practical value in acquainting ourselves with what others think about well-being—with e.g. the philosophical accounts of goodness we find in Plato, Aristotle, and other ancient schools; or with the conceptions of good and evil that we find in literary works or popular culture.

[9] The passage cited lists a number of ways in which first principles are learnt: induction, perception, habituation. I assume that, in his opinion, ethical first principles are learnt through a process of habituation.

or pursue various pleasures; to be faced with a problem of justice.[10] These are things he must experience at first hand, if he is to become a good judge of what philosophers like Aristotle have to say about well-being. If the student's own experience is too narrow or elementary, he will have too little basis for determining the plausibility of what others say about well-being. If he is suggestible, he might be overawed by the seeming profundity of a serious thinker, and adopt, at least for a short while, a questionable new system of ideas about well-being (I.4 1095a25–6). The proper approach, then, is to go through a long period in which one encounters at first hand the typical problems and goods of human life. It is only after one has accumulated this personal knowledge of life that one occupies a favorable position for moving beyond one's own experience, and evaluating the opinions about good and evil put forward by others. Well-being might turn out to consist in goods that are not yet familiar to the student, when he begins his study of this subject; but he will be in a poor position to recognize that those unfamiliar goods really are good unless he already has some ideas, based on his own experience, about which things are good. The right method is to start with what one is familiar with, and then to enlarge upon one's experience, by reflecting on what others have said about well-being.[11]

Aristotle coveys the importance of personal experience by saying that the student of well-being develops an understanding of the ultimate end through a certain process of habituation (I.7 1098b3–4). The term 'habituation' (*ethismos*) conveys the thought that we become familiar with the goods and problems of social life only when certain patterns repeat themselves. We know what problems of justice are like, or what it is to receive the goodwill of others, only when we encounter these things many times and in many different ways. Through the recurrence of the same sorts of circumstances, the impression forms in us that certain things are generally good or bad. A few of those impressions may be mistaken; but if one has been properly guided by good parents and a decent community, and one's exposure to social phenomena is varied and lengthy enough, then it cannot be the case that all of those impressions are wrong. This process of habituation therefore gives one a basis for

---

[10] These examples are my conjecture about the sort of phenomena Aristotle expects his students to be familiar with; they are not his examples.

[11] See *EE* I.8 1218a15–22 for Aristotle's criticism of philosophers who make the mistake of arguing from questionable premises about unfamiliar goods to conclusions about undisputed goods.

determining which ideas about well-being—including unfamiliar ones—to accept.

Of course, there are some things that one can reasonably assume, because others have experienced them, and one has no reason to discount their reports. Consider, for example, Aristotle's statement that no one—unless he were going to an extreme to defend a thesis—would consider a person who is suffering the greatest misfortunes to be happy (I.5 1096a1–2). One can be assured that certain things are great evils, even though one may have no first-hand acquaintance with them. The student of well-being does not need to have lost children to disease, to have been severely punished for a crime he did not commit, or to have been defeated in war. He knows that many others have suffered these misfortunes, and have judged them to be great evils. Since their experience shows that these things are bad, the rest of us know that there must be something wrong with any argument, not itself based on experience, that attempts to reach the conclusion that (for example) the death of one's children is a matter of indifference and is compatible with a perfect life. Mere reasoning that makes no contact with human life as it is lived and felt cannot be trusted. Aristotle is confident that his own conception of well-being, including his defense of the philosophical life, does not go wrong in this way (X.8 1179a20–2).[12] For in holding that the best human activity consists in contemplation, he does not deny that if great misfortunes befall a person who is devoted to this activity, his life would be very far from ideal. His defense of the philosophical life adds to the inventory of goods we make when we first begin our investigation of well-being, but it does not reject the validity of impressions of good and evil that are widely experienced.

As we have just seen, one kind of mistake to avoid in any investigation of well-being is to place too little weight on what one experiences or what others experience, and to give reason, uninstructed by experience, too much weight. But Aristotle also points out the rather more common mistake of putting too little stock in the power of reflection to make improvements in the way one lives one's life. There is a certain kind of person (and Aristotle thinks that young people often fall into this category) who takes his emotions and feelings to be the only reliable indicators of how he should act (I.3

---

[12] For a discussion of this passage, see Kraut, 'Aristotle on Method and Moral Education', pp. 274–5.

1095a4–8). He devotes himself to the expression of his passions, and does not ask himself whether his fears and bouts of anger might be excessive or unwarranted. If such a person tried to justify his way of life by claiming that, when reason operates in isolation from one's experience of life, it should not be trusted, Aristotle would have to acknowledge his point. But of course it would be a non sequitur to infer that our ability to reflect on what we feel or experience should not be cultivated at all. The fact that we need something other than our power of reasoning to determine how we should live does not lend any support to the idea that we should make no use of that power. Neither our habits nor our passions will by themselves reveal to us everything we need to know in order to live well. The benefits of reflection are constantly revealed to us in everyday affairs: we know all too well that at times anger, fear, envy, and other passions lead people astray. And if we discover, by a process of trial and error, that philosophical reflection about human well-being can lead us to a better understanding of what our ends should be, then that would be the most convincing possible demonstration of the benefits of practical reasoning.

3.5. 'Brought Up Well'

Aristotle holds that because the student of well-being must begin with what is already familiar to him, he must come to his investigation of this subject with a certain background: 'he must have been brought up well in his habits' (I.4 1095b4).[13] In saying this, he is not merely making the point that the student must have a certain *amount* of experience of life, and must draw upon that experience in his inquiry. He is also saying that the student's experience must be of the right sort: he must have been brought up *well*. But precisely what is involved in being 'brought up well' in one's habits?

We receive some help in answering our question when Aristotle makes a list, several chapters later, of the things that we choose for themselves: 'honor, pleasure, understanding, and every virtue we choose for themselves, for if nothing resulted from them we would choose each of them' (I.7 1097b2–4). He is not claiming here that all human beings, or all of his contemporaries, regard these items as

---

[13] A fuller discussion of this statement is contained ibid.

desirable in themselves. When he says that "we" choose them, he is referring to himself and anyone else who has been brought up well. So one of the lessons learnt by those who have been properly trained is that certain things are good in themselves, and that among these things are honor, pleasure, understanding, and all of the virtues. Their long exposure to these things has taught them that they are good in themselves. They have developed many of the habits of a virtuous person, and on the basis of their experience, they judge the virtues to be good qualities to have, aside from the advantages they bring. Aristotle does not say in this passage which qualities he takes to be virtues, but there can be no doubt that they are the ones that he explores at length in the rest of the *Ethics*: *sophrosunē* ('temperance', 'moderation'[14]), courage, *eleutheria* ('liberality', 'generosity'), and so on. Although Aristotle's students have not yet learnt from him what these qualities involve, they have already acquired, to some degree, the dispositions of a temperate, courageous, liberal person.

He cannot mean that they have completed their moral education, or that they fully possess these virtues. For he says that his audience is conducting this investigation 'in order to become good' (II.2 1103b28), and that of course means that they are not yet good—not completely, at any rate. We should take Aristotle to mean that his students are well on their way towards acquiring the virtues. They have developed the right habits, but they have not yet carried out an examination of well-being. Once they arrive, with Aristotle's help, at an understanding of what well-being is, and put that understanding into practice, they will have become completely good.

Why does he think that only such students will benefit from reflecting on what he has to say about well-being? Why doesn't he believe that he will be able to lead anyone who pays attention to him, regardless of that person's upbringing, to accept the conception of well-being put forward in the *Ethics*? The answer is contained in points we have already made. Aristotle holds that the proper way to improve our beliefs about what is good is to start with what already seems good to us. One must draw on one's own experience of life, at least to some degree. He infers from this that someone whose experience of life is limited in certain ways is unlikely ever to arrive

---

[14] The Greek term conveys the idea of soundness of mind. For a helpful discussion, see Young, 'Aristotle on Temperance'.

3.5. 'BROUGHT UP WELL'

at a proper of understanding of well-being. Consider, for example, someone who regards justice and other virtues as mere means to further ends—someone who does what is just only in order to avoid punishment, or to win the rewards of a good reputation. His aim in life, let us suppose, is to possess as much power and wealth as possible, and he takes virtue (which he equates with mere adherence to certain social rules) to be an occasionally useful means towards these ends. Such a person has nothing in his personal experience that would incline him to accept Aristotle's conception of well-being. He does not know what it is like to be a virtuous person, and does not regard virtue as one of the many things that are good in themselves. His current projects—to maximize his enjoyment of power and wealth—would have to be curtailed were he to try to transform himself into a virtuous person. What are the chances that he will read with an open mind a philosopher who takes as one of his starting points the intrinsic goodness of virtue? Were he to ask himself what well-being is, and to draw on his own experience in answering this question, he would have no basis for arriving at the conclusion that Aristotle proposes. He would fall back on a stock of assumptions that prevent him from seeing any plausibility in one of Aristotle's central starting points—that virtue is in itself a good thing.

By contrast, the audience to which Aristotle addresses himself has no such handicap. They *do* know what it is like to be virtuous, and they take the virtues to be among the things that are good in themselves. Therefore, when they consider the question of what their ultimate goal should be, their experience of life will not prevent them from reaching the right conclusion, because they will be open to the possibility not merely that virtuous activity is one good among many, but that it ought to become their ultimate end. When they enter Aristotle's classroom, they have not yet reflected in a philosophical way on the various ends they have; but they can easily put together a list of things that seem good to them, and the virtues are on that list. These are the people that Aristotle thinks are in the best position to make improvements in their beliefs about how to lead their lives, and to put what they learn into practice. Once they have arrived, with Aristotle's help, at a fuller understanding of what virtue is, and see that it is not merely a good but *the* good, their firm recognition of what their ultimate goal should be will make them all the more adept at hitting their target.

Aristotle is right to suppose that he will have no influence on certain kinds of person. His arguments will not receive serious consideration from those who evaluate ideas about well-being solely on the basis of their own experience, and have never experienced virtuous activity as something enjoyable or worthwhile in itself. But he is wrong to assume that the only sort of audience that will be receptive to his ethical works is one that is already convinced, on the basis of its own experience, that virtuous activity is in itself a good thing. After all, there are people who are open to the suggestion that their experience of life has thus far been too limited, and are prepared to make a change. They may be willing to consider the possibility that it would be good for them to acquire the virtues, not as means to further ends, but simply because they are among the things that are good in themselves. They may realize that there are people who do enjoy acting virtuously, and they may be willing to transform themselves so that they can enjoy this good as well. (Recall a point made in 3.4: we learn from the sufferings of others; we do not have to experience great misfortunes to know that they are awful. In the same way, we can recognize that our experience of good things is limited, and can learn from the example of others.) What Aristotle ought to have said is that if certain members of his audience do not, on the basis of their own experience, take virtuous activity to be good in itself, they ought to accept the reports of those who have had a different experience—namely, those who have been 'brought up well' in their habits.

In any case, the audience to which Aristotle addresses himself is rather large. Many people take pride in their social skills and accomplishments, and consider it a good thing to treat others with fairness, generosity, and honesty. In any decent society, only a small minority regards every good deed as a mere means to further ends. Normally, people want to be of some help to others—not all others, to be sure, but some of them. When they assist their friends, they are not doing so merely for the sake of their friends. They also enjoy such activity, and would take it to be a significant loss to themselves if they were prevented from being of any value to others. Nearly all of us are attracted, at least some of the time, to the idea that virtuous acts can be good in themselves for the person who performs them. We of course do not regard the exercise of the virtues to be the only good thing in life. Before we turn to philosophy, we are unlikely to have fixed ideas about how the goodness of virtuous activity compares with the goodness of many other sorts of things. We are the people whom Aristotle is most eager to address.[15]

3.6. The Function Argument: First Thoughts

Thus far, we have been examining those portions of Book I of the *Ethics* in which Aristotle describes the problem that he wishes to solve and the method he will use to solve it. The problem, as he poses it in sections I.1-2, is this: what should we place at the top of our hierarchy of ends? The method he then proposes, in I.3-4, for answering this question is to draw upon the thoughts of those who have been brought up well—people who have a broad experience of life and its many intrinsic goods, and are able to bring their actions in line with their reflections. Then, starting in I.5, he begins to explore a number of different ways in which other people have tried, unsuccessfully, to answer his question. He argues against the view that the human good can be identified with physical pleasure, or honor, or virtue, or wealth. These are popular ideas about how we should lead our lives—'popular' in the sense that each proposal enjoys broad support. In I.6, he examines theories put forward by philosophers—such people as the Pythagoreans, Speusippus, and the

---

[15] My understanding of the restriction Aristotle places on his audience (to those who have been 'brought up well') should be contrasted with the one proposed by McDowell in 'Two Sorts of Naturalism', pp. 194-5. He contrasts two ways in which confidence in ethical beliefs may be threatened or challenged: First, there is 'a peculiarly modern threat to confidence, posed by neo-Humean naturalism' (p. 194), which requires a grounding for all of our ethical beliefs in non-ethical natural facts that can be recognized even by those who lack those ethical beliefs. Second, a threat to our confidence can arise whenever we scrutinize our ethical beliefs from a standpoint internal to those beliefs. McDowell thinks that Plato takes this second sort of challenge seriously, but that Aristotle does not. 'Aristotle ... gives no sign that he is so much as aware that ethical confidence is fragile, let alone concerned about the fact. He simply stipulates, in effect, that he is addressing only people in which the value scheme he takes for granted has been properly ingrained' (pp. 194-5). By contrast, I take Aristotle to be just as concerned with the second threat as Plato. The restriction he places on his audience is based on the idea that if one begins with too small an inventory of goods, one will not be able to expand it. That restriction does not prevent him from seeing that when one starts with an inventory large enough to include the virtues and many other goods, critical reflection can raise questions about how much weight should be attached to the virtues, and whether they might not be goods after all. McDowell's reading comes into conflict with his own observation that Aristotle occupies 'a line of descent from Socrates' commendation of the examined life' ('Some Issues in Aristotle's Moral Psychology', p. 36; see 2.n.10). For further discussion relevant to McDowell's interpretation, see 4.6-7 and 7.1. (See too 4.9 and 4.n.37 for the Platonic background to Aristotle's portrait of the man who is unjust in the narrow sense of the word.) For reasons given in 4.7 and 7.1, I am not convinced that the first sort of threat McDowell discusses is peculiarly modern.

Platonists—and finds these no more adequate than the popular ideas. Finally, in I.7, after making several further remarks about the sort of good he is searching for, he presents and begins to defend his own answer: if we consider the 'function' (*ergon*) of human beings, we will discover that the human good consists in virtuous activity of the parts of the soul that have reason. In the chapters of Book I that follow I.7, he advances a number of diverse considerations that he takes to confirm the conclusion he has reached. And then, having satisfied himself that his argument is on the right track, he begins, in I.13, to explore the topic to which his conception of the good has led him: since the good consists in virtuous activity, we must examine the nature of the virtues. And that becomes his central topic in Books II–VI.

It is clear from this summary that the function argument of I.7 plays a central role in Aristotle's thinking about well-being. But it is also important to realize that some of the arguments he uses before he presents the function argument are intended to lead the way towards an acceptance of his theory. We are meant to see some of the merits of his conception of well-being by first recognizing the shortcomings of rival accounts. (His critique will be discussed in 3.7.) Furthermore, we should continue to bear in mind that the conclusion of the function argument is put forward as a mere sketch of Aristotle's conception of the good (1098a20–1). It is something he means to fill in, as he proceeds; and therefore we cannot fairly assess the plausibility of his account until we see how he works out the details. (This aspect of his theory will be discussed in 3.10 and 3.11.) Important as the function argument is, it cannot be evaluated in isolation from the rest of Aristotle's defense of his theory of well-being.

That theory, as I have said, has considerable force, although not every component of it need be accepted. One of its central insights can now be recognized. We have already observed, in our discussion of Aristotle's methodology, that he addresses himself to adults who have been brought up well. Childhood should be devoted to the acquisition of certain habits, and adulthood is a time in which we draw on the skills that were learnt during that earlier period of preparation. Notice that these simple and obvious methodological remarks contain the rudiments of a theory of proper human development, and therefore of human well-being. A good life for a human being is one in which we develop from early childhood to adulthood according to a certain pattern. If a human life were cut off at too

3.6. THE FUNCTION ARGUMENT: FIRST THOUGHTS

early a stage, it would not yet have fulfilled its potential to become a good life. And that by itself tells us something about how we should live. The best pattern for a human life is one in which we first prepare ourselves (with considerable help from others) for adulthood and then, as adults, exercise the kind of self-mastery for which we have been trained. Certain powers that are inchoate in a child need to be nurtured, for his own good; the well-being of an adult consists in exercising them. It is not difficult to say, in general terms, what those powers are. Childhood is a time when our emotions and ability to reason are limited by our lack of experience and training. The goal for which the child should be prepared, for his own good, is an adult life in which he exercises, on a regular basis, certain skills of thought, emotional response, and action. A good life for an adult human being is therefore one in which we have the resources needed for the full exercise of those mental powers for which our childhood training has prepared us.

Described in this way, Aristotle's general framework is one that agrees with common ways of thinking about human life. The development and training of thought and emotion from childhood to adulthood is something that parents already care deeply about, if they love their children. They do not need to read Aristotle in order to learn that this must be their central concern as parents. Their devotion to the well-being of their children is expressed primarily in their efforts to give them the mental skills they will need to live good lives as adults. Anything that would impair the growth of reason and feeling would be regarded as a grave misfortune that must be avoided at all costs. Forced to choose between the loss of a child's finger and the loss of his mind, no sane parent would be in doubt about what to do.

Perhaps in certain extreme circumstances, parents can reasonably wish that their children might remain within the limited intellectual and emotional horizons of childhood. When the social and material circumstances of adults are ghastly, and children are not yet exposed to the horrors that will come with adulthood, then parents may well wish that their children could remain free of the dreadful burdens of adulthood forever. They would reasonably reject Aristotle's remark that 'no one would choose to live with the mind of a child throughout his life' (X.3 1174a1–2). But the circumstances in which children and their parents can understandably wish that they might avoid adulthood are those of a world that has become inhospitable to human well-being. When conditions are favorable for human life, our good lies in making a successful transition from childhood to adulthood, and this requires a training that equips us with complex intellectual, emotional, and social skills.

3.7. Honor and Virtue

In several of the arguments Aristotle gives against popular conceptions of well-being, he prepares the way for his idea that the proper exercise of our cognitive powers plays a central role in a well-lived life. In I.5, he briefly criticizes the thesis that the good for human beings consists in honor—that is, in holding positions of great status such as political office, or other tokens of high regard. Aristotle remarks that such a good is 'more superficial than what we are seeking; for it seems to depend on those who honor rather than the one who is honored, whereas we surmise that the good is something of our own and hard to take away' (I.5 1095b23–6). Honors are bestowed by others, and can be withdrawn as easily as they are given. Aristotle does not mean to deny that they can be good to have, but he claims that they are inappropriate candidates for our ultimate end, because our highest good must be 'something of our own and hard to take away'. But that is precisely what is valuable about a cognitive power that we have developed over a long period of time: it is our own accomplishment, it has become part of who we are, and so it is something we will not easily lose. Aristotle thinks his readers will agree with him, even before they encounter his own conception of well-being, that what is most important to our lives is something that is in some sense within us, something that has become a part of ourselves and cannot be withheld by others. His thesis that our highest good consists in the full exercise of our powers of thought and feeling is a development of a widely shared point of view.

He points out, several lines later, that we can fall short of having a good life even when we possess a good that lacks the superficiality of honor, and has become part of us through our efforts and training. He appeals to an imaginary case (1095b31–1096a2): suppose someone who has become virtuous (has, in other words, perfected his skills of thought and feeling) falls asleep, or in some other way becomes inactive, for the rest of his life, and furthermore suffers great misfortunes. It should be evident, Aristotle says, that such a person is not living well, even though he has acquired the cognitive skills for which his childhood prepared him. Our highest goal cannot merely be the perfection of our powers of thought and feeling; for those powers, having been developed, may lie unused, and in that case we are missing something of the greatest importance. Aristotle's language hints at what it is: such a person is inactive (*apraktein*: 1095b33). What our childhood should prepare us for is a life in which we regularly and frequently actualize the powers we have developed; merely having developed them is not by itself sufficient. This component of Aristotle's thinking is present in the conclusion of the function argument: our good, he says, lies in 'activity of the soul in accordance with virtue' (1098a16–17). The term 'activity' (*energeia*) is doing important work here: our highest goal is not merely to develop certain cognitive skills, which might then lie dormant, but to do something with them—to bring them to bear on the world. What is within us must be brought into contact with other human beings and the material resources we need.

3.8. The Function Argument: Reason

Having rejected a number of rival conceptions of the good, Aristotle turns in I.7 to a presentation and defense of his own theory. He argues that human beings have a function (*ergon*) and sets out to discover what it is. Through a series of steps, he comes to the conclusion that the human good consists in virtuous activity of certain parts of the soul—the parts that think or are responsive to thought. Several components of the argument that he presents here—for example, his claim that human beings have a function—are questionable (as we will see in 3.12). Even so, there are other aspects of the argument that are defensible. Before we decide what to retain and what to reject, let us review the steps of his argument.[16]

One important component of this argument is expressed in terms of distinctions he makes in his psychological and biological works. Aristotle thinks of the soul as that aspect of a living thing that causes it to interact with the world in a certain manner. Things that grow and reproduce do so because their bodies are organized in a certain way; the organization that is the basis for that capacity is the

---

[16] For discussion of the function argument, see Irwin, *Aristotle's First Principles*, pp. 363–72; Reeve, *Practices of Reason*, pp. 123–38; Whiting, 'Aristotle's Function Argument: A Defense'; Gomez-Lobo, 'The *Ergon* Inference'; Lawrence, 'The Function of the Function Argument'. Other helpful essays are cited in Barnes, *The Cambridge Companion to Aristotle*, p. 360.

nutritive soul. It is not itself a further material component of a living thing, but rather its form—just as the shape of a statue is not a material component of it, but the way in which its matter is arranged. Plants have a rather simple sort of soul (the nutritive soul), but all other living things are capable of more complex ways of interacting with the world: they can move (and therefore, Aristotle thinks, have a locomotive soul); they can perceive (and thus have a perceptive soul); and certain kinds of animal—human beings—are capable of reasoning and responding to reasons.[17]

The most important aspect of Aristotle's argument is his claim that what sets human beings off from other living creatures is our capacity to reason. It is important not to misunderstand what he means by this. We should not take him to be saying that no other animal can rightly be called intelligent. On the contrary, in the *Ethics* he notes without dissent that some non-human species are taken to have practical intelligence (*phronēsis*, VI.7 1141a26–8), and in his biological works he points out several times that various other kinds of animal exhibit some adeptness in thought and learning.[18] Rather, when he says that human beings alone possess reason, he means that we alone engage in such activities as these: deliberating about what to do, looking for and demanding reasons for and against proposed courses of action, assessing our emotional responses and altering their strength, investigating why the world appears as it does, developing theories that explain the facts, arguing that certain theories give better explanations than others. Not every human being engages in each of these activities. But every adult human being whose rational capacity has been nurtured by his community is brought into the realm of practical reason: he is asked to give reasons for his actions, he joins in deliberation with others, and he makes reasoned choices between alternatives. Many human beings are born with the capacity to develop these mental skills, and with the

---

[17] The core of Aristotle's theory of the soul is presented in *De An.* II.1–3. For brief overviews, see Irwin, 'Aristotle's Philosophy of Mind' and Everson, 'Psychology'.

[18] *Hist. An.* IX.5 611a15–16, IX.7 612b18–31, IX.39 623a7–8, IX.46 630b18–21. See too *Gen. An.* III.2 753a7–17; *Met.* I.1 980a27-b25. Nonetheless, at *De An.* III.3 428a19–24 and *Mem.* 450a15–16 he denies that animals have beliefs. For discussion, see Labarrière, 'De la phronèsis animale'; Sorabji, *Animal Minds and Human Morals*, pp. 12–16. For a recent overview of evolutionary theory that attributes intelligence to many other species, see Jolly, *Lucy's Legacy*. A more cautious position is taken by Hauser, *Wild Minds*. Much recent philosophy has cast doubt on whether beliefs are the sort of thing that non-linguistic creatures can have. See e.g. Stich, 'Do Animals Have Beliefs?'; Davidson, 'Rational Animals', and Putnam, *Renewing Philosophy*, pp. 28–31. For a critique of this position, see MacIntyre, *Dependent Rational Animals*, pp. 11–61.

proper sort of upbringing, they engage in these practices, albeit with different degrees of success.[19] No other kind of animal strives to live a life of this sort. And it is widely agreed that those human beings who are born without the capacity to develop these skills, or who have the capacity but never develop it, are extraordinarily unlucky. When we remind ourselves of these differences between human beings and other animals, we are calling attention to an aspect of human life that we are constantly enacting, and would not wish to eliminate.

It must also be emphasized, however, that Aristotle distinguishes two different components of the soul that can be said to have reason. One of them, he says, obeys reason; the other has reason and engages in reflection (1098a4–5). What he has in mind here is a psychological phenomenon that was first explored by Plato in the *Republic*: our thoughts about what to do are capable of influencing our emotions, although they are not always successful in doing so. Our mental life can be the scene of conflict. To take a simple example, we may be thirsty but at the same time realize that it is best not to drink. Our recognition of what we have reason to do can influence the force of our passions and appetites, and this shows that human passions and appetites are the sorts of thing that in some sense have reason. That too, Aristotle thinks, sets us off from the rest of the animal world. When he says that human beings alone have reason, he is making a point not only about our capacity for theorizing and deliberating, but also about our ability to reshape our emotional lives by examining whether our feelings and appetites are reasonable.[20]

3.9. *The Function Argument: Virtue*

There is one other aspect of Aristotle's argument in I.7 that should receive our attention. He plausibly denies that the mere activity of reasoning is good by itself; it is a good activity for us to engage in only if we are good at it—only if we reason well. To have reached

---

[19] Aristotle holds, notoriously, that two types of human beings lack the potential to develop fully as rational beings. We will explore his account of the slave's rational deficiency in Ch. 8; see 8.n.22 on the deficiency of women.

[20] For discussion of Aristotle's analysis of the emotions, see Cooper, 'An Aristotelian Theory of the Emotions'; Frede, 'Mixed Feelings in Aristotle's *Rhetoric*'; Leighton, 'Aristotle and the Emotions'; Nussbaum, 'Aristotle on Emotions and Rational Persuasion'; and Striker, 'Emotions in Context: Aristotle's Treatment of the Passions in the *Rhetoric* and in His Moral Psychology'.

adulthood is not necessarily to have become good at deliberating and making choices; on the contrary, it happens all too often that those who are old enough to engage in the activity of practical reasoning and to shape their emotional responses are not particularly adept at either task. So the conclusion Aristotle arrives at is that our highest goal is to engage in an activity of the soul—or rather, the rational parts of the soul—in accordance with *aretē* ('virtue', 'excellence').

Aristotle tries to persuade his readers of his point by drawing on an analogy with playing an instrument: Although it is the function of a lyre-player to play the lyre, it is the function of a *good* lyre-player to do so well. To succeed in his task, the good musician must develop and exercise certain skills. Similarly, since our highest aim as human beings is not merely to live, but to live well, we must develop and exercise the skills that constitute aptitude in reasoning and responding to reasons. Our highest end, therefore, consists in exercising those skills—'virtues'—that make us good at reasoning and responsive to reason.

We may not agree with Aristotle that human beings have a function; that is an issue we will take up in section 3.12. But we need not accept this thesis in order to agree with one of the simple points he is making: it is better for us to be skilled at finding, weighing, responding to, and acting on reasons than to be incompetent reasoners and unresponsive to thought. The sort of cognitive training we think a child should receive, for his own good, is one that goes beyond making him someone who is barely able to engage in the practice of deliberating and reasoning; he is better off if he becomes excellent at this activity. Aristotle is right to conclude that for our own good we need certain virtues of thought and responsiveness to thought.

3.10. Virtue: Further Developments

That is as far as the function argument of I.7 takes us. It does not specify which powers of the mind are virtues. But Aristotle very soon mentions such qualities as justice and liberality (I.8), temperance and courage (I.13). Nothing in the function argument shows that these traits are in themselves good for us to have, but presumably Aristotle is aware of this limitation in his argument. As we have noted before, in I.7 he describes himself as having given a 'sketch' of the good (1098a20–1). Since he does not want to rest content with a mere outline, we should expect to find, in later material, considerations designed to convince us that exercising such cognitive skills as courage and temperance is in itself a great good. And of course there is no better place to look for that material than his discussion of the ethical virtues, in Books II–VI.

When we read this portion of the *Ethics*, Aristotle's strategy becomes apparent. It emerges that his doctrine of the mean plays a central role in convincing us that such qualities of mind as justice, temperance, and courage are great goods. The 'doctrine of the mean' is the phrase often used to designate his thesis that corresponding to every ethical virtue there are two vices: one involving an excess of something, the other a deficiency of that same thing, and the corresponding virtue in some way or other falling between these two extremes.[21] For example, one way of living one's life badly is to be excessive in one's feelings of anger: one becomes angry more often than one should; on many occasions, one's anger is stronger than it ought to be, and lasts longer than is appropriate. Alternatively, one may be too pliant and docile in one's relationships with others: such a person feels no anger when he should, and often feels and expresses too little anger. The person who has the virtue of handling anger well avoids both of these extremes. When ethical virtues are described in this way, it becomes obvious that they are good qualities for us to have. Assuming that it would be bad for us to suppress or eliminate anger at every point throughout our lives, and also that there is such a thing as too much anger for our own good, it becomes undeniable that it is good for us to have the virtue that deals with anger. Exercising that virtue is part of what it is to live well.

More generally, how we control our emotions and integrate them into our practical reasoning is of central importance in any well-lived life. Since Aristotle conceives of the ethical virtues as the qualities we put into action when we handle our emotions well, he has strong grounds for thinking that an important component of human well-being is the skill we bring to bear on the activities in which we reason and are responsive to reason.

We should also notice another aspect of the ethical virtues, as Aristotle conceives them: he describes them in such a way that there can be no such thing as having too much of them for one's own good.

---

[21] The doctrine is presented in *NE* II.6–9. We should distinguish (a) the thesis that each virtue lies between two vices, and (b) the thesis that the virtuous agent aims to do what is in some sense intermediate. For discussion, see Broadie, *Ethics with Aristotle*, pp. 95–103; Hardie, *Aristotle's Ethical Theory*, ch. 7; Hursthouse, 'A False Doctrine of the Mean'; Urmson, 'Aristotle's Doctrine of the Mean'.

Consider liberality (*eleutheria*), for example—the virtue (analyzed in *NE* IV.1) that has to do with acquiring, preserving, and spending wealth. To have this excellent quality of mind is to be skillful in deciding what level of wealth we need for ourselves, which projects deserve our financial support, when it is appropriate to give or receive money, and the like. So defined, there is no such thing as having an excessive amount of *eleutheria*. Once one agrees that the value of wealth can be both overemphasized and underemphasized, and that avoiding these distortions requires skill in deliberation, as well as control over one's emotional response to wealth, then one must also agree not only that *eleutheria* is a quality one needs in order to live well, but that one cannot have too much of it. We should therefore take care not to confuse this virtue with the quality we call 'generosity'. To be generous is merely to be disposed to use one's resources to help others. And since a person who has this disposition might give others too much, or too often, or with too little discrimination, it is possible to be generous to a fault. Generosity as we conceive it does not require striking a proper balance between oneself and others. But since *eleutheria* as Aristotle defines it does strike such a balance, no amount of it can be excessive.

One other aspect of the ethical virtues, as Aristotle conceives them, should be noticed: they are not merely one component of a good life among others; rather, they exercise control over other components, including the other goods in our lives. The virtue that has to do with anger, for example, enables us to govern this emotion, so that it is neither weaker or stronger than the occasion demands. Similarly, courage governs fear, temperance physical pleasure, liberality wealth, and so on. When the thing controlled by virtue is itself a good—for example, wealth (governed by liberality) or honor (governed by magnanimity)—then there is a great difference in the value of the virtue and that of the good under its control. Consider wealth, once again. Aristotle assumes that its goodness is limited: at some point, additional riches make no further contribution to well-being. It would therefore understate the relative worth of *eleutheria* and wealth, if one merely said that *eleutheria* is the more valuable of the two. That would ignore the striking fact that no increase in wealth is worth the permanent loss of one's ability to make intelligent decisions about how much wealth is worth having. Since wealth is not something to be maximized, or given priority over all other goods, it is sometimes better to accept a lower level of it, and we therefore need to make decisions about when it is worth giving up,

3.10. VIRTUE: FURTHER DEVELOPMENTS

and when it is not. So it would be foolish to make an exchange in which we gain a certain sum of money, however large, but lose the ability to know whether this and all future exchanges are worthwhile.

The same point applies to any good that no longer contributes to well-being, when it is pursued in excess. We must, through long experience, develop those deliberative and affective skills that enable us to determine, case by case, when we have enough. There is no saying, once and for all, how much wealth it is good to have, or how much physical pleasure, or how many friends. What one needs, in order to make sound judgments about these matters, are the character traits that Aristotle takes to be virtues.

Of course, most of the practical problems we face are not quantitative in nature. It would be foolish to suppose, for example, that friendship is a homogeneous good, equal in value wherever it occurs, and that the only question we need to ask about it is how much of it to have. There are different kinds of friendships and in order to live well we must develop a sense of which among these relationships are worth developing and sustaining. That is a commonplace, but it is no trivial matter to examine systematically the many different kinds of friendship there are, and to say why some are better for us than others. Aristotle takes up this project in Books VIII and IX, where he argues that the most valuable kind of friendship—a long-lasting and stable relationship built on trust, admiration, and genuine love—is possible only among people who have acquired the virtues. It is not surprising that he should come to this conclusion, for the virtues are, in part, social skills: they enable us to size up the character of others, and they prevent the development of emotional handicaps (envy, spite, greed, unjustified anger) that would make it difficult for us to sustain healthy relationships. By calling our attention to these aspects of the virtues, Books VIII and IX give us further assurance of the goodness of the kind of life Aristotle is proposing to us. Happily, we do not have to choose between exercising the virtues and having the kinds of friend worth having. On the contrary, since the virtues are in part social skills, they help us sustain our friendships.[22]

That same strategy is deployed in Aristotle's discussion of another

---

[22] For discussion of Aristotle's theory of friendship, see Price, *Love and Friendship in Plato and Aristotle*, chs. 4–5. For more detailed analysis, see Pakaluk, *Aristotle: Nicomachean Ethics Books VIII and IX*. Cooper, 'Aristotle on the Forms of Friendship' and 'Friendship and Good in Aristotle' are fundamental contributions.

topic he considers at length: pleasure. Like friendship, this is not an undifferentiated good, equal in value wherever it is found. Pleasure, as Aristotle conceives it, is not a single kind of sensation that happens to be produced by a variety of sources; rather, just as the things in which we take pleasure differ—playing games, being with friends, listening to music—so too the pleasures themselves differ (X.5 1175a21–b1). Since they differ in kind, they presumably also differ in value; the enjoyment of a minor good is itself a minor good (b24–6). In fact, Aristotle suggests that some kinds of pleasure may not be good at all (X.3 1174a9), and therefore an ethical refusal to indulge in certain kinds of pleasure takes nothing away from the value of an ethical life. (Recall that we broached this issue in 2.5.[23])

Whether Aristotle is right about this or not, we ought to recognize that his investigation of pleasure, like his examination of friendship, is an attempt to lend further support to his thesis that the life of a virtuous person is an attractive one. Both a life devoid of fellow feeling and a life without enjoyment would have grave defects, and it counts in favor of an ethical life that it cannot have these deficiencies. That is because virtue is the sort of good that presupposes and brings with it other components of a well-lived life. Because of the kind of complex social skills the practical virtues are, they can be acquired only with the help of intimate relationships;[24] and once we possess them, they help us make and keep the best sorts of friend. Similarly, there is a close connection between virtue and pleasure: one cannot have the former without the latter. That is because one would not be a just person unless one took pleasure in promoting the common good of one's community; nor could one possess the virtue that governs wealth unless one delights in using one's resources to help others (I.8 1099a7–21). And since the virtues are skills and their exercise an accomplishment, all virtuous activity is accompanied by pleasure; for it is always a pleasure to do what we have managed, through long training, to become good at doing (X.5 1175a29–1175b1).

We have seen how the virtues lead to other goods (for example, the

---

[23] For Aristotle's analysis of pleasure, see Broadie, *Ethics with Aristotle*, ch. 6; Gosling and Taylor, *The Greeks on Pleasure*, chs. 11–17; and Hardie, *Aristotle's Ethical Theory*, ch. 14.

[24] Aristotle argues in *Politics* II.2–4 that the education of small children should be left in the hands of parents, because they alone give the sort of care that children need (9.5). But he offers no guarantee that someone who acquires the virtues will possess, at every point in his life, the other goods without which a life cannot be happy. A good person can, for example, lose friends and family to death (*NE* I.8 1099b5–6, I.9 1100a5–9).

best kinds of relationships, and attractive pleasures), but it should be kept in mind that the causal relationship moves in the other direction as well: when we have other goods, we are better able to exercise the virtues. 'It is impossible or not easy to do fine things, if one lacks resources' (I.8 1099a32–3). The virtuous person is not concerned solely with the quality of his thoughts and feelings, and indifferent to the world around him. On the contrary, thought and feeling are for the sake of successful action, and that requires equipment of all sorts. A just person, for example, does not simply keep himself innocent of injustice; he seeks justice in his community, and that requires him to improve his social world, or to keep it from deteriorating. And to bring this about, he often needs resources of various kinds: friends, wealth, and power are likely to come in handy. Aristotle of course does not mean that friends and other resources are merely of instrumental value. A virtuous person seeks the well-being of his friends for their own sake (a point emphasized throughout Books VIII and IX), and promotes justice because it serves the good of the community. Aristotle's point in emphasizing the instrumental value of friends, power, and wealth is to assure his audience that a plan of life that includes virtuous activity will have to include many other types of goods as well, and will therefore be a life that is rich in the variety of goods it contains.

I have been emphasizing that large portions of the *Ethics* carry out the program that Aristotle announces in I.7. The function argument leads to the conclusion that we should live in a way that gives expression to our mastery of certain intellectual and emotional skills; but it gives us only the barest sketch of the kind of life Aristotle is proposing to us. The rest of the *Ethics*—with its fuller discussion of the virtues, friendship, and pleasure—explains more fully which sorts of skill Aristotle thinks we need to exercise, and develops his argument that such a life is worthwhile and appealing. But our survey of the range of topics covered by the *Ethics*, and contributing to its elucidation of the well-lived life, is not yet complete: the one further topic discussed at length (besides the virtues, friendship, and pleasure) is *akrasia* (sometimes translated: 'incontinence' or 'weakness of will'). Here too it should be evident that Aristotle's discussion advances his general program of spelling out in detail the attractive features of the life of an ethically virtuous person.

Continence and incontinence, as Aristotle conceives them in VII.1–10, are closely related internal disorders that we all wish to avoid—although they are not categorized as vices. Both continent and incontinent people tend to experience some degree of psychological counter-pressure, after they have made certain kinds of decisions.[25] An appetite for pleasure, or anger, or some other emotion opposes their rational resolve, and so they experience a troubling internal tension. Continent people are those who are typically better able to resist these counter-rational pressures than is the average person, and who therefore often succeed in acting as they had planned; those who are worse than most at resisting these internal pressures, and often fail to stick to their resolutions, are incontinent (VII.10 1152a25–7). Aristotle's interest in these deficiencies derives in part from the philosophical puzzle that incontinence presents.[26] He realizes that it is no trivial matter to explain why human beings do not necessarily pursue whichever of their options reflection reveals to be their best. But in reading his analysis of continence and incontinence, we must not dwell exclusively on the theoretical problem of how incontinence is possible, and overlook the point that he is led to this topic because it fits into the general plan of his treatise: his general goal is to demonstrate not only that those who are ethically virtuous are better off than those who are thoroughly vile and wicked, but also that their condition is superior to those whose condition is intermediate between virtue and vice—the continent and the incontinent. Certain kinds of internal tension are fruitless, and among them are those desires and emotions that press against our resolution to do that which is in fact best for us. One of the accomplishments of a virtuous person is that he has so mastered himself that such pointless forms of resistance to his resolve do not occur. A great advantage of the virtues is that they free one from the irrationalities that so often afflict ordinary people.

3.11. *Contemplation, Science, and Other Activities*

After Aristotle completes his investigations into virtue, *akrasia*, pleasure, and friendship—each of which develops the conception of well-being proposed in Book I of the *Ethics*—he returns for a second

---

[25] To be more precise, this is only one kind of *akrasia*. Another kind (impetuosity) consists in acting so hastily that no time is allowed for deliberation. When that kind of incontinent person acts, he feels no counter-pressure. See VII.7 1150b19–28.

[26] Aristotle's treatment of this puzzle is notoriously difficult. For discussion, see Hardie, *Aristotle's Ethical Theory*, ch. 13; and Broadie, *Ethics with Aristotle*, ch. 5.

3.11. CONTEMPLATION, SCIENCE, AND OTHER ACTIVITIES

look at well-being (X.6–8), and takes up a thread he had left hanging. He had said, in I.5 (1096a4–5), that the best sort of life, on one account, is *theōrētikos*—'theoretical' or 'contemplative'. In X.7–8, that idea receives his full consideration and wholehearted endorsement. He puts forward a series of arguments to support the thesis that the best activity for a human being is contemplation: an activity in which one brings to mind truths that one has come to understand through a properly systematic investigation of the highest causes of the cosmos.

His audience has already been given a hint of this idea, for in his discussion of *sophia* ('wisdom', 'theoretical wisdom') in VI.7, he has said that the best thing to learn and think about is not oneself or others, because human beings are not the best thing in the cosmos (1141a20–2).[27] Which things are better? The uniformly moving and eternal causes of change that we see in the heavens; and the unchanging, unseen, and divine first cause on which all change depends. In order to understand these causes—and therefore to contemplate them—we must put ourselves through the entire course of study that is conveyed to us in Aristotle's theoretical works. We must understand the nature of causation, and the most important kinds of cause: souls. And to do this, we must see them at work throughout plant and animal life. To possess and exercise theoretical wisdom therefore requires a knowledge of all of the sciences, and of the philosophical underpinnings of those sciences. Perhaps Aristotle's students and readers have not begun to explore these subjects. That would not be surprising, since the only prerequisite for this course of study is that one should have been brought up well in one's habits; nothing in these works requires a knowledge of science or a prior study of causal notions. Those among his students who are unacquainted with these matters will learn from Aristotle that they are missing something of the greatest value. The highest good is something they have not yet begun to acquire. (Recall our discussion in 3.3.)

Few of Aristotle's present-day readers are persuaded by the arguments he offers in X.7–8 for the conclusion that contemplation is the highest human activity. But even if we agree that this part of the

---

[27] Aristotle leaves room for the possibility that one kind of virtue is superior to all others when he concludes the function argument with the words: 'and if there are many virtues, [the human good is activity of the soul] in accordance with the best and most perfect' (1098a17–18). 'Best and most perfect' might refer to the composite of all virtues, but I think that it refers to a single virtue, which turns out to be theoretical wisdom. For further discussion, see Kraut, *Aristotle on the Human Good*, pp. 241–4.

Ethics falls short of its mark, it would be wrong to infer that the intellectualist component of his conception of well-being is entirely misguided. Aristotle's defense of the contemplative life is in part a defense of the intrinsic value of science, a good that is now widely appreciated. Every prosperous nation of the modern world seeks to give its citizens a basic scientific education. No doubt that policy rests, to a large extent, on the assumption that economic prosperity requires a skilled workforce, and that the best way to produce an adequate supply of engineers, accountants, health professionals, and the like is to introduce the young to science and mathematics at an early age. But many parents are eager to have their children learn these subjects for a different sort of reason. They rightly encourage and reward the natural curiosity of their children in the world around them; they plausibly assume that it is in itself a good thing to pursue causal inquiries; in their opinion, the mastery of a rigorous intellectual discipline that explains natural phenomena is a worthwhile accomplishment, and a successful career in science can be one important ingredient of a well-lived life. These reasonable ways of thinking about science are not distant from Aristotle's high regard for contemplation. What unites them is the idea that something of great value is missed by those who are indifferent to the causal order of the universe. To take no interest in causal questions and inquiries is to fail to participate in one of the most complex and satisfying reason-giving practices that human beings have devised. Such indifference leaves one of the great powers of the mind undeveloped. It is therefore one of the merits of Aristotle's conception of well-being that he does not restrict his account of proper mental development to social, emotional, and deliberative skills. The realm of what is worth knowing is not restricted to that which enables us to cope with human relationships.

Aristotle holds that an eternal, incorporeal, and imperceptible being—a god—is ultimately responsible for the beautiful causal structure that science studies. When he lays out his plan for an ideal constitution, in Books VII and VIII of the *Politics*, he therefore leaves room for traditional religious institutions—priests, temples, worship, and the like (6.4). Science and philosophy, properly pursued, reveal the shortcomings of some traditional beliefs about the gods, but they do not destroy religion root and branch. Correctly understood, these three aspects of human life—science, philosophy, and religion—can be brought together. Whether we accept this optimistic picture or not, at least this much of Aristotle's thinking is

3.11. CONTEMPLATION, SCIENCE, AND OTHER ACTIVITIES

plausible: a conception of divinity must be evaluated in the light of our ideas about what it is to live well. The study of human well-being is continuous with the study of perfection, and therefore the theory of the good and theology are kindred subjects. Aristotle's way of linking these domains illustrates this point. His first cause is an eternal soul that thinks—and surely it must be a perfect thinker; what we do intermittently and with effort, it does ceaselessly, easily, and with great pleasure (*Met.* XII.7 1072b13–30). There is therefore a kinship between the philosophical life and the life of Aristotle's god. Christianity and other religious traditions attribute to divine being a far richer array of qualities—ethical attributes (love, compassion, forgiveness) being the most important among them. What a religious outlook cannot do, if it is to have any appeal or plausibility, is to put forward a conception of well-being that conflicts with human experience and reflection. A so-called god whose imitation or worship required us to destroy our minds, humiliate our neighbors, or let our children fend for themselves would be the greatest sort of devil. A religion devoted to such a conception of the good would create havoc in the political community.

Aristotle's discussion of contemplation in *Ethics* X.7–8 brings to the fore large and important areas of human life—philosophy, science, religion—though he does not take them to be separate spheres. Even so, we might wonder whether his account of the human good is one-sided. There are many other activities that are often thought to be of great value in themselves, but do not, at first glance, seem to fall within the categories carved out by his conception of well-being —for example, the exercise of skills in creating or responding to poetry, music, drama, dance, and art. Just as parents reasonably encourage the natural curiosity of children in the causal order, so they foster their children's proclivities to explore symmetries and asymmetries of sounds, images, words, pictures, and the like. Anyone who appreciates these aspects of human life counts them as parts of living well. Does Aristotle's theory of well-being overlook them?

Not at all—though he says far less than we would like. In the *Poetics* and Book VIII of the *Politics*, he tries to explain the value of these representational activities within the terms of his own account of well-being. Tragedy and comedy (which for Aristotle encompass poetry, music, and dance) are not forms of activity that are divorced from the social and emotional issues that we face in our everyday lives. He holds that these representational practices enhance our ethical outlook. Furthermore, he likens certain kinds of musical enjoyment to philosophical contemplation: when we listen with pleasure to beautifully expressed ideas accompanied by musical instruments, our delight in the truth merely for its own sake is akin to the philosopher's contemplation of the workings of the universe.[28] Perhaps we would conclude, upon examination, that Aristotle's way of thinking about drama and kindred activities fails to bring out what it is about these social practices that makes them so valuable to us. But it would be surprising if the emotional responses elicited by these activities were irrelevant to their worth; and one of the merits of Aristotle's account of well-being is the central role it assigns to properly felt emotions. The adequacy of his account of the arts is not a matter we can consider here. But we should give him credit for at least this much: he recognizes that an account of human well-being should explain why children should be educated not only to have the ethical virtues, and not only to have a love of science and philosophy, but also to be participants in such institutions as poetry, music, and dance.

One sphere of human life to which Aristotle devotes little attention is athletics—even though this was an important part of Greek civic life. It might be said, against Aristotle, that this omission is revealing: it shows that his conception of well-being is biased against the body. He of course recognizes the importance of physical health, but that does not rebut the charge. A critic might argue that the body should not be looked upon as a mere tool that needs to be kept in good condition in order to serve various purposes; good physical condition, it might be said, is no less valuable than any of the goods that receive Aristotle's attention. He overemphasizes cognitive skills at the expense of physical well-being and excellence—or so it might be said.

In fact, however, when we think about what it is about sports that arouses enthusiasm, we realize that cognitive skills and accomplishments play a central role. In many kinds of game, a player must make smart decisions quickly—often in an instant. A stupid player is a bad player, whatever the condition of his body. Many games demand extraordinary control over one's emotions. A player who lets anger, fear, or impatience get the better of him will fail; overconfidence and dejection brought on by a string of successes

---

[28] Aristotle's thoughts about the role of music in a well-lived life are found in *Pol.* VIII.3, 5–7. For further discussion, see below, 6.3; DePew, 'Politics, Music, and Contemplation in Aristotle's Ideal State'; Lord, *Education and Culture in the Political Thought of Aristotle*.

3.11. CONTEMPLATION, SCIENCE, AND OTHER ACTIVITIES

and failures must be avoided. Part of the background knowledge that fans bring to a game is their realization of how much mental discipline success requires—how much the body must respond to the extreme demands of the mind. In team sports, both selflessness and the ability to take charge are admired. It should be evident that athletic contests are shot through with moral qualities. They are regulated contests designed to express in a concentrated and emotionally charged form some of the qualities that are admired in everyday life. Without this ethical dimension, they would lose much of their hold on us. And so they can be fitted quite comfortably into an Aristotelian framework. They show that thinking with ethical categories is a nearly ubiquitous feature of human life. Even when we turn away from our workaday social activities and enter the artificial world of physical rivalry, we find that what engages us, whether we are players or spectators, are the familiar virtues, expressed in dramatic and physical form—intelligence, courage, fairness, endurance, patience, and the like.

The richness of Aristotle's account of well-being makes it a fruitful framework for normative reflection on the conduct of our lives. It takes us beyond a mere listing of goods and evils, by proposing as the central value of human life the mastery of various skills of thought, emotional response, and social interaction. Philosophy, science, poetry, music, and the sacred are treated as various ways in which our cognitive powers unfold. Wealth, honor, families, friendships, and political communities provide the resources and institutional frameworks that allow our cognitive powers to be nurtured and expressed. Of course, there are many ongoing questions about these institutions that Aristotle has not definitively answered. His conception of what scientific understanding consists in, or what divine being is, or the value of poetry and music, or the virtues of social life, are open to reconsideration and revision. That is the nature of a rich and living philosophical system: its central insights require modification and development. But even if our own thinking about the value of science, philosophy, poetry, and the virtues of social life departs significantly from Aristotle's, his general framework, which takes the excellent deployment of our cognitive powers to be the highest good, should continue to guide us.

3.12. Return to the Function Argument: Metaphysics and Science

One important aspect of Aristotle's conception of the good has not yet received our attention. It plays a role in the function argument that he gives in *Ethics* I.7, but we passed over it, when we discussed that part of our text (3.6, 3.8, 3.9). We should now turn back to it.

Before he tries to show what our function is, he gives two reasons for thinking that we human beings must have some function or other (1097b28-33). First, builders, shoemakers, and all sorts of craftsmen have functions; it would be odd, then, if there were no function for human beings. Second, eyes, hands, and many other parts of the body have functions; so we should expect that some function, different from those of bodily parts, can also be ascribed to human beings.

At least this much can be said in support of these inferences: functions are often hierarchically nested. Tools provide an excellent example. The threads of a screw, for instance, allow it to enter and remain fixed in a solid object. Both parts (threads) and whole (screw) have functions, and these are related to each other; the function of a part allows the whole to serve its function. So it is a reasonable principle that whenever one comes across a part or whole that has a function, we should look for a corresponding object (the whole to which a part belongs, or a part that contributes to the whole) that also has a function. These things don't exist in isolation; they come in groups.

Aristotle's audience is introduced at the very start of the *Ethics* to the notion that crafts are hierarchically organized. The maker of bridles serves the horse-trainer, who in turn serves the general. The military leader studies methods for producing victory; but victory is for the sake of peace, which provides the conditions in which we carry out the activities that make it worthwhile to have defended the community against aggressors. Those peacetime activities will be ones that are good for any human being (not merely for craftsmen) to undertake, and therefore there must be some function that we possess precisely because we are human beings. This train of thought rests on the assumption that when one finds a nested series of functions, they ultimately serve one highest function. The various functions of craftsmen must ultimately serve some higher function—and what else could that be but our functioning as human beings?

3.12. RETURN TO THE FUNCTION ARGUMENT

The second argument, which moves from the function of bodily parts to the function of human beings, proceeds according to the same logic. Here the analogy between the parts of a tool and the parts of a body is one that Aristotle would welcome. Tools are designed to be put to use; there is something that they do—or that we do with them; that use is the tools' function, which is in turn supported by the sub-functions of their several parts. Similarly, the parts of the body are organized in ways that support the activities characteristic of living things. The matter of the eye, for example, has a certain structure, without which the power to see would be lost. If that matter is altered in ways that impede the eye's operation, we count that as an injury, and not a mere alteration, because seeing is good for the organism. Now, the good of a human being cannot be equated with the proper functioning of any single part of the body; rather, we should expect the human good to consist in something that is supported by all parts of the body working together. That activity, whatever it turns out to be, will be our function, because the sub-functions of parts always serve some further function beyond themselves.

Having reached this point in his argument, Aristotle then relies upon one of the principal ideas of his metaphysics: the function of the body and its various parts is to serve the soul, for the soul is not some corporeal stuff (some mixture of earth, air, fire, and water), but rather the potentiality possessed by certain kinds of matter to operate in ways characteristic of living things—growing, reproducing, moving, perceiving, and thinking.[29] Therefore, to discover what the function of human beings is, we need only consider which of these activities of the soul is most plausibly taken as the ultimate end served by the parts of our body. And surely that must be the activity of the part of the soul that possesses reason, because this power sets us apart from plants and other animals.

Notice that these ideas about well-being and the parts of the body apply with equal force to other kinds of living thing besides humans. The snout and tail of a dog should also have functions, if Aristotle's argument is worth anything. Furthermore, there must be an activity of the dog's soul that is ultimately served by the proper functioning of its bodily parts. The bodily organization of dogs and all other species of living things serves the operations of their souls, and the function and well-being of an organism consists in an activity of its

---

[29] The principal text is *De An.* II.1–4. See 3.n.17.

soul, or some part of it. Accordingly, when we study plants and other animals, the question we should ask ourselves is how their corporeal parts enable them to grow, reproduce, move about, and perceive. We should ask, in other words, how their bodies serve their souls. Since a scientific understanding of anything consists in grasping its causes, one cannot acquire this kind of knowledge of living things until one sees why their bodies are organized in a way that serves the good of the whole organism. Just as we cannot understand what the human hand is, until we recognize how its organization serves human thought (*Part. An.* IV.10 687a7–23), so we cannot grasp the matter of any living thing, unless we see how it promotes the soul's proper functioning. The science of plant and animal life cannot be possessed by those who know nothing about the well-being of plants and animals.

Having looked beneath the surface of this component of the function argument, we have found that it rests on Aristotle's metaphysics and his approach to the study of living things.[30] Now that we recognize this connection between his ethical theory, his metaphysics, and his science, we must ask ourselves: would successful objections to his metaphysics and his methodology for the study of living things undermine his conception of well-being?

That is not an idle question. Aristotle's conception of the soul as a non-corporeal cause of the body is a piece of metaphysics that many philosophers—beginning with the ancient Stoics and Epicureans—have rejected.[31] Furthermore, the life sciences, as they are now practiced, refrain from making assumptions about what is good for plants and animals; even though survival and reproductive fitness play an important role in biological explanation, biology need not assert that it is good for an organism to survive and reproduce.[32] Modern scientists take themselves to be in the business of describing and explaining what exists or has existed, not evaluating what is better or worse for living things. Accordingly, from the point of view of contemporary science, Aristotle's conception of scientific

---

[30] This aspect of Aristotle's ethical theory is fully discussed by Irwin, *Aristotle's First Principles*, esp. chs. 15–18. For a briefer presentation, see Irwin, 'The Metaphysical and Psychological Basis of Aristotle's Ethics'.

[31] The viability of Aristotle's framework for the philosophy of mind continues to be a matter of controversy: see the essays in Nussbaum and Rorty, *Essays on Aristotle's De Anima*.

[32] The notion of function is retained in modern biology, but its proper interpretation is a matter of dispute. See Sterelny and Griffiths, *Sex and Death*, pp. 220–4, and p. 251 for further reading.

3.12. RETURN TO THE FUNCTION ARGUMENT

understanding is an unsustainable hybrid: because he holds that corporeal organization is caused by an animal's good, he illegitimately brings together two spheres that must be kept apart—the normative and the explanatory.

For these reasons, the metaphysics and the scientific framework that lie beneath the surface of one part of the function argument are open to question. What sort of response to these objections can be given on Aristotle's behalf? One strategy would simply be to launch a defense of his metaphysics and his conception of proper scientific method.[33] But, whatever the prospects for such a defense are, we should recognize that a different kind of strategy can be successfully pursued: it can be argued that Aristotle's conception of well-being is still viable even when it is detached from his conception of the soul as the cause of the body and his teleological approach to the study of living things. That is the strategy I have pursued here. I have revived those components of the function argument that do not depend on Aristotle's teleology and metaphysics.[34] By reflecting on our ideas about proper human development from childhood to adulthood, and the central role played in a well-lived life by skills of thought, feeling, and social interaction, Aristotle's conclusion—that well-being consists in the skillful deployment of our capacity to give and respond to reasons—can be sustained (3.6, 3.8, 3.9.) I have also argued that his conception of well-being should be evaluated not solely on the basis of what we find in the function argument of I.7,

---

[33] For a comprehensive interpretation and defense of Aristotle's essentialism, see Charles, *Aristotle on Meaning and Essence*.

[34] I have not rested my defense of Aristotle's conception of the good on his thesis that each of us is essentially a human being, and that we should be defined as rational animals. That is because I take his ideas about the essence and definition of human beings to rest in part on a normative assumption: that it is best for us live in accordance with reason. He does not attempt to derive conclusions about how we should live from a normatively neutral division of living things into species, or from a value-free scientific theory of what explains human behavior or development. See Hurka, *Perfectionism*, chs. 2–4, for an attempt, inspired by his reading of Aristotle, to do what I believe Aristotle himself did not do: draw conclusions about how we should live from premises about what it is to be human—premises that do not themselves presuppose ideas about what is good. For criticism of Hurka's approach, see Kitcher, 'Essence and Perfection'. At 3.14 I return to questions about Aristotle's essentialism; and at 7.3, 7.9, and 7.11 I consider the metaphysical basis for his thesis that the political community is prior to each of its members. For a brief introduction to Aristotle's concept of essence, see Barnes, 'Metaphysics', pp. 99–101; and the bibliography to his *Cambridge Companion to Aristotle*, p. 351. For a full discussion of whether Aristotle's teleological approach to politics is defensible, see Salkever, *Finding the Mean*, pp. 3–104. Interest in this subject has been heightened by the statement of MacIntyre that 'Aristotle's ethics, expounded as he expounds it, presupposes his metaphysical biology'. See *After Virtue*, p. 139. See too Broadie, *Ethics with Aristotle*, pp. 49–50; Antony, 'Natures and Norms'; and Nussbaum, 'Aristotle, Politics, and Human Capabilities', pp. 116–24.

but in the light of everything he says about the virtues and their relationship to such other goods as friendship and pleasure (3.10, 3.11.) If these aspects of Aristotle's practical philosophy continue to be attractive, then his conception of well-being will not come undone, whatever the fate of his metaphysics and science.

3.13. Well-Being and Other Species

There is one other debatable component of Aristotle's philosophy that lies in the background of his function argument: he holds that human beings are superior to all other animals because we alone can deliberate, give and demand reasons, modify our emotions when we find them too weak or strong, search for causal explanations, and the like. If reason is the capacity for engaging in these activities, then human beings are the only species that possesses reason; and this, Aristotle supposes, makes the lives we lead better than those of plants or any other animals.[35]

This assumption lies behind his statement that our function cannot consist in nutrition, growth, or perception. These are activities of the human soul, for they are some of the operations that the parts of our bodies enable us to carry out. But, Aristotle says, they are activities that are not peculiar to us: other animals take in nourishment, grow, and perceive. And therefore the human function cannot consist in carrying out these activities (I.7 1097b33–1098a3). Surely his conviction that we are not on a par with all other living things is playing a role here. His tacit assumption must be that if nutrition, growth, and perception were our function, our lives would be no better than those of other living things. But, he supposes, the level of well-being we can achieve, if we live our lives properly, is far superior to the level attainable by other living things. Therefore, the activities we share with other species cannot be our function. He is looking for an activity of the soul that is peculiar to human life, because only that will explain what makes it possible for human lives to be superior to those of other organisms.

Even though the thesis of human superiority lies behind

---

[35] Only gods and human beings can be *eudaimōn* (I.9 1099b32–3, X.8 1178b24–8), though other living things can live well, to the extent that their lives distantly resemble divine life (*De An.* II.4 415a26–b2, III.12 434b22–5). The cognitive superiority of human beings to other animals is the major theme of *Met.* I.1. Aristotle says at *Pol.* I.8 1256b15–22 that plants and all other animals exist for the sake of human beings.

3.13. WELL-BEING AND OTHER SPECIES

Aristotle's elimination of nutrition, growth, and perception as candidates for our function, it is important to realize that his conception of human well-being can be freed from its dependence on so controversial a claim. He can set aside his assumption that the lives of human beings can be better than those of other animals, and substitute for it the far weaker thesis that each species has its own peculiar way of living well. Horses, for example, have the potential to live a life that makes good use of their equine bodies, and of their unique physical and cognitive powers; if they lose that potential, because of disease or injury, they cannot make good their loss by leading instead the life of a dog or a cat or a human being. Similarly, one can say on Aristotle's behalf that a good life for a human being makes use of powers that are peculiar to us. A human being who loses his capacity to deliberate, alter his emotions, cooperate with others, or understand the world cannot develop in their place the skills of a different kind of animal. His uniquely human body and peculiarly human kit of psychological tools have equipped him to lead a certain kind of life. The development of those resources is where his good lies, and should they be lost, there is no possibility of living instead the life of a mere plant or animal.

When we reconstruct Aristotle's argument in this way, we can justify his thought that human well-being consists in the exercise of capacities that are peculiarly human—our deliberative, social, emotional, and intellectual skills. We can say, as he does, that we should live a life that no other kind of living thing can live—but not (as he thinks) because we are superior to them; rather, we should live a peculiarly human life because it is a general truth, applicable to all species, that well-being consists in the development and use of powers that are not fully available to members of other species.

It follows from this way of looking at the well-being of living things that the good of any individual organism is to a large extent species-specific. We can say little of interest about what is good for things in general; but we can say a great deal more when we divide the world into species, and separately consider the well-being of each of the different kinds of living thing. In the same way, little can be said about what is good or bad for all craftsmen, or all tools, or all parts of the body. We must specify which sort of craftsman we are talking about, or which tool, or which part of the body; only then can we say in detail what is good for it. In general, the good of X is determined by the kind of thing X is.

But it is important to make this point more precise. To clarify matters, it will help to return to the example I used in the previous chapter (2.4) of a man who learns from a friend how to appreciate the beauty of the natural world. Suppose he had failed to respond, emotionally or intellectually, to his environment. If we are reasonably confident that there is nothing amiss in his friend's efforts to educate him, then the proper diagnosis should be that, for whatever reason, he has a deficiency that cannot be removed. There is no reason for us to withdraw our judgment that he would be better off were he to enjoy his walks. His incapacity to do so does not undermine the idea that he is missing something valuable.

But now consider other kinds of living thing—birds, for example—who also lack a sense of beauty. Are we to say that this lack is also a loss to them? I am not asking the complex question whether on balance their lives are better or worse than human lives. My question is whether it makes sense to make comparisons across species at least to this extent: can we say that one respect in which they are not as well off as human beings is that they lack a sense of beauty? An affirmative answer would not prevent us from saying that there are other respects in which we are not as well off as they. Nor would an affirmative answer commit us to making an overall judgment about whether human life is better than any other kind of life.

If we refuse to think that birds are missing out on a good thing because of their incapacity to appreciate the beauty of their songs, but agree that the absence of a sense of beauty in a human being is a deficiency, then we are adopting the principle that 'good-for-X' is always an abbreviation for the fuller expression: 'good-for-X-of-kind-Y.' According to that principle, we cannot create a list of good and bad things until we have first divided the world into species. Once we have worked out our taxonomy, we can put a sense of beauty on the list of good things for human beings, thereby committing ourselves to saying that any human being is to some extent worse off if this sense is missing. But we are not committing ourselves to saying that the members of other species are worse off for lacking the good things that human beings have.

I see no reason why our judgments about value should be biologically fragmented in this way. If the incapacity of a human being to enjoy beauty is bad for him, then it is arbitrary to hold that when this incapacity is species-wide it is no longer a loss. Furthermore, there is no good reason to abandon the sensible thought that the life of a human being who has developed normally is richer than the life of certain other organisms—those, for example, that have only a

3.13. WELL-BEING AND OTHER SPECIES

single cell. We are not so different from all other living things that *all* cross-species comparisons of well-being are impossible to make. It is open to us to reject Aristotle's thesis that we are superior to all other animals, while retaining the far weaker claim that we can have better lives than at least some other species.

For all that, it remains the case that the good of an individual living thing depends to a large extent on the species to which it belongs. In ministering to the well-being of an organism, it would be madness to ignore the kind of thing it is. Our rough and ready classification of living things into kinds gives us a good sense of what their capacities and limitations are, and the only reasonable way to promote the good is to take these broad differences into account. When we care for human beings by promoting their rational agency, we can be guided by the thought that the excellent exercise of reason is a good thing for whomever and whatever can achieve it. It so happens that, so far as we can tell, the only biological species that is capable of sapience[36] and moral development is our own. In the same way, in ministering to the good of horses, we need only be guided by the thought that certain kinds of equine behavior, which make good use of that animal's psychology and body, are good for any animals that can achieve it—and we can leave open the question whether any other kinds of animal can do so. In this way, we transform the idea that the good for members of a species is to be found in some activity that can be found *only* in that species. In its place, we can say that the world of living things offers to us a large number of patterns of normal development, and corresponding to the successful unfolding of these developmental patterns are many different kinds of good life. We thereby bring our conception of the good of human beings under the heading of a larger theory about the good of all living things.

By revising Aristotle's theory in this way, we can abandon the least viable component of his conception of kinds. He seeks a scientific understanding of each species in terms of its good, and the taxonomy I have presupposed requires no such conflation of scientific and normative enterprises. Biology as currently practiced need make no claim about what is good for dogs, mice, or human beings; it

---

[36] I borrow this use of 'sapience' from Brandom, *Making It Explicit*, pp. 3–5. It designates our capacity to be 'subject to the authority of reasons' (p. 5), a capacity that must be contrasted sharply with the sentience we share with other animals. Recall the point made in 3.8: it is reason in this sense, not intelligent behavior, that sets us off from other animals, according to Aristotle.

replaces the notion of what is good for an organism with that of its fitness, and fitness plays a purely explanatory role as a theoretical construct of evolutionary biology. Nothing I have said in my defense of Aristotle requires that my division of the world into kinds competes with the taxonomy that biologists settle upon for their purposes. For my division of organisms into kinds is not intended (as Aristotle's was) to serve a scientific purpose. It is a normative rather than a scientific taxonomy: it holds that when we consider the normal development and well-being of different types of individuals, we find that they come in clusters that correspond more or less to the species recognized by common sense.

By contrast, the subjectivist approach to well-being that we considered in Chapter 2 must give a bifurcated account of well-being, for it holds that what is good for human beings is created by their volitions or other psychological attitudes, but it cannot tell anything like this story about other living things. Human subjectivity does not create the good of other creatures. The only plausible approach to the good of an animal or plant is one that speaks in terms of its normal development and operation, where 'normal' is not a statistical but an evaluative matter. The subjectivist must accept this, but is at the same time committed to giving an entirely different account of the well-being of humans: this is something that is brought into existence through our psychological attitudes, whatever they happen to be. Aristotelianism agrees with subjectivism that there is a great discontinuity between human beings and other living things, but it explains that discontinuity by saying that in our own case normal development consists in the education of rational agency, whereas the normal development of other living forms is nothing like this. There is no mystery, for Aristotle, about why the contours of a good human life are so different from those found in any other species: that is because we alone are sapient. By contrast, subjectivism is saddled with a puzzling contrast: for so many other species, well-being is a matter of proper development and operation, but in one case only, the human case, goodness is created by each individual. Instead of viewing human beings as a very different kind of animal, the subjectivist takes a page from the book of those philosophers who locate all value in the will of God: the subjectivist says that, godlike, we create our good; but concedes that the good of a living thing is not generally the sort of thing that is created.

3.14. Essence

Aristotle believed in the fixity and eternality of species, and that of course is a component of his system that must be abandoned. Does this create a difficulty for his thesis that there is an account of well-being that holds true for all members of our species at all times? It might be claimed that since all species are likely to change, sometimes radically so, it is reckless and naïve to advance a thesis about what is eternally good for all human beings (or, for that matter, any other species).

A further complaint can be made: since we agreed in Chapter 2 (2.4, 2.8) that the ideas we have about what is good for us may at any time be incomplete, and that our lives may suffer because we have too narrow a conception of the good, we ought to leave open the possibility that future experience and reflection will reveal to us more important goods than the ones Aristotle places at the center of human well-being.

These two objections can be put together in the following way. As human beings change over hundreds of thousands of years, it is likely that new capacities will unfold, old capacities will die, and ways of living that cannot be imagined now will emerge. What has been good for us for a mere few thousand years will at that distant time no longer be good for us, or even possible for us. And so we should reject any theory of well-being, like Aristotle's, that commits itself to the existence of a single human nature and human good that persists without change through time.

A contemporary defender of Aristotle might reply that the scenario just imagined is impossible: it simply cannot happen that at some point human beings will evolve in such a way that it is no longer part of their good to exercise reason, master their emotions, and engage in social activities. That is because it is part of our essence that we are reasoning, emotional, and social animals. And so, even if we did evolve in a way that gave rise to a species that lacks sapience, we could not properly count that new species as human, because it would lack the defining characteristic of our species.

But that is not the line I would wish to take. There is no point arguing about what we would or should say in circumstances utterly remote from the ones in which we live. We should instead take to heart Aristotle's point that ethics and politics are to be studied for the sake of action (*NE* II.2 1103b26–9), and that in these areas we should leave aside anything that makes no practical difference. Since the dispute just described about who is to be counted as a human being can make no difference to the way we live now, we should banish it from our study of ethics. If it is an appropriate matter for metaphysical discussion, that is not a branch of metaphysics that can make a difference to ethics. There is, in any case, a far simpler way to respond to the objections put forward. The mere possibility that scientific theories that have so far been entirely successful might be undermined by future discoveries gives us no reason to withhold assent from them; and for the same reason, the mere possibility or even likelihood that millions of years from now human beings (if there are such things) will have evolved into who knows what gives us no reason to change our ideas about how we should live.

3.15. The Political Life

Aristotle announces near the beginning of the *Ethics* (I.2 1094a26–8) that the science whose job it is to study the ultimate end of human beings is *politikē* ('politics', 'political science'). The audience he is addressing will use what they learn from him to guide their work in the public arena. Having sharpened their ideas about what the human good is, they will go forth and promote the good of the several communities in which they exert some influence. Political science, so conceived, deserves to play a uniquely influential role in civic life. Students of other practical disciplines carve out some limited task for themselves, and do not ask themselves, as part of their course of study, what is good for all human beings, or what it is to live well. A military expert, for example, learns everything he can about how to win battles. His studies begin with the assumption that victory is good, and he learns various ways to produce it. But his expertise does not tell him what to do with victory once it has been achieved. In a well-governed community, military experts are placed under the control of those who understand the proper uses to which war should be put. At any rate, if generals do happen to have some insight into such matters, they are not the only ones who do so. They may deserve to cast their votes about matters of war and peace, but the authority to make these decisions does not rest with them alone.

The same holds true of all others who develop an expertise in

3.15. THE POLITICAL LIFE

some narrow area of human life. Doctors and architects know something about how to produce health and buildings, but that does not entitle them to apply their expertise to whomever they choose, whenever they choose. There is nothing about their technical training that would prevent them from using their skills to do harm rather than good. These crafts need to be regulated and overseen, so that they are used in ways that benefit rather than injure the public. The power that plays this supervisory role will therefore exercise supreme authority over the entire community: it will make the final decision about which activities should be fostered or hindered, required or forbidden. The authority to make those decisions resides in those who hold political power.

People who exercise such supreme oversight should have an understanding of the proper role played by medicine, architecture, and other crafts and disciplines in a community. More generally, since their job is to promote the well-being of the citizens, they should have reflected on the proper place of many sorts of good in a well-lived life. Aristotle's political works are an attempt to improve the decision-making skills of those who wish to play this role in public life. The members of his audience are assumed to be interested in something beyond mere self-improvement; having been brought up well, they already take an interest in the well-being of others—and not merely their family and friends. When they learn from Aristotle that the name of the subject that they are examining is *politikē*, they do not close their books or leave his school, because that is precisely what they wish to study. They agree with Aristotle that they will be better equipped to participate in the affairs of their communities once they have learnt, through reflection on his treatises, what the proper standard is for making public decisions. And what standard could be more appropriate, for their purposes, than human well-being?

But an understanding of well-being is not the only thing one needs if one is to do some good for one's community. One must also know something about how political communities have been, or might be, organized. One must have some familiarity with the strengths and shortcomings of different constitutional arrangements, the degree to which they are capable of improvement, and the dangers to which they are exposed. That is why Aristotle concludes, in the final chapter of the *Ethics*, that the next topics to which his students should turn are the ones discussed in the treatise known to us as the *Politics*. He conceives of these two works as components of a single project: the first describes the nature of well-being, and the second portrays the many different ways—some better, some worse—in which cities can be organized.[37] Once they have learnt both components of the science of politics, his students will possess a general understanding of how to benefit whole communities in a wide variety of circumstances. They will not only know what is good for human beings in general, but will be familiar with the various obstacles to well-being created by defective political arrangements. They will not only understand which sort of political system is ideal, but will also have developed a realistic sense of how much or little change can be expected, within the limitations of ordinary political life.

Should they successfully apply the lessons they have learnt, by promoting the good of entire cities, they will have gone as far as it is possible for a human being to go in the exercise of the practical virtues. Their aptitude as practical reasoners, their mastery over their emotions, and their social skills will have been developed and successfully deployed in a way that cannot be surpassed, because there is no greater accomplishment, in the practical realm, than to improve the lives of all members of one's community. Of course, from the point of view of one's own well-being, there is a better alternative to the successful exercise of political power: as Aristotle tries to convince his audience in X.7–8, those who devote themselves to mastering philosophy and the sciences, and to contemplating the truths that they have discovered, will live better lives than do political leaders. Members of Aristotle's school who arrived at his door in a state of uncertainty about whether to devote themselves to theoretical studies or the practical life are advised that their own well-being will be best served by the former alternative. But Aristotle assumes that only a handful have the intellectual aptitude needed to pursue a life of science and philosophy. For all others, the best sort of life is one in which their social, emotional, and intellectual skills are challenged by the most difficult and therefore the most rewarding of practical tasks: the improvement of civic life. 'If it [the good] is the same for both one [human being] and for the city, it seems to be greater and more complete to attain and preserve that of the city. For although one should be satisfied [to do so] for even

---

[37] It is sometimes said that for Aristotle there is no distinction at all between ethics and politics; they are not closely related subjects, but one and the same. But in fact he does sometimes distinguish them. See 1.5.

3.15. THE POLITICAL LIFE

one [human being] alone, it is finer and more divine [to do so] for a nation and for cities' (I.2 1094b7–10).[38]

No doubt such a life will inevitably have its troubles and anxieties. That is one reason why Aristotle thinks the political life is inferior, from the point of view of one's own well-being, to the philosophical life (X.7 1177b4–15). Political action always tries to shape the future, but the consequences of one's actions are never a matter about which one can be certain; by contrast, the contemplation of truth is always under one's control, since it does not aim at some state of affairs beyond the present. Nonetheless, the burdens of a political life are not so great that they will make someone leading it regret that he chose to develop and exercise his cognitive powers as fully as a human being can.

Aristotle says several times in his practical writings that man is by nature a political animal.[39] We will examine that idea more fully at a later point (7.2), but we should recognize immediately that he cannot mean by this that the best life for a human being is to lead a political rather than a philosophical life. His point, rather, is that a good life for a human being is one in which one participates in various kinds of activity with others—and not only with one's blood relations and friends, but with many other members of the political community (I.7 1097b9–11). Human beings are given to working in large groups, not only in small units; and it is good that this should be so, because participation in those large groups allows us to develop our cognitive powers more fully. A good life for a human being consists, in part, in good relationships with other human beings, including those who are outside one's circle of family and friends. That is why all of the qualities that Aristotle takes to be practical virtues are skills whose exercise constitutes having good relationships with others. Other human beings are not mere instruments or obstacles with whom one must come to terms, in order to preserve a private space within which to pursue one's good. On the

---

[38] For an alternative interpretation, see Mulgan, 'Aristotle and the Value of Political Participation', esp. pp. 200 and 211. He argues that the ethical virtues can be fully exercised without active political participation, and that Aristotle 'articulat[es] the growing mood of quietism and withdrawal from public life that developed during the fourth century' (p. 211). I believe that the passage cited (I.2 1094b7–10) provides evidence against this interpretation; so do Aristotle's characterization of his treatise as a political work (I.2 1094a27–8; see above, 1.5), his conception of justice (4.3, 4.4, 4.8), and his thesis that, aside from the philosophical life, the political life is the best available to human beings.

[39] The phrase is used seven times: *Pol* I.2 1253a7–8, III.6 1278b19; *NE* I.7 1097b11, VIII.12 1162a17–18, IX.9 1169b18–19; *EE* VII.10 1242a22–3; *Hist. An.* I.1 487b33–488a13.

contrary, they are fellow participants in the social activities that are in themselves good for us to pursue.

It would be a mistake to infer from this that, according to Aristotle, there can be no genuine conflict between one person's good and another's. We need others, and not as mere instruments; but in certain circumstances we can also get in each other's way. That is because it is not enough for us just to think and feel in a certain manner: the full exercise of our cognitive powers requires material resources, and those resources can become scarce. When they do, one person's good can easily come into conflict with another's. The only way for me to feed my children might be to take from someone else who needs these provisions as much as I do. Accordingly, one of the tasks of a well-governed community, as Aristotle recognizes (*Pol.* II.6 1265b10–12), is to make sure that its citizens are not driven by necessity to take such desperate measures. No one should be so poor that he must break the law in order to have the resources needed for living well. It is only in certain kinds of community that each of us can pursue his good without coming into conflict with the good of others. One of the many tasks of Aristotle's students is to use their influence to insure that each citizen has adequate material resources.

But that can be only one small part of their job. Material resources are a necessary condition for well-being, but they are not what well-being consists in. The most important task of Aristotle's students is to learn how to create conditions favorable to the development of virtue within their fellow citizens—or, if that is too high a goal in certain communities, at least something akin to genuine virtue (*Ethics* X.9 1179b18–20).[40] Although Aristotle takes each person to be responsible for the traits of character he acquires (III.5 1113b6–7), he shows an acute awareness, in the closing chapter of the *Ethics*, of the role that the family and the larger community play in shaping the outlook of their members. A city's mode of organizing itself, its unwritten norms of conduct, and its legal system have a profound effect on the manner in which its citizens interact with each other. A certain way of life takes hold in a community and becomes difficult to dislodge. Over the years, as one generation succeeds another, modes of thought and emotional response become second nature to the citizens; and these patterns are the product of their

---

[40] The passage cited will play an important role in my interpretation of the *Politics*. See esp. 10.7 and 12.2.

3.15. THE POLITICAL LIFE

city's norms, laws, and way of governing itself. The principal task of Aristotle's students is to do what they can to shape these institutions, which in turn have so great an influence on the well-being of individuals. When laws, both written and unwritten, are not too distant from ideal justice, and have genuine force in a community, then many of the citizens will themselves be just, more or less. Their habits of thought and feeling will lead them to interact with each other in a way that constitutes a well-lived life, or something approximating that goal. That is the ultimate end studied and promoted by the science of politics.

4

Justice in the *Nicomachean Ethics*

4.1. A Complaint

No virtue is of greater importance in political philosophy than justice, and it is therefore appropriate that in the *Nicomachean Ethics*—a treatise that presents itself as a political work—this is the virtue that receives Aristotle's fullest attention. And yet his discussion is likely to disappoint or bore many of his readers. I would guess that when teachers of the *Ethics* are forced to omit some portion of the treatise from their courses, it is Book V that they most often choose to ignore. Students who do read it probably consider it the least interesting component of his ethical theory. By the time they arrive at this book in their study of the *Ethics*, they may have grown weary of the doctrine of the mean, and will have little patience for Aristotle's attempt to show that justice can be made to conform to this doctrine. The other principal ideas of Book V may seem obviously false or uninteresting. Aristotle holds that in the broad sense justice is lawfulness; and that in the narrow sense it is equality or proportionality, which comes in three kinds (distributive, corrective, and reciprocal). The idea that justice can be equated with lawfulness may seem preposterous, whereas the distinction between distributive, corrective, and reciprocal justice appears to be acceptable but unexciting. The remainder of Book V is devoted to several further themes—a distinction between natural and conventional justice, a discussion of equity, and a puzzle about whether one can voluntarily be treated unjustly—but they seem a disorderly assortment. Aristotle appears to be putting together a series of loosely related remarks, and this suggests that he lacks a cohesive and systematic theory of justice. An unfavorable comparison with Plato springs to mind, for the *Republic* is nothing if not systematic in its full-scale analysis of this virtue. Whether we accept Plato's picture of a just society or not, he at least gives us a comprehensive and detailed theory of what a just person and a just community would look like. That is what we miss in Book V of the *Ethics*.

Our disappointment will be all the greater because justice is a subject that continues to arouse deep disagreements that cry out for philosophical analysis and resolution. We hope to find in a philosophical account of justice some attempt to show how the deep divisions within and among nations ought to be resolved. We would like to know which institutions and laws a just society must have, and which among our current practices ought to be reformed or abandoned. Since Aristotle himself demands that ethical theory serve a practical purpose, and not be pursued solely for its own sake (*NE* II.2 1103b26–9), it seems fair to hold his own treatment of justice to this standard, and ask whether it can provide us with a guide to action. Yet it is difficult to find anything of practical value in the theory he presents in Book V of the *Ethics*—not merely for us modern readers, but for his contemporaries as well.

In fairness, we must not expect more of Book V than it is meant to deliver. It does not try to offer a complete political theory or even a complete theory of justice. Aristotle realizes that he is leaving some of the most important questions of justice unresolved in Book V, for several times he alludes to points that are developed more fully in the *Politics*.[1] But it is not much of a defense of his treatment of justice in the *Ethics* to say that we must go elsewhere for his really interesting material.

---

[1] The distinction made at *NE* V.2 1130b26–9 between a good man and a good citizen is developed in *Pol.* III.4. The principal dispute about distributive justice, mentioned at *NE* V.3 1131a25–9, is treated in *Pol.* III.6–18. And *Pol.* VII–VIII defends the claim, made at *NE* V.7 1135a5, that there is one naturally best city. Do these passages show that the *Politics*—or, at any rate, these portions of it—were composed prior to Book V of the *Nicomachean Ethics*? Not necessarily. We could take them as indications that when Aristotle wrote Book V, he had it in mind to write a political treatise (or a series of political essays) that would elaborate on some of the points made quite briefly in his discussion of justice. Alternatively, Book V of the *Nicomachean Ethics* might be a second draft, the first draft having been written for the *Eudemian Ethics*, and revised after the composition of the *Politics* so as to include references to questions discussed in that work. See 1.5 for discussion of the chronology of Aristotle's practical writings.

I have begun with these negative thoughts about Book V because my aim will be to undo them. As I read him, Aristotle has a theory of justice that rivals Plato's in scope and depth, and provides a plausible alternative to it. We do not get his full picture until we read the *Politics*, but nonetheless, I hope to show that Book V of the *Ethics* is of far greater interest than my initial remarks make it out to be.

This will be a lengthy chapter (the longest in this book), and it will not shy away from some of the intricacies of Aristotle's analysis of justice. It may help, therefore, to say something about the broad contours of the discussion to come. Aristotle's analysis of justice, we shall see, is in many respects a critique of Plato's approach to the same subject—even though Plato is never mentioned explicitly in Book V of the *Ethics*. Plato holds in the *Republic* that justice is a unitary psychological phenomenon, that it is at bottom a relationship one has to oneself (or, more precisely, a relation among the parts of one's soul), that it is most fully exhibited by philosophers, and that it is best understood by being placed in the context of an ideal society. Aristotle rejects all of these claims. His disagreement with Plato is not merely over the analysis of a concept, but about the proper place of political philosophers in the social world. Plato's conception of justice leads to the conclusion that it is only in the most unusual circumstances that philosophers should entangle themselves in the practical affairs of their cities. One can preserve the justice of one's soul only by remaining aloof from everyday political matters; small-scale political amelioration is at best a waste of one's time, at worst corrupting. Aristotle decisively rejects the idealistic aloofness of Plato's approach to politics. He holds that the approximate forms of justice that can be negotiated by hostile political factions are significant achievements. One way to lead a worthwhile life is to promote some modicum of legality and justice in highly defective regimes.

This activist component of Aristotle's anti-Platonism is most evident in the *Politics* when he asserts that political theory must examine not merely the best possible city, but cities of every possible variety, including those that are locked into deformed structures that severely limit the possibility of improvement (IV.1).[2] But it is not only in that portion of his political writings that we can find a deeply anti-Platonic strain in his thinking. His conception of justice in Book V of the *Ethics* rests on the thesis that justice requires active participation in the affairs of one's political community, even when

---

[2] This feature of Aristotle's thought will be discussed in 12.1.

4.1. A COMPLAINT

it offers limited opportunities for reform. Ethical life, as Aristotle portrays it, is inevitably a social matter—a coming to terms with the rules, customs, norms, and laws of one's political community. Justice is not a relationship of the parts of one's soul but a relationship among separate human beings, and political justice (the most important aspect of this virtue) requires that one treat others in ways that accord with the rules of one's community—defective though that community may be. Withdrawal from one's city's affairs may, in certain circumstances, be justified; but even so, the paradigm of a just person is not a philosopher contemplating the eternal order of abstract objects, but an expert on constitutional and legal matters who knows how important it is to prevent bad political systems from becoming worse, and who can use his expertise to promote the good of ordinary citizens in ordinary cities—someone like Aristotle himself.

Not everything of importance and value in Book V of the *Ethics* is designed to contribute to this anti-Platonic theme. One of Aristotle's main concerns in this book is plain enough, and has little to do with his opposition to his teacher: how to fit justice into his general framework for thinking about the virtues as characteristics that fall between two undesirable extremes. That may strike us as a dull exercise, but in fact Aristotle's analysis grapples with deep questions that every political philosophy must try to answer. Does justice require strict adherence to legal requirements and general rules? And if so, should justice sometimes be set aside, in favor of more important considerations? Can a legal system allow its citizens to use their discretion in making judgments about what the laws require? Is it characteristic of justice that it treats all wrongdoing according to strict and uniform rules? If one refrains from doing all that one can to resist unjust treatment, is one departing from the virtue of justice? These questions arise because there seems to be a tension between two attractive lines of thought: justice requires adherence to generally accepted rules, but a genuine virtue enables one to respond flexibly to the particular details of each situation. Part of the interest of Aristotle's analysis of justice lies in his attempt to recognize the validity of both of these thoughts, and to show how they can be reconciled.[3]

---

[3] Before moving on, the reader should be warned that editors and translators disagree about where certain passages of Book V belong. Irwin's translation differs from Ross's at three places: V.4 1132a29–30 is moved back to a32; V.4 1132b11–18 is moved forward to a14; and V.5 1133b29–1134a23 is moved back to V.7 1135a5. The third of these passages is of

4.2. Broad and Narrow Justice

We will begin with the principal theme of Book V, Chapters 1 and 2: that *dikaios* ('just') has both a broad and a narrow sense, and is not univocal in meaning. We can already see, at this early stage, that Aristotle is distancing himself from Plato, because the very fact that this ambiguity exists shows that Plato had misunderstood his subject. The *Republic* defines justice as doing one's own,[4] but Aristotle takes this to be so obviously wrong that he does not even make an effort to refute it. Justice, he says, is best understood by means of two definitions; and in neither of them do we hear anything about doing one's own.[5] The *un*just person is, in one sense, lawless; in another, unequal; correspondingly, the *just* person is, in one sense, lawful; in another, equal.[6]

Aristotle does not take the meaning of these simple equations to be obvious, for he goes to some length to explain how they should be understood. He is particularly eager to defend his idea that equality constitutes one form of justice, because this is the formula that allows him to apply his doctrine of the mean to the virtue of justice. The unjust person is someone who is not satisfied with an equal share for himself: he wants more, and is pleased to leave others with less. That shows that the just person, who is satisfied with an equal share, chooses something between what the unjust person allocates to himself (too much) and what he leaves for others (too little). Aristotle explains and defends this idea by showing how it can

---

considerable importance, because it is here that Aristotle explains why justice is not a mean in the same way as the other virtues. My references to this passage will treat it as a part of V.5; readers of Irwin's translation should look for it in his V.7. See Hardie, *Aristotle's Ethical Theory*, p. 184, on some of the textual difficulties. His chapter (pp. 182–211) is a helpful guide to much earlier literature.

[4] See 433c–434a, 443c–444a.

[5] Aristotle does not deny that *ta hautōn echein* ('having one's own') or similar words can be applied to justice. See e.g. *NE* V.4 1132b17. What he denies is that such words explain what justice is.

[6] Many scholars call justice as lawfulness 'universal' or 'general' justice, and justice as equality 'particular' or 'special' justice. I find these tags misleading, and prefer to describe Aristotle's distinction as one between a broad and a narrow sense of the word. To speak of one type of justice as 'universal' or 'general' and the other as 'particular' or 'special' might suggest that the former is observed in all or most communities, whereas the latter is more restrictive. But that is not at all what Aristotle's distinction is meant to suggest. Another terminological point: in some translations, Aristotle is made to say that justice in the narrow sense consists in equality, and that the person who has this quality is fair. But Aristotle does not use two different Greek terms, one corresponding to 'equal', the other to 'fair'. He uses *isos* and its cognates both of the virtue and of the person who has the virtue. His thesis, as I will put it, is that justice in the narrow sense consists in equality, and the just person is equal (not 'fair').

4.2. BROAD AND NARROW JUSTICE

be applied to three particular areas: distributive justice, corrective justice, and justice as reciprocal exchange. In each case, we can see that justice consists in equality and is therefore a mean between two extreme and undesirable conditions.

But it would be a mistake to think that the other definition Aristotle offers of justice—the equation of justice with lawfulness—is one in which he loses interest, once it has been separated off from justice as equality. After he has completed his examination of the three forms of justice as equality (justice in distribution, correction, and reciprocal exchange), he turns to several other topics, and as we will see, his discussion of them gives us considerable help in understanding his claim that justice in one of its senses means lawfulness. Furthermore, his equation between justice and lawfulness is in a way the more basic of his two definitions. For he tells us that justice as lawfulness and justice as equality are not unrelated: justice in the sense of lawfulness is the whole of justice, whereas justice as equality is only one portion of the whole (V.2 1130b10–14). There are, in other words, just acts that are neither equal nor unequal; their justice is a matter of their lawfulness. By contrast, there are no equal acts that are not at the same time lawful. So lawfulness is the one characteristic that all justice has in common.[7] Evidently, Plato was not wrong in his belief that human justice can be characterized by means of a single formula—he merely proposed the wrong formula. In addition, he made a further mistake in that he overlooked a further feature that many (though not all) just acts and people have in common: they are equal.

Since all of justice is lawfulness, it is of the greatest importance to understand what this equation means. And it should be admitted from the start that this simple formula seems to be vulnerable to an obvious objection: there are such things as unjust laws, and so lawfulness cannot provide a standard of what is just. Even if we obey the law, we may be doing what is unjust, because the law itself may be unjust. And for the same reason, even if we disobey the law, our action may be just. Does Aristotle disagree? Or do we misunderstand him?

---

[7] The proposal that justice be defined as lawfulness can be found in an earlier author: Xenophon attributes it to Socrates at *Memorabilia* IV.4. For discussion, see Morrison, 'Xenophon's Socrates on the Just and the Lawful'. Plato characterizes Socrates as a man who has great respect for the law—so much so that he would rather die than commit an unlawful act. The idea that respect for the law is a precious quality was widely accepted in the classical world. (See e.g. Herodotus 7.104.4; Thucydides 2.37.3; Demosthenes 24.5. For more passages and discussion, see Dover, *Greek Popular Morality*, pp. 184–7.) By contrast, it was not at all a commonplace that lawfulness is precisely what justice consists in.

Not everyone would accept the claim that laws can be unjust. Hobbes, for example, holds that no sovereign power can be guilty of injustice, because injustice consists in the violation of a covenant, and no sovereign makes a covenant. Hobbes seeks a solution to the interminable debates among political theorists and rivals for power about the nature of justice, and proposes that the only practicable standard consists in the edicts of those who have the power to make and enforce the law. He might find nothing wrong with Aristotle's thesis that all justice consists in lawfulness.[8]

But this Hobbesian point is not the one Aristotle can be making when he writes that justice in its broadest sense consists in lawfulness. For he agrees with the claim I made, two paragraphs ago, that there can be and have been foolish and unjust laws.[9] At one point in the *Politics*, he ridicules the barbaric laws of archaic societies (II.8 1268b38–1269a3), and in another passage he implies that every defective regime—and there have been many of them—has unjust laws (III.11 1282a41–b13). Furthermore, as we will see (4.7), he holds in V.7 of the *Ethics* that there is another kind of justice besides legal justice, one that is based on nature, and not dependent on human legislation or convention. That suggests that there is a standard of justice that can be used to determine whether the enactments of a legislature or of any other kind of ruler are just. And surely this conception of justice is the one we would expect Aristotle to adopt, for his whole approach to human well-being and virtue reflects his conviction that ethics and politics are a search for the proper way to live our lives. Acting and living can go well or badly, and one can be mistaken about where the difference between them lies. In fact, it is possible for a whole community to live in accordance with a misguided conception of well-being, and to misunderstand the nature of virtue. Sparta was precisely such a community, as Aristotle tells his audience several times.[10] So it is no surprise to find him saying that rulers can be wrong about what justice is, and that laws can be unjust.

That leaves us with a puzzle: why does he define justice, in its broadest sense, as lawfulness?

---

[8] See *Leviathan* I.15: 'injustice is no other than the not performance of covenant'; and I.18 for the thesis that the sovereign can do no injustice. Ironically, Hobbes's defense of this point in I.18 depends on the premise, first defended by Aristotle, that no one can be unjust to himself. See 4.15 below for discussion.

[9] For the contrary view—that a morally objectionable resolution cannot be characterized as a law—see Plato's *Minos* 314e.

[10] For references to his critique of Spartan militarism, see 1.n.13.

4.3. Justice as Lawfulness

To solve our problem, we must bear several points in mind. To begin with, we should realize that the Greek term that is translated as 'law'—*nomos*—covers not only the enactments of a lawgiver or legislature but also the customs, norms, and unwritten rules of a community. The noun *nomos* is cognate to the verb *nemein*, one of whose senses is 'to believe'. Whatever conduct a community believes to be fitting—its proper and customary way of doing things—constitutes the *nomoi* (plural of *nomos*) of that community.[11] There can be no such things as *nomoi* in which no one believes; for a *nomos* to exist is for it to be recognized and observed by a group of people.[12]

Our own term 'law' lacks this feature. It is not an impossible use of this word to say that moral laws exist whether or not people recognize their validity or obey them. We might say, for example, that slavery is contrary to the moral law, and that this law existed before the wrongness of slavery began to receive general recognition. It seems reasonable to say that slavery was always a violation of the moral law, and that what came into existence was not the law itself but rather its general acknowledgement and observance. At any rate, this claim does not abuse the word 'law'. By contrast, the Greek term *nomos* was not used in this way by Aristotle's contemporaries.

Accordingly, when he says that a just person, speaking in the broadest sense, is *nomimos*, he is attributing to such a person a certain relationship to the laws, norms, and customs generally accepted by some existing community. Justice has to do not merely with the written enactments of a community's lawmakers, but with the wider set of norms that govern the members of that community. Similarly, the unjust person's character is expressed not only in his violations of the written code of laws, but more broadly, in his transgression of the rules accepted by the society in which he lives.

There is another important way in which Aristotle's use of the term *nomos* differs from our word 'law': he makes a distinction

---

[11] *Nomos* is 'what the people as a whole regard as a valid and binding norm'. See Ostwald, *Nomos and the Beginnings of Athenian Democracy*, p. 54. This statement expresses the conclusion of a lengthy examination of texts, pp. 20–61. Although, as Aristotle tells us (*Rhet.* I.10 1368b8–9), there are certain unwritten laws that seem to be accepted in all communities, a *nomos* need only be accepted by one community—not by all. In fact, even if only a segment of a community abides by a practice, its members can claim to be obeying a law. Thus when Empedocles says that it is unlawful to kill anything that has a soul (*Rhet.* I.13 1373b14–17), he is reporting (and endorsing) the practice of a religious sect.

[12] This is why law is characterized as *doxa* ('belief', 'opinion') in Plato's *Minos* (314e).

between *nomoi* and what the Greeks of his time called *psēphismata*—conventionally translated as 'decrees'. A decree is a legal enactment addressed solely to present circumstances, and sets no precedent that applies to similar cases in the future. By contrast, a *nomos* is meant to have general scope: it applies not only to cases at hand but to a general category of cases that can be expected to occur in the future. If a legislature grants citizenship to one person, because of the great services he has rendered the city, it has enacted a decree, because it does not bind itself to any general principle. But if it resolves that the child of a citizen is himself a citizen, then it has adopted a law, because the general scope of the rule it has adopted makes a commitment to a definite way of proceeding in the future.[13]

Aristotle holds that it is typical of tyranny to rule by a series of edicts rather than by a stable system of law, and he likens the worst forms of democracy and oligarchy to tyrannies.[14] In all three systems —a tyranny, a democracy led by demagogues, and an oligarchy dominated by a tiny elite of great wealth—the rulers are so contemptuous of others that they do not provide the city with a general and stable legal framework of legitimate expectations. Because such rulers have no concern for consistency over time, what they resolve today may be reversed tomorrow. In all three systems, the law has no authority, and it is individuals who rule. The favored kind of enactment in democracies of this sort is the decree, precisely because these make no commitment to long-term principles. Although there is nothing objectionable about decrees in themselves, excessive use of this device is incompatible with the existence of an orderly body of rules that citizens can confidently expect to be in force.

We can now begin to see why Aristotle thinks that justice in its broadest sense can be defined as lawfulness, and why he has such high regard for a lawful person. His definition embodies the assumption that every community requires the high degree of order that comes from having a stable body of customs and norms, and a coherent legal code that is not altered frivolously and unpredictably. Justice in its broadest sense is the intellectual and emotional skill one needs in order to do one's part in bringing it about that one's community possesses this stable system of rules and laws.

It must be emphasized that the just person as Aristotle conceives

---

[13] Aristotle makes the distinction between laws and decrees at *NE* V.10 1137b13–32. In doing so, he is following customary fourth-century usage. See MacDowell, *The Law in Classical Athens*, pp. 43–6.

[14] See *Pol.* IV.4 1292a4–37, IV.6 1293a30–4.

him is not a merely passive follower of rules. It is not sufficient to know what the norms of one's community are, and to abide by them, for as he points out, that is an easy task that practically any adult can perform (V.9 1137a4–17), whereas any real virtue is a difficult achievement that requires practical wisdom (VI.13 1144b30–2). The virtue of lawfulness is not a mere matter of being law-abiding.[15] To see how demanding a job it is to be a just person, we must keep in mind a further point Aristotle makes in a passage at the end of *NE* V.1: whoever is just in the broad sense of the word will possess every other ethical virtue as well (1129b25–1130a10). We will soon discuss this passage more fully, but for now we need only notice that this commits Aristotle to saying that anyone who is just in the broad sense will also possess the virtue of justice in the narrow sense of the word: he will be an equal as well as a lawful person. Justice as equality is further divided into distributive and corrective justice, and therefore the lawful person must be skillful in distributing goods and resolving disputes.[16] His most important decisions, as a distributor of goods, are made when he plays an active role in the politics of his city, for this is the arena in which the most significant distributive questions—how should power and honor be divided?—are decided. He takes part in corrective justice when he volunteers to serve on juries and gives a fair hearing to contending parties in the courts. A fully just person, then, is not merely a follower of rules, but is also a competent maker and adjudicator of the law, and his decisions reflect his understanding of the great benefits that come from having a stable system of rules and norms.

We can now see how great a mistake it would be to assume that when Aristotle defines justice in the broad sense as lawfulness, he is proposing that to determine what is just in any community we need only look to its laws, since those laws are precisely what justice consists in. A legislator who is trying to determine how goods should be distributed in his community is exercising the virtue of justice as lawfulness—justice as equality is part of justice as lawfulness—but since he is making law, he cannot decide how to distribute goods by looking to an already existing law. Similarly, although a jury member who is deciding whether a defendant should be punished must look to the law that has allegedly been violated, that law

---

[15] Hence Ross's translation of *nomimos* as 'law-abiding' is misleading. Irwin's 'lawful' is better.

[16] These forms of justice in the narrow sense, as well as justice in reciprocal exchange, will be discussed more fully below (4.11–13).

by itself cannot determine what his verdict should be. Aristotle cannot have intended his equation between justice and lawfulness to be a way of determining what is just in all cases, because it simply cannot play that role in many of the most important situations that call for justice. What he must therefore be proposing, when he equates justice with lawfulness, is that this is the sort of person we should strive to become: a person who serves his community by means of its legal system and its pattern of norms. We will soon fill out this portrait of a just person in greater detail.

It should come as no surprise that Aristotle's definition of justice in the broad sense does not give us a criterion for deciding how to act in particular cases. For none of his definitions of the virtues is meant to serve this purpose. When he explains what temperance, courage, and other moral skills are, he describes the kind of person we should try to become, but does not offer a formula for making decisions about particular cases. That is how we should understand his equation of justice with lawfulness.

4.4. Equity in V.10

There is another reason why the laws of a community cannot always be used as a criterion for determining which particular actions are just. Aristotle tells us that by their nature laws are broad in scope: they are generalizations, and that is precisely why they are so valuable. But this great advantage, he insists, carries with it a certain disadvantage, because it is impossible for legislators to address themselves to all of the complications and exceptions that may become relevant in particular circumstances. Laws are not only general; they are inevitably *too* general. That defect is unavoidable, because the details that would be needed to make laws exceptionless cannot be foreseen in advance. Of course, some legislators anticipate the future better than others, and the rules they construct are less in need of supplementation or revision.[17] But even the best of them will

---

[17] Notice a distinction Aristotle makes in *Rhet.* I.13: equity is sometimes needed because of involuntary legislative errors and sometimes because of voluntary errors (1374a28–33). A voluntary error is one that cannot be eliminated, because of the need for universality and the impossibility of making endlessly complex rules; an involuntary error derives from a legislator's inability to foresee what could have been anticipated by a more competent drafter of laws. In *NE* V.10, Aristotle mentions only the former case, presumably because of its greater theoretical interest. Equity must always be part of the equipment of a just person, because every legal system needs correction.

4.4. EQUITY IN V.10

sometimes pass a law whose deficiencies emerge when violators are brought to court. In these cases, Aristotle says, a juror must call upon the virtue of 'equity' (*epieikeia*), a skill that enables him to see how to correct those deficiencies of the laws that result from their over-generality.[18] An equitable juror will refuse to punish someone even if he has violated a law, if the defects of the law are revealed by the case in hand. In these circumstances, the judge is not showing contempt for those who made the law, because he can reasonably say that they themselves would not have intended this particular defendant to be punished. To use an illustration drawn from the *Rhetoric*: the law may call for higher penalties if one person strikes another with a metallic object (I.13 1374a35–6), but if the only piece of metal involved is a finger-ring, the equitable juror should vote for acquittal, because this is not the sort of case to which the legislators intended to attach a stiffer punishment. Perhaps wiser legislators could have foreseen this case and have drafted a more precise law, but an equitable juror will not make defendants bear the costs of such legislative deficiencies. He will consider it a matter of justice to correct the deficiencies of the law, and to refuse to apply the law, in its uncorrected form, to the case before him.[19]

Notice that since justice in the broad sense is defined as lawfulness, what the equitable judge does must be lawful. This virtue does not require but in fact forbids casting a blind eye on the deficiencies of the law and mechanically doing whatever it requires. Justice consists not in obeying each and every law, but in supporting the legal framework as a whole. It is adherence to the law, but not to every particular law, however deficient. The equitable juror plays a valuable role in his community by protecting individuals from the deficiencies that laws are bound to have, even when legislators are all that they should be. He is a lawful person, and his equitable acts are lawful, because they make the legal system better than it would

---

[18] Other translations are 'decency' (Irwin's translation of the *NE*) and 'fairness' (Kennedy's translation of the *Rhetoric*).

[19] When Aristotle says at V.10 1137b21–2 that legislation needs judicial correction whenever it leaves something out, he is referring to omitted details that would restrict the scope of the law. We must not take the legislator's omission to consist in his failure to forbid a certain kind of behavior that should have been forbidden. Were that Aristotle's point, he would be saying that sometimes the laws are not general enough, and that the juror must punish certain kinds of behavior that the legislator failed to condemn. For further discussion, see Shiner, 'Aristotle's Theory of Equity'. It follows that where equity is called for, it always consists in leniency—acquittal or a smaller punishment than the one demanded by the prosecutor. It is not the juror's role to be more severe than the legislator, by punishing behavior that the legislator neglected to forbid.

be were he to follow the law blindly. The legal system works best when legislators know that defects in their products will not necessarily result in injustice, because equitable jurors will be on hand to recognize the exceptions that were overlooked when the laws were adopted. It would be futile for them to try to anticipate every imaginable exception to the rules they formulate; they should instead allow the important exceptions to emerge when the law is put into practice. The equitable juror is therefore not an opponent of the legislator, but an ally. It is not as though he refuses to enforce the law because he personally dislikes it, or thinks that there are no cases in which the law should be applied. Rather, although he recognizes that his role as juror is subordinate to that of the legislator, and that he must apply even those laws that he himself would like to be repealed, he sees that the legislators themselves did not intend the punishment to be applied to this particular case. He is supporting the legislators' own point of view, not substituting his for theirs, and that is why his equitable judgment sustains rather than undermines the legal system. He can therefore be characterized as a lawful person, and his equitable decision can be called lawful, even though it fails to do what the law requires. Paradoxically, lawfulness can occasionally require violating the law. Little wonder, then, that being a lawful person and doing what is lawful are no easy matters. One needs considerable understanding to determine what the virtue of lawfulness calls for on particular occasions.

Aristotle's approach to equity provides no justification for violating a law merely on the grounds that it is unjust and should never have been adopted in the first place. He assumes that a juror can rightly refuse to enforce the law only when he sees that legislators did not intend it to be applied to the case in hand. But a citizen who refuses to obey a law simply because it is unjust is trying to do something quite different: he concedes that the legislators intended the law to apply to him, but insists that it should not have been adopted in the first place, because of its injustice. He claims that he sees what the legislators do not—that the law is unjust—and this makes his thesis more difficult to sustain than the one Aristotle defends. For the individual violator of the law cannot expect the legislators to agree with him that he is acting properly, whereas this is precisely what Aristotle's equitable judge expects of them. The individual who breaks the law because he takes it to be unjust sets himself up as a rival to the body that has the authority to make the laws. He says that he can see where justice lies and it cannot; and that his actions should be guided by his own judgment rather than theirs. That is a radical challenge to the legal system, not the modest correction that Aristotle calls for. As we will see (10.6), he has no sympathy for those who seek to undermine the whole legal framework of a city. He holds that cities in which citizens seek gradual and modest improvements by lawful means are far better places to live than cities in which warring factions with rival conceptions of justice undermine the legal system rather than accommodate themselves to perceived injustices. When he defends the thesis that at times one must, as a matter of justice, refuse to comply with legislative errors, he is defending a policy that poses no threat to the rule of law.

4.5. 'Everything Lawful Is in a Way Just'

After Aristotle distinguishes the broad and narrow senses of justice, and briefly elucidates his idea that injustice in the narrow sense is motivated by a desire to have more than one's share (V.1 1129a26-b11), he returns to his conception of justice as lawfulness, and makes several further remarks about it:

A. 'Since the lawless person is unjust and the lawful person just, it is obvious that everything lawful is in a way just' (1129b11-12).

B. 'For the things determined by the science of legislation (*nomothetikē*) are lawful and each of these, we say, is just' b12-14.

The first of these two statements might at first seem to be highly objectionable. For suppose we take Aristotle to be assuming:

C. Whatever is required by an existing law is lawful.

In that case, he would be committed to saying that whatever is required by an existing law is in a way just. That might strike us as a consequence that Aristotle could not have accepted, for as we saw earlier (4.2), he recognizes that defective and unjust laws are all too common. In fact he points out, several lines below the passage cited above in (A) and (B), that some laws are badly made (1129b25). So we might be reluctant to take him to be tacitly accepting (C). Furthermore, statement (B) can be used as evidence that he rejects (C)—provided that we take (B) to mean:

D. *Only* the things determined by the science of legislation are lawful, and each of these is just.

Although Aristotle does not tell us in this passage what 'the science of legislation' is, he presumably means that it is the field that his students of politics should master.[20] It requires an understanding of the material we find in Aristotle's ethical and political works: the human good, the nature of the virtues, the variety of political systems, and so on. And, as the term *nomothetikē* implies, it is a study that prescribes a system of legislation—a system of laws based on a proper understanding of human well-being and political reality. So, (D) takes Aristotle to be saying that only those acts are lawful that would be prescribed by laws adopted by experts in the art of politics—laws that are, in this sense, without defect.[21] That way of understanding 'lawful' (*nomimos*) takes the bite out of Aristotle's statement in (A) that 'everything lawful is in a way just'.

But that way of reading our passage does not explain why Aristotle says, in statement (A), that 'everything lawful is *in a way* just'. The emphasized phrase indicates that he does not mean that everything lawful is *unqualifiedly* just. Yet there would be no reason for him to qualify his statement if he were counting only those acts as *nomimos* that would be adopted by superbly trained legislators. Surely such acts would be supremely and unequivocally just—not 'in a way' just. So, Aristotle's unwillingness to say quite simply that all lawful acts are just indicates that he is not restricting 'lawful' to ideal laws. A second reason for questioning the interpretation under consideration is that statement (D) goes far beyond what Aristotle says. He tells us that what is determined by legislative science is lawful, but not that *only* those enactments are lawful.

There is a third reason for resisting this way of reading our passage. If a just person were someone who serves and obeys only those laws that are without defect, he could play only a limited role at best in his political community. He could not, for example, serve as a juror, because in that case he would have to apply 'laws' that he takes to be unlawful, since many of them would not be prescribed by the science of legislation. (Recall our discussion in 4.4: the equitable juror plays a role that is subordinate to that of the legislator; he can correct the law only when legislators would themselves agree that they have been overly restrictive.) But if a lawful person refused to serve as a juror, and refrained from participating in other aspects of his community's political life, there would be little scope for his

---

[20] We are told at *NE* VI.8 1141b23–5 that the science of legislation is the controlling branch of political science, and that it is the same state as practical wisdom.

[21] This is the reading of Irwin, *Aristotle's First Principles*, p. 623 n. 1.

4.5. 'EVERYTHING LAWFUL IS IN A WAY JUST'

justice. Someone who is just in the broad sense (a lawful person) must be just in the narrow sense as well (an equal person), and the virtue of equality is exercised in the political arena—in the legislature and the courts, where the most important distributive and corrective decisions are made. But if he withdraws from the political life of his community, because he takes many of its norms to be unlawful, he would be hard put to exercise the virtue of justice as equality. Aristotle cannot be advocating such resignation. As we will see in Chapters 10–12, he is training his students to be politically active in a wide variety of circumstances, and to make what small improvements they can in the defective cities over which they have influence. One of his reasons for undertaking this project is his belief that all but the worst cities have at least this much to be said for them: they abide by the law.[22] He takes the rule of law to be a commendable feature of many non-ideal cities, and this speaks against our taking him to mean that only those things are lawful that are prescribed by the science of legislation.

Let us search for an alternative reading by seeing how our passage continues:

E. 'The laws address all matters,[23] aiming at the common advantage of all or of the best or those who have power based on virtue or on some other such thing'[24] (1129b14–17).

F. 'So, in one way we call just those things that produce and preserve happiness and its parts for the political community' (b17–19).

---

[22] See *Pol.* IV.4 1292a1–6, IV.5 1292b4–7.

[23] I take Aristotle's point to be one that he elucidates at 1129b19–25: the laws address all matters, in that for every ethical virtue there is a law that requires action in accordance with that virtue. Contrast Irwin's translation of 1129b14–15: 'In every matter that they deal with, the laws aim . . .' On his reading, Aristotle does not claim that the law's scope is universal.

[24] In the Oxford Classical Text (OCT), Bywater brackets *kat'aretēn* at 1129b16. Ross, accepting this emendation, translates: 'the common advantage either of all or of the best or of those who hold power, or something of the sort.' Irwin proposes a different way of emending the text: he would omit *ē tois aristois* at b16, and thus translates: 'the common benefit of all, or at the benefit of those in control, whose control rests on virtue or some other such basis.' The translation I have given retains the reading of the OCT. There is a further problem, because the Greek of the OCT (and of Ross's and Irwin's emendations) can be read in two ways: 'common' can be distributed over each alternative (thus Ross: 'the common advantage either of all or of the best . . .') or it can be attached solely to the first alternative (thus Irwin: 'the common benefit of all, or at the benefit . . .'). My translation adopts the first of these alternatives. But I do not think that the differences between these construals of the text and the meaning of the Greek are of major interpretive significance. I take Aristotle to be saying that, however narrowly or broadly the political community is defined, justice in the broad sense produces and preserves happiness for the whole of it. This, I think, is Irwin's interpretation as well. See *Aristotle's First Principles*, pp. 424–5.

Notice that these claims are about actual laws in all sorts of existing communities. Some of those communities may be worse than others (and may therefore enact worse laws): that is implied by the point, made in (E), that laws are devised for the benefit of different groups in different cities. Power might be based on virtue in some cities, but in others it might be based on wealth, or free birth, or some other qualification. Can the laws adopted and observed in all of these different kinds of political community be lawful, even when they are defective and would not be adopted by ideal legislators? Aristotle does not explicitly address that question, but it is clear that in (E) and (F) he has not yet moved away from the topic of lawfulness and its connection with justice. For in (F) he is still presenting his conception of justice in the broad sense: when he says 'in one way we call just those things that produce and preserve happiness,' the phrase 'in one way' (*hena tropon*) refers to justice as lawfulness (as distinct from the other way in which things are called just—justice as equality). That shows that he takes his comments in (E), about the broad range of existing laws and their beneficent aim (in many different communities, even defective ones), to support his idea that because justice is lawfulness, 'everything lawful is in a way just'.

The conclusion we should draw is that when Aristotle says 'everything *nomimos* is in a way just', he is using the term *nomimos* to apply both to what would be enacted in an ideal city by fully trained political leaders, and to laws that are in force in existing cities. He is, in other words, using two sorts of consideration to show that there is a connection between lawfulness and justice: First, the products of the science of legislation (*nomothetikē*) are rightly called *nomimos* (the verbal similarity between *nomothetikē* and *nomimos* suggests as much), and they are obviously just.[25] (How could they not be, since they are ideal?) Second, existing laws (*nomoi*) can also be rightly called *nomimos* (here too Aristotle is guided by a verbal similarity), and when we attend to some of their positive features, we find that they too are just (or, at least, in a way just), even when they have certain defects.

Aristotle has more to say, as our passage continues, about what it is about existing laws that leads him to characterize them as just, or at any rate qualifiedly just. For his next step is to explain and expand

---

[25] Note that something can therefore be called *nomimos* even if it is not practiced in any existing city: it is enough that it is proposed by the science of legislation. Contrast the way the word *nomos* works (as noted in 4.3, first paragraph): to call something a *nomos* implies that it is put into practice in some community.

4.5. 'EVERYTHING LAWFUL IS IN A WAY JUST'

on the claim he makes in (E) that 'the laws address all matters'. He now adds (1129b19–23): The law 'commands us to perform the acts of a courageous person—not to leave our position, or run away or throw away our arms; and of a temperate person—not to commit adultery or acts of aggressive assault; and of a gentle person—not to strike or verbally abuse another', and so on. Aristotle is here making a general observation about the content of existing codes of law. All cities that have legal systems possess a common core of legislation that prevents their citizens from doing great harm to each other. That is why he does not need to specify which city he is talking about when he says that the law commands us not to run away in battle, not to commit adultery, and so on. Something good is achieved for all members of the community whenever a city is regulated by law. To repeat the words used in (F) above: all legal systems, even defective ones, have some degree of justice, because they are able to some extent to 'produce and preserve happiness and its parts for the political community' (1129b17–19).[26]

Significantly, Aristotle explicitly calls our attention to the existence of defective legislation, immediately after he has finished making his point that the law commands us to perform the acts of a courageous person, a temperate person, and so on. He says: '(the law) commands some things and forbids others—one rightly laid down does so rightly, one laid down in an off-handed way does so worse' (b24–5). A law made 'in an off-handed way' is one that has not been carefully thought through, and is therefore not something that would have been adopted by ideal legislators. Aristotle is here reminding his audience that the laws regarding military service, adultery, assault, slander, and the like may be far from perfect. He does not deny that there may be injustices in these and other laws—in fact, his claim that 'everything lawful is *in a way* just' is so qualified in order to make room for the point that existing laws can also contain considerable injustice. But the defects and injustice of a law

---

[26] See *NE* VIII.9 1159b26–31 for the claim that every community is just to some degree. This theme is taken up again in VIII.11. Note especially Aristotle's claim that justice exists to a small degree in deviant constitutions (1161a31–2), and that it is more fully present in democracies than tyrannies (1161b8–10). Compare his thesis that even those who have mistaken ideas about what sort of political system is best have a partial grasp of what justice is (*Pol.* III.9 1280a9, 1281a9–10). It should also be kept in mind that, according to Aristotle, the best forms of democracy and oligarchy are those that are ruled by law (*Pol.* IV.4 1292a1–6, IV.5 1292b4–7). Presumably this is because the respect for law shown in these constitutions mitigates their injustice. The rule of law, in other words, is by itself a just institution, and offsets to some degree the injustice inherent in rule by the rich or the poor.

do not show that it does no good whatsoever, and do not keep what it commands from being lawful. A just person, being a lawful person (someone who serves his community by means of its legal system), will comply with lawful commands. He will not adopt the perfectionist attitude that the only laws we have reason to obey are those that would be adopted by legislators who have fully grasped the science of politics. He will abide by his community's legal system, even when those who govern do not possess the science of legislation, and laws are made 'in an off-handed way'; and he will do so because the legal system, despite its deficiencies, promotes human well-being to some degree.

That does not mean that he will do whatever he is commanded to do by someone who has power over him. Aristotle believes that some sorts of act are never to be done and can never be made lawful, because they are entirely destructive of human well-being.[27] He must therefore hold either that a command that requires such terrible acts can never qualify as law, or that there are some laws that prescribe what is unlawful.[28] When he says that 'everything lawful is in a way just', he cannot mean that even the orders of a tyrant (or a tyrannical group) are in a way just. Lawful acts must meet certain minimal tests of decency; they must, to some degree, 'produce and preserve happiness and its parts for the political community' (1129b17–19). That is why Aristotle maintains that, whatever their defects, they are in a way just.

The thesis that all legal systems aim at the good of the political community is based on a simple and powerful idea: the rules by which cities organize themselves are not pointless regulations that deserve obedience simply because they exist. The rule against assault is not an arbitrary command for which nothing can be said except that it is a traditional prohibition. It serves an obvious purpose: people do not live well when others are free to attack them. Similarly, there is a rule that prohibits adultery, because relationships between couples do not prosper in the absence of fidelity, and the health of such relationships is an important component of human well-being. Accordingly, Aristotle must be assuming that when a lawful person obeys the law, or enforces the law as a jury member, or helps create a law as a member of a legislative assembly,

---

[27] We should accept death rather than perform certain acts: *NE* III.1 1110a26–7. The enslavement of those who are not natural slaves can never be lawful: *Pol.* VII.2 1324b22–7.
[28] If Aristotle accepts the second of these alternatives, he admits exceptions to (C): Whatever is required by an existing law is lawful.

4.5. 'EVERYTHING LAWFUL IS IN A WAY JUST'

he does so because he is trying to serve the good of his city. Lawfulness is not a matter of respecting the rules that are in force simply because they are the customary way of doing things. Even when a lawful person obeys a law that he takes to be a bad law, his reason for doing so cannot simply be that this is the law, and nothing more need be said. On the contrary, Aristotle would insist, there is a great deal more to be said: although this law may do little or no good, the legal system as a whole promotes the good of the community to some degree, and legal systems cannot exist unless citizens are willing to obey the rules favored by those who are not entirely wise and just. Human beings can do little good for each other unless they do so in socially structured ways. They must live in accordance with rules that create a reliable system of expectations about what each person will do for others and refrain from doing. There must be some procedure for resolving questions about how goods should be divided, and there must be juridical bodies that redress wrongs. The only way to promote the good of the political community is to abide by the regular procedures that have been established in each city for doing so. Nothing can be accomplished if one tries to live in accordance with a set of rules that are not recognized and obeyed by others.

One other feature of Aristotle's discussion in V.1 should be noticed: justice in the broad sense does not merely promote the well-being of someone or other: it promotes the good of the political community at large. Recall the words of (F) above: 'in one way we call just those things that produce and preserve happiness and its parts for the political community' (1129b17–19). Of course, as Aristotle points out in (E), some communities are more restrictive in their membership requirements than others, and the distinctions made between included and excluded groups vary from one city to another. The laws 'aim at the common advantage of all or of the best or those who have power based on virtue or on some other such thing' (1129b14–17). Even so, justice in the broad sense is a virtue that benefits all members of the community, however broadly or narrowly it is defined. The examples Aristotle gives of acts that are just in the broad sense bear this out: all cities have laws that require citizens to defend the community against aggressors, forbid assault and certain kinds of sexual relation, and so on. Such regulations as these promote the welfare of all members of the community. And this has an important consequence: it implies that a person who is just in the broad sense must have a concern for the well-being of all members of his community. For example, if the citizenry includes both rich and poor, someone who proposes legislation designed to benefit only one of these groups, and opposes all legislation designed to benefit the other, because he has no concern for that second group, could not be counted as a lawful and just person. The lawful person's goal is not to obey rules merely for the sake of obedience; it is to promote the good of the entire community. Accordingly, when his city contains both rich and poor citizens, he must have some concern for the well-being of both groups. Justice is never a matter of merely doing good; it involves distributing the good over a certain range of people, according to some definite pattern. When Aristotle discusses justice as equality, that pattern becomes quite precise: good must be balanced against good, and evil against evil, according to a strict proportion. But even justice in the broader sense involves a certain structure. Promoting the common good need not take the form of achieving a precise proportion of benefits, but it does always involve seeking the good not just of this or that segment of the community, but of all of its components.

The English word 'justice', like equivalent terms in many modern European languages, conveys the idea of some appropriate distribution of benefits and burdens. A just outcome is one in which the interests or rights of *all* parties receive due attention, and no one enjoys benefits or suffers burdens in an arbitrary way. It should be obvious that the Greek word *dikaios*, as Aristotle understands it, has this same feature, both in its narrow and in its broad sense. To be *dikaios* in the narrow sense is to know how to achieve proportionality in goods and evils; it is to know when someone has more good or evil than he should have, and how to avoid or rectify this situation. And as we have just seen, *dikaios* in its broad sense also has something to do with maintaining a certain structure or pattern among people. This virtue is not merely a matter of doing good to others: the good one aims at must be the good of all.[29]

4.6. Justice as the Whole of Virtue

Aristotle's final point in *NE* V.1 is that justice in the broad sense is an extraordinary quality, because it is 'complete' or 'perfect' virtue (1129b25–6). But then he immediately adds that it is not

---

[29] Plato's use of the term in the *Republic* has this same feature: to be just is to have concern for all components of the political community. See esp. 419–421c.

4.6. JUSTICE AS THE WHOLE OF VIRTUE

complete or perfect in an unqualified way, but rather in relation to others (b26-7). What he means can best be conveyed by way of example. The actions of a temperate person can be divided into those concerned solely with his own affairs and those that bear on his relations with others. For example, there are times when the exercise of his ability to refrain from overeating benefits no one besides himself; when there is an abundance of food, he need not confine himself to a modest portion for anyone's sake but his own. But when there is just enough food to go round, temperance benefits others as well; by taking modest portions, the temperate person leaves others their due. Similarly, there may be times when a courageous person benefits no one but himself. For example, in isolated hand-to-hand combat, his control over fear may enable him to save his life, even though no one else besides himself is at risk. But on many other occasions, courage enables one to save the lives of one's comrades.[30]

When an act of temperance or courage is done for the good of the political community, then it is not only an act of temperance or courage, but an act of justice as well (1129b17–19). For that is precisely what justice in the broad sense is: the exercise of the other ethical virtues in accordance with law for the good of the political community. Notice how different it is from those other virtues. It is not exercised on its own, but is always tied up with the employment of one of the other moral skills. A courageous act is not at the same time a temperate act or a generous act. But an act that exercises justice in the broad sense always expresses one of the other ethical virtues at the same time: it is courageous, or temperate, or just in the narrow sense, and so on. That is what Aristotle means to convey when he says that justice in the broad sense is the whole of virtue. Justice involves every other virtue, because just acts are not only just but also temperate (on some occasions), courageous (on other occasions), and so on; and every other virtue exercised for the sake of the good of the political community is at the same time an act of justice.[31]

---

[30] Is there such a thing as an act of generosity that is not generous towards another person? Aristotle can reply that when a generous person attends to the preservation of his own resources, his generosity is for the moment trained on himself, even if his motive is to have enough to give to others at a later time (IV.1 1120a34–b3). Acts of generosity are directed at others only when one is actually helping them.

[31] The special nature of justice in the broad sense cannot consist in the fact that a just person has all of the other practical virtues. For one can equally well say: a courageous person has all the other virtues, a temperate person has all the virtues, and so on. To have any such virtue is to have them all (*NE* VI.13 1144b32–1145a2). It should also be noticed that as justice is a super-virtue, so injustice, in the broad sense, is a super-vice (*NE* V.1

Why does Aristotle think that lawfulness bears this relationship to the other ethical virtues? Surely his thesis derives from a thought he has already expressed: 'the laws address all matters' (1129b14–15), and prohibit citizens from engaging in acts of cowardice, intemperance, ill-temper, and so on. To be a lawful person, therefore, is to have an all-around skill: it is to have the proper attitude towards the law not only in matters that require proper control over some single emotion, like pleasure, fear, or anger, but in all of these areas. Each of the other ethical virtues—temperance, courage, and the like—is narrow in scope, because each is defined in terms of one or two emotions. But when we call someone just in the broad sense, we indicate that he has a comprehensive ability to conduct himself properly in his relation to all other members of his political community, and this broad skill presupposes mastery over the entire range of his emotional engagement with others. Justice as lawfulness does not have its own special emotion, but that is not because it has nothing to do with the emotions; on the contrary, to call someone just in the broad sense is to say that he has mastered all of them. In this respect, justice in the broad sense is to be contrasted with justice in the narrow sense, for justice as equality involves mastery over the desire for having more than one's share. Any emotional disorder can deflect us from lawfulness, but it is only the desire for more that undermines equality.

If we read Aristotle carelessly, his statement that justice, construed broadly, is the whole of virtue in one's treatment of others might, paradoxically, lead us to underestimate its significance. For we might mistakenly take this to mean that justice has no identify of its own, and is nothing but a composite whose components are each a slice—the other-regarding slice—of the other ethical virtues. So understood, justice would be nothing other than courage towards others plus temperance towards others, and so on. And in that case, there would be no reason to give it much attention. Having understood the nature of the other ethical virtues, there would be nothing new to learn from a study of justice in the broad sense.

1130a10). This thesis (unlike the claim that justice is a super-virtue) does seem to be a point about one character trait entailing all the others. To say that someone is unjust in the broad sense means that he is utterly distant not merely from this or that virtue but from all of them. A coward need not have other vices (although he cannot have any ethical virtues); but to call someone unjust in the broad sense implies not only that he is defective in every other area, but that those defects are so grave as to constitute vices. (Here I rely on a point Aristotle makes in his treatment of continence and incontinence: these states are not vices, though they of course are not virtues either. See VII.8 1150b29–1151a10.)

4.6. JUSTICE AS THE WHOLE OF VIRTUE

But this cannot be Aristotle's meaning, for he defines justice in the broad sense as lawfulness, and no other virtue is defined in this way. The best way to appreciate the distinctive nature of justice as lawfulness is to notice the difference between complaining about someone's injustice and pointing out some other ethical deficiency. When we say, for example, that someone's behavior on the battlefield arises from his cowardice, our meaning, according to Aristotle's analysis, is that he suffers from an excess of fear and a lack of confidence. If we add that this lack of courage is a vice, our meaning, according to Aristotle, is that he is not living his life well (*NE* II.6 1106a15–24). Notice that, in making these statements, we have not yet called attention to the effect his action and character have on others. If, however, we go on to say that he has not only acted with cowardice, but in doing so he was also unjust, we are complaining about him and his action from the point of view of the whole community. Our claim that he is unjust does not allege that he suffers from some specific emotional disorder. It rather criticizes him for violating a social norm that serves the well-being of the city. Of course, these two points are related: it is because he suffers from some emotional disorder that he is disposed to give short shrift to such norms. And since justice is a virtue, its exercise is a component of living well. Nonetheless, when we criticize someone for his injustice, what we mean is not that his own life is deficient, but that he shows too little regard for the community's norms and the well-being of its members.

Notice how Aristotle differs from Plato in this regard. In the *Republic*, Plato defines justice as the condition of the soul that allows each of its components to do its own work: reason rules, spirit serves as its ally, and the appetites obey. He arrives at this definition by portraying a community in which each of his three classes (philosophers, soldiers, workers) does its own job; but he insists that this conception of justice as an interpersonal relationship should be used as an image that helps us see that at bottom justice is really a relationship that exists entirely within each person (443c–d). When someone reasonably decides to refrain from eating, but appetite rebels against this command, the internal tension that results is, according to Plato, an example of injustice—even if no one else, on this particular occasion, is injured by this disharmony. For Aristotle, however, injustice is exhibited only when one person harms another by failing to abide by a useful social norm. Justice is a virtue that by its nature bears on one's relations to others. Plato's mistake, as Aristotle sees it, is to conceive of the social aspect of justice as a mere image of the relationship one has to oneself.

Plato makes justice the centerpiece of the *Republic* because it has a special status among the virtues. It is not one good quality alongside others; rather, it is the highest virtue, and yet at the same time the most problematic virtue, because it seems to benefit others but not the person who possesses it. In Aristotle's terms, then, the topic of the *Republic* is justice broadly conceived—justice as lawfulness, not equality. For it is justice of this broad sort that is generally considered to be 'complete virtue' (V.1 1129b26). But how can it be shown that exercising justice in this broad sense is a component of a well-lived life? Plato's guiding idea is that justice is one and the same psychological condition, wherever it occurs: it is a harmony between reason, spirit, and appetite; and because it unifies the soul and makes it balanced, it is, like every other kind of harmony, a good condition to be in. Furthermore, justice in the soul is a super-virtue because it is the source of the goodness of all other virtues. A person is wise because he is ruled by reason—because, in other words, reason does its job. Similarly, he is courageous because spirit does its job; and temperate because the appetites do not try to usurp the role of reason. Justice is a greater virtue than any other because of the important causal role it plays within the soul: as the principle of specialization is the cause of all goodness in social relations, so the psychological analogue of this principle is the cause of all internal goodness.

By contrast, for Aristotle, justice in the broad sense is not a unitary psychological state. The motives that lead to injustice are many and diverse: excessive anger, fear, appetite, love of money, love of honor, and so on. A just person has learned how to avoid all of these extreme states (as well as the corresponding deficiencies), but that is not because there is some single emotional skill that he has developed. There is no one fund of energy on which the just person draws, no unitary psychological state that explains why he is able to master his anger, his fear, and other such emotions. For, according to Aristotle, justice in the broad sense is not related to some single emotional condition, as courage is to fear, temperance to pleasure, and so on. Rather, the unity of justice lies in one's external relations: it is the skill that allows us to promote the good of the political community by respecting social norms.

Why is it part of a person's own good to possess and exercise this comprehensive political skill? Aristotle does not raise that question,

4.6. JUSTICE AS THE WHOLE OF VIRTUE

just as he does not ask why it is good to be courageous, or why it is good to be temperate, and so on. But that should not lead us to conclude that he thinks there is nothing worthwhile to be said in answer to such questions. When we consider in turn each of the qualities he takes to be virtues, we can understand why he thinks they are central components of a well-lived life—and therefore why he calls them virtues. Recall what was said earlier (3.10) about anger, for example: It seems obvious that there is such a thing as being angry more often than one should for one's own good, or being incapable of experiencing or expressing as much anger as one ought to feel. And the same holds true of appetite, fear, and many other feelings. The emotions are the stuff of any human life worth living, and handling them well is therefore part of what it is to live well. Furthermore, the proper functioning of our emotional lives cannot be separated from success in our relationships with others, for what counts as too much or too little with regard to certain emotions depends on what it is to have good relationships with our neighbors. Someone who constantly suppresses anger, or feels none, thereby develops a subservient relationship to others, and that is precisely why it is bad for him to have a deficiency of this emotion. Similarly, feeling more anger than is appropriate, and for longer periods of time than is called for, is unhealthy precisely because it constitutes a relationship with others that is incompatible with friendship, good will, trust, and cooperation. Such attitudes towards others are not mere instruments to be used for the accomplishment of some non-social and private good. They are constitutive of a well-lived life.

Now, if Aristotle is on firm ground in his conviction that it is part of one's own good to master all of the emotions that affect one's connections to others, then he has already gone a long way towards showing that it is part of one's good to have and exercise the virtue of justice. For justice presupposes mastery of the emotions that provide the material of the other virtues (courage, temperance, and so on): it is a comprehensive skill, and therefore its value to oneself is no less than the combined value of all of the other ethical virtues. And we should add to this Aristotle's further point that we are political animals: it is good for us to work in larger groups that take us outside the bounds of our small circle of family and friends (*NE* I.7 1097b9–11; further discussion at 3.14 and 7.2). To be a just person in the broad sense is not only to master the emotional skills that constitute the other virtues, but to use these skills and one's knowledge of civic life and legal systems to advance the well-being of all other members of one's political community. Someone who is able to achieve that much for others will also have developed his own practical cognitive powers to the fullest possible extent. (And here we have the beginnings of an answer to the question of why one should be just in the narrow sense, and not merely in the broad sense: for if it can be shown that the whole community is best served when good is distributed according to various kinds of proportionality, then that constitutes a sufficient reason for being an equal person—a person who strives for such proportionality.)

We should note one further point: Aristotle is committed to saying not only that whenever one acts unjustly in the broad sense, one also displays some other vice as well, but also that whenever one displays any of these other vices in one's treatment of others, one has violated some existing social rule or norm. For example, when one acts in a cowardly or intemperate way in one's treatment of others, one is also being unjust in the broad sense, and therefore acting in a way that is contrary to what is lawful. The fact that the cowardly and intemperate treatment of others is unlawful is not a point Aristotle makes when he discusses these virtues in Book III of the *Ethics*; rather, it is something we learn for the first time in Book V, when he points out that justice as lawfulness is a whole of which such virtues as temperance and courage are parts. I take his meaning to be that the proper treatment of others always takes place against a background of social expectations that are encapsulated in the form of rules. Although he emphasizes that in practical life we sometimes have to recognize exceptions to general rules, and that an ethically virtuous person has the ability to perceive what is to be done on each occasion, these points allow a large role to be played by general norms, rules, principles, and laws.[32] (In the same way, the fact that

---

[32] For the point that ethics is an inexact discipline, because what it studies holds only for the most part, see *NE* I.3 1094b13–27, I.7 1098a26–32, II.2 1103b34–1104a7, III.3 1112a34–b11, IX.2 1164b27–1165a18. Something like the faculty of perception is necessary, in part because it allows us to apply rules to particular cases and in part because it helps us determine when an exception is required; see II.9 1109b20–3, III.3 1112b33–1113a2, VI.11 1143a35–b14. For discussions of the role of perception in Aristotle's ethics that give less weight to generalization, rules, and long-term plans than I do, see Nussbaum, 'The Discernment of Perception', esp. p. 68; Sherman, *The Fabric of Character*, pp. 13–55; and several essays of McDowell: 'Deliberation and Moral Development in Aristotle's Ethics', pp. 21–2; 'Some Issues in Aristotle's Moral Psychology', pp. 27–8; 'Virtue and Reason'. For a forceful critique of the idea that Aristotle's recognition of ethical inexactitude leads him to refrain from seeking general principles, see Irwin, 'Ethics as an Inexact Science: Aristotle's Ambitions for Moral Theory'.

equity is sometimes needed in the courtroom does not mean that jurors may, if they choose, ignore the law, and judge each case as though it had no connection with any other.) Social norms and rules, both in the law courts and outside them, ought always to figure in our deliberations, even if on occasion they are not applicable to the case at hand. In serving the community, one should always try to apply existing social norms as best one can, like a juror who is guided by existing legislation; it is only in exceptional circumstances that one needs to invent solutions to practical problems entirely by one's own lights, and without reference to established practices and the expectations of others. Those who care little about the good of the community or their friends typically give laws and social norms too little attention in their thinking, and are all too willing to violate them. The coward violates the rule that requires him to come to the defense of his community; the stingy person violates rules that require him to help friends and those in need; the excessively angry person speaks ill of others and is physically abusive; the lover of pleasure may commit adultery or disappoint the legitimate expectations of his family and community in other ways. It is this conception of how people are tied together by means of rules, and how their well-being is best advanced by means of laws and norms, that lies behind Aristotle's assumption that justice is a super-virtue: whenever the parts of virtue (temperance, courage, and so on) are exercised, lawfulness is expressed as well, because to be virtuous is to be a skillful user of social rules.

4.7. *Natural and Legal Justice*

We should now examine some other important distinctions that Aristotle makes between different kinds of justice. He says, in the opening sentence of V.7: 'Of political justice, one part is natural, the other part legal [*nomikos*]' (1134b18–19). The remainder of the chapter explores this distinction, and that will be our main concern here. But before we turn to that topic, we should ask what Aristotle means by political justice, for the distinction between natural and legal justice falls within this general category.

To understand what is meant by political justice, we should turn to Aristotle's discussion in V.6. Here he tells us that he is inquiring into both justice without qualification and political justice, and then he explains the latter by saying that it pertains to those who 'share in a life led with a view to self-sufficiency, being free and equal either proportionally or arithmetically' (1134a26–8). Political justice is what governs the relationship of all full-fledged members of the political community. It therefore excludes both those who live in other cities and those who live within one's city but wholly or partially lack citizen status (slaves, women, children, resident aliens). The city is an association that can more or less provide for its own needs, and that is why its full members are spoken of as those who 'share in a life led with a view to being self-sufficient'. Some of these citizens may be more deserving than others of the city's positions of power and honor; they are 'proportionally equal' in that the different roles they play in the city vary according to their qualifications for playing these roles. And they are 'arithmetically equal' because in certain situations the difference in their qualifications ought to be ignored and they should be treated alike. Aristotle will discuss these kinds of equality more fully when he treats justice in the narrow sense, and they will occupy him in much of the *Politics*. For now, the important point is that political justice is the kind of justice that organizes relationships among full members of the polis, each of whom has some role to play in governing the community. It is called *political* justice precisely because it brings together all full members of a single *polis*. There is a special kind of lawfulness that obtains between these free and equal citizens, because each of them plays some role in making the laws that govern their association. These people possess and exercise their natural capacity to make and apply the law.

But there is such a thing as justice among individuals not all of whom are equal members of a polis. There is, for example, a kind of justice—household (*oikonomikos*) rather than political justice—that governs the relationship between husband and wife (V.6 1134b15–17), for a good wife is qualified to play an important role in ruling the household, and a husband ought to give her some degree of authority in these matters (VIII.10 1160b32–5). And there is yet another kind of justice that obtains between an adult citizen and his children, or between him and his slaves (V.6 1134b8–15). Certain norms govern their association, and so these are relationships in which it is possible for one party to be unjust towards the other. But this sort of justice is different from the kind that should obtain between equal citizens, because neither the young child nor the slave participates in any form of governance, as a wife does in the household.

Aristotle also points out that a child and a slave are like parts of

4.7. NATURAL AND LEGAL JUSTICE

oneself, and no one chooses to harm himself (b9–12). His idea is that a father's self-interest generally makes him give at least minimal care to his children and his property. He realizes that if he does not watch after them, his own affairs will suffer. Aristotle's remark seems to be offered as an explanation of the fact that most legal systems do not greatly concern themselves with the proper treatment of children and slaves. By contrast, people often do find it difficult to treat their fellow citizens or their wives properly; that is because they do not see these others as parts or extensions of themselves. And so there is a special need for cities to determine what justice requires among citizens, and between husband and wife. Self-love, in an extended form, will prevent most people from harming their children and slaves, but will not restrain people from injuring their fellow citizens or wives.

Accordingly, when Aristotle says, 'of political justice, one part is natural, the other part legal' (1134b18–19), he is making a distinction within the category of justice as it applies to equal citizens. Natural justice, he tells us, is that part of political justice that 'has the same force everywhere, and does not depend on what is thought to be so or not so' (b19–20). By contrast, legal justice is 'that which at first makes no difference whether it is done one way or another, but does make a difference, after it has been established' (b20–1). Some examples of legal justice are then given: it costs one mina to ransom someone; a sacrifice consists in one goat rather than two sheep. Later in the chapter, Aristotle says that legal justice depends on agreement and expediency (1134b35), and compares it to the variability of measures: 'the measures for wine and corn are not everywhere equal, but in wholesale markets are larger, in retail markets smaller' (1135a1–3).

Legal justice evidently has three characteristics. First, it exists only by virtue of being recognized and practiced by some human community. This is the force of calling it 'legal' (*nomikos*); Aristotle is here drawing on the connection between *nomos* and *nemein* that we noted earlier (4.3). Second, any rule of legal justice has a number of close cousins that could have served the community as well. There is no reason why a measure of wine has to be precisely this size or that, or why the ransom of a prisoner must be exactly this sum rather than another. Anything within a certain range would have done as well. In this sense, there is something arbitrary in all legal justice. It is a matter of indifference whether a sacrifice consists in one goat or two sheep. (Nonetheless, some or all of the members of the community may fail to recognize that their way of doing things is not uniquely correct. Blind habit may incline them to suppose that only one goat will please the gods.[33]) Third, because legal justice rests on an arbitrary choice within a certain range, we will often find variations in what is legally just in different communities. It would in fact be surprising if all communities had the same practices, when their norms depend on some arbitrary starting point. (Even so, different communities may not realize that their variant practices are equally good alternatives. Each may think that only its way of doing things is correct.)

Legal justice (we might also call it 'conventional justice') 'at first makes no difference whether it is done one way or another, but does make a difference, after it has been established' (1134b20–1). The fact that this form of justice rests to some degree on an arbitrary selection of one rule rather than another does not undermine the importance of abiding by the convention that is in force in one's community. It would be absurd to argue that since some of the practices of one's city are not uniquely correct, but are just only by convention, one need not abide by them. Such an argument would ignore the obvious fact that there are great advantages in having a common way of interacting with each other, despite the initial arbitrariness involved in conforming to this rather than that scheme of expectations. For once a convention is established in a community, the common good is best served when its members abide by that convention; the initial arbitrariness of doing things this way rather than that does not rob the rule of its validity and value. When it comes to legal or conventional justice, the practices of other members of one's community determine where justice lies. And therefore the fact that other cities live by some other rule does not detract from the importance of doing what one's own city has established as just.

But Aristotle insists that there is another kind of justice—natural justice—and he argues against those who claim that all justice is conventional. Here the term 'natural' (*physikos*) is simply used to mark a contrast with 'legal' or 'conventional' (*nomikos*): no rule counts as just in the conventional or legal sense unless it has

---

[33] The examples of legal justice that Aristotle gives in *NE* V.7 may mislead us into supposing that these conventions always regulate matters of little concern, and that their arbitrariness is easily recognized. But that may not be the case. For example, at *Pol.* VII.16 1335b19–25, he implies that prohibiting the exposure of normal infants is a matter of legal but not natural justice. See Kraut, *Aristotle: Politics Books VII and VIII*, pp. 154–5.

4.7. NATURAL AND LEGAL JUSTICE

actually been put into practice by some existing community; by contrast, a rule is naturally just if its justice does not depend on its being accepted in any city. As Aristotle says, when he makes the distinction between natural and conventional justice: the former 'does not depend on what is thought to be so or not so' (1134b20). Although a law depends for its existence on its being accepted in some community, its natural justice does not consist in its being thought just. When a law is naturally just, its justice is inherent in the law itself, and does not derive from its being accepted or practiced; by contrast, when a law is legally or conventionally just, its justice is not inherent (since some alternative would have served as well), but derives from its being taken as valid.

Why do some people think that there is no natural justice, and that all justice is conventional? Aristotle's diagnosis is that they have too simple a conception of the natural. As they understand this concept, the natural is that which is 'unchangeable and everywhere has the same force [*dunamis*]' (1134b25–6).[34] The nature of fire is to burn, and it burns wherever it exists, whether in Greece or Persia. So, according to those who doubt the existence of natural justice, if some things were naturally just—if, for example, it were naturally just for virtuous people to rule—then we would find that practice everywhere we go. But since no practice is universally adopted, they infer that there is no natural justice.

Aristotle concedes that these critics of natural justice have a point: they are correct in their claim that no rule is naturally just in the way in which fire naturally burns. No institution has the kind of power that would make it a moving force in all communities. Justice does not itself make things happen, as does the heat of fire. And so the defender of natural justice must concede that it is changeable, just as conventional justice is changeable ('all is changeable', 1134b29–30). Conventional justice changes, in that the legal justice that holds sway in one community does not hold sway in another. Natural justice, it must be admitted, is also subject to this variability. Even if there were some city that abides by natural justice, there are many others in which such justice has no force. If having force is a matter of having an effect on the lives of real people, then

---

[34] Irwin uses 'validity' to translate *dunamis* throughout V.7. Aristotle is thus made to say: 'the natural is unchangeable and equally valid everywhere—fire, for instance, burns both here and in Persia.' But validity is a normative notion, and it is hard to see how to apply it to the heat of fire. 'Force' can more easily be found in both causal and normative contexts (the 'force' of the better argument), and Aristotle seems to be using *dunamis* to play both these roles. I return to this point in the final paragraph of this section.

neither natural nor conventional justice has the same force everywhere.

Aristotle is nonetheless unwilling to concede that all justice is conventional, because he employs a conception of natural justice that differs from the one used by those who deny its existence. As he uses the term 'natural' (*physikos*), what makes some laws naturally just is the fact that their justice 'does not depend on what is thought to be so or not so' (1134b20). Why is he so confident that some laws are just in this way? He says that the right hand is by nature stronger than the left, even though it is possible for all men to become ambidextrous (b33–5). His idea is that habituation (frequent exercise of the left hand) can overcome natural propensities, and so we cannot make inferences about what is natural simply by looking at people as we find them, bad habits and all. This is a valid point, but it does not take us far enough. Aristotle is right to say that we should not base our idea of what is natural entirely on the way the world actually is. But this does not tell us why we should agree that there is a kind of justice that is independent of what people believe.

A more telling indication of the way Aristotle thinks about natural justice can be found several lines later, when he says that although there are many different kinds of political system, there is 'one alone that is everywhere naturally best' (1135a5). Here he is alluding to a program carried out in Books VII and VIII of the *Politics*, where he gives us the contours of the city he claims to be ideal.[35] By alluding to this program, he is in effect telling his audience that a concrete and detailed conception of what natural justice calls for is not something they will read about in Book V of the *Ethics*. To develop a full account of what natural justice is, one will need to construct an answer to the question of how people are best governed —a project Aristotle undertakes in the *Politics*, but not in the *Ethics*. By contrast, if we simply want to know what is conventionally or legally just, we may confine our investigation to existing cities, because although not everything that exists is just, only what exists can be counted as legally or conventionally just. That is not the case when our topic is natural justice: here, we cannot confine our discussion to what exists, because questions about natural justice are questions about how cities ought to be ruled, not how they are in fact ruled.

---

[35] I do not believe that this passage provides evidence that this portion of the *Politics* had already been written. See 4.n.1.

4.7. NATURAL AND LEGAL JUSTICE

Of course, some of the rules we already follow in existing cities would be accepted in ideal cities as well, because there is no good alternative to them. For example, whether a city should have laws that punish some kinds of assault is not a matter of indifference; without such laws, the common good cannot be achieved. And so a rule prohibiting certain kinds of physical attack is naturally just, and we do not have to wait until we develop a detailed picture of the ideal society in order to assure ourselves of this. Even so, there is a connection, in Aristotle's mind, between natural justice and the 'naturally best' constitution: all laws that are naturally just would be found in an ideally ruled city, and such a city would adopt every rule that is naturally just. We are not utterly removed from such an ideal, because, despite the pathological condition of existing cities, we can find some degree of natural justice among them, as well as conventional justice.

We should now be able to see why Aristotle conceives of natural justice as something that 'does not depend on what is thought to be so or not so' (1134b20). When a philosopher puts forward a conception of an ideal city and claims that it is a perfectly just community, it would be absurd to object that this description of perfect justice cannot be correct, because it describes practices that are not found in existing cities, and are not presently thought to be just. That reaction to the utopian project would simply be a confusion, because the whole point of the project is not to describe the laws that are in force but to imagine a better collection of laws and institutions. Although some of the rules that exist may be naturally just, the test of natural justice cannot be what is thought just or actually practiced—'what is thought to be so or not so'. The only legitimate way to think of natural justice is to free it from the confines of what people have already practiced or described, for if we do impose these limits on it, it becomes impossible for us to improve on what already exists. It is conventional or legal justice that is confined to what is already thought and practiced; so if there were no kind of justice but that, it would be impossible to discover new rules to promote the common good. 'Natural justice' is simply Aristotle's phrase for the system of laws, norms, and rules that would ideally govern our lives; it includes some of the rules we currently observe, but is not confined to 'what is thought to be so or not so'.

We should notice one telling detail in the way Aristotle expresses himself in this chapter: When he says that there is a constitution that 'is everywhere naturally best' (1135a5), the word 'everywhere' (*pantachou*) should remind us of the way he speaks of natural justice, in the opening sentence of V.7, as that which 'everywhere has the same force' (1134b19). In effect, the argument of this chapter implicitly distinguishes two senses of 'force' (*dunamis*), and has conceded that natural justice 'everywhere has the same force' in one sense but not the other. If having force is a matter of being practiced, then there are elements of natural justice that have almost no force at all. But if having force is something possessed by any goal for which we should be striving, then the ideal constitution does have force, and it has this force everywhere. Wherever we live, if we are to make improvements in our political institutions, we ought to be guided by a conception of the best city, and in that sense natural justice will everywhere control the way we act.[36]

4.8. Withdrawal or Engagement?

A remarkable difference can now be recognized between the attitudes adopted by Plato and Aristotle towards the requirements of justice and their conceptions of what sort of person a just human being is. The difference between them is not merely a theoretical matter; rather, they propose competing ideas of how one should live one's life. Plato thinks that it is only in the most unusual circumstances that justice requires one to play an active role in the politics of one's community. Ordinarily, one can be a just person only by withdrawing from the corrupt practices of everyday civic life. Plato sees no point in seeking small improvements in our workaday political structures, or tinkering with the details of legislation. For he thinks that normal politics is poisoned by the pathologies of human nature; it resists significant improvement, so long as the human soul

---

[36] For an interpretation radically at odds with the one presented here, see Yack, *The Problems of a Political Animal*, pp. 128–174. He denies that the city portrayed in *Pol.* VII–VIII is Aristotle's paradigm of natural justice. It is the best city, but Aristotle does not conceive of it as a just city (pp. 169–70). This is a difficult thesis to accept, because one would expect the most just city to be the one in which the citizens most fully succeed in finding laws that promote the common good. And surely the city proposed in *Pol.* VII–VIII meets that description. Because Yack takes conventionally just laws to be the ones about which *the citizens* are indifferent (though in fact Aristotle only says that it makes no difference whether the law says this or that), he proposes that naturally just laws are the ones about which the citizens are not indifferent: they are matters of concern and controversy (p. 143). This interpretation does nothing with Aristotle's principal characterization of natural justice as that which 'does not depend on what is thought to be so or not so' (1134b19–20).

4.8. WITHDRAWAL OR ENGAGEMENT?

is governed by the love of riches, empty honors, and domination over others. The only city we should try to establish, and in whose political life we should participate, is the ideal city described in the *Republic*, or something close to it. If we cannot do so—and that is the situation of most human beings—then 'to do one's own' is to mind one's own business, keep to one's own affairs, and wall off the corrupting influences of the world.

This counsel of withdrawal emerges in Book VI of the *Republic*, where Plato explains why those who have a talent for philosophy and political leadership are so easily corrupted. It is only extraordinary circumstances that have prevented a few of these exemplary people from entering political life and destroying their souls. Some live in exile; others are citizens of small cities; Theages has been saved by his physical weakness, Socrates by his divine sign (496b–d). Each has for some special reason taken refuge from the storm of political life, and each 'does his own' by keeping himself aloof from the lawlessness and madness around him (496d–e). This policy of withdrawal is endorsed once again later in the *Republic*, when Plato comes to the end of his description of the perfect city and the ideal condition of the human soul. He says that his portrait of the best city will retain its value even if it never comes into existence, because we can use it as an image of the harmony we should try to establish in our souls. He then adds one further thought: political activity must be shunned whenever it is corrupting, and therefore the politics of the ideal city are the only politics we ought to practice (592b). We are here given a final warning not to misinterpret the politics of the *Republic*: though much of it is about civic matters, the deeper subject is the soul, because it is only in extraordinary conditions that we should participate in political life. In all but the rarest of circumstances, the description of the ideal city is to serve no practical purpose other than to be the model we look to, as we withdraw from politics in order to save our souls.

Aristotle's account of justice is not entirely at odds with Plato's. For example, as we have seen, he opposes those who recognize no other justice than conventional and legal justice, which depends for its existence on what human beings in fact do and think. Furthermore, he believes that in order to understand natural justice, we must develop a conception of the 'naturally best' constitution (V.7 1135a5), as Plato does in the *Republic*; and a sizeable portion of the *Politics* is devoted to precisely this Platonic project. Nonetheless, when he makes his distinction between natural and legal justice,

Aristotle is not only trying to leave space for the project of describing an ideal city; he is at the same time creating room for something Plato refuses to acknowledge. For Plato believes that the only justice worth talking about is natural justice. The only city that is just is one that does not and probably never will exist, and the only just laws are ones that would be in force there. He would therefore say that Aristotle's so-called legal or conventional justice is no justice at all. For such 'justice' is by definition a creation of human beings, and does not exist apart from their activities and thoughts. What is conventionally just is at first a matter of indifference, and then it comes to seem just only because it is widely accepted in a community. Plato can have no use for such a notion. According to his way of thinking, whatever is just is so apart from what we do or say. We cannot make a practice just merely by participating in it; rather, we must participate in it because it already is just.

By contrast, Aristotle thinks we must recognize both categories—both natural and legal justice. Some justice exists apart from human activity, but some is created by us. The arguments he gives in V.7 are addressed to those who wish to eliminate one of these categories—natural justice—but we should recognize that he is equally opposed to the Platonic move in the opposite direction. And we should also notice that his examples of legal justice suggest that Plato's portrait of ordinary political life as a cesspool of corruption is highly exaggerated. Aristotle has no trouble at all in giving examples of existing practices that are just: they are as mundane and simple as the price of ransom or the price of an animal to be sacrificed. The justice of these practices consists simply in the fact that they promote the common good in existing cities. There is no need to show that they would be adopted in some ideal city, in order to certify that they really are just. (In fact, they might not be adopted in an ideal city, because, as Aristotle points out, some close cousin of these practices would serve their purpose equally well.)

Aristotle's general point, then, is that if we take the world as it is, we should have no trouble finding examples of just laws. No doubt there is considerable injustice as well, for, as he acknowledges right from the start of *Ethics* Book V, not everyone agrees about who should be served by the legal system (1129b15–16), and some conceptions of the common good are presumably more just than others; in any case, no one would be so foolish as to deny that there are ill-considered laws (1129b25). But Aristotle believes that it is a serious mistake—one made by Plato—to draw a uniformly dismal picture of

4.8. WITHDRAWAL OR ENGAGEMENT?

ordinary civic life and to claim that whoever gets involved in it will inevitably lose his soul. Even if it is conceded that on balance existing cities are unjust, we can find some justice in them, in all but the most extreme cases. (Recall our discussion in 4.5 of the point, made at V.1 1129b12, that 'everything lawful is in a way just'.) Furthermore, if there is already some degree of justice in cities that have legal systems, surely there can be more, especially if those who have a deep understanding of this virtue play an active role in civic affairs.

Plato's thesis that in the world as we find it justice requires withdrawal from political life comes into conflict with Aristotle's entire conception of a virtuous person. Aristotle holds, for example, that the virtue of courage is most fully displayed when one defends one's city on the battlefield and preserves the freedom of one's fellow citizens (III.6). In the private realm, one can exercise only a diminished and partial courage. This virtue reaches its fullest employment when one is faced with the most serious of dangers: the loss of a free way of life not only for oneself but for one's entire city. And so to be a fully courageous person, one must join one's fellow citizens in battle. Similarly, the person who most fully displays the virtue of magnificence is someone who knows how to support major civic projects (IV.2 1122b19–23); and although the magnanimous man will not be eager to perform mundane services, he does not hold back entirely from public service, but performs great deeds when his skills are most needed (IV.3 1124b24–6). Justice in the broad sense requires aiming at the good of the political community in a lawful way, and cannot exist in isolation from courage, magnificence, and magnanimity. These virtues must be exercised in cities as we find them, with all their defects and injustices. If we 'do our own', that is, if we keep to ourselves and leave public matters to others, we can at best develop a partial and diminished kind of justice.

This conflict between Plato and Aristotle is as complex as it is profound. To some extent, it involves a deep normative issue: does one owe it to one's community to participate in its affairs? But their disagreement also poses a largely empirical question, which cannot be resolved in the same way at all times and places: what can virtuous people actually accomplish in the political arena, without compromising their principles and losing their souls? Plato's counsel of withdrawal is understandable, for there can be no doubt about the power of politics to subvert moral integrity. At the same time, withdrawal often comes at a great price: political passivity allows moderately bad political systems to degenerate into increasingly evil forms.

As we will see when we turn to the *Politics*, Aristotle holds that cities typically contain an unstable mixture of justice and injustice, but that these mixtures are not of a piece: some are far more destructive of the common good than others. When decent people stay aloof from public life in order to 'do their own', they may find themselves at the mercy of regimes in which it is impossible to live the life of a good person.

4.9. Pleonexia

Aristotle uses two terms to characterize injustice in the narrow sense: the unjust person is *pleonektēs* (translated as 'greedy', 'grasping'), and he us unequal (V.1 1129a32–3). The just person, by contrast, is equal. Let us now consider these characterizations in greater detail.

Pleonexia literally means 'having more', and so the unjust person is someone who strives to have more. But more of what? Aristotle replies: more of the goods on which good and bad fortune rest (1129b2–3). No one seeks more goods—more clothing or houses or tools—unless he thinks such items will in turn bring him what he takes to be a better life. He acts for the sake of gain or profit (*kerdos*), trying to increase his share of such things as honor, money, and safety (1130b2); and he takes pleasure in such gain (b4). In V.2, Aristotle uses the following example to explain what he has in mind: a man who plans an act of adultery in order to make a profit, and does so in the absence of strong physical desire, is guilty of injustice; whereas someone driven to adultery by physical appetite, realizing that he will suffer financial losses, exhibits intemperance rather than injustice in the narrow sense (1130a24–8). The unjust person does take pleasure in what he does, but it is pleasure in profit (1130b4), not in the senses.

But since profit can take many different forms—it includes honor and safety, no less than money—injustice in the narrow sense need not be caused by avarice. It is easy to think of other examples that fit Aristotle's description. For example, suppose someone wrongly leaves his post on the battlefield without feeling the slightest degree of fear, and solely for the sake of safety. His action does not count as cowardice, because Aristotle conceives of this vice as a state caused

4.9. PLEONEXIA

by excessive fear. Rather, the defect he exhibits is injustice. His act is unjust both in the broad and narrow sense, since it exhibits his disrespect for the law and is motivated by *pleonexia*—a desire for a larger share of safety than is his due.

Similarly, someone who lays claim to an honor he knows he does not deserve is greedy for honor. The gain or profit he seeks from his injustice is not money but the good opinion of others. He is a lover of honor, just as the man who acts adulterously for profit rather than fun is a lover of money, and the man who coolly leaves his wartime post loves a life of safety. But there is a difference in these cases as well: the usual motive for adultery is pleasure rather than gain, and those who run away from their post are usually full of fear. We should not infer, however, that whenever there is injustice in the narrow sense, the motivation for the act is different from what is normally expected. On the contrary: those who are lovers of honor and therefore knowingly take more than their fair share of it act with precisely the motivation we would expect of those who commit such acts.

As Aristotle reminds us several times, however, injustice in the narrow sense is sometimes expressed by a desire for less of something rather than more. *Pleonexia* can manifest itself in a desire to have fewer evils, but even so, the unjust person is seeking some gain, because he profits by having fewer bad things (1129b6–10). If someone wrongly tries to shift blame from himself onto others, he is seeking both less and more: less blame, more blamelessness. Though *pleonexia* is always the motive for injustice in the narrow sense, we must remember, throughout Aristotle's discussion, that in some cases such injustice involves shifting burdens onto others, and in this sense having less.

We must now discuss a puzzle: since injustice is caused by a great desire for money, honor, or some other good, why cannot Aristotle treat all cases of injustice as the manifestation of one of the vices he has already discussed in Books II–IV of the *Ethics*? Too great a love of wealth is a disorder analyzed in IV.1–2; too great a love of honor is discussed in IV.3–4. Why does Aristotle need to recognize yet another vice, in Book V, when he considers acts motivated by these excessive attachments to external goods? Perhaps he ought to have said that injustice in the narrow sense is not a distinct vice, but merely an amalgam of the vices of excess having to do with money, honor, and other forms of gain. Admittedly, not every case of injustice can be handled in this way, as our example of the man who coolly flees for safety shows. But this is an example that we have supplied, not one that Aristotle himself produces. Since he does not call our attention to it, he must have some other reason for thinking that injustice is a separate virtue, and that his discussion of it does not merely repackage material he has already presented.

I suggest that Aristotle takes *pleonexia* to be a distinct vice because he tacitly assumes that it involves a desire to have more *at the expense of others*. The unjust person doesn't merely want to have some good, such as money, honor, or safety. In addition, he is not at all displeased that others will suffer as a result of his greed. In fact, when he takes pleasure in his gain, part of what pleases him is his profiting at the expense of others: he is glad that they are losing as a result of his gain. To return to Aristotle's example: the man who commits adultery in order to make a profit does not merely love money, for if that were the only emotional disorder his act displayed, it would merely exhibit the vice of excessive love of wealth. Rather, as Aristotle says, he takes pleasure in his gain (1130b4). What he means is that the unjust person is glad that his gain comes at the expense of another, because causing that suffering is part of his motive.

Similarly, to return to the other examples we used: the man who coolly flees his post is pleased that as a result the burdens of others will increase. And the man who wrongly claims an undeserved honor is glad that his rivals have been robbed of their due. It is not characteristic of the coward that he wants to shift risks onto others; nor is it part of the vice having to do with dishonor that it wants to rob others of their deserts. Those who seek to gain at the expense of others—whether the gains and losses come in the form of wealth, honor, or safety—suffer from a single emotional disorder, one that is separate from excessive love of these goods. So the kind of *pleonexia* Aristotle discusses in Book V is a highly pernicious desire for more: it is the desire to have more at the expense of others.

We must bear in mind that injustice in the narrow sense is a species of injustice in the broader sense. That is, when someone exercises the vice of *pleonexia*, he does so by violating a law or rule that is generally observed in his community. He regards such rules as illegitimate restraints on his behavior. He has no admiration for his fellow law-abiding citizens, but regards them as mere fools and weaklings. The pleasure he takes in getting the better of them derives from his general contemptuousness towards the law and those who respect the law. His injustice is an expression of his sense of superiority to others, and the pleasure he takes in his act derives not only from gaining some good (money, honor, safety) but from the satisfaction he takes in expressing his contempt for others.[37]

By contrast, someone who falls short of justice in the broad sense but is not unjust in the narrow sense has a less antagonistic attitude towards others. Consider, for example, someone who decides to commit adultery because he loves sexual pleasure and pursues it as a great good. He has too little regard for the law and therefore is not a just person in the broad sense. But since he is (by hypothesis) not unjust in the narrow sense, he is not trying to make others suffer and does not take pleasure in their loss. He acts for his own good and has less concern than he should for the common good. He allows others to suffer, because this is a cost he is willing to pay in order to get more pleasure. By contrast, someone who is unjust in the narrow sense does not regard the suffering of others as a cost, but as part of the appeal of acting unjustly.

I have attributed to Aristotle the idea that some people take pleasure in making others suffer. But do we have evidence that his picture of human nature is really so dark? Rest assured; it is. The idea that it is pleasant to injure one's enemies was a commonplace of Greek popular morality, and Aristotle takes note of it in the *Rhetoric* (I.12 1373a4–5). In fact, the Greeks have a word for it: their term for spite —*epichairekakia*—literally means 'joy in evil'. It names the happy sensation one gets when evils befall others. So Aristotle certainly recognized that some people take pleasure both in hearing about and in contributing to the misfortunes of others. We are not going beyond his conception of human nature in attributing to him the assumption that when the unjust person takes pleasure in gaining at the expense of others, his pleasure arises not only from his own gain but from their loss.

Aristotle briefly discusses spite and related emotions in II.7 of the *Ethics*, and applies his doctrine of the mean to them. The intermediate state is *nemesis* ('righteous indignation', 'proper indignation'): it is the disposition to feel pain when someone does well undeservedly. Since such a person *sometimes* feels pain at another's good fortune, obviously the corresponding vice that goes to excess is one that involves feeling pain *too often* at another's good fortune—

---

[37] The attitudes described in this paragraph should be familiar to readers of Plato's *Gorgias*: they form part of the ideal proposed by Callicles.

and this is what an envious person is like. He feels pain at someone else's good fortune even when it is deserved.

But what would the related deficiency be? Aristotle might have replied that this is the condition in which one *never* feels pain at the good fortune of others and perhaps even feels pleasure whenever others fare well, whether they deserve to or not. But for some reason this is not the reply he gives. He says instead that the deficiency related to *nemesis* and envy is spite (1108b3–6). Perhaps he was taken in by the twofold verbal opposition between envy and spite: envy is pain at good fortune; spite is pleasure (the opposite of pain) at bad fortune (the opposite of good fortune). Or perhaps he thinks that the envious person feels pain too often (whenever others fare well) and the spiteful person too little: rather than being pained when others fare ill, the spiteful person is instead delighted. But the problem with his scheme is that the excess of the envious person and the deficiency of the spiteful person are directed at two different things, and so it cannot be said that one has too much and the other too little of the same emotion. The emotion felt by the envious person is pain at good fortune; that felt by the spiteful person is joy at bad fortune. These are not opposites, and do not follow the pattern of the other vices. The vices that have to do with fear, for example, involve having either too much or too little of it. One cannot be in both of these states at the same time. By contrast, envy and spite can easily be combined: one can regularly feel pain at the good fortune of others, and joy at their bad fortune.

In any case, even though Aristotle fumbles in treating these emotions as opposites, it should be apparent that they play a significant role in his conception of injustice in the narrow sense. The *pleonektēs* does not merely seek an excess of such goods as money, honor, and safety; he also takes pleasure in profiting at the expense of others, and can therefore be characterized as spiteful and envious. When his victims escape his clutches, he is pained by his failure to cause them some loss; and when he succeeds, he delights in their misfortune. Even when he is not active in the world, but merely surveys the other members of his community and contemplates their successes and failures, he is downcast when others fare well and delighted when they do poorly.

Aristotle of course approves of people he describes as intermediate between the envious and the spiteful—those who experience *nemesis*, and are pained when success comes to those who do not deserve it. When a criminal fares well, for example, by executing his plan

4.9. PLEONEXIA

without mishap, observers of his success ought to be displeased. (Conversely, those who witness the deserved success of others should be gratified.) But we should notice that mismatches between success and desert do not figure at all in Aristotle's discussion of justice. He takes justice and injustice to be something that human beings do to each other, rather than something that is present in the world in the absence of human action. If the virtuous suffer grave misfortunes for which no one is responsible—if, for example, they become extremely ill, or their friends die before their time—then those who observe their plight ought to be pained by their losses, but no one should think that some injustice has been done to them. The fact that they did not deserve their losses does not mean that they suffered an injustice, if in fact no one treated them unjustly. Aristotle's gods have no other activity besides contemplation (*NE* X.8 1178b8–22), and therefore cannot selectively intervene in or even care about human life. So they cannot be accused of injustice on the grounds that they allow bad things to happen to good people. They allow nothing and bring nothing about, because they are not moral agents. And so the undeserved misfortune for which no human being is to blame is simply that—undeserved—but not unjust. Aristotle recognizes that the world is sometimes a harsh environment, made all the worse by unjust people. But injustice comes only from other people, not from the world.

This completes our discussion of *pleonexia*. There is no doubt that this complex psychological syndrome—a combination of spite, envy, and greediness for profit—is real, and causes a great deal of the world's injustice. It should be kept in mind, however, that this is only one component of Aristotle's account of what leads people to do wrong in the broad sense. His basic idea is that unjust behavior consists in disregard for the rules that promote the common good, and that any number of psychological disorders can lead to such disregard. Excessive appetite, or fear, or anger, or any of the other pathologies discussed in Aristotle's analysis of virtues and vices can become the cause of injustice. *Pleonexia* is only one part of the picture. It plays a special role in his theory because he singles it out as the characteristic emotional disorder of someone who is unjust in the narrow sense—someone who tries to overturn the proportionality that ought to obtain in human relationships.

4.10. Objections

We should now take note of several objections that might be made against Aristotle's theory.[38] To begin with, consider a juror who is biased by his friendship for a defendant. Knowing that his friend is guilty, he nonetheless votes for acquittal, out of a desire to see him fare well. He is not moved by excessive physical appetite, or anger, or any of the other emotions that Aristotle discusses in Books II–IV of the *Ethics*. Nor does he seem to be motivated by *pleonexia*. His fault lies in the bias and partiality that move him, when he ought instead to be serving the larger community. And yet Aristotle's conception of the psychological sources of injustice does not seem to recognize this all too common phenomenon.

But in fact, he does mention this sort of case, in the opening pages of the *Rhetoric*: jurors can and do cast their votes out of feelings of friendship and hatred, without regard to the merits of the case (I.1 1354b7–11). Furthermore, the theory of justice he proposes in the *Ethics* can be extended to account for these examples. He need only point out that the feeling of friendship, like any other feeling, can be excessive, and manifest itself at the wrong time and place. (He implies as much at *NE* VII.4 1148a30–1, where he notes that one can be overly concerned about one's children or parents.) In general, a virtuous person must not only love others, but love them in the right way. In particular, he must not favor his friends on those occasions when doing so might undermine the good of the community. Jurors who acquit their guilty friends violate a rule that is central to the well-being of the political community, and they do so because of an emotional disorder. They lack justice in the broad sense, and they have this defect because there is some other virtue that they are also lacking—the virtue that enables some people to hit the mean in matters having to do with friendship.

The act of knowingly acquitting a guilty friend is also a violation of justice in the narrow sense, for it is an unequal act: it fails to correct an injustice, and allows some to have more and others less than they deserve. (This form of injustice will be discussed more fully in 4.12.) But Aristotle is not required to say that all acts of injustice in the narrow sense are caused by the peculiar emotional disorder that he calls *pleonexia*. Just as acts of adultery do not necessarily flow from an excessive love of pleasure, but can be caused by

---

[38] My thoughts in this section have been stimulated by Williams, 'Justice as a Virtue'.

4.10. OBJECTIONS

other emotional disorders (for example, a love of gain), so acts that are unjust because unequal need not be caused by *pleonexia*, but can arise from other excesses or deficiencies of feeling. The motive that makes someone an unequal *person* is the desire for more, but it does not follow that this is always the motive that leads to an unequal *act*.

Even so, Aristotle's theory can reasonably accuse the juror who unjustly acquits his friend of exhibiting *pleonexia*, if that is the motive that led to his friend's violation of the law, and the juror shares in that motive. Suppose his friend committed a crime not only for some material advantage, but also because he wanted to experience the pleasure of gaining at the expense of another person; and that in helping his friend get away with his crime, the juror enjoys contemplating his friend's success and the misfortune of the victim. Even if he receives no money or other reward from his friend for his biased vote, the juror can plausibly be accused of an extended form of *pleonexia*: he takes pleasure in contemplating his friend's unjust gains and the victim's losses. He wants his friend to have more, at the expense of someone else; and that is close enough to what Aristotle calls *pleonexia* to deserve the same name. And of course it would not at all be surprising for the juror to receive some reward from his friend in exchange for his vote, and in that case, his motive is *pleonexia*, plain and simple. (Aristotle discusses such a case at V.9 1136b34–1137a4.)

Another objection can be made against Aristotle's account of the motives that underlie injustice in the broad sense. He seems to hold that the cause of such injustice is always some emotional disorder— whether it be *pleonexia*, excessive anger, immoderate desires for honor or money, or the like. But it might be claimed, against this, that injustice can arise because people hold false theories or make false judgments about justice, and that these can be merely intellectual mistakes that are not rooted in any emotional disturbance.

Aristotle does recognize this possibility, however. He says in V.9 that if someone who is distributing goods 'made a judgment in ignorance, he does not do injustice with respect to legal justice, and his judgment is not unjust, but there is a way in which it is unjust. For legal justice and primary justice are different' (1136b32–4). Suppose one is serving as an arbitrator in a dispute, and one decides badly, because one ignores some salient feature of the case. Aristotle's point, when he says that 'one does not do injustice with respect to legal justice', is simply that the arbitrator has committed no injustice that can be remedied by the legal system. He cannot be prosecuted merely on the grounds that his decision was mistaken and based on ignorance. On the other hand, Aristotle points out that there is a sense in which the arbitrator's judgment is unjust: the distribution he chose is not a just distribution. For our purposes, the important point is Aristotle's recognition that justice can arise solely from ignorance. The arbitrator who makes an unjust distribution need not be guilty of *pleonexia*, or partiality, or any other emotional deficiency. He may simply have overlooked some of the facts of the case.

Nonetheless, Aristotle does not mean to suggest in this passage that a considerable portion of the world's injustice arises from ignorance. His point rather is that citizens and legal officials may make occasional errors because of their ignorance of the facts. But when they treat others unjustly on a regular basis, he believes that the underlying causes for their doing so are emotional. He recognizes (*Politics* III.9) that people put forward competing ideas about what justice is, and that often their theories of justice are misguided, and therefore lead to injustices. He thinks that the theories of justice put forward by defenders of oligarchic and democratic regimes are equally mistaken. Oligarchs sometimes mistreat the poor, because their conception of justice holds that the poor should be excluded from civic life; and conversely, democrats sometimes wrong the rich, and seek to distribute the property of the wealthy among themselves. But Aristotle holds that this conflict is not purely intellectual; it is fueled by the excessive desires of the rich, and the spite and envy of the poor.[39] Each party to the dispute adopts a conception of justice that serves its own interests and disregards the legitimate claims of others. So, when they treat each other badly, they are not merely acting in ignorance. Rather, their ignorance about what justice demands is the result of emotional disorders.

Whether or not Aristotle is correct about the sources of this particular rivalry, he ought to have recognized the possibility that mistaken ideas about justice can by themselves do great harm, even in the absence of emotional deficiencies. His attempt to justify slavery (to be discussed in Chapter 8) is a case in point. He argues that, although there may be people who are unjustly enslaved, there is

[39] The enmity between rich and poor is one of the main themes of *Pol.* IV–VI, and will be examined in Ch. 12. See e.g. V.9 1310a9–10 for the oath taken by the wealthy elite of certain cities to harm the poor. *Pol.* III.10 is an introduction to this conflict. For the point that theories of justice often reflect a bias in one's own favor, see III.9 1280a14–16.

nothing intrinsically unjust about the institution of slavery itself. Provided that the slave is naturally inferior to the master, his enslavement is not an injustice but is in fact advantageous to both slave and master. Slavery makes possible a life of virtue for slave-owners, and slaves benefit from their service to a superior person. In making this claim, Aristotle was speaking in ignorance: he failed to recognize that no group of people has the rational deficiency that, he claims, qualifies them for slavery. But must it be the case that some emotional defect within Aristotle led him to adopt his disastrous defense of slavery? At any rate, there is no reason to assume that he must have had the psychological profile he attributes to an unjust person—that he tried to justify the institution of slavery because he himself was driven by an excessive desire for wealth, power, honor, and the like.

Perhaps it will be said that Aristotle's discussion of slavery reveals a culpable lack of compassion or sympathy for the condition of slaves, and therefore the injustices he helped perpetuate by defending this institution were the product not only of his intellectual errors but his emotional inadequacies as well. I have no doubt that he is guilty as charged: he shows no sympathy for the suffering of slaves. But would sympathy have saved him from moral error? Compassion for slaves might lead to efforts to alleviate their suffering, but it can coincide with the conviction that there is nothing inherently unjust about this institution.[40] Emotional health cannot by itself protect one from doing great harm by accepting a false picture of the world. It is best to admit, then, that adherence to misguided theories of justice can by itself be a powerful cause of injustice. Aristotle is right that *pleonexia* and kindred emotional disorders account for much of the world's injustice, but these are by no means the only sources of evildoing.

4.11. *Equality in Distribution*

Aristotle says that the unjust person (in the narrow sense) is both *pleonektēs* and unequal (V.1 1129a32–3). We have seen what sort of thing *pleonexia* is; now let us turn to the just person's other defining feature—his inequality. Aristotle's principal idea here is that we

---

[40] Seneca, for example, urges Nero to treat slaves mildly, but he sees nothing unjust about slavery. See 'On Mercy', I.18.

must recognize several different kinds of equality and inequality. First, there is equality in the distribution of goods and evils. Here the problem of justice is how one or more people playing the role of distributors are to allocate goods or evils among several potential recipients of those goods and evils, based on their merits. The distributor's job is to arrange matters so that one ratio is equal to another: the ratio between one recipient and the good he receives must be made equal to the ratio between a second recipient and the good he receives. To the extent that the first recipient is superior to the second, to that same extent the good he receives should be greater. If the recipients are of equal merit, they should receive an equal amount; otherwise, their shares must be unequal. Nonetheless, Aristotle says that even when the right allocation is one that distributes shares unequally, this sort of justice can be called equality, because the ratio on one side of the equation is made equal to the ratio on the other. This is proportionate or geometrical equality (V.3 1131a29–32), rather than the strict arithmetic equality that calls for equal shares for all alike, regardless of their merits (V.4 1132a1–2).

Surprisingly, Aristotle does not consider the point that sometimes only one good is available for distribution. There may be only one prize, and each potential recipient may have some degree of merit. In this case it will be impossible to achieve equality among the ratios: one person will get the whole prize and the other nothing, even though they may be close in merit. Aristotle is not troubled by this possibility, because he is concerned principally with a political problem: how should positions of power and honor be distributed among citizens (1131a27–9)? Even if there are only a small number of high offices, qualified citizens can be rotated in and out of office, and in this way all those who are equally qualified to receive these honors can share them on an equal basis. The good of public office is divisible over time.

Aristotle also ignores the point that sometimes distributions are based not on merit, but on some other criterion. If food and other resources are available for distribution to the needy, then justice requires that larger amounts be given to those who have greater needs. Aristotle ignores this point in *Ethics* Book V because he does not regard the threat of starvation and extreme poverty as the primary issue faced by the polis. (He acknowledges in *Politics* II that such problems are the collective responsibility of the community.[41])

[41] See 9.n.29.

4.11. EQUALITY IN DISTRIBUTION

The principal question of justice, he thinks, is: who should have power? He holds that those who are better qualified for office should have greater power, but recognizes that this point by itself does not tell us enough, because different political factions propose different criteria of merit. Democrats, for example, think that merit consists in having the status of a free man rather than a slave, and that power should therefore be distributed equally among the non-slave male population. And there are other criteria of merit as well (V.3 1131a27–9), one favored by oligarchs (wealth), another by aristocrats (virtue). Aristotle makes no attempt to resolve the issue in the *Ethics*, but takes it up in Book III of the *Politics*. The principal point that will emerge there is that the choice among competing criteria of merit is to be made by considering what it is for citizens to live well. If, as Aristotle believes, the ultimate goal of the community should be to create and sustain conditions favorable to the full exercise of the intellectual, emotional, and social powers of all citizens, then high offices should be filled by those who are best able to achieve this. They should be fully realized human beings—not merely free men, and not necessarily rich men—because such individuals are best equipped to make sound political judgments.

Aristotle holds, in other words, that although merit is the basis on which distributive questions should be resolved, the kind of merit that must be taken into account is a matter to be determined by looking to the common good of the whole community. His general approach to distributive questions has many different applications. For example, if a community wants to honor those who have written the best poetry, or who have excelled in athletic contests, its ultimate reason for holding these civic ceremonies must refer to the good of the whole community, and not merely the recipients of the honors—the poets or athletes. The justice of an institution that distributes goods is a twofold matter: first, the institution must contribute to the common good, and second, the distributions must be made in accordance with the criterion of merit that is appropriate, in light of the common good that is to be achieved. If an institution undermines the well-being of the community, then it does not serve the goal of justice, even if it succeeds in distributing goods according to the criterion of merit it uses. For example, it would not be fair for poets to receive greater public honors than others, unless rewarding good poetry makes a particularly important contribution to the life of the community. Similarly, if athletes are given public rewards for their victories, but the contributions made by philosophers to the common good receive no public recognition, then, as Socrates recognized (*Apology* 36d–e), the city is an unjust distributor of honor.

4.12. Corrective Justice

Aristotle's second category of justice in the sense of equality has to do with the rectification of wrongs done either in transactions that are voluntary among all parties (sales, loans, promises) or in transactions in which one party has participated involuntarily (theft, adultery, assault). When he discusses this aspect of justice in V.4, he makes much of the point that in these cases the distributors of justice (the jurors) look only to arithmetic and not to proportionate equality. In the case of distributive justice, the question is always: how do the potential recipients of justice compare with each other in terms of merit? But when a court faces the question whether one person has stolen from another, and if so, what the punishment is to be, it does not ask how the complainant and the defendant should be compared on some scale of merit. The law treats these two parties as equals (1132a5), and asks only whether the defendant has done the wrong of which he has been accused.

Aristotle obviously approves of such equal treatment, but why so? Why should the law not direct the jury to consider whether a thief is a better person than his victim, and to decide whether he deserves the goods he has stolen, as a reward for his greater virtue? Surely Aristotle would reply that such a law would undermine the good of the political community. It would encourage anyone who has a favorable opinion of his own virtue to take the property of those he takes to be his inferiors. Obviously no stable political system would be possible if the law allowed individuals to redistribute wealth in this way. Aristotle's assumption, then, is that a city best promotes the common good when the same legal rights are assigned to all citizens, whether they are good human beings or not. There is nothing 'intrinsically' unjust about a good person taking from a bad person, any more than there is something 'intrinsically' just about a good person receiving more honor than a bad person—if 'intrinsic' means 'apart from the common good'. For the virtue of justice can be expressed only through a system of rules that promote the good of the whole community.

Aristotle holds that corrective justice restores the two individuals involved to a position of equality, a position that has been disturbed by the unjust act (1132a24–7). They are equals, so far as the law is concerned: the system of rules prohibiting certain actions applies equally to both, and both know that they will be punished if they violate the rules. If one harms the other, the first party has gained and the second has lost (1132a9–14). By punishing the guilty party, the jurors restore them to a position of equality. What Aristotle means is that if the city does not provide for the punishment of the guilty party, then in effect the two individuals are no longer being treated by the law as equals. The person who has committed the injustice has gained, in the sense that he now has a status higher than others: he is being allowed to treat others as he pleases. And those who are forced to accept such treatment have been demoted to the status of inferiors. In order to maintain a system of law in which all are treated as equals, something must be done to the person who has caused another person's suffering. The punishment takes something away from him, in order to make it the case that he is not someone who is allowed by the legal system to do as he pleases. He cannot be allowed to take on the status of a superior person, rather than an equal in the eyes of the law. The more serious the injury he has done, the more he must be made to suffer; for if serious crimes receive only light penalties, then the legal system in effect invites some to make victims of others, and thereby to demote them to an inferior status. The city becomes divided into brazen criminals and their victims—tyrants and subjects—and is no longer a community of citizens who are equal before the law. Crime must be punished, then, because it serves the common good to maintain a legal system in which all citizens, whatever their defects or merits as human beings, are treated alike. It is not 'intrinsically' just to make someone suffer a loss because he himself has done this to another person. The justice of returning evil for evil can only be seen when we view punishment as part of a system that treats people as equals, and understand the benefits of having such a system.

The basic idea underlying Aristotle's approach to corrective justice is that a community will not succeed in achieving its goal—the well-being of all—unless its members regard each other as equals, despite differences among them in power, wealth, education, and the like. Distributive justice requires distinctions based on merit, and it serves the good of all to have such hierarchies, when they are in fact based on merit. But it would be a serious mistake to allow such distinctions to permeate the legal system, for example, by giving some greater access to the courts, or by requiring some to obey the laws but not others. Dividing the community into two kinds of citizen—those who are treated favorably by the law and those who are not—would undermine the sort of cooperation that cities need in order to achieve their goals. When citizens can say to each other that they are equals, and the courts treat all of them alike, despite their differences in merit, then politics can accomplish something worthwhile.

Those whose unjust behavior is motivated by *pleonexia* (recall our discussion in 4.9) pose a particularly serious threat to the egalitarianism of the legal order, because their crimes are not merely attempts to get an advantage for themselves, but are also intended to get the upper hand over others. A man who commits adultery in the absence of physical desire, in order to take pleasure in having made someone else worse off, does not treat his victim as an equal. To be unjust in the narrow sense is to be an unequal person—it is to have an attitude that threatens the equality of citizens. By contrast, when it is physical desire that leads to adultery, the adulterer is not expressing a sense of superiority over another person, by gaining at his expense. The act is unjust in the broad sense, since it violates a law that promotes the common good, but it is not unjust in the narrow sense. The man who commits adultery from passion of course foresees that someone else will suffer as a result of his act, but he may regret that fact, even as he acts. There is a sense in which he is seeking a certain gain for himself (he is satisfying his appetite and feeling pleasure), and he realizes that his gain will be another's loss. Aristotle can therefore apply his theory of punishment to him: those who voluntarily perform acts that upset the equality among citizens, by seeking gain for themselves and thereby bringing loss to others, must themselves be made to suffer a loss, in order to undo the inequality they have caused. But when a passion like physical appetite or anger is what leads to an unjust act, the punishment need not be as severe as it is in cases caused by *pleonexia*. For the person driven by such emotions cannot be called an unequal person. He allows himself to cause undeserved suffering to others, but undermining the good of others is not one of his aims.[42]

---

[42] Aristotle is concerned at several points in *NE* V with distinctions that might be relevant to the severity of punishment. See e.g. V.6 1134a17–23 and the whole of V.8.

4.13. Commercial Reciprocity

Aristotle's account of justice in distribution and punishment applies to the two main arenas in which citizens govern themselves. They both distribute and receive goods when they vote for public officials, occupy civic offices, and adopt legislation; and they make decisions about how to correct past injustices when they serve as magistrates, jurors, and arbitrators.[43] But when Aristotle turns, in V.5 of the *Ethics*, to the third of the three kinds of justice in the narrow sense—reciprocal justice—he focuses on the commercial activities in which both citizens and non-citizens participate: buying, selling, lending, renting, and the like.

No doubt, one reason why he discusses this aspect of just relations lies in the opportunity it gives him to show in yet another way that justice consists in some sort of equality, and that the doctrine of the mean can therefore be applied to this virtue. But it is possible that he has a further motive for including commercial relations in his account of justice. We should recall that in Plato's *Republic*, the idea that justice consists in doing one's own is first illustrated by means of the division of economic labor. Justice in social relations consists in each person doing the job for which he is best suited. When this principle is applied to craftsmen, it requires them to contribute to the justice of the city by working at their special crafts, and leaving the jobs for which they are ill suited to others. We find nothing corresponding to this idea in Aristotle's writings. Although he would certainly agree (who would not?) that craftsmen benefit others by providing for their material needs, he does not claim that in doing this useful work, craftsmen are acting justly. This refusal to follow Plato's lead is reasonable: after all, just acts are not simply those that benefit others, or those done for this purpose. Political justice in the broad sense consists in promoting the good of the whole community by means of laws and rules—that is, by making law, adjudicating disputes, and obeying the laws and norms of the community.[44] But there is no rule or law that requires one to be a builder, a shoemaker, or a farmer. So it is hard to see why the justice of a craftsman should consist precisely in sticking to his craft. If we ask what justice demands of craftsmen, farmers, and others who

---

[43] On the various kinds of judicial office that existed in the Greek city, see Harrison, *The Law of Athens*, ii. 1–68.

[44] Such justice is 'political' in the sense explained in 4.7; other kinds of justice govern relations among members of the household.

engage in economic activity, surely the sensible answer is that they must refrain from cheating and other unfair practices in their commercial relations. It is more plausible to say that justice is shown by respect for these commercial norms than to claim, as Plato does, that practicing one's craft is in itself a just activity.

The basic idea behind Aristotle's analysis of justice in the economic sphere is that goods should be exchanged for goods on an equal basis. The complexity of his analysis in V.5 derives from his attempt to show what sort of equality this is, and how it is achieved. People do not merely exchange one good for another: they pay attention to how many goods of one sort they are giving in return for a certain quantity of goods of another kind. They insist upon giving and receiving the right amounts, and Aristotle's goal is to show that in a certain way these are equal amounts—even when they give one unit of X in order to get many units of Y.

Commercial exchange is a form of reciprocity—what each party to a transaction gives is in some way equivalent to what he has received—but before Aristotle presents his own ideas about this form of justice, he briefly criticizes a conception of reciprocity proposed by certain Pythagoreans.[45] Reciprocity can be taken in two ways: it might mean not only that good should be returned for good, but also that evil should be returned for evil. But if one interprets the latter maxim in the wrong way, one is led to the *lex talionis*—the dictum that an eye should be taken for an eye. That is the conception of justice proposed by the Pythagoreans. Their maxim is: 'should one suffer the things one did, right justice would be done' (V.5 1132b27).

Aristotle's complaint about this conception of justice can be divided into two separate points.[46] First, the Pythagoreans go wrong because their definition of justice is unqualified (1132b21–2): they equate justice with reciprocity, as though that were the whole of this virtue. Aristotle does not waste any time telling us why this is a mistake; he takes it to be evident that distributive and corrective justice cannot be subsumed under reciprocity. But why is this so obvious? In particular, why can we not view what goes on in the courtroom as a case of reciprocity, that is, a case of returning evil for

---

[45] At least one member of the Pythagorean school (Archytas, early fourth century) was active in the politics of southern Italy, and so it is not surprising to hear of a Pythagorean conception of justice.

[46] In thinking about this portion of *NE* V.5, I have been helped by Scaltsas, 'Reciprocal Justice in Aristotle's *Nicomachean Ethics*', esp. pp. 249–53.

4.13. COMMERCIAL RECIPROCITY

evil? Why call it corrective justice and distinguish this from reciprocity? Aristotle's reply can be inferred from his treatment of corrective justice in V.4. If we view courtroom justice as a matter of heaping evil upon evil, we will miss the elementary point that when we punish, we do so in order to *correct* what has gone awry. The penal system is a system of correction, not a device with no aim other than causing people to suffer in the same way they have made others suffer. The courts try to restore equality among the citizens; they aim at this good in human relations, and not at evil for its own sake. The punitive aspect of justice must be understood within the larger framework of justice as a system of rules designed to promote the common good. That is why the kind of justice the Pythagoreans discuss is better thought of as corrective justice rather than as reciprocity.

The second component of Aristotle's critique of Pythagorean justice is that their formula—'should one suffer the things one did, right justice would be done'—gives us bad advice in particular cases (1132b28–30). To use Aristotle's example, that formula can be taken to mean that an officeholder and ordinary citizen are on a par: if an officeholder strikes someone, he should be struck in turn; and vice versa. Aristotle thinks this is obviously wrong, but his point requires some elucidation. What he has in mind, when he gives this example, is this. Suppose A is an official whose job is to take B to prison, and B resists.[47] If A needs to hit B, in order to do his job, it does not follow that A should be struck by B or anyone else. Conversely, if B strikes A, in order to resist arrest, then it is not only the case that A would be right to defend himself by striking back; it is also the case that B should be punished for using violence against an official. ('If he struck the official, it is necessary not only that he be struck, but that he be punished as well', 1132b29–30.) Aristotle agrees that in some sense evil should be returned for evil: those who do injustice deserve to suffer some punishment. But this is because justice requires a restoration of status that serves the public good—not merely the piling up of harms.

We can now turn to Aristotle's discussion of the exchange of goods for goods in commercial relations. Suppose a builder and a shoemaker want to exchange their products. What underlies their relationship is need: if neither had any use for the other's product, they

---

[47] On the role of imprisonment in Athenian law, see MacDowell, *The Law in Classical Athens*, pp. 75, 126, 166–7, 239, 256–7.

would not enter into negotiations (1133a25–9). But exchange will not take place on just any terms. If the shoemaker proposes that one pair of shoes should be given in return for one house, there will be no exchange. If they were bartering, the shoemaker would have to offer the builder many pairs of shoes in exchange for one house. In this sense, these two craftsmen are not equals; the more shoes it takes to exchange for one house, the greater the superiority of the builder in commercial relations (1133a7–24). But once money has been introduced as a medium of exchange, there is no need for these two workers to negotiate an exchange between shoes and buildings. They can propose an exchange of coins for their products. If a house commands a price 3,000 times higher than the price of a pair of shoes, that is equivalent to a trade between a house and that many pairs. Money has made it easy for them to exchange, although the need of each for the other's product is also an essential factor in explaining how and why one sort of good is given in return for another. Furthermore, when a certain number of coins are exchanged for a certain number of goods, a full analysis would reveal that there is always a four-term proportion that lies in the background (1133b23–6). One pair of shoes is exchanged for 30 drachmas, but this would not happen unless those 30 coins are equal to all sorts of other goods. The shoes exchanged for coins equal a certain quantity of other goods, and not just those coins.

But we might wonder: what has any of this to do with justice? Or, to put the same question in different terms: what is it to perform an unjust act, in this sphere? That is an easy question to answer, when it is posed about distributive or corrective justice. To commit injustice in distribution is to seek some honor, office, or other advantage that one knows one does not deserve. To commit corrective injustice is to acquit someone one knows is guilty, or to convict someone one knows is innocent. But what sort of injustice does Aristotle have in mind when he discusses reciprocity in commerce?

We should recall that when he introduces the notion of corrective justice, he divides it into two kinds (V.2 1131a1–9). In one kind of case, both of the contending parties who appear in court have voluntarily engaged in the transaction that has led to the complaint: a sale or some other commercial action has gone awry, or so it is alleged. In the second kind of case, one party has involuntarily come into relation to the other: he is the victim of theft, adultery, or the like. It is the first of these two categories that Aristotle has in mind when he discusses justice in exchange. He is talking about commercial cases

4.13. COMMERCIAL RECIPROCITY

that have come to court, not about the initial setting of terms among those who exchange goods. At least one of the parties to the legal dispute alleges that he has not received the goods that are due him. For example: A has finished making his payments to B, but B still has not delivered any goods to A. A has too little, B too much, and the court is asked to play an equalizing role. The dispute is not about what the terms of exchange should be—how much money should be paid for a certain product. That is something that has already been worked out. The terms are not the problem, because each has agreed to them. Had both lived up to their agreement, justice would have been done. What each gave would have been equal to what each received. But one party claims that the other knowingly gave less than an equal amount, and asks the court for redress.

It might be asked whether Aristotle's diagnosis of the situation can be greatly simplified: perhaps he ought to have said that what goes wrong here is that one person has violated an agreement. B said he would do something for A, and has not performed. And it might be said, against Aristotle, that this is where the injustice lies, not in some failure of reciprocity. Can we explain why he does not analyze commercial disputes in these terms?

He of course does not tell us why he makes no reference to the role of agreement in determining the quantities involved in commercial exchanges. But it is not difficult to understand why he concentrates on reciprocity and leaves agreement in the background. Suppose A agrees to pay B 30 drachmas for a pair of shoes. A gets his shoes, but B has not received his drachmas, and goes to court. We ask why the court should force A to pay B. If the only response we make is that A agreed to pay 30 drachmas in exchange for the shoes, we fail to mention a crucial point: A has received the good he bargained for, and yet he has given nothing in return. It is the absence of reciprocity that explains why the city should take the trouble to rectify matters. The agreement between A and B explains *what* one owes the other, but the reason *why* A should pay B the amount agreed upon is that A has already received something of value from B. It is the present inequality between the two traders that shows that an injustice has been done, not the fact that they agreed upon terms.[48]

---

[48] It is significant that in the *Crito*, Socrates endorses the thesis that just agreements should be kept—implying that not every agreement should. If one asks why agreements should sometimes be honored, the answer cannot appeal to the fact of agreement. Perhaps this helps explain why Aristotle does not make agreement the basis for commercial exchange: he assumes that the mere fact of agreement never by itself establishes a point about justice, because agreements can themselves be unjust.

It should be kept in mind that justice in reciprocity, like all forms of equal justice, is a species of justice in the broad sense. All of the varieties of justice in this sense are ways of respecting rules that promote the common good. And so the justice of requiring someone to make an equal return for a good he has received can only be recognized when one looks at that transaction from a larger perspective. We saw in the previous section that there is nothing intrinsically right about making someone suffer for an injustice, if intrinsic rightness is a matter to be determined in isolation from the common good. In the same way, there is nothing intrinsically unjust about failing to make an equal return for a good received. The courts should be used to enforce such exchanges because, in the absence of this system of justice, human needs become far more difficult to fulfill. Similarly, there would be no reason for the city to maintain a currency that serves as a medium of exchange, unless this served as a tool that promotes human well-being. Aristotle holds that there can be no happiness unless people have an adequate supply of material resources, and they cannot achieve this level of prosperity unless they exchange goods with each other, using a form of currency to facilitate their trades. Furthermore, they will not trade unless they can be assured that they will get an equal return. They must be able to protect themselves against people who relish getting a larger than equal share. Those who are recognized to be just in commercial relations can be relied upon to give an equal return for what they receive, and it is such people who help support an economic system that meets our needs. Those driven by *pleonexia* in commercial relations do not merely harm the people they cheat; they also undermine the common good, because the distrust and resentment they create make it difficult for citizens to engage in the commercial transactions that meet their needs. Justice in economic relations is not exemplified by builders building and farmers farming, but by citizens and non-citizens alike abiding by the rules of exchange that serve the common good.

4.14. *Justice as a Mean*

The opening sentence of V.1 asks 'what sort of mean justice is' (1129a4–5), and we begin to get an answer in the first line of V.3: 'since the unjust person is unequal and what is unjust unequal, it is obvious that there is also something intermediate between what is unequal; this is what is equal' (1131a10–11). Aristotle's idea is that whenever injustice in the narrow sense is done, one person has less of something than he should have, and another person has more. The unjust person aims precisely at this imbalance, because of his *pleonexia*. Conversely, the just person is someone who seeks to avoid these extremes by going between them. He assigns to each person the amount of good or evil that he should have, neither more nor less.[49]

Now that we have examined the three different varieties of equal justice that Aristotle explores, let us spell out what the doctrine of the mean amounts to, when it is applied to the virtue of justice. First, consider justice in distribution. The unjust person gives more honor (or some other good) to one person and less to another than they deserve. The person to whom he gives more is often himself, since he is driven by *pleonexia*. By contrast, when the just person distributes honor or other goods among others (or between himself and others), he avoids both extremes. We can compare these two allocations in the following way. The unjust distributor of goods gives certain people more than they deserve and others less; because the *just* distributor would give those same two groups the right amount, that would leave the first group with less than they had received through an unjust allocation, and the second group with more. In this sense, justice requires giving an intermediate amount. Of course, there is no mechanical procedure for determining what the right amount is. But whatever the right amount is, just people know how to find it, whereas unjust people avoid it by making certain portions too large and others too small.

The doctrine of the mean can be applied to reciprocal justice in precisely the same way. A builds a house for B in exchange for 10 minas, but after it has been built and occupied, A still has not received payment, because B is trying to cheat him. B is assigning a larger share of goods than is right to himself and a smaller share than is right to A. He is trying to have both a house and 10 minas, and is giving nothing at all to A. A just person would go between these extremes: in comparison with the allocation arranged by B, he would assign less to himself and more to A.

---

[49] Aristotle says at II.7 1108b7–9 that both kinds of justice are intermediate states, and this might be thought to contradict Book V, which appears to hold that only justice in the narrow sense is a mean. Contradiction can be avoided, however, if we take Book V to be saying that justice in the broad sense is a mean because all the other ethical virtues are its parts, and each of these parts is a mean.

What of corrective justice? Suppose A has assaulted B, gaining a position of superiority, and B has suffered as a result. Or suppose A has cheated B in a transaction, so that he has more than he should and B less. An unjust juror does not care: he allows A to have more than he should and B to have less. By contrast, a judge devoted to justice wants something intermediate: the superior position of A must be diminished, and the loss suffered by B must be rectified. Furthermore, since *pleonexia* is the motive that lies behind an unjust disposition, we can add that the unjust juror wants more for himself than he should have. By serving as a juror, he receives a certain amount of power, honor, and perhaps even money (if his city pays citizens for jury service). But that is not enough of a gain for him; he accepts a bribe, and takes pleasure in allowing the loss of the injured party to go uncorrected. By contrast, the just person cannot be bribed: he seeks only as much good from jury service as is right, and this is less than what the unjust juror seeks. And because the just juror refuses to be corrupted, he assigns to the victims of injustice precisely what is owed them, and thus gives them more than what they receive from unjust jurors.

But as Aristotle points out, there is also an important difference between the ways in which the doctrine of the mean applies to justice and to the other virtues (V.5 1133b32–1134a13).[50] 'Injustice is both excess and deficiency' (1134a8–9). That is, we have one and the same name for the two conditions between which justice is intermediate. In saying this, Aristotle is making two points. First, every act of injustice is both an excess and a deficiency. When an unjust politician gives certain people more power than they deserve, he at the same time treats other people unjustly, because they should have been given some of that power. When a court case is wrongly decided, this injustice leaves one person with more than he should have and another with less. The other vices do not exhibit this pattern. When someone expresses too much anger at an offense, he is not at the same time expressing too little anger. When someone spends too much money on a banquet, he does not at the same time spend too little. In these cases, an act is either excessive or deficient, but not both at the same time. By contrast, unjust acts are always both excessive and deficient. That is because their injustice consists in a disproportionate relation between two or more people: someone gets too little precisely because someone else gets too much. The

---

[50] As noted in 4.n.1, some place this passage in V.7.

4.14. JUSTICE AS A MEAN

excess cannot exist unless the deficiency is present at the same time.

There is a second way in which justice is a different kind of mean. To see this, we should bear in mind that the doctrine of the mean is twofold: it holds not only that each virtuous act aims at a mean between two extremes, but that the state of mind of the virtuous person is intermediate between two undesirable conditions. Courage, for example, is intermediate between cowardice and recklessness. The coward is apt to have too much fear, the reckless person too little; but the brave person is not susceptible to either excess or deficiency. One cannot say that the condition of the cowardly person, or that of a reckless person, is both an excess and a deficiency. Cowardice is only a deficiency, recklessness only an excess. By contrast, as Aristotle points out, injustice is both excess and deficiency (1134a8–9). The word 'injustice' names both what is suffered by those who get less and the condition of those who take more. These two people are in a sense opposites, because one of them seeks too much and as a result the other receives too little. But the opposition between them is not like the opposition between the coward and the reckless man. How so? Aristotle does not make this point explicit, but presumably that is because it is so obvious: cowardice and recklessness are opposite *vices*, but although doing and suffering injustice are opposites, in that one is the deficiency caused by the other's excess, they are not opposite vices, because only one of them is a vice. Justice, in other words, differs from other virtues because, although it is a mean between two states that should be avoided, it is not intermediate between two vices.

Remarkably, nothing Aristotle says suggests that he is the least bit troubled by this. He takes himself to have successfully integrated justice into his larger framework, because he allows himself a certain degree of flexibility in specifying how each virtue is a mean. Justice is a mean both because the just person aims at something between excess and deficiency and because his virtue is intermediate between two undesirable conditions. Although Aristotle acknowledges that it is not a mean in the same way as other virtues, he is so impressed with the similarities between justice and other virtues that the differences do not bother him at all.

He says no more than this about how justice differs from other virtues with respect to the doctrine of the mean. But had he wished to devote more time to this topic, he might have pointed out a further difference. Each of the other trios—excess, intermediate, deficiency—consists in a relation to one or two emotions. Recklessness, courage, and cowardice are all conditions that have to do with fear and confidence. Similarly, generosity and its corresponding vices have to do with emotional responses to wealth. In each case, there is some emotion that needs to be mastered, and vices arise because there are two opposed ways of failing to master that emotion. But this is precisely what is lacking in Aristotle's analysis of justice and injustice. The emotional state that makes someone an unjust person in the narrow sense is *pleonexia*. But being a just person is not a matter of having that same emotion to the right extent; rather, it is a matter of not having such an emotion at all. The just person has no desire to gain at the expense of others, and to enjoy their losses. His virtue does not consist in handling well the emotion that the unjust person handles poorly. Of course, he does have an emotional response to injustice and justice: he loves and takes pleasure in the latter, and is pained by the former. But the emotions he feels are not proper amounts of the very same emotions felt immoderately by the unjust person. They are completely different emotions.

Had Aristotle wished to assimilate justice more fully to the other virtues, he could have proposed the following analysis. Some want more than their fair share, others are willing to accept less, but the just person avoids both excess and deficiency by seeking exactly what is due him. Had Aristotle proposed this idea, he could have claimed that justice is intermediate between two vices. And *pleonexia* would then fit the same general pattern as other defective emotional conditions: it would be an excessive amount of an emotion that we should feel to the right degree. We should be pleased to have exactly the right amount, and pained by anything more or less. To be pleased by having more than others is *pleonexia*; to fail to be pained by having less is the opposite emotional deficiency. Such a scheme seems so obvious that it is hard to believe that it never occurred to Aristotle. What reason might he have had for not adopting it?[51]

---

[51] For a defense of the claim that Aristotle does adopt such a scheme, see Curzer, 'Aristotle's Account of the Virtue of Justice'. Though I depart from his interpretation, I have learned much from his discussion. Grotius (1583–1645) criticizes Aristotle's doctrine of the mean on the grounds that although accepting less than belongs to oneself may, in certain circumstances, be a fault, it can never be an injustice, because injustice consists in taking what belongs to another. Evidently, Grotius mistakenly takes Aristotle to mean that a just person aims at getting what is neither too much nor too little for himself. See 'On the Law of War and Peace', in Schneewind, *Moral Philosophy from Montaigne to Kant*, i. 94–5. Grotius's point that unjust acts are always offenses against others is precisely the point Aristotle makes against Plato.

4.15. Choosing Less

Aristotle has no quarrel with the suggestion that one can go astray by assigning oneself too small a share of goods or allowing others to give one too small a share. If, for example, one gives away one's money too readily, and leaves too little for oneself, then one lacks the virtue that has to do with spending and acquiring wealth (IV.1 1120b2–3, 1121a12–13). Similarly, if one underestimates one's own excellence and fails to accept honors that one deserves, that too is a defect of character (IV.3 1125a19–27). But Aristotle would say that these are not cases in which one is doing an injustice to oneself, for he holds that injustice always involves two different parties. When we accuse someone of injustice, we presuppose that there is one person who does the injustice and another who is unjustly treated. Were we to charge the person who leaves too little wealth or honor for himself with injustice, we would be saying that he is both the willing perpetrator and the willing victim of injustice. Aristotle finds that an intolerable paradox (V.11 1138a4–26). Furthermore, if one could voluntarily treat oneself unjustly, then one could also voluntarily be treated unjustly—and he finds that a paradoxical concept as well (V.9 1136b6, V.11 1138a23–4).

There is nothing puzzling in the idea that people voluntarily *harm* themselves. Aristotle gives a simple example (V.9 1136b9–13): Glaucus made a foolish trade with Diomede, giving gold for bronze. His voluntary act was disadvantageous. Nonetheless, as Aristotle points out, he caused no injustice and was not unjustly treated, because he gave away what was his own to give. Perhaps Glaucus did not realize that he was harming himself, but it is perfectly possible—in fact, it is rather common—for self-injuries to be voluntary. Every *akratic* (incontinent) act is a case of voluntarily harming oneself.[52] But Aristotle holds that injustice is always a transaction among people, and that *akrasia* is therefore not unjust.

Is this merely a piece of dogma on his part? Does he have any argument to show that akratic acts are not examples of injustice to oneself? Aristotle raises this issue at V.9 1136a31-b9, but to understand his treatment of it, we should turn first to some points he makes later, in V.11. In that chapter, he supports his interpersonal conception of justice by appealing to the twofold conception of justice that he has been using throughout Book V. In the broad sense,

---

[52] See 3.10 for an explanation of what Aristotle means by *akrasia*.

injustice is unlawfulness: it is a lack of respect for the rules by which a community promotes the common good. But obviously *akrasia* is not unjust in this broad sense. No community enforces a rule against acting against one's better judgment. And that is precisely because *akrasia* does not injure the community. It is a personal, not a social, flaw.

Might *akrasia* be unjust in the narrow sense? It is easy for Aristotle to prove that it is not. But before we turn to his simple and devastating argument, we should consider a tangential but fascinating question that he raises at this point in V.11: he considers the objection that injustice towards oneself occurs when someone takes his own life. Suicide may be wrong in certain cases, and if so, that might provide an argument against Aristotle's thesis that injustice always involves two parties. For suicide seems to involve only a single person who plays the dual role of agent and victim (V.11 1138a4–14). We can see from Aristotle's discussion of this objection that some Greek cities legally prohibited citizens from killing themselves in certain circumstances, and punished those who violated this law by depriving them of rights—presumably burial rights—normally granted to citizens.[53] So the objection to Aristotle's theory is that suicide is unjust in the broad sense—it is a violation of the law—but there is only one person implicated in the injustice: the suicide is being unjust to himself.

We should be careful to notice, however, that Aristotle takes the law to prohibit not taking one's own life in general, but rather taking one's life when one is carried away by anger. That is, the person who wrongfully kills himself is assumed to have been moved by a passing but powerful feeling of anger at himself, caused no doubt by a sense of failure and shame. Rather than allowing time to pass and looking at his failure from a rational perspective, rather than letting others determine the appropriate punishment for his failure, he ends his

---

[53] Aristotle specifies the punishment—loss of civic rights—at 1138a12–14, but gives no further details. In Plato's *Laws*, those who unjustifiably kill themselves are disgraced by being assigned distant and nameless graves (873c–d). It is reasonable to assume that some cities had such a law, and that this is what Aristotle is referring to. The text at 1138a6–7, as translated by Ross, is: 'the law does not command a man to kill himself, and what it does not command it forbids.' But the rest of the passage shows that there was a legal prohibition of suicide; Aristotle is not merely making an inference (a treacherous one) from the silence of the law. Joachim, following Cook Wilson, proposes that Aristotle wrote *ouk eai* ('does not allow', i.e. forbids) rather than *ouk keleuei* ('does not command'), and that the remainder of the sentence ('and what it does not command it forbids') is a later insertion. Irwin, following Joachim, translates: 'we are legally forbidden ... to kill ourselves', and omits the rest of the sentence. I too accept Joachim's proposal. See his commentary, *Aristotle: The Nicomachean Ethics*, p. 161.

4.15. CHOOSING LESS

life and deprives others of the contributions he might have made to the city. In such circumstances, Aristotle claims, it is entirely appropriate for others to blame him, and for the law to dishonor him. For the role of the community has been usurped and its members have been injured by his impulsive act. That is why Aristotle thinks the objection to his theory fails: although this kind of suicide is unlawful and therefore unjust in the broad sense, it is not an injustice in which there is only one victim. It is the whole community that suffers.[54]

To complete his argument that one cannot treat oneself unjustly, Aristotle next turns to injustice in the narrow sense (V.11 1138a14–20). This always involves a deviation from equality or proportionality: two quantities are involved, one higher and the other lower than it should be. Now, if injustice and justice did not require two different parties, a doer and a sufferer, then it would be possible for this imbalance to reside within a single person—the person who does injustice to himself. If *akrasia* were unjust in the narrow sense, then the akratic person would get both too much and too little of the same thing at the same time. And that would be a contradiction.

So much, then, for the argument that one cannot treat oneself unjustly. Aristotle also tries to show, in V.9, that no one is voluntarily treated unjustly (1136a10–b14). In the example he gives, one person voluntarily harms a second, who voluntarily succumbs, not because he has a rational wish to be harmed (no one can have such a wish: 1136b7–8) but because of a non-rational emotion or appetite. To provide greater detail to the case Aristotle is considering, we might imagine that one person is trying to inflict an injury on another by offering him a bad deal, and the second party accepts it, recognizing that he will be worse off, because he has an appetite for one of the items on offer. Aristotle's treatment of this case turns on the point that since the second person has accepted the terms of the transaction, the situation cannot be described as a full-fledged example of injustice. He makes a distinction (1136a27–8) between doing what is unjust (*t'adika prattein*) and acting unjustly (*adikein*), and similarly between suffering what is unjust (*adika paschein*) and being treated unjustly (*adikeisthai*). When one person tries to harm another but does so only with the consent of the other, he is doing what is unjust (voluntarily trying to harm another) but not acting

---

[54] For a helpful discussion of this passage, see Cooper, 'Greek Philosophers on Euthanasia and Suicide', pp. 19–23. I do not follow his suggestion that Aristotle treats suicide as an injustice in the narrow sense.

unjustly, because what he does is what the other wants him to do. Because consent has been given, this cannot be described as a case of voluntarily being treated unjustly.

We can now turn to a different sort of case—one that is conceptually less difficult but far more significant, because it provides an answer to the question we raised in the preceding section: why is *pleonexia* not treated as an excess to which there is a corresponding deficiency? Aristotle says that on certain occasions taking less than one deserves, and thereby leaving more for others, may be the right thing to do. At V.9 1136b20–1, he briefly alludes to a person who is prepared to take such a loss, and says that because he 'opts for less' (*ellattōtikos*) he is a 'decent' fellow (*epieikēs*). Presumably he is thinking of a situation in which leaving more for others and less for oneself does not harm anyone, for otherwise he could not approve of such a distribution. His assumption is that in some circumstances one does no harm, to oneself or others, by allowing them to have more than they deserve. Here is an example that will bring out his point. It is sometimes impossible to divide goods with such precision that each party gets exactly what he should have, no more and no less. When exact justice cannot be achieved, the person who makes the distribution may best avoid creating bad feelings by taking the smaller share for himself and giving others the larger shares. He cannot be accused of doing an injustice to anyone, nor can he be blamed for voluntarily suffering an injustice. For, as Aristotle has pointed out (1136b4–5), to do an injustice is to act against the rational wish of the person to whom the injustice is done. But by assigning himself the smaller share, the moderate and decent person is not coming into conflict with his own rational wish. On the contrary, he is expressing it.

Furthermore, in taking the lesser share, he need not be doing himself harm. Though he may deserve just as much as the others, the smaller amount may suit his needs perfectly. Rather than make a fuss, he assigns the lesser share to himself, even though there is no reason why it is he who should get it rather than others. His action may not be what justice requires, but neither is it unjust.

This explains why Aristotle thinks of the unjust person as someone who is driven by the desire to have more, but does not propose a general scheme according to which both the desire for more and the desire for less are extremes to be avoided, and the desire for equality is the mean between these extremes. He shows no inclination to adopt this taxonomy, even though it would allow him to describe justice as a mean in the very same way that other virtues are intermediate states. Such a taxonomy would distort the facts, for although it is sometimes a fault to accept less than one deserves, there are also occasions when such a distribution is praiseworthy. And so, rather than characterize *pleonexia* as an excess of an emotion that one should feel to the right degree, Aristotle chooses instead to admit that justice is not a mean in exactly the way that the other virtues are.

But now it might seem that he is vulnerable to a different sort of objection: what has become of his idea that to be a just person (in the narrow sense) is to be an equal person? Equality is a mean; it lies between more than the right amount and less. But, as we have just seen, sometimes the right thing to do is to assign oneself an amount that is less than one deserves, and to allow others to have more. If that is not unjust, then what meaning can be attached to the idea that justice consists in equality or proportionality? Has this become an empty phrase?

Aristotle seems to anticipate this objection, because after he points out that the decent person sometimes takes less, he adds a qualification: by taking less of one sort of good, the virtuous person is expressing his desire to get a larger amount of a different type—reputation, or 'what is fine without qualification' (1136b22). There is a sense, then, in which this is an equal division after all. It is not an equal division of money, or some other single type of good; but it is an allocation in which an unequal distribution of one type of good is offset by a corresponding inequality in the division of a different type. Someone gets fewer material goods, and so it is only right that he be compensated with a different type of benefit. Even though there is no way to express this balance in exact arithmetic terms, it is rough equality nonetheless. And so the person who takes less can be described as someone who is aiming at a certain kind of equality after all.

Hume, in a well-known phrase, speaks of justice as a 'cautious, jealous virtue', implying that it is not without its blemishes.[55] Presumably his idea is that to the extent that we are motivated by

---

[55] *An Enquiry Concerning the Principles of Morals*, s. III, pt. I, para. 3. Sandel uses Hume's ideas about the limitations of justice as a virtue to question Rawls's thesis that justice is in all cases the foremost virtue of social institutions: 'justice is the first virtue of social institutions not absolutely, as truth is to theories, but only conditionally, as physical courage is to a war zone.' See *Liberalism and the Limits of Justice*, p. 31. Aristotle's way of thinking about justice is completely at odds with the suggestion that we should wish that the circumstances that call forth this virtue could be eliminated.

justice, we will not allow others to have a larger share than what they are entitled to; we will even be glad (as jealous people are) when someone loses his undeserved surplus—even if that loss does no good to others. But Aristotle's characterization of the just person as a 'decent' fellow who sometimes 'opts for less' provides us with a way to resist Hume's suggestion. We need not think of justice as a tendency to apply principles of distribution in a mechanical fashion, and of a just person as someone who cannot abide the thought that others might be getting even a bit more than the rules allow. For if justice is a genuine virtue, it cannot be a blind disposition that operates in isolation from good judgment about what circumstances call for. When we see that, on a certain occasion, it is best to opt for less than we deserve, we realize that justice does not always call for a strict arithmetical division of material goods. It is part of the virtue of justice to refuse to adhere in all cases to strict proportionality, and so there is no need for something that stands watch over justice and reins it in.

4.16. Equity Again

We can now recognize a striking parallel between what Aristotle says in V.9 about the person who assigns himself a smaller share and what he says in V.10 about the juror who recognizes a deficiency in the law. The moderate person who opts for less cannot be used as a counter-example to the thesis that justice consists in equality, and this corresponds to Aristotle's idea that the equitable juror who corrects the law is not a counter-example to the thesis that justice in the broad sense consists in lawfulness. The equitable juror decides the case before him by ruling in accordance with what the legislator would say about it; that is why he can be called a lawful person, even though he does not blindly follow the letter of the law. The virtue of lawfulness requires a certain degree of flexibility and good sense, and is not a matter of following a list of rules, however long. And as we have now seen, justice as equality requires the same kind of attentiveness to detail, and a willingness to strive for proportionality in the broad rather than the narrow sense. There are times when giving oneself or accepting a smaller share of goods is appropriate, but there is no way to specify in advance when that is so. And, in a sense, the person who is skillful in making these decisions lives up to an ideal of equality

4.16. EQUITY AGAIN

after all. He accepts a loss with respect to one kind of good, but by doing so wins a different kind of advantage, and thus he and his neighbors achieve a rough kind of equality. Justice is a matter of both lawfulness and equality, but if either notion is interpreted too narrowly, the result will be blind obedience to bad rules and an inflexible adherence to strict proportionality. One of the most appealing features of Aristotle's investigation of justice is his recognition that the very stuff of justice—law and proportionality—can sometimes lead us astray.

Aristotle calls the person who sees when to assign himself the lesser amount *epieikēs*—a word that can be translated 'decent' or 'equitable', depending on the context. He never proposes that it has a double meaning, but instead regards it as a single virtue that manifests itself in different ways in different situations. In a juror, it involves the ability to recognize defects in the law and to insure that defendants are not burdened by them. But if a juror is truly equitable em;if he realizes that this virtue has applications outside the courtroom—then he has learnt the larger lesson that there are times when looking for precision about what is just leads us astray. Someone who demands an inflexible exactness about justice will abide by the law, even when the legislator himself would not wish to do so, and will refuse to take less than an equal share, even when it would serve the common good to do so. A just person must know how to be lawful and equal without falling back on some easy and inflexible formula for making just decisions. That is why justice cannot be achieved entirely through the existence of just laws and obedient citizens; those citizens must also become adept at knowing when the law should be set aside, and when it is right to accept less than they deserve.[56]

We are told in the *Rhetoric* that the equitable person 'puts up with

---

[56] It is sometimes thought that in V.10 Aristotle discusses two different conceptions of the equitable person, without realizing that they have nothing to do with each other: an equitable person is (a) a judge who knows how to correct deficiencies in the law, and (b) a citizen who settles for less. See e.g. Georgiadis, 'Equitable and Equity in Aristotle'. Against this, Brunschwig, 'The Aristotelian Theory of Equity', argues that V.10 is concerned only with the equitable judge, and proposes that we take 1138a1–2 to mean that the equitable person 'does not stick to the letter of the law when it is for the worse, and . . . mitigates [the punishment of the accused], although he has the law on his side [sc. if he wished to apply it rigorously]' (p. 138). This takes *ellatōtikos* at 1138a1 to mean 'applies a lighter sentence' (or, as Brunschwig says, 'mitigates') rather than 'takes less than his share' (as Ross translates). The interpretation I have proposed is compatible with Brunschwig's proposal, but does not require it. The crucial point is that a single state of mind leads both to mitigating punishment and to taking a smaller share for oneself.

unjust treatment' (I.13 1374b18). Since this work is a compendium of common opinions, we are not entitled to assume that Aristotle himself believes that this is an appropriate characterization of the equitable person. As we can see from his discussion in *Nicomachean Ethics* V.9, he would say that if the phrase 'to put up with injustice' is interpreted in a certain way, it rests on a confusion. One can voluntarily be *harmed*, if one accepts bad treatment against one's better judgment, but doing so can never be praiseworthy, and so this cannot be characteristic of the equitable person. Nor can the equitable person be described as someone who is voluntarily treated unjustly, because when someone willingly consents to an act, even one that harms him, the complaint that can normally be made against mistreatment is no longer valid.

Nonetheless, there is an important sense in which Aristotle can approve of someone who occasionally 'puts up with unjust treatment'. The victim of injustice must decide how to respond to it, and there are times when the right decision is to do nothing. Admittedly, on some occasions, an immediate response in the heat of the moment can be justified (V.8 1135b26–1136a1). At other times, the proper decision will be to wait, and seek corrective justice in the courts, because in that way the common good will be served. But should every injustice be met with anger or prosecuted in court? A magnanimous person will pay no attention to minor injustices, for, as Aristotle says, he is not 'mindful of wrongs' (IV.3 1125a3).[57] Just as there are times when it is best for a distributor of goods to assign himself a smaller portion, and for a juror to vote for acquittal even though the law has been violated, so Aristotle can say that there are times when it is best to 'put up with unjust treatment' by making no effort to undo it. It is easy to think of cases in which this would be the appropriate response. The wrongdoer may have already suffered from his crime; he may pose no further threat to oneself or others; one's loss may be of no real consequence; valuable time may be lost; more important cases may need to be heard. Though justice consists in lawfulness and equality, we have seen that these formulas cannot be interpreted mechanically. If one has lost nothing through being treated unjustly, and nothing is to be gained by bringing a case to court, then lawfulness and equality are best served by making no response. In these circumstances, one promotes the common good by investing one's

---

[57] Note too that the generous person is vulnerable to unjust treatment (IV.1 1121a5) and the mild person is not inclined to get even (*timōrētikos*: IV.5 1126a2).

4.17. Aristotle versus Plato

Having noticed, several times in this chapter (4.2, 4.6–8, 4.13), significant differences between Aristotle's conception of justice and Plato's, let us now explore more thoroughly what sets them apart. It may be useful to begin by reviewing the points about which they disagree.

Plato holds that all justice is one and the same, whereas Aristotle distinguishes a broad and a narrow sense, and neither of his two definitions (justice as lawfulness and as equality) corresponds to the single definition Plato proposes (justice as each part doing its own). Aristotle analyzes justice as an interpersonal relationship: to be just is to be just to other people, and since justice in the broad sense is composed of other virtues, there is no single motive that underlies the just person's actions. By contrast, Plato takes justice to be at bottom an intrapersonal relationship: it is the condition in which reason, spirit, and appetite are properly related, and the way a just person treats others is merely a consequence of this inner harmony. He also holds that justice is entirely independent of human practices and beliefs, whereas Aristotle's distinction between natural and legal justice rests on the assumption that some practices become just practices because they are adopted by one's community. Plato insists that the just person must withdraw from the corrupting influences of ordinary cities; ideal politics is the only politics worthy of his attention. By contrast, a just person, as Aristotle conceives him, makes improvements in ordinary cities—for example, by serving as a juror and correcting the law when legislative deficiencies become apparent. Even justice in the commercial sphere is treated differently by our two philosophers: Plato holds that a craftsman contributes to the justice of the city simply by sticking to the work for which he is suited, whereas Aristotle holds that it is not by keeping to himself but by engaging in proportional exchange with others that a craftsman contributes to a city's justice.

Remarkably, Aristotle never names Plato as one of his adversaries in Book V. But his opposition to Plato becomes all but explicit when he says, near the end of V.11, that in a way there is justice within the human soul: although one cannot be just to oneself, we can say, if we wish to speak by way of metaphor and analogy, that the reasoning part of the soul and the part that lacks reason are able to treat each other justly or unjustly (1138b5–13).[58] What Aristotle means by this is that there is a proper relationship between the part of us that makes decisions and the part that cannot deliberate but can respond cooperatively or uncooperatively to our deliberations (3.8). Reasoning ought to govern our emotions and appetites (as Plato pointed out). And, if we like, we can say that when these parts of ourselves are in their proper order, then justice prevails among them. Aristotle remarks that this is the kind of justice that characterizes masters (i.e. slave-owners) and households (b7–8). In other words, to say that there can be just or unjust relations between the part of the soul that reasons and the part that should listen and obey reason is in effect to say that reason should be related to the emotions and appetites as a superior person (a husband or a slave-owner) is related to an inferior (a wife or a slave).[59]

The comparison between justice in the soul and the justice of masters and husbands in relation to their slaves and wives underscores Aristotle's point that the fundamental use of 'justice' is to name a relationship among people, and it is only by analogy that we can apply the word to something that exists within a single person. Aristotle is entirely unpersuaded by Plato's attempt to show that it is really the other way around—that justice within a person is fundamental, and justice among people derivative (*Republic* 443c–d). Of course, he agrees with Plato that it is not enough to perform just acts—one must also be a just person. But a just person is one who is

---

[58] See *Republic* 444a–b: injustice is the misappropriation by one part of the soul of what belongs to another part. That is, injustice is a relation that exists entirely within the soul; it is not only an interpersonal relation. See too *Laws* 863e: injustice is a 'tyranny in the soul on the part of anger, fear, pleasure, pain, envy, and appetites'. Although Aristotle does not mention Plato, he makes it clear in V.11 that he is criticizing someone else's words: '*in these discussions*, the part of the soul that has reason is distinguished from the part that is without reason' (1138b8–9). Another passage in *NE* V.11 makes it evident that Plato is on Aristotle's mind. At 1138a28–b5, he takes up the question of Plato's *Gorgias*: is it worse to suffer injustice or to do it? The fact that Aristotle treats the question so briefly, and says that theory can go only so far in answering it, implies that he regards the *Gorgias* as a work devoted to a question of little moment.

[59] Compare *Pol.* I.5 1254b4–6: the control exercised by understanding over desire is comparable to political or kingly rule; by contrast, the rule of the soul over the body is comparable to the power exercised by a slaveowner over his slave. The passage provides further evidence that Aristotle is willing to make analogies between interpersonal and intrapersonal relations. I take him to mean that we should keep our bodies in good condition merely because they are useful to us (that is how masters treat slaves), but we should keep our desires in good condition because that is worthwhile in itself (this is the way equal citizens should treat each other, and the way kings should treat their subjects).

lawful and equal, and these terms refer to interpersonal relations. By contrast, Plato proposes that a just person be defined as someone who has the right relationship to himself—or rather, as someone whose parts are properly related to each other.

This opposition between Plato and Aristotle is rooted in their contrary attitudes towards the politics of ordinary cities and in their metaphysical differences. As we have seen (4.8), Plato advocates withdrawal from everyday politics. He holds that if one cannot participate in an ideal regime, or something very close to it, then one can 'do one's own' only by removing oneself from civic life and devoting oneself to philosophy. Furthermore, he insists that even when the philosopher withdraws from the so-called 'real world', and focuses his attention on the realm of the forms, he remains a paragon of justice. Aristotle would protest: how can someone who withdraws from social relations and engages in solitary pursuits deserve to be lauded as a person of great justice? Admittedly, Plato's apolitical philosopher refrains from doing injustice—but is that enough to justify calling him a just man? Should we not expect a just person to bring benefits to large numbers—to be a champion of the common good, and not merely to refrain from doing harm? Aristotle can concede that, in ideal circumstances, Plato's philosopher would re-enter the social world and become an accomplished leader. But does that show that he is a person of great justice even now, when he has nothing to do with his fellow citizens, and fails to promote the common good? Aristotle holds that justice in the soul must be exercised through just action, and just action consists in treating other people justly. He concedes (V.11 1138b5–13) that one can say, speaking metaphorically, that the rational part of the philosopher's soul treats his emotions with justice. But if Plato's philosopher refuses to make what improvements he can in his political community, and practices justice only in a metaphorical sense, then Aristotle cannot agree that he is a paradigm of justice.

Plato has a response to this line of questioning, but it is not one that will persuade Aristotle, because it rests on a component of Plato's metaphysics for which he has no sympathy. Plato holds that it is not only human beings that can be characterized as just: the word also can be applied to the eternal and non-perceptible abstract objects he calls 'forms' (*ideai, eidē*), and indeed, such objects exhibit the highest degree of justice (*Republic* 500c). Justice consists in orderliness; therefore, objects that undergo no alteration but are fixed eternally in a harmonious pattern possess the highest kind and degree of justice. Human beings can at best approximate the orderliness of the forms, and they most fully assimilate themselves to these abstract objects by studying the relationships among them. The philosopher is more fully ruled by reason than any other human being because when he develops a passionate understanding of the forms, his soul assimilates itself to their orderliness.[60] When he withdraws from ordinary politics and studies the forms, he is acting justly, not merely because he abstains from the corrupt practices of ordinary politics, but because his study of the forms is itself a just activity. In fact, his pursuit of philosophy is the highest form of justice available to human beings, because only in the philosopher does reason truly do its proper job, which is to understand and imitate the forms. The justice of his soul could be of enormous benefit to others, but the everyday political world turns a blind eye to his extraordinary qualities as a leader, and he cannot be blamed for their indifference or hostility to him (*Republic* 488a–489e). Although it is contrary to the common way of using words to speak of an act as just even though it benefits no one but the agent, Plato sees no reason for adhering to conventional usage in this case. For once we see what justice really is, we will realize that the philosopher's contemplation of the forms is the highest kind of justice there can be.

Aristotle refuses to accept this way of thinking because he believes that Plato is deeply confused in his metaphysics. Although he agrees with Plato that there are other kinds of objects besides the ones we observe by means of the senses, he has no temptation to think of these objects as paradigms of orderliness, beauty, and justice. Justice is necessarily a quality of the human realm: it applies to human beings, the cities and constitutions that they construct, and the actions they perform. There simply are no objects besides these that can be called just or unjust. Accordingly, when we study what lies beyond the ken of the senses, we cannot claim to be performing just acts, for we are not entering into a relationship with anything that can be called just. If a philosopher wants to do what is just, then he must turn his attention to the changeable world of human beings, and seek improvements in those less than perfect objects. And he will find that his study of a world beyond the senses makes him no better able to pursue justice in this world than anyone else. It is

---

[60] For a fuller presentation of these ideas, see my 'Plato's Defense of Justice' and 'Return to the Cave: *Republic* 519–521'.

practical wisdom one needs, in order to do justice in the world of the polis, not theoretical understanding.

Plato holds that ordinary cities leave no room for improvement. If one works within the framework of an oligarchic or democratic constitution, one will inevitably become corrupt. That is why he advocates withdrawal: no harm is done to cities when philosophers withdraw from them in order to do their own, because those cities are incapable of significant improvement so long as they maintain their current constitutions. By contrast, as we will see, Aristotle's *Politics* rests on the assumption that Plato's pessimism is unfounded. Aristotle believes that although oligarchies and democracies are filled with injustices, it is nonetheless important to make moral distinctions among these regimes, because some are far worse than others. And he also believes that there are ways for a good person to make improvements in these constitutions, or to prevent them from becoming even worse, without corrupting his soul. If Aristotle is right, then he has a serious charge to make against Plato and his followers: those who refuse to participate in the politics of imperfect but moderately decent cities not only fail to be paragons of justice—they can even be accused of *in*justice. They are in a position to make significant improvements in civic life, but rather than doing so, they stand by, as these cities grow increasingly corrupt. Although they refrain from doing injustice, that is not enough to qualify them as just people, because they care nothing for the ordinary legal systems in which the common good can be promoted, and some degree of lawfulness and equality achieved.

We should mention one further difference between the accounts of justice proposed by these two philosophers—one that is entirely obvious but nonetheless worth reflecting on. Plato embeds his account of justice in a description of the ideal city, whereas Aristotle's fullest analysis of this virtue, in Book V of the *Ethics*, leaves aside the question of which constitution is best. In order to understand Aristotle's conception of justice more fully, we must turn to the *Politics*—not only to Book III, where disputes about justice are aired, but also to Books VII and VIII, where he gives us his fullest description of the city in which the common good of all citizens is fully achieved. Nonetheless, even though these parts of the *Politics* complete the account he begins to give us in the *Ethics*, it is highly significant that according to Aristotle a great deal can be said about the virtue of justice even before we take up the questions discussed in the *Politics*. The reason why that is so should be clear by now:

there is as much work for a just person to do in ordinary cities as there would be in the best city, and so we do not need to imagine an ideal constitution in order to see the just person in action. He is a lawful and equal person, and since these are qualities that can be exercised in all but the worst among existing cities, we can learn a great deal about what justice is without constructing a perfect constitution.

By contrast, Plato needs to set the philosopher in the context of an ideal city, in order to convince his readers that he really is the paradigm of justice. He realizes that a person of great justice must be capable of promoting the good of a whole community, and he argues that the philosopher, properly understood, is such a person. But there is only one kind of city in which such a person can promote the common good—an ideal city that accepts his authority. Although the soul of the philosopher will be just regardless of the city he lives in, his power to do good to others will lie dormant until circumstances are ideal. To prove that the inner harmony he is describing really is justice, Plato needs to show how socially beneficial that inner state will be, when conditions are right, and so he must set his portrait of the philosopher in an ideal state. That is because in all other conditions, the philosopher withdraws from politics, and the interpersonal manifestations of his justice are limited to cases in which he refrains from treating others badly. We can see most clearly how just he is when we envisage him at work in the ideal state, because it is only there that he promotes the good of all. The political backdrop to Plato's discussion of the just soul is therefore not merely serving the purpose of illustration; it is not simply giving us an easy-to-see and large-scale model of the invisible justice that lies within us. The politics of the *Republic* is part of Plato's attempt to prove to us that there can be no greater servant of public well-being—and therefore no better paradigm of justice in this world—than the philosopher-king.

4.18. Aristotle versus Socrates

We can find another portrait of justice in Plato's dialogues: in the *Apology* (23b, 31c-e) and the *Gorgias* (521e), Socrates describes himself as a man who withdrew from ordinary civic life and yet nonetheless practiced a unique kind of politics. He did not retreat into an isolated circle of like-minded philosophers, but entered into

4.18. ARISTOTLE VERSUS SOCRATES

conversation with his fellow citizens, challenging them to become more critical of their own moral beliefs and the practices of their community. When his death is described at the end of the *Phaedo* (118a), he is proclaimed to be the most just man of his time, and we can understand why: not only did he uphold the great value of justice and the other virtues in conversation, but he made it his business to serve his whole community through his practice of philosophy. He promoted the common good of Athens by provoking his fellow citizens to reflect on their love of power and wealth, and to entertain doubts about their conception of virtue and well-being.

If we agree with Plato that Socrates was an admirable person, or perhaps that he was the most just man of his time, we can raise a powerful objection to Aristotle's conception of justice. In some respects, Socrates satisfied Aristotle's description of a just person: he was lawful—or at any rate, he is portrayed in the *Crito* as someone who has great respect for the laws of Athens. Furthermore, he devotes his life to philosophical activity, and regards this as a great good for the whole of Athens, and not merely for some small portion of the citizenry. In other respects, he does not qualify as a just person, by Aristotle's standards—but that may lead us to wonder whether those standards are reasonable. For as we have seen, according to Aristotle, a just person in the narrow sense is someone who distributes such goods as power and honor on the basis of merit, and who restores others to a position of equality when they have been wronged. He must therefore attend meetings of the assembly, where distributive issues are debated; and he must serve on juries, where corrective justice is determined. Aristotle's just person, in other words, participates in the ordinary civic life of his community, whereas Socrates rarely took part in these activities. So, if he managed to be a paragon of justice despite—or perhaps because of—his withdrawal from ordinary politics, something has gone wrong with Aristotle's understanding of what this virtue is.

We can understand why Aristotle would not feel threatened by this objection: although Socrates may have aimed at the common good of Athens, he in fact did very little to improve the lives of his fellow citizens. As such dialogues as the *Euthyphro* and *Gorgias* show, Socrates often failed to persuade his interlocutors to change their minds about how to live their lives. One of his best-known students, Alcibiades, was notorious for his immorality; in the *Symposium* he is portrayed as someone who occasionally falls under the spell of Socrates, but does not make any permanent improvement

(216a–b). And the most damaging fact of all is that Socrates was sentenced to death by his own city. He was so far from success in his project of improving his fellow citizens that he could not convince a majority of them that he posed no threat to their religious practices. At most, he benefited a few of his admirers—such people as Plato, Xenophon, and several interlocutors named in their works. But if it is the mark of a just person to accomplish a great deal for his community, then Socrates cannot serve as a paradigm of justice, despite Plato's high praise for him.

Plato's admiration for his teacher derives in part from Socrates' rejection of normal politics. Socrates holds that no community can make significant improvements in its political affairs unless citizens enter into philosophical dialogues about the good life. In this respect, the Socrates portrayed in the *Apology* is a close cousin of the kind of reader for whom the *Republic* is intended: someone who loves to pursue questions about justice and the good, but who has no intention of participating in the ordinary political affairs of highly defective cities. Aristotle must say, therefore, that Plato overrated the character of Socrates: though he was certainly far from being a bad person, he accomplished little for his community, precisely because he stayed away from the assembly and the courts, the very places most in need of just men.

From Aristotle's point of view, it was no accident that Socrates accomplished so little. If one stands in the marketplace and tries to reason with ordinary people—people who rarely listen to argument—one cannot expect to change many minds about what is worthwhile or admirable. If one wants to influence the way most people live, one must attend to the formation of their habits, because once these have developed, they are rarely altered by reasoning. But improving habits is a long-term project, and requires careful attention to legislation and the constitutional framework in which laws are passed. This is the anti-Socratic theme with which Aristotle brings the *Ethics* to a close: having completed his investigation of the virtues, he admits that few people will be persuaded by what he has said (X.9 1179b4–20). Since ethics is a practical undertaking, the members of his audience are urged to study legislation; for when good laws are established and accepted, they have a powerful effect on character (1179b31–1180a24). In reading the *Ethics*, we are trying to become good people (II.2 1103b26–9), but this is a project that cannot be completed until we finish our study of Aristotle's writings, depart from his school, and apply what we have learned to the highly

4.18. ARISTOTLE VERSUS SOCRATES

imperfect realm of everyday politics. Only that immersion in the details of political life, informed by a general study of legislation, will allow us to exercise the virtue of justice as lawfulness.

But what of Aristotle himself? How can he meet his own standard of what it is to be a just person? He attends no meetings of the assembly, and has never served as a magistrate or juror. Lacking citizen status (1.2), he is an outsider barred from political activity. Despite these handicaps, he shows that there is a way in which even a non-citizen can promote the common good—and not only of one community, but of many. By making a comparative study of constitutions, and proposing ways in which they can be improved, or kept from deterioration, he seeks to influence the way in which politics is practiced in many different kinds of cities. By systematizing the study of legal systems, and giving political advice to those who seek it, Aristotle tries to show how philosophical inquiry, properly conducted, can both make one a more just person and contribute to the well-being of ordinary people living in ordinary cities. He seeks to heal the rupture created by Socrates and Plato between philosophy and the politics of the everyday world.

PART II

5

Introduction to the *Politics*

5.1. *The Organization of the* Politics

Having examined Aristotle's conception of well-being, virtue, and justice in the *Nicomachean Ethics*, we are now ready to follow the instructions he gives his audience in the final sentences of the *Ethics* (X.9 1181b12–23). We are about to bring to completion the 'philosophy of human affairs' (1181b15) begun in the *Ethics*, by examining the work to which the *Ethics* is a prolegomenon. But before we enter the terrain of the *Politics*, we should raise some questions about its internal consistency and its principle of organization. Because Aristotle wrote voluminously about diverse topics over the course of his lifetime, it would not be surprising to find him modifying his positions, or perhaps even changing his mind quite radically about certain matters. As I noted earlier (1.5), there are at least subtle shifts in Aristotle's thinking, as he moves from the *Eudemian* to the *Nicomachean Ethics*; otherwise, he would not have bothered revising his work. Perhaps each of these two treatises is entirely self-consistent and unified (although doubts have been raised about this);[1] but even so, we know that his thinking evolved as he rewrote the book he refers to as *ta ēthika*. That should lead us to wonder

---

[1] I have in mind Aristotle's advocacy of the philosophical life in *NE* X.7–8, which has been thought by several scholars to fit poorly or not at all with the rest of the treatise. See e.g. Ackrill, 'Aristotle on *Eudaimonia*'.

about his political writings: can we also find inconsistencies—perhaps minor, perhaps radical—among the various books of the *Politics*? Is there an organizing principle that gives this work some degree of unity? We cannot settle that question in this chapter, but it will be helpful to have a preliminary discussion of the way this treatise (or collection of essays, if that is a better way to describe it) is arranged.

The general question of whether or how Aristotle's thought evolved came to the fore almost a century ago, when Werner Jaeger argued that although Aristotle accepted, at the earliest stage of his philosophical career, some of Plato's favorite doctrines—the existence of transcendent forms and the survival of the individual soul—he soon began to develop a distinctive metaphysics and theology of his own, and eventually, in the final stage of his development, pursued empirical investigations of the sensible world and, in direct opposition to Plato, fully accepted them as a proper subject for philosophy. The *Politics*, according to Jaeger, combines material from Aristotle's transitional period, when he took himself to be pursuing a Platonic project in spite of his disagreements with Plato, with material composed during his later period, when he had given up Plato's quest for a single ideal and pursued instead a program of empirical research far more tolerant of diversity. The studies of utopias in Books II, III, VII, and VIII belong to one phase of Aristotle's career, and are at odds with the more realistic and empirical study carried out in IV–VI, when Aristotle was most fully opposed to Platonism.[2]

Jaeger's picture of Aristotle's philosophical development is controversial,[3] and his division of the *Politics* into conflicting empirical and utopian parts cannot be sustained, as we will discover in later chapters.[4] It is unlikely that at the end of his philosophical career

---

[2] Jaeger's developmental approach to Aristotle's *Metaphysics* was published in German in 1912, and his analysis of the whole corpus was published in 1923. An English translation, *Aristotle: Fundamentals of the History of his Development*, appeared in 1934, its 2nd edn. in 1948. Ch. 10 is devoted to Aristotle's development as a political thinker.

[3] Wians, *Aristotle's Philosophical Development* contains many excellent papers on the questions raised by Jaeger. For a brief presentation of Jaeger's main ideas see Code, 'Owen on the Development of Aristotle's Metaphysics'. For criticism of Jaeger's picture of Aristotle's development as a political thinker, see Rowe, 'Aims and Methods in Aristotle's Politics'. More recently, Rist has argued in favor of an early date for Book VII. See *The Mind of Aristotle*, pp. 146–64. For criticism, see Pellegrin, 'On The "Platonic" Part of Aristotle's Politics'. Ober argues that Books VII and VIII of the *Politics* were late developments (composed in the 330s), inspired by Macedonian conquests and fresh possibilities for the establishment of new colonies. See *Political Dissent in Democratic Athens*, pp. 339–51.

[4] See esp. 10.7, 12.1–2.

5.1. THE ORGANIZATION OF THE *POLITICS*

Aristotle turned away from his early idealism in order to adopt a more empirical approach to politics. For, as we have seen (1.5), he wrote much of the *Nicomachean Ethics* after the *Politics*; and in that later work he begins by describing political science as a subject that reflects on the highest good and the highest ideals of character, and then closes with the recommendation that his audience put these reflections together with the empirical study of constitutions, so that they can understand what the best political system is.[5]

But even if we reject the specific content of Jaeger's developmental hypothesis, his more general point—that we should not dogmatically assume that Aristotle's philosophy forms a unity, that we look for change and perhaps even conflict in his writings—is one that students of the *Politics* must take seriously. For this work seems, at first sight, to be oddly arranged. It is not at all clear whether its disparate parts fit together into an organized whole, or whether it is an aggregate of unrelated and perhaps even conflicting essays.

There are eight books of the *Politics*, but in some cases these partitions are artificial. Books VII and VIII form a single treatise on the ideal constitution, and its division into separate books marks nothing of significance. Similarly, Books V and VI pursue a single, connected project, namely the examination of inferior constitutions. That is a theme Aristotle begins to explore in Book IV, and so we might think of IV, V, and VI as a single unit. Book II is closely connected to VII and VIII, since it is an attempt to show the defects in cities that have been proposed by others as ideal. So we can reasonably view II as belonging together with VII and VIII. But the remaining books do not seem to have a natural place or sequence. Book I is a discussion of the natural development of the polis out of the household, and of the elements of the household (especially slaves and other forms of property). Book III discusses such assorted topics as citizenship, constitutions (both 'correct' and 'deviant'), justice, and kingship. A modern editor might therefore be tempted to reconfigure the *Politics* into four unrelated parts:

---

[5] It should be emphasized that the closing passage of the *Ethics* urges students to examine 'the collected political systems' (1181b17-18)—i.e. the 158 accounts of constitutional arrangements gathered by Aristotle's school. This, Aristotle says, will lead to a better understanding of the system that is ideal. Obviously, when he wrote these final words on politics, he saw no conflict between careful and exhaustive empirical study and the design of the best possible constitution. Note too that one of the passages of the *Politics* that refers back to the *Eudemian Ethics* (and therefore precedes the *Nicomachean Ethics*) is from Book IV (1295a36)—one of the books that Jaeger claims to belong to the final (anti-utopian) stage of Aristotle's thinking.

I: household and city[6]
II–VII–VIII: ideal constitutions
III: citizens and constitutions (both ideal and deviant)
IV–VI: non-ideal constitutions[7]

Furthermore, a modern editor might reasonably feel uncertain about the order in which these disparate parts should be arranged. Should Book III come first, because it is a general discussion of all kinds of constitutions, both good and bad? What should come next? A treatment of ideal cities, or of non-ideal constitutions? Where should Book I be placed?[8]

Some students of the *Politics* might reply that it matters little where the various components of this work are placed, because it is intended to be nothing more than a collection of essays on diverse political topics. According to this line of thinking, there is no organizational principle that drives the flow of ideas in the *Politics* from beginning to end, no destination towards which it is moving. It is not a real treatise, but a collection of diverse essays on political themes.[9]

This much can be said in favor of reading the *Politics* as a mere compilation: a philosophical work does not have to be unified or tightly organized in order to achieve its aim. We should therefore resist the a priori assumption there must be must be some key that unlocks the secret of why the *Politics* is arranged as it is. Its ideas are no less interesting, even if they are loosely related to each other.

But we would be missing an important feature of the *Politics* if we

---

[6] The final sentence of Book I (1260b20–24) announces that the next topic will be the best constitution. In this sense Books I and II are continuous, and the segregation of I from II unjustified. But the bridge that the final sentence of I builds to II is entirely artificial, for the ideal constitution is not a topic that flows logically out of the material in I. In that sense, I is a unit that stands apart from the rest of the treatise.

[7] This description of IV–VI oversimplifies, because IV also contains some discussion of one of the kinds of constitution that Aristotle calls 'correct', and in this respect IV carries forward a discussion inaugurated in III. Should we, for that reason, take III and IV–VI to form a single and continuous unit? That would, I believe, be a legitimate way of organizing the *Politics*, even though IV.1 seems to make a fresh start. Other scholars would object, as we are about to see: they hold that III should not be juxtaposed to IV, because the proper position of VII and VIII is between III and IV.

[8] One reasonable principle of organization is that books in which Aristotle refers his audience back to something he has already said should be placed later than the books to which he refers. On this basis, VII and VIII should come somewhere after (though not necessarily immediately after) III. See VII.14 1333a3–6 (which refers back to III.6 1278b32–7 and III.7 1279a25–b10) and III.14 1333a11–13 (which refers back to III.4 1277b7–11).

[9] For this reason, Pellegrin prefers *Les politiques* to *La Politique* in his translation. See his introduction, p. 5; also pp. 6–14, entitled 'Un "traité" divers, au texte chaotique, établi par une tradition manuscrite infirme'.

5.1. THE ORGANIZATION OF THE *POLITICS*

read it in this way. If we look more closely, we will discover that in fact there is an organizational principle that lies behinds its traditional arrangement. Whether that arrangement was Aristotle's own idea or is instead due to later editors of his manuscripts, it is possible to discover a certain kind of logical progression that the treatise follows. The movement of thought in the *Politics* takes us from what is rudimentary, undeveloped, and defective to what is more fully realized and excellent. Just as adult living things emerge out of their imperfect childhood forms, and artifacts are constructed out of disorganized materials, so cities have evolved out of more rudimentary communities. In parallel fashion, the *Politics* takes us from these lesser social formations, examines the sorts of cities (of varying quality) with which we have become familiar, and concludes with the depiction of a city that would provide the locus for the perfection of human life. We move, in other words, from bad to better to best.

To be more specific: Book I begins with the institutions from which the city developed and which form the equipment needed by every well-governed city: slaves, other forms of property, and the family. Early communities contain the imperfections of anything that is young and rudimentary; and even though slaves and the household are necessary components from which all political communities are made, they cannot on their own provide human life with the goods that constitute well-being. Book I is a discussion of the matter needed for political life, but not of political life itself.

In Book II, we examine another kind of imperfection: false ideals. Just as an examination of the imperfect communities from which cities emerge can teach us something about what they are and how they should be governed, so we can learn something about what the best kind of constitution is by critically reviewing what others have said about this subject. Philosophical inquiry typically starts with something that contains defects; we must sift through what seems or is thought to be the case, in order to arrive at a systematic theory that is free of the problems that others have not been able to resolve. So a study of politics must examine the mistakes other thinkers have made in their proposals for constitutional reform, as well as the flaws in the institutions of well-regarded cities.

In Book III Aristotle provides his audience with a third preliminary study. It prepares us for the examination of both ideal and non-ideal constitutions by exploring several general, connected questions about citizenship and constitutions. What is a citizen?

What is it to be a good citizen? What are the different kinds of constitution? How do those that are well governed differ from the rest? Aristotle introduces a sixfold classification of constitutions that will guide his analysis throughout Books III–VI: three of them correct (kingship, aristocracy, polity), and three deviant (tyranny, oligarchy, democracy). In the final chapters of Book III, he claims that it is better to be ruled by one or a few (a king or a small group of aristocrats) than to be ruled by the many—provided that the one or the few are greatly superior to the many.

But Book III is only the beginning of his examination of the variety of political systems. For deviant regimes are capable of improvement, and their amelioration is as important a component of political science as the examination of the best constitution. Inferior regimes admit of better and worse versions—and the better versions are superior to the lawless communities that existed in pre-civic times and continue to arise today. Political leaders must know how to choose the lesser evil, and Books IV–VI help them do so, by distinguishing the varieties of badness among constitutions.

Finally, in Books VII and VIII, Aristotle presents his portrait of the regime that is without qualification the best that can be achieved, when all of the human and material resources that one can hope for are at hand. It is not a city governed by one or a small number, and therefore it is even better than the kingship and aristocracy championed at the end of Book III. Rule by a single superior individual or by a few best is indeed superior to polity and deviant political forms (as Book III maintains), but the most that we can hope for is a community in which *all* citizens possess the correct understanding of well-being and have the equipment needed to live a life of excellence.[10]

The *Politics* is not the only Aristotelian treatise that follows a movement of thought that culminates in the depiction of an ideal form of life. Both the *Eudemian* and the *Nicomachean Ethics* end with an account of the best life possible for a human being; and the search for highest causes initiated in the first book of the *Metaphysics* eventually leads to an understanding of a substance that is without matter or change—the divine substance described in Book XII. Aristotle's guiding assumption in these treatises is that we can best understand perfection if we begin with more easily comprehen-

---

[10] See 10.1 for a defense of this way of interpreting the relationship between Books III and VII and VIII.

sible but defective forms. That is why he says, in the concluding lines of the *Ethics*, that our next task must be to study existing political systems: by doing so, we will be able to see which sort of constitution is best (1181b15–22). Here he provides us with the basic organizational principle of the *Politics*: when we learn to recognize the worthwhile institutions of well-governed cities, and the derangements of corrupt regimes, we will be in the best possible position to understand which type of city, among those that are possible to achieve, would be best. Aristotle does not mean by this that the *only* worthwhile question for a student of politics to examine is: which constitution is best? We rarely, if ever, have the resources needed for building the best possible community. That is why he insists, in *Politics* in IV.1, that political theory must have a wider compass than ideal theory. Even so, the *Politics* is not a shapeless compilation of loosely related essays. It never loses its normative focus, never analyzes politics simply for the sake of knowledge or explanation. Even its examination of defective communities is attentive to distinctions between greater and smaller defects. The culmination of this systematic exploration of the good and the better, the bad and the worse, is an understanding of the best. In this sense, all of the books of the *Politics* are preparatory to VII and VIII.[11]

5.2. *The Final Sentence of Book III*

There is, however, a radical alternative to this way of understanding the organization of the *Politics*. Some scholars believe that the traditional arrangement of the books should be rejected, because it overlooks explicit instructions Aristotle gives, at one point, about how we ought to read his work. At the end of Book III, he writes: 'These matters having been settled, we must now try to say, regarding the best constitution, in what manner it naturally arises, and how it is constituted. It is necessary for one who intends to make a proper investigation of it . . . '—and here the manuscripts break off (III.18 1288b2–6). These words indicate that the next topic that will

---

[11] Books VII and VIII are incomplete. We know that because at several points they promise to return to a certain topic, but fail to do so. See VII.5 1326b32–6, VII.10 1330a3–5, VII.10 1330a31–3, VII.16 1335b2–4, VII.17 1336b24–6, VIII.3 1338a32–4, and VIII.7 1341b38–40. No other books of the *Politics* show such unmistakable signs of incompleteness, but I do not believe that this gives us a weighty reason for inferring that these books were written last. Perhaps they were; but my claim is that they lie at the end of a movement of thought that can be reasonably attributed to Aristotle, not that they were composed last.

be addressed is the one that Aristotle explores in VII and VIII. And, in fact, the opening words of VII are nearly identical to the ones just cited in III ('It is necessary . . .'). It is tempting to infer that Aristotle wanted his audience to move directly from III to VII. In that case, the *Politics* ought to be organized differently: VII and VIII should be placed immediately after III; and IV, V, and VI should come after that. That is the order that some editors and translators have adopted. Accordingly, what has traditionally been called Book VII is instead renumbered as IV—and so on. The *Politics*, so arranged, does not culminate in a description of ideal life (as do the ethical treatises). It ends, instead, with a discussion of oligarchy and a final chapter on the various kinds of political office.[12]

The case for rearranging the *Politics* in this fashion rests heavily on the final sentence of Book III. But it would be wrong to assume that we have no choice but to obey that sentence's instructions about what to look for next, in our copies of the treatise. Here is a hypothesis that provides us with an alternative: We can see from Aristotle's writings that the final sentences of books are often used to tell the reader what to look for next. These sentences need not have been composed by Aristotle; they could easily have been added later by an editor or scribe.[13] Accordingly, we can conjecture that the final sentence of Book III of the *Politics* was not written by Aristotle, but was added by someone who was preparing a short edition of the *Politics*, one that omitted Aristotle's account of the imperfect constitutions analyzed in Books IV–VI.[14] We can understand why someone might want to produce such an edition: the entire work moves gradually towards an understanding of the best constitution, and some of its readers might have no need to learn about corrupt regimes, or no interest in working their way through a lengthy and detailed analysis of such political systems. An audience that is not being trained to reform defective regimes but simply wishes to understand the best constitution is well served by a short edition of the *Politics*, one that omits Books IV–VI. It is not far-fetched to

---

[12] See the editions of Susemihl and Hicks and of Newman. Lord believes that VII and VIII were 'dislocated' from their proper position, between III and IV, by a 'mechanical error' (see his translation, p. 16). Simpson's translation inserts VII and VIII between III and IV and therefore assigns new numbers to everything after III. See his introduction, pp. xvi–xx.

[13] Jaeger, recognizing that alternate books of the *Metaphysics* contain pointers to the beginning of the next book, hypothesized that they were added to tell the reader which roll (each roll containing two books) to read next. For a brief account, see Ross, *Aristotle's Metaphysics*, i.33.

[14] This hypothesis was proposed to me in conversation by Stephen Menn. Readers who like it should credit him; others should criticize me for making use of it.

suppose that the edition that has been handed down to us contains a version of Book III that was part of such an abbreviated edition of the work.

There is of course no way to prove or disprove the hypothesis that the final sentence of III was composed for this purpose. But since it is a possibility that cannot be dismissed, it serves a useful purpose: it allows us to see that we are not forced, like it or not, to conclude that VII and VIII are misplaced. If we think that the traditional order of the books falls into a pattern that was congenial to Aristotle, we may reasonably retain it. And doing so has the advantage of allowing the final lines of the *Ethics* to correspond to the order of subjects examined in the *Politics*.

There is a one further way to test the hypothesis that Book IV is properly placed after Book III. In IV, Aristotle occasionally tells his audience that he is presupposing or building on points made earlier. If these references are best understood as allusions to passages in VII and VIII, then that would constitute excellent evidence that those books ought to be relocated to a position between III and IV. On the other hand, if, as I believe, these references are best understood as allusions to points made in III, and none of them rests on doctrines found in VII or VIII, then that would constitute excellent grounds for believing that IV is meant to follow III, and that VII and VIII need not be interposed between III and IV. Discussion of these backward references in Book IV is best postponed.[15] On balance, I believe that the case for overturning the decision of whoever it was that put the *Politics* into its present order is weak.

5.3. *Why Books VII and VIII Are Next*

Although there is (as I have just argued) good reason for preserving the traditional organization of the books of the *Politics*, it does not follow that our study of that work must begin with Book I, and then march through the remainder of the treatise in order. Even if we read the *Politics* by beginning at the beginning and ending at the end—a perfectly reasonable way of making one's first acquaintance with the work—we need not, when we return to it for more serious study, follow that same order. Since the treatise has a direction, one that culminates in the depiction of an ideal city in Books VII and VIII, we

---

[15] See 10.n.9 and 12.n.1 for details.

might choose to begin our study with that final stage, and then examine the way in which Aristotle has arrived at it.

That is the order of discussion that appeals most to me. For there is something unsatisfactory about Aristotle's postponement of his discussion of the ideal city to the end of his treatise: he asks his audience to wait a long time before he comes to the destination for which he has been preparing them. (Here I express some sympathy for the editor who, according to my conjecture in 5.2, prepared a short version of the work.) It is in Books VII and VIII that we find Aristotle's fullest and most detailed account of how a city is best organized. The material that precedes these books tells us much about what is bad, but little about what is good.[16] We learn mainly about what to avoid, or how to make the best of a bad situation; but we do not find in these books a lengthy and extended exposition of what a good political community would look like. (We do have brief discussions of good regimes: in the final chapters of III on kingship and aristocracy, and in IV.11 on polity.) The treatise is nearly over before we learn at length and in detail about the institutions that Aristotle favors. Our study of his political thought would inherit this shortcoming in the organization of the *Politics*, if we were to follow him and save this subject for last.

There is a further reason for us to turn first to Books VII and VIII: our examination of Aristotle's political philosophy began with a study of his conception of the good (Chapters 2 and 3), because one of his central tenets is that the highest order of business for the political community is to look after the well-being of its citizens. In turning to the *Politics*, we will want to see how Aristotle's theory of the good is worked out in concrete terms. What sorts of social arrangement does he think we need if we are to live well? Does his theory of the good appear less attractive or more attractive, once we discover the politics to which it leads? Since these are the questions we will be pursuing, it makes good sense for us to turn immediately to the portion of the *Politics* in which his theory of well-being is

---

[16] In this respect, the organization of the *Ethics* is more successful. Having learnt in I.7 that virtuous activity is the central element of well-being, we soon begin to explore what the various kinds of virtue are. We are not asked to wait until the conclusion of the treatise before reading a detailed description of the qualities we need to live well. Virtues and vices are depicted together (two vices for every virtue); we do not first learn about deformations of character and only later about excellence. Had Aristotle devoted several books to continence and incontinence, and only then described the virtues, he would have produced an ethical treatise parallel in structure to the *Politics*. (This of course provides no reason for producing editions of the *Politics* that reorder its books—just as a weakness in a philosopher's theory does not allow us to rewrite his sentences.)

most clearly in play, and that is his discussion of the ideal city in Books VII and VIII. Here alone, in the *Politics*, he argues for his conception of happiness; having done so, he depicts for his audience the sort of community that can be created for people who live a life that embodies that conception of well-being. (In Books IV–VI, by contrast, it is difficult to discern what role—if any—his conception of happiness is playing. That is one of problems we will address, when we turn to that material, in Chapter 12.) Since we have identified his conception of the good as the central element of his political theory, let us turn next to the portion of the *Politics* that most fully depends on it—notwithstanding Aristotle's desire to save it for last.

6

Politics VII and VIII: The Ideal Polis

6.1. *The Practical Value of Utopia*

The task Aristotle sets himself in *Politics* Books VII and VIII is to present a detailed portrait of the best possible city—a city that is the most one could hope or pray for.[1] He is not dreaming up a state of affairs that he knows could never be realized. On the contrary, he restricts himself to what can actually be accomplished: everything that exists within this hypothetical community should be capable of realization (VII.4 1325b39).[2] He acknowledges that anyone who tries to bring his ideal society into existence will require the cooperation

---

[1] The Greek term is *euchē*: see II.6 1265a18, VII.4 1325b36, VII.5 1327a4, VII.10 1330a26, VII.11 1330a37, VII.12 1331b21, VII.13 1332a29. Not all translations seek to render this aspect of the Greek. The cumulative effect of these occurrences of *euchē* is to emphasize that Aristotle is not forming intentions or making decisions about what to do. Hopes and wishes are not the same things as plans. By allowing himself to describe the best that he can hope or wish for, Aristotle brackets questions of likelihood. His frequent use of *euchē* may also be a signal that he wants to put some distance between his approach to the construction of an ideal city and Plato's. For Plato uses this word 4 times in the *Republic* (450d1, 456b12, 499c4, 540d2) to insist that he is not merely describing an imaginary realm but devising strategies for its implementation. Aristotle, by contrast, tells his audience: this city, the best we can hope for, is possible; but nothing further need be said about how one should go about establishing it. Plato is eager to show that his city is something more than a prayer; Aristotle uses the same term to indicate that his city need be nothing more than a prayer—so long as it is possible. I am grateful to Myles Burnyeat for calling to my attention Plato's use of *euchē* to affirm the practicality of his ideal city.

[2] See too II.6 1265a17–18 for his insistence that the best constitution should contain nothing impossible. See below 6.3 and 6.10 for further discussion of this limitation.

6.1. THE PRACTICAL VALUE OF UTOPIA

of good fortune (VII.12 1331b21–2, VII.13 1332a30–1). But of course luck is not all that is needed; the construction of an ideal society requires considerable resources, material and human. It would be no objection to his scheme that, at the moment, those resources are not available. That would not undermine his claim that the city he describes is the best that is possible. Nor would it be an objection that it is *unlikely* that such resources will ever be available, or that his blueprint is *difficult* to put into practice. If we acknowledge that there is nothing contrary to human nature in his proposals, that the resources with which he provides the citizens of his ideal city are not impossible to acquire or sustain, and that such a community would be superior to any other that is possible, then we have granted everything about the city of Books VII and VIII that Aristotle asks us to accept.

Nonetheless, we might wonder why he would bother with this project, unless he thought that the resources for establishing the community described in VII and VIII are ready to hand. He tells us that we should study ethics for the sake of action (*NE* II.2 1103b26–9), and no doubt he would agree that the same dictum applies to politics. But if the ideal city is something that cannot be established now, or during our lifetime, then it might seem that describing it is a pointless exercise.

Aristotle does not consider this objection to his way of proceeding. He simply takes it for granted that one proper task for political theory is to describe the best possible civic community. But we can make a reasonable guess about how he might respond to this challenge to the utopian component of his practical philosophy. To begin with, he can point out that even if at present there is no possibility of bringing the best city into existence, it may be possible to alter our circumstances so that we are not quite so distant from the ideal as we once were. The practical value of studying the ideal community lies in its furnishing us with a goal that can be approached to some degree; even if we know that we have no chance of establishing and living in such a community, we can use it as a guide to reform. If, over time, communities can be improved or kept from deteriorating by people who are inspired by a vision of a utopian constitution, then the portrait of that ideal community will have proved its worth.[3] Furthermore, a utopian blueprint, if properly constructed,

---

[3] For example, Aristotle's ideal city is one in which all citizens share power equally, and no elites dominate civic life (6.10). Perhaps no sizeable community can fully achieve such equality, but if we think that Aristotle's description of the best constitution is correct in

can help clarify what is wrong with existing cities. It might even engage our emotions: by revealing to us how good a community can be, it can increase our dissatisfaction with the cities in which we now live, and that dissatisfaction can fuel a desire for political change.

In any case, by Aristotle's lights, political theory would be too limited an undertaking if it merely identified which kind of city is worst, and advised us to settle for anything superior to that. There are many kinds of political arrangement that are not quite so bad as tyrannical regimes, and some of them are farther removed from tyrannies than others. In fact, some kinds of cities are more or less well governed; though they have imperfections, they are on the whole good. But how can we be secure in making such distinctions between good and bad constitutions, and between better and worse among those that are bad, unless we ask ourselves what sort of city would be ideal? If we want to think systematically about civic life, and in this way move beyond our first impressions, we need to explore the full range of political possibilities. That means that we must try to develop a theory about what is best, not merely what is bearable or intolerable. Distinctions between bad and good, worse and worst, good and better cannot be validated unless they are brought to completion by an account of what is best. Aristotle's assumption that he owes his audience an account of the ideal constitution derives in part from his conviction that a genuine theory must be systematic.

Of course, his conviction that this is a proper matter for political philosophy derives to some degree from the fact that several earlier thinkers—Plato chief among them—had proposed blueprints for ideal societies. They did so partly because, in the Greek world, the establishment of new cities was a common phenomenon, and these new communities sometimes sought the advice of philosophers or leaders who had given serious thought to questions of constitutional design.[4] Perhaps Aristotle was also encouraged by recent Macedonian conquests in Asia to ponder the question of how a new model city might be established.[5] (In that case, his reply to the objection

---

this respect, we can try to approximate it by curtailing the power of elites. (The interpretation I propose here rests on a disputed assumption: that there is a fundamental continuity between the ideal and non-ideal components of Aristotle's political thought. See 10.7 and 12.2.)

[4] On Greek colonization, see: Graham, *Colony and Mother City in Ancient Greece*; Malkin, *Religion and Colonization*; Dougherty, *The Poetics of Colonization*.

[5] Thus Ober, *Political Dissent in Democratic Athens*, pp. 339–51.

under discussion might have been that in fact his ideal city could be established with resources ready to hand.) But even if contemporary political realities were not part of his motivation for depicting an ideal constitution in Books VII and VIII, he would have had reason enough for undertaking this project.

6.2. Uncoerced Consensus about the Good

Disagreement is an eliminable part of political life. No community—certainly no sizable community—can expect to achieve unanimity, or anything close to it, at all times. And so one of the central goals of political institutions is to develop and safeguard fair and effective procedures for the resolution of conflicts.

These familiar ideas are congenial to Aristotle, as we will see later in this chapter (6.11). Even his ideal city is the locus of disagreement. But he would certainly reject a more specific thesis about politics, namely that disagreement *about final ends* is a necessary component of every political community. He assumes that when conditions are right, it is possible for an entire city to have a common and correct understanding about what human well-being is, and for this common understanding to be transmitted from one generation to another through normal and reasonable methods of education. In fact, he would insist that a city would fall far short of being ideal if it lacked such a common understanding. He equates the search for the best city with an inquiry into the best constitution, and a constitution is not only a way of distributing political power, but also a way of life (1.4). It includes both the means used for collective decision-making and the ends that guide political deliberation. Therefore, part of what makes a city the best city is that it is guided by the best ends. In such a polity the citizens aim, both individually and collectively, at virtuous activity sufficiently equipped with external resources. They aim at this goal not because they think that excellent rational agency is a means to some further end, but simply because this is what well-being is.

Aristotle realizes that in existing cities there is significant disagreement about what the highest good is (11.4). He never proposes that one of the tasks of political leadership is to re-educate the citizenry and teach them the correct conception of happiness. Rather, he assumes that when adult citizens misconceive their good (as they often do), it is usually too late to correct their errors. They have become accustomed to a certain way of thinking about their well-being, and that outlook is embodied in their emotions. Their whole way of life has become fixed, and it is therefore unlikely that they will listen to argument or be influenced by the example of others (3.5). The false conceptions of well-being that prevail in these defective communities are handed down from one generation to another, and are embedded in their legal systems. Political leaders faced with a populace of this sort must settle for something less than a radical change in its ethical outlook; they must instead devise strategies for making citizens less hostile to each other and for mitigating the harm they do themselves. These defective cities, which Aristotle studies in Books IV–VI, can be improved, but only to a limited degree. They can become better oligarchies or better democracies, and such changes are worth making; but one cannot take an oligarchy or a democracy and transform it (even by degrees) into a perfect constitution.

Utopia cannot be created out of misshapen human resources. If one seeks to form a perfect society, one must therefore begin afresh. The founders of an ideal community must already possess the proper understanding of well-being, and they must establish institutions that will foster that understanding in future generations. Because a fresh start is being made, the ideal city will be constructed on a new site, carefully selected for its advantages. Those who become its citizens will be leaving their homes and establishing a new polity. We can safely assume that they join the new community voluntarily, and do so because they already share the conception of happiness on which it is based. Since Aristotle expounds his moral philosophy in his school and through his writings, and has friends in high places, it would not be absurd for him to suppose that a new city could be formed by a group of associates and admirers who would like to start a community based on his ideas. They would bring their families with them and would instill a love of virtue in their children, who would in turn inculcate these habits in their own children.[6]

Aristotle assumes that this new polity could sustain itself indefinitely, provided that it continues to possess the material resources it needs, and is not defeated by hostile cities. He does not take himself to be describing, in Books VII and VIII, a fragile institutional

---

[6] Aristotle's depiction of the ideal city is often expressed in terms of a legislator or political leader who selects its site, citizenry, and fundamental institutions. See Kraut, *Aristotle: Politics Books VII and VIII*, p. 66. But we need not take him to mean that the establishment of this regime is a task for one person only.

structure that makes extreme demands on citizens and is therefore bound to deteriorate as time goes by.[7] On the contrary, once the ideal community is well established, it should continue to receive the voluntary allegiance of its members. They take great pleasure in their way of life—that is part of what makes it ideal.[8] There would be no need to keep them from learning about the way other cities are managed, or to bar them from moving to those cities, if they chose to do so. Aristotle portrays the politics of existing cities as a dismal affair, as we will see (Chapter 12); they are filled with faction, corruption, and the pathologies that arise when people have too much wealth or too little. The citizens of the ideal city will therefore have no interest in living elsewhere. Having been educated by their parents and other members of their community to understand where their well-being lies, they will see no reason to leave. They will freely affirm the superiority of their community to all others.

6.3. Philosophy, Education, and Leisure

Since Aristotle argues (*NE* X.7–8) that the best kind of life is that of a philosopher, he seems to be committed to the thesis that the best possible city is one in which every citizen devotes at least some time to philosophical activity. For surely the best community one could hope for is a city in which each citizen is leading the best possible life.

But is this in fact a thesis he explicitly endorses in *Politics* VII and VIII? To answer this question, we need to be more precise about what is meant by 'philosophy'. Aristotle sometimes uses *philosophia* and its cognates loosely to designate *any* kind of inquiry, although the term most often applies to a study that is general in scope and not a mere means to other ends.[9] But at times he has something more limited in mind: philosophy, strictly speaking, is the search for a systematic understanding of the first causes of the universe. Beginning with what we observe in nature, and examining the most widely accepted or prominent theories of the day, it leads eventually to an understanding of the subjects investigated in the

---

[7] Compare Plato's admission that the ideal city of the *Republic*, though resilient, will inevitably devolve into a less perfect constitution (546a).
[8] See *NE* I.8 1099a7–31, II.3 1104b3–13; *Pol.* VIII.5 1339b18–19.
[9] See *Pol.* VII.11 1331a16; *Met.* I.2 982b11–19; *Poetics* 9 1451b5–7.

Metaphysics: substance, essence, form, and the unmoved mover.[10] Someone who has completed this investigation has acquired wisdom (*sophia*) in the strict sense, and the exercise of this intellectual virtue is the activity Aristotle equates with perfect happiness in *Ethics* X.7–8.

In this strict sense of 'philosophy', only a handful of people were occupied with philosophy in Aristotle's time. There would not have been enough of them to constitute the citizenry of an entire polis, for a city would have needed about 1,000 citizens to have an army large enough to protect itself against invasion. If Aristotle's ideal city is to be composed of citizens who are all philosophers in the strict sense, then it would need to take special steps to provide them with a philosophical education. It could not expect so many people to become philosophers on their own initiative. Now, although Aristotle does devote a large portion of Books VII and VIII to prescribing a common education for his citizens, he never says that they are to investigate the first causes of substance and eventually contemplate the unmoved movers (about which more will be said in 6.4). When they are young, they are trained to read and write, to sing and play an instrument; between the ages of 14 and 17, they undertake various other studies (about which more later), and then they receive military training. Beyond that, no further subjects are prescribed for them[11]—although far more would certainly be required if they were to become philosophers in the strict sense. So it looks as though they are not being prepared to engage in the highest kind of activity. Apparently, Aristotle assumes that in any community there will only be a few who have the ability and interest needed to complete the long training required of philosophers.

Does this create an intolerable paradox, because in the best city, where people are as happy as possible, at most a few will achieve the perfect happiness Aristotle equates with philosophical contemplation? No, because there is a broader use of such terms as *philosophia* and *sophia*, and the citizens of the ideal city will engage in philosophical activity in this looser sense.[12] When they are adults, they

---

[10] See *Met.* IV.2 for this use of *philosophia*.

[11] Books VII and VIII are incomplete, as we can see from the promises they leave unfulfilled (5.n.11), but these contain no suggestion that Aristotle intends his citizens to become contemplators of the unmoved mover. At one point (VII.14 1333a24–9) he strongly implies that not all citizens will be capable of theoretical activity.

[12] This broader use of the term is not peculiar to Aristotle. See e.g. Pericles' funeral oration in Thucydides' *Histories*, 2.40: 'we cultivate the mind (*philosophoumen*) without softness.'

6.3. PHILOSOPHY, EDUCATION, AND LEISURE

engage in activities that are akin to philosophical contemplation in the strict sense, and so, although they are not philosophers, they come as close to this condition as can be reasonably expected. In this community, citizens are as happy as *possible*, because there is no realistic possibility that a large proportion of them will be philosophers in the strict sense.

To see more fully what Aristotle has in mind for his adult citizens, let us consider in greater detail the kind of education he says the city should give them when they are children. Until they are 7 they remain at home, where their parents (supervised by officials) will educate them through stories and games.[13] Between the ages of 7 and 14 they are instructed by teachers, appointed and paid by the city, in reading and writing, gymnastics, music, and drawing. At 14 they move on to other subjects, though Aristotle does not say what they are. And then, between the ages of 17 and 21, they receive intensive physical training that will prepare them to be good soldiers.[14]

It is possible to make an educated guess about what subjects they learn between 14 and 17. Aristotle says that they should be taught to read and write not only because these are useful skills, but also 'because many other studies [*mathēseis*] become possible through them' (VIII.3 1338a39–40). And he adds that they must be taught to draw because this makes them contemplate the beauty of bodies. 'To search everywhere for what is useful is what least suits those who are great in soul and free' (1338b2–4). In light of this, it is plausible to suppose that between the ages of 14 and 17 students will read certain works not because they are useful but because they reveal certain symmetries and harmonies that are intrinsically appealing. Treatises in mathematics (construed broadly to include astronomy) will show them the order and beauty of shapes and

---

[13] Should both father and mother play a role in educating them? And should girls also receive some education in the home? Aristotle does not directly address either question in VII and VIII, but it is likely that he would give an affirmative answer to both. He insists at the end of I.13 that women must be properly trained (I.13 1260b13–20)—and surely the place where such training takes place is the household. (Note too his complaints about Spartan women at II.9 1269b12–1270a15.) Presumably the stories heard by boys and girls are told to them not only by their fathers but their mothers as well. In recommending that during pregnancy women should rest their minds (VII.16 1335b16–18; cf. VIII.4 1339a7–10), Aristotle implies that at other times then they must be mentally active. His tacit assumption is that mothers have a supervisory role to play in the household; and surely the education of their daughters is one of their responsibilities. See too NE VIII.10 1160b33–5. Of course, he assumes that daughters need not be taught to read and write, and more generally, that their education should be different from and inferior to that of sons.

[14] On the first stage of education, see VII.17 1336a3–b2; on the second (ages 7–14), VIII.1 and VIII.3 1337b22–7; on subsequent education, VIII.4 1339a4–7 (with VII.17 1336b37–40).

natural phenomena.[15] Like philosophers who completely understand the universe and contemplate its order, these students develop a rudimentary knowledge of the organized universe, and in this way they approximate the condition of philosophers.[16]

What will these citizens do when their education has been completed? At some point in their adult lives they will spend a significant amount of time engaged in political activity (6.10). But this cannot be their only occupation, for the assembly to which they belong will be in session only during certain periods, and although they will occasionally hold other offices as well, these responsibilities will rotate.[17] They will not have to work for a living (6.8). They will therefore have a considerable amount of free time: what will they do with it?

Part of the answer is that they will relax by amusing themselves. Aristotle holds that although political activity is worthwhile in itself, it is also arduous, and whenever we work hard, we need to relax in pleasant ways, so that we will be able to refresh ourselves and get back to work.[18] But he thinks that, ideally, life should have some other element in addition to the cycle of work and relaxation. Work can and should be worthwhile in itself, but the very fact that it is arduous means that it is not entirely to be loved. Relaxation does not supply the missing element, because even though it is pleasant, its role is to help us get back to work. It is subordinate in value to work, because its place in life is to refresh our energies and thus to revive our ability to work well. Aristotle's idea is that there should be a period of leisure in which we are not merely getting ourselves ready to go back to work, but doing something that is entirely pleasant and worthwhile because it is not arduous. Every well-lived life must have regular periods of leisure devoted to some entirely lovable activity.[19] If one has the special talent and training of a philosopher, then one will devote one's leisure to philosophy, for this is a purely

---

[15] Recall that arithmetic, geometry, and astronomy are among the studies Plato prescribes for his rulers in the *Republic* (522c–531d). Plato calls these subjects *mathēmata*—a term that Aristotle's *mathēseis* (1338a40) brings to mind.

[16] See too 6.n.70 for the conjecture that Aristotle's ideal citizens receive *paideia* (education) but do not possess scientific knowledge (*epistēmē*).

[17] See VII.4 1326b6–7 on the herald who must be heard by all when the assembly is convened, and VII.14 1332b26–7 on rotation of offices. Further discussion can be found in Kraut, *Aristotle: Politics VII and VIII*, comments on VII.14 1332b12–1333a16.

[18] The relation between work and relaxation is discussed in *NE* X.6 1176b27–1177a1; see too *Pol.* VIII.3 1337b38–1338a1, VIII.5 1339b25–31.

[19] On the distinct roles of leisure and relaxation, see *Pol.* VIII.3 1337b29–1338a6, VIII.5 1339a14–26. For discussion, see Kraut, comments on VII.5 1326b30–9, VII.14 1333a30–b5.

6.3. PHILOSOPHY, EDUCATION, AND LEISURE

enjoyable activity unsullied by the stress inherent in political activity (*NE* X.7 1177b12–15).[20] But what of ordinary citizens, who do not have this special training and talent? With which purely enjoyable activities should they fill their leisure?

Aristotle finds his answer in one of the most generally enjoyed activities of Greek culture: music. In their homes and in dramatic festivals financed by the city, the citizens of the ideal city, like many ordinary citizens everywhere, will listen to recitations of poetry sung with musical accompaniment. They will have been taught to sing and accompany themselves when they were young, because this training was designed to enhance their ability to make good choices of singers and songs when they are adults. And although Aristotle holds that these musical activities provide a needed respite from the hard work of governing a city, and also provide an outlet for emotional distress, their most important value lies simply in the fact that they are an excellent way to pass one's leisure time. They are good in themselves, and not merely a means to a further end.[21]

When the citizens enjoy listening to musical performances, are they doing something akin to what philosophers do when they contemplate the order of the universe? Such a comparison may seem farfetched, unless we remind ourselves that Aristotle is not referring to unaccompanied music, but to poetic or dramatic words that tell a story, and that such stories may embody a kind of truth. He is not talking about the sheer pleasure of sound, abstracted from all content, but about musical words that represent the world. When reality is well represented in song, we rehearse in our minds a species of correctness, and in this respect something like philosophical activity is stimulated by musical performances. Aristotle assumes, in other words, that traditional stories conveyed in song express a form

---

[20] It would be reasonable for Aristotle to assume that a small number of his ideal citizens will be philosophers in the strict sense. For he regards philosophy as a natural outgrowth of human curiosity (*Met.* I.1–2): when there is sufficient leisure, some human beings will seek an understanding of the highest causes. And certainly when a city educates all of its citizens in the sciences, as the ideal city does, it can be expected that a few of them will, on their own, pursue these studies further, during those periods when they are freed from political responsibilities.

[21] At VIII.5 1339b13–15 Aristotle says that music is valuable because it promotes education, provides amusement, and is the proper way to spend one's leisure time. These ideas are more fully developed at VIII.3 1337b28–1338a13 and throughout VIII.5. Because of the close connection between well-being and leisure (emphasized at VIII.3 1337b28–1338a13), it is this last role of music that is most important. At VIII.7 1341b38–41, he adds purification to his list of the benefits of music. For discussion, see Kraut, comments on 1341b36–1342a16.

of wisdom, and that part of the joy we take in music is due to our perception of the truths embodied in these tales.[22]

It must be emphasized that Aristotle's ideal polis plays an important role in shaping the citizens' enjoyment of leisure. His city not only guides the development of ethical virtue but promotes something comparable to the intellectual virtue of the philosopher. The city provides *all* children of citizens with an education so that as adults they can fill their leisure with good music. Learning to sing and play an instrument is not a privilege confined to the wealthy or the talented, but is part of the basic equipment everyone needs to live well. In this respect, the ideal polis is radically different from any that had ever existed, for in Greek cities education was not publicly supported and music lessons were not provided to all.

Though his proposal is radical, Aristotle is in a way merely extending an idea that was prevalent in his culture. It was widely assumed in the ancient world that one of the city's tasks was to organize various kinds of festival—religious, athletic,[23] dramatic, and musical. The Greek city did not concern itself solely with such mundane matters as building docks and ships, or protecting citizens from bodily assault and foreign invasion. It was also heavily implicated in their cultural and spiritual lives. Aristotle's idea, which he derives from Plato, is that because the city already plays an active role in organizing these ennobling activities among adults, it makes good sense for it to go one step further, by preparing children for the higher activities they will engage in when they become adults.

---

[22] See VIII.5 1339a25–6: music contributes to wisdom; note too Aristotle's statement that one needs to fill leisure with philosophy (VII.15 1334a23, 32; cf. II.5 1263b40). See Kraut, *Aristotle: Politics Books VII and VIII*, comments on VII.14 1333a16–30, VIII.3 1337b22–33. The expressions I use in this paragraph ('a kind of truth', 'a species of correctness', a 'form of wisdom') correspond to Aristotle's statement that although poetry aims at 'correctness', it is not the kind of correctness that can be achieved in politics or other productive activities. See *Poetics* 25 1460b13–15, and compare his view that the pleasures of poetry are pleasures of learning (*Poetics* 4 1448b12–15), as well as his thesis that poetry is more philosophical than history, because it deals with universals (*Poetics* 9 1451b5–7). For discussion, see Halliwell, *Aristotle's Poetics*, pp. 3–4, 24–7. It should also be kept in mind that the word Aristotle often uses for philosophical activity—*theōria* ('contemplation')—is cognate to a word commonly used of spectators at the theater (*theomenoi*, from *theaomai*: 'to view, observe'). In fact, *theōria* refers to observation generally, and not merely the kind of mental reflection that Aristotle prizes.

[23] But note that Aristotle is critical of the way athletes are trained (VII.16 1335b5–7, VIII.4 1338b9–11). Although the city provides gymnasia and physical training (VII.12 1331a36, VIII.3 1338b6–7), it prohibits the distorted physical development that wins athletic contests but interferes with military fitness.

6.4. Religion

In the ancient city, temples were built with public funds, sacred festivals were organized by the city, and participation in religious ceremonies was a widely accepted civic obligation. So it should be no surprise that in Aristotle's ideal city there is no attempt to keep religion out of public life or to make it a matter of individual conscience and private choice. Rather, he assumes that it is proper for citizens to honor the gods collectively and that the city is to organize such ceremonies. There will be sacred buildings (VII.12 1331b6) and priesthoods filled by older men who are past their mental prime (VII.9 1329a27-34).

Aristotle spends little time on this subject—far less than he does on music. He asks what role music is to play in civic life, but it never occurs to him to ask why the city should appoint priests and build temples. We therefore have to speculate about how he would answer these questions: How are the citizens to conceive of the gods? Why is it beneficial for them to participate in religious ceremonies?

He thinks that there are divinities: they are the eternal, changeless, non-corporeal substances on which all change in the universe depends.[24] But although these unmoved movers resemble the traditional gods of Greek religion in some respects—they never die, and they are the causes of all the natural phenomena we observe—they are radically different from Zeus and other ordinary divinities, because as Aristotle conceives them they have no ethical characteristics. They do not guarantee that justice will be done, or punish those who violate their agreements, or respond favorably to sacrifice and prayer. Aristotle's eternal substances take no interest in human life or in each other; they are simply isolated living beings who endlessly think true thoughts.[25] The philosopher who understands the structure of the universe and occasionally reflects on it bears some resemblance to these unmoved movers; for his contemplation is like their non-practical thinking. But since the gods do not respond to prayers or sacrifice and do not intervene in any other way in human

---

[24] On Aristotle's theology, see Ross, *Aristotle's Metaphysics*, i, 'Introduction', pp. 130–54; Gerson, *God and Greek Philosophy*, pp. 82–141; and Reeve, *Substantial Knowledge*, pp. 190–239. Bodéüs, *Aristotle and the Theology of the Living Immortals* presents an unorthodox interpretation, according to which Aristotle accepted the existence of beneficent gods who are pleased by our good conduct.

[25] For Aristotle's conception of the divine, see *Met.* XII.7 1072b13–1073a13, XII.9; *NE* X.8 1178b8–25.

life, it is difficult to see why Aristotle thinks that there ought to be temples, priests, and public worship. The citizens of the best community can imitate the gods by taking pleasure in philosophical thought: why is that not religion enough?

These questions presuppose that the citizens of Aristotle's ideal polis share his conception of the gods—but we have already seen reason to question this assumption. He does not provide them with an education beyond the age of 17, and does not portray them as philosophers in the strict sense. So we should not suppose that they will themselves adopt the metaphysics and physics that led Aristotle to his austere conception of the gods. It is more likely that they think of the sun, moon, planets, and the other heavenly spheres as the supreme gods, for this is a traditional part of religion that Aristotle treats with respect (*Met.* X.8 1074a38–b14).[26] He takes the heavenly spheres to be eternal, to admit of no change other than motion, and to be the causes of seasons and other meteorological phenomena. Citizens who worship the sun and moon as divinities interrupt their everyday routine in order to honor the most basic causes of their world, and in doing so they come very close to the truth—for the precise truth is that these corporeal bodies, important as they are, are less worthy of honor than the non-corporeal and unmoving substance that is the highest god.

As we have seen (6.3), the citizens of the ideal polis develop, at an early age, an appreciation for the beauty and order of the natural world by learning the rudiments of mathematics and science. It is a reasonable conjecture that this education is preparatory to their religious life. For what would the point of that education be, if it were no longer used by adults? Mathematics and science awaken a child's love of order in the world; and then the world—or its orderly part—is honored by adult citizens in celebrations sponsored by the city. Aristotle's civic religion is not an abnegation of the self or the world, and is not embodied in a specific creed or an affirmation of a life to come. It is simply a public celebration of the unchanging causes of the world's order.[27]

---

[26] He agrees that the heavenly bodies are divine, but takes them to be inferior to other gods, on whose motionless activity they depend.

[27] Why does Aristotle assume that such celebrations should be public? Why would it not be enough to worship the causes of the universe in private periods of devotion? It would be anachronistic to think that Aristotle consciously recognized this alternative and opposed it because he wanted religious practices to foster social solidarity. Rather, he assumes that we should worship the divine collectively in civic festivals because that is how the gods were celebrated in his society. He approves of this feature of traditional religion not because he is

We now live in societies that possess far more religious diversity than was present in the Greek polis, and holy wars have taught us the dangers of too great a civic involvement in religious life. In the modern world, the state can legitimately appoint priests and organize religious life only in those communities where such practices are widely embraced and equally promote the good of all. These conditions are not easily or often satisfied. But this does not mean that Aristotle's city is flawed because of its involvement in religious life. In the ancient world, there was no good reason to separate politics and religion. Aristotle's ideal city oppresses or offends no one by organizing the worship of the gods. On the contrary, he may well be right that the state should offer children an education in mathematics and science because this training enables them to enter into the right relationship—a relationship of reverence—with the invariant forces of nature.

6.5. VII.2 and 3

Aristotle devotes a significant portion of Book VII (chapters 2 and 3) to a debate between two parties: one opposes the political life because it thinks that it must consist in aggressive domination of others; the other opposes the philosophical life on the grounds that it is inactive and useless. He argues that both parties are wrong: the political life need not be tyrannical, and the philosophical life is active. But why does Aristotle enter into this debate? How do these chapters prepare us for what is to come in later portions of VII and VIII? Are they a digression, serving no further purpose?

To a degree, these questions are easy to answer. All of the citizens of Aristotle's ideal city lead a political life, because all participate equally in ruling the city (6.10). So it is obvious that Aristotle needs to say something against the anti-political party if he is to convince the reader that the city he is presenting is ideal. If politics were inevitably a corrupting business, as some allege, then an ideal city would either be impossible or would be managed by as few dirty hands as possible. Since Aristotle's citizens devote a considerable

indifferent to the truth in religious practices and regards them merely as a civic bond, but because he sees in them a good measure of truth. This does not mean that he is unaware of the unifying effect of common religious practices. The point rather is that he does not consider the sociological value of religious practices in isolation from their philosophical significance.

amount of time to public service, he is eager to emphasize from the start that politics is not merely the locus of relationships of domination and submission.

But what of the other part of our question: why does Aristotle defend the philosophical life at this early point in Book VII? A possible answer, parallel to the one we have just given, is that his citizens will all be philosophers; but we have seen (6.3) that strictly speaking this is not so. A better answer is that Aristotle is addressing himself to future political leaders, and wants these statesmen to be hospitable to philosophy. This is not because he hopes that these leaders will themselves *be* philosophers, but because philosophy cannot endure in a hostile political climate.

We can now see that there may be a further reason for defending philosophy at the beginning of Book VII: although Aristotle does not propose that citizens receive a philosophical education in the strict sense, his citizens are broadly educated in mathematics, science, and music. They engage in activities that express a kind of wisdom, and so they can be described as philosophers in a loose sense of the word. These highest activities are useless. Listening to music accomplishes nothing; its goal is achieved during the time it is enjoyed, and it is not a means for arriving at some further end. The same is true of a reverential perception of the order of the world. If it were true that philosophy in the strict sense ought to be avoided because it is useless, then these activities, so akin to philosophy, would also be discredited. Aristotle's reason for opposing the anti-philosophical party is parallel to his reason for opposing the anti-political party. His citizens will engage in both political and quasi-philosophical activity, and a defense of both aspects of their lives is needed.

6.6. *Education, Freedom, and the Common Good*

In Aristotle's time, no polis provided the sort of education he prescribes in Books VII and VIII for the children of citizens. Sparta organized the training of children, but the education it promoted was designed above all to promote warriors, not the cultured and thoughtful citizens that Aristotle favors.[28] In Athens, education was exclusively the responsibility of parents. Typically, if they had

---

[28] For Aristotle's criticism of Spartan militarism, see the passages cited in 1.n.13.

6.6. EDUCATION, FREEDOM, AND THE COMMON GOOD

enough money, they hired teachers who instructed their sons in reading, writing, and music.[29] So, in proposing that all future citizens of a certain age be sent from their homes and enter a common system of education, Aristotle was advocating a radical departure from contemporary practices.[30]

The argument he gives for it is quite brief: 'Since there is one end for the whole city, clearly it is necessary that education too be one and the same for all. ... [I]t is necessary, when things are a common concern, that preparation for them also be made common ... [No citizen] belongs to himself; rather all of them belong to the city, for each is a part of the city. And it is natural that care for each part should look to care for the whole' (VIII.1 1337a21–30).[31] The one end for the whole city is of course happiness—a life of virtuous activity sufficiently equipped with resources. Citizens will not be able to live such a life unless they start preparing for it when they are children. If the city does not require education—if it leaves this as an option to be individually elected or rejected by each household—then it creates a risk that only some future citizens will be capable of participating in cooperative political arrangements and common cultural pursuits. And it creates this same risk if it merely requires some sort of education, but leaves it entirely open to parents to determine what the content of that education must be.

Aristotle's statement that 'no citizen belongs to himself; rather all of them belong to the city' is an expression of the idea that citizens must do what they can to serve the common good, and cannot simply live as they please. It is not appropriate for a parent's decisions about his children's education to be entirely within his control, because this is a matter that affects everyone in the community. Similarly, Aristotle assumes that decisions about military service, payment of taxes, and participation in political life should not be left to each individual, but should be made collectively. His point about the need for public education is an application of the more general thesis that in matters that affect the good of all, collective decisions take precedence over individual preferences. This

---

[29] See *Pol.* VIII.3 1337b23–5, Plato's *Protagoras* 325c–326c. A good recent discussion can be found in Harris, *Ancient Literacy*, ch. 4. See esp. pp. 106–111 on the extent of female illiteracy.

[30] Here he follows Plato, who, in both the *Republic* and the *Laws*, urges the city to take control over the education of its citizens.

[31] For a detailed analysis, see Curren, *Aristotle on the Necessity of Public Education*.

is the practical import of his statement that the 'citizens belong to the city'.[32]

It is hard to quarrel with some components of Aristotle's thesis: we think, for example, that no government can make taxes a matter of personal discretion; and military service is obligatory when a nation is in great danger. But he imposes more civic obligations on the citizens of his ideal city than we modern citizens are accustomed to bearing. In his city, participation in public education is mandatory, since private schools are not permitted. He would require people to hold office and to vote, whether they want to or not.[33] He thinks the community should oversee the ages at which people marry and the way they bring up children (VII.16–17).

What lies behind these regulations is his rejection of a conception of freedom that has become widely (though not universally) accepted in modern liberal democracies. According to this common way of thinking, certain parts of our lives are no one's business but our own. Within this private realm, we escape public accountability. We should of course be prevented from doing positive harm to others, and so laws against violence, theft, fraud, and the like are legitimate. But so long as we respect these prohibitions, we should be allowed the largest possible liberty to live as we choose. Admittedly, we might make a poor use of our freedom. But it would be a violation of our rights if the political community tried to keep us from misusing our freedom—even if, in doing so, we injure ourselves and become incapable of contributing to the common good. One of our most important rights is the right to be left alone—to decline to serve the community, if we choose not to. The political community must not force or induce its members to be community-minded.

These are ideas to which Aristotle is deeply opposed. His thought is not that the polis should be *everything* to us—that it is the *only* community to whose members we owe a strong allegiance and to whom we are accountable. For he argues in Book II of the *Politics* that families, close friendships, and other small associations have a special role to play in a well-lived life. (That will be our subject in Chapter 9.) But his reason for regarding these smaller circles as valuable is not that they are places into which we can retreat and escape

---

[32] A related thesis—that the city is prior to the individual (*Pol.* I.2 1253a18–29)—will be fully discussed in Ch. 7. See esp. 7.10.

[33] See II.9 1271a11–12: someone qualified to rule must do so, willing or not. Note too IV.13 1297a17–19 (taken with a38–40): to achieve a balanced mixture of rich and poor, one must fine certain citizens for not attending the assembly. We will discuss Aristotle's policy of mixing rich and poor in 10.4–6 and 12.6.

6.6. EDUCATION, FREEDOM, AND THE COMMON GOOD

from the burdens of public responsibility. Rather, he believes that these smaller units provide goods that the political community cannot. Our association with fellow citizens, for example, cannot give us the same pleasures and benefits that we derive from intimate friendships; and the family meets the needs of small children in a way that the city cannot. Families and friendships are associations worth preserving not because they create a private realm into which we can escape from the claims of the polis, but because they supplement the city's contribution to well-being.

Aristotle realizes that many of his contemporaries favor a far less restrictive way of arranging civic life. He takes proponents of democracy to be advocates of a large measure of freedom, and he understands them to mean that citizens should be allowed to live in whatever way they please.[34] These democrats do not go so far as to say that each person should be allowed to harm others; they mean, rather, that there is a private realm in which citizens should be exempt from having to give an account to others of the choices that they make.[35] Aristotle's opposition to this conception of freedom is based on his conviction that if the political community allows its members to withdraw into a private world in which their responsibilities and their accountability to their fellow citizens is suspended, then it permits the growth of psychological forces that will eventually undermine the good of all. When people are given a large zone of freedom, and no public efforts are made to encourage certain ways of life and discourage others, then the worst features of human nature—greed, envy, love of domination—are likely to flourish and to poison civic life.[36] The ideal city avoids this, but not because it is peopled by citizens who are made of better stuff than ordinary mortals. Its citizens do not have an extraordinary natural talent for virtue. Rather, the ideal city avoids the common dangers of civic life because it

---

[34] See V.9 1310a28–36, VI.2 1317a40–b17. Aristotle's attitude towards democracy will be more fully discussed in 12.4–5 and 13.2–3.

[35] Thus Pericles interprets Athenian freedom to mean that there is a distinction between what is public and what is private, and in the later realm 'we are not angry with our neighbor if he does what he wants'. Thucydides 2.37.2–3. For recent discussion of the conception of freedom prevalent in classical Athens, see Hansen, 'The Ancient Athenian and the Modern Liberal View of Liberty as a Democratic Ideal'; Wallace, 'Law, Freedom, and the Concept of Citizens' Rights in Democratic Athens'; Cohen, *Law, Sexuality, and Society*, pp. 70–240. Note too Cohen's assertion that Aristotle's regulation of the private realm in his ideal community makes him 'far more hostile to democratic principles than is often thought to be the case' (*Law, Violence, and Community in Classical Athens*, p. 43).

[36] 'The freedom to do whatever one wants cannot guard against the evil in every human being' (VI.4 1318b39–1319a1). Man becomes the worst of animals when he lacks law and virtue (I.2 1253a31–7). See too II.7 1267a41–b5, VII.15 1334a25–8.

requires all children to be properly educated, and because, among adult citizens, it encourages the kinds of common activity (drama, worship, common meals) that bring out the best in human nature.

I have said that, in his construction of an ideal society, Aristotle does not seek to create a private realm in which the obligation to contribute to the common good is suspended, and the citizen is allowed to do as he pleases, even if in doing so he harms himself. But it might be objected that the distinction he makes between work and leisure, which we discussed in 6.3, is much the same thing as a distinction between public and private. After all, during periods of leisure the citizens of his ideal city are relieved of their political responsibilities. While they listen to music, they seem to be doing nothing for the common good. So perhaps Aristotle in effect agrees with democrats that the claims of the city do not extend beyond a fixed limit.

But it would be a mistake to take him to mean that citizens should do as they please when they are at leisure, or that they are not to be criticized by other citizens if they misuse their time. Periods of leisure are to be used well; this is not a realm in which one is at liberty to harm oneself or engage in activities that make one a less useful member of the community. On the contrary, he thinks that listening to music is a good way to fill one's leisure not only because music conveys a kind of wisdom and truth that is valued for itself, but also because it provides relaxation and thus allows one to return to work.[37] The arduous business of public deliberation is enhanced, not undermined, when citizens enjoy a period of relaxation in which their thoughts are occupied by the words of poets and dramatists. Even if, during these periods of relaxation, they are not deliberating about the good of their fellow citizens, they will be better able to discharge their public role when they return to it, because they have recently enjoyed a period of leisure.

6.7. Utilitarianism and the Common Good

We have just taken note of a powerful strain in modern thought that parts company with Aristotle and sides with the ancient democrats. But we should also recognize that there is a modern philosophical school—utilitarianism—whose doctrine resembles Aristotle's in

---

[37] See e.g. VIII.5 1339b10–31; for other passages, see 6.nn.18 and 19.

6.7. UTILITARIANISM AND THE COMMON GOOD

some respects. Its ultimate principle, roughly expressed, is that each action must be aimed at the maximization of the good of the whole.[38] Like Aristotle, the utilitarian does not recognize the existence of a realm in which we are free to make whatever decisions we wish, even if this hurts ourselves or diminishes our contributions to the larger whole. Accordingly, the utilitarian would have to agree with him that if allowing parents to educate their children as they please is less advantageous for the community than requiring all to attend public schools, then private education should be forbidden. What Aristotle and the utilitarian share is the principle that the individual should regard himself as a part of a larger whole and should lead his life in a way that enables him to promote the good of the whole. They do not urge the individual to count himself as nothing; after all, he is one part of the whole. But they agree that we should live not just for ourselves or for our intimate friends and family; we should look upon ourselves as a part of a wider community, and rather than build a wall to protect ourselves from the demands of that community, we should actively promote its good.

It is just as important, however, to notice some major differences between Aristotle and the utilitarian. To begin with, Aristotle holds that the good we are to aim at is the good of our political community. Some people will be members of it, but others will not; it is only the former who are included in the common good. Utilitarianism, by contrast, makes one a citizen of the world: it is the good of all human beings (or perhaps all rational beings, or all sentient creatures) that one must serve. Even if we are seldom in a position to benefit others because of their great distance from us, we are in principle required to exclude no one as a possible object of beneficence. Aristotle's moral universe is limited and closed; the utilitarian's is infinite.

Second, utilitarianism holds that how the good is distributed is not in itself a relevant moral consideration. It does not insist that in each of our actions we benefit all, for as we have just noted, there is no limit to who is included in 'all', and we are seldom if ever in a position to perform an act that does some good for everyone. Rather, the utilitarian's goal is to produce the largest possible aggregate of good over evil. It does not matter how many benefit and how many

---

[38] A principal text is Mill's *Utilitarianism*. Although his highest ethical principle is to maximize the good—a principle that in itself permits interfering with freedom—his substantive conception of the good and his sociology lead him to believe that in the right conditions the good is maximized by leaving people a significant zone of freedom.

lose, so long as we achieve the highest sum, after subtracting losses from gains. Doing a great deal of good for just one person would be better than doing a small amount of good for many, if the benefit concentrated in the one is larger than the aggregate spread out over many.

By contrast, the smaller community of Aristotle's philosophy makes it a feasible idea that the good of *all* members should be each citizen's target. He insists that the *common* good is the proper goal of public life (III.7 1279a28–30), and this means the good of all citizens, not the highest aggregate of gains over losses. It must be emphasized that the common good at which the citizen ought to aim includes his own—it is not merely the good of others. One would not be aiming at the common good if one's political deliberations excluded one's own well-being from consideration. By contrast, the ultimate principle of utilitarianism requires individuals to make great sacrifices in their own happiness (or anyone else's), if that is what it takes to maximize the good.

The willingness of utilitarianism to sacrifice some for others, if doing so maximizes the good, is one of its troubling features. Since it looks only to the sum total of good accomplished, it permits the thought that the world should be divided into winners and losers, if the combination of gains and losses produces the largest sum. By contrast, Aristotle's idea that the polis should promote the good of all citizens does not allow a division of the city into winners and losers. Such factionalism would be the death of a city. But even though this aspect of Aristotle's social thought is highly appealing, it has an ugly corollary, which has already been mentioned: those who are excluded from citizenship receive little or no attention. Citizens and political leaders are to promote the good of other *citizens*—not other human beings. The well-being of the community requires that it be limited in population (VII.4), and those who are outside it are of no direct concern. At most, the city will try to keep resident aliens satisfied because it needs their services. Utilitarianism, to its credit, requires us to have a wider concern than this.

A plausible moral theory must try to combine Aristotle's emphasis on the common good with the utilitarian's broader reach. It would recognize our responsibility to contribute to the good of our local communities, but would also require us to be good members of more global communities. Although Aristotle is wrong to devote so little attention to those excluded from citizenship, we can

6.7. UTILITARIANISM AND THE COMMON GOOD

state in general terms how his error ought to be corrected: although the condition of one's own country and one's fellow citizens should be a matter of great concern, they should not be all one cares about.[39]

One other point must be emphasized, before we return to our examination of the ideal polis. As we saw in the preceding section, Aristotle sometimes speaks of the citizen as a part of a larger whole. We need a common education, he says, because no citizen 'belongs to himself; rather all of them belong to the city, for each is a part of the city' (VIII.1 1337a27–9). There are a number of other passages in which he goes farther and compares the whole city to an organism and each of the citizens to differentiated parts.[40] This way of talking appeals to him because it makes the point that each of us should contribute to the political community, as a hand contributes to the whole body. And the analogy with organisms also conveys the suggestion that different kinds of citizen have different contributions to make; just as hands and feet do different jobs, so too do young and old, rich and poor. But we should not take this comparison between a city and an organism to mean that the well-being of the city is something other than the well-being of its citizens. As Aristotle says, a number can be even without its parts being even, but the happiness of a city exists only by virtue of the happiness of all or most of its parts (II.5 1264b17–22).[41] In a city of 5000 happy citizens, there are not 5001 happy things: the citizens plus the city. The city's

---

[39] Admittedly, this statement is too general to resolve the question of how strong one's cosmopolitan obligations are, in comparison with one's commitments to one's own political community. For discussion, see the contributions in Nussbaum, *For Love of Country*. I am in agreement with Walzer's statement: 'A particularism that excludes wider loyalties invites immoral conduct, but so does a cosmopolitanism that overrides narrower loyalties' (p. 127). But as he recognizes ('the argument needs to be cast in different terms'), this does not get us very far.

[40] See e.g. I.2 1253a20–5, III.4 1277a5–6, IV.4 1290b23–39, V.3 1302b33–1303a2, V.9 1309b18–35. (The gist of these passages is given in 7.n.18.) At VII.4 1326a35–b1, he compares the city both to living things and to artifacts, because the point he is making (the city must be neither too large nor too small) is illustrated equally well by both analogies. In all but one of the passages referred to in the first sentence of this note, Aristotle could have used an analogy between the polis and an artifact to make his point, which is simply that the city is composed of unlike parts. The exception is the first passage: I.2 1253a20–5, which compares the relation between citizen and city to that of hand and body. Here it is crucial to Aristotle's point that a so-called hand that is separated from the body is a hand in name only. The precise meaning of that analogy will be our subject in Ch. 7. But, whatever his point is, it is not one that he believes he could make equally well through an analogy with artifacts. For he does not claim e.g. that the mast of a ship is only a mast so-called, when it is separated from the ship.

[41] See too VII.9 1329a22–4.

happiness is just another way of referring to those 5000 happy citizens. Like the utilitarian, Aristotle aims at the general good by aiming at the good of individuals.[42]

6.8. Non-citizens

Women, manual workers, and slaves are denied citizenship in the ideal city.[43] Slavery will fully occupy us in Chapter 8. Our present concern is Aristotle's basis for not allowing manual workers to play a role in managing the political institutions (the assembly and courts) of this community.

But we begin with a word about the exclusion of women from the political realm—not merely from the politics of the ideal city, but from the political life of any of the constitutions that Aristotle considers. Although Plato had proposed that in an ideal city political office would be open to women, Aristotle denies them a civic role, both in ideal and non-ideal polities, because he holds the view, prevalent in his time, that they are not as capable as men (Greek men, that is) in the realm of politics. They have the mental capacity to oversee certain household tasks (6.n.13), but Aristotle says that their deliberative faculty lacks authority (I.13 1260a13), and he takes this to be an unalterable deficiency. It is unclear what sort of deficiency he is talking about. Precisely what is the deliberative faculty? In what way does it lack authority in women? These questions (particularly the first) will be discussed in the next chapter, when we turn to Aristotle's justification of slavery, for his defense of this institution depends on his thesis that those who are slaves by nature *entirely* lack the deliberative faculty (I.13 1260a12). We can learn something about what he thinks is wrong with women if we

---

[42] For a fuller discussion of this issue, see Miller, *NJR*, pp. 53-6, 194-224. I agree with his conclusion that Aristotle is a 'moderate individualist' (pp. 198-204) in this sense: the good of the whole city consists simply in the good of all the citizens—though this is not something they can achieve in isolation from each other or by treating each other as mere means to their own ends.

[43] As citizenship is defined in III.1, Aristotle refuses this status to women, since he thinks that there is no city in which they should be allowed to participate in the assembly or the courts. But there is a secondary sense in which he does count them as citizens, since he favors restricting citizenship to males whose fathers *and mothers* are citizens (VI.4 1319b9-10; cf. III.2 1275b33, III.5 1278a28). Accordingly, the definition of citizenship in III.1 must be regarded as a definition of full citizenship, and this is the status denied to women. See 10.n.10 and Keyt, 'Aristotle and Anarchism', pp. 140-1.

6.8. NON-CITIZENS

concentrate on a kindred deficiency that he thinks is more severe in slaves.[44]

Unlike women, manual workers did participate in the political process of many Greek cities. But Aristotle excludes all those who work for a living—farmers, craftsmen, unskilled laborers, and the like—from membership in the ideal city. He often speaks of craftsmen as 'banausoi' ('the vulgar'), and his distaste for them was widely shared in the ancient world.[45] Why does he exclude them from citizenship and forbid his citizens from doing such work? He does not claim that they have any natural deficiency, as do women and slaves. They have the capacity to deliberate and to control their emotions. But this makes it mysterious that they should be excluded from political life.

Aristotle says little to justify his policy; he simply remarks that their activities make it impossible for them to develop and practice virtue.[46] That is, although they had the natural capacity for virtue when they were born, their training, habits, and daily occupations

---

[44] It is possible that Aristotle's statement about women at 1260a13 means that although they are equal to men in deliberative capacity, the unruliness of their emotions limits the kind of power that should be entrusted to them. But I doubt that he is willing to pay that high compliment to their rationality. See 8.n.22 for my further thoughts on this topic. For further reading, see: Cook, 'Sexual Inequality in Aristotle's Theories of Reproduction and Inheritance'; Fortenbaugh, 'Aristotle on Slaves and Women'; Matthews, 'Gender and Essence in Aristotle'; Modrak, 'Aristotle: Women, Deliberation, and Nature'; Mulgan, 'Aristotle and the Political Role of Women'; Nichols, *Citizens and Statesmen*, pp. 31–2; Salkever, *Finding the Mean*, pp. 178–204; Saxonhouse, 'Family, Polity, and Unity'; Smith, 'Plato and Aristotle on the Nature of Women'; Swanson, *The Public and the Private in Aristotle's Political Philosophy*, pp. 44–68.

[45] The term has some elasticity, and can be applied to anyone who relies too heavily on the body and leaves the mind underdeveloped (musical virtuosos, VIII.6 1341b8–18; Spartan warriors, VIII.4 1338b29–36). But typically Aristotle uses it far more narrowly. At *Pol.* I.11 1258b25–7, he distinguishes a banausos, who has some skill, from an unskilled worker (so too III.4 1277a39–b1), but several lines later, at b37, he says that the more an employment uses the body the more banausic it is. Banausoi are distinguished from farmers, traders, and unskilled workers at IV.4 1290b39–1291a6; see too *EE* I.4 1215a28–32. For a brief account of this widespread prejudice, see Austin and Vidal-Naquet, *Economic and Social History of Greece*, pp. 11–18. In several passages, Aristotle distinguishes between those who have mastered the intellectual component of a craft like medicine and those who practice medicine or any other craft without understanding its rationale. See e.g. *NE* I.13 1102a21–3 and *Pol.* III.11 1282a3–5; these passages are discussed at 8.6 below. He does not include the former group among banausoi, and does not believe that they must be excluded from citizenship in his ideal city or any real city.

[46] See *Pol.* III.5 1277b33–7, VII.9 1328b33–1329a2, VIII.2 1337b8–15. For the view that Aristotle's refusal to give citizen status to craftsmen violates his own principles, see Nussbaum, 'Nature, Function, and Capability'. My own view is closer to that of Charles, 'Comments on M. Nussbaum'. These issues are discussed by Mulgan, 'Was Aristotle an "Aristotelian Social Democrat"?' For Nussbaum's reply, see her 'Aristotle, Politics, and Human Capabilities', pp. 108–116.

have blocked the development of virtue. But why does Aristotle assume that working for a living has this effect? He expects his audience to agree with him so readily that he wastes no time justifying himself. Even so, we can form a reasonable conjecture about what stands behind his prejudice.

First, although a craftsman or a farmer uses reason in his work, he gives this faculty a very narrow employment: he is trained from childhood to think about how to achieve a predetermined end—building a ship, or making a pair of shoes. Certain kinds of workers do not use their minds at all, but are entirely occupied with hard physical labor. But all of those whom Aristotle calls banausoi work solely in order to make money, for they would gladly give up their work if they did not need to make a living (*NE* I.5 1096a5–7; *EE* I.4 1215a25–37). None of them has sufficient time to take thought about the larger issues that face the polis. They spend their days selling their labor and their bodies for money, and this colors their approach to political issues. Since their day-to-day relations with others are largely instrumental, and their minds have not been enlarged by an education befitting a free person, they are highly imperfect participants in discussions of public issues.[47]

Nearly every society stigmatizes certain kinds of work. The job of hangman, for example, is dishonored even where hanging is widely accepted as a method of punishment. Similarly, the feeling that it is degrading to sell one's body for sexual use is common in many societies. Athens was no exception: any male who had ever engaged in homosexual intercourse for gain was in effect deprived of his citizen rights.[48] Such transactions were thought to make one unfit to participate in civic affairs; if one was willing to sell one's body, surely one could be bribed or bought in all sorts of other ways. What lies behind Aristotle's prejudice against banausoi is an extension of this way of thinking. To be forced by the necessities of life to use one's

---

[47] Aristotle holds in *Pol.* III that in a well-governed polis citizens deliberate about the common good and do not treat politics as a source of personal enrichment or an arena of domination. The conjecture I make in this paragraph is that he wishes to exclude banausoi from membership in an ideal city because their work makes it difficult or impossible for them to live up to this standard. Note that one goal of Aristotelian education is to prevent the formation of a narrow utilitarian outlook; children study music and drawing because 'to search everywhere for what is useful is what least suits those who are great in soul and free' (VIII.3 1338b2–4). Presumably he thinks that because banausoi have not received this breadth of education, they have no skill in any other form of practical reasoning except instrumental reasoning.

[48] For discussion, see MacDowell, *The Law in Classical Athens*, p. 126; Cohen, *Law, Sexuality, and Society*, p. 176.

6.8. NON-CITIZENS

body or one's mind principally as a means of survival does not befit a free citizen.

In explaining Aristotle's prejudice in this way, I am not proposing (absurdly) that we should instill in ourselves the feeling of disgust or contempt that he and many other members of his society felt towards manual work. But I suggest that there is something in that prejudice that still bears thinking about: Aristotle may be right that good public discussion requires those participating in it to have an outlook that is not fostered, and may even be undermined, by certain kinds of training and work. If one's occupation and one's preparation for it are entirely dominated by the need to make money and accumulate possessions, what effect will this have on the way one looks at issues facing the polis? It cannot be easy to shift perspectives: to be occupied, for much of the day, with maximizing one's profits and outdoing one's competitors; and then to adopt a cooperative and non-commercial outlook when one reflects, as a citizen, on the good of the whole community. Aristotle's concern about mixing politics and money-making is understandable. Ideally, one does not want to live among fellow citizens who evaluate political issues solely from their own narrow financial perspectives.[49]

But even if we agree, at least tentatively, that Aristotle has a point, the social structure of his ideal city might seem repellent. It is sharply divided into haves and have-nots. On the one hand, there are the citizens: they have inherited enough property (in the form of land, slaves, and the like) to be free of the need to work for wages. They do not till the soil, or buy and sell for profit, or engage in craft activity.[50] Nothing they do is done merely in order to earn a living. Furthermore, they are the ones who make political decisions (6.10). Other inhabitants lack citizen status, have no political power, and do all of the arduous physical work.

It seems obvious that this arrangement is unjust. Can anything be said in Aristotle's defense? There is no point asking whether he is right to have his citizens depend on slave labor, or to exclude women

---

[49] See 12.8 and 13.2 for further discussion.

[50] See *Pol.* VII.9 1328b39–41, 1329a17–26. According to Davies, *Wealth and the Power of Wealth in Classical Athens*, pp. 9–37, Athens contained about 400 men in the fifth century, and 300 in the fourth, who belonged to the leisure class and bore the financial burdens of the city. Aristotle's ideal city will presumably have more citizens than that. (A fighting force much smaller than 1,000 would make the city vulnerable to conquest; see 1.4, 6.3.) Perhaps he is assuming that his citizens will not need resources so great as those of the Athenian leisured class, in order to be relieved of the necessity to work. In fact, some of them will require the financial assistance of their fellow citizens, even though they are wealthy enough to live in leisure. See 6.9, esp. 6.n.61.

from citizenship. We know that Aristotle is wrong about these issues. (We will ask in Chapter 8 what sort of mistake he made, in his attempt to justify slavery.) The more interesting question is whether there is anything *else* objectionable about his ideal city, once we set these errors aside.[51] Is it wrong, for example, for some people to have so many resources that they do not have to work for a living? That would not be a plausible complaint about Aristotle's model city. For everyone who is retired is in this enviable position, and surely there is no moral objection to retirement. But perhaps what bothers us about the citizens of his utopia is that they have all inherited considerable wealth at birth. They never had to work for a living. But why should we object to that? Suppose *all of us* had enough wealth to escape the need to choose a line of work merely as a way of making money. And suppose our resources could be handed down from one generation to another. Would that not be an ideal situation?

Perhaps the real problem with Aristotle's scheme (aside from its dependence on slavery and the subordination of women) is that his wealthy citizens are living off the backs of non-citizens who are far less fortunate. It can be conceded that a group of people who have enough resources to avoid the burdens of earning a living are doing nothing wrong—provided everyone on whom they depend is equally free of these burdens. It is unjust for some to do well, if they do so at the expense of others. That seems to be one of the fundamental moral principles that Aristotle is violating, in his construction of an ideal city.

A defense of Aristotle would have to proceed along the following lines. Suppose that the craftsmen, farmers, retailers, and unskilled laborers who move to the new city work for wages and are not slaves. Let us assume that they have freely chosen to reside and work there rather than elsewhere, because this is a peaceful community, wages are high, and working conditions are not harsh. They have been told, before arriving, that they will not be allowed to

---

[51] It should be kept in mind that although Aristotle hopes to find enough slaves to do the farm work, he mentions a second-best alternative to this arrangement: the farmers might instead be 'foreigners who live in outlying areas' (*barbaroi perioikoi*, 'non-Greek subject peoples' in Reeve's translation). See VII.6 1327b11–12, VII.9 1329a26, VII.10 1330a25–31. Sparta, Crete, and many other Greek cities depended on the farm labor of *perioikoi*. See Kraut, *Aristotle: Politics Books VII and VIII*, pp. 116–17. We should have no doubts about the injustice of Aristotle's second-best alternative; though *perioikoi* were not property, their status was one of servitude. The question I am pursuing is whether there would still be an injustice in Aristotle's ideal city if its farmers and laborers were neither slaves nor *perioikoi*, but *free* non-citizens.

6.8. NON-CITIZENS

participate in the collective decision-making processes of the new city, and they gladly accept these terms. Is it clear that, in these circumstances, Aristotle's citizens would be doing well at the expense of non-citizen workers?

Aristotle's restrictions on who may be a citizen of his model community are not arbitrary. Since he is constructing the best possible city, he is justified in making great demands on his citizens. Citizenship in this city is a major responsibility that requires a certain level of education and a large commitment of time. Citizens are office-holders of the highest order, not mere voters in occasional elections (6.10). They should undertake no pursuits that would interfere with their full realization as human beings, or that would undermine their ability to deliberate as free and independent persons seeking to promote the common good. If one spends most of one's time working at a job that one is forced to accept only as a way of making money, one is quite distant from a life that meets anyone's idea, let alone Aristotle's, of well-being. Were citizenship granted to all residents, or to all those on whom the city depends for resources, the quality of public decision-making would decline markedly, and the city would no longer be ideal.

It is understandable that Aristotle should be far more restrictive in granting citizen rights than are ordinary cities and states. But in fact, no political community offers rights of citizenship to all who request it. Modern nation-states make few demands on their citizens, but even so, applicants for citizen status are required to meet certain standards. Those who have criminal records, for example, are normally disqualified. Nor do states give citizenship rights to all those on whom they economically depend. Most of them would collapse were it not for the imported goods made by the workers of foreign nations, and yet foreign workers are not allowed to vote. The state is by its very nature an exclusionary organization: it makes a distinction between insiders and outsiders, and does not allow outsiders the privileges of insiders.[52]

---

[52] We should also keep in mind how much the educational institutions of modern states, both public and private, seek to insure that future citizens will acquire the moral attitudes that will make them acceptable as citizens. Note the way Rorty addresses hypothetical parents who resist having their children read certain books: 'There are credentials for admission to our democratic society, credentials which we liberals have been making more stringent by doing our best to excommunicate racists, male chauvinists, homophobes, and the like. You have to be *educated* in order to be a citizen of our society, a participant in our conversation, someone with whom we can envisage merging our horizons. So we are going to go right on trying to discredit you in the eyes of your children, trying to strip your fundamentalist religious community of dignity, trying to make your views seem silly

Suppose the world's material resources were far more abundant, and machines did all of our work for us.[53] Suppose all human beings had the wealth and education that Aristotle prescribes for members of his ideal community. If we think that, in these circumstances, a life organized along the lines of Books VII and VIII would be splendid, then we have accepted a great deal of Aristotle's political philosophy. He does not imagine a world made up of many ideal cities, each with sufficient resources to support a well-lived life for every citizen. Instead, when he expresses his hopes for the future, he thinks in terms of a single ideal city, one that has relations—possibly hostile—with highly imperfect cities, and economically supported by people who do not have the potential, or no longer have a chance, to live a good life. That single city is the most he can realistically wish for, and because he does not envision a radical transformation of the world, but a practicable scheme, his city contains a citizen class that depends for its resources on non-citizen inhabitants who are far less well off. But he would rejoice at the creation of a world in which many ideal cities exist, and every human being meets his high demands for citizenship. And he would reject the idea that no single ideal city should be constructed, until the world is blessed with as many cities as are needed to support the full realization of the entire human race.

Perhaps, then, our dissatisfaction with Aristotle's utopia can be put this way: he expresses no hope for the entire human race, but only for a small portion of it. He assumes that the most we can realistically wish for is that a small fraction of humankind will understand their good, and will have the resources needed to live together in a self-governing community. When he envisions the best possible future, his vision is occluded, because he cannot see any possibility that all people might live as his ideal citizens do.

6.9. Common Meals and Equal Citizens

Aristotle says that each citizen is to own one plot of land near the urban center and another closer to its perimeter (VII.10 1330a9–25,

---

rather than discussable. We are not so inclusivist as to tolerate intolerance such as yours.' See 'Universality and Truth', p. 22.

[53] Remarkably, Aristotle notes that slaves would not be needed if tools could follow our instructions on their own (*Pol.* I.4 1253b33–1254a1). His point, however, is that this can never happen; the need for slaves is permanent.

6.9. COMMON MEALS AND EQUAL CITIZENS

discussed more fully in 6.11 and 9.7). The language of this passage calls for the territory to be divided in certain ways, and there is no mention of its sale or purchase. In other words, parcels of land are distributed to citizens according to a certain pattern, and are not bought from previous owners or put up for auction. It would be reasonable to assume, in these conditions, that there will be an initial division of land into *equal* lots, at least if there are no variations in the quality of the soil or other significant differences. There is no reason why one citizen should have more than another.[54] What we know about Greek colonies confirms this conjecture. Some of them, at any rate, were established by means of founding decrees that call for an equal division of land.[55]

Although citizens of the ideal city do not need to acquire the necessities of life, they are not likely to have equal economic resources. Some of them will surely enter their new community with more money, slaves, or other forms of property than others. At any rate, Aristotle says nothing to suggest that those who have more must leave their excess behind, when they join the colony. And even if they happened to be equal in wealth when they joined the new community, it is unlikely that this situation will persist. As Aristotle recognizes, chance plays a role in determining how many external resources one has.[56] Fortune smiles on some more than others, and so citizens will eventually have unequal resources, unless the city maintains such equality by making constant adjustments. There is no evidence that Aristotle favors such ongoing enforcement of economic equality, and some evidence to the contrary. In II.7 he criticizes a certain Phaleas, who proposed equality of holdings (9.20). In Book VII there is a passage, to which we will now turn, in which Aristotle calls for the support of citizens whose households fall on hard times. Evidently, his approach to economic misfortune is to alleviate its effects whenever it occurs, not to maintain a constant equality of resources.

Economic assistance is discussed briefly in connection with a Greek social institution called *syssitia*, 'common meals', which took different forms in different cities. In Athens, the members of the council (the body that prepared the business of the assembly of

---

[54] 'It is reasonable to think, with respect to external resources that have not been acted upon by anyone, that no one has more right to them than anyone else does, and that equal rights in them should therefore be instituted.' Thus Cohen, *Self-Ownership, Freedom, and Equality*, p. 110.

[55] See Graham, *Colony and Mother City in Ancient Greece*, p. 59.

[56] *NE* I.8 1099a31-b7, I.9 1100a8–9; *Pol.* VII.12 1331b19–22.

all citizens) ate their meals together. In some other cities—in Sparta, Crete, and Carthage, for example—the institution encompassed all citizens, or at any rate those who could afford the expense. Aristotle proposes that in the ideal city all male citizens should participate, regardless of their economic position. He does not advocate one large mess hall, but rather several smaller arrangements—some for soldiers, others for magistrates, and so on.[57] Each citizen is to be a member of one of these smaller communities.

What is the purpose of this institution? Aristotle says at one point that he will answer this question (VII.10 1330a3–5)—but this is one of several promises made in VII and VIII that are not kept (5.n.11). We can be certain, however, that the sole or principal function of common meals is not to get food into the stomachs of the citizens. The citizens normally have adequate resources; they live in their own houses and own their own land. They can therefore usually feed themselves and their families, and do not have to rely on the city for the necessities of life. Admittedly, Aristotle says, at one point in VII.10, that 'none of the citizens should be in need of food' (1330a2)—suggesting that at times some citizens may fall on such hard times that they will need food from others, and that this should be provided to them. But his very next words ('as for common meals', a3) suggest that the provision of food to those in need and common meals are two independent aspects of the ideal city. Since the citizens are normally wealthy enough to live at leisure, only occasional and extreme misfortune could force them to turn to others for food; and that sustenance could easily be supplied by friends or communal methods of distribution.[58] Common meals would be an absurdly extravagant institution if their sole or principal purpose were to address the occasional problem of poverty.

It is more likely that they are primarily meant to serve a social purpose: to provide a regular occasion for citizens to associate with each other and to discuss common concerns. At VII.17 1336b9–10, Aristotle talks of 'reclining' at the common meals, implying with the use of this term that on some occasions the common meals are followed by *symposia*, which traditionally offered an occasion for

---

[57] On common meals in the ideal city, see VII.10 1329b5–1330a13, VII.12 1331a19–28, b4–6; in Athens, *Ath. Pol.* 42.3, 43.3; in Sparta, *Pol.* II.9 1271a26–37, Plutarch, *Lycurgus*, XII.1, 4, 7, Xenophon, *Lacedaimonian Constitution*, 5.7: in Crete, *Pol.* II.10 1272a1–21; in Carthage, II.11 1172b33–4.

[58] Does Aristotle believe that those in need must rely on the voluntary support of friends, or does he favor the use of tax money for this purpose? We turn to that question in 9.18.

6.9. COMMON MEALS AND EQUAL CITIZENS

discussion, poetry, music, and relaxation.[59] At V.11 1313a41–b6, he says that tyrants often forbid the *syssitia* and other institutions of leisure, because they want the citizens to be unfamiliar to and distrustful of each other. So he sees common meals as a way of fostering civic friendship and trust.[60] He does not say that participation in this scheme is required, and that non-participation is to be punished. But presumably this is because his citizens will be happy to associate with each other in this way.

At one point (VII.10 1330a5–7) he says of the common meals: 'All of the citizens ought to share in them, although it is not easy for those without resources to contribute the payment from their private holdings and to manage the rest of their household in addition.' His point can best be understood if we compare what he says here to a complaint he makes (II.9 1271a26–39) about the Spartan system of common meals: the Spartans require each citizen to pay for what he consumes at these meals, and make no provision for those who are too poor to afford them. The result is that some citizens do not participate, and this undermines the democratic intent of the institution. (Conversely, at II.10 1272a12–26 he praises Crete for making the common meals available to all citizens at public cost.) There is no doubt, then, that Aristotle wants the common meals of his ideal city to be available to all of his citizens, and he proposes that they be publicly funded (VII.10 1330a9–13), in order to insure the participation of those whose resources have become insufficient. His assumption is that economic hardship cannot always be avoided, even among those who start off with abundant resources and have been diligent and cautious in overseeing their property. His solution to this problem is not to impose on all citizens a periodic equalization of their resources, but to free all of them from the burden of having to contribute individually to the cost of the common meals. That allows every citizen to feel confident that economic misfortune will not force him to sever his social ties and become a second-class citizen. Should some of them fall into poverty so extreme that they cannot even feed themselves, then the common meals can be used to play a double role. They will not only enable

---

[59] See Hornblower and Spawforth, *The Oxford Classical Dictionary*, s.v. 'symposium', 'syssitia'.

[60] See too II.5 1263b31–1264a1, where he advocates common meals as a way of promoting the proper kind of civic unity. Civic friendship will be more full discussed in Chs. 9 (esp. 9.5, 9.6, 9.10, 9.16, 9.22) and 12 (12.3, 12.9).

these citizens to continue to share fully in the social life of the community, but will also put food in their mouths.

These are not the only ways in which the ideal city protects those who become poor.[61] Education is provided to the children of all citizens, as we have noted (6.3). Even if a father's resources are depleted, he can be assured that his children will receive the same education as all others. The musical festivals funded by the city are also available to all citizens, regardless of their resources.[62] And of course no citizen will be required or allowed to give up his political activities because of his poverty. In all these ways—in their common meals, schools, festivals, and political assembly—citizens will be equals, whether they are rich or poor. If they have few personal resources, they will be no worse off, at least in these respects, than those who have more. In the ideal constitution, economic differences have little significance. Since citizens have a common understanding of their good, each regards wealth as a mere instrument that contributes to well-being only to the extent that it can be used to promote excellent activities. Because civic arrangements guarantee each citizen sustenance and an equal role in communal life, those who have less will not envy the rich, and the rich will have nothing to fear from the poor. Class conflict—the common poison of ordinary civic life (12.3–9)—is entirely absent.

6.10. Governance

We have discussed some of the educational, social, and economic arrangements of Aristotle's ideal city, but have said nothing so far about what surely ought to be the most important institutions of all, particularly in a work called *Politics*, namely the political structures

---

[61] Here 'poor' is used to refer to anyone whose resources are not fully adequate for civic purposes. Aristotle does not balk at saying that some of his citizens may be *aporoi*, 'lacking in resources', and this is the term he often uses as the opposite of *euporoi* ('wealthy', 'great in resources'). See VII.10 1330a6, and cf. II.9 1271a30. But these 'poor' citizens have enough slaves to avoid the need to labor on their land or work for wages, and Aristotle's contemporaries would therefore have considered them rich. See Ober, *Mass and Elite in Democratic Athens*, pp. 194–5. If we ask whether the less fortunate citizens of Aristotle's ideal city are 'really' poor or 'really' rich, the answer of course is that there is no fact of the matter. But there is something to be said for Aristotle's idea that when one's resources require one to rely on transfers mandated by one's city, that is a kind of poverty.

[62] Aristotle does not discuss the way in which the ideal city will fund musical performances, but he presupposes that they will be paid for, as they were in Athens, by wealthy individuals who are expected to undertake expensive projects (known as 'liturgies') that serve the common good. See 9.9 for further discussion.

of the best constitution. How will decisions be made? What sort of offices will there be? How will power be distributed? These are major issues in some parts of the *Politics*, particularly in Books III–VI, but they do not preoccupy Aristotle in VII and VIII. For example: in IV.15 and VI.8 he enumerates the kinds of office that cities need, and the various methods of filling them (a topic that Plato had treated extensively in the *Laws*); but in VII and VIII he says almost nothing about this. He happens to mention the minor position of forest warden (VII.12 1331b15)—but says nothing about the selection of generals, financial officers, juries, and so on. The major political organizations and offices of the ideal city are not described, nor does Aristotle promise that he will write about them at a later point. The most likely explanation for this gap is that he expects his readers to apply to the ideal constitution many of the points that are made about offices in other books of the *Politics*. A fresh treatment is not needed in Books VII and VIII, because offices needed in all cities are obviously necessary in the ideal city as well.

But Book VII is not entirely silent on the question of who should rule. Aristotle begins his discussion of this topic in VII.14 with the remark that if there were a group of individuals who manifestly surpassed, in body and soul, their fellows by as much as gods and heroes surpass us human beings, then that group should permanently rule, and all others should obey. But, he immediately adds, there are no such superhuman beings. He might have posited their existence—after all, he is constructing an imaginary community, and is not confined to using only those resources that currently exist—but he does not do so. Presumably that is because he is building the best *possible* city, and he interprets this limitation to mean that it must not depend on the existence of an entirely new species—a race whose better-than-human soul would require a better-than-human body in which to operate.[63] There are no such extraordinary beings, and there is no reason to believe there ever will be. They are therefore outside the realm of practicability.[64]

---

[63] For a contrasting view, see Vander Waerdt, 'Kingship and Philosophy in Aristotle's Best Regime'. He holds that since, at the end of Book III, Aristotle takes kingship and aristocracy to be the best regimes, he must be making this assumption in VII and VIII as well; the rotation scheme of VII.14 is therefore intended as a second best, to be used when kingly individuals are not available. But as I read Book III, it merely affirms the superiority of kingship and aristocracy to polity, but refrains from comparing rule by one or a few with the constitution described in Books VII and VIII. We will return to this issue in 10.1 and 11.13.

[64] When Aristotle says that this manifestly superhuman race is 'not easily found' (1332b23), I take him to be understating his point for humorous effect. There are many

But there have been *some* good human beings—people, that is, who possess the ethical virtues as Aristotle describes them in the *Ethics*. And if there have been some, there is no reason why there might not be more. The best feasible community we can hope for is one that is filled with the sort of people who fully measure up to Aristotle's standards of excellence. Since it is far better for *all* of the adult male citizens of this community to be virtuous than for some of them to fall short in this respect, the ideal city will be a society of people who have equal moral skills. They are equal in their ability to deliberate about the affairs of the community, and Aristotle therefore says that it would unjust for one of them to be given more power or authority than any other (1332b26-9).

Of course, this regime of equal power does not apply to the young. Aristotle assumes that they do not yet have the ability, experience, or knowledge necessary for governing the city. Their contribution to the polis is military rather than deliberative (VII.9 1329a6-17), and since they know that eventually they will be admitted to positions of power, they will have no reason to complain about their temporary powerlessness. The adult citizens will rule and be ruled by turns (VII.14 1332b26-9); the young will join this system of rotation when they reach the proper age.

Aristotle tacitly assumes that the most important decisions of the ideal city are made collectively by an assembly of which all male citizens are members. We know that there will be such a body, because when he discusses the size of the citizen population in VII.4, he says that there should not be so many that they cannot all hear the herald's voice (1326b5-7). The herald is the officer who opens and closes meetings, and calls speakers to the platform,[65] so Aristotle must be assuming that the citizens will regularly meet together as a group. What powers does this body have? In Athens, the assembly of all citizens was the supreme decision making power of the city; its agenda was prepared by a council of 500, but it was the assembly, not the council, that had the power of legislation, and it was therefore the more important body.[66] Aristotle never mentions

---

components of the ideal constitution that are 'not easily found', but that does not prevent Aristotle from including them in his construction. He does not impose on himself the limitation that the ideal city must be one that is easy to establish. We will return to the superhuman race in 6.11 and 11.14.

[65] See Hansen, *The Athenian Democracy*, p. 142.

[66] See Ober, *Mass and Elite in Democratic Athens*, p. 21. In the late fifth century, Athens made it more difficult to introduce new laws. See MacDowell, *The Law in Classical Athens*, pp. 46-52.

such a council in Books VII and VIII,[67] so even if he is tacitly assuming that there will be one, he is unlikely to have it in mind to assign it powers that significantly limit the authority of the assembly. For the collective authority of his citizens does not need to be restrained by some other civic body; they are all equally good men, so there is no need to pick out some small number of them to serve as a restraint on the rest. It is safe to assume, therefore, that the assembly to which all citizens belong is the supreme authority of the ideal city. This is the body that Aristotle has in mind in VII.9 when he says that there must be a deliberative body that makes decisions about what is advantageous and just (1329a2–4).

However, the assembly of all citizens cannot be the whole of the city's governmental apparatus. Aristotle assumes elsewhere that every city will need juries and a large number of officials, as we recently noted.[68] Some positions will be more important than others (generals and treasurers, for example), but in the ideal city, where citizens have the same education and moral skills, all will be equally capable of filling any of these offices. This does not mean that no job requires special training; generals, for example, must have a knowledge of strategy (NE I.1 1094a9). But Aristotle assumes that any citizen has the capacity to acquire such expertise. When he says that the adults will share in ruling and being ruled by turns (VII.14 1332b26–7), he means that no one will hold high office indefinitely; all will yield to others, through a system of rotation. It does not matter, then, that some offices are more powerful than others. All citizens have the same chance of being allotted high or low office. They have not only equal power as members of the assembly, but also an equal chance to participate at all levels in the apparatus of government.[69]

Throughout his discussion of governance in VII.14, Aristotle takes it for granted that positions of power (including the power of a member of the assembly) must be merited. That is precisely what we should expect of him, in light of the conception of distributive justice he puts forward in *Ethics* V.3 (4.11). His assignment of equal power to all citizens is not based on any assumption that the

---

[67] Elsewhere (IV.15 1299b30–1300a4, VI.8 1322b12–17), he makes a distinction between councils that are democratic and those that are oligarchic; the former merely serve the larger assembly, whereas the latter limit the authority of the people.

[68] See IV.14 1297b35–1298a3. Offices are most fully enumerated in IV.15 and VI.8.

[69] The contrast with the hierarchical governing structures prescribed by Plato's *Laws* is striking. For a brief account of these mechanisms, see Saunders, 'Plato's Later Political Thought', pp. 474–6.

external goods or resources needed for well-being should always be equally divided; on the contrary, as we have just seen (6.9), although he probably intends to divide parcels of land equally, he takes no steps to prevent some citizens from being wealthier than others. His citizens are equally entitled to participate in public discussion and to hold individual offices because they are equally qualified to do so, by virtue of their equal moral skills and education. This point emerges clearly when Aristotle says that because our minds are not at their best when we are old, the elderly should serve the city by holding religious rather than political offices (VII.9 1329a27–34). Positions of considerable power are not entitlements or rewards for past accomplishments; they must be merited by one's present qualifications. When those qualifications diminish, offices must be relinquished.

Aristotle is here making a remarkable assumption, and it is important not to overlook it. His ideal constitution assigns all major political responsibilities to citizens who are, in a certain sense, people of ordinary human ability. They have no exceptional natural talents, and are given no extensive training in specialized subjects, such as mathematics or law. The only geometry or science they have learnt, for example, is the kind that any 17-year-old can understand (6.3). Admittedly, they have developed a kind of wisdom—but this is wisdom about practical, not theoretical, matters; it does not require any exceptional facility in the study of mathematics or the natural world. The only inborn qualification for citizenship and high office in the ideal city is that one's reason should not be impaired—that one should not be a natural slave or a woman. Of course, the citizens of the ideal polity have received a good education and have developed good moral habits—an upbringing that Aristotle thinks is all too rare. Even so, he believes that any normal free child who is given a chance can learn what these ideal citizens have learnt. Their intellectual competence can be found among free men everywhere in Greece. What is remarkable, then, about Aristotle's ideal city is that it is ruled by amateurs: people of ordinary ability who have learnt no abstruse science accessible only to those of rare intellectual talent. The contrast with the ideal constitution of Plato's *Republic* is striking. No less significant is the contrast with the governance of modern nation-states, which depend so heavily on professionals who have received their technical training and credentials from academies that deny admission to all but a few. Modern democracies involve a complex interaction between elites and masses;

they assign considerable power to experts, and could not function without them. By contrast, Aristotle's ideal city is run by its citizens: they can read and write and have a non-specialist's grasp of the science of their times, but their principal qualifications are the ethical virtues and practical wisdom.[70]

Aristotle does not claim that the capacity to philosophize—and that includes the ability to write treatises on ethics, politics, and constitutional history—is found in a large part of the free population (6.3). He takes himself to have extraordinary political insight, and although he seeks to transmit it to a select group of students through his writings, he never suggests that the citizenry of the ideal community must be his equal in intellectual ability or accomplishment. But should Aristotle's writings and personal influence ever lead to the establishment of an ideal city, its government can be sustained without relying on Aristotle, or his talented students, or any other intellectual elite. So long as the corrupting influences of human nature are kept in check through education, the best city can flourish with nothing but ordinary human beings for its guide.

6.11. Disagreement

One of the arrangements that makes it easier for the citizens to live on friendly and just terms with each other is the division of privately owned land into two plots for each household, one on the outskirts of the territory, and the other near its urban center (VII.10 1330a9–23). This partition is necessary, Aristotle says, because if each citizen owns just one plot, and these vary significantly in their proximity to the outskirts, then some will be more exposed than others

---

[70] It is a reasonable conjecture that the citizens of the ideal city receive a general education in the Aristotelian sense: 'For every study and investigation, both humble and grand, there seem to be two levels of skill. One is rightly called scientific knowledge (*epistēmē*) of the subject, the other as it were a certain kind of education (*paideia*) in it. For it is characteristic of someone who has been educated in a certain manner to be able to distinguish successfully between what a speaker explains well and what he does not. That is the sort of person whom we think has a general education' (*Part. An.* I.1 639a1–7). A similar distinction is made at *Pol.* III.11 1282a3–4 between a doctor who has mastery over his subject and someone who is 'educated in the craft'. See too *NE* I.3 1095a1–2. Aristotle's citizens will presumably seek the advice of specialists who have scientific knowledge. Their exposure to the sciences will enable them to make good judgments about the quality of the advice they are getting. They never cede their decision-making responsibilities to experts in the sciences and crafts. (Of course, the broad education they receive between the ages of 14 and 17 will be far more rudimentary than the sophisticated general education Aristotle imparts to his own students in his scientific writings.)

to the dangers of military invasion, and this will create division when questions of war and peace are debated. We should take note of his assumption that even when people share a common conception of the good and are educated in ways that foster cooperation and civic friendship, their self-love and partial perspectives can set them at odds. The ideal city eliminates one source of bias and conflict among the citizens by making each equally exposed to military attack. Aristotle does not say: since these citizens are virtuous, nothing can divide them. Rather, he assumes—realistically—that moral education does not by itself eliminate conflict. Whenever possible, social arrangements should reduce the number of factors that make it difficult for citizens to live harmoniously with each other on terms they recognize as just.

Does Aristotle think of his ideal city as a place that has found a way to eliminate *all* disagreements among citizens about matters of common concern? Will everyone think alike not only about which goals are worthwhile, but about the best way, in any particular situation, to realize those goals?

We can make these questions more specific by asking what sort of voting rule will be used by the assembly of all citizens, whose job it is to 'make decisions about what is advantageous and judgments about what is just' (VII.9 1329a2–4). Obviously, there would be no need for such a deliberative body, if each citizen already knew, on his own and in isolation from others, which communal actions ought to be undertaken. Each would simply do his share to carry out the course of action that is obviously called for, and there would be no need for an assembly. Its meetings would be a waste of time. The very fact that the citizens do need to assemble and deliberate presupposes that they sometimes collectively face problems of some complexity—problems to which there is no single best solution immediately apparent to all. Aristotle's theory of deliberation emphasizes this point: we do not deliberate about what is straightforward and obvious (for example, how to write the letters of the alphabet), but only about those matters about which we feel divided and uncertain. Typically, our difficulties arise when we are dealing with matters that do not fall under exceptionless rules, and are subject to the unpredictability of the future (*NE* III.3 1112a34–b11).

We can assume, then, that when a meeting of the assembly begins, there is a deliberative problem whose solution is not evident to any of the citizens, even though they share the same goals and are men of practical wisdom. But what does Aristotle expect to occur, as their

6.11. DISAGREEMENT

meeting continues? Does he think that inevitably they will arrive at a plan of action that receives unanimous acceptance? Does he assume that they ought not to make a collective decision until they reach unanimous agreement? Unfortunately, he says nothing about this matter. He does not prescribe a voting rule for his assembly.

He does tell us, outside of Books VII and VIII, that the principle of majority rule is used in nearly every type of Greek political system—not just in democracies, but in oligarchies and aristocracies as well. (Needless to say, the rule is not used in a kingship.[71]) In one passage (IV.4 1290a30–1), he points out that democracy should not be defined as the political system in which the majority (*plēthos*) has authority. The reason why this characterization will not work is that 'in oligarchies and everywhere else the greater [*pleon*] part has authority' (a31–2). His point is that even when a few rule, they arrive at conflicting conclusions about what needs to be done, and to resolve these disagreements they use the principle of majority rule. Several chapters later, in IV.8, Aristotle repeats the point, and applies it to aristocracies no less than oligarchies and democracies. Here he characterizes aristocracy, oligarchy, and democracy in terms of their defining marks (*horoi*)—that is, the way of life or goal supported by their institutions. Aristocracy is defined in terms of virtue, oligarchy wealth, democracy freedom (1294a10–11). In all of them, 'whatever is thought by the majority [*pleiosin*] holds sway in every case. For in oligarchy, aristocracy, and democracy, whatever is thought by the major part of those who share in the constitution has authority' (a11–14). What is most significant about these lines, for our purposes, is the observation that even when a political system has virtue for its goal, the citizens are not always unanimous, and they therefore accept the principle of majority rule as the legitimate way to make decisions about matters of common concern.

These passages, however, do not give us a decisive answer to our question: they do not prove that, in Aristotle's opinion, the ideal city will also need to rely on the principle of majority rule. For the sorts of existing political system that Aristotle calls aristocracies in Book IV are not ideal constitutions.[72] They make room for the recognition

---

[71] I believe that this is why Aristotle ranks kingship above all the other constitutions in his usual sixfold taxonomy. See *NE* VIII.10 1160a35–6 and below, 11.15.

[72] Aristotle does not call the constitution of Books VII and VIII an aristocracy, but it has all the characteristics that he elsewhere associates with this kind of constitution: it denies citizenship to banausoi (III.5 1278a17–21), aims at what is best (III.7 1279a36), takes virtue for its goal (IV.8 1294a9–11), and requires rulers to be educated (*Rhet.* I.8 1365b33–4).

231

of moral excellence in their methods of distributing offices, but they also accord considerable power to ordinary free men as well as to wealthy elites (IV.7 1293b7–21). They are called aristocracies, but they might more properly be called mixed regimes, and in any case they are certainly inferior to the constitution Aristotle describes in Books VII and VIII. So it would be possible for him to say that although the so-called aristocracies that exist (for example, in Carthage and Sparta) rely on majority rule, the far superior aristocracy constructed in VII and VIII will not need this principle, because its citizens will always come to the same conclusion, whenever they deliberate together.

It would be possible for him to say this—but it would also be extremely foolish. It should be obvious to everyone, including Aristotle, that assemblies do not have unlimited amounts of time in which to make difficult decisions. They must often make do with partial information and ambiguous evidence. It is only to be expected that the initial differences of opinion and uncertainties with which collective decision-making begins cannot always be resolved within the time allotted, even when all participants are people of good will and practical intelligence. If an assembly fails to choose one of the alternatives under consideration, its failure to act will often make everyone worse off. So everyone benefits, over the long run, if they accept some procedural rule that allows their deliberations to issue in action, when differences of opinion persist.

It is highly unlikely that Aristotle failed to recognize these points, for the commonplaces just rehearsed are not at all foreign to his way of thinking. As we noted earlier in this section, he recognizes the uncertainties with which deliberation must cope (*NE* III.3 1112a34–b11). He describes it as a process that inherently resists routinization: whatever can be done by means of an exact science is not a matter that requires deliberation. He realizes that when we deliberate, we must make do with the unpredictability of the future. He suggests that even though the past often gives us some guidance, the generalizations that we have been able to formulate frequently admit of exceptions, and we must look to see whether the situation with which we are confronted has features that make this case exceptional. The aspects of deliberation that Aristotle explicitly recognizes ought to lead him to the conclusion that collective decisions cannot always be expected to be unanimous, even when those who make them are good people of considerable practical intelligence. Some rule will be needed, even in his ideal city, for

6.11. DISAGREEMENT

coping with situations where unanimity cannot be achieved in the time allotted. As we have seen, he is familiar with the widespread use of the principle of majority rule. Unless he is a fool, we can plausibly take him to be tacitly assuming that in his ideal city the assembly, like the decision-making bodies of countless Greek cities, will abide by that same principle. We need not attribute to him the idea that majority rule is the best or only method for making collective decisions in the face of disagreement. Rather, we can simply take him to be assuming that the ideal city will need some such method; and since he himself points out the prevalence of majority rule, he is likely to be taking it for granted that this method will be employed in the ideal constitution as well.

We should recall, at this point, that when Aristotle begins his discussion of governance in VII.14, he does not immediately announce that all citizens should share alike in holding office (6.10). Instead, he first engages in a bit of fantasy: suppose there were a race of superhumans who manifestly differed from their fellows, in body and soul, as much as gods and heroes differ from us. If we could find such a clan, they should be permanent rulers, and everyone else should gladly accept their superiority. But in their absence, the citizens of the best community ought to share offices equally (1332b16–27). Aristotle does not explain how those imaginary beings might be superior even to the citizens of his ideal city—and in fact, the very possibility of such superhumans might seem to create a puzzle. How can anyone be more qualified to rule than a citizen of the ideal city? After all, such a citizen receives an education designed to inculcate the ethical virtues. If that education is successful, he eventually acquires practical wisdom. How is it possible to improve on that?

We are now in a position to answer that question, if we take Aristotle to be assuming that his ideal citizens will often be uncertain and divided in their collective decision-making. We can say that their practical wisdom is not a superhuman ability to see quickly and clearly precisely what needs to be done in any situation. The governance of the ideal city will have to make do with the principle of majority rule, because its rulers are limited in their ability to foresee all of the consequences of their actions. A race of superhumans would be one in which this limitation was removed. For them, no practical problem would be difficult. They would possess an exact science of reasoning about practical matters, and the rest of us would leave the job of governance to them and occupy ourselves with other matters—drinking (moderately) with friends, listening to music and poetry, attending the theater, learning the sciences, beholding divinities, and discussing philosophy. But such superhumans, Aristotle gently reminds us, are not easy to find. The best city that is practicable is one in which all citizens spend only part of their time in leisurely pursuits, and for the rest, join together as equals to work out, as best they can, the solutions to their common problems.

6.12. *Assessing Aristotle's Ideal*

Undeniably, there are grave defects in the city that Aristotle thinks is ideal. It is a community that does great wrong to the slaves on whom it depends. Women are restricted to the home and denied equal status as citizens. Both injustices stem from Aristotle's disastrous underestimation of the moral and intellectual capacities of a large part of the human race. He fails to do what moral philosophers should do: see past the prejudices of their time and place.

Aristotle's prejudice against banausoi does not similarly underestimate the capacities of those who work with their hands. On the contrary, he holds that naturally free men who earn their living as craftsmen are born with the capacity for full moral development. To say that they are by their nature free men rather than slaves entails that they have this capacity. But Aristotle thinks that over the course of their lives their ethical outlook has become severely constricted by their need to work for a living (6.8). As we will see (Chapter 12), he does not wish to deny them a place in the politics of ordinary Greek cities. He recognizes that they have a useful though limited role to play: they can keep a watchful eye on powerful elites, and prevent the wealthy from exercising undue influence. But in the ideal city, Aristotle thinks, all citizens have sufficient resources to be released from the burden of filling their days with work that would keep them from fully exercising their intellectual, emotional, and social skills—work they would not choose to do, were they wealthy enough, and which detracts from their ability to perform the major civic responsibilities that self-governing citizens must undertake.

We can reasonably say, against Aristotle, that it is possible to work with one's hands and to exercise one's mind and ethical dispositions at the same time. There are many forms of manual labor that are not

6.12. ASSESSING ARISTOTLE'S IDEAL

by their very nature impediments to the exercise of one's cognitive powers, and do not necessarily give one a narrowly selfish perspective on civic matters. Even so, we ought to concede that there is a grain of truth in his denigration of certain kinds of hard physical labor (as there most certainly is not in his low opinion of the capacities of women and natural slaves): he is right to think that certain kinds of work are debilitating, and leave no time or energy for active citizenship; and he is right to think that when the need to work for a living leads citizens to adopt a selfish and wholly pecuniary perspective on all civic issues, the life of the political community deteriorates.

Suppose we altered Aristotle's ideal community by including within it those whom he wrongly excluded. Assume that women are full and equal members of the assembly of all citizens, and responsibilities for raising children and caring for the household are shared equally by both sexes. Imagine too that the material resources of the city are provided entirely by machines rather than slaves. Our thought experiment need not be completely unrealistic: we can assume instead that individual and collective resources must be husbanded and wisely allocated. The women and men of our ideal community must therefore address the same sorts of questions as do the members of Aristotle's ideal city—questions about the adequacy and distribution of the food supply, the availability of clean water, and the like. But we are supposing that in our Aristotelian utopia technology has succeeded in eliminating mindless and debilitating work. No one's daily labor is so burdensome that he cannot participate as an equal in the political life of the community.

By eliminating those parts of Aristotle's blueprint for an ideal society that are morally objectionable, have we succeeded in depicting a genuinely perfect community? It would be foolish to suppose that we have accomplished that much. Aristotle's ideal city is based on his conception of human well-being, and although that theory provides us with an attractive framework for thinking about our lives (if the arguments of Chapters 2 and 3 were correct), it almost certainly needs to be modified and developed in various ways. If, for example, we want to know what sorts of religious belief and practice would exist in an ideal community, and what politics should have to do with religion, we will need to move beyond Aristotle. Even if we want to arrive at the conclusion that the members of an ideal community would be religious people (because a wholly secular outlook excludes something of great value), and that the legal system would help sustain their religious practices, we must move towards these conclusions with ideas and premises that take us far beyond Aristotle. We must also move beyond him if we want to resist these conclusions.

Nonetheless, we can say this much in favor of his proposal for an ideal city—or rather, the transformation of that community that results from the inclusion of women and the use of machines to eliminate mindless and debilitating work: it is a city that is very good indeed. No one's life is disfigured by joyless labor; instead, everything the citizens do engages their powers as thinking, feeling, and social beings. The ethical and intellectual capacities of citizens are developed by a system of education provided to all. Although some have more resources than others (because good and bad fortune are not equally distributed), no one need be concerned that some day he may no longer possess the basic necessities of a good life. If some citizens fall on hard times, they suffer no loss of political power, and participate fully in the social and cultural life of the community (6.9). Their children will still receive the same education as all others. Differences in economic resources are never extremely large, because each household has an equal amount of land. Because all citizens are literate and have been taught the sciences in their schools, they develop a basic understanding of the physical universe and perceive its beauty (6.4).

The rulers are not a distant and corrupt power: they are the citizens themselves. Governing (that is, participating in the assembly and holding various offices) is a matter of concern to all, because each develops an interest in the well-being of the whole community. The assembly is a deliberative body that arrives at its decisions after holding a public discussion to which all can contribute. All citizens agree that justice requires an equal sharing of political power (6.10). This distribution of power is one that we would not hesitate to call democratic, though Aristotle would not himself use that word for it, because he equates democracy with rule by the poor, that is, those who have to work for a living (12.4). His ideal city contains no elite that acquires a preponderance of power, because none of his citizens is power-hungry, and none shirks the responsibility of helping to govern the community. Nor are there political factions, as there are in nearly all other Greek cities, because all citizens of the ideal city share a common conception of well-being, and their resources are great enough to provide for all (6.2). Although there will be differences of opinion about how to achieve the city's goals (6.11), the

6.12. ASSESSING ARISTOTLE'S IDEAL

rancor that poisons the civic life of so many cities does not exist in this one. Each citizen admires the character of the others, and assumes that when different viewpoints persist, that is because practical decisions are often filled with uncertainty and imprecision, and the truth is therefore difficult to discern. No citizen regards any other as a superior being whose judgments must always be followed, or as an inferior to whom no attention need be paid. They subject each other to questioning and criticism. Disagreements about political issues may not always be resolvable, but they do not arise out of or create animosity.

Participation in the deliberations of the assembly is not a full-time job, however. When the citizens are not participating in politics, they are busy with many leisurely pursuits. At least a small number of them can be expected to develop more fully their interest in learning about the world. All human beings by their nature have a desire to learn (*Met.* I.1 980a21), and universal literacy and education are likely to lead at least some of the citizens to develop a strong interest in mathematics, science, and philosophy. Those who are so inclined devote their leisure to inquiry, and come to a fuller understanding of the cosmos and its ultimate causes (6.3). Religious festivals, including theater and other events that feature poetry and music, are sponsored by the city and are meant for the entire community (6.4). All citizens learn to play an instrument when they are children, and this enhances their appreciation for and understanding of the music and drama performed at public festivals. A strong sense of community is created by widespread participation in these religious and musical events. In addition, there are publicly supported common meals: although they are not city-wide events (rather, the community is divided into several smaller groups, each with its common messes), they too create social ties that bring citizens together with those who are not members of their families. When citizens become too old to participate on an equal basis in political life, they are given religious duties, and in this way they remain honored and active members of the community.

However, some of the most important activities of the citizens will involve only their own children, their intimate friends, and their household property. Aristotle opposes Plato's proposal to abolish the family and private property in an ideal community, in part because he believes that our lives would be diminished if everything we did were part of a community-wide effort. In his ideal city, personal friendships and family life flourish. There is pleasure to be had in taking care of what is our own—our own child, our own property, our own friends. The political community, despite its great importance, must not be the only community we care about; and the resources that belong to us collectively must not be the only resources at our disposal. So, Aristotle would claim, one of the attractions of the city depicted in Books VII and VIII is that its citizens enjoy owning their own things and caring for their friends and family. There are both public and private pleasures in his ideal city: citizens participate not only in the political community but in intimate groups as well. They act both collectively as citizens but also as individual decision-makers who control their own resources. (We will explore these ideas more fully in Chapter 9.)

It should be kept in mind that Aristotle's ideal community is not imposed on anyone against his will. It is established by a group of volunteers who leave their homes and set themselves up in a new territory (6.2). We can reasonably assume that they know what their lives in this new community will be like, and that they gladly choose to uproot themselves in order to live in a better world. But, of course, if this city is to sustain itself for long periods of time, it will have to educate future citizens so that they too will gladly cooperate with each other in governing their city. The city will no longer remain ideal, for example, if young citizens take little interest in politics, and only a few of them are willing to do their share in ruling. Similarly, later generations will have to develop a love of poetry, music, and drama if the civic institutions of the founders are to flourish.

But here lies a difficulty that Aristotle does not discuss, and does not fully appreciate. Poetry, music, drama, and many other complex human activities heavily imbued with thought and feeling are not static. They evolve and sometimes change radically; and it would be fruitless and oppressive to try to prevent them from doing so. Politics itself requires new institutions, as economies and technologies change. But Aristotle's principal idea about politics is that it should be made to serve something that does not change from one generation or century to another: human well-being, that is, the full development and exercise of our capacities as reasoning, feeling, and social beings. The inevitability of social change therefore poses a great challenge to the practice of ideal politics as Aristotle conceives it. Members of an Aristotelian ideal community must possess considerable creativity and imagination, if they are to find ways in which their current circumstances, which are never the same for

6.12. ASSESSING ARISTOTLE'S IDEAL

very long, allow them to achieve the goals that have always been and will always be central to human flourishing.

Aristotle realizes, of course, that there is no magical formula whose discovery could put an end to our need to deliberate about practical problems. He insists that practical reason, even when it is wise, is always confronted with fresh difficulties to which past experience is an imperfect guide (*NE* III.3 1112a34–b11). What he could not see was how much the institutions of the Greek polis would need to adapt to changing circumstances. There is a general lesson to be learnt here: highly specific descriptions of ideal societies inevitably become dated and lose their value as blueprints. But we should not infer that utopian proposals can be of no value to those who read them centuries after their conception. Their great worth resides in the way they vividly convey to us the general ideals that their authors urge us to adopt. The concrete detail with which an ideal society is described gives us a better grasp of the general goals that such a community is meant to serve. How to form a polity that best promotes Aristotle's highest ends—the full realization of our powers as reasoning, feeling, and social beings—is a problem that must always be re-examined, as social circumstances change. It cannot be solved simply by copying the institutions and practices described in Books VII and VIII of the *Politics*.[73]

---

[73] The critique of utopianism expressed here is extremely mild in comparison with the anti-utopianism of some recent thinkers. For a highly influential attack on the very idea that there can be an ideal society, see Berlin, 'The Pursuit of the Ideal' and 'The Decline of Utopian Ideas in the West', both in *The Crooked Timber of Humanity*. For an overview of this aspect of Berlin's thought, see Gray, *Isaiah Berlin*, pp. 5–75. One fundamental premise of Berlin's anti-utopianism is that since the most important values are inherently incompatible with each other, a community can at best embody some of them. Because it will entirely lack some of the highest goods, it will be far from ideal. Berlin's thesis, when applied to Aristotle's utopia, means that no society can have all the features we have been discussing in this chapter (democratic rule, civic friendship, justice, philosophy, music, poetry, etc.), because they are by their nature at war with each other; or that Aristotle's ideal community is deeply flawed, because it makes it impossible for citizens to achieve certain other goods that are no less important than the ones they can obtain. That complex claim should not be accepted without argument. In any case, if Berlin is right, that would only show that there are several equally good ways of answering the question, 'What kind of community is the best that is possible?' The availability of several good answers would not indicate that the question is confused or not worth asking. For an extensive analysis of utopianism, which treats it as perversion of humane values, see Kolnai, *The Utopian Mind*. For a subtle discussion of anti-utopianism, see Kateb, *Utopia and its Enemies*. See Nozick, *Anarchy, State, and Utopia*, pp. 293–334, esp. 310–11, for a defense of the thesis that there is no single community that is best for all. The decline of utopian politics is denounced by Jacoby in *The End of Utopia*, 1999.

7

Politics I: Nature, Political Animals, and Civic Priority

7.1. 'Every City Exists by Nature'

Aristotle realizes that the city did not always exist. In *Politics* I.2 he tells a story about how it arose: although human beings have never lived in total isolation from each other, there has been a gradual development of increasingly complex social organizations. Households (composed of a man, a woman, children, and slaves) came together to form villages, which in turn grew to become cities. These changes occurred because people perceived that it was easier to survive and secure the necessities of life by forming larger and more complex units. The city, as Aristotle says, came into existence for the sake of life (1252b29–30). But once this more complex mode of social organization was established and the necessities of life were secured, the polis took on a new dimension: it began to provide not merely the resources for survival but also the opportunity to live well (b30), though this larger role had not been envisioned by those who made the transition from the pre-political period to the polis. Now that the necessities of bare existence have been secured, we members of a political community have the opportunity to choose between different ways of life. Those of us who are lucky enough to

7.1. 'EVERY CITY EXISTS BY NATURE'

live in the age of the polis can do far better than any of our predecessors, if we choose a life of virtuous activity, and misfortune does not deprive us of the resources we need.

Aristotle thinks this process of development is inevitable. Human beings have an impulse to live with others rather than in isolation (1253a29–30).[1] Our desire to survive and to join with others to achieve mutually advantageous goals propels the process by which larger and more complex associations are formed. Isolated households give rise to villages, but villages are not a fully satisfactory solution to the problems of securing the necessities of life, and so their inhabitants are bound to seek and discover a more complex mode of social organization. The polis is an outgrowth from households and villages so obviously rational that we can expect this process to occur whenever conditions are favorable. In fact, Aristotle thinks that human civilization goes through repeated cycles of birth and destruction, and that the polis will always be re-invented.[2] Alternating periods of moisture and dryness lead to the creation and destruction of civilizations, but in each period the same pattern recurs: families give rise to villages, villages grow into cities, and despite their best efforts to survive and flourish, these cities are eventually destroyed and the process begins again.

During one of these stages, conditions are right for human beings to live their lives as they should be lived. The earliest communities—scattered households—were devoted solely to the provision of everyday needs (1252b12–14), but the greater material abundance that is possible in the polis relieves us from the struggle for existence and makes available a rich variety of goods that were lacking in earlier times. Friendships and satisfactory family relations, the musical enactment of poetry, the full exercise of our moral and intellectual skills—all of these goods presuppose sufficient material resources and at least a modicum of leisure. Had we examined human beings and institutions at a stage prior to the birth of the polis, we would never have guessed how much human life has to offer. Only in the polis can we see all that we can become. Only here can we be fully realized.

Aristotle describes the process that leads from the household to

---

[1] See too *NE* IX.9 1169b16–19; *Pol.* III.6 1278b17–21. These and related passages will be discussed in 7.2.

[2] See *Pol.* VII.10 1329b25–7; *De Caelo* I.3 270b19–20; *Meteor.* I.3 339b27–30; *Met.* XII.8 1074b10–13. For discussion, see Kraut, *Aristotle: Politics Books VII and VIII*, comments on *Pol.* VII.10 1329b25–31.

the city as one of *natural* development. Nature (*physis*), the central concept of *Politics* I.2, is already in play in its opening sentence: 'If one could view things as they grow [*phyomena*] from the start, as one does in other cases, one would study them in the best way' (1252a24–6). (The verb translated 'grow' is cognate to the noun, *physis*.) The household is the result of a natural desire to have children (a29); the village arises from the household by nature (b17); and the city exists by nature (b30), because it is the final stage in the realization of the goals of more primitive natural communities. Throughout this chapter, the *physis* of a thing refers both to that from which it originates and to the proper end towards which it moves, as it develops properly.[3] The city arises out of a feature of our psychology that is neither chosen nor inculcated by habit, but is fixed by our nature—namely our desires to survive, meet our everyday needs, and procreate.[4] Just as a seed has an inherent tendency to develop properly, and will do so in appropriate conditions, so primitive human communities grow according to a fixed pattern, thus achieving greater self-sufficiency at each later stage. When desires for ordinary and simple goods can easily be satisfied, their secure possession allows human beings to focus their attention on better goods, and in this way the desire for mere life, which is the dominant impulse of primitive communities, gives rise to a peculiarly civic desire, namely the desire to live a life of one's own choosing, a life that is not forced on one but instead reflects one's conception of well-being. When all goes well and we choose wisely, we will realize that a well-lived life is a political life (1253a2–3), one that acknowledges the priority of the community to the individual (a19–20). The fixed nature that ties us together in primitive communities eventually leads to the full realization of our nature in a life permeated by collective deliberation.

Aristotle's thesis that 'every city exists by nature' (1252b30) contains both a normative and an empirical component. Its normative element consists in his assumption that the process that leads from the primitive household to the city is a process of *proper* development. The city is the best stage of history, but it is not the

---

[3] See *Physics* II.1 for Aristotle's fullest presentation of this twofold aspect of nature.

[4] Here I draw on the trichotomy (nature, habit, reason) that Aristotle works with in *Pol.* VII.13 1332a39–b11. 'Nature' refers to those parts of human psychology that are unalterable and normally present from the start. Their presence in our make-up is not up to us, and we therefore cannot be praised or blamed for them (*NE* VII.5 1148b31–3). For discussion of Aristotle's use of the concept of nature in his ethical and political theory, see Annas, *The Morality of Happiness*, pp. 142–58.

7.1. 'EVERY CITY EXISTS BY NATURE'

last stage, because, as noted earlier, periods of cataclysmic destruction leave a small remnant of primitive communities, and the cycle of growth begins anew. It is Aristotle's conception of well-being that lies behind his claim that one recurring phase in this pattern of endless repetition can be picked out as the proper goal of the process. We cannot validate our conception of the good by setting it to one side and looking instead to history to see where it leads, because it leads just as much to one part of the cycle as to any other.

The empirical component of the claim that the city exists by nature consists in the assumption that impulses not of our own choosing—in many cases, impulses we are born with—are the psychological forces behind the development of the city. The founders of cities (mentioned at the close of I.2: see 1253a30–1) were driven by the same motives that had led to the establishment of smaller and less complex communities: their goal was to find a more secure way to defend themselves against enemies, to have an adequate supply of food, to nurture future generations, and so on. It was not habit or ratiocination, but nature, that produced these needs. Once those needs are met, however, city-dwellers cannot help but want something more from their lives; the desire for mere life is replaced, at a certain stage in history, with the desire for a good life. Aristotle implicitly assumes that the desire to live well is every bit as natural as the desire to survive. It arises in us only when certain other desires have already been satisfied, but it is a desire that inevitably grows in us, once certain conditions have been satisfied. We do not arrive, by means of reasoning, at a desire to live well. Nor do we acquire such a desire because, after we start living well and do so for a time, the force of habit makes us want to continue doing so. Rather, the desire arises in us because it is our nature to want to be happy, once we securely possess the necessities of life. The cities in which we now live have a fair measure of stability because they help us satisfy, to some degree, this natural desire for well-being. That is one reason why Aristotle says that cities exist by nature: the desires that created them and continue to sustain them are natural desires.

There is a second basis for this claim: like plants and animals, all cities began from small and simple organizations that were gradually propelled to grow according to certain fixed patterns into larger, more complex, and better organizations. Plants and animals exist by nature because something within them has moved them forward from their embryonic stages to their adult forms (*Physics* II.1 192b8–15). But cities have also arisen through such a process of growth, and so they exist by nature as well.⁵ As we have seen, the engines of their growth are the natural desires of human beings to live and meet their basic needs. These natural desires cause associations of households to grow larger, and eventually they lead villages to grow into cities. But the emergence of a city is not merely an accumulation of more and more people. Like all genuine growth, it also involves the evolution and transformation of structures: more matter is gradually acquired, but the matter is always organized in a way that allows certain goals to be achieved, and these organizing structures can themselves be transformed and become more complex. Pre-civic social organizations exhibit a structure that bears a rough similarity to the constitutions of mature cities: the relationships that exist between husbands and wives, parents and children, brothers, masters and slaves exhibit certain patterns of dominance and equality that can be found in kingships, aristocracies, polities, and their deviant analogues.⁶ Of course, Aristotle does not believe that cities are living things. Their growth is not propelled by their possession of a nutritive soul.⁷ But not everything that grows is ensouled, and Aristotle has no hesitation in saying that cities emerge from less complex social organizations through a process of growth. One of the most striking features of our passage is its insistence that we should look at the genesis and perfection of human beings, horses, and cities in precisely the same way (1252b32-4).

It might be objected that this way of thinking about cities is incompatible with an obvious fact: cities do not come into existence in the absence of human planning.⁸ Families join together to form villages, and villages combine with each other to form cities, not through some mindless process of social cohesion, but through the plans and decisions of heads of households and village leaders. Aristotle himself fully recognizes that human choice plays a crucial

---

⁵ For readings that differ from the one proposed here, see Yack, *The Problems of a Political Animal*, pp. 90-6; and Miller, *NJR*, pp. 37-45.

⁶ See *Pol.* III.3 1276a30-b15 for Aristotle's thesis that the constitution of a city is its form, and its citizens its matter. See *NE* VIII.10-11 for the idea that different kinds of constitutions have analogues in various relationships within the family. The emergence of cities through a process of growth is therefore one in which constitution-like family relationships develop into full-fledged constitutions.

⁷ A soul is a certain kind of power, and the nutritive soul can exist only in matter of a certain kind (*De An.* II.2 414a17-28). A statue lacks the powers of the soul because it is not made out of the right sort of matter, and similarly a city's material component is not of the right sort to make it a living thing.

⁸ For this objection, see Keyt, 'Three Basic Theorems in Aristotle's *Politics*'. He argues that Aristotle cannot reconcile the role played by human design in the construction of cities with the thesis that they exist by nature.

7.1. 'EVERY CITY EXISTS BY NATURE'

role in the formation of cities; in this very chapter, he pays tribute to the founder of cities (1253b30–1). But if cities are the products of human planning, should they not be put into the same category as the other things we make—houses, ships, and statues? They are the products of human craft, and no such product comes into existence by means of a process of growth.

This objection overlooks the fact that many processes of growth are overseen and influenced by human beings. As seedlings grow, we protect them, so that they will not become diseased or stunted. We breed certain kinds of plant and animal, so that they will best serve human needs. Whole species may owe their existence to human intervention. There is no incompatibility in saying that something owes its existence both to a process of growth and to human beings. So Aristotle's thesis that cities arise in a manner that parallels the growth of living things is entirely compatible with the fact that they are founded by human beings. They come into being because their growth from primitive social organizations into more complex forms has been guided by human beings. No product of craft comes into existence in this way. Each house is devised anew by its builder. Houses do not emerge out of proto-houses because of the influence of some propelling force within them. But cities do emerge from proto-cities, as plants develop from seeds, and the fact that human desires and plans are part of their causal story should not stop us from saying that these are processes of growth.

Such are Aristotle's reasons for holding that 'every city exists by nature' (1252b30). It is a reasonable conjecture that he is interested in advancing this claim because he wants to oppose those who look to what is natural as a guide to life, and who think that the only things that are natural in human beings are desires that are unaffected by social influence. According to this way of thinking, we should discover what is natural by looking to the behavior of animals. What we find, it might be supposed, is a world in which the strong dominate the weak and satisfy their appetites without restraint, a world devoid of common goals and cooperation. A man who lives according to nature, therefore, will pay little heed to civic obligations or the good of others, for the laws of the city are merely human conventions, and have nothing natural about them. And if civic laws are not natural, then surely the same should be said about cities themselves: they are places where our natural desires to dominate others are held in check by unnatural legal restrictions.

These are the ideas expounded by Callicles in Plato's *Gorgias*

(483a–d), and no doubt they represent a line of thought that had some currency in the fifth and fourth centuries.[9] We get a glimpse of this conception of the natural in the *Ethics*, when Aristotle reports that noble and just things exhibit so much variation that they are thought to exist merely by convention, and not by nature (I.3 1094b14–16). And as we have seen (4.7), the expectation that whatever is natural has the same invariant force everywhere leads some to the conclusion that nothing is just by nature (*NE* V.7 1134b24–7).

The passage we are now examining in the *Politics* shows how Aristotle criticizes those who use this conception of the natural to attack the norms of political justice. First, if we call desires 'natural' only if they are unaffected by habituation and rational control, we ought to recognize how urgent are the desires that bring people together for the purpose of achieving common goals. Natural desires lead to the existence of the family and larger cooperative organizations. Cities cannot be unnatural, because they are the outcome of a process that is initiated by nature. Second, if we look to non-human living things for our ideas of what is natural, we cannot ignore the fact that growth is an omnipresent feature of their lives. Plants and animals progress towards their good as they exhibit normal growth and arrive at the final stage of their development. Therefore, cities and their legal systems cannot be contrary to nature, for they too come into existence by means of a process of growth. Third, if we insist that invariance is the mark of the natural, then we can find a high degree of invariance in civic life, and not merely in the heat of fire and the wetness of water. The process that leads from household to city is inevitable, so long as nothing impedes it. In favorable conditions, small and simple social organizations tend to produce larger and more complex units, until they reach the size where they are finally able to achieve their good. All natural things proceed to their good according to a regular pattern, and since the process that leads to the existence of cities exhibits that kind of invariance, cities too must be counted as natural. The denigration of cities and civic life on the grounds that they are contrary to nature rests on a false conception of what nature is and how cities arise.

---

[9] The contrast between nature and *nomos* (convention, law) is one of the elements of the intellectual trend fostered by the sophists. For overviews of what this contrast involves, see Guthrie, *The Sophists*, pp. 55–134; and Kerferd, *The Sophistic Movement*, pp. 111–30.

7.2. 'A Human Being is by Nature a Political Animal'

Having argued that 'a city is among the things that exist by nature' (1253a2), Aristotle immediately adds that the same considerations lead to the conclusion that 'a human being is by nature a political animal' (1252a2–3).[10] Let us try to determine what he means by this, and why he thinks it is supported by the points he has been making in *Politics* I.2.[11]

As we noted in 7.1, Aristotle uses 'nature' and its cognates to refer both to the matter from which a growing thing begins and to the proper end towards which it moves, as it undergoes normal development. This same dual sense is present in his claim that we are by nature political animals: human beings have something in them right from the start—a political impetus or impulse—that propels them towards civic life; furthermore, the good towards which this impulse propels them is civic life. In other words, the statement that we are political animals contains both a normative component (a claim about where our good lies) and an empirical component (a claim about what propels us towards this good). It is good for us to live in cities, and we have an impetus (*hormē*: 1253a29–30) that leads to the development and ongoing existence of cities. The very considerations that lend credibility to Aristotle's claim that cities exist by nature also support this further thesis about the nature of human beings. Cities do not exist at all times and places; rather, they have a history, and emerge from primitive social forms. They would not exhibit this pattern of development were it not the case that something in human beings inclines them to join together with others to form social groups, and were it not the case that in doing so they are better able to achieve their good.

Let us try to say more precisely what Aristotle means when he says that 'by nature the impetus for such a community [that is, a city] exists in everyone' (1253a29–30). Part of his meaning is simply that every human being has an inclination to reject solitude and seek some kind of association with others. This component of the claim

---

[10] The phrase is used 7 times: *Hist. An.* I.1 487b33–488a14; *NE* I.7 1097b11, VIII.12 1162a17–18, IX.9 1169b18–19; *EE* VII.10 1242a22–3; *Pol* I.2 1253a7–8, III.6 1278b19.

[11] For further discussion of this passage, see Keyt, 'Three Basic Theorems in Aristotle's *Politics*', esp. pp. 123–6; Kullmann, 'Man as a Political Animal in Aristotle'; Miller, *NJR*, pp. 27–36; Saunders, *Aristotle: Politics Books I and II*, pp. 69–70; and Cooper, 'Political Animals and Civic Friendship', pp. 224–7.

that we are political animals might be expressed by saying that we are *sociable* animals. That simply means that we cannot abide isolation for long; we seek to live together with others. As Aristotle says in the *Ethics*: 'No one would choose to be by himself and have all of the goods. For a human being is political and by nature lives with others' (IX.9 1169b17–19). We find the same point being made later in the *Politics*: 'It has been said in our first discourses ... that by nature human beings are political animals. That is why, even when they do not need assistance from each other, they have no less of a desire to live together' (III.6 1278b17–21). Aristotle's historical account of the development of the polis does not begin (as does, for example, Rousseau's[12]) with a story about how human beings first lived in isolation from each other, and then joined together in couples. He thinks such a story is incompatible with what we know about human nature. We have an instinct for social life that has been operative in all the stages of our historical development. There was no asocial phase of human life that preceded the family, because we are political animals: we have an innate desire to live together with others.

But there are passages in which Aristotle is making a somewhat different empirical claim, when he says that by nature we are political animals. For example, he says in the *Nicomachean Ethics*: 'human beings are by nature couple-forming [*sunduastikon*]—more so than political, inasmuch as the household is prior to and more necessary than the city' (VIII.12 1162a17–19). Similarly, he says in the *Eudemian Ethics*: 'human beings are not merely political animals but also householding animals' (VII.10 1242a22–3). The claim that *by nature* we are couple-forming or householding animals means both that we have an instinct to form couples and set up a household and that it is good for us to do so. So, if we ask, 'Why wasn't there a stage of human history in which we roamed the earth as isolated individuals?', Aristotle will reply both by giving a highly general answer (we cannot abide isolation: we are political animals) and a more specific answer (we have a desire to form couples and have children). Furthermore, in the passage just cited from the *Nicomachean Ethics*, he contrasts the low intensity of our political drive with the higher intensity of the householding drive. We feel a greater need for procreation than for civic life, and this couple-forming drive was present in us before we joined together in cities. In

---

[12] *Discourse on the Origins of Inequality.*

7.2. 'A HUMAN BEING IS BY NATURE A POLITICAL ANIMAL'

saying this, Aristotle is taking our political nature to be something that first began to operate after the household had already been formed. In other words, he is, in this passage, positing a drive to form social units larger than the household and the village, and he calls that motive 'political' because it is a desire to conduct one's life in a social organization as complex as the city. In this sense, calling human beings 'political animals' refers not to our highly general desire to escape isolation and form social ties of some form or other, but to our more specific desire, which arises at a certain moment in history, to live in a community in which we can lead a richer and more complex life than is available in the household. Our nature as political animals, in this specific sense, is expressed when we are not content with mere life, or with the limited range of goods that can be achieved within the confines of a household or village, but wish for something better, something that can be achieved only in cities.

Because Aristotle uses the claim that we are by nature political animals to refer both to our general desire to be with others and to our more specific desire to be part of the political community, he can say, without contradiction, both that all human beings are political animals and that only some are. All human beings—including women and natural slaves—naturally want to join with others in some sort of community, whether that community be a household or something larger. No human being can abide isolation. But only free men are political in the more specific sense; only they (Aristotle wrongly supposes) have an impetus to participate in civic life.

Aristotle acknowledges, at one point in his biological writings, that human beings both are and are not political animals. In the opening chapter of the *History of Animals*, he describes some of the differences in the modes of life of various species: 'Some of these are gregarious; others (footed, winged, and seafaring) solitary; others dualize. And among those that are gregarious, some are political, others dispersed. . . . Human beings dualize' (487b34–488a7). Here, human beings are placed in the category of animals that are gregarious (*agelaia*)—or, as we might say, social. Such animals live in groups rather than in isolation. Social animals are further divided into those that are political and those that are not, and Aristotle claims that human beings fall into both categories. Although he gives no explanation of his claim that we 'dualize' (*epamphoterizein*) in this way, we can easily explain what he means. Women and male natural slaves are social but not political, whereas free males are both social and political. Slaves and women are 'dispersed' in that their nature is to spend their days in small, isolated living units. They do not leave those units in order to join together in communities that have a common purpose, and so they fail to satisfy the definition Aristotle gives in the lines that follow: 'Political [animals] are those for whom one common thing is the task of all. Such are man, the bee, the wasp, the ant, and the crane' (488a7–10).[13]

It might seem odd that Aristotle is perfectly content to apply his term *politikos* to other species besides our own. (He continues to speak this way in our own passage. At 1253a7–8, he says: 'man is a political animal in a higher degree than bees or other gregarious animals.') After all, what can it mean to call a bee a political animal? Surely the association formed by bees is not a polis in the strict sense. For one thing, bees do not have a constitution. Nor are they citizens of their hives, since they do not engage in the characteristic activities of citizens—deliberation and judgment.

But it would be wrong to suppose that for Aristotle the word '*politikos*', when applied to bees, loses its connection with the polis. A better way to think about his linguistic practice is to recognize that his name for an animal's drive (whether that animal is human or not) refers to the highest goal to which that drive eventually leads. We have observed this phenomenon already, when we learnt that, according to Aristotle, human beings reject a solitary life because they are political animals. Our aversion to solitude is named after the best institution to which we are led by that aversion. In this sense of *politikos*, even slaves are political animals, for they have no less of a desire to live with others than any other human being. The fact that slaves can never be citizens does not prevent Aristotle from saying that, in a way, they are political animals; for they too have the same impetus that, in other kinds of human beings, creates and sustains the polis. Similarly, bees count as political animals, because the instinct that causes them to join together in one common task is the very instinct that, in human beings, leads free men to want to join together in a common association that takes them outside the household. Bees are not citizens and do not live in a polis, but there

---

[13] Alternatively, we might take the claim that human beings are politically dual to mean that each has a householding impulse (exhibited at certain times) and a political impulse (exhibited at other times). (This reading was proposed to me by Mark Philp.) But Aristotle cannot be saying that *all* human beings—even women and slaves—are at times political, in that they participate in the common task of the polis; and his statement that humans dualize seems to be meant as a claim applicable to all members of our species. See Balme, 'Aristotle's Use of Division and Differentiae', pp. 85–6 for a brief discussion of Aristotle's notion of dualization in biology.

7.2. 'A HUMAN BEING IS BY NATURE A POLITICAL ANIMAL'

is something in them that propels them to form societies and not merely couples; like us, they are led by their nature to form large groups that serve a common purpose. Man is more political than the bees, Aristotle thinks, because we alone have the capacity to learn a language and to talk and reason with each other (1253a9–18).[14] Language gives us the ability to reflect on and choose our common task, and to pursue it, in cooperation with others, with greater intelligence than is possessed by any other animal. We can choose to make collective deliberation part of our highest goal, and not a mere means to the satisfaction of apolitical desires.

I conjectured in 7.1 that what lies behind Aristotle's attempt to show that cities exist by nature is his opposition to those who look to the lives of animals for their conception of what is natural in human beings, and who find in animals a model of indifference to the needs of the community. Aristotle's remarks about the political nature of certain kinds of animal can also be construed as an effort to combat this picture. Other animals besides human beings join together to help each other avoid pain and pursue what they find pleasant, and they communicate with each other for these purposes (1253a10–14). They seek to cooperate, but the range of goals they can pursue cooperatively is severely limited by their nature. What we find among some of the animals is not a model of how to live, but a defective version of what we human beings do much better. We should regard our ability to think and speak to each other about what is just and good not as a liability, but as a characteristic that takes human life to an entirely better level than any other animal can attain.

There is one other passage in which Aristotle affirms the political nature of human beings. In I.7 of the *Nicomachean Ethics*, he suggests that we will be able to discern where our good lies if we recognize that the highest good must in some sense be self-sufficient. But before he explains what he means by self-sufficiency, he warns us not to misunderstand the idea he is proposing: he is not trying to suggest that the kind of life a human being should lead is an isolated life. Whatever self-sufficiency amounts to, it must be sufficient for someone who is living in the midst of others. As he says: 'By self-sufficient we do not mean what is sufficient for someone alone, living a solitary life, but what is sufficient also for parents, children,

---

[14] For further discussion, see DePew, 'Humans and Other Political Animals in Aristotle's *Historia Animalium*'.

wife, and in general friends and citizens, since by nature human beings are political' (1097b8–11).[15] Here, the claim that we are by nature political is offered as a reason why we should envisage the person who is doing well as someone who lives among his family, friends, and fellow citizens. In calling us political animals, Aristotle is referring not to the psychological make-up that propels us into the polis, but to the goal to which we are propelled—the kind of life that is good for us to live. Just as it would be a diminution of our lives if we lost our friends and family, so it would be a significant loss to be without a city, and to have no fellow citizens. Aristotle should be taken to mean that engaging in common pursuits with fellow citizens is one element of a good life, just as it is a component of a good life to share it with families and friends. Part of the goal of all human beings is to be active as political animals—not merely to make use of what a city has to offer (security, the necessities of life, dramatic festivals), but to be active participants in the deliberations and judgments that citizens need to make collectively. Women and natural slaves cannot reach this goal; they benefit by living in cities, but they can never become active political participants. Aristotle can count them as political animals only because they too are propelled by the instinct to live with other human beings, and so they share the psychological make-up that leads to and sustains the existence of cities.

One further question should be raised. In saying that human beings are by nature political animals, does Aristotle mean that cities as they presently exist, with all their strife and so little justice, are places where we fulfill our nature? Or does he instead mean that it is our nature to live in true cities—cities that do not yet exist, but that we should try to build?

A full answer to this question cannot be defended at this point, since more must be said about the distinction Aristotle makes between correct and defective constitutions. But when we have completed our discussion of the material in Books III–VI that pertains to this distinction, a simple answer will emerge: many existing cities do partly fulfill our nature, because they are complex mixtures

---

[15] The Ross translation (revised by Ackrill and Urmson) renders this as: 'man is born for citizenship' (p. 12). Their translation, included in the Revised Oxford Translation published in 1984 by Princeton University Press, edited by Barnes, has been changed to: 'man is sociable by nature.' As we have seen, Aristotle's claim that we are by nature political can be used to make both of these points: we are sociable, and are born for citizenship. But at 1097b8–11, it is the latter point that he has in mind.

of good and bad elements. Admittedly, when their injustices take an extreme form, as happens in pure democracies and oligarchies, they can hardly be called cities at all, and we are no better off living in them than we would be dwelling in pre-political associations.[16] When man is 'deprived of law and justice, he is the worst of all animals' (1253a32–3); living in lawless cities, he lives in misery. But most cities are or can manage to be better than this. Even if they are sites of injustice and strife, they do not completely depart from norms of justice (4.5), and they allow their citizens some small measure of well-being. Furthermore, there are usually ways in which they can be significantly improved. To say that we have a polis-nature means that the closer a polis comes to being what it should be, the more worthwhile it is to be an active citizen, and the closer we come to leading good lives.

7.3. *Cities and Other Composites*

Having explained and defended his idea that human beings are by nature political animals, Aristotle proposes a further thesis: 'the city is prior by nature to the household and to each of us' (I.2 1253a19). That has the sound of a deep and provocative dictum. But precisely what does it mean? It will take the remainder of this chapter to answer that question.

We can understand these words only by seeing how they fit their context, so let us begin by taking in the rest of the passage. Aristotle immediately adds, by way of explanation, that 'the whole is necessarily prior to the part'.[17] This is not the first time in the *Politics* that he has spoken of the city as a whole made out of smaller units. He has already told his audience, in the opening chapter of this work, that the city must be understood by the method we apply to any composite (*syntheton*): we break it down into its components, until we arrive at the smallest and indivisible parts of the whole (1252a17–23). The city is made out of households and individual

---

[16] See III.9 1280b6–12 for the idea that a city truly so-called must make virtue one of its concerns. See 11.3 for further discussion and 10.n.15 for a related point about the term *politeia*.

[17] Reeve translates: 'a whole is necessarily prior to its parts.' The Greek uses the singular—*tou merous* (part), not *tōn merōn* (parts); and, as we will see, that makes a significant difference. Aristotle says that when we compare the city with any single component of it, the former is prior to the latter. That does not mean that when we compare the city with all of its components, the former is prior to the latter.

human beings. Not only did it arise from smaller units, but it ought to continue to serve them. In Book II, Aristotle will use this point as a weapon against Plato, whose proposal to abolish the household (through the abolition of private property and traditional marriages) he condemns as an attempt to undermine the very nature of the city. The political community, Aristotle thinks, is and ought to be a composite, and Plato's radical measures are therefore wrong-headed and futile attempts to turn the city into something that it cannot be (II.1 1261a13–22). In Book III, the idea that the city is to be analyzed in terms of its components is exploited once again: the parts in terms of which a city must be understood are its citizens, and so political theory must ask what it is to be a citizen (III.1)—and accordingly, what it is to be a good citizen (III.4).

We will turn later to these dimensions of Aristotle's attempt to understand cities in terms of their parts. What is central to our current purposes is not the bare idea that a city is a composite of parts but the far more provocative claim that the city is prior by nature to that from which it is composed: the household and the individual citizen. Aristotle thinks that this priority thesis is built into the nature of the relationship between parts and whole. Because an individual citizen is part of the city, he is posterior to it. He immediately offers an example, to help explain and defend this thesis: when the body is destroyed, neither the foot nor the hand will exist, except in a 'homonymous' way.

'Homonymous' literally means 'alike in name', but Aristotle always uses this term to talk about things that not only are alike in name but also have different natures. His interest in this phenomenon reflects his conviction that progress in philosophy requires attention to the different ways in which we use our words. We should not assume that all of the things named by a single word are to be defined in precisely the same way. To take the example he uses in our present passage: both a stone-shaped hand produced by a sculptor and a hand that is a functioning part of the human body are called by the same name, but they merely have a shape in common, and that is a superficial similarity. A hand should be defined in terms of what it can do; a stone 'hand' cannot perform that same or any other biological function, and so it is a hand in name only. Similarly, Aristotle says in our passage, a dead body is made up of 'hand', 'foot', and other such parts only in a certain manner of speaking: these terms cannot be applied to parts as they once were, because they no longer designate items that have the capacity to contribute to a larger whole. A dead 'hand' is a hand in name only, because it can no more perform the function of a hand than can the sculptor's 'hand' of stone.[18]

Having explained this point, Aristotle returns to his thesis that the city is prior to each of us (1253a25–6), and adds the following thoughts, to support his claim: 'For if each is not self-sufficient, having been separated, he will stand in the same relation to the whole as do other parts, and he who is not capable of community, or has no need of one because of his self-sufficiency, is no part of a city, and is therefore a beast or a god' (a26–9).

What sense can be made of all this? We need answers to the following questions:

A. How are we to understand Aristotle's conclusion? That is, what kind of priority is he talking about when he says that the city is prior in nature to the household and each of us?

B. What argument or arguments does he offer for this conclusion? How does the analogy between the city and the body support the priority thesis? What contribution to the argument is made by the thesis that a dead hand is called a hand homonymously? How does the fact that human beings are not self-sufficient support the conclusion?

C. What are the practical consequences of this conclusion? Civic priority sounds like a thesis that should make a difference to the way we conduct our civic lives. But precisely how should we act, if we agree that the city is prior to each of us?

7.4. Priority: Two False Starts

When Aristotle says that the city is by nature prior to each of us, what sort of priority does he have in mind? He points out in several

---

[18] Homonymy is defined at *Cat.* 1 1a1–6. The concept is applied to the body at *De An.* II.1 412b17–22. See too *Meteor.* IV.12 389b31–390a16; *Part. An.* I.1 640b29–641a5; *Gen. An.* II.1 734b24–31. For general studies of this concept, see Irwin, 'Homonymy in Aristotle'; Shields, *Order in Multiplicity* (esp. chs. 1 and 5). For other passages in which Aristotle makes use of a comparison between the city and a living body, see *Pol.* III.4 1277a5–6 (the city is composed of unlike parts, as an animal is composed of soul and body), IV.4 1290b23–39 (as bodies need many different kinds of organs, so cities must assign citizens to different roles), V.3 1302b33–1303a2 (bodily parts must grow proportionately, and similarly the ratio of rich to poor cannot change dramatically), V.9 1309b18–35 (extreme constitutions are like ugly noses), VII.4 1326a35–b2 (cities and bodies must be of a certain size, in order to serve their purposes). In the latter passage, cities are compared both to ensouled bodies and to artifacts. At III.4 1277a5–10, the analogy drawn is between the city's composition out of dissimilar parts and other relationships among dissimilar things (soul and body, reason and desire, man and woman, master and slave). See too 6.n.40.

of his theoretical writings that there are a number of different ways in which one thing can be prior to another. Do any of these passages help us with our question? Do they call to our attention a use of 'prior' that allows us to make good sense of our passage?[19] Consider the following possibilities:

A. Some things are prior to others because they are in some way closer to a reference point. For example, one time can be called prior to another because it is closer to the present. Or, to take a different example, when one member of a chorus is selected as primary, the others can be called prior or posterior to each other because of the way they are arranged in relation to that first individual. (*Met.* V.11 1018b9–29; cf. *Cat.* 12 14a26–9)

If Aristotle is saying that the city is prior to each of us in this sense, then his meaning must be that the city predates the existence of each of the citizens of which it is composed. No doubt that is true in many cases. Cities normally endure for many generations, and later generations of citizens are younger than the city to which they belong. But it should be obvious that cities are not always prior in this sense, and Aristotle realizes this. Cities come into existence, and are created by individuals (*Pol.* I.2. 1253a30–1). Those founders are temporally prior to the city they establish.

B. If one thing can exist independently of another, but not vice versa, then the first is prior in existence to the second (*Met* V.11 1019a1–4; cf. *Cat.* 12 14a29–35). Aristotle attributes this use of 'prior' to Plato, presumably because he takes Plato to claim that forms can exist independently of things that participate in them, but not vice versa.

If Aristotle has this kind of priority in mind in our passage, then he is saying that the city can exist independently of each of its citizens, but that no citizen can exist apart from the political community of which he is a member. But the second half of this claim is obviously false, and Aristotle cannot have failed to realize this. An individual citizen can move away from his city and survive. In fact, as Aristotle insists in *Politics* I.2, the cycle of history always contains a stage in which there are individual human beings, but no cities.[20]

---

[19] Types of priority in Aristotle are helpfully distinguished and discussed by Keyt in 'Three Basic Theorems in Aristotle's *Politics*', pp. 126–7. Keyt holds that the doctrine of civic priority draws on several different types of priority distinguished in Aristotle's theoretical works, but that he ought to have recognized that the city is prior in none of these senses.

[20] In 'Three Basic Theorems', Keyt holds that Aristotle is misled by his analogy between citizens and hands: because hands cannot exist separately, Aristotle supposes that no individual human beings can exist apart from a city (see pp. 135–40). For discussion, see Miller, *NJR*, pp. 47–50. Mayhew takes Aristotle to mean that 'the city can exist without any particular individual, but every individual requires a city in order to exist (as a human)'

7.5. Definitional Asymmetry

Some things are defined in terms of others, but not vice versa. For example, Aristotle believes that right angles are prior in definition to acute angles, because the latter are defined in terms of the former, but not vice versa (*Met.* VII.10 1035b4–7). Similarly, things in the category of substance are not defined in terms of their qualities or quantities, whereas the definition of items in non-substantial categories must contain a reference to substance in their definitions (*Met.* VII.1 1028a32–6).

Now, human beings are by nature political animals, as we have been told shortly before our passage begins (1253a2–3). Furthermore, we can reasonably take Aristotle to be saying, in *Politics* I.2, that the definition of human beings ought to refer to the political activity they engage in, when they have perfected themselves. Just as a hand is defined in terms of the task it has (that is why a dead hand is a hand in name only, 1253a23), so human beings are defined in terms of their task and highest end, and this includes the civic activity they undertake as citizens. Therefore, a reference to the city must be incorporated into the definition of a human being—just as a reference to the right angle must be included in the definition of an acute angle.

It might be thought, however, that this type of priority cannot be what Aristotle has in mind, because he defines cities partly in terms of the parts of which they are composed—namely, human beings. Cities are communities of human beings, organized by means of a constitution. The constitution is the form of a city, and its individual citizens are its matter.[21] So, even if it is true, as Aristotle claims, that one must define a human being as a political animal, thus incorporating a reference to the city in our understanding of what a human being is, that does not establish the priority of the city. For human beings are as much a part of the definition of the city as the city is part of the definition of a human being.[22]

(*Aristotle's Criticism of Plato's Republic*, p. 18). But if someone is separated from his community and manages to survive, he exists and is human. Is that not 'to exist (as a human)'? Admittedly, he does not live well. But if the thesis of civic priority merely means that each of us needs a city in order to live well, then in the same sense food, shelter, and clothing are prior to each of us.

[21] Cities necessarily consist in a multitude of human beings (II.2 1261a18–23) or citizens (III.1 1274b41, 1275b17–21) or those who are free (III.6 1279a21). The inhabitants are compared to matter at III.3 1276a30–b13.

[22] For this reason, Miller, *NJR*, p. 47, holds that Aristotle cannot mean that the city is prior in definition to the individual.

But we should be careful here. Aristotle's thesis is that the city is prior to *each* of us (1253a19). Take each citizen one by one and you can say in each case: the city is prior in definition or knowledge to him. Aristotle does not say, and it does not follow, that if we gather up all of the human beings from which a city is composed, we can say: the city is prior (in this sense) to all of them. Similarly, the body is definitionally prior to the hand, as well as to the foot, and the nose, and so on. But Aristotle never suggests that when we consider all of these parts collectively, the body is prior to all of them. It is not clear what sense could be attributed to such a thesis.

So, the proper question to ask is this: does Aristotle believe that although each human being is to be defined in terms of a city, no city is to be defined in terms of any particular human being? And the answer to this question must surely be yes. He thinks that if we ask who Socrates is, the answer will be: a human being (*Cat.* 5 2b31–3; *Met.* VII.1 1028a16–17). And if we ask what a human being is, the answer will be: a political animal. So, to know Socrates, one must know what sort of thing a city is. We know who Socrates is by identifying him as a member of a species, and that species is defined in terms of the kind of life its members should be leading, namely a political life. In that sense, an individual human being cannot be understood apart from the city of which he is a part. By contrast, to understand what a city is, we do not have to make any reference to Socrates in particular. We need only refer to the human beings whom cities ought to serve. So there is, after all, a definitional asymmetry between each one of us and the city to which we belong.

But can that be the conclusion Aristotle is trying to reach in our passage? The fact that he accepts this asymmetry does not mean that it is the one that he is trying to establish here. We should take the definitional priority of the city to be Aristotle's conclusion only if the argument he gives in our passage is well designed to establish that conclusion. And in that respect, the interpretation under consideration is weak. For in order to understand our passage, we must see why Aristotle bothers to make the point that the hand of a dead body is a hand in name only. But in fact it is difficult to see why he needs to make that point, if he merely wants to persuade us that the city is definitionally prior to any single citizen. It would have been sufficient for Aristotle to say: 'Any single part is defined in terms of the whole, but no whole is defined in terms of a single part. For example, the hand must be understood as something that serves the body; but the body is not defined by reference to the hand. Similarly, an individual human being must be understood as a political animal, whereas no city is defined in terms of some single individual.' Aristotle's argument, so stated, has no need of the premise that a dead hand is a hand in name only. And yet it is difficult to believe that we have understood our passage, if we are forced to the conclusion that this thesis can simply be dropped.

There is another defect in the interpretation under consideration: the thesis that the city is definitionally prior to any individual citizen is rather uninteresting, for it hardly goes beyond the point that human beings are political animals. It tells us that (A) because an individual human being is by nature a political animal, he is to be defined in terms of his city; but (B) no city is to be defined in terms of any single citizen. The significant component of this double thesis is (A); by contrast, (B) is trivial. But that in effect means that Aristotle's priority thesis, so understood, would add nothing important to what he has already established.

7.6. *Priority in Development*

One of the most common kinds of priority mentioned in Aristotle's theoretical works is what he calls priority 'in nature' or sometimes 'in substance'. A fully developed plant or animal is in this sense prior to that from which it came to be—a seed or embryo. An adult is also prior in this sense to the child from which it has grown. In developmental processes, things that are prior in time are posterior in nature and substance. Their existence is only a preparation for something that they will lead to: they exist for the sake of the later stages to which they lead.[23]

This might at first seem to be precisely the sort of priority Aristotle has in mind in our passage. After all, his thesis is that 'the city is prior *by nature* to the household and each of us' (1253a19). The phrase 'by nature' might be construed as an indication of the sort of priority he is talking about. But on reflection, this interpretation cannot be correct, for it overlooks the obvious point that a city is not related to a citizen in the way that a perfected organism is related to that from which it has developed. An individual human being is not

---

[23] See *Physics* VIII.7 261a13–14, VIII.9 265a22–4; *Part. An.* II.1 646a24–7; *Gen. An.* II.6 742a19–22; *Met* I.8 989a15–18, IX.8 1050a4–b6. Miller, *NJR*, pp. 50–3, argues that it is in this sense that the city is prior to the individual. He is followed by Saunders, *Aristotle: Politics Books I and II*, p. 70.

something that turns into a city, as a seed becomes a tree or a boy becomes a man. A human being does not exist for the sake of the city into which he will develop—for there is no such developmental process. Of course, there is this much similarity between the two cases: an individual who has never lived in a city must be imperfectly developed, and in that respect he is like an embryo, or a seed, or a child. He is not as fully realized a human being as a city-dweller who has taken advantage of what a city has to offer. But that does not mean that he *is* a city in inchoate form. Therefore, he cannot be said to have a natural posteriority to the city, if natural priority and posteriority mean what they mean in Aristotle's theoretical works.

The only way to salvage this interpretation would be to take Aristotle to be making the following point, when he affirms the priority of the city: the first cities emerged from the joining together of villages (and the households and individuals that they contained), and this developmental process is analogous to the formation of an adult from the child or seed from which he came. No single individual is a city in inchoate form, but certain groups of individuals moved from being non-city dwellers to being city-dwellers. Taken collectively, they were the material from which a city emerged. And therefore the city that they formed is prior to the communities and individuals from which it emerged, just as an adult organism is prior to the developmentally inferior stages from which it emerges.

But if this were Aristotle's point, he would not have expressed it by saying: the polis is prior by nature to *each of us*. Those words advance a thesis about my relation to the polis in which I live, your relation to the polis in which you live, and so on. It applies to each individual citizen of every city, not to the collective body of individuals who formed the first cities. And although, long ago, a large group of individuals formed the first cities, it cannot be said of each individual citizen that he is (or ever was) an early stage of an entity that emerges from him, namely, the city.

Another way to recognize the weakness of this interpretation is to recall that our passage depends heavily on a comparison between the individual city and any part of the body. However we understand the priority of the city in relation to the individual human being, that kind of priority must be precisely the priority the body has in relation to the hand. But Aristotle cannot be making the claim that the hand is posterior to the body in the way that a seed or an embryo or a boy are posterior to the fully developed organisms that they become. For a hand is not a developmentally inferior stage of the body.

7.7. Citizens and Hands

We have not yet found a satisfactory way to understand what sort of priority Aristotle has in mind, when he claims that the city is prior by nature to the household and to each of us. We should therefore try a different approach: let us set aside, for the moment, the problem of determining what 'prior' means in our passage. Instead of concentrating on Aristotle's conclusion—his priority thesis—let us consider more carefully the analogy he uses to establish that conclusion. Perhaps when we know how Aristotle understands the premises he uses to arrive at the conclusion that the city is prior to the individual, we will be in a better position to know how to interpret that conclusion.

He focuses on certain facts about the relationship between the body and any one of its parts, and asks us to accept an analogous point about the relationship between the city and any one of its parts. More specifically: when the body dies, the hand can no longer function, and is a hand in name only. What is the political analogue of this point about the body?

That depends on what it is for a city to die. Obviously, according to one scenario, a city ceases to exist when it is attacked by enemy forces, and all of its citizens are put to death. If that is what Aristotle has in mind, then the upshot of his analogy between the city and the body is that when a city is destroyed, the human beings that once constituted its citizenry have become human beings in name only. That sounds plausible, but it seems too tame a point to be the one that Aristotle is driving at. In any case, it is possible for a city to be destroyed even if all those who were once its citizens remain alive. Suppose they flee from the enemy, disperse, and take refuge in many other cities. Their native city no longer exists, but it hardly follows that each of the citizens from which it was composed has become a human being in name only.

Here is a better way to understand what Aristotle is trying to convey. The analogy he wants us to draw is between a 'hand' made of stone or a dead 'hand' and a 'human being' who may in some respects seem human, but who is really either a beast or a god, and therefore a human being in name only. What sort of so-called human would not really be human? He tells us in so many words: someone 'who is not capable of community, or has no need of one because of his self-sufficiency' (1253a27–9). Someone who cannot make any contribution to the good of others is not capable of being a member of a community—he is a beast, not a genuine human being. Similarly, someone who can, on his own, possess and use all of the goods that are needed for a well-lived life, would have no reason to join a community—he is a god, not a genuine human being. The analogy with stone or dead 'hands' is meant to correspond to the point that a 'human' who cannot contribute to a larger whole is really a beast and not a human being. Perhaps Aristotle also means to suggest that a dead hand, like a stone hand, has no needs, and therefore cannot be served by other parts of the body. It is both beastlike and godlike in its isolation: unlike genuine bodily parts, it can give nothing to and receive nothing from other parts of the body.

We can now understand one further detail of our passage. After Aristotle points out that hands made of stone or dead hands are only homonymously hands, he returns to his claim that the city is prior to each of us, and adds: 'For if each, having been separated, is not self-sufficient, he will stand in the same relation to the whole as do other parts.' His point is simply that, by imagining someone living in isolation ('having been separated'), we can easily recognize the dependency of each human being on others. When you separate someone—that is, when you completely isolate him from society—many of his needs can no longer be met. He might or might not be able to survive; that depends on whether he is a child or an adult, and on many other circumstances. But in either case he is not self-sufficient, because even if he does manage to stay alive, the quality of his existence will be severely diminished, and many of his needs will go unmet.

At this point, however, Aristotle's analogy between an individual human being and a non-functioning part of the body breaks down. For the corporeal analogue to a socially isolated human being is a severed hand: it too has needs that cannot be met. A severed 'hand' that remains severed cannot continue to function, and is a hand in name only. In that respect, it is not analogous to an isolated human being, because someone who is cut off from all other human beings might manage to stay alive for some time, if circumstances are favorable. But the existence of this disanalogy does not require us to suppose that it somehow escaped Aristotle. We need not take him to be presupposing or committing himself to the implausible thesis that no human being can survive in isolation. Instead, the point he is trying to get across, when he remarks on what isolation reveals—namely, our inability to meet all of our needs on our own—and compares it to the dependence of any part of the body on the whole, is simply this: if we are genuine human beings, and are not so called homonymously, we need the help of others. Someone would be a human in name only not by being isolated from others, but by needing nothing from them, and therefore not suffering from isolation.

Aristotle expresses some of these same ideas earlier in *Politics* I.2, about fifteen lines before he puts forward and defends his civic priority thesis. He says: 'man is by nature a political animal, and one who is without a city because of his nature and not by chance is either an inferior being [*phaulos*] or better than human' (1253a2–4). This classification of naturally cityless individuals into two categories—those inferior and those superior to normal human beings—is evidently an expression of the very idea that we have been examining: someone who is incapable of community or has no need of one is either a beast or a god (a27–9). But in the earlier passage, Aristotle makes it completely clear that he is making such a claim only about someone who is 'without a city because of his nature and not by chance'. He is not reclassifying as subhuman those unfortunate people who lived in pre-political times, and therefore had to devote their whole lives to the bare necessities of life. Aristotle never claims, and it would be absurd to think, that those earlier generations lacked the *capacity* to be members of a political community. They were without a city because households and villages had not yet started joining together, and the era of material prosperity had not yet begun. They had the capacity to contribute to others—in fact, they exercised it, in small ways, in their dealings with their families and other members of their tiny, struggling communities. Although they could exercise that capacity only in limited ways, it would be absurd to suppose that they were not really human beings, or that they were human to a smaller degree than city-dwellers. Aristotle never says anything to suggest otherwise.[24] The point of the analogy he draws between parts of the city and parts of the body cannot be that certain living things are wrongly called 'human', even though they had (or have) a human appearance: namely, pre-political household and village dwellers, and citizens who have been forced

---

[24] Here my interpretation should be contrasted with the one proposed by Miller, *NJR*, pp. 50–3. He takes Aristotle to be saying that if one does not have the training or opportunity to exercise the virtues, then one is human to a lower degree.

into social isolation. For he has no reason to doubt that these individuals have the rational faculty and the capacity to join with others in mutually beneficial cooperative relations—features that make it proper for them to be classified as human. Unless they are natural slaves, their capacity to reason is entirely intact. And since Aristotle does not say even of natural slaves, whose rational capacities he takes to be defective, that they are only apparently human, or that they are less human than others, he has no basis for saying of those who fully possess the rational faculty that they are only homonymously human.[25]

7.8. The Civic Good is Prior to the Individual Good

We have, I think, finally begun to make some progress in arriving at a satisfactory reading of our passage. We have a better grasp of the way in which Aristotle wants to make use of the analogy between a dead hand and someone who is human in name only. But, unfortunately, that by itself does not show us what Aristotle means by 'prior', when he says that the city is prior by nature to each of us. We must therefore return to this issue and continue our search for a satisfactory reading of this thesis.

Our earlier failure (7.4–5) to find an account of the kind of priority Aristotle is talking about suggests that we were looking in the wrong places for our clues. We mined his studies of nature and metaphysics for distinctions he makes among the various senses of 'prior', but in doing so we overlooked the possibility that in ethical discourse

---

[25] There is one passage in which Aristotle says that certain creatures should not be classified as genuinely human, despite their similarity in outward form to human beings: At *NE* VII.6 1149a9–11, he says: 'Among those who are foolish [*aphrones*], those who by nature lack reason [*alogistoi*] and live by means of perception alone are brutish [*thēriōdeis*], as are some kinds of distant foreigners.' What Aristotle has in mind, as the context indicates, are creatures who are said to engage in savage acts, such as killing pregnant women in order to eat their children (1148b20–1). Presumably his idea is that, if certain reports are to be believed, some creatures are to be classified, not as extremely evil human beings, but as non-human, because not only do they fail to abide by the laws observed in human communities, but they lack reason. They merely look like human beings, but are not really such. Much of VII.6, by contrast, is a discussion of *human beings* who are brutish. They act like brutes—that is the point of calling them brutish [*thēriōdeis*]; but because they possess reason, they are nonetheless to be classified as human. It is only at 1149a9–11 that Aristotle takes the more radical step of affirming that some apparent human beings entirely lack the faculty of reason, and live entirely through perception, like animals. This passage therefore confirms the general point that I am making: it is only in very rare instances that we find Aristotle reclassifying an apparent human being as non-human. And when he does so, it is not because of their behavior, but because they entirely lack the faculty of reason.

7.8. THE CIVIC GOOD IS PRIOR TO THE INDIVIDUAL GOOD

'prior' takes on a different meaning—a meaning that Aristotle does not exploit in his theoretical works, because it is not pertinent to the points he wishes to make in them. Perhaps we should try a different strategy: we should investigate the possibility that 'prior' has an evaluative meaning—one that Aristotle thinks will be grasped easily enough by his readers, provided they realize that politics is not a theoretical discipline, and that its vocabulary sometimes takes on its own distinctive meaning.

In fact, Aristotle sometimes warns his audience to separate questions and terms that belong to ethical inquiry from those that belong to the scientific study of nature. For example, in his opening remarks about friendship in the *Nicomachean Ethics*, he reports that, according to Euripides, certain elements love other elements; and according to Heraclitus, harmony can arise from discordance. But he mentions these ideas only to dismiss them, because they are not at home (*oikeia*) in his present inquiry, which has to do with human matters (VIII.1 1155b1–10). We should study human friendship, not friendship in the cosmos, because the study of ethics has a distinct subject matter.

Furthermore, in one of his discussions of the various meanings of 'prior', Aristotle describes one way of using the term, but then dismisses it as 'most alien' (*allotriōtatos*). 'What is better and more to be honored is thought to be prior by nature. Even the many are in the habit of saying that those who are held in higher regard and are loved more by them are prior, as far as they are concerned' (*Cat.* 12 14b4–8). When Aristotle says that this sense of 'prior' is 'most alien', he should be taken to mean that it is the manner of speaking that has least to do with the subject under discussion in the *Categories*: things predicated, and the various kinds of priority that hold among items in different categories. To say that substance is prior to the other categories does not mean that it is to be preferred or better loved. Rather it means that (for example) a thing need not be white in order to exist, although white cannot exist unless something is white. The ethical meaning of 'prior' is not at home (*oikeion*) in this sort of discussion.

But of course it is quite at home in a discussion of ethics and politics. We should therefore consider the possibility that when Aristotle says that the city is by nature prior to each of us, he means that it is better and more to be honored. My hypothesis, to be more precise, is that the city is by nature prior to each of us in that its good is greater than the good of any single one of its citizens. That is true *by nature* rather than convention because it is the nature of the political community to serve the good (not the apparent good) of a large multiplicity of human beings, whereas it is the nature of each of us to be, not a community, but only one human being.[26]

So read, the civic priority thesis has important practical implications. It commits Aristotle to saying that if a choice must be made between promoting the good of a single individual and promoting the good of the whole city (that is, the other members of the community), the latter alternative should be selected. And similarly, if we are forced to choose between a bad outcome for one individual and a bad outcome for all the others, we must opt for the former.[27]

The interpretation I propose also attributes to Aristotle the thesis that the good of the body is greater than the good of any one of its parts. Forced to choose between the destruction of a single part of the body—a hand or a foot, to take the examples Aristotle uses—and the destruction of the body (that is, the rest of the body), one must choose the former.

So understood, Aristotle's thesis that the body is prior to any of its parts is undeniable. His argumentative strategy in this passage is to convince us that what holds true of the body ought to hold true of anything that is structurally similar to it. If anything is an organization of elements that can fare well or badly, and if the parts can also fare well or badly, then the good of the whole is superior to that of any single part. The city and the body are such organizations. And so the good of the whole city (like that of the whole body) must be given priority over the good of any single one of its parts.

There can be no doubt that, according to Aristotle, the aim of the city, and those who are responsible for its governance, is to promote the common good, not the good of merely one individual or household. That is one of the guiding ideas of Book III of the *Politics* (III.6 1279a17–21). His taxonomy of constitutions rests on the distinction

---

[26] Recall that at *Cat.* 12 14b4–8 Aristotle says that if one thing is more to be honored than another, then it is prior *by nature*. I take him to mean that anyone affirming that something has this kind of priority is not merely saying that he likes one thing more than another; rather, his claim is that the nature of the thing makes it more choiceworthy.

[27] We might instead take Aristotle to be saying that the good of the part is inferior to the good of the whole that includes the part. In other words, when given a choice between the good of X and the good of X and everyone else, we should choose the latter. But that would turn the civic priority thesis into a triviality that no one in his right mind could reject. It is more likely, I suggest, that Aristotle takes himself to be making a more substantive claim. Later in this chapter (7.10) we will discuss the connection between the doctrine of civic priority and Aristotle's defense of the institution of ostracism, which allows the good of one individual to be sacrificed for the good of the rest of the community.

between those that accept this principle (kingships, aristocracies, polities) and those in which the ruling faction uses power in purely self-serving ways (tyrannies, oligarchies, democracies). But his idea that the common good must be the aim of constitutions commits him to saying not only that rulers must not be entirely self-serving, but also that no small portion of the community—certainly no single person or household—must be the sole object of a ruler's concern. Translated into the language of Book I, this means: the city is prior by nature to the household and each of us. That thesis has great plausibility in its own right. But it gains even more plausibility when it is recognized as an instance of a more general truth, one that applies to the body no less than the city: the good of any whole is naturally prior to the good of any of its parts.

7.9. *Homonymy Again*

Let us now take a second look at Aristotle's point that when the body is destroyed, its parts are no longer such things as hands and feet, unless these terms are used homonymously. How does that point fit into the argument of our passage, if we take its conclusion to be that the good of the city is prior to the good of the individual citizen?

Suppose one must choose between two evils: the destruction of a hand (and nothing more), or the destruction of the rest of the body. Which is worse? We might think that the only factor that should figure in our answer to this question is size: the hand is only one small part of the body, and it is better to save more parts than fewer. Aristotle does not deny that these quantitative considerations are significant, but one of the main points of our passage is that when we compare a whole and a part, in order to choose between them, we must not ignore the mutual dependence that exists among the parts. The body is not a mere concatenation of elements, for the good of each part is dependent on the good of the others. In fact, this mutual dependence among parts of the body is so extreme that the very existence of a part is undermined by its separation from the whole. An attempt to sacrifice other parts in order to save one is bound to fail, because when the rest of the body is destroyed, each single part is replaced by some other thing that merely looks like it. The good of a living thing is not enhanced by its dying and turning into something else.

How should we apply these points to the relationship between a citizen and his city? It might be thought that Aristotle's analogical argument is utterly and obviously misguided, because individual human beings are not like parts of the body in the relevant respect, as Aristotle himself realizes. A human being who is separated from the rest of his city and lives on his own is nonetheless a human being.

But there is a way to read Aristotle's argument that makes him invulnerable to this objection. We can take him to be thinking along the following lines. It is worse for a whole city to be destroyed than for any single member of the community to be destroyed, and not merely because it is better to save many than to save one. For when we bear in mind what a human being is, and define each thing in terms of its ultimate goal, we will recognize how radically misguided it would be to save one human being at the cost of the destruction of the rest of his community. A human being living in isolation from others would suffer two kinds of loss: he could not receive the aid that all human beings need from others; and he could not employ his capacity to give aid to others and thereby to exercise the other-regarding component of the ethical virtues.

These two kinds of loss are far from trivial. We can see how important they are by reminding ourselves that creatures that have no capacity to serve or no need of support from other members of their community cannot be counted as human beings. Therefore, when a human being is separated from his community, he cannot exercise a capacity without which he would not be human. Since there is no value in having a capacity unless one can exercise it, an isolated human being could not take advantage of being human. Excellent interaction with others, the defining goal of human life, would be unavailable to him. In that respect, saving a single part of the city at the cost of its other components is comparable to saving a hand at the cost of the rest of the body. A hand's good cannot be served in this way because it is what it is only when it operates together with like parts. Similarly, a single citizen's good cannot be served in this way, because he is what he is only by virtue of his ability to interact with other members of his city. Aristotle's point is not ruined by the fact that a human being can exist in isolation, as a hand cannot. For the more important point remains: an isolated human being loses the good of being human and therefore might as well not be human, just as a severed hand cannot attain the good of a hand.

We can therefore make good sense of Aristotle's argument, provided that we take him to be using his notion of homonymy to make similar points (but not precisely the same point) about parts of the body and individual members of the community. A dead hand is no hand. A human being who has no capacity to serve others is no human being. In both cases, Aristotle uses a definition to show that the priority of the whole to the part does not presuppose that there must be or typically is a conflict between whole and part. On the contrary, he is assuring us that the good of the part cannot exist in isolation from the good of the whole to which it belongs.

We can distinguish three lines of thought that make Aristotle confidently affirm the priority of the city. First, he is taking for granted one of the principal themes of Book III of the *Politics*: the aim of those who govern ought to be the good of the whole community rather than the good of any portion of it. Surely if that assumption is correct, then the good of the city is prior to the good of any single household or citizen. Second, the thesis of civic priority is one instance of a more general thesis, which applies to bodies no less than to cities: the good of the whole is always prior to that of any part. Third, it would be absurd to assign the good of a part more importance than the good of the whole, because no part can fare well in isolation from the whole to which it belongs. A hand separated from the body cannot flourish as a hand because it no longer is one. Similarly, an isolated human being cannot fare well because he can no longer exercise the capacity without which he would not be classified as human. Or, if he can carry on just as well, despite his isolation, then he is not a human being after all.

7.10. *The Practical Import of Civic Priority*

What is the practical significance of the thesis of civic priority? If one believes that thesis, how should one show one's acceptance of it, in one's practical thinking and one's actions? I said in 7.8 that, according to the thesis of civic priority, if a choice must be made between the good of a single individual and the good of the other members of the community, the latter alternative should be selected. And similarly, if one must choose between a bad outcome for one individual and a bad outcome for all others, one must opt for the former. The priority of the body to a hand entails that the body should be saved rather than the hand, if one must choose between these alternatives; and similarly, if the loss of a single soldier's life would lead to the preservation of his city, then he should accept that personal loss. Of course, it rarely happens that a city's preservation depends entirely on the actions of just one individual soldier. But nonetheless, it makes an enormous difference to an army's effectiveness if all soldiers accept the priority of the city, and are willing to accept a loss to themselves for the good of their community. An army of soldiers who reject this thesis, and who would serve their own good rather than the good of others, should they conflict, would make a poor fighting force indeed.

It is important to emphasize, nonetheless, that the doctrine of civic priority does not presuppose or entail that there must be or sometimes are conflicts between the good of a single citizen and the good of the rest of his community. It merely commits Aristotle to saying that *if* there are such conflicts, they should be resolved in favor of the whole rather than the part. If in fact there are no such conflicts, the thesis of civic priority still has practical significance.

To see why this is so, we should remind ourselves that, according to Aristotle, living well consists in exercising cognitive skills that aim, principally or exclusively, at the good of others. Courage, for example, can be displayed in the defense of one's own life, but its best manifestations arise on the battlefield when one comes to the defense of one's city. The practical thinking of a genuinely courageous person must have a certain structure: it takes as its starting point the good of the whole community, not the good of the practical agent alone. Someone who fights fiercely in ways that happen to save the lives of others, but who does so primarily to save his own skin, has not acquired the virtue of courage.

A similar point holds true of justice. In both its broad and narrow senses, it cannot be exercised in the absence of a system of laws, assemblies, and courts. The practical thinking of a just person cannot take as its starting point some conception of his own well-being that makes no reference to the good of his community. Rather, to have become just is to have become the sort of person whose thinking about his life locates it in the larger context of the whole community to which he is dedicated. When he confronts practical problems, he thinks first of what can be done for his city and what he owes to it. He deliberates about his household and friends within that larger framework, because often what he does with his house-

7.10. THE PRACTICAL IMPORT OF CIVIC PRIORITY

hold and friends is to provide services to the whole community;[28] and in any case, he will not form plans that bring him into conflict with communal goals, if he can avoid doing so. He has shaped his character so that he makes the good of the whole city his first priority, and he pursues his own good in ways that allow him to honor that priority. To revert to Aristotle's analogy between citizens and parts of the body: an embryonic hand that could deliberate about its own growth and operation would form itself by looking first to the needs of other parts of the body, and would then attend to its own needs only in ways that allow it to operate as harmoniously as possible with those other bodily parts.

Aristotle assumes throughout his political writings that a citizen can be called upon to obey the law and serve his political community in many different ways, and he almost never pauses to offer a justification for this far-reaching assumption. Perhaps that is because he believes that such a justification is already contained in the doctrine that each citizen is a part of a whole that is prior to him. Because the good of the community is superior to the good of any of its members, a citizen can be called upon to risk his life in order to preserve his city, make contributions to the public treasury, obey the laws, and participate in deliberative and judicial institutions. All of these are widely recognized by Aristotle's contemporaries as components of a citizen's obligations, and the doctrine of civic priority helps explain why a citizen should serve his city in these and other ways. Each citizen must serve the larger community both because his own good is less valuable than the good of the whole (as the good of a hand is less important than that of the entire body) and also because his own good consists, at least in part, in serving the whole (as the good of the hand consists, to a large degree, in its service to the body). If, in certain situations, a citizen is called upon to sacrifice his good for the sake of the rest of the community, he must do so, because he must recognize that his well-being is less important than the good of the entire city. But that should not mislead us into supposing that such conflicts between one's own good and that of others are typical. That is why the passage in which Aristotle affirms and argues for the doctrine of civic priority stresses the analogy between a dead hand and an isolated citizen. Without the body, the hand cannot achieve its good—it cannot even be a hand; and similarly, without the city, we cannot achieve our good,

---

[28] This theme will be more fully developed in Ch. 9. See esp. 9.13, 9.15.

because our good consists in virtuous activity, and a major component of virtuous activity is our service to the political community.

Although Aristotle does not explicitly reaffirm the doctrine of civic priority in passages other than the one we have been examining, that thesis lies close to the surface in several other parts of the *Politics*. In III.13, he asks what cities should do about individuals who are in some way so outstanding or powerful that they cannot be treated as merely one citizen among many.[29] Some Greek cities, Athens among them, had a way of dealing with this problem: they periodically asked whether any citizen should be ostracized—that is, sent into exile for a fixed period (five or ten years)—because his presence in the city was thought to be injurious to it. Aristotle says that cities should try to govern themselves so that they never need to ostracize anyone (1284b17–19), and he also notes that often this procedure has been used by factions to promote their own interests rather than the common good (b4–5). Even so, he holds that in certain situations, it is the best remedy for an imbalance in power (b19–20). Sometimes, the presence of a powerful individual in a community makes it impossible for other citizens to achieve their legitimate goals, and in these instances, ostracism does serve the common good. Aristotle never mentions the doctrine of civic priority when he discusses and endorses ostracism, but it should be evident that there is a close connection between these two components of his political theory. His justification of ostracism does not claim that this practice serves the good of the person who is ostracized—and such a claim would lack plausibility. Rather, Aristotle's argument is that this practice serves the good of everyone except the person who is ostracized. One person's good is sacrificed for the good of the city—just as a body might be saved by the amputation of one of its limbs. The justification of ostracism evidently presupposes that the good of the whole is prior to the good of any singe part.[30]

There is one other passage in which Aristotle clearly presupposes the doctrine of civic priority. In VIII.1, he argues briefly that in the ideal city the education of children should be a matter of common concern, and should not be left to each household to provide or fail to provide, as each sees fit. The education of children affects the whole community, and therefore should be under the control of the whole community (6.6). Having said this, he adds: 'At the same

---

[29] Ostracism is also on Aristotle's mind at III.17 1288a25, V.3 1302b18, V.8 1308b19.

[30] For further thoughts on Aristotle's discussion of ostracism, see Kraut, *Aristotle on the Human Good*, pp. 90–97.

time, one should in no way think that any of the citizens belongs to himself; rather all of them belong to the city, for each is a part of the city' (1337a27–9). (More literally: 'one should in no way think that any of the citizens is of himself; rather all of them are of the city.') Someone who thinks that he 'belongs to himself' or is 'of himself' must be opposed to the public supervision of education. He thinks that he need not act in a way that serves the common good, if he chooses not to. Aristotle's response to that thought is that no citizen can be given the authority to decide whether or not he shall contribute to the well-being of others. We 'belong to the city' or are 'of the city' in the sense that we are not free to ignore the good of the rest of the community. When Aristotle backs up his reply to the opponent of common education with the further remark that 'each is a part of the city', he uses the language of civic priority. In effect, he is saying that individuals can be required to serve the city by educating their children in ways approved by the community, because in doing so they serve the common good, and the good of the whole is prior to the good of any of its parts. It is unlikely that he means that there is, in this case, a conflict between the good of an individual household and the good of the city, as there is when an individual is ostracized. His point, rather, must be that the good of an individual household consists partly in the contribution it makes to the good of the city, and in this sense is posterior to the city's good. It cannot be good for a household to educate its children in isolation from the rest of the community, just as a hand cannot properly develop except by taking on a function that serves the whole of which it is a part.

7.11. Body and City

One of the most striking features of the passage we have been examining is the analogy it draws between bodies and cities: each of us is to the political community of which we are a member as a functional part of the body is to the whole of which it is a part. A hand needs support from the rest of the body; so too, a citizen relies on his city for the resources he needs. The proper functioning of a hand consists, to a large degree, in the good it does for the rest of the body; so too, the good of a citizen consists, to a large degree, in what he does for the rest of his community. A single part of the body should be sacrificed in order to save the whole body; so too, the well-being of a single individual should be sacrificed, if doing so is necessary for the good of the city. Aristotle assumes that each of these claims (three about the body and three about the city) has independent plausibility. But nonetheless the analogy he draws is intended to have argumentative force. He thinks that each point takes on additional plausibility when it is seen to be an instance of a more general rule about the relationship between parts and wholes.

Aristotle has other grounds for supposing that it is helpful to think of cities as analogous to bodies, though these further points of comparison do not figure in his argument for civic priority. The parts of a body are not uniform: hands and eyes, for example, have different needs and make different contributions to the well-being of the body. And yet the body is not a mere aggregate of unlike parts that happen to be housed within a skin that separates them from the rest of the world. Rather, the functionally different parts cooperate with each other and form a cohesive material unit. These two complementary aspects of bodies—their diversity and unity—can be found in cities as well, Aristotle thinks; and he will insist on this point in Book II, when he criticizes Plato's abolition of the family and private property. He agrees with Plato that cities need to be unified in some way or other—but not in a way that seeks to make all of their parts alike. The body serves Aristotle as an illuminating model of the city not only because hands and eyes depend on each other, but also because they cooperate with each other in ways that make use of their differences. Too little differentiation will destroy a city, as it will any complex living organism.

Of course, Aristotle is not committed to saying that citizens and parts of bodies are alike in *all* important respects. He would never say, for example, that the parts of the body treat each other justly— even though it is true that each part both serves others and is served by them. Justice requires thought and choice, and can be exhibited only by human beings in their relation to each other. The kind of reciprocity that ties citizens together, each receiving benefits from others and bestowing them in turn, has an analogue in the corporeal realm, but Aristotle shows no temptation to call its physical counterpart a kind of justice.

What he emphasizes, rather, is that there are homonymous ways of speaking about both the body and the city: a dead 'hand' merely looks like one, and a 'human being' who had no need of others and no capacity for community would not really be human. This feature of our passage draws on a doctrine that Aristotle puts to use in his theoretical works, but it is important to see that the doctrine of civic priority does not stand or fall with the success of Aristotle's doctrine of homonymy as applied to the parts of the body. It must be admitted that this piece of Aristotelian metaphysics runs counter to common ways of thinking and talking about things that have functions. A ship that has lost its seaworthiness is still called a ship, as a dead hand is still called a hand. Aristotle's doctrine has a bizarre consequence: when the body dies, a hand is transformed into something new; a different kind of hand arises at the moment of death. Why not stay with common sense and say that because the living and the dead hand have such strong material continuities, they are both really hands?

We need not pursue this metaphysical question. For our purposes, the important point is that civic priority is not a doctrine Aristotle arrives at merely by way of inference from his metaphysical thoughts about dead or stone hands. Even when we set aside those metaphysical thoughts—in fact, even when we entirely set aside Aristotle's analogy between body and city—we are left with a thesis that cannot be dismissed as an absurdity. The doctrine of civic priority, as we have seen, holds that the good of the city is prior to the good of any single individual. Good practical thinking, in other words, has a certain structure. It attends to the good of the agent by first examining the ways in which he can promote the good of the whole community, and then, within that context, by examining the ways in which he can promote the good of smaller groups—his friends, his household, himself. Should circumstances require an individual to choose between the good of his household or his own good and that of the larger political community to which he belongs, it is the latter that must be given priority. So understood, the doctrine of civic priority rests partly on the eminently plausible idea that the good of a single individual is no match for the good of a great multitude, but it also rests on the specific contours of Aristotle's conception of human well-being. A good life consists, among other things, in treating other people justly, and that in turn consists in the active pursuit of the common good of one's community. The very nature of justice requires that one make demands on others only in ways that are compatible with the good of the whole community. It is these ideas, elaborated in Aristotle's *Ethics*, that lie at the heart of his doctrine of civic priority. What Aristotle seeks to do, in our passage, is to give that doctrine additional support, by pointing out that the whole body has an analogous priority to each of its parts. No doubt he is right that a single part of the body should be sacrificed to save the whole. No doubt he is also right that we would resist calling a creature 'human', if it had no need of humans. The weakest link in Aristotle's argument is the one that depends on his doctrine of homonymy, namely his thesis that a dead hand is a hand in name only. But his case for civic priority is not one whose plausibility is only so great as its weakest component.[31]

One further point should be kept in mind: the doctrine of civic priority should not be confused with the thesis that the commands of anyone who has power over a city, or any large collective body, must be obeyed. Aristotle's assumption throughout *Politics* I.2 is that the proper goal of a city is the well-being of its citizens. Though cities long ago came into being for the sake of life—mere survival—increasing prosperity allowed them to secure, to some degree, the conditions in which human beings can not only live but live well. It is only because cities genuinely promote the good of all citizens that they should be given priority over the individual. Priority is not to be given to what merely seems good to someone in a position of power or authority. Aristotle fully recognizes, in *Politics* V.8, that tyrants or tyrannical groups use their positions of power to oppress people and serve their own interests. Their commands are not genuine laws but mere decrees, their regimes are not constitutions in the proper sense of the word, and they do not constitute a city.[32] When Aristotle affirms the priority of the city, he is claiming that when there is some degree of justice in a polis, when it has a genuine legal system, and its government is not a mere device for sustaining the power of the most powerful faction, then each citizen should plan his life in a way that gives precedence to the good of the whole community.

---

[31] For a contrasting view, see Barnes, 'Aristotle and Political Liberty'. He holds that the analogy Aristotle draws between human beings and parts of the body blinds him to the fact that we are independent individuals. As he reads the *Politics*, the bad metaphysical reasoning of I.2 produces in Aristotle a tendency towards totalitarianism—the view that the state is always entitled to intervene in our lives. 'Aristotle's implicit totalitarianism rests ultimately on a questionable inference from a metaphysical untruism' (p. 263).

[32] On the contrast between edicts and laws, see 4.3; for the thesis that tyrannies are not genuine constitutions, see the references at 10.n.15; for the idea that whatever counts as a city must have a concern with the character of citizens, see *Pol.* III.9 (discussed in 11.3).

8

Politics I: Slavery

8.1. *How Could He Have Believed It?*

We must now turn to a topic that looms large in the remainder of Book I of the *Politics*: Aristotle's attempt to show that the enslavement of certain kinds of people is just. That he defended an institution that is inherently debasing and often brutal is a deeply disturbing feature of his political thought, and our repugnance increases when we learn that his attempt to justify this practice played a significant role in its perpetuation. Two millennia after the *Politics* was written, Aristotle's assertion that some people are slaves by their very nature figured prominently in debates in Spain about the legitimacy of enslaving indigenous peoples of the New World.[1] And in the American South, the existence of slavery in Greece and Rome—and the defense of slavery in the *Politics*—gave comfort to apologists for this institution.[2]

What led Aristotle to make this horrendous error? We cannot reply that the thought of abolition never occurred to him, for his

---

[1] A brief account of the debates held in 1550–1 between Sepúlveda (an apologist for enslavement) and Las Casas (an opponent) can be found in Davis, *The Problem of Slavery in Western Culture*, pp. 172–3. For more detail, see Pagden, *The Fall of Natural Man*, pp. 109–45. Las Casas argued, within the framework of Aristotle's *Politics* and Aquinas's commentary on it, that the American Indians deserved paternal treatment, not enslavement.

[2] See Tise, *Proslavery: A History of the Defense of Slavery in America, 1701–1840*, p. 340. I owe this reference to Garnsey, *Ideas of Slavery from Aristotle to Augustine*, p. 16 n. 35 (hereafter cited as *IS*). For further information on the use of Aristotle to support slavery, see Davis, *The Problem of Slavery*, pp. 94–6, 175, 195, 247; and Campbell, 'Aristotle and Black Slavery: A Study in Race Prejudice', pp. 283–302.

attempt to defend slavery is a response to unnamed opponents who argue that it is an unjust institution, lacking a basis in nature and depending entirely on force for its existence (I.3 1353b20–23).[3] Aristotle concedes that in a way these critics are right (I.6 1255a4–5)—but, as we shall see, the main thrust of his argument is that the institution of slavery needs to be reformed, not abolished. His cardinal premise is that some people by their nature deserve to be slaves, and so there is nothing intrinsically wrong with slavery as an institution. This idea, though far from receiving universal acceptance, was revived from one age to another, and the authority of Aristotle lent it considerable support.[4]

We need to understand how Aristotle was able to talk himself into believing that slavery as he knew it was a just institution. Why did he not see what is so obvious to us today? The answer I wish to give is that his justification of slavery rested to some degree on the limited empirical evidence available to him, and the false premises on which he relied were not ones that could easily have been refuted by his contemporaries. Although nothing could be farther from my agenda than to defend slavery, I believe that Aristotle's framework for thinking about this subject was internally consistent and even contained a limited amount of explanatory power. It was a coherent way of looking at the social world that could not, at that time, have easily been undermined by armchair theorizing.[5]

---

[3] Whom did Aristotle have in mind? One possibility is Alcidamas (a student of the sophist Gorgias), who wrote: 'the deity gave liberty to all; nature created no one a slave.' See Garnsey, *IS*, pp. 75–6. Similar statements can be found in Antiphon (a fifth-century sophist) and Philemon (a comic poet somewhat younger than Aristotle). See Brunt, 'Aristotle and Slavery', pp. 351–2. Cambiano, 'Aristotle and the Anonymous Opponents of Slavery', is skeptical that we can identify those opponents. He takes Alcidamas's 'all' (*pantas*) to refer to the Messenian helots, who had been freed as a result of the Theban victory over Sparta in 371.

[4] There was in antiquity a strong tradition—one that runs from Philo through Roman jurists and early Christian thinkers—that rejected the attempt to base slavery on nature. See Garnsey, *IS*, pp. 14, 64. These writers were not in favor of the abolition of slavery; rather, they supported its legitimacy while rejecting the Aristotelian thesis of natural inferiority and superiority. Similarly, although Stoic thinkers emphasized the common rationality of all human beings, they did not oppose slavery. See Garnsey, *IS*, pp. 128–52. According to Garnsey, pp. 80–85, 240, Gregory of Nyssa (fourth century AD) was the only figure of antiquity to condemn the existence of slavery. It should also be noted that the Hebrew and Christian Bibles accept slavery. See e.g. Exod. 21:1–6, Gen. 25: 23, Lev. 25: 44–6, 1 Cor. 7: 20–4, Col. 3: 22–4.1; with discussion in *IS* at pp. 27, 155–6, 163–71, 174–86. On the medieval Church's acceptance of slavery, see Davis, *The Problem of Slavery*, pp. 83–111. Had Aristotle never written in favor of slavery, attempts to defend it by appeals to authority could have relied entirely on sacred texts.

[5] My reading is less condemnatory than those proposed by other scholars. Garnsey, for example, says that 'natural slavery as presented by Aristotle is a battered shipwreck of a theory' (*IS*, p. 107). 'The essential characteristics of the theory' are neither 'plausible nor

No doubt, Aristotle believed that slavery was justified in part because that was a convenient tenet for him to hold. Had he come to the opposite conclusion, he would have been forced to announce to the Greek world that its political institutions, which he greatly valued (however much he also he criticized them), rested on resources that could not be justly acquired or used. The all too human tendency to avoid upheavals of thought and revolutions in social practice certainly played a role here. But it would be a mistake to suppose that because Aristotle was a victim of these complacent habits of mind (a terrible fault in a philosopher), we need not pay careful attention to the theory he used to defend slavery. One cannot talk oneself into believing anything whatsoever, however absurd, and however much it conflicts with appearances—even if one might, by doing so, realize one's fondest dreams. In order for Aristotle to have arrived at the sincere conviction that slavery was just, his social world had to present itself to him in a way that supported that thesis. We cannot understand how he talked himself into accepting slavery unless we try to look at this institution through his eyes.

8.2. Slavery in Greece

Before we examine his theory, let us look at some of the major features of this institution as it had developed in Athens during the fifth and fourth centuries BC. We will be able to understand his discussion better if we know something about what he was trying to defend.

The slave population was considerably larger than the number of adult male citizens. According to one estimate, there were 100,000 slaves in Attica (Athens and its surrounding countryside) in 431 BC, as compared with 50,000 adult male citizens; and 50,000 in 317, as compared with a citizen population of 21,000.[6] What percentage of

easy to establish by philosophical or scientific argument. Aristotle's arguments in support are feeble' (p. 125). Similarly, Williams finds the theory 'incoherent'. See *Shame and Necessity*, p. 117. I respond to Williams in 8.nn.26 and 38. For a full presentation and defense of the thesis that Aristotle's theory does not hold together, see Smith, 'Aristotle's Theory of Natural Slavery'.

[6] Joint Association of Classical Teachers, *The World of Athens* (hereafter *The World of Athens*), p. 157. See too Fisher, *Slavery in Classical Greece*, pp. 34–6. As several authors stress, it is difficult to make reliable estimates. See Wood, *Peasant-Citizen and Slave*, pp. 43–6; and Hansen, *The Athenian Democracy in the Age of Demosthenes*, p. 93. The latter author says: 'The Athenians... did have a conception that there were a lot of slaves, more than the free, and in that they may well have been right.' Note too the report of Thucydides (8.40) that, aside from Sparta, the island of Chios had more slaves than any other Greek city.

the citizen population owned slaves is a matter of controversy, but many scholars believe that they were affordable by a large spectrum of Athenian citizens and were not owned exclusively by a wealthy minority.[7] Although Greeks enslaved other Greeks, for the most part slaves were foreigners (*barbaroi*) who came from regions north or east of Greece.[8] It was a common practice for the survivors of a defeated city to be sold by the victorious army to slave-dealers, who would in turn sell them in the market places of slave-holding cities. There were other paths to slavery as well: for example, one might be kidnapped by pirates and sold into slavery; a child might be sold by impoverished parents; or one might commit a legal offense for which the punishment was enslavement. Someone whose parents were slaves was also a slave, and although manumission was a recognized practice, it was not a usual occurrence.[9]

Slaves were chattel and could not themselves exercise ownership rights. Marriage was a civic procedure unavailable to them, and the children of slaves could be separated from their parents and put up for sale. They could not take legal action in the courts, and were therefore vulnerable to beatings and maltreatment from their masters. Many slaves resided within the household of their owners, performing household services (including the care of children and the elderly) and menial farm work—and these are the slaves that Aristotle has in mind when he tries to show that slavery is a just institution. Other slaves lived apart from their masters and worked at some trade, paying to their owners a portion of their earnings. Some of the richest Athenians accumulated wealth from the silver mines of Laureion (in south-east Attica), which were worked by slaves. Other slaves were collectively owned and performed police functions.[10]

Because slaves played so many roles in Athenian society, it is hard

---

[7] See e.g. *The World of Athens*, p. 186, on the cost of slaves. For the view that slaves were owned primarily by an elite, see Wood, *Peasant-Citizen and Slave*, pp. 42–80. For further discussion, see Osborne, 'The Economics and Politics of Slavery at Athens'; Fisher, *Slavery in Classical Greece*, pp. 37–47. Surely slaves were owned by a larger number of families than the 300–400 who bore the primary financial burdens of the city, according to the estimate of Davies in *Wealth and the Power of Wealth in Classical Athens* (see above, 6.n.50).

[8] See Garnsey, *IS*, p. 6, n. 14.

[9] See MacDowell, *The Law in Classical Athens*, pp. 79–83; Garlan, *Slavery in Ancient Greece*, pp. 73–84; Fisher, *Slavery in Classical Greece*, pp. 67–70.

[10] On the work of slaves, see Garlan, *Slavery in Ancient Greece*, pp. 60–73; MacDowell, *The Law in Classical Athens*, pp. 79–83; *The World of Athens*, pp. 186–7, 228.

to generalize about how hard a life they had.[11] But their legal status—or rather, lack of status—placed them at the bottom of the social hierarchy. Aristotle has no illusions about this. His encapsulation of what a slave is—an ensouled piece of property, an ensouled tool[12]—reveals how lowly and degraded the status of a slave is. And yet he thinks that it is just to assign this role to a certain kind of human being.

8.3. Some Puzzles

It is easy to state some of the principal ideas behind Aristotle's attempt to justify slavery. His main points are that (A) some human beings are by nature slaves, (B) others are by nature masters, and (C) the relationship between a natural slave and a natural master is mutually beneficial.

When Aristotle says that slavery is beneficial to the master, there is no mystery about what he has in mind.[13] The slave performs services for the master that allow the latter to devote his time to better activities. The master need not toil away at hard physical labor, or perform routine or trivial tasks that would dull his mind. By owning a slave, he is able to live a life befitting a free man: he can devote himself to politics, philosophy, poetry, music, and the like. Although slaves were a form of wealth, Aristotle has no interest in defending this institution by appealing to the property rights of owners or the wealth-producing effects of slavery. When he claims that slaves are useful to their masters, he is appealing to his own theory of well-being, which insists that a good life is one taken up with excellent uses of the mind. Slavery relieves the master from

---

[11] Thus Garnsey, *IS*, p. 5: 'many slaves in ancient societies ... were more secure and economically better off than the mass of the free poor, whose employment was irregular, low-grade and badly paid.' For further discussion of the ways in which slaves were treated, see Fisher, *Slavery in Classical Greece*, pp. 70–77.

[12] *Pol.* I.4 1253b32; *NE* VIII.11 1161b4.

[13] The claim that slavery benefits both master and slave is first made at I.2 1252a31–4, but here Aristotle is discussing a relationship that existed prior to the development of the city. Although at that stage of history the slave performed physical services for the master, the master nonetheless had to devote himself to survival and had little time for higher activities. It is only with the rise of the polis that the physical services of the slave allowed the master to live well, and not merely to live. When Aristotle later says that the slave is 'a servant in matters related to action' (I.4 1254a8), he is using his distinction between action and mere production (see *NE* VI.4–5, esp. VI.5 1140b6–7) to indicate that the best use of slavery in the polis is not to allow the owner to produce more goods, but to make possible a life of ethical or intellectual action.

physical toil, and gives him the leisure he needs to engage in ethical, political, and intellectual activities.[14]

We can see immediately that this point would not by itself allow Aristotle to conclude that slavery is justified. For it could be objected that the benefits obtained through slavery are available in other ways. Rather than own slaves, one can hire workers to perform the same services. One of the questions we must ask is why Aristotle thinks that the benefits of slavery could not be equally well secured in some other way.

We will also need to ask what Aristotle means when he says that there are *natural* slaves and masters.[15] At least this much is clear and uncontroversial: he thinks that at birth some people are suited to be slaves. Nothing they do as children or adults can undo the deficiency with which they are born. They lack the faculty by which normal human beings reason (I.5 1254b22–3), and no amount of training or education can remedy this impairment. A natural master, on the other hand, is simply someone who does not suffer from this handicap; he is in full possession of his rational faculties. One of the major difficulties in understanding Aristotle's theory of slavery is to determine what sort of rational incapacity he is talking about. And we must also ask what evidence he relies on when he assumes that many people—tens of thousands in Attica—suffer from this impairment.

There is another puzzle: why does Aristotle think he needs to assert that there are natural slaves and masters, in order to reach the conclusion that slavery is justified? Surely it would be sufficient to show that this relationship is beneficial to both parties. (The institution of trade, for example, is justified because both parties profit; there is no need to show that the farmer who brings his goods to market is suited by birth to be a farmer.) Why does Aristotle take on the additional burden of trying to show that some people are suited at birth to be slaves and others to be masters?

And finally there is this question, which is perhaps most perplexing of all: What makes Aristotle think that slaves benefit from slavery?

---

[14] That is why it is household slavery that Aristotle focuses on in *Pol.* I.3–7. Perhaps he would not go so far as to say that this is the only kind of slavery that is justified. But in any case, he thinks that the strongest argument for slavery can be made when the slave relieves the master of the need to engage in physical toil or the management of the household.

[15] The principal passage is I.5 1254b16–23, which is the conclusion of an argument that begins at 1254a17. See too VII.2 1324b36–41.

8.4. Childlike Helplessness

Perhaps the most important statement Aristotle makes in his defense of slavery is that someone is a slave by nature if he 'shares in reason insofar as he perceives it but does not have it' (I.5 1254b22–3).[16] Here he relies on a distinction he makes in several works between two parts of the human soul: one of them has reason in itself; the other does not, but is merely capable of listening to and being persuaded by reasoning.[17] Aristotle most fully explains what he has in mind when he says (NE I.13 1102b13–29) that sometimes we rationally decide on one course of action, but another part of us—the part responsible for our feelings and passions—urges us to do otherwise. When such conflicts occur, our passions might listen to reason, or might rebel, but in either case, we must recognize that there is an element in the human soul that is rational in a limited way: it does not itself engage in reasoning, but listens to what reason has to say, and reacts favorably or unfavorably. This passionate part of the soul obviously understands what reason tells it—and in this sense, it can be counted as rational, despite the fact that it is not what does our thinking for us. No animals other than human beings have either of these parts of the soul, for they neither actively carry out a process of reasoning nor understand such reasoning when it is presented to them.

Natural slaves, then, share in the defining feature of human nature: they are rational—but only in a limited way. As Aristotle puts the point, they 'perceive [reason] but do not have it' (I.5 1254b22–3).

What does this mean? The thought immediately suggests itself that according to Aristotle the natural slave is a helpless mental invalid. He needs constant attention and direction because, without the guidance of another, he would be unable to cope with any human task that requires even the smallest degree of self-direction and intelligent initiative.[18] His cognitive dysfunction is not total, because he can obey orders and can understand the reasons for those

---

[16] Here and throughout, I use the masculine pronoun to refer to a slave, but it should be kept in mind that a large proportion of the slave population—particularly those who worked in the household—was female.

[17] See NE I.7 1098a4–5, I.13 1102a26–1103a10; EE II.1 1219b28–31; Pol. VII.14 1333a16–18.

[18] This, or something close to it, seems to be the reading adopted by Schofield, 'Ideology and Philosophy in Aristotle's Theory of Slavery'. See pp. 12–14, where the terms 'childlike' and 'feeble-minded' are applied to Aristotle's portrait of the slave.

orders. But that is the only way in which he can be considered a reasoning being. Left to himself, he would be helpless. Nonetheless, Aristotle thinks, people who suffer from such severe mental disability are often capable of performing routine physical tasks, and so they can contribute to the good of others, despite their severe limitations.

It is understandable that we should be tempted to read Aristotle's portrait of the slave in this way. For such a portrait makes it easy to see why it is good for a natural slave to be ruled by someone who is fully rational: without the supervision of a normal adult, he would barely manage to cope with the everyday world. Nonetheless, it is difficult to understand how Aristotle could have convinced himself that such a portrait was realistic.[19] As we noted earlier, there were more slaves in Attica than citizens. Did Aristotle believe that all or many of them were helpless mental invalids? Some slaves worked as craftsmen and lived apart from their masters;[20] obviously they did not suffer from massive cognitive disabilities. Many slaves were victims of war and obviously had had no trouble, prior to their enslavement, living on their own without close and constant supervision. The portrait we have drawn of a natural slave fits only a tiny portion of any sizable community. If Aristotle intended to defend the institution of slavery in anything like the form it took in the ancient world, he ought to have admitted that natural slaves have far more mental competence than is allowed by the portrait we have just composed.

But perhaps we should reconsider our assumption that Aristotle *was* trying to defend slavery as it was practiced in his time. Perhaps the *Politics* is simply trying to show that in principle slavery can be justified—namely, when the slave suffers from cognitive failures so deep that he needs constant direction. Let us evaluate this hypothesis by following it to its logical conclusion: if Aristotle means that

---

[19] Here I disagree with Schofield, 'Ideology and Philosophy in Aristotle's Theory of Slavery', who holds that Aristotle is indifferent to the applicability of his theory to contemporary practices. 'Does [Aristotle] need to ask whether the slaves in the society of his day were natural slaves? Clearly not. And of course, he does *not* ask the question. ... his concern is with the essential character of the master–slave relation, not with slavery as it actually was in fourth-century Greece' (p. 21). It is true that Aristotle does not raise the question, 'Are there any natural slaves today?' but that is because he assumes, and takes his audience to assume, that the answer is so obvious that the question need not be addressed. To support his theory of slavery, he cites with approval the widespread Greek assumption that foreigners are naturally inferior (I.2 1252b5–9, I.6 1255a31–b4).

[20] See Garlan, *Slavery in Ancient Greece*, pp. 64–5, 70–1. On the role of slaves in banking activities, see pp. 67–8.

it is only this kind of person who is a natural slave—someone so mentally impaired that he needs constant care—then in effect he was offering a radical critique of slavery as it was practiced in his society. For in fact the overwhelming majority of slaves were not so severely handicapped, as Aristotle surely must have realized. So, according to the hypothesis we are considering, Aristotle puts forward a theory about what it would take for slavery to be justified, leaving it to his readers to infer that these conditions do not obtain in the real world. His tacit conclusion is that slavery should be abolished in all but a few cases.

This is not a credible hypothesis. Had Aristotle wanted to lead his readers to conclude that slavery as it was practiced in Greece was, with few exceptions, a great injustice, because natural slaves were seldom to be found, he would have had no reason to conceal his point or to leave it unstated. Although he acknowledges that the critics of slavery have a point (I.6 1255a3–7), it is best to take this as his concession that in fact *some* who were enslaved should not have been so.[21] But it is implausible to read him as a radical critic of slavery as it was practiced in his time and place. On the contrary, as we are about to see, the evidence suggests that his defense of slavery does not call for far-reaching changes in the institution of slavery as it is practiced by his contemporaries. He seeks to show that most of those who serve as slaves in Greece are justly enslaved.

8.5. Two Kinds of Deliberative Incapacitation

As I read Aristotle, he attributes to natural slaves far more mental competence and autonomy than was described in the preceding section. He thinks that slaves lack only the capacity to acquire advanced intellectual skills. But he believes that they do possess the human ability to live on their own, to find means to their quotidian ends, and to go about their lives in ordinary ways.

My argument for this interpretation begins with the observation that in *Politics* I.13 Aristotle is more specific than he had been at I.5 1254b22–3 about what the slave is missing: what he wholly lacks, we are told at I.13 1260a12, is the faculty of deliberation (*bouleutikon*). To understand what sort of deficiency a natural slave has, we must determine what this faculty enables those who have it to do.

---

[21] See 8.nn.31 and 45.

It will be helpful to divide the deliberative faculty into two parts. In doing so, we are making use of a distinction Aristotle draws in Book VI of the *Nicomachean Ethics* between deliberating well in a strict or unqualified sense (*haplōs*) and deliberating well in relation to a particular end (VI.9 1142b29). Both kinds of deliberation are directed at ends, but Aristotle says that excellent deliberation in the strict sense succeeds in discovering our goal in the strict sense, whereas deliberation in the lesser sense merely succeeds in arriving at a specific goal (b30–1). What he means is this: when we say that someone is a good deliberator, and do not add any qualification about the kind of goal his skillful deliberation is directed at, we should be taken to mean that he can deliberate well about how to achieve the highest end of human life. If we mean instead that he is a good deliberator because he knows how to attain some more specific end like wealth, or because he can deliberate well about how to craft a product, then we should spell out this limitation in our compliment by calling him, not a good deliberator without qualification, but a good deliberator in relation to that particular goal.

This distinction between two kinds of excellence in deliberation corresponds to two different kinds of intellectual faculty that Aristotle discusses in Book VI. The capacity to engage in *practical* reasoning is one of them; the capacity to engage in *productive* reasoning is the other. The former is perfected when one acquires practical wisdom (VI.5); the latter is perfected when one acquires the knowledge of a craft—medicine, building, navigation, and so on (VI.4).

Aristotle says at *Politics* I.13 1260a12 that the slave wholly lacks the deliberative faculty. Does that mean that he wholly lacks both the intellectual capacity to acquire a craft and the intellectual capacity to reason about his highest ends? The word translated 'wholly' (*holōs*) does not by itself answer our question: it merely tells us that whatever it is that the slave lacks, his lack of it is not partial.[22] Nonetheless, as we will discover, there is good reason to

---

[22] *Holōs* is used in this line in order to contrast the defect of slaves with that of women, who do have the deliberative faculty, even though it is 'without authority' (*akyron*: 1260a13). Precisely what does that female deficiency amount to? I take Aristotle to mean that women cannot deliberate about matters that are removed from the sphere of the household. They can oversee slaves and the work that must be done in the house, but cannot become skilled as political deliberators, because, like slaves, their reason has a natural deficiency. Free women are in possession of only one part of the deliberative faculty (the part that lacks authority), whereas slaves (male and female) entirely lack it. Their deliberative faculty is without authority because the sphere in which they can develop competence as deliberators is subordinate to the authority of the polis. Of course, what this means cannot become fully clear until we determine what Aristotle thinks the deliberative

take him to be saying that the slave's thorough deliberative incapacity is twofold: he cannot acquire intellectual excellence as a fashioner of artifacts, nor can he deliberate well about how he should lead his life.

That does not commit Aristotle to saying that if you see someone working on the construction of a house, or helping to heal a sick person, or making a pair of shoes, then you can infer that he has the deliberative faculty, and that he is not by his nature a slave. As we will now see, it is much more difficult than that to tell, by simple observation, who is a natural slave and who is not.

8.6. *Craft as an Intellectual Power*

Aristotle thinks that someone who does what is just is not necessarily a just person. He is just only if he knows what he is doing, chooses the act for itself, and does so because of his firm and unchangeable character (*NE* II.4 1105a31–2). To confirm this point, Aristotle points out that something similar applies to other spheres of life: saying something grammatical or musical does not prove that one has knowledge of grammar or music (1105a22–6). For 'it is possible to produce something grammatical by chance or at the direction of someone else' (a22–3). He does not elaborate on the requirement that one should not be acting 'at the direction of someone else', but he makes it clear enough in other passages that he has something rather demanding in mind. He hints at this briefly at *Ethics* I.13 1102a21–3: 'Among doctors those who are refined take a great deal of trouble as regards their study of the body.' That implies that there are unrefined doctors who have not studied the body. We hear more about this at *Politics* III.11 1282a3–4: 'A doctor is a common worker [*dēmiourgos*] or a master craftsman [*architektonikos*] or third someone who has been educated [*pepaideumenos*] in that field.'[23] In other words, one sort of doctor has not made a study of the

---

faculty is. For an alternative reading, see Fortenbaugh, 'Aristotle on Slaves and Women', pp. 138–9. He takes Aristotle to be saying that women are equal to men as deliberators, but are inferior to men only because it is their emotions, not their reason, that govern their actions. Still another reading is proposed by Saxonhouse, *Women in the History of Political Thought*, pp. 74–5: she takes Aristotle to be making the merely empirical point that women are not granted political authority. Both of these readings implausibly take Aristotle to be making an astonishing concession to the intellectual powers of women.

[23] The context is a discussion of whether the many (as opposed to the few who have expertise) should have power. The elitist argues: only a doctor can determine whether a patient has been treated correctly. Aristotle sees a way for the anti-elitist to respond: one

body, and administers medicine under the direction of a supervisor. A second sort has made such a study, and tells his medical assistants what to do. And a third falls between these two extremes: he has not made a special study of medicine, but he is an educated person, and is in a better position than the mere assistant to assess the quality of a doctor's advice.

This passage from the *Politics* is likely to have been written with an eye to a distinction Plato makes in the *Laws*: 'There are some who are doctors, as we call them, and others who are assistants to doctors, though we of course call them doctors too. . . . Whether they [the assistants to doctors] are free men or slaves, they acquire their craft at the command of their masters and through observation and experience—but not through nature, as do free men who have made a study on their own and taught these things to their students. . . .'[24] (720a). The passage goes on (720b–c) to say that the inferior doctor gives the patient no account (*logos*) of what he is doing or recommending. He merely tells the patient what to do, and does not teach him about his condition. Presumably that is because he himself does not know his subject; he is merely following a fixed rule that he has learnt from someone else, or is carrying out a command.

The passage just cited from the *Politics* builds on Plato's distinction between these two kinds of doctor, by adding an intermediate category, but it nonetheless accepts Plato's basic idea. One kind of craftsman has knowledge of his subject, and can give an account of why he acts as he does. Another has made no such study, and acts as he does because he is following the recommendations or commands of someone else. In either case, the results are the same: a patient is healed, a pot made, a building erected. But what lies behind these products is in one case the knowledge of a craft, and in the other an ability to follow a pattern laid down by another. The mere maker of products—the common worker (*dēmiourgos*)—does not possess a craft (though he can be called a doctor, a builder, and the like), because craft is a form of knowledge and is accompanied by reason (*NE* VI.4 1140a3–5).[25]

---

need not have a specialist's knowledge of medicine in order to evaluate doctors; one need only have received a sufficiently broad general education. For Aristotle's notion of general education, see 6.n.70.

[24] See too *Apology* 22d and *Gorgias* 465a. These passages assume that a genuine craftsman has mastered an intellectual skill, and is not merely good at creating a product.

[25] Note too *Met.* I.1 981a5–12: 'Craft knowledge comes to be when from the experience of many notions one universal judgment [*hypolēpsis*] arises concerning like cases. For to make the judgment that when Callias was sick this helped with this disease, and so too

8.6. CRAFT AS AN INTELLECTUAL POWER

Let us now return to the statement that the natural slave wholly lacks the deliberative faculty (I.13 1260a12). It is not immediately apparent what that means, because, as we saw in the previous section, there are two kinds of deliberation, one directed towards living well, the other aimed at such products as ships, buildings, and health. Aristotle does not say, in Book I of the *Politics*, whether slaves lack the capacity for both kinds of thought. Of course, there can be no doubt that, in his opinion, a natural slave lacks the capacity to learn how to make wise judgments about well-being. For surely Aristotle believes that this is the most important deliberative skill a human being can possess, and he cannot afford to agree that slaves have it. At most, he might admit that slaves have the capacity to learn how to deliberate well about craft matters.

But the passages we have considered in this section are evidence that he would not want to concede to them even that less exalted component of the deliberative faculty. For these passages indicate that craft-knowledge and craft-deliberation are significant intellectual accomplishments. Someone who has acquired knowledge of a craft, and does not merely make things by following the instructions of someone else, must have made a study of the goal of his craft, and must have learnt how to achieve that goal by deliberating well. Deliberative skill, as Aristotle describes it in *Ethics* III.3, is not a mere matter of finding instrumental means to simple ends—going to the market in order to get food, cooking food to prepare a meal, cutting leather to make shoes. It involves the adaptability and ingenuity that are needed whenever fixed rules cannot always be relied upon, and decisions must be made under conditions of uncertainty (1112b2–9). That flexibility cannot be developed in the absence of a proper understanding of the end at which the craft aims, and that understanding is acquired only through careful investigation. It is plausible to take Aristotle to be assuming that these are among the intellectual skills that a slave can never acquire, because of his natural debility. A natural slave can certainly think successfully about how to make things, but Aristotle believes that he can never rise above the level of an ordinary worker, who manages to get the job done only because he follows rules and models laid down by others. Although a slave can make the same product day in and day

for Socrates and the many other particulars: that belongs to experience. But to make the judgment that among all those of a certain sort who have been marked off as a kind and are sick with this disease, it helped (for example among all those who are phlegmatic or bilious or feverish): that belongs to craft knowledge.'

out, he cannot train his mind to acquire knowledge of a craft, no matter how much instruction he receives, and no matter how much he tries. He can live on his own and earn his daily bread well enough. He can feed himself, clothe himself, and set aside provisions for the winter, for these humdrum activities require no knowledge of any craft. Observation of his daily activities would not by itself reveal his intellectual deficiencies.

8.7. Greek Superiority

In order to justify the institution of slavery as he knew it, Aristotle needs to show that there are a large number of people—corresponding roughly to the slave population of his time and place—who not only *do not* deliberate (in his sense of the word) but *cannot* do so. He cannot rest content with the assertion that as a matter of fact there are many people who do not deliberate about the highest ends of human life, and are not master craftsmen. Those empirical claims are plausible enough. After all, few people are sufficiently thoughtful to ask themselves what their highest goals should be, and to choose the kind of life they lead on the basis of these reflections. And in any sphere of craft activity, there are few who have mastered their subject. But these points will not by themselves prove that the reason why many people are not deliberators is that they lack the deliberative faculty. (Many people do not knit, but that hardly shows that they lack the capacity to do so.) What evidence does he rely on, when he assumes such widespread cognitive incapacity?

Aristotle attributes to the Greeks a sense of superiority to their northern and eastern neighbors, and thinks that their attitude is entirely justified (I.2 1252b5–9, I.5 1255a31–b2).[26] His view is that

[26] The class solidarity of the poor in Athens was especially dependent on their sense of superiority to foreigners and slaves, and was fed by the pride they took in their citizen status. See Ober, *Mass and Elite in Democratic Athens*, pp. 261–4. I believe that this casts doubt on the thesis, advanced by Williams, *Shame and Necessity*, p. 123, that all Greeks but Aristotle thought that the distinction between slaves and free men was an arbitrary matter. According to Williams, enslavement was for the Greeks (Aristotle excepted) a mere matter of bad luck, something for which no justification could be given (pp. 116–17). Aristotle's very idea that it could be justified brings him greater discredit than is deserved by his contemporaries, who merely accepted it as a necessity (p. 111). Yet Williams acknowledges the existence of 'Greek prejudices about the slavish nature of barbarians' (p. 115). In any case, if Williams were right that all Greeks but Aristotle took slavery to be an arbitrary misfortune, one would have expected the Athenian legal record to indicate some willingness in the popular assembly to improve the condition of slaves, or to manumit them in limited numbers, or to grant them citizen status. But what evidence we have points in the

8.7. GREEK SUPERIORITY

natural slaves are to be found among certain foreigners, and that the Greeks are by nature a free people, a people not fit to be enslaved (III.14 1285a19–22).[27] So he thinks that there is a rough and ready test for determining whether someone is a natural slave: if he is a native of an area to the north or east of Greece, he probably is; if he is a native Greek, he almost certainly is not.[28]

That sounds astonishingly simple-minded—but there is more to what Aristotle is saying than meets the eye. To see what he is getting at, we must turn to *Politics* VII.7, where he claims that meteorological conditions foster the development of different types of people in different regions.[29] The climate of Greece is intermediate between that of Europe (the area to the north) and Asia (to the east). These conditions favor the growth of intelligence (*dianoia*) and spirit (*thymos*) in Greece; by contrast, the climate of Europe is favorable to the development of spirit but not intelligence, whereas Asia produces a population that is intelligent but lacking in spirit (1327b23–36).

Here Aristotle is treating 'spirit' as a disposition to resist domination, and he is saying that the peoples who live to the north of Greece (Scythians, Thracians, Celts) have a strong antipathy to occupying subordinate positions. For the most part, they resist slavery, and when they are enslaved, they are difficult to manage. On the other hand, these peoples are rather deficient in 'intelligence and craft' (b24–5); that is why they are 'apolitical' (b26) and do not occupy themselves with making things. They lack the sort of intelligence needed to be rulers (b26–7)—in other words, they do not have the faculty of deliberation—and so they qualify as natural slaves. Even so, Aristotle's description of them implies that it is generally best to look elsewhere for slaves, because the spirit of these northerners is apt to make them difficult to manage.

What of Persians and other peoples of the east? Do they qualify as

---

opposite direction. In late fifth-century Athens, a proposal that would have granted citizenship to metics and slaves who had helped overthrow the Thirty Tyrants was defeated. See Ober, *Mass and Elite in Democratic Athens*, p. 97. For a brief account of the Thirty Tyrants, see Hornblower and Spawforth, *Oxford Classical Dictionary*, s.v. 'Thirty Tyrants'.

[27] For Plato's endorsement of this idea, see *Republic*. 469b–c, 471a. The Greek sense of superiority derives from their success in the Persian Wars, as Garlan notes (*Slavery in Ancient Greece*, pp. 120–1).

[28] 'Rough and ready' because Aristotle acknowledges exceptions (I.6 1255b3–4). See too 8.n.31.

[29] Aristotle's thoughts about climate and character were influenced by the Hippocratic treatise, *On Airs, Waters, Places*. See esp. chs. 12–24. Cf. Montesquieu, *The Spirit of the Laws*, bks. 14–17.

slaves, and do they make good slaves? Aristotle says that they lack spirit (b28), implying that they do qualify as good slaves. But he also says that they 'have souls that are intelligent [*dianoētika*] and skilled in the crafts [*technika*]' (b27–8), and his recognition that they are intelligent might be taken to mean that he credits them with the capacity for deliberation. Such a reading cannot be correct, however, for we know that, according to Aristotle, Asians are the people who are naturally most suited for slavery (III.14 1285a19–22). What he must mean, then, when he says that Asians are 'intelligent and skilled in the crafts' is that they have the low-level capacity that is needed in order to learn how to make buildings, pots, shoes, and so on. The second component of Aristotle's phrase—'skilled in the crafts'—spells out what he means by the first component, 'intelligent'. The evidence on which he is relying is that the peoples to the east possess a technologically advanced civilization. Like the Greeks, they are the beneficiaries of humankind's discovery of the crafts in all of their variety. But in making this concession to the intelligence of Asian peoples, Aristotle is not granting that they have either of the two components of the deliberative faculty. What he says in VII.7 is compatible with his belief that the Asian world is filled with natural slaves. They have enough intellectual ability to learn how to make things, when they are told by others how to do so. But that does not show that they have the capacity to become master craftsmen or to deliberate about the highest ends of human life. When we read our passage in this way, we can explain why he thinks that easterners are excellent candidates for slavery. By and large, they have no rational capacity more impressive than their ability to become ordinary craftsmen. Like northerners, they have no deliberative capacity; unlike northerners, they are submissive. And so they make the best slaves.

Putting all of this together, we can identify the empirical evidence Aristotle would cite to support his claim that the Greeks rightly count themselves superior to other peoples. The Greeks clearly do have deliberative skills, for they are a people who govern themselves, and governance requires deliberation about the highest ends of human life. Although kingships were common in Greece at an early point in its political development (III.15 1286b8–10), they were replaced by oligarchies and democracies, as the number of men who had some deliberative skill increased. Major decisions about what the goals of the city should be, and how those goals should be pursued, were put in the hands of collective bodies, and this development could have taken place only among a people who have the native capacity to reason together about the highest goals. That many Greek cities were ruled democratically confirms Aristotle's point: all Greek men are capable of participating to some degree in the governance of their cities. (And since they have this deliberative skill, they also have the capacity to become master craftsmen—though few of them in fact develop this capacity.)

Europe and Asia, by contrast, were the sites of quite different patterns of political development. The peoples of Europe showed no talent either for the crafts or for political governance. There were no self-governing cities in these northern areas. Similarly, the peoples of Asia show only a limited rational capacity: the crafts flourish in these eastern locales, but Asia has always been dominated by tyrants, and the people have always accepted a subservient role. How can this differential pattern of political development be explained? Aristotle's hypothesis is that character traits and rational capacities do not float free of physical influence. The body's heat and moisture must affect the development of the soul, and the body in turn is likely to be influenced by the heat and moisture in the world around us. Aristotle's hypothesis—that environmental differences explain the prevalence of self-rule in Greece and its absence elsewhere—was not incoherent or devoid of explanatory power.

We can now answer the question we raised earlier: what evidence can Aristotle cite to support his thesis that those whom he took to be natural slaves really do lack the capacity to deliberate? His response is that we need only look to Europe and Asia and compare these regions to Greece. Consider the systems of self-rule that have arisen in Greece over several centuries, and contrast this with the absence of self-rule in those other areas. If the northerners and easterners have a capacity to deliberate, why has there been so little evidence of this capacity for such a long period of time? Why do we find such abundant evidence of this capacity in Greece, and so little elsewhere? Why have habits of subservience to mediocre kings and oppressive tyrants been short-lived in Greece but not in other parts of the world? These are legitimate questions, and Aristotle's answer to them is not preposterous.[30] Differences in natural capacity

---

[30] There is one weakness in Aristotle's theory that his contemporaries should have been able to detect: it seems to predict that the children of Asian slaves born in Greece should be capable of becoming excellent deliberators. (After all, they spend their formative years in a moderate climate.) If Aristotle wishes to claim that the parents' inability to deliberate is inherited even when their children are born and raised in Greece, he needs to add this

sometimes do explain differences in accomplishment. Aristotle is not flying in the face of reason or the evidence available to him and his contemporaries when he maintains that for the most part those who serve as slaves in Greece—Asians and Europeans—do not deliberate about the highest ends because they lack the capacity to do so.[31]

Aristotle's hypothesis about why different parts of the world have developed in such different ways has been conclusively refuted. Climate may have some effect on character, but not in the way he proposes. History how shown that the political intelligence he was talking about can develop in every region of the world and is not confined to Greece or to any other area. Whenever a group of people has been denigrated by others as intellectually inferior, empirical evidence has shown that such allegations are baseless. Science has helped us to set aside our prejudices and blinders.[32] That is why it is

hypothesis to his theory: although the physical basis for rational incapacity is at first meteorological, that incapacity becomes unalterable and is then transmitted across generations. The admission that meteorology does not by itself account for inequality would make Aristotle's theory more complex, but not untenable.

[31] I say 'for the most part' because Aristotle thinks it is the business of science to understand not only what happens universally but also what is the case *hōs epi to poly*, 'for the most part'. For representative passages, see *Physics* I.5 197a19–20; *Gen. An.* IV.10 778a4–9; *Met.* VI.2 1027a20–1; and for discussion, Reeve, *Practices of Reason*, pp. 13–22. Pointing to a number of exceptions would not by itself undermine Aristotle's thesis that Asians are natural slaves (just as exceptions would not undermine the claim that old age brings gray hair). It is possible that when Aristotle says that slaves often have the souls of free men (I.5 1254b32–4), he means that although most Asians are slavish, a significant number are not; but perhaps he is only alluding to the fact that Greeks are enslaved, although for the most part free. In a parallel passage, he says that although nature tends to make it the case that good people are born of other good people, it is often unable to do so (I.6 1255b1–4). The idea seems to be that in certain cases a child's innate tendencies make him resist the best efforts of good parents to inculcate the virtues. (Moral education requires the cooperation of nature, habituation, and reason, and so one must begin with a soul of a certain sort: VII.13 1332a38–42.) The converse idea would be that sometimes a child's innate goodness leads him to become virtuous, despite his lack of good parental guidance. By parity of reasoning, Aristotle can agree that some inhabitants of Europe and Asia are not natural slaves.

[32] For a recent attempt to explain the vastly unequal development of technology and political organization in different regions of the world, without resorting to an Aristotelian hypothesis of innate inequality, see Diamond, *Guns, Germs, and Steel*. Diamond's question—'why weren't Native Americans, Africans, and Aboriginal Australians the ones who decimated, subjugated, or exterminated Europeans and Asians?' (p. 15)—is similar to Aristotle's question about why different regions of his world exhibit unequal political development. But we are now in a better position than Aristotle was to give defensible answers to such questions. To be sure, it is not merely our science that has improved; we also have undergone moral changes—for the better. Many of us would be disturbed by apparent evidence for significant innate inequalities. We want it to be the case that people have equal capacities for political, moral, and technological development. The members of Aristotle's social world had no such desire.

so much easier for us than it was for Aristotle to see that slavery lacks a justification.

8.8. Why Slavery Benefits Slaves

Suppose, for the sake of argument, we were to allow Aristotle to reach the conclusion that certain people by their nature lack the capacity to deliberate. What would follow from this about how these people should be treated? Would this premise lend any support to the conclusion that they should be slaves?

To answer this question, we should distinguish two different features of the relationship between masters and slaves, as Aristotle understands it. First, the master rules over the slave, whereas the slave exercises no legitimate power over the master. A slave is not a partner in decision-making—not even a junior partner. The master gives commands; the slave obeys. Second, the master owns the slave. He can sell the slave, transfer him to another, or free him, if he so chooses.

The independence of these two features of slavery should be obvious. In a modern legal system, a court may judge someone mentally incompetent and give a guardian extraordinary powers to make decisions on his behalf. Even so, the ward is not a piece of property. Decision-making authority does not entail ownership rights.

Aristotle's claim that some human beings lack the capacity to deliberate might give some support to his conclusion that others should exercise control over them. The lives of those who are incapable of thinking wisely about their ends might go better if their decision-making authority were restricted in certain ways. But even if we were to agree with Aristotle about that, we would balk at drawing the further conclusion that the institution of chattel slavery is justified. Even if the slave requires careful supervision, it does not follow that he must be owned.[33] What Aristotle must show is that both the slave and the slave-owner benefit from the property–owner relationship that exists between them. Why would not both of them be better off if slavery were abolished and replaced by a system in which those who lack the deliberative faculty have the right to determine whether to sell their labor to this or that person? Let us grant, at least for the sake of argument, that the interests of

---

[33] For this point, see Smith, 'Aristotle's Theory of Natural Slavery', p. 154.

slave-owners would not be served by abolition. But why was it not clear to Aristotle that the transformation of slaves into wage-laborers would have been good for them?

In order to arrive at an answer to this question, we must try to understand precisely what sort of benefit Aristotle thinks slaves derive from their status as owned and supervised beings. He says that a master exercises 'foresight' (I.2 1252a32) and relies heavily on the idea (I.5 1254b2–16) that it is always beneficial for something or someone who is naturally inferior to be ruled by a superior. To convince of this, he relies on examples: as the soul rules the body, reason rules appetite, husband rules wife, and man rules other animals. But these analogies tell us little about how slaves are supposed to benefit from their enslavement.

It might be suggested that since the slave is incapable of deliberating about the highest ends of human life, the master benefits him by telling him what these highest ends are. He teaches him the lesson to be learnt from Aristotle's ethical works: that happiness consists in virtuous activity, adequately supported by external goods, over the course of a lifetime.

A slave would gain nothing, however, from simply being told that this is so. It would be useless for him to listen to this formula if he had no understanding of what it means and why it is true. Yet if the slave is to acquire that understanding, he will become practically wise—which, of course, Aristotle denies that he can do, since he lacks the capacity for deliberation.

Here is another possibility: Aristotle might mean that by living under the direction of a master, a slave will enjoy better health and a greater degree of prosperity than he otherwise could attain. In the household of the master, he is well fed and need not worry about how to support himself. Should he be freed, he will quickly discover how hard it is to work for wages and to acquire the basic necessities of life. He will recognize how much better off he was to be a slave.[34]

But this cannot be what Aristotle is getting at either. For it is contrary to his ethical theory to suggest that any real gain in well-being comes from the mere possession of such external goods as

---

[34] Recall the point made by Garnsey, *IS* (8.n.11). Note too the criticism Epictetus makes (*Discourses* 4.1.37–8) of the slave who receives his freedom and then longs for slavery: 'He says, What evil did I suffer? Another clothed me, another supplied me with shoes, another fed me and looked after me in sickness ... But now a wretched man, what things I suffer, being a slave of many instead of one' (translated, with slight modification, by Garnsey, *IS*, p. 49).

8.8. WHY SLAVERY BENEFITS SLAVES

health, shelter, and food, or from the mere enjoyment of the pleasures of the body.[35] He holds that well-being consists in excellent activity, and although such activity requires resources, the mere presence of those resources does not by itself make one better off. Whether one benefits from having external goods depends on how they are used, and this point of course applies to slaves no less than to other human beings. A wealthy master who has more slaves than he needs, and assigns some of them no work, allowing them to live a life of idle amusement, would be corrupting, not benefiting, them.

The only way a slave can have a life worth living even to a small degree is for his master to inculcate some measure of virtue in him. And Aristotle thinks that this can be done. In I.13 he admits that the question whether slaves can be virtuous is full of difficulties, but he resolves the issue by concluding that a slave needs 'little virtue—so much as keeps him from failing in his tasks through intemperance or cowardice' (1260a35–6). The slave benefits from slavery, then, because, were he not a slave, he would lead a life of idleness, dissolution, and petty immorality. The supervision of a master (at any rate, a good master) will keep his worst qualities in check. Properly disciplined, he can acquire a small portion of virtue, and although his life can never be a good one, since real virtue is beyond his capabilities, his subordination to a master makes him less distant from this ideal than he otherwise would be.[36]

It is entirely compatible with this picture of slavery that at some point the slave might deserve to be given his freedom and to live a life of independence. If a slave develops good habits, if he is disciplined, obedient, and shows a measure of temperance over a long period of time, then he may no longer need the daily supervision of a master, and it may do him no harm to live on his own. So it is understandable that Aristotle should say, in his depiction of an ideal city, that slaves should be offered freedom as a reward for their good behavior (VII.10 1330a32–3).[37] Here he must be assuming that even

---

[35] Well-being needs the goods that we acquire in part through good fortune, but it is a mistake to identify it with good fortune or with these external goods. Rather, it consists in making an excellent use of them. See NE I.8 1099b6–8, I.10 1100b8–11; EE I.2 1214b24–7.

[36] I take Aristotle to be saying that in order to instill some degree of virtue in a slave, one must not merely issue orders, but must explain the reason for those orders. This seems to be the gist of his criticism of Plato at I.13 1260b5–7 (apparently directed at Laws 777e–778a). For discussion, see Fortenbaugh, 'Aristotle on Slaves and Women', esp. pp. 136–7.

[37] He promises to say more about this, but does not do so. The pseudo-Aristotelian Economics says that slaves will work harder if they are promised freedom as a reward (I.5 1344b15–17). According to Diogenes Laertius, Lives of Eminent Philosophers (hereafter Lives) V.14–15, Aristotle's will provided for the manumission of his slaves. My views on

in well-disciplined slaves the desire for freedom will be present to some degree. Otherwise the offer of freedom would not be an attractive goal.[38] But it is not necessary to take him to be making the further assumption that when they are freed, slaves will be worse off.[39] It is compatible with his theory of slavery to say that if a master's discipline takes hold in the slave's soul, his habits will keep him on a steady course even after he wins his freedom. The slave, we must recall, is not a helpless mental invalid. Although he cannot deliberate about the highest ends, he can get by with less, if he has been properly trained.[40]

But the only way for him to get this training, Aristotle supposes, is for him to live for a long period of time under the close supervision of someone who has considerable power over him. A wage-laborer who lives outside the household and can terminate his relationship with his employer at any time cannot be overseen and disciplined in the way a slave can. That is why Aristotle thinks the abolition of slavery would not serve the interests of those who lack the deliberative faculty.

We should be careful not to misstate Aristotle's position. He must not be taken to mean that when a master gives orders to his slaves, he does so, or should do so, for the purpose of inculcating a small degree of virtue in him. Giving orders to slaves is not and never can become a noble calling; its purpose is not to provide the slave with a moral education, but to take care of the necessities of life so that one

---

this matter should be contrasted with those of Smith: 'even Aristotle was ultimately uneasy with his own theory, for he provided in his will that his own slaves be freed' ('Aristotle's Theory of Natural Slavery', p. 144).

[38] For this reason, Aristotle should be acquitted of the charge that he denies the obvious: slavery rests on coercion. For this accusation, see Williams, *Shame and Necessity*, p. 117. Aristotle is of course eager to show that slavery does not rest on coercion *alone*. But he recognizes and makes use of the point that no one wants to be a slave, and this allows him to hold that although this institution is just, it must be backed by force. There is no inconsistency in his thesis that slavery is both natural and forced; slavery accords with the nature of certain people, but since no one wants to be a slave, the institution cannot exist without coercion.

[39] This is an assumption I wrongly made in my commentary on 1330a31–3. See Kraut, *Aristotle: Politics Books VII and VIII*, pp. 117–18.

[40] Aristotle should not be taken to mean that in an ideal city all slaves will be good slaves. See VII.17 1336a39–41 for evidence to the contrary. His idea is simply that promising freedom as a reward will be effective in some cases but not all. He assumes that as a rule slaves are and will always be vulgar people. Note his remark that citizens who violate social norms act in a way 'characteristic of slaves' (VII.17 1336b12). This low opinion of slaves was widely shared; see Dover, *Greek Popular Morality in the Time of Plato and Aristotle*, pp. 114–16; Ober, *Mass and Elite in Democratic Athens*, pp. 270–2; Garnsey, *IS*, pp. 72–4.

8.8. WHY SLAVERY BENEFITS SLAVES

is free to pursue higher activities.[41] The master treats the slave as an instrument, and is not trying to promote the well-being of the slave for the slave's own sake.[42] It is crucial to Aristotle's defense of slavery that slaves not be harmed by their enslavement, for if they were, his own theory of justice would force him to admit that slavery is a questionable institution. Justice consists in a proportionate exchange of good for good or evil for evil; if the slave received nothing good from his enslavement, but merely provided goods to others, Aristotle's attempt to defend this institution would fail to meet his own standards. But although he needs to show how slaves benefit from their condition, he need not claim that the motive of the slaveholder is or should be to benefit slaves for their sake. He holds, on the contrary, that it is self-interest that underlies the master's treatment of the slave. The slave is to be treated like any other tool: he is to be cared for, because a badly treated instrument will not get the job done.

Let us now consider an objection to Aristotle's attempt to show that slaves benefit from their slavery. We shall continue to concede, for the sake of argument, that someone who cannot deliberate about the highest matters would benefit from being placed in a subordinate position to a wise master. Even so, Aristotle would admit that few have ever met his high standards of wisdom, and it is unlikely that more than a few will ever do so. But doesn't this concession

---

[41] If one devotes oneself too fully to ordering slaves about, one is no longer living a life suitable for a free person: 'The life of a free person is better than that of a master. For there is nothing grand about employing a slave as a slave; for giving orders about necessities has no share in what is noble' (VII.3 1325a24–7).

[42] The slave is compared to a tool at I.4 1253b32–3; see too *NE* VIII.11 1161b4–5. I take Aristotle's meaning to be, not simply that it is advantageous to own slaves, but that the master rightly treats the slave in the way all tools should be treated: they should be taken care of, not for the sake of the tool, but for the owner's sake. See *EE* VII.9 1241b17–22 and *Pol* III.6 1278b32–7. That is why he thinks the relationship of master to slave is comparable to that of tyrant to subject (*NE* VIII.10 1160b29–30; cf. *Pol.* III.6 1279a19–20). A tyrant, unlike a king, treats those over whom he rules as means to his own ends (III.7 1279a32–b7). Another analogy Aristotle proposes is that master is to slave as soul is to body (I.5 1254b4–5, I.6 1255b9–11). The soul cares for the body, not for the sake of the body, but for its own sake. Aristotle says that there is a kind of friendship between a natural master and a natural slave, although such friendship does not exist when their relationship is based solely on convention and force (I.6 1255b12–15). I take him to mean that when a master-slave friendship exists, it rests on mutual advantage; but when the slave is by nature a free person, he does not benefit from being enslaved, and therefore no friendship exists between him and his owner. Aristotle says that there can be no friendship for a slave insofar as he is a slave, though there can be friendship for him insofar as he is a human being (*NE* VIII.11 1161b5–6). That is, tools (axes, bridles, and the like) are not the sort of thing that receive benefits from their owners, and so putting a slave into the category of tools does not represent him as the sort of being who can be treated as a friend. It is not because a slave is a tool that he can receive benefits, but because he is a human being.

undermine his efforts to defend the institution of slavery as it was practiced by his society? For slave ownership was not restricted to the virtuous. We need not answer the difficult historical question whether slaves were owned primarily by a wealthy elite or by a much larger number (8.n.7). In either case, Aristotle holds that only a handful of those who actually own slaves meet the high standard of virtue that he describes at length in his ethical works. So, it might seem that even if he had succeeded in showing that slavery is justified in principle, he fails to produce a successful defense of slavery as it was actually practiced.

But Aristotle can easily respond to this criticism. Recall what he takes the benefits of slavery to be: if a slave is kept busy with tasks, is prevented from acting in an intemperate or cowardly way, and develops habits of obedience, then he develops a modicum of virtue. It would not be extraordinarily difficult for a slave-owner to confer these benefits. It does not require a high level of virtue or an understanding of the ultimate end of human life to give slaves enough work to keep them out of trouble. So a slave does not need a perfectly virtuous master to benefit from slavery: he only needs someone whose level of virtue is higher than his own, and Aristotle thinks that most Greeks meet this undemanding standard.[43] By and large, the Greeks are a people who have sufficient virtue to rule themselves (VII.7 1327b29–33). Though some of them sink to the level of beasts—and such people corrupt their slaves rather than improve them—the ordinary Greek citizen has the potential to become a virtuous man, and if he lives under a constitution that does not deviate too greatly from the correct standards of justice and decency, he realizes this potential to some degree.[44] The level of virtue achieved by the ordinary Greek is therefore frequently a cut above that of the typical inhabitant of the lands to the east and north. That is why the Greeks are qualified to own slaves.

Aristotle can admit that not every Greek slave-holder does in fact benefit his slaves. Some may be so harsh and arbitrary in their

---

[43] In order to make his case for slavery, Aristotle assumes that the master is virtuous (I.5 1254a36–b2). But this should be taken to mean that the case for slavery is most obvious in this instance—not that it is valid in this instance alone.

[44] See I.2 1253a31–5 for the remark that human beings can become the worst of animals; I.5 1254a39–b2 and I.6 1255b9 for the observation that the rule of a bad master is bad for both master and slave. I rely on *NE* X.9 1179b18–20 and *Pol.* V.9 1309b21–33 to support my claim that, according to Aristotle, ordinary Greeks can achieve a small but significant degree of virtue, so long as the constitutions of their cities are not extremely corrupt (below, 10.4, 10.7, 12.2).

demands that their slaves become increasingly rebellious or dissolute; others may be so lax that their slaves remain lazy and undisciplined. But these examples, so long as they are not too numerous, would indicate only that slavery does not always work as it should. They would show that individual slave-holders need admonishment, not that the practice itself is corrupt. Aristotle's defense of slavery as he knew it rests not on the idea that it works to perfection, but on the modest assumption that it is not difficult for most ordinary Greeks to participate in the exchange of benefits that constitutes the justification of this institution.

8.9. Natural Slaves

Most of the questions we raised earlier (8.3) have now received answers. We asked what sort of rational deficiency the natural slave suffers from, and we have seen that although he can become an ordinary craftsman and think about how to achieve rather specific goals, he lacks both the capacity to engage in that context-sensitive and creative adjustment of means to ends that Aristotle calls deliberation and the capacity to engage in the far more important intellectual activity that occurs when one reflects well on the highest ends of human life. The slave's mind is not grossly dysfunctional, but he cannot acquire practical wisdom. His lack of the deliberative faculty makes him especially susceptible to bad habits, but if he is placed under the close supervision and control of a master, and is ruled properly, he will develop a modicum of virtue, because the tasks he performs will keep him out of trouble. When all goes well, a slave who is properly disciplined and has acquired good habits no longer needs the constant supervision of a master, and can be granted his freedom. But whether or not he is eventually freed, he benefits from being owned, not because there is in itself something beneficial about being a piece of property, but because the owner–property relationship gives the master the kind of control over the slave that should, in favorable circumstances, be beneficial to both.

But there is one further question we raised earlier, to which no answer has yet been given. We asked why Aristotle thinks that he needs the assumption that there are *natural* slaves and masters, in order to reach the conclusion that slavery is justified. Why should it matter to him that some people are suited to be slaves because of their very nature at birth?

To see what is at issue here, let us imagine someone whose capacity for deliberation is completely intact. Given the mental equipment he is born with, there is no reason why he should not develop into a perfectly virtuous man. Nonetheless, let us suppose, he develops bad habits when he is a child, and by the time he reaches adulthood, he is, by Aristotle's ethical and intellectual standards, a poor excuse for a human being. Aristotle's theory does not count him a natural slave, because there is nothing wrong with his capacity for reasoning. His problem is that he has chosen a life that has not fully developed this capacity. No mental impairment holds him back from being the sort of person who deliberates about the highest human ends, but he has not become that sort of person. Instead, blind passion and the force of habit have led him to acquire his fundamental goals.

The question I am raising is this: why is this person not as good a candidate for slavery as someone who was born without the capacity to deliberate? For surely if Aristotle thinks that the natural slave can benefit from supervision, then he has every reason to think that the poor specimen just described can benefit in precisely the same way. Why does he not simply say that slavery is justified whenever it is imposed on those who can benefit from the careful supervision of a master, whether or not they have the capacity for deliberation? Were Aristotle to follow this suggestion, he could simply drop his assumption that some people are slaves by nature, and his theory would be less vulnerable to objection. He could divide the world into two classes: good people, who are qualified to serve as masters; and everyone else, who are suited to be slaves. Whether one is placed in the latter category because of bad habits or a natural incapacity would be a matter of indifference.

This proposed revision of Aristotle's theory would in one way suit his purposes, but in another way it would not. It would simplify his attempt to show that slavery is justified, because it would allow him to drop his assumption that some people are slaves by nature. On the other hand, it would rob his theory of its relevance to the world in which he lives. Aristotle is not interested in defending the abstract proposition that slavery can in principle be justified. Rather, he wants to show that slavery as it is practiced in his society, or something rather like it, is a just institution.[45] Most slaves were not

---

[45] I say 'something rather like it' because Aristotle's theory does not justify the enslavement of Greeks, although some of them were in fact enslaved. Like Plato's (8.n.27), his theory of slavery supports reform: Greeks should enslave only foreigners, not other Greeks.

Greeks, but foreigners from the east and north, and the Greeks thought that these *barbaroi* were inferior beings. If Aristotle cannot show that, by and large, the Greeks are suited to be in a position of superiority over other peoples—if he can only show that perfectly good people deserve to be masters over others—then his defense of slavery would in effect be a radical critique of the institution of slavery as it was practiced in his time. We may wish that he had offered such a critique, but it is evident that he did not. He claims that there are natural slaves and natural masters because he thinks that in fact there is empirical support for this proposition, and because the institution of slavery as it was practiced in his time and place rested on the assumption of Greek superiority. The thesis that by their very nature Asians and Europeans lack the capacity for deliberation suits his purposes perfectly: it locates the superiority of the Greeks in their capacity to deliberate, a capacity made evident by the greater maturity of Greek politics, as compared with the primitive politics of Asia and Europe.

8.10. *No Slave Lives Well*

Aristotle holds that slavery is justified in some cases but not others. Naturally, our attention is drawn to one side of this thesis—the horrible side that upholds slavery—but it is important not to overlook the other. We should not lose sight of a striking fact about his approach to this subject: he thinks that it is unjust to enslave anyone who has the capacity to deliberate. When we drop his assumption that there are whole peoples in whom this incapacity is widespread, we emerge with the result that slavery is an unjust institution. This is not Aristotle's conclusion, but it is the conclusion to which his political philosophy is driven, when it abandons his empirical claim about the natural slavishness of Europeans and Asians.

Another feature of his theory deserves emphasis: Aristotle recognizes that the life of a slave is utterly removed from what is best for human beings.[46] Ethically and intellectually, the slave's existence is confined to a narrow sphere. He follows a path laid down by others. He does not intelligently reflect on or discuss the highest human goals, either as an individual or as a member of the community. He

---

[46] No slave lives well: *Pol.* III.9 1280a31–4; *NE* X.6 1177a8–9.

takes no part in the deliberations of his city, and is cut off from all but the simplest kinds of music and poetry.[47] Although he can acquire low-level craft skills, his comprehension of the universe is confined to the truths embodied in myth and common sense.[48] Although his cognitive impairment does not make him a helpless invalid, he is confined to a constricted and stunted life. To force such limitations on a human being who is capable of more would be a grave injustice, for slavery is defensible only if it benefits slaves as well as their owners. This is why Aristotle concedes that the critics of slavery are in a way right (I.6 1255a3–7).[49] It is only those who would not in any case lead a better life who may be enslaved.

We should give Aristotle some credit for recognizing just how impoverished the life of a slave is, even as we deplore his idea that whole peoples can do no better. This aspect of his attitude towards slavery should be contrasted with the thesis, proposed by some Stoic and early Christian writers, that legal enslavement is not incompatible with a well-lived life.[50] The Stoics hold that virtue is the sole constituent of well-being and that it is as available to those who are slaves (legally speaking) as it is to the free (legally speaking). True freedom—the real thing, not the legal status—is the possession of those who are virtuous, and all who fall short of this ideal are truly slaves, even if they are 'free' in the legal sense. Our most important goal is to keep the mind from being enslaved to passion, false opinion, or anything external to itself; and those who occupy the social role of slaves can reach this goal.[51] Since so-called 'slaves' can practice the virtues and live well, it is not a matter of the greatest importance to put an end to slavery, even if it is not an institution

---

[47] Aristotle distinguishes between free and crude theater-goers; the latter takes pleasure in nothing but spectacles and competitions (VIII.7 1342a18–28).

[48] Although Aristotle says that the slave is incapable of deliberation, and this is an impairment of practical—not theoretical—reason, I take him to be assuming that the slave also lacks the capacity to acquire theoretical wisdom.

[49] As the remainder of this passage shows, Aristotle's meaning is that it is not an adequate defense of enslaving someone to say that he or his city was defeated in battle. The only way to justify this institution is to establish that there is a deficiency in certain people that makes them suitable to be placed in a subordinate role.

[50] For the attitude of some Stoics towards slavery, see Garnsey, *IS*, pp. 128–52; for early Christian thought, see pp. 153–6, 173–219.

[51] 'It is a mistake for anyone to believe that the condition of slavery penetrates into the whole being of a man. The better part of him is exempt. Only the body is at the mercy and disposition of a master. The mind, however, is its own master' (Seneca, *De Beneficiis* 3.20.1, trans. Garnsey, *IS*, p. 66).

that rests on natural differences among human beings.[52] Even if a Stoic believes that all human beings fully possess the capacity to reason, and that those who are enslaved are just as capable, intellectually and morally, as those who are (legally speaking) free, that thesis does not commit him to speaking out against slavery as a great evil.[53]

Perhaps the Stoics are right to say that a kind of self-mastery is possible even for those who are owned by others. Even so, the slave's severely diminished opportunities to develop his capacities by participating in the valuable institutions of his community must be counted as a severe handicap. This is a point that did not escape Aristotle. His account of why slavery is a miserable condition correctly identifies one of the ways in which the life of a free person is so greatly superior to that of a slave. The kind of virtue a slave can develop and exercise is a pale imitation of the excellence available to human beings at their best. Aristotle's failure consists in his assumption that it is the slave's nature rather than his community that limits his development and his opportunities. Even so, any account of the wrongness of slavery that leaves aside the Aristotelian point that a well-lived life requires the full development of human capacities fails to recognize one of the central objections to this institution.

---

[52] Here I follow Garnsey. 'The category of semi-rational subhumans, fitted for and benefited by slavery plays no part in Stoic discourse' (*IS*, p. 150). '[T]he doctrine of common rationality and fellow-feeling was not a springboard for a critique of slavery' (ibid.). See too Griffin, *Seneca: A Philosopher in Politics*, pp. 459–60.

[53] Can the Stoic notion of 'preferred indifferents' be used to show that slavery should be abolished? Something is a preferred indifferent if it is neither good nor bad, but is by its nature to be chosen over its opposite. Examples proposed by the Stoics include: life, health, pleasure, beauty, strength, wealth, and reputation. See Diogenes Laertius, *Lives* VII.101–3. For this and related passages, see Long and Sedley, *The Hellenistic Philosophers*, pp. 354–9. A Stoic might reasonably hold that when a slave is offered freedom, it accords with nature for him to choose it. But that would not constitute an objection to slavery as an institution; for the Stoic might also hold that it is in accordance with nature for someone to prefer owning a slave to not owning one. (After all, slaves are a form of wealth, and it accords with nature to prefer wealth to poverty.) Similarly, living at leisure might be naturally preferable to having to work for a living, but that does not create an objection to hiring a worker. Evidently, the concept of a preferred indifferent does not contain the resources for posing an objection to the institution of slavery. Diogenes Laertius attributes to the Stoics the theses that one kind of slavery consists in subordination (*hypotaxis*); that a kind of ownership is correlative to such slavery; and that both of these are objectionable (*Lives* VII.121–2). But subordination and its opposite in an owner may consist in a certain pair of attitudes (servility and arrogance); in that case, what is to be avoided is not the institution of slavery but undue deference and its opposite. For a more radical reading, see Erskine, *The Hellenistic Stoa*, pp. 43–63. For Seneca's attitude towards slavery, see Griffin, *Seneca: A Philosopher in Politics*, pp. 256–85, 458–9. She argues that some of Seneca's philosophical principles could have led to a condemnation of slavery, but that he deliberately avoided reaching this conclusion.

9

Politics II: Family, Property, and Civic Unity

9.1. *Some Themes in Book II*

Aristotle often places near the beginning of his works a critical examination of what others have said about the subject under investigation.[1] Thus his inquiries into knowledge, nature, and soul (in the *Metaphysics*, *Physics*, and *De Anima*) turn immediately from brief general statements about these subjects to surveys and critiques of earlier theories. Since the *Politics* culminates (or, at any rate, terminates) in a depiction of the best possible city, it is not surprising that one of its books is devoted entirely to an examination of what others have thought about the ideal constitution—that is, about the institutions a city should ideally have, and how its citizens should live. Book II contains a critique both of utopian schemes proposed by individual thinkers (Plato, Phaleas, Hippodamus) and of existing cities that have a reputation for being well-governed (Sparta, Crete, Carthage). Aristotle's investigation of these constitutions, imaginary and real, is not meant to stand on its own;

---

[1] A much briefer version of this chapter appeared in my 'Aristotle's Critique of False Utopias'. I have also altered, to some degree, my interpretation of Aristotle's complaint that Plato's program for unifying the city would, if fully carried out, destroy it (9.3-4).

9.1. SOME THEMES IN BOOK II

his purpose, rather, is to prepare the way for his own ideas, as he presents them in Books VII and VIII, about the ideal city.

Book II covers many diverse topics—the family, private property, the gap between rich and poor, the proper distribution of political power—but amidst this variety we find a common theme. The utopian thinkers whom Aristotle considers and the real cities he examines are all concerned with the problem of how citizens are to be integrated into a single community and kept from dividing into hostile factions. Aristotle's approach to this issue is evident at an early point in his discussion. He says that a city is by its nature a 'plurality' (*plēthos*, I.2 1261a18), for not only is it made up of many human beings, but they are people 'of different kinds' (a22–3). And although he insists, against Plato, that we must preserve this plurality, he nonetheless agrees that it creates a problem that every city must address. Although the city needs diversity, it must, by means of education, be made 'common and one' (II.5 1263b36–7). Here Aristotle tips his hand about how he intends to solve the problem of creating an integrated community out of a diversity of human types: through education. But his agenda in Book II does not require him to elaborate on this idea. He leaves that project for Books VII and VIII; in Book II, his limited goal is to show how various thinkers and cities have stumbled in their own efforts to solve this problem.

The most radical solution Aristotle discusses (II.2–5) is the one proposed by Socrates in Plato's *Republic*: if the family is abolished and private possessions are prohibited, then, Socrates thinks, the citizens will form a single large family, each will attend to the welfare of all, and the domination of one class over another will be abolished. A different way to eliminate these factions is the one proposed by Phaleas (II.7): citizens are allowed to have private possessions, but they are allotted equal amounts of wealth. And the problem of unifying the city is not dropped, when Aristotle turns to a critique of the constitutions of Sparta, Crete, and Carthage (II.9–11). He agrees that the good reputation these cities have in certain circles is deserved (II.11 1273b26), for each includes several different constituencies in the life of the city. Mass and elite share power; a common education is provided to all; and all male adult citizens are eligible to participate in a unifying institution: they participate in common meals, and thus relax together and discuss issues of common concern. Although Aristotle is critical of these regimes, he nonetheless borrows from them when he constructs his own ideal city.

But Book II is not merely a preparation for Aristotle's discussion of the ideal constitution of Books VII and VIII. It also contains material that will be taken up again in his analysis of less than perfect political systems. One of the ideas explored in these chapters is that 'the best constitution is a mixture of all constitutions' (II.6 1265b33–5). Many of the constitutions discussed in Book II—Plato's Magnesia (the city described in the *Laws*), Sparta, Crete, Carthage, and Solon's Athens—strive for stability by making room for aristocratic, oligarchic, and democratic elements, and thus giving some measure of power to all citizens. Although Aristotle insists that these regimes are far from ideal, he takes an interest in the way they mix varying elements, because he recognizes that the notion of a mixed constitution provides a helpful guide for the reform of existing cities. That component of his thinking will come into prominence in Book IV.

Had Book II been lost, we might reasonably accuse Aristotle of remarkable complacency about such traditional institutions as the family and private property. The account he gives in Book I of the rise of the city seems to rest on the assumption that we must not make any alteration in the traditional household, because it has always existed and is therefore natural. When he portrays an ideal city, in Books VII and VIII, he simply assumes, without argument, that his citizens should be allowed to own property, and that they will marry and raise children. But, as Book II makes clear, Aristotle realizes that the questions Plato raises about traditional practices deserve an answer, and cannot be dismissed simply because they are radical. He points out: 'In general, what all seek is not the traditional but the good' (II.8 1269a3–4). People will want to change their habits and reconfigure their communities if they become convinced that current practices are impediments to their well-being. Aristotle has learned this much from earlier thinkers: everything that exists must be examined in order to determine whether it has merely become customary, or whether it can be shown to merit a place in a well-lived life. If we should continue to uphold the institutions of marriage and private property, then Plato's doubts about them must be addressed. It must be shown that there is no better way to manage human affairs.

9.2. Plato's Abolition of the Family

In the ideal city of the *Republic*, rulers are not allowed conventional marriages or families; sexual liaisons are arranged for them, and their offspring are raised collectively by supervisors (457c–461e). Plato's astonishing proposal is meant to produce several results. First, children will be more talented and therefore better able to help the polis if their parents have been selected for eugenic purposes. Second, when people do not develop special affective ties to their families, their allegiance to the whole community will become stronger and more impartial. Once the family is abolished, it becomes impossible to do special favors for brothers, parents, children, and so on. Citizens will instead be educated to be impartially and equally dedicated to the good of all. Plato's concern about factionalism is increased by the extraordinary power he gives to his rulers. Just as the abolition of private property among the guardians is intended as a safeguard against their corruption, so the abolition of the family is meant to assure ordinary citizens that the power of the rulers will not be compromised by favoritism.

Aristotle devotes Chapters 2–4 to Plato's abolition of the traditional family, and Chapter 5 to his abolition of private property. Although there are similarities in the ways he criticizes both proposals (9.11), we will consider them separately. It will be useful to begin with a summary of the reasons he gives for retaining the traditional family and rejecting Plato's alternative to it:

A. Socrates abolishes the family in order to create the greatest possible unity of the city, but maximal unity is not an appropriate goal of constitutional design. A city is by its nature a plurality, and excessive unity will destroy it (II.2 1261a15-b15).

B. Even if maximal unity were possible or desirable, this goal could not be achieved by abolishing the family, because such a measure would bring about only a weak degree of unification. The affection each citizen would have for all other members of the community would be so diluted as to be negligible in value (II.3 1261b16–32, II.4 1262b15).

C. The abolition of the family would not only fail to achieve some good; it would actually bring about harm. For children would be neglected if they were shared by all, just as collectively owned property tends to deteriorate, because everyone assumes that it will be looked after by someone else (II.3 1261b32–40).

D. It would be impossible to obliterate evidence about blood relations, because strong physical resemblances can be observed between people, and in any case those who remove newborn children from their parents would have such knowledge (II.3 1262a14–24, II.4 1262b24–9).

E. When people do not know who their blood relations are, they are in danger of having sex with or killing members of their own family. Socrates' scheme would make it impossible to expiate these crimes (II.4 1262a25–40).

F. Abstaining from adultery is an expression of ethical virtue. Socrates' proposal would make that exercise of virtue impossible (II.5 1263b9–11).

In none of these points does Aristotle address himself to the eugenic advantages Plato claims for his proposal. But we can safely assume that he is unimpressed with this aspect of Plato's scheme. From Aristotle's point of view, the polis has no reason to breed extraordinary individuals. Since ruling does not require mathematical talent, philosophical understanding, or any other purely intellectual skill, all that a city needs, to function well, is normal, healthy, rational citizens. He takes it to be obvious that the city has no reason to match sexual partners in the way Plato advocates.[2] He therefore focuses principally on the questions Plato raises about the relationship citizens should have with each other. Should there not be a strong sense of unity among them? And would not the attachment citizens feel for each other be enhanced if it did not have to compete with family feeling? Aristotle's replies to these questions are contained in points (A), (B), and (C); and they will therefore be the focus of our discussion. (D) and (E) will be set aside. (F) is an afterthought that parallels a point Aristotle makes about property, which will be considered in 9.17.

9.3. The Plurality of the City

Aristotle thinks that the crucial premise on which Socrates relies when he proposes the abolition of the family is that 'it is best for the whole city to be one, so far as possible' (1261a15–16). To this he objects: 'the city is by nature a certain kind of plurality' (a18). Therefore, any attempt to give a city as much unity as Plato proposes will in the end lead to its destruction. Aristotle returns to this claim in

---

[2] In VII.16, Aristotle prescribes measures that produce healthy babies (1335a11–22, a24–8, b5–19) but it does not enter his mind to propose that marriages be arranged for eugenic purposes.

9.3. THE PLURALITY OF THE CITY

II.5: the process of unification proposed by Plato will at first make the city a worse city, and one that is nearly not a city at all; when the process proceeds even farther, the city will in fact be destroyed (1263b32–4).

In order to understand and assess Aristotle's argument, we must determine what he means by his claim that 'the city is by nature a certain kind of plurality'. He provides some help when he adds, several lines later: 'the city is made not only of many human beings, but of those who differ in kind' (1261a22–4). He goes on to explain what he means by these differences in kind. Citizens cannot all be in power at the same time; some must rule, and others obey; even when they are equal, offices must rotate among them, and therefore at any time some of them will hold office and others will not. So, Aristotle's point at a22–4 is not only that a city contains a plurality of people, but that they must occupy different roles. This tells us that prior to a22 his claim does not depend on the idea that there must be some differentiation in the roles played by citizens. Even if all members of the political community played the same role, it would still be true that they form a plurality; and this by itself shows that there is something amiss in Plato's premise that the best city is the one that has the highest possible degree of unification.

It is tempting to take Aristotle to be making an elementary point, and to be supposing that this by itself overthrows Plato's abolition of the family. The elementary point is that a city is a community that contains more than a handful of members. No matter how small it is, it must contain more members than does a household. How does that show any defect in Plato's proposal to abolish the family? Well, Plato's proposal is based on the assumption that the closer a city comes to oneness or unity, the better off it is. What is meant here by oneness or unity? Uncharitably, Aristotle takes this to be a mere matter of counting human beings. A city has less oneness than a household, because, in order to be a viable city, it must contain many hundreds of citizens. The maximal degree of unity would be achieved by a single human being, because a human being is necessarily one human being. That is what Aristotle is getting at when he points out: 'we would say that the household is more one than the city, and the one [human being] than the household' (1261a20–1).

If we choose to understand Aristotle's argument in this way, then it must be admitted that, at best, he has won a verbal victory against Plato. He has forced Plato to admit that he does not seek to give the ideal city every possible kind of oneness: he does not want to transform it from a plurality of human beings into a single human being. But surely Plato's main idea would not be touched by Aristotle's argument, so interpreted. Plato does not propose that the citizens of his ideal city somehow be melded together so that they become a single person. He does not regard it as a shame that there is more than one human being, and his search for civic unity is not an attempt to come as close as possible to that kind of oneness. Rather, what he is proposing to create in an ideal city is a plurality of individuals who have the highest possible degree of sympathy and single-mindedness. The members of his ideal community would remain a plurality of people, but they would speak and feel with one voice. Aristotle's elementary point that a city must contain a plurality of human beings does not by itself show that a harmony of beliefs and feelings among all citizens is impossible to achieve. Still less does it show that it is not a goal that we should strive to achieve, so far as possible. In fact, it is a goal that Aristotle embraces. As we noted above (9.1), he agrees with Plato that measures must be taken to insure that a city becomes 'common and one' (II.5 1263b36-7). And he agrees with Plato that the high degree of concord of thought and feeling that he seeks to instill in his citizens would be a fine thing—if only it were possible (II.3 1261b31).

There is no doubt that Aristotle is basing his critique of Plato on the elementary point that cities must be composed of a large number of human beings, but we would be underestimating his objection if we took his entire argument in lines 1261a15-22 to consist simply in that single premise. We can make far better sense of his argument in these lines, if we take him to be relying on two further tacit assumptions as well. First, he is taking Plato's criterion of constitutional design to be extremely simple: the *only* question we need ask about the excellence of a city is a question about its oneness. For that is the *only* feature that makes a city good.[3] Second, he assumes that as the size of a group diminishes, its potential to be a locus of disagreement and ill feeling also declines.[4]

The logic of Aristotle's argument, supplemented with these two

---

[3] Aristotle might point to *Republic* 462a-b as his basis for attributing this assumption to Plato. For there Socrates says that the greatest good of the city—the good to which the legislator looks, in constructing the ideal city—is the unity of the citizens. Aristotle reasonably takes this to mean that all civic institutions and human relationships should be constructed in a way that maximizes unity.

[4] Recall our earlier point (6.11) that Aristotle recognizes the widespread use of the principle of majority rule, and probably accepts the need for such a principle even in the assembly of his ideal city.

9.3. THE PLURALITY OF THE CITY

premises, can be put as follows. If Plato is seeking unity of opinion and sentiment in his ideal city, and that is his sole criterion of its excellence, then he ought to establish the smallest possible city—for the larger the population, the greater the possibilities for disagreement. But since Plato's ambition is to achieve the greatest harmony of opinion, and he is willing to do whatever it takes to reach that goal, then he has every reason to establish a smaller community than a city. Why not establish the best possible household, rather than the best possible city, if the smaller unit provides greater possibilities for maintaining unity of opinion? And of course, the logic of the argument does not stop there: 'as it becomes more unitary, it will go from a city to a household, and from a household to a human being' (1261a18–20). Perhaps this process of gradual diminution in size will be difficult to put into practice (can we persuade people to leave the community, or must we force them?), but that of course is irrelevant. The point is that Plato's overly simple criterion of constitutional design will create unity at the cost of destroying the very thing he is trying to perfect. 'Therefore, even if it were possible for someone to do this, he should not do so; for he will destroy the city' (a21–2).

A defender of Plato can respond by saying that he seeks a unified *city*—not unity of feeling, regardless of how few people have those feelings. But that response plays into Aristotle's hands, for he can now point out that the only reason to establish a unified *city* (and not some smaller object that has greater unity) is that something becomes possible in a city that is not possible in smaller, more unified groups: a good life for the citizens. The ultimate goal of constitutional design cannot simply be unity of feeling; it must rather be excellent activity of the rational soul, adequately supplied with external goods. No doubt, unity of opinion is something Aristotle wants in a city, but he does not make it the sole criterion of good civic design—the crucial error that lies behind Plato's abolition of the family and private property. By attacking Plato's overestimation of the importance of unity, he sets the stage for the rest of his discussion in Book II. The most important question to be asked as we investigate Plato's proposals is not 'What will create the greatest unity?' but 'What will make the lives of citizens go best?'

In the next few chapters of Book II, Aristotle goes on to deny that Plato's ideal city would be harmonious and free of conflict. He thinks that the like-mindedness that Plato seeks by the abolition of the family is largely a verbal matter: citizens might say 'this child is mine', but the feeling that normally accompanies those words will be absent (II.3 1261b30–2). Furthermore, he will claim, in II.5, that the abolition of private property would increase, not diminish, the hostility among citizens. But these later objections to Plato do not make it less important for him to start his discussion by showing an even more basic weakness in Plato's approach to constitutional design. Unity of feeling is an important matter, but it is not nearly as important as Plato makes it out to be. It is not the sole test of how to construct social groups. For if it were, the best such 'group' would be a single individual.

9.4. Differentiation of Roles

Aristotle goes on to say: 'Not only is the city made of many human beings, but of those who differ in kind; for the city does not come from those who are alike' (1261a22–4). That is because citizens should rule and be ruled in turn, when they are equals (a30–b6). Aristotle thinks that this constitutes a second objection to Plato's thesis that unity is the sole criterion of the excellence of a constitution. His point is that if we really want a city to be as unitary as possible, we will make every citizen as much like every other citizen as we can. That would require each citizen to play precisely the same role in civic life. If any one of them holds high office, then all of the others should simultaneously hold equally high offices. Obviously, that would be an absurd form of government.

Once again, it is tempting to suppose that Aristotle's objection is a failure, because it does not squarely address Plato's proposal to create emotional and rational harmony among the citizens. Plato recognizes—in fact, insists—that different citizens of the ideal city must play different roles: some must be philosophers, some soldiers, some craftsmen and farmers. A city should not be made unitary if unity means that all citizens have the same task. But, having made this concession to Aristotle, Plato can point out the obvious: this is not the kind of unity he has in mind, when he says (to use Aristotle's words) that 'the best city is the one that is most of all one' (1261a15–16). Rather, as Aristotle well knows, the kind of unity Plato endorses is a unity of feeling and belief. The citizens should care for each other, and it is no objection to that idea that there must be some degree of role differentiation.

If this were our diagnosis of the dispute between Plato and

Aristotle, then we would miss the excellent point Aristotle is making: since there are a number of different kinds of unity, and Plato is recommending only one of them, he must be aiming at something other than unity when he constructs his ideal city. After all, what entitles Plato to assume that unity of feeling is the proper test of a city's excellence? Why not some other kind of unity instead? The answer must appeal to something besides unity itself. Aristotle agrees with Plato that some kind of like-mindedness among citizens is desirable, but that is because the well-being of a citizen consists in virtuous activity adequately supported by external goods, and that goal requires civic friendship. Unity itself is not the test of an ideal constitution—for otherwise we would have to say that every kind of unity (even uniformity of roles) is desirable. That shows that we must reject Plato's guiding assumption that 'the best city is the one that is most of all one'.

9.5. Family, Attachment, and Care

In II.3 Aristotle claims that even if all adult citizens were to say of each young person, 'this is my child', the city would not be unified in the way that Socrates seeks. Socrates wants all of the adults to say 'all of these children are mine', meaning by this, 'each child is mine'. In that case, each and every child would be loved in the way that children are loved by their parents in traditional families. But, Aristotle suggests, what would in fact happen if the family were abolished is this: when all of the parents say 'all of these children are mine', they will mean not that each child, taken one by one, is mine, but that the collection of all children, not any one of them in particular, is mine. Aristotle makes his charge against Socrates by saying that there is an unnoticed slide from one sense of 'all' to another—from 'all' used individually to 'all' used collectively (1261b20–30). But his point might have emerged more clearly had he said that there is a slide from one use of 'mine' to another. Socrates wants 'mine' in 'this child is mine' to convey the same strong attachment that the phrase now possesses, and he wants all parents to apply it to all children. But, Aristotle claims, a 'mine' that applies to all would carry with it a far looser sense of attachment. It would of course be desirable for all parents to love all children in the way they now love the members of their families; but this is impossible (1261b30–1). What would in fact happen if one tried to put Socrates' scheme into practice would not be particularly attractive. Concord would not result (b31-2); friendship would be watery (II.4 1262b15).

It is difficult to tell which of these two points Aristotle has in mind:

A. Currently, one loves one's own children more than other children in the community. It is impossible to have this same attitude towards all children, for one cannot love all children in the community more than all other children in the community.

B. Currently, one loves one's own children a great deal. It is impossible to love every other child to this same extent, because it is beyond human nature to feel love for more than a few. If one is trained to have the same level of affection for all, it will have to be a low level, because intense attachment can be felt towards only a few.

Point (A) would serve Aristotle's purpose, if he aims to show that it is valuable to give a few people one's special attention. Logically, *special* attention cannot be given to all—for what is given to all singles out no one. Point (B), by contrast, makes a psychological claim about how far it is possible to feel a close attachment to others. The two points are of course compatible, and Aristotle may mean to make both. In any case, his idea is that if we were to abolish the family, we would be needlessly destroying something that is of great intrinsic worth. A well-lived life includes activities carried out jointly by a small group of people among whom there is a strong sense of friendship. Plato's city would destroy this good. By trying to enlarge the group towards whom this close relationship is carried out, the intimacy and therefore the value of their relationship would be undermined.

It is important to distinguish this point, which rests on the intrinsic goodness of loving, from another, which rests on the importance of being loved. (Recall the distinction between (B) and (C) in 9.2.) After Aristotle completes his argument that Plato's abolition of the family rests on an equivocal use of 'all', he makes the further claim that in such a regime sons would be equally neglected by all, just as communal property receives less care than private property (II.3 1261b32-40). When many individuals share responsibility for attending to things and other people, they face the difficulty of coordinating their efforts. Each tends to assume that others will take charge, and so there is a danger that no one will put forward the effort required. Accordingly, even if mature adults had an intense concern for each and every member of the next

9.5. FAMILY, ATTACHMENT, AND CARE

generation, the young might suffer from neglect. The chances that this will happen are all the greater if in fact the older generation takes only a mild interest in the younger generation.

In making this point, Aristotle relies on the assumption that, according to Plato, the responsibility for raising children should be placed on no single individual or small group, but instead assigned to all of the citizens taken as a whole. Surely Aristotle is right that such a scheme would lead to serious neglect. But it is reasonable to assume that Plato has something different in mind: the offspring of the ruling class will be placed under the special care of a few adults who are not their biological parents, but are specially trained to perform this task. Who are these foster parents? How are they selected? Do they care for children in small groups? Plato does not say.[5] But one thing is certain: he is not proposing that the sole group charged with the care of small children is the whole civic community (or the entire class of guardians).

The most plausible component of Aristotle's argument is his insistence that every child receive extraordinary care from a small number of loving adults. Certain people must take on the special responsibility of nurturing a manageable number of children; no community is viable if it assigns to all adults the task of caring for all children, with no particular children assigned to any particular adult. But this allows for many different ways of caring for children. It does not show that biological parents should be the ones who take on the task of loving and caring for the children they have produced. Perhaps care of the young should be the special responsibility of those who have been trained for the job, not those who have produced them. Aristotle is evidently assuming that as a rule children are most likely to be loved by their biological parents, and therefore these adults are normally the ones who should be entrusted with the job of raising them. More generally, he holds that the intense feelings of family members for each other makes it appropriate that adult children give special care to their elderly parents, and that siblings take special responsibility for each other.

He is aware that the intense feelings of family members towards each other sometimes become embittered, and that family strife can be more terrible than any other kind.[6] But he assumes that these are the exception rather than the rule, and that there is no need to

---

[5] All that Plato says about this is contained in *Republic* 460c, which merely assigns to nurses the task of nurturing the children of good parents.

[6] See *Pol.* VII.7 1328a1–16, *Rhet.* II.2 1379b2–4.

abolish the family simply to avoid these evils. Tensions among family members are not outside the sphere of influence of the political community, because the quality of family life can be affected by social expectations. The customs of the polis influence the age at which men and women marry as well as the age at which property is transferred to children; and these in turn influence the quality of personal relationships between husbands, wives, and children.[7] In the ideal city, the community does what it can to relieve some of the normal tensions inherent in family life. There is no need to go so far as to abolish the family because of these personal strains; nor is this the problem that led Plato to his radical proposal.

9.6. Friendship and Partiality

What is uppermost in Aristotle's mind when he discusses the community of wives and children is the special care that must be given to children. But he does not want to limit his argument to this case alone; rather, the general point he wants to make is that the family is needed because of all of the special relationships it involves: husbands and wives, parents and children, siblings, and so on.[8] But this creates a problem: even if we concede, at least for the sake of argument, that biological parents are generally the ones who will best care for children, we may not wish to grant the more general point that we need to receive special care from family members throughout our lives. Perhaps we all benefit from intimate ties with a small number of people—not only during childhood, but throughout life. In these little communities, we pay special attention to the other members. But why should we look to the family to meet these needs once we have become adults? Why not look instead to our closest friends? Aristotle's defense of the family presupposes that biological ties matter, and this may perhaps be true in the case of parents and children. But is it true in other cases as well?

Aristotle has no desire to argue that the family can give us all that

---

[7] Aristotle discusses these matters in VII.16. Note his interest in minimizing disputes about procreation between spouses (1334b32-8) and about property between fathers and sons (1334b38-1335a4).

[8] At II.3 1261b32-1262a5, Aristotle's worry is that children will be neglected if the family is abolished, but in the lines that follow his concern is that the value of all family connections will be lost. Similarly, at II.4 1262b17-35 he emphasizes the relationship between fathers and sons, but also mentions the closeness between brothers and between mothers and their children.

9.6. FRIENDSHIP AND PARTIALITY

we need in human relationships. As his lengthy discussions of friendship in the ethical treatises show, he assumes that we have a deep desire and need for relationships that we choose on the basis of character, and not merely the relationships of blood that exist within the household.[9] One thing missing from Book II of the *Politics* is an account of why these voluntary and non-biological ties are no substitute for family ties.

It is important to recognize, nonetheless, that Plato, Aristotle's chief opponent in this part of the *Politics*, is not proposing that the institution of intimate friendship be retained in the ruling class of the ideal city as a substitute for the family. Plato is as opposed to the factionalism of friends as he is to the factionalism of the family. In his ideal community, the rulers are to have no favorites at all: not only are they to treat all children alike and vice versa, but no guardian is to become more dedicated to certain members of the community than to others.[10] For special relationships formed outside the family pose the same dangers to the common good as do blood ties. In Plato's *Symposium*, Diotima describes the proper course of love as one in which we ascend from attachments to this or that person to a general appreciation of what all such objects of love have in common (210a–212a). Here and in the *Republic*, the goal of education is to induce individuals to give up a special concern for one or a few individuals, and to develop a comprehensive regard for all. Aristotle, by contrast, holds that we need to enter voluntarily into intimate relationships with a few friends, just as we need special relationships

---

[9] *Philia*, the subject of *NE* VIII and IX and *EE* VII, encompasses relationships both among family members and between friends, and is therefore a broader phenomenon than the conventional English equivalent, 'friendship', implies. (In fact, it is still broader than this, since it also applies to those who associate with each other for mutual advantage or pleasure, even if they are not what we would call 'friends'.) But Aristotle insists that the perfect kind of *philia* is one that holds between those who are equally virtuous and choose to associate with each other because of their mutual admiration, emotional ties, and shared interests (*NE* VIII.3 1156b7–32, IX.4 1166a1–10, IX.12 1172a1–15). It is therefore not a relationship between fathers and sons or husbands and wives, since these are unequal (VIII.7 1158b11–17). (Note, however, that mothers are exemplary in their love of their children: IX.4 1166a5–6, 8–9.) There is nothing that prevents brothers from having this perfect kind of relationship (VIII.11 1161a25–7), but neither is there reason to expect that perfect friends will typically or frequently be brothers. Aristotle assumes that generally one must look outside the family for the best kind of relationship.

[10] This is implied by the ideal of impartiality advocated at 420b–421c: no single component of the city is to be singled out for extraordinary happiness, if this injures others. Just as the city's founders must favor no group, so its guardians must favor no faction or individual (463b–c). Justice is not helping friends and harming enemies (332d–335e); rather, it is precisely this division of the community into warring factions that must be avoided (417a–b, 464a–465e).

with members of our family. The political community to which we belong is no substitute for either of these smaller communities.

Although our untutored sympathies may lie with Aristotle rather than Plato, it is important not to lose sight of the problems that underlie Plato's fear of special relationships. If I have an intense attachment to a small number of people, will I be inclined to give them more favorable treatment than others, even when doing so would be unjust? If I care greatly about a few, does this leave me enough time and energy to devote to the rest of the community? If everyone's primary allegiance is to friends and family, will there be too few who care about the whole community? Can political life flourish when people care most of all about their narrow social enclaves?

These are issues Aristotle ought to have addressed in his examination of Plato's proposal to abolish the family. Even if he is right that children need special care, he should have asked whether special ties carry with them a special danger, and how that danger can be lessened or eliminated. So there is a gap in his argument. Nonetheless, he is not without resources to fill it—if we make use of material he provides outside of Book II.

First, all citizens of the ideal city believe that well-being consists in virtuous activity—and they believe this deeply, because their emotions are in full accord with this conviction.[11] Justice is one of the virtues they have been taught to love, and their sense of justice leaves no room for the idea (common in the ancient Greek world) that this virtue is a matter of helping friends and hurting enemies.[12] Rather, they take justice to consist in distributing goods in accordance with the objective merits of individuals and their circumstances. So, when they serve as magistrates or jurors or vote in the assembly, they treat people according to their deserts, regardless of whether they are friends or family members. Because they see no conflict between their own well-being and treating others justly, they are not even tempted to do a special favor for a close personal relationship, when they see that this would be wrong.[13]

---

[11] Aristotle often contrasts genuine virtue with the condition in which the reasoning and non-reasoning parts of the soul are not in full harmony. See e.g. *NE* I.13 1102b25–8. To become wise, what one learns must inform one's emotions and become part of one's nature (VII.3 1147a19–22). For other indications of the kind of psychic unification Aristotle has in mind, see I.8 1099a7–20, IX.4 1166a13–19; *Pol.* VII.15 1334b6–12.

[12] See Blundell, *Helping Friends and Harming Enemies*, pp. 26–59.

[13] Note Aristotle's statement that it is by means of education—not abolishing the family or private possessions—that the city is made 'common and one' (II.5 1263b36–7). The kind

9.6. FRIENDSHIP AND PARTIALITY

Furthermore, when they raise their children at home, they give them the rational and ethical skills they will need for a life of active citizenship and public service. The close attachments of the household do not detract from civic life but enhance it.

Second, the citizens of the ideal city meet each other at common meals, and their participation is guaranteed, regardless of their economic status. The point of this institution, as we have seen (6.9), is not solely or primarily to feed the citizens, but to foster social ties. The common meals are places where various groups regularly meet to share in discussion and entertainment. This institution is not meant to foster special interests—like music clubs or book groups— but brings citizens together because they are fellow citizens and have common problems to discuss. They are united not only because they have a common conception of the good and a common love of justice, and not only because they spend time with each other in the assembly and at religious or musical festivals, but also because they converse in a comfortable setting that fosters civic friendship. Although the relationships they form with fellow citizens cannot be as intimate as the ones they have with their family and friends, they still have some sense of affiliation with the larger body of citizens. A fellow citizen is not a stranger; he is someone whose company one regularly enjoys.[14]

Third, although the citizens of the ideal city own their own land and oversee its cultivation, those of them who have sufficient resources will use their wealth for public purposes. (We will consider these 'liturgies' in more detail in 9.9.) 'The things of friends are common' is a proverb Aristotle cites with approval, and he adds that in an ideal city the use of property will be common because the citizens are virtuous (II.5 1263a29–30). Though intimate friends do special favors for each other, all of the citizens are united by the sense that the possessions of each are for the benefit of all.[15]

---

of education he has in mind is, among other things, a moral education; when the ethical virtues are inculcated, the social conflicts and legal battles that Plato despised will be eradicated.

[14] Aristotle takes it to be characteristic of close personal friends that they share each other's joy and sorrow (NE IX.4 1166a7–8, IX.10 1171a6–8), and denies that this can exist among fellow citizens (IX.10 1171a2–20). Nonetheless he wants there to be a kind of friendship among fellow citizens, because even though it is diluted in emotional intensity, it prevents the citizens from dividing into factions (Pol. II.4 1262b1–9). His allusions to common meals at II.5 1263b41 and 1264a8 suggest (when taken in context) that he regards them as a means of unifying the city.

[15] Note that at II.5 1263b40–1264a1, the common meals of Sparta and Crete are treated as one application of the general principle that possessions should be available for general use.

Fourth, through intermarriage, the families of a polis overlap to a considerable degree, and so citizens develop increasingly complex connections with each other. The parents and siblings of a child who marries develop new ties to members of the spouse's family, and as this pattern recurs throughout the city, more and more citizens develop at least some sense of connection with each other. When patterns of intermarriage are not artificially constricted, the city will not divide into a small number of disjoint and hostile clans.[16]

9.7. Land Distribution

The rulers of the city described in the *Republic* do not own gold, silver, or other possessions. They receive food and other resources from farmers and craftsmen, and therefore have no need of land or other forms of wealth (416d–417b). Before we turn to Aristotle's discussion, in *Politics* II.5, of Plato's proposal, we should review his own ideas, in *Politics* VII, about the distribution of land. So far as possible, we should read his critique of Plato in Book II in a way that is consistent with what he says later.

In Aristotle's ideal city, some but not all of the land is privately owned. Each citizen has two allotments: one near the urban center, the other near the outskirts of the territory. The rest is held in common, and the produce of this land is used to support common meals and religious sacrifices (VII.10 1330a3–13).

It is important to recognize that this scheme places limits on the freedom of the citizens to buy, sell, and exchange. Since some of the land is held in common, it cannot be bought by or sold to any individual. The size of this common territory is presumably determined by the needs of the community: it must be large enough to grow the crops and nurture the animals needed for common meals and religious worship. Furthermore, citizens do not have the freedom to sell or give away their two private allotments of land. The scheme of dual allotments is intended to shape the political deliberations of the community, and so the city must forbid citizens from undermining it through individual transactions. Someone who sold one of his two

---

[16] See III.9 1280b35–1281a1, where Aristotle mentions this as a cause of civic friendship. At II.5 1264a6–7, kinship groups are mentioned along with common meals as a way of dividing up the citizens into groups, and therefore destroying the extreme unity of Plato's ideal city; but presumably what Aristotle has in mind is that both of these institutions create more civic friendship than does the abolition of the family and private property. We will return to the theme of civic friendship in 12.3 and 12.9.

9.7. LAND DISTRIBUTION

plots would diminish his value as a citizen, since his contribution to public discussion would be biased, or at any rate he might be suspected of bias. For the same reason, the system of transferring property to children must be carefully supervised so that the proper division is maintained by future generations. Obviously a father cannot leave one of his lots to one son and the other lot to another son. Childless people and parents who have only one child will have to coordinate the transfer of their allotments with the transfers made by other families. An individual's freedom to acquire, sell, or transfer is limited by whatever laws are needed to insure that a certain pattern of property distribution is maintained.[17]

That Aristotle should be willing to limit individual citizens in this way should not be surprising. For his theory of the good holds that the possession of property beyond a certain measure is not in a person's interests, and he designs the ideal city so that it promotes the good of the citizens. If one citizen is not allowed to increase his holdings by buying a second citizen's allotment of land, no objection can be made, because no harm is done. The first citizen would not benefit from having more; and the whole city would be harmed if such transactions were allowed.

We should also bear in mind that Aristotle conceives of his ideal city as a new city established in a new location. The citizens move to the territory as a group, not as isolated individuals; and they do so because they want to establish a constitution guided by a common conception of the good (6.2). So, although there will be private property, this is because it is recognized by all that the system of individual ownership that will be in force is one that serves the legitimate needs of citizens and does not undermine any common purpose. No one has a prior claim to a certain piece of land; rather, land is distributed by the community to individual citizens in conformity with a plan that caters to the needs of all. Each member of the community recognizes that he will receive an individual allotment because such a pattern of distribution benefits all equally.

We might compare those who are founding the ideal city to a group of scholars who establish a new college by taking over an abandoned group of buildings. They might agree that some parts of

---

[17] The plots of land allocated to each citizen are therefore not their 'own', in the sense of *Rhet.* I.5 1361a21–4, because they cannot be given away or sold. Aristotle's aim in this passage is not to prescribe a system of ownership but to describe what is normally meant by wealth. The passage is, however, sometimes used as evidence that Aristotle wishes to guarantee an unrestricted right of transfer. See Miller, *NJR*, p. 312; and Mayhew, 'Aristotle on Property', p. 820.

the campus should be accessible to all without restriction, but that some spaces should be turned into private offices. Such offices cannot be used by their occupants in any way they please; they cannot be bought, sold, transferred, or destroyed. When someone says, 'this is my office', he means that he can decide on his own when to use it and what to put in it; furthermore, others can use it only with his permission. But he has only some of the rights that normally accompany ownership in the modern world.

That is a useful model to keep in mind, as we read Aristotle's discussion of Plato's *Republic*. His rejection of Plato's proposal to abolish private property among the guardians should not be taken to mean that, in his opinion, citizens of the best community should have the full set of rights and freedoms that were associated with property in the Greek world (and still prevail in much of the modern world). Although he argues that individuals should have private possessions, the rights of ownership that the best constitution would accord to individuals are far more restricted than the ones to which owners are accustomed.[18]

9.8. Power and Trust

Another point that should be kept in mind is that the disagreement between Plato and Aristotle regarding private property is connected to a more basic difference between them. Plato's abolition of private property is not an isolated measure but part of a larger political scheme. The leading idea behind his radical social innovations is that statesmanship requires intensive study of abstruse subjects culminating in comprehension of the deepest structures of reality. The science of politics cannot be understood or properly practiced by mere amateurs, but requires special expertise. As we have seen, Aristotle rejects this proposal entirely. Although the *founders* of his ideal city have made a special study of ethics, politics, and

---

[18] Here I agree with Nussbaum, 'Aristotelian Social Democracy', p. 232. I take it for granted that property consists in a bundle of rights and powers, and that legal systems can differ markedly in their specification of what is included in that bundle. The mere fact that the members of his ideal community cannot sell or transfer their lots as they please does not mean that they do not own the land on which they live. It means, rather, that their ownership rights are more narrow than they are in other legal systems. For recent philosophical studies of property, see Waldron, *The Right to Private Property*; and Harris, *Property and Justice*.

constitutions, the *citizens* need nothing more than ordinary practical reason and a good education (6.10).

This difference is part of the reason why Plato and Aristotle diverge in their views about property. Plato gives immense power to an elite and must guarantee that it not be abused. He must assure ordinary citizens that they have nothing to fear from their rulers. The abolition of private property among the rulers is designed to win the trust of those over whom they rule. In Plato's ideal city, political power cannot be used as a means to personal enrichment because there are no personal riches. By contrast, in Aristotle's ideal city, the most powerful body is the assembly of all citizens; those who are chosen for special offices have far less power than do Plato's guardians, and far less power than the whole body of Aristotelian citizens (6.10). Furthermore, there are many features of Aristotle's ideal city that tend to create trust: the citizens share a single conception of well-being, receive the same education, and frequently interact with each other at the common meals. Offices rotate, so no official serves for very long. This does not mean that it is unnecessary to keep a watchful eye on public officials; but there is no need to go so far as to abolish private property among the rulers, because an ordinary level of caution should be sufficient to guard against the abuse of power. Abolishing private property among Aristotle's rulers would be a radical measure indeed, since every citizen eventually shares in holding office. In effect, the abolition of private property would prevent *every* citizen from owning property throughout most of his adult life.

9.9. *Liturgies*

One further point should be made before we consider Aristotle's arguments in favor of allowing private property. He assumes that many citizens of his ideal city will use a portion of their wealth to support public projects. This point is not explicit, but it lies behind a statement we find in VII.8: here Aristotle says that various tasks—economic, military, religious, and deliberative—must be performed in the ideal community, and that one of them is 'a good degree of wealth' (1328b10). It may strike us as odd that wealth is called a 'task' (*ergon*, b5). What Aristotle means to convey by his use of this term is that the city cannot flourish unless it has a great deal of money at its disposal, and therefore one of the tasks that must be performed by the citizens is to provide the city with the financial resources it needs.

He goes on to mention one particular task: military expenditure (b11). What he has in mind is not the equipment needed by a hoplite soldier (shield, spear, sword), for he has already mentioned this as a separate category (b7–10). He is thinking instead of the need to pay for constructing and equipping ships. In Athens, these extraordinarily expensive projects were undertaken by individual citizens, who were expected, if their assets were sufficiently large, to serve the city by performing a 'liturgy' (*leitourgia*). Ships were not the only expensive items that were funded in this way; religious festivals, including dramatic and athletic contests, were also paid for by the wealthiest citizens.[19]

Aristotle's ideal city will have to pay for all of these items, and it will have the additional expense of public education. All of these undertakings will be the responsibility of individual citizens. Since some of them will not even be able to contribute to the expense of the common meals (VII.10 1330a5–8), we can safely assume that not all citizens will be expected to perform liturgies. On the other hand, it is certain that many will. Since the privately owned territory of the ideal city is divided equally among citizens, liturgies are not likely to be the responsibility of a small number of extremely wealthy citizens (as they were in Athens). Resources will be widely dispersed, and so a large number of citizens will contribute to civic projects.[20]

This means that the privately owned wealth of citizens is not entirely within their power to keep or use as they see fit. They can possess gold, silver, and other forms of property, but their

---

[19] For further discussion of this institution, see Austin and Vidal-Naquet, *Economic and Social History of Greece*, pp. 121–3; MacDowell, *The Law in Classical Athens*, pp. 161–7; Joint Association of Classical Teachers, *The World of Athens*, pp. 228–9, 272–3, 300; Ober, *Mass and Elite in Democratic Athens*, pp. 199–202, 226–33. In Athens, liturgies were assigned by magistrates, though there was a complex system of exemptions and legal challenges available to those who did not wish to perform them. See MacDowell, *The Law in Classical Athens*, pp. 161–3. In addition, property taxes (*eisphorai*) were imposed on wealthy citizens and metics. See Hansen, *The Athenian Democracy in the Age of Demosthenes*, pp. 112–15.

[20] Performance of liturgies by the wealthy is listed at IV.4 1291a33–4 as one of the necessary tasks that must be performed in any city. (The list begins at IV.4 1290b39.) Contributions to the expense of common meals is called a liturgy at II.10 1272a20, as is the support of religious customs at VII.10 1330a12–13. Aristotle sometimes makes the point that the expenses demanded of the wealthy are wasteful (V.5 1305a5, V.8 1309a18, VI.5 1320b4), but he is not opposed to the institution itself. See V.11 1314b14 on the value of this practice in a tyranny, and VI.7 1321a33 on its value in an oligarchy.

freedom to dispose of their goods in a manner of their choosing is restricted, for some of those possessions must be devoted to the common good, and are subject to the control of collective decisions. The institution of private property that Aristotle is defending in Book II must therefore be a system of rights that is subject to this restriction. Each citizen can decide how to improve his land and his house, how many slaves to purchase or sell, which individuals to lend to and which to refuse, and so on. But Aristotle cannot have it in mind to grant to each citizen the legal right to refrain from performing liturgies for the city. He does not specify how his ideal city will organize the performance of liturgies—who will be in charge of making these assignments, and on what basis they will be made. He regards these as details of little importance. The essential point is that many citizens will have to accept their responsibility to make financial contributions to public projects.

We should also recall what Aristotle says in VIII.1 in support of a single system of education: this must be a common project, and therefore no citizen is allowed to keep his children at home and given them a private education (1337a21–30). The education their children receive is collectively controlled and not a matter to be determined by individuals in isolation from each other. Though a child belongs to and is cared for by his parents, their power over him is not complete, even during his early years. We can easily understand why Aristotle takes a similar position regarding property. Which public projects are to be undertaken is not a matter to be individually determined by wealthy individuals acting in isolation, but is a matter subject to the authority of the assembly. Though each citizen owns and cares for his own property, no one has complete control over its disposition.

9.10. *Individual Ownership, Common Use*

When we turn to Aristotle's discussion of property in II.5, we find a brief positive proposal regarding the distribution of property in the best constitution, and a lengthier critique of Plato's arrangement in the *Republic*. Aristotle begins the chapter by noting several possibilities: both ownership and use can be either private or communal (1263a2–3). Of the four possible arrangements this creates, he explicitly mentions only three (a3–8):

A. Land is owned individually, but its produce is put into a common pool for consumption.
B. Land is owned and farmed communally, but its produce is distributed for private use.
C. Both land and crops are communal.

Having listed these possibilities, he begins his critique of communal ownership, and therefore of options (B) and (C). Nothing is said against (A), for it is the system that he goes on to endorse: property should be private, he says, but its use should be communal (1263a38–9). He again proposes such a system when he constructs his own ideal constitution: 'possessions should not be held in common ... but should be common in their use, as befits friends, and none of the citizens should be in need of food' (VII.10 1329b41–1330a2). His ideal city, as we have seen, requires that some land be owned communally, although nothing in Book II explains what the advantage of that arrangement is. All of the arguments Aristotle gives in II.5 are in favor of private ownership—although he insists that the *use* of property should in some sense be communal. If we wish to read him in a way that avoids contradiction, we must not take his conclusion in II.5 to be that nothing should be collectively owned. Rather, his conclusion must be that each citizen should have his own land, houses, slaves, money, and the like. He is opposed to making everything collectively owned, but not in favor of making everything privately owned.

Aristotle leaves it unclear whether, in (A), each individual takes from the common pool as he chooses, or there is instead some central system of distribution, presumably based on need. System (C) involves the same method of distribution, but differs from (A) in that the land is communally owned and farmed. In (B) too, land is communally owned and farmed, but it is not immediately obvious what Aristotle means by the distribution of produce for private use. Private use cannot mean consumption by individuals, for of course in any system of ownership the produce of the land is consumed by individuals. Perhaps what Aristotle has in mind in (B) is this: the resources extracted from common lands are entirely distributed among those who have worked on them, according to some pattern that has been agreed upon; and anyone who has needs that have not been met by that allocation must seek aid from this or that individual. In other words, a system of private use is one that leaves decisions about who will receive aid entirely up to individuals acting 'privately', that is, non-collectively, in isolation from each other. By

9.10. INDIVIDUAL OWNERSHIP, COMMON USE

contrast, in (A) and (C), those who are in need do not have to appeal to this or that individual for aid, but can draw upon resources made available to them by the community acting as a collective unit. That still leaves it unclear whether someone in need can simply draw upon a common pool as he sees fit, or whether the community makes collective decisions, on a case-by-case basis, about who is to receive aid. But in any case there is a clear contrast between (B) and the other two systems: (B) contains no social mechanism for distributing food to those in need, whereas the other two schemes do.

Aristotle says that system (A), the one he favors, is practiced by several peoples (*ethnē*, 1263a4–5), and later in II.5, he tells us that Sparta has a system that is similar to the one he prefers (a30–40). Here, he reports, citizens have their own property, but use each other's slaves, dogs, and horses as though they were their own. If they need food on a journey, they take from their neighbors' fields. But he also indicates that no existing city possesses precisely the system he is talking about, although some come close to it. 'Even now, this sort of thing exists in some cities in outline form, because it is not impossible; and particularly in those that are well managed some parts exist and others might come about' (a30–3). When Aristotle discusses Sparta later in Book II, we learn why he denies that it is a perfect model of distribution: those Spartans who become impoverished are excluded from participation in the common meals (II.9 1271a26–37). It seems, then, that Aristotle is proposing a system of private ownership in which all citizens know that if they are ever in need, they can count on support from others. They are guaranteed by the community that the privately owned resources of others can be made available to them. In this way, the evils of all-encompassing communal ownership will be avoided, and communal use will guarantee that the needs of all citizens are met.

This way of reading Aristotle allows us to see what he has in mind, when he says, in VII.10, that 'possessions should not be held in common . . . but should be common in their use, as befits friends, and none of the citizens should be in need of food' (1329b41–1330a2). Common use, civic friendship, and the hardships of poverty are connected in his mind: no one need fear the harsh burdens of poverty, because when the doctrine of common use is widely accepted among citizens, each is assured by this common understanding that he will have the use of the property of others. That common understanding arises out of and contributes to a sense of civic friendship.

Aristotle's doctrine of common use deserves fuller analysis (9.16–18), but let us set it aside for now. Our next task is to consider his arguments against a scheme of ownership that seems far friendlier than the one he endorses: common ownership and common use. If Aristotle thinks that common use is desirable in part because it expresses a form of civic friendship, then why not develop an even greater sense of civic friendship, by abolishing private property?

9.11. The Evils of Collectivism: Property and Family

Aristotle believes that once we recognize that property can and should be *used* communally, we will be disabused of the thought that collective *ownership* is the best way to establish friendship among citizens (II.5 1263b15–16). For collective ownership has several disadvantages:

A. When all property is collectively owned, each individual assumes that others are taking care of it, and it suffers from neglect (II.3 1261b33–8). Conversely, property that is individually owned receives closer attention and better care (II.5 1263a28–9).

B. Collective ownership gives rise to quarrels about how produce is to be distributed. Those who work more are resentful when those who work less take more (II.5 1263a8–21).

C. The recognition that something belongs to oneself is a great pleasure. Self-love is a natural and useful attitude, and is wrongly censured (II.5 1263a40-b5).

D. It is a great pleasure to use one's own resources to help one's friends, guests, and companions (II.5 1263b5–7).

E. If one has no private possessions, one cannot exercise the virtue of generosity, which consists in making good use of one's own possessions (II.5 1263b7–14).

Several of these arguments repeat or adapt points that Aristotle makes about the value of the family and deep emotional ties to small communities within the city. Just as it is a great good to have a strong tie of affection to other people, so it is a great pleasure to have control over the material resources one needs in order to live well. The abolition of the family would make certain expressions of temperance impossible, and similarly the abolition of private property would undermine the virtue of generosity. Both property and children that are communally tended will suffer from neglect.

The desire to abolish private property, like the proposal to abolish the family, arises from a misguided plan to give the city a unity that it cannot achieve and should not strive for, and so in II.5 Aristotle reaffirms his point that not every kind of unification is desirable (1263b29–37).

When we compare Aristotle's arguments in favor of the traditional family with the points he makes in favor of private ownership, certain broad themes become apparent. Preserving these institutions has three kinds of advantage.

First, private property and the small family are the most effective means by which the community can tend to things that need special care: children, elderly parents, the food supply, and other resources that must be handed down from one generation to another.

Second, human relationships become less satisfying and more difficult to maintain if people are prevented from having a special degree of concern for a small number of people or a small parcel of land. Without small associations, we will have no strong affection for others; if all property is collectivized, our relationships with fellow citizens will be filled with strife. A city cannot function well unless something binds its citizens together, but since the strongest ties cannot be universal—we cannot love all people and all pieces of property equally—the best way to maintain good civic relations is to allow people to give particular care to their own things and to people with whom they are close.

Third, the traditional family and private property play an important role in any well-lived life. Well-being consists in excellent activities adequately supplied with resources. If we have no close emotional ties with others, then one important sphere of virtuous activity—the way we treat our friends and family—is diminished. If we do not have our own resources for living well, but must always depend on receiving provisions from friends or the political community, then we cannot feel the pleasure that comes from a confident sense that we control our own lives.

9.12. *Property and Disagreement*

The first point Aristotle makes against communal ownership in II.5 is that it will create fewer difficulties if the citizens are not themselves farmers (1263a8–10). As he goes on to point out, when people are not only joint owners but also joint *workers*, there will inevitably be disputes about how to divide the products of their labor: those who work more will want a greater share, and it is difficult to resolve disagreements about who deserves more (a10–15). What is surprising about this remark is that in Aristotle's ideal city the citizens are not engaged in physical labor on the farms they own; furthermore, in Plato's *Republic* the farmers individually own their land and produce, and private property is abolished only in the upper two classes.[21] Since Aristotle is asking whether ownership should be collective in the *best* city, his point about the quarrels of those who actually labor on farms seems irrelevant.

Presumably he would reply that even if a system of communal ownership is *less* troublesome when citizens do not farm, it is still objectionable enough to warrant choosing a system of private ownership. For the same problems will arise. If you and I jointly own land and we also own slaves who do the farm work, how should we divide the crops and the income produced by their sale? If we work equally hard at *supervising* the farm, then should we share the results equally? Who is to say whether we are working equally hard at our supervisory tasks? Furthermore, suppose I have four children and poor parents, but you have only one child and rich parents: how should that affect our distribution of the produce? If we were actually working the land together side by side on a daily basis, such disputes would be especially vexing; but Aristotle can say, with some plausibility, that even if we are owners and supervisors but not workers, the same sorts of issue will divide us. The solution seems obvious: let each citizen own and oversee his own territory. In that way, we eliminate a source of conflict.

As a criticism of Plato's abolition of private property, what Aristotle says here would be completely off the mark. Plato's rulers are completely free of any responsibility to manage farms and divide their produce. And so they have no quarrels about how to divide resources. But we need not take everything Aristotle says here to be directed against Plato. He also needs to settle the problem of ownership in his own ideal city. If joint ownership is often a source of disputes, there is good reason to adopt a system of individual ownership in the ideal city.

---

[21] Aristotle expresses uncertainty about how extensive Plato's abolition of private property is (II.5 1264a14–17). See Mayhew, 'Aristotle on the Extent of Communism in Plato's *Republic*'. He argues that Aristotle is right to be uncertain, because Plato leaves this matter unclear.

9.13. Selfishness and Self-Love

It may seem that Aristotle's point is superficial, because it ignores the possibility that human beings, when properly educated and socialized, might be less selfish and less inclined to quarrel over the proper division of the produce of jointly owned property. In fact, Aristotle himself reminds his audience, in II.5, of the harmonizing effects of education. He says that although land should be individually owned, its produce should be distributed to one's friends, guests, and companions (1263a37–b6). What will make citizens inclined to share in this way? He replies: customs, and an education that will instill in them a sense of friendship and unity (1263b36–1264a1). Here one might protest: if it is legitimate to say that citizens will freely share with each other when they are properly educated, why not also say that when citizens are trained to be less selfish, the quarrels that have often occurred in the past among those who own land in common will not arise?

At this point it is tempting for a defender of Aristotle to say that human beings simply are incapable of that degree of selflessness. They can't help but want some things to be their own; they can't be indifferent to various ways of dividing the fruits of their work. However, Aristotle can make a stronger argument than this: he can reasonably claim not only that it is difficult or impossible to devise an upbringing that would eliminate this aspect of human nature, but that it would not be desirable to do so. Expressions of self-love are not merely tolerable but desirable, provided it is the right kind of self-love. For a certain way of caring more about oneself and what is one's own is not only in one's own interest but in the interest of others as well. Were we to succeed in suppressing this feature of human nature, the result would be less attractive, not more. Aristotle sees that at bottom this is the issue, for he asserts in II.5: 'Self-love is justly censured, but this consists not in loving oneself, but in loving oneself more than one ought' (1363b2–3).

An analogy with anger may help. Aristotle is aware of how dangerous an emotion this is, but he does not urge his readers to eliminate it completely, because he believes that it would be contrary to one's interests to become totally pacific. Someone incapable of anger would be perceived as servile, and would become a target of insults and attacks.[22] When others perceive one's willingness to strike back,

---

[22] 'People seek to return evil; otherwise, they are thought to be slaves' (NE V.5 1132b34–1133a1).

one is less likely to be wounded. So, some degree of self-assertion is all to the good—provided that it is fully responsive to reason. To eliminate anger entirely would be to overreact to the threat it poses. The best type of education, difficult though it may be, is not to suppress anger entirely but to harmonize it with reason.[23]

In the same way, Aristotle is saying that a certain kind of bias in one's own favor is not to be regretted; it is all to the good—not only one's own, but that of others. This bias must be of the right sort: it must not be a desire to have more external goods than others, or to exercise control over as many people as possible. But suppose instead each of us competed for the honor of having served our friends and our community better than anyone else: would we not all benefit from such ambition? Instead of suppressing one's desire for one's good, one should cultivate one's self-love in the proper way: one should want to live well by excelling in ways that help others.[24] No one who competes with others in this benign way would be terribly upset if he 'merely' did as well as everyone else, but no better. One's *greatest* desire ought not to be for a happiness that surpasses anyone else's, or for superiority to everyone else as a public benefactor; rather, what we should want most of all is to live well by serving our community. But that does not mean that one should have *no* desire to outdo others as a benefactor.

This is the kind of thinking that lies behind Aristotle's proposal that land be privately owned and that its products be used for the good of others. The basic idea is that it is good, both for me and for the whole community, for there to be certain things that are mine rather than everyone's. 'In terms of pleasure, it can't be said how much difference it makes to believe that something is one's own' (II.5 1263a40–1). This is a remark about the pride of ownership. When the land whose cultivation one oversees is productive and well tended, one can take special pleasure in one's success. A mere stranger who looks at the land and observes how well managed it is might be pleased about this, but this can hardly be compared with the sense of accomplishment one has when the land is one's own and one is responsible for its care. If land that is owned and

---

[23] See *NE* IV.5 for Aristotle's principal discussion of how anger should be handled. Unfortunately, he finds it so obvious that anger should sometimes be felt and expressed that he does not argue against a hypothetical opponent who advocates its elimination. The latter view was adopted by the Stoics; see esp. Seneca, *De Ira*.

[24] See *NE* IX.8 for Aristotle's defense of the proper form of self-love. For the competitive nature of this self-love, see Kraut, *Aristotle on the Human Good*, pp. 115–19.

supervised by everyone were capable of being well managed (contrary to Aristotle's hypothesis), all would take some pleasure in their joint accomplishment. But Aristotle claims with some plausibility that it is not in human nature to be as pleased by this collective accomplishment as it is by the individual accomplishment of having managed one's own property well. If a prize is granted to the communal garden managed by a committee of 1,000 each member of the committee will receive some pleasure, but the pleasure of the sole manager of a small but successful garden will be far greater.

9.14. *Common Meals and Collective Ownership*

Let us now return to the point, recalled earlier (9.7), that in Aristotle's ideal city not all property is individually owned. Some of the land—the part used to support common meals and to meet religious needs—is owned by the whole community (VII.10 1330a9–13). Why do Aristotle's arguments against collective ownership not apply here?

The answer must be that sometimes the circumstances that provide reasons for private ownership do not obtain, or are overridden by countervailing considerations. Suppose the common meals were supported by dedicating certain *privately* owned lands to this purpose. In that case, citizens whose land is restricted to this use suffer a great personal loss: they have been made poor and must depend on others for provisions. Perhaps instead the common meals should be supported by distributing the burden among all citizens: each landowner is to set aside a certain portion of his land to support the common meals. But this creates the need for an elaborate system of supervision and collection. It would be far more efficient to have all of this work located in one place. Aristotle is evidently assuming that whenever the alternatives to collective ownership are inequitable or inefficient, then ownership must not be private. The pleasures of common ownership are not as great as those of private ownership, but this is just one consideration among many, and in certain cases there are overriding reasons for collective ownership. Aristotle's thesis in II.5 is that in a well-organized community, *some* things—but not all—ought to be privately owned.

How much should be privately owned, and how much communally owned? And by what criterion are we to decide? Aristotle does not say how much of the territory of the ideal city is to be set aside for communal ownership, and obviously he is right to be silent. This is a matter of detail that can be answered only when one knows more about how much food is needed, the quality of the land, the number of farmers, and so on. But clearly Aristotle is committed to saying that this question is to be answered by considering the needs of the whole community. Suppose it were discovered, as the ideal city is being founded, that private ownership would leave certain needs unmet; that after another generation there would not be enough trees (for example) to provide the material for warships. And suppose the most fair and efficient method for meeting this need is to make less of the territory available for private ownership and to set aside a larger amount for communal development. Aristotle has every reason to endorse this solution. His defense of individual ownership is an attempt to show that it is best that some things be individually owned, not that this form of ownership be as extensive as possible.

9.15. *Individual Effort, Public Service*

It will be helpful at this point to recall another part of Aristotle's defense of private ownership: such an arrangement, he says, calls forth greater effort. More attention is usually paid by an individual owner to privately held objects than is paid by a large group to its collective possessions (II.5 1263a27–9). What Aristotle is implying when he says this is that, as a rule, the output of privately owned land will be greater than the output of collectively owned land. For when land and crops receive attention, the yield is greater. But of course he cannot mean that the ultimate goal of encouraging individual attention and effort is to allow each citizen to maximize profits and accumulate personal possessions. The aim of the community in dividing land and allowing some of it to be privately held is to serve the common good, and this goal is achieved when resources are abundant enough to allow all citizens to live well. Aristotle favors a certain amount of private ownership, but ownership is for the sake of use, and the use of private possessions is to be common (II.5 1263a37–9). Each citizen of the ideal city will take pride in the way he has managed his own piece of land, but he will then make some of his produce available to the whole community, for the point of having a system of private property is to redistribute resources so that all can live well.

9.15. INDIVIDUAL EFFORT, PUBLIC SERVICE

Aristotle's conception of how property should be distributed will be difficult for us to grasp if we cling to the idea that it is self-interest alone that attaches people to things. When we find him saying that people care more for what is their own than they do for communal property, we might infer (unjustifiably) that, in his opinion, people are not motivated to take care of things by any thought of the good of others. We may take him to mean that I take care of my house because it will give *me* (or *my* family and friends) pleasure and comfort; if I thought of myself as doing a public service in looking after it, my efforts would flag. But if we read Aristotle in this way, we cannot make sense of his thesis that there should be *communal* use of individually owned property (1263a25–6, a38–9). And so we may be puzzled: how can my efforts be called forth by the thought that this is *mine*, if I am to care for what is mine in order to benefit everyone else? Or, to put the question the other way round: if I realize, as I oversee my property, that I will be using it for the good of others—not just for my friends, but for the common good—why wouldn't I oversee it just as well if it belonged not to me alone but to the whole community?

What we must supply, in order to understand Aristotle, is the idea that public-spirited people take pride in making *individual* contributions to the common good. The contribution they make is their own, and is recognized as such by the community; but their intention is to use their private resources for the good of all. To take an example from our age rather than Aristotle's: someone might beautify her house with the intention of leaving it to the public when she dies. The house is hers, because she alone has the right to live in it and to make decisions about how to improve it. But her motivation for taking good care of it might be her devotion to the common good. Aristotle's conception of an ideal system of property contains the thought that citizens should be trained in a way that makes them care for their possessions in this public-spirited way. He assumes that education can never entirely eliminate our desire to have some things that are ours and not others. But there is no reason to regard this as a regrettable feature of human nature. The desire to own a piece of the world can be put to good public use, and so we are all better off if we give this aspect of our psychology some free play.

9.16. The Common Use of Property in Sparta

As we saw in 9.10, Aristotle cites with approval the Spartan practice of allowing others to use their slaves, horses, dogs, and crops, as needed (1263a33–9).[25] He cannot mean that they sometimes decide to make gifts of their property—that custom is nearly universal. Rather, his point is that the Spartans have an unusual social practice, one that teaches us an important lesson about the public use of private property. They make use of the property of others as though that property were their own, and do so with the knowledge that no one, not even the owner, will object. The Spartan citizen expects others to make use of some of his property without asking permission to do so. The common knowledge among Spartans that this is their practice makes it unnecessary to ask for the owner's permission. Accordingly, when a Spartan oversees his farm, he knows that some of what he owns or grows will be used in ways that lie beyond his decision and his control—and he has no objection to that use of his property. In fact, if he has a friendly feeling towards his community, then he will have decided to grow some of his crops and to purchase some of his horses in order to allow others to use them when they wish, without asking his permission.

We need not take Aristotle to be recommending precisely this arrangement. He introduces his discussion of the Spartan practice by saying: 'Even now, this sort of thing exists in some cities in outline form, because it is not impossible; and particularly in those that are well managed some parts exist and others might come about' (1263a30–3). He cites this Spartan practice because it shows that it is not contrary to human nature for someone to take good care of his property, while expecting control over a portion of it to be exercised by others. In Sparta, that control is exercised by individuals as they travel or find themselves in need from time to time. But there is an obvious way to modify the Spartan practice: the whole community might deliberate collectively about what use to make of a portion of each person's property. The collective use of individual resources, as determined by the decisions of an assembly, is simply a way to make a more systematic use of the Spartan attitude towards property. If other individuals besides the owner can make good use of the owner's property and need not rely on his permission to do so, then

---

[25] For another report on this Spartan practice, see Xenophon, *Constitution of the Lacedaimonians* VI.3–5.

the whole community can justifiably do the same. It is a reasonable conjecture, then, that Aristotle's favored economic system is one in which a portion of each citizen's property is put to public use in a manner decided upon by citizens in common. Our earlier discussion of liturgies (9.9) and Aristotle's threefold classification of systems of ownership (9.10) fit well with this conjecture. For as we have seen, he takes it for granted in Books VII and VIII that his ideal city will require its citizens to use their private resources to perform liturgies for the community, and in II.5 he favors a system of property in which the produce of individually owned land is put into a common pool for consumption (1263a3–4). All of our evidence points in the same direction: decisions about the best use of private property for public purposes are to be made collectively by the whole community.

9.17. *Generosity and Friends*

Although Aristotle's doctrine of 'private ownership, common use' allows the assembly of all citizens to allocate private property for public purposes, he assumes that the city is not entitled to take so much from individuals that it undermines their ability to live well. It can tax wealthy citizens, but it must leave them resources sufficient for a life of rational activity in accordance with virtue. And in particular, because citizens must be able to exercise the virtue of generosity, they must not be taxed too much. Their financial resources must not become so meager that they are no longer able to help their friends and companions, for such aid is an important component of generosity.

If the city overtaxed its citizens, Aristotle's endorsement of the common use of private property would run afoul of one of the objections he makes against Plato's abolition of private property, namely that it would make generosity impossible (II.5 1263b5–14). This aspect of his critique of the *Republic* draws upon his initial objection to Plato's underlying premise that civic unification is the sole criterion of good constitutional design (II.2 1261a15–22). As we saw (9.3), Aristotle's basic point in II.2 is that Plato exaggerates the importance of unity. Such institutions as the family and property must be arranged in a way that promotes well-being, and the unification of the city should be pursued only to the point where it serves that ultimate goal. In II.5, he twice returns to this objection

(1263b7–9, b29–37): Plato goes too far in his desire for civic unity, for the kind of unification he seeks would undermine the possibility of virtuous activity, the very thing for the sake of which the city exists. By contrast, his less intrusive scheme, which allows the city to use a portion of each citizen's private property, does not undermine generosity, provided that the community does not take so much from wealthy individuals that they can no longer exercise this virtue in the support they give to their friends and family.

This part of Aristotle's discussion of private property presupposes the success of his earlier argument against Plato's abolition of the family (II.2–4). He assumes in II.5 that intimate ties between family members and friends must be left intact, because the community of fellow citizens is not an adequate replacement for these smaller and more affective associations. Once he has shown the need for these intimate communities, he believes he has secured his case for allowing people to have sufficient resources to give not only to the city but to their family and friends as well. It is part of the nature of these relationships that family members and friends look to each other in time of need and share with one another on special occasions. Leaving such ties intact requires allowing citizens to have the material resources they need to sustain a special form of closeness.

When Aristotle makes the point that the abolition of private property would make it impossible to exercise the virtue of generosity, he corrects an impression that might be created by the rest of his discussion. He argues that joint ownership would create quarrels, that private ownership calls forth greater effort and therefore makes more resources available, and that we take a special pleasure in what is ours. What he adds, when he makes the further claim that abolishing private property would also destroy generosity, is that such a radical measure would diminish well-being itself and not merely the resources needed for a happy life—because, of course, well-being consists in virtuous activity. If the best life is the one in which we actualize not just a narrow range of moral capacities but all of them, then making generosity among family and friends impossible diminishes the range of excellent activities we can undertake and therefore diminishes our well-being. The point is important because it shows that the case for allowing some property to be private does not rest simply on the value of pleasure (the pleasure of ownership) and the efficient production of resources. These advantages of private property are important, but not as important as well-being itself.

Aristotle is entitled to make this same point about his argument

9.17. GENEROSITY AND FRIENDS

that jointly owned property creates strife. Conflicts with others are not merely unpleasant; they impede excellent activity. The more conflicts of interest we create by badly designing institutions, the more difficult it will be for us to treat each other justly. Recall Aristotle's reason for giving each citizen two widely separated lots: this removes a source of difficulty in arriving at unbiased and just decisions that promote the common good (VII.10 1330a15–23). We must not assume that when people are virtuous they can constantly overcome all obstacles to their arriving at fair collective decisions. Even a community of good people should design their institutions to avoid needless tensions. Quarrels created by the abolition of private property would strain the virtue even of those who are qualified to live in an ideal community.

It might seem, nonetheless, that Aristotle is wrong to suppose that abolishing private property would destroy the virtue of generosity. After all, even if all material resources were collectively owned, individual citizens would still need to participate in making collective decisions about how those resources should be managed and exploited. Why could not generosity be shown by each member of the assembly, since each participates in the debates of this body about ways and means?[26] Admittedly, if private resources were abolished, generosity could not be shown in one's individual relationships with friends and family members, since generosity is a virtue essentially tied to the use of external goods. But Aristotle seems to exaggerate when he says that generosity would be *destroyed* by the abolition of private property (1263b8); at best, he is entitled to say that its sphere of operation would become more limited.[27]

But on second thought, it is not obvious that Aristotle is vulnerable to this criticism. In any large assembly there will frequently be divisions of opinion—a point that did not escape Aristotle, for, as we saw earlier (6.11), he points out that the principle of majority rule is used in all political systems. If he assumes, realistically, that this principle will be needed even in an ideal polis, then many of that community's decisions about how to use the public treasury for the common good will be opposed by some citizens. When the city decides to undertake a project that did not receive unanimous support in the assembly, who can claim to act generously? Only those

---

[26] Aristotle believes that it is important not only to be a generous person and to act generously, but also to *show oneself* to be generous (II.5 1263b11–12). If one's concern for others remains unknown to them, then a valuable element of human relationships is lost.

[27] For this objection, see Irwin, 'Aristotle's Defense of Private Property', pp. 222–3.

who favored the resolution? (If so, those opposed are harmed by the abolition of private property, because it is only through collective action that they can be generous.) Or should we say that all who participated in the vote expressed their generosity—even those opposed? (After all, the minority is committed to accepting the outcome of the vote, because it accepts the principle of majority rule.) Should gratitude to the city for its aid be shown only to some members of the assembly, and not others? And how should such gratitude be expressed? We lack answers to these questions because public expenditures are not normally regarded as expressions of generosity: this is a virtue that is expressed by individuals in their personal transactions and face-to-face encounters, not by collective bodies. This point does not apply across the board to all virtues; practical wisdom, for example, can certainly be exercised by a collective body. But many other virtues are exercised chiefly or entirely by individuals, as they bring their deliberative skills and feelings to bear on their social relations. Perhaps Aristotle ought to have said that generosity would be greatly diminished—rather than destroyed—by the abolition of private property. Even so, he is right to think that each citizen should be left with enough resources to show generosity to his family and friends.

9.18. *Taxation and Individual Choice*

Immediately after Aristotle describes the Spartan convention that allows citizens to use the property of others as though it were their own, he says: 'It is the distinctive task of the legislator to make them that sort' (1263a39–40). What he means is that nothing resembling the Spartan system of making common use of private possessions will work, unless those who participate in the system have a character suitable to it. They must be so disposed to each other that they welcome the common use of their private property. The job of someone who is building an ideal city is to design institutions that foster these feelings of friendship and public spirit. If the citizens do not have these attitudes towards each other and the common good, they will not make or accept collective decisions to use their private property for public purposes.

But Aristotle's words might be given a different interpretation: we could take him to be implying that his favored way of allocating property—individual possession, common use—is not to be made a

9.18. TAXATION AND INDIVIDUAL CHOICE

legal requirement, but is to be fostered solely through the inculcation of good habits. The task of the legislator who wishes to foster the common use of private property is simply to create conditions favorable to the development and exercise of ethical virtue among the citizens. He should, for example, create public schools that encourage habits favorable to the growth of generosity. He should encourage adult citizens to give generously to civic goals. If he is successful in creating a certain sort of citizenry, then individual property-holders will voluntarily use their resources for public purposes. But, according to this way of understanding Aristotle, the city should never *require* anyone to use his property to serve the public good. How each citizen allocates his private holdings—whether to spend it on himself, or his children, or his fellow citizens—is a matter that must be left to his decision. Of course, Aristotle thinks that the right way for him to spend it is to contribute a sizable portion of it to the common good. That is what any citizen will in fact do, if he is a virtuous person. But the legislator should bring about that result through indirect methods, not through coercive legislation.[28]

That, however, cannot be Aristotle's meaning. Greek cities had the power of taxation, and he implicitly assumes that they cannot survive unless they use it. In fact, when he turns, in Book II, to a discussion of Sparta, one of the points he makes against it is that it is lax in overseeing the contributions its citizens are required to make to the public treasury (II.9 1271b10–17). Elsewhere in Book II, he says that poverty and food shortages are sometimes the outcome of poor civic planning, and that it is the city's job to avoid these problems or address them when they occur.[29] These passages show that he takes poverty and the threat of starvation to be matters of collective concern. They are to be addressed by those who govern, and cannot be left entirely to wealthy individuals to resolve, if they so choose, through the generous use of their private resources. He takes it for granted that the uncoordinated efforts of private individuals will not provide effective solutions to these problems. They are civic matters, and if the assembly chooses to solve them by taxing wealthy citizens, it is acting in accordance with the doctrine that private property should be used for the common good. Of course, if the citizens have not developed certain habits of thought and

---

[28] This line of thought is suggested by Mayhew, 'Aristotle on Property', pp. 819–20, 827–9. Cf. his *Aristotle's Criticism of Plato's* Republic, p. 107. So too Reeve in the introduction to his translation, p. lxxviii.

[29] See II.6 1265a38–b16, II.7 1267a9–10, II.9 1270a34–b6.

feeling, their city will not try to address the problems of poverty through a system of taxation, or it will not be effective in doing so. They must have an abiding concern for the common good, and there must be a sense of friendship among them. That is something the Spartans do not fully possess, despite the fact that they allow others to take their crops and animals without asking permission. They accept a system in which individuals freely take from each other, but do not see the need to enlarge the public treasury. So, when Aristotle says about the Spartans that 'it is the distinctive task of the legislator to make them that sort' (1263a39–40), he must be taken to mean that although they have the bare elements of the system of private property that he favors, the creation and successful governance of an ideal city will require people of far better character.

Recall that in VIII.1 Aristotle argues that the education of children should be overseen by the city, and not left to each household to manage entirely on its own. Since his ideal city does not allow parents to have complete control over their own children, we should expect him to think that the city must be equally willing to take control over private property. After all, as we noticed earlier (9.11), Aristotle's discussion of family relations and of property are remarkably alike. So it would be out of keeping with his general approach to these subjects for him to suppose that the city must allow individual citizens the right to decide whether they shall or shall not use their financial resources for public purposes.

Recall too that concern for the common good lies behind many of the economic restrictions imposed by the best constitution: citizens cannot buy, destroy, or sell their allotments of land. Some land is unavailable for private purchase, because it is dedicated to such public goods as common meals and religious activities (9.7). Citizens who can afford to do so will be required to provide funds for military equipment and other purposes (9.9). So it would make no sense for Aristotle to oppose the use of the public treasury—funds taken through coercive legislation from private holdings—to help those in need. We should not attribute to him the idea that the city's only way to help the poor is to foster the growth of virtue, and to hope that each citizen will give generously to those in need.

It might be thought, however, that there is a conceptual difficulty here. Note, to begin with, that if someone is legally required to contribute to a common pool, then he is not free to refrain. But Aristotle insists that only voluntary acts can be virtuous and deserving of praise (*NE* III.1 1109b30–2). Furthermore, he says that a virtuous

9.18. TAXATION AND INDIVIDUAL CHOICE

person will choose virtuous acts for themselves, and will not undertake them merely because they are means to some further end, such as the avoidance of punishment or some other external result.[30] It might seem to follow from these points that a city will destroy or severely restrict the virtue of generosity, if it taxes individuals and in this way requires them to contribute to the common good. According to this way of thinking, the payment of those taxes, or the performance of any other legally required services to the city, cannot be an expression of the virtue of generosity, or any other genuine virtue. And so, if Aristotle wishes the citizens of his ideal city to express the virtue of generosity in their dealings with the city, he cannot *require* them to make donations to the public treasury, or to use their private resources for public purposes. Those who establish the ideal city must confine themselves to encouraging such public-spiritedness. That, it might be supposed, is what he has in mind when he says, after describing the Spartan system of sharing: 'It is the distinctive task of the legislator to make them that sort' (1263a39–40).

But the line of reasoning taken in the preceding paragraph cannot be right. As Aristotle's analysis of voluntary and involuntary acts shows, any act that results from an agent's decision counts as voluntary, provided he has knowledge of the circumstances of his act (*NE* III.1 1109b35–1110b9). When a tyrant threatens to kill one's parents unless one does his will (1110a5–7), one is faced with a choice among several terrible alternatives, but it is one's decision that will determine which of them one will do, and so one's act is voluntary. For this same reason, an act that is required by law is not rendered involuntary by that requirement. Therefore, when a city tells a citizen that he must contribute some of his resources to a public project, his compliance can be given voluntarily, even though he lacks the legal freedom to do otherwise. And since he can voluntarily obey the law and contribute to the common good, his act can be praiseworthy, and can exercise such virtues as justice and generosity. A citizen who is required to perform a financial service for the city is able to arrive at his own views about whether there are good reasons to comply with that requirement. He might come to the conclusion that in order to be a good citizen and a good human being, he should obey the law, even if he thinks it is far from ideal. Or he may decide that the law is a good one, and that it is best both for him and the

---

[30] See *NE* II.4 1105a31–2, II.5 1106a3–4, III.2 1111b5–6, VI.2 1139a22–7.

community to do what it requires. He might even decide that he would have good reason to perform the act required by the law, even if his city were not demanding that he do so. In all of these cases, his performance of his legal duty can be an expression of virtue. What he cannot do, if he wishes his act to exercise a virtue, is to obey the law only because doing so is a means to some external goal, such as the avoidance of punishment. But from the fact that the city threatens to punish those who do not comply with its laws, it does not follow that an act of compliance cannot be an expression of generosity, justice, or any other moral excellence.

So, Aristotle would have made a grave philosophical error if he had left his citizens legally unrestricted, on the grounds that otherwise they could not make choices. And we know that he does not make this mistake, because even in the ideal city of VII and VIII he calls for the punishment of those who violate certain rules.[31] The citizens of the best city are virtuous, but Aristotle does not think he must leave them free to do as they please. Nowhere in his discussion of justice in Book V of the *Ethics* does he show the least concern that legal coercion might pose a threat to the expression of virtue. The law, he says, commands us to perform the actions of a virtuous person: to stay at our post in battle, to refrain from adultery, to forbear from assault, and so on (V.1 1129b19–25). To be just in the broad sense consists in having the right attitude towards these and other laws (4.3). A philosopher who sees so close a connection between justice and obedience to the law cannot believe that the existence of a legal requirement to perform or refrain from a certain kind of act makes it impossible for that performance or restraint to exercise a virtue. Aristotle cannot believe that when a magistrate assigns a citizen the job of financing and overseeing a public project, that activity, when properly executed, cannot be an expression of virtue.

9.19. *Communism for Defective Cities*

As we have seen (9.12), Aristotle holds that joint ownership leads to strife, and this is one of his reasons for favoring private property (II.5 1263b23–5). But there is an obvious objection to what he says: the fragmentation of the world into separately owned parcels has also

---

[31] See VII.16 1335b38–1336a2, VII.17 1336b8–12; cf. III.15 1286b27–33.

9.19. COMMUNISM FOR DEFECTIVE CITIES

caused one of our deepest social divisions—that between rich and poor. The have-nots envy the haves; the haves fear and therefore hate the have-nots. Aristotle might reply that private property need not *inevitably* lead to class conflict. In his ideal society there are some who have less than others, but even so there is no class division among the citizens (6.9). Nonetheless, even if we concede that in ideal conditions the conflicts caused by unequal private possessions can be avoided, we should ask: when conditions are far from ideal, as they have always been, would it not be better to abolish private property? Doing so would have at least one great advantage, since it would eliminate the strife between rich and poor. Why allow private property to exist in current conditions, when it leads to immense social problems?

Aristotle does not address this question in Book II, because this part of the *Politics* merely examines various conceptions of an ideal constitution, and does not seek solutions to the problems of defective cities. But when he does consider their problems in Books IV–VI, the strife between rich and poor is very much on his mind, and yet he never considers the abolition of private property as a solution. Why not? Does he assume that the city would be overstepping the limits of its legitimate authority if it required people to give up their possessions and place them in a common pool? That cannot be the answer, because we have seen that he gives the city considerable power to use private possessions for public purposes. He favors private ownership not because he thinks there are limits on the authority of the state, but because he thinks the best way for individuals to serve the common good is through a system of private ownership. So, if the common good were better served by taking from all and putting everything in a common pool, he would have no reason to object. And the suggestion we are now considering is that in cities where there is rampant strife between rich and poor, the common good might best be served by abolishing private property. Where there is no individual ownership, there are no rich and poor—and so no conflict between rich and poor.

It is unlikely that it simply never occurred to Aristotle that class division might be avoided in this way. Such conflict is one of his major themes, and Plato's communism one of his main concerns. It would not have taken much imagination to put the two ideas together and to take communism to be the right solution not to the problem of the ideal but to the problem of the real. And yet, although Aristotle devises many schemes in Books IV–VI for making the rich and the poor get along better with each other, the abolition of property is never mentioned as a possibility. Why not?

I suggest that he gives no thought to communism as a solution to current problems because he does not want to waste words on what he assumes to be obviously unworkable. It is worthwhile to imagine a new city in which all property is held in common, and to ask whether such an institution would be desirable; but it is quite another matter to impose communism on an existing city afflicted with class conflict. How would such a proposal be regarded by the citizens? Needless to say, the rich would not give up their possessions without a fight. Perhaps the poor would also oppose the abolition of property, for they might prefer having small portions of the pie to having none at all. Even if such a scheme could be forced on the populace, there would be constant pressure to return to the previous system of ownership. Aristotle believes that there are effective ways of alleviating the conflict between rich and poor in existing cities without radically altering the distribution of wealth or abolishing private property altogether.

9.20. *Equal Division*

Consider another possible solution to the conflict between rich and poor: instead of abolishing private property, we might equalize it. Something like this proposal is considered in II.7 of the *Politics*: Phaleas of Chalcedon advocated equal division of *land*, though not of all property whatsoever (1267b9–10). Aristotle is interested in the broader question of economic equality, and therefore considers a generalization of Phaleas's proposal. He asks: should an ideal city require equality of wealth, and should we try to approximate this goal in existing cities?

His answer is negative, but on the surface his opposition to equal shares seems superficial. He says: (A) It is possible for shares to be equal and yet too small or too large. (B) Even if shares are moderate in size, this will serve no purpose, unless all have an equal education. (C) And even if all have the same education, it might nonetheless be a bad education (1266b24–35).

Aristotle's argument seems disappointing because he takes the egalitarians to mean that the *only* thing an ideal community needs is equality. He may be right that other things are required as well, but he seems to overlook the point that even if equality is not sufficient

9.20. EQUAL DIVISION

for perfection, it may nonetheless contribute to perfection. Granted, resources and education must be of the right size and the right sort; but why not take seriously the idea that *one* of the elements of an ideal society is equality of possessions?

Part of Aristotle's answer to this question should be apparent from his definition of well-being as virtuous activity *sufficiently* equipped with external resources (*NE* I.10 1101a15). What a community should aim at, when it manages its resources, is that every citizen have *enough*—enough to live a life of virtuous activity. Once a citizen reaches this level, an increase in resources is, by hypothesis, not necessary for a good life. So it does not seem to be a matter of urgency or significance to arrange matters so that all citizens have the same amount. It is not even true that it does *some* good to equalize wealth; provided each has enough, it does no good at all.[32]

This response to the egalitarian will not quite do, however. For Aristotle must admit that a person who has large resources can carry out major projects for the good of the city, whereas someone who has just enough to live well is limited to making smaller civic contributions. The rich person who uses his wealth wisely exercises virtue on a grand scale, and therefore has a better, more successful life than does the person whose resources are moderate.[33]

Aristotle can deflate the force of this objection, to some extent, by reminding us of the egalitarian features of his ideal community: all citizens have the same education, share equally in the common meals, and participate as full equals in offices and the assembly. Those who have fewer resources are not limited to making minor contributions to the city, because in the public forum they can serve just as well as anyone else. So, if the rich have an advantage over the poor because they can perform larger liturgies, their advantage will not be as great as we might have imagined. All citizens can perform great public services, even though it is true that the range of services provided by the rich is wider than that available to the poor.

One other consideration makes the gap between rich and poor still less significant: when a new city is established, the division of land is a matter to be determined by the whole community, and there is

---

[32] In this respect there is a similarity between Aristotle's doctrine and the view defended by Frankfurt, 'Equality as a Moral Ideal'. For a contemporary defense of the view that equality among human beings requires an initial allocation of equal material resources to all citizens, see Dworkin, *Sovereign Virtue*, pp. 1–303. From an Aristotelian perspective, Dworkin overemphasizes the importance of equal wealth.

[33] See *NE* IV.1–2 on the distinction between liberality and magnificence. For a helpful discussion, see Irwin, 'Disunity in the Aristotelian Virtues', pp. 62–4.

no reason to give some citizens smaller lots than others, provided there are no complicating factors, such as differences in soil quality (6.9). Although some will have greater resources than others (more cattle, slaves, and so on), these differences cannot be very great, because one of the most important components of wealth—land— will be equal.

A strict egalitarian would say that this is still not *ideal*. It is good that in the city of Books VII and VIII the gap between rich and poor is small—but why should *any* differences be allowed, if they are eliminable and enable some to be better off than others? After all, Aristotle is trying to describe an ideal society, not just a pretty good one. Would it not be ideal to eliminate economic differences entirely?

It is not clear how Aristotle would respond to this objection, but a defense could be developed on his behalf, using many of the points he himself makes. It is important at this point to bear in mind that the kind of egalitarianism Aristotle examines in II.7 does not merely require that citizens initially receive equal resources, but also demands that this equal division be maintained in perpetuity, through periodic redistributions. Little would be accomplished if there were equal resources among the members of one generation but changes in population and patterns of inheritance produced inequality in the next generation (II.6 1265a38–b16, II.7 1266b8–24). The egalitarian does not seek equality at some one moment in time, but equality through time.

To maintain a constant regime of equality, there would have to be some mechanism for redistributing shares on a regular basis. Some would have to part with some of the tools, oxen, and slaves they had purchased, and with some of the money they still possess after the performance of liturgies. When the economy is frequently disrupted in this way, might not the total output decline? Will people care for their tools and slaves so well when they must be given up at the end of each year? Will there not be quarrels because some think they worked harder than others, and yet have equal shares in the end? Will there not be a temptation to spend excessively in the performance of one's liturgies, because what one does not spend will be given to someone who has less? Would it not better serve the common good to allow those who have successfully managed their farms (and have therefore made large public contributions) to retain whatever resources are still left to them? Aristotle says that the best flutes should be played by the best flute players (III.12 1282b31–1283a3), for the goal of musicians is to give listeners the best performance.[34] Similarly, he would say that economic resources should be distributed equally only if doing so is the best way to foster the common good. A pattern of distribution is a device, not an end in itself. And it is unlikely that the best way to promote the common good is to guarantee that each will receive equal resources, regardless of past performance, and regardless of the use he is likely to make of them in the future.

These are reasons Aristotle could give for holding that the best city would not embrace a policy of strict economic egalitarianism. But what of non-ideal cities? Though equal shares may not be a perfect arrangement, they might seem to provide an instant solution to a problem that greatly troubles Aristotle. The strife between rich and poor would be eliminated at a stroke, when all have the same resources.

The solution is illusory, however, because in effect it simply means taking from the rich and giving to the poor. The latter would be pleased, but not the former. A city that tries to solve its economic problems in this way simply exchanges one kind of difficulty for another: instead of fearing a revolution of the poor, it must fear a revolution of those whose property has been appropriated (II.7 1267a37–41).

It would be a mistake to take Aristotle to favor whatever distribution of wealth happens to exist in cities. As we have seen, he believes that citizens should be required to contribute some of their resources to the common good, if they can afford to do so. This is a significant transfer from rich to poor, and it is backed by the force of law. What he opposes is a transfer carried out merely for the sake of equality of resources—a transfer, in other words, that makes no concrete contribution to the common good. When the ideal city requires the performance of liturgies, it does so as part of a more general arrangement that fosters the well-being of the whole community; and its combination of economic, political, and educational institutions is a model to be imitated by less than ideal cities. To leave aside the common good, and to move resources around simply so that all have the same, accomplishes nothing worthwhile. That is the mistake made by Phaleas and other economic egalitarians.

---

[34] 'Flute' is the common translation for *aulos*, but the instruments to which Aristotle refers had single or double reeds, and were in this respect more like clarinets and oboes than flutes.

9.21. Aristotle's Conservatism

Aristotle's approach to utopian planning, slavery, the family, and property all reveal a certain kind of conservatism. In saying this, I mean not that he adheres to some distinctive political philosophy that goes by this name (if in fact there is one), but simply that he has a conservative cast of mind.[35] He thinks that social problems are often to be solved not by extreme changes, but by moderate steps that preserve the best features of long-established institutions.[36] This penchant for moderation is what lies behind his thesis that typically our alternatives can be located along a continuum and that the best solution lies at some distance from the two extremes. The best-known example of this thesis is the doctrine that every virtue lies in a mean between two vices.[37] Similarly, Aristotle's cast of mind inclines him to think that any radical transformation of our customary institutions goes too far, and throws out much good as well as some bad. Between the extremes of radical transformation and simply adhering to whatever is traditional lies the better course: modifying present practices in ways that preserve their good features and eliminate their faults. This is why he says, in his criticism of Plato's radical proposals, that it is unlikely that institutions that have such a long history ought to be entirely abandoned (II.5 1264a1–5). Aristotle's ideal city makes use of social practices of great antiquity—assemblies, courts, marriage, property, common meals, music, gymnastics, and so on. Their great age does not by itself prove their acceptability, and Aristotle leaves room for the possibility that there are still some discoveries to be made (VII.10 1329b34–5). But he does not think of himself as living at the dawn of a new age that

---

[35] For the idea that conservatism is a distinctive political philosophy, see Scruton, *Conservative Texts*, esp. pp. 1–28. Note too Dworkin, *A Matter of Principle*, pp. 181–2, 198–201. When Wood and Wood describe Aristotle as a 'tactician of conservatism' (*Class Ideology and Ancient Political Theory*, ch. 5) they simply mean that he hates the poor and loves the rich. Note that Aristotle lacks some of the attributes sometimes used to characterize conservatism. 'To be conservative . . . is to prefer . . . the actual to the possible . . . ' (Oakeshott, 'On Being Conservative', p. 408), but Aristotle prefers his ideal city to any that has ever existed.

[36] Such conservatism can be found in a large number of Athenian texts, and is not a peculiarity of Aristotle or his social class. See Boegehold, 'Resistance to Change in the Law at Athens.'

[37] See 3.10, 4.9, 4.13, 4.14. As we will see (Ch. 12), Aristotle treats democracy and oligarchy as constitutions that are unbalanced in opposite ways, so that the best feasible arrangement is to find something that lies between them. At *Pol.* IV.11 1295a35–b5, he suggests a link between his thesis about the intermediate nature of the virtues and the moderation of good regimes.

calls for bold new experiments in living. Utopia need not be postponed to a distant millennium, nor does it require a radical transformation of human nature. The ideal city is possible now, because human nature is already good enough and all the institutions we need lie ready to hand. The kind of unity that cities need can be achieved without abolishing the family or private property; systems of sharing already exist in such places as Sparta, and many cities require liturgies. All that is missing is the special combination of circumstances that would allow us to put the best of these materials to work.

9.22. *The Individual and the Community*

When we consider Book II and Books VII and VIII together, we find in them both a kind of individualism and a recognition of the value of community. When citizens of an ideal city attend the assembly and decide how to vote, they do so not in order to represent their family, clan, or any other party. They come as individuals to evaluate the strengths of competing arguments, not as partisans of a sub-community who seek to protect or enlarge their turf. Their goal as citizens is always to promote the good of the whole community, not some favored section of it. Their concern for the good of the whole is not expressed only in the assembly, however. When they care for their children, and oversee their property, they do so in part because they recognize that these endeavors contribute to the well-being of all. But their commitment to the well-being of the whole polis is not based on a blind allegiance to the group. Their education has given them an independence of mind that allows them to evaluate arguments on their merits, and they also possess an objective standard of human welfare that allows them to assess the merits or deficiencies of their political community. They like the community they belong to because the goal at which it aims—virtuous activity, sufficiently equipped with resources—really is the ultimate good at which human beings should aim. Their commitment to their community is based on their own reflective decision about what kind of community is best.

If the label 'communitarian' is to be attached to Aristotle, the justification for doing so must lie in the large role played by the whole polis in the thinking of his ideal citizens.[38] Modern citizens are obliged to do little for the polity: they must obey the law, serve in the military when necessary, appear for jury duty, and pay taxes; but for the most part, they can think entirely of themselves and their clan. By contrast, the citizens of Aristotle's ideal city are legislators, judges, and officers. Even when they are at home with their families, they are not beyond the reach of communal concerns. They take to heart Aristotle's principle, examined in 7.3–10, that 'the city is prior by nature to the household and to each of us' (I.2 1253a19).

But it must be emphasized that Aristotle does not look to the community as the ultimate arbiter of values and standards. In fact, as we noted at the beginning of this chapter, he thinks that 'what all seek is not the traditional but the good' (II.8 1269a3–4). Communities abandon earlier practices when they realize how defective they are; their standard of evaluation in these cases cannot be tradition—because then they would never change—but something that can show the defects of tradition: the good. Much as we cling to our habits, we also want what is good for us, not merely what seems good because we are used to it. Over time, rational criticism brings about social change.

There is one other kind of misunderstanding that must be avoided, if we want to think of Aristotle as a communitarian. Our word 'community' suggests a special kind of social relation, one in which people do not treat each other as mere instruments but instead express some degree of genuine concern for other members of the group. This is what we look for when we seek to instill a spirit of community in our organizations. We want people to develop a sense of belonging, a feeling that they are integrated into a larger whole. And we want them to pursue the common aims of the group, not merely to interact with others strategically and for their own isolated ends. This characterization of a community certainly applies to Aristotle's ideal polis, and for this reason it is appropriate to call him a communitarian. But we should be careful not to make the mistake

---

[38] The word has entered the vocabulary of contemporary political philosophy, and applies to those who emphasize the value of communal ties and reject the individualism of the liberal tradition. Aristotle, Rousseau, and Hegel are often regarded as important sources for this movement. Leading writers to whom the label is applied are: MacIntyre (*After Virtue*), Walzer (*Spheres of Justice*), Sandel (*Liberalism and the Limits of Justice*), and Taylor (*Philosophy and the Human Sciences*). For a discussion on what Aristotle can contribute to the evaluation of contemporary communitarianism, see Yack, *The Problems of a Political Animal*, pp. 25–87. For an introduction to the issues, see Avineri and de-Shalit, *Communitarianism and Individualism*; Bell, *Communitarianism and its Critics*. A related current of thought centers around the contribution made to a flourishing society by voluntary organizations that inculcate public spirit and good habits of citizenship. For a collection of essays on this theme, see Eberly, *The Essential Civil Society Reader.*

9.22. THE INDIVIDUAL AND THE COMMUNITY

of thinking that the very term we translate as 'community' (koinōnia) has the same warm association as ours. Aristotle applies the term koinōnia to any group of persons—travelers and commercial partners, for example—who work together to achieve a common goal.[39] The term conveys the idea that they have something in common (koinon), namely the advantage they jointly seek. But people can share a common aim without being a community in our sense of the term: two people who regularly barter with each other share the common aim of exchanging goods, but each views the other merely as a means to his own ends. Aristotle would not hesitate to call such a commercial relationship a koinōnia, whereas we would be reluctant to apply the word 'community' to it.

Because the Greek term koinōnia coveys nothing more than the idea of a common purpose, and every polis, whether defective or perfect, does foster some common goal, Aristotle takes the polis to be a koinōnia (I.1 1252a1–7). If we use 'community' to translate his term, we should be careful to screen out the word's usual associations. Aristotle's ideal city is a community in our sense of the term; this is not because he calls it a koinōnia, but because he thinks that the polis should be an association in which citizens care not only for themselves and their families, but for all the other citizens as well.

At one point Aristotle draws on the connection between 'common' (koinon) and 'community' (koinōnia) to make the point that the more people have in common, the more they form a community (NE VIII.9 1159b31–5). Brothers and intimate friends have more of a community, because there is so much that they share; in these deepest forms of friendship we join in each other's joys and sorrows, and pass our days together (IX.4 1166a6–8). Citizens have far less in common with each other than this, and so the friendship of one

---

[39] The notion that the city is a community is introduced in the opening lines of Book I of the Politics (1252a1–7): it is the community that has authority over others (e.g. over villages and the family). A community consists in a number of persons (as few as two) working together (perhaps temporarily) to achieve a common benefit. See NE VIII.9 1160a29–30, and note Aristotle's references to such communities as travelers (Pol. I.5 1263a17, NE VIII.9 1159b28) and commercial partners (NE V.5 1133b5–6, b14–16; VIII.14 1163a31). He says at Pol. IV.11 1295b24–5 that community is philikon ('friendly'), 'for people do not want to share (koinōnein) even a road with their enemies'. Here the term philikon conveys nothing more than a cooperative will that is strong enough to achieve a common goal. Members of a community need not be friends in any more robust sense of the word. For an alternative view, see Cooper, 'Aristotle on the Forms of Friendship'. He argues that, according to Aristotle, even relationships based on mutual advantage (e.g. commercial partnerships) contain an altruistic component: each party wishes to benefit the other for the sake of the other. For criticism of Cooper's interpretation, see Price, Love and Friendship in Plato and Aristotle, pp. 149–161; Pakaluk, Aristotle: Nicomachean Ethics Books VIII and IX, pp. 62–3.

citizen with another, even in an ideal community, cannot be as great as a close personal friendship. The goal of politics should not be to bind citizens together as tightly as possible, by having them live together as one family, since civic friendship should not and cannot perform the same role as other personal relationships. But neither should the city go to the opposite extreme: it should not be a merely commercial or protective association, one in which the partners have nothing in common beyond their limited aim of making money or deterring aggression (III.9 1280a25–b36).[40] The polis should be as much of a community as it needs to be: one in which the citizens share a single conception of the good and a single education, but in which they live in separate houses and share their joys and sorrows with different families and friends.[41]

---

[40] This text will be discussed in 11.3.

[41] Some of the most intriguing statements Aristotle makes about the social glue that holds cities together are found not in Book II of the *Politics*, nor in the other portions of this work, but in his ethical writings. 'Friendship seems to hold cities together, and legislators are more concerned with it than with justice' (*NE* VIII.1 1155a22–4). 'In each of the constitutions there appears to be friendship to the extent that there is justice as well' (*NE* VIII.11 1161a10–11). These statements are about cities in general, not merely about the ideal city, and so we will be in a better position to understand the kind of relationship Aristotle calls 'political friendship' after we have studied his entire taxonomy of constitutions. We will return to this theme when we have completed our discussion of ideal and non-ideal cities (12.9).

10

Politics III: Citizenship, Stability, and Obedience

10.1. *A Change of Ideals?*

The *Politics* has a wealth of introductory material—which is a polite way of saying that the traditional arrangement of the treatise defers (perhaps for too long) the positive core and rich detail of Aristotle's political theory.[1] The topic of Book I is not the polis and its organization, but the household; by insisting that the individual and the household are secondary in importance to the city (I.2 1253a19), Aristotle conveys the point that this book is merely a prelude to political theory. Book II also serves as an introduction to later material: it tells us how others have stumbled in their thinking about the ideal constitution, and thus sets the stage for Aristotle's own utopian ideas. Furthermore, as we have just seen in Chapter 9, the household continues to occupy Aristotle's thoughts throughout much of Book II, for his discussion of Plato's utopianism is, for the most part, an attempt to show that family and property are indispensable components of civic life.

It is not until we arrive at Book III that we come to the heart of

---

[1] Recall (5.3) that for this reason we began our discussion of the *Politics* with Books VII and VIII.

political theory, as Aristotle conceives it. In many ways this is the central book of the *Politics*, for it introduces and defends principles of political philosophy that are fundamental to Aristotle's outlook: that the city should be organized for the common good; that offices should be awarded on the basis of merit; and that virtuous activity should be the city's goal. Book III is the most lively and philosophically engaging part of the *Politics*, because it struggles with one of the deepest problems of political theory: who should rule? Instead of dogmatically affirming his own answer to this question, Aristotle surveys the merits and deficiencies of rival views. His own position is not always easy to discern, but because he recognizes the difficulty of the problem and the merits of rival alternatives, Book III is one of the most appealing parts of the *Politics*. It is also an indispensable introduction to Aristotle's reflections on non-ideal political systems, for his treatment of that theme in Books IV and VI draws heavily on concepts and distinctions introduced in III.

The topic of Book III, announced in its opening line, is not the ideal constitution, or bad constitutions, but constitutions in general. This leads immediately to a discussion of what a city is, which in turn raises the question of what a citizen is. These transitions—from constitution to city, and from city to citizen—feel natural to Aristotle and his audience, because of the close linguistic relationship between the corresponding Greek terms: *politeia* (constitution), *polis* (city), and *politēs* (citizen). Once we know what a citizen is, we can determine what good citizenship consists in, and how the virtues of good citizenship differ from those of a good human being: that is the topic of III.4, one of the most difficult and important chapters of the *Politics*, and therefore one to which we will devote considerable attention.

The virtues of citizenship vary, Aristotle thinks, according to the political system in which one lives, and so he is naturally led, in III.6, to a taxonomy of constitutions: three that are labeled 'correct' (kingship, aristocracy, polity[2]) and three that he considers 'deviant' (tyranny, oligarchy, democracy).[3] Those labels are anything but

---

[2] The Greek term for this political system is *politeia* (the same word Aristotle uses for all constitutions). I have at times used 'polity' not as a translation of the Greek word for this particular type of regime but in its normal English sense, which designates all political units. An alternative equivalent, 'republic', is used by some translators.

[3] We will discover that this sixfold classificatory scheme is a first approximation and eventually leads to more sophisticated distinctions. The difference between kingship and aristocracy becomes insignificant (see 11.10 and 11.15, esp. 11.nn.29 and 43); recognizing that oligarchies and democracies have different sub-types and that some are more akin to

10.1. A CHANGE OF IDEALS?

neutral. To call such regimes as democracy and oligarchy 'deviant' is to take a stand in the debates between the rival factions of Greek cities, and so Aristotle's normative taxonomy of political systems brings him to the core question of Book III: who or what should be the authoritative element (*to kurion*) of the city (III.10 1281a11)? Some hold that rule by one person is best, and Aristotle has himself classified kingship as one of the correct forms of rule. The final five chapters of Book III therefore turn to an analysis of the forms of monarchy, and canvass arguments for and against this form of government. In the end (III.17–18), Aristotle claims that if one person is outstanding in virtue, or a small number are, then he or they should rule. And so Book III, which begins as an investigation into the nature of the polis and citizenship, comes to the conclusion that although three constitutional forms are correct, two of them— kingship and aristocracy—are superior to the third. Rule by one or a few is better than rule by many.[4]

That conclusion might seem to be at odds with the portrait Aristotle draws of the ideal city in Books VII and VIII. Obviously, that utopian community is not ruled by *one* person. As we saw earlier (6.10), the supreme power of the ideal city is the assembly of all citizens, and all of them take turns occupying the city's most important offices, because they are each other's equals. For precisely this reason, it would be misleading and inappropriate to say that the ideal community of VII and VIII is ruled by a *few*.[5] It seems far better

---

polity than others becomes more important than distinguishing oligarchies from democracies (see 10.6). We also learn that one kind of oligarchy and democracy is not a constitution at all, just as a tyranny is not a constitution (see 10.n.15). In the *Nicomachean Ethics* (VIII.10–11), Aristotle continues to use his sixfold scheme, and ranks kingship above aristocracy. See 11.15 for discussion.

[4] The superiority of kingship and aristocracy to polity is affirmed at III.17 1288a15–29 and III.18 1288a32–b2, but Aristotle has already anticipated this conclusion at III.13 1284b22–34. In fact, as we will soon see (10.3), he is already assuming in III.4 that in the best city there will be permanent rulers who never rotate out of office. And note the implication at III.5 1278b4 ('by himself') that there might be just one permanent ruler. We will later discuss Aristotle's reasons for affirming the superiority of kingship or aristocracy to other regimes (11.12).

[5] It might be objected that the territory of the best city will contain more non-citizens than citizens, and is therefore ruled by few. It is certainly true that when women are included in the count, the number of non-citizens (women, slaves, foreigners) is larger than the number of citizens. But this way of counting yields the conclusion that every city, not just the ideal city, is ruled by few. Obviously this cannot be Aristotle's way of counting, when he says that some cities are ruled by many and others by few. Furthermore, it is important to realize that Aristotle urges every city to keep the number of male non-citizens smaller than the number of male citizens. He recognizes that it is dangerous for there to be a large number of able-bodied inhabitants who are not part of the community (*Pol.* III.11 1281b28–31; see

to say that it is ruled by many: for those who constitute the principal ruling element are the entire body of citizens. If, as Aristotle insists (II.2 1261a18), a city cannot contain only a small number of parts, but is necessarily composed of many, then surely he must agree that those who share rule in the ideal city are not one or a few, but many. The ideal city can be called an aristocracy, because Aristotle sometimes uses that term for any city ruled by citizens of outstanding character.[6] But in Book III, an aristocracy is necessarily a constitution that assigns authoritative power to a few rather than to many. In that sense of the word, the ideal city of VII and VIII is not an aristocracy.[7] Still less is it a monarchy. So, if we were forced to use the taxonomy of Book III, and to place the city of VII and VIII into its framework, we would have to call it a polity.[8] And in that case, we would have to say that the conclusion Aristotle draws in the closing chapters of Book III is at odds with the picture he paints in VII and VIII. One part of the *Politics* says that rule by one or a few is best; another part holds that ideally all citizens should rule.

There is, however, an easy way to defend Aristotle against this accusation. Book III is an examination of traditional political systems, as are Books IV–VI. Their aim is not to devise a new way of organizing civic life, but to examine constitutions with which the Greeks are already familiar, to make judgments of better and worse among them, and to choose, among those that are better, those that are best. Therefore, when Aristotle comes to the conclusion, in III.17–18, that kingship and aristocracy are the best constitutions, he

---

Miller, *NJR*, pp. 285–93). For this reason, he recommends that the property qualification for citizenship be altered so that the number of citizens remains larger than the number of non-citizens (IV.13 1297b1–6, VI.6 1320b22–8; see below, 11.n.8). Aristotle would presumably apply this idea to kingship and aristocracy: here too, the number of inhabitants who are not members of the community should be kept smaller than the number of citizens. Even so, he is committed to saying that in these two regimes only a few rule—namely the king or a handful of outstanding men. What makes them constitutions ruled by a small number is the relation between the quantity of supreme rulers and the quantity of those on whose behalf they rule—not the quantity of inhabitants or male inhabitants. It follows that the ideal city of VII and VIII is ruled by *many*, not few. Every single adult citizen (except those who are too old) is a ruler. So, this city is not an aristocracy, when this concept is partly defined in terms of the number of rulers, as it always is in Book III.

[6] More fully: a constitution counts as an aristocracy if it is ruled by the best, or by those who aim at the best (III.7 1279a36); or if its goal is virtue (IV.8 1294a9–11); or it is devoted to education and requires that all rulers be educated (*Rhet*. I.8 1365b33–4); or if craftsmen are excluded from politics (III.5 1278a17–21).

[7] Alternatively, one might call it an 'aristocracy of all citizens', to adapt the title of Barber's *An Aristocracy of Everyone*.

[8] Yet there are decisive reasons for rejecting that designation: Aristotle's full treatment of polity comes in IV.11, not in VII and VIII (see below, 12.3).

10.1. A CHANGE OF IDEALS?

should not be taken to mean that they are better even than a political system constructed out of the best possible materials. He is rather making a comparison among the six basic forms of government that exist or have existed, and with which he and his readers are already familiar. Kingship and aristocracy are better than rule by the many: when Aristotle affirms this thesis, in Book III, he is thinking of the many as ordinary people who have not undertaken a philosophical examination of the nature of human well-being, and who have not been brought up as children in a controlled environment by those who understand where the human good lies. Only so much can be expected of rule by people who lack that extraordinary training. More, Aristotle thinks, can be achieved by a political system in which at most a few people rule, provided those few possess the virtues of character and intellect that most people lack.

If we read Book III in this way, it does not contradict Aristotle's conception of the ideal city in VII and VIII. We can take him to mean that the best political arrangement is one in which all citizens are trained to excel as human beings. To achieve that, conditions would have to be ideal. A fresh start in a new location would be needed. A group of colonizers would have to band together, and their material resources would have to be of the highest order. They would need to establish something entirely new under the sun: a common and public educational system, one that prepares citizens for a life of active citizenship and the proper use of leisure. Property arrangements would have to foster a sense of community, and the division of society into factions and elites would have to be abolished. Book III contemplates none of these radical changes in Greek civic life. In that sense, it is not a search for the ideal city. It does not take up the topic left hanging at the end of Book II (if these cities are not ideal, which is?), but makes a fresh start on a new topic: what is the polis? That is why the conclusion it reaches—that kingship or aristocracy would be best—must be understood in a restricted way. They are the best of the six political systems under consideration in Book III, but that does not mean that nothing better can be achieved. Kingship and aristocracy are better than rule by the many, but when Aristotle makes this claim at the end of Book III, the many he has in mind are not the many who have the special qualifications needed to be citizens of the utopian community described in VII and VIII.[9]

---

[9] Having seen that the city of Books VII and VIII does not fit into the classificatory framework of Books III–VI, we have an excellent reason for resisting the proposal (discussed in 5.2) that VII and VIII be repositioned between III and IV–VI. See too 12.n.1.

10.2. Good Citizens: Aristotle's First Argument

Aristotle devotes the early chapters of Book III to the question of what a polis is, because such an investigation will help develop a taxonomy of constitutions, and this will in turn enable him to examine the conflicting claims of those who compete for positions of power and authority. In III.1, he quickly transforms his question about what a polis is into a question about what a *politēs* (citizen) is, and he replies that a citizen is someone who is allowed to participate in deliberating or making decisions (1275b18–20).[10] A polis is a multitude of such persons, and a *politeia* (constitution) is the way these citizens live their lives and divide their powers. Different political systems—democracies, oligarchies, and so on—are so many ways of arranging the lives and powers of citizens.

Throughout this book (as well as in IV–VI) Aristotle is preoccupied with the question: who should be a citizen? He assumes that in any city there will be many non-citizen residents who have few, if any, legal powers and privileges. Since those powers and privileges are assets that often make a great difference to the quality of one's life, it matters a great deal to most people whether they are granted the status of a citizen. In practice, as Aristotle points out (III.2 1275b22–34), this status is determined by birth: a citizen is someone both of whose parents are citizens (although in some circumstances this standard is relaxed). But that does not really answer the question: who *ought* to be a citizen (1275b37–9)? For it could be argued that one's parents ought to have been granted citizenship, though they were not; or conversely, that although they were citizens, they should not have been. Political systems differ not only in how they distribute power among citizens, but in how they draw the distinction between those who ought and those who ought not to be citizens.

These ideas and questions are presented in the first two chapters of Book III and pose few serious difficulties of interpretation. In Chapter 3, Aristotle asks what it is for a polis to remain the same through time, and argues that this depends on the continuity of the constitution. Even if all of the citizens die and new citizens take their place, the city remains the same, so long as it has not changed its political system. Again, the reader is in untroubled waters. When

---

[10] On the several attempts made in III.1 to define citizenship, see Miller, *NJR*, pp. 143–8.

10.2. GOOD CITIZENS: ARISTOTLE'S FIRST ARGUMENT

we reach Chapter 4, however, we encounter a major interpretive difficulty. Here Aristotle argues that we should make a distinction between being a good citizen and being a good person. What does this distinction amount to and what is its point? It will be worth our while to discuss these questions at some length.

The opening question of III.4 is this: is the virtue of a good man the same as the virtue of a good citizen? To answer this question, Aristotle proposes that we formulate a general description of what a good citizen's task is. Although they may have different roles, citizens nonetheless aim at a single end: as the sailors try to preserve the ship, so the goal of a citizen is to preserve his political system (1276b21–9). But, Aristotle adds, there are different kinds of constitution. Therefore, the excellent qualities required to preserve one kind of constitution will differ from the virtues needed in a different kind of constitution. What counts as the virtue of a citizen varies according to the constitution. By contrast, the qualities of a good man do not vary in different circumstances. A good man has perfect virtue, and this virtue is one and the same everywhere. Therefore, it is possible to be a good citizen without having the perfect virtue possessed by a good man (b30–4).

One striking feature of this argument is its assumption that the task of a good citizen is to preserve his city's political system. Aristotle does not argue for this claim, and yet it is certainly open to challenge. Why should a good citizen not try to *improve* his city's constitution? In fact, if it is a bad constitution, why should he not get rid of it entirely and establish a different kind of political system? Is Aristotle expressing here a kind of conservatism more pernicious than the variety we have seen at work in other parts of his political thought (9.21)? That is, does his penchant for preserving institutions that have stood the test of time and resisting radical changes lead him to embrace the status quo, even when he admits that existing political forms are defective? Does he have any good reasons for defining good citizenship in the way he does?

We will be able to answer these questions eventually, but for the moment we must set them aside. The only way to make progress in developing an answer is to see what Aristotle does with the concept of a good citizen. So let us now attend to the details of his argument in III.4.

Part of what he is saying is easy to grasp. The virtues of a good man are those described in his ethical writings, and these are intellectual and emotional skills worth having in all conditions; they do not become virtues in some cities and cease being virtues elsewhere. By contrast, the good qualities needed to preserve one kind of city are specific to the kind of constitution it has, and would not equip one to preserve a city with a different kind of constitution. Civic virtue varies, perfect virtue does not; therefore they are not the same quality; and it also follows that one can have a citizen's virtue without having perfect virtue.

The argument is difficult to assess because it is so abstract and compressed. We would like to know what it is about democracies and oligarchies, for example, that leads Aristotle to say that the qualities that enable one to preserve one of these regimes would not serve so well in the other. Why not say instead that in spite of the many differences among political systems, knowing how to preserve one of them is knowing how to preserve them all? Furthermore, for all that Aristotle has said, it might be true that in order to know how to preserve any constitution, one must have the virtues of a good man. Even if we concede, for the sake of argument, that civic virtue and perfect virtue are different qualities, it does not follow that one can have the former without the latter.

Since this first argument seems so disappointing, we should look at the other arguments Aristotle gives in III.4, in order to discover which further premises he is taking for granted. That is not an easy task, as anyone who has struggled with this material quickly discovers. But if we persevere, we can find a reasonable interpretation.

10.3. *Good Citizens in the Best City*

Aristotle claims that even if we consider the best constitution, we will come to the conclusion that one can have civic virtue without having perfect virtue (1276b35–7). This may strike us as a dubious strategy: for how do we know, at this early stage of Book III, what the best constitution is? Aristotle might reply that some assumptions about the best regime can be made at this early stage of his argument, provided that they are sufficiently obvious. More specifically, he assumes that in the best city all citizens must be good *citizens* (1277a1–3), for this is part of what it is for a city to be best. But, he claims, the virtues of a good *man* cannot belong to them all, for it

10.3. GOOD CITIZENS IN THE BEST CITY

is impossible for a city to be composed entirely of good men (1276b37–8).[11]

That assertion sounds highly dubious. Why is it *impossible* for all the citizens to be good human beings? Suppose we grant that no existing political community is composed entirely of good people, and that no such city has ever existed. Would that show that such a community is impossible? And in any case, Aristotle of all people should not be saying that no such city can exist. For in Books VII and VIII, he himself proposes that the best *possible* city is one in which all members of the community are good human beings. So, there seems to be a stark contradiction between Book III and Books VII and VIII: one part of the *Politics* says that a city composed entirely of good human beings is impossible, and another part says that it is possible.

But if we keep in mind the sort of project Aristotle is undertaking in Book III, this apparent inconsistency disappears. Recall the point recently made in 10.1: Aristotle's goal in Book III is different from the one he sets himself when he proposes an ideal constitution in Books VII and VIII. In Book III, he is not looking for an entirely new way of organizing civic life, but is merely sorting through traditional political systems—kingship, aristocracy, and the like—in order to assess their strengths and weaknesses. He contemplates no thoroughgoing transformation of the polis. He is not talking about making a fresh start in a new land, under the guidance of enlightened leaders who have the resources to establish a common and public

---

[11] The words I use here do not merely report what is in Aristotle's text, but interpret it. A literal translation of the lines cited (1276b37–8) is as follows: 'For if it is impossible for a city to be composed of all those who are excellent . . . ' Two matters of interpretation must be resolved. First, does Aristotle agree, at least in Book III, that this is impossible? Or is he merely recording an argument that uses this statement as a premise? Second, does this premise hold that it is impossible for a city to consist entirely of excellent *citizens*? Or that it is impossible for a city to consist entirely of excellent *men*? As for the first question: We might think that since Books VII and VIII describe a city in which all the citizens are excellent men and excellent citizens, Aristotle cannot here accept the premise in question (on either of its two interpretations). But III.4 (see too III.5 1278b1–5) presents arguments for a conclusion that Aristotle endorses—namely, that one can be a good citizen without being a good man, unless one is a ruler in the best city—and so he must be using premises he also endorses. One of those premises asserts the impossibility of a city's consisting entirely of those who are good. That brings us to the second question: does 'those who are good' refer to good men or good citizens? That question is answered decisively at 1277a1–3: surely, Aristotle says, in the best city all citizens must be good citizens. So his claim is that in the best city all citizens are good *citizens*, but in no city can all citizens be good *men*. He emphasizes his reliance on this premise when he says, several lines later at 1277a4–5: 'if it is necessary that not all the citizens in the excellent city are good men'. My reading of 1276b37–8 differs from the one endorsed by Pellegrin's translation, but accords with those of Reeve and Lord.

educational system for the children of all citizens. And so, when he says in III.4 that it is impossible for a city to be composed entirely of good men, he should be taken to mean that no such city can be constructed out of the limited materials available. If we consider all of the human beings that populate existing cities, or have ever done so, we can find only a small number who have fully developed their capacity for ethical and intellectual excellence. That, Aristotle thinks, cannot be an accident. The traditional constitutions to be examined in Book III simply cannot create a community that consists in nothing but good human beings. They do not start from scratch, but make do with the limited materials at hand. Given these limitations in even the best of the traditional regimes, it is impossible for a city to be composed entirely of good men.

Aristotle assumes in III.4 that the best that can be hoped for, given ordinary resources and within the framework of traditional political systems, is a community that contains a small number of outstanding individuals. That starting point brings him fairly close to the conclusion that he will eventually reach in III.17–18: that it is better for those few (or one of them) to rule than for the many to hold supreme power. Although he does not explicitly arrive at that conclusion in III.4, this chapter takes it for granted that in the best regime there will be hierarchies of merit and authority. Those who are best qualified to hold high office will do so permanently. They will receive an education that sets them apart from ordinary people. Others will participate in the governance of the city, but they will rotate into and out of the lower positions they hold. Aristotle thinks we should not be surprised or offended by these differences among the few who rule permanently and the many who occasionally hold lesser offices, for such hierarchies are nearly ubiquitous: we find them, for example, in the relation between soul and body, reason and desire, man and woman, master and slave (1277a5–12).

If we accept the idea that hierarchies of authority will be present even in the best (traditional) constitution, that provides us with a second argument for the conclusion that the virtue of a good citizen is one thing, the virtue of a good man another. For surely in an ideal constitution those who hold supreme power should not only possess the qualities needed to be good citizens of that regime; they should also possess the virtues of good men. By contrast, although those who occupy lower positions of authority must be good citizens (otherwise their city would not be the best possible), they need not be good men. In fact, they *cannot* all be good men. Unlike Aristotle's

10.3. GOOD CITIZENS IN THE BEST CITY

first argument (examined in 10.2), this one does not depend on the assumption that the virtue of a good citizen will vary from one kind of constitution to another. It rests instead on the premise that in the best constitution some will deserve more power than others, and only a few will be qualified for the highest offices.

The remainder of III.4 elaborates on the differences that will exist among the two kinds of member of the ideal city—rulers and citizens. The excellent ruler must possess practical wisdom (1277a14–15), since he is a good human being, and one cannot fully possess the ethical virtues without also possessing this intellectual virtue (*NE* VI.13 1144b14–21). Aristotle never speaks of this ruler as someone who is, during certain periods of his adult life, ruled by others. He is assuming, in other words, that he will hold office permanently, and that his position will be one of supreme authority. By contrast, he speaks throughout this chapter of the excellent citizens of the ideal city as individuals who are good at both ruling and being ruled. Although he does not make this point explicit, he seems to be assuming that when an excellent citizen rules, he does so for a limited period of time, and that the position of power he occupies is subordinate to those held by men of practical wisdom. That explains why the excellent citizen does not need practical wisdom, but merely right opinion (1277b28–9): his decision-making skills need not be of the highest order, because he occupies a lower office, and he is overseen by wiser men.

It must be emphasized that those citizens of the ideal city who lack practical wisdom are not merely passive. Their civic duty does not consist solely in unthinking acceptance of the orders they receive from others. This cannot be Aristotle's intention, because he says that a good citizen must be able to rule and obey well (1277a25–7, b14–17). We are told that the virtue of a good man is a ruling sort of virtue, whereas the virtue of a good citizen involves both ruling and being ruled; both are praiseworthy capacities, but the former is more so than the latter (1277a27–9). That should be taken to mean that the good rulers of the ideal city do nothing but rule (they are not ruled by others), whereas the good citizens do some ruling and some obeying. Of course, those who have supreme authority acquired their wisdom by going through a period in which they were ruled (1277b7–13)—presumably when they were children. When they become adults and occupy the highest offices, they rule not over slaves, but over free men and good citizens, that is, over people who have the ability to rule and be ruled.

If we read Aristotle in this way, we can make sense of the distinction he draws between the perfect virtue of a good man and the virtue of a good citizen; and we can better understand the argument he gives for saying that one can have the latter without the former. Civic virtue is not a vice, just as right opinion is not an error. It is somewhat praiseworthy, because it involves doing things well— being ruled well and ruling well. But the offices it equips one to occupy are not demanding. They do not require real understanding or the kinds of quality Aristotle describes as virtues in the ethical works. Most members of the best community will occupy and excel at these moderately demanding roles, but the highest offices must be filled by permanent rulers who fully possess the virtues.

10.4. Moderation and Noses

Let us now take a second look at the opening argument of III.4—the one that moves from the variability of civic virtue and the invariability of perfect virtue to the conclusion that they are different, and that one can have the first without the second (1276b16–34). There are two different ways to read this argument, and these should now be distinguished, for choosing between them makes a great difference to our understanding of Aristotle's political thought.

We might take him to be presupposing a point he will soon make explicit in Book III, namely that there are several kinds of correct and deviant political systems. Furthermore, he might also be assuming that part of what distinguishes good regimes from bad is that the good ones have good goals, the bad ones bad goals. For, as we noted long ago (1.4), Aristotle holds that a constitution is a city's way of life, and he distinguishes among them by assigning them different ends. The goal of oligarchy, for example, is wealth; of democracy, freedom; of aristocracy, virtue.[12] Accordingly, we might read the first argument of III.4 to rely implicitly on the following premise: in a regime that has a bad goal (for example, wealth or freedom), one will be a good *citizen* if one promotes that goal as fully as possible,

---

[12] On oligarchy, see IV.8 1294a11, V.10 1311a9–10; democracy, IV.8 1294a11, V.9 1310a28–34, VI.2 1317b11–14; aristocracy, III.17 1288a9–12, III.18 1288a32–41, IV.8 1294a10–11. For the general principle that constitutions have goals, see IV.1 1289a15–18, IV.11 1295a40–1295b1. We will discuss the kind of freedom that is characteristic of democracies at 12.4–5. Plato too speaks of wealth and freedom as the organizing goals of oligarchies and democracies (*Republic* 562b–c).

10.4. MODERATION AND NOSES

since this will preserve the constitution. When we supply this premise, we can easily see how Aristotle arrives at the conclusion that the skill needed to be a good *citizen* is, in certain constitutions, different from the skill needed to be a good *person*. In fact, these qualities are incompatible, not merely different, because a good person will not try to maximize wealth or freedom. It follows that it is possible (in deviant political systems) to be a good citizen and to fall short of being a good man—so far short, in fact, as to be a bad man.[13]

We should notice an immediate problem for this interpretation, however: Aristotle says in III.4 that although a good citizen does not need practical wisdom, he does have right opinion about practical matters (1277b25–9). But, according to the interpretation we are considering, good citizens of bad regimes have opinions about practical matters that are decidedly false: they think they should pursue money or freedom without limit. When Aristotle says that to be a good citizen one need only have right opinion, he seems to be saying what all good citizens have in common; this is one of their characteristic features, along with their ability to rule and be ruled, and to preserve the constitution.

Furthermore, if we look at the opening of the next chapter, III.5, we find Aristotle claiming that if a city allows craftsmen to be citizens, then not all citizens will be able to be good citizens (1278a8–11). He means, in other words, that a craftsman or a farmer cannot be a good citizen of *any* city.[14] But he ought not to say this, if he assumes in III.4 that being a good citizen of a democracy is simply a matter of promoting the highest possible degree of freedom. For a craftsman is certainly capable of doing that.

But if we reject this interpretation, what can we put in its place? The idea suggests itself that a good citizen of a democracy or an

---

[13] Thus Barker, *The Political Thought of Plato and Aristotle*, p. 287: 'in a State which does not pursue a moral purpose, but has made wealth its aim and goal ... to be a good citizen is simply to seek and accumulate wealth; and consequently, in such a State, the good citizen would be a bad man, and the good man a bad citizen.' The same reading is proposed by Mulgan in *Aristotle's Political Theory*, p. 57; and Newman, *The Politics of Aristotle*, iii. 155. An alternative reading—one that accords with my own—is proposed by Simpson, *A Philosophical Commentary on the Politics of Aristotle*, p. 145.

[14] Does Aristotle mean that even master craftsmen, who must use their deliberative faculty in order to achieve the goals of their craft, cannot be good citizens of any city? Or does he mean that ordinary craftsman, whose work is a matter of routine and leaves no room for variation, cannot be good citizens? (For his distinction between these two levels of skill, see above, 8.6.) My guess is that he is making only the latter claim. Craft work that regularly employs the deliberative faculty makes use of the very mental skill that is needed in politics. By contrast, it is easier to see why Aristotle thinks that those whose daily practice leaves no room for deliberative ingenuity will be deficient as citizens.

oligarchy is someone who tries to moderate the defects of such regimes. Instead of supposing that such a person pursues the democratic goal (freedom) or the oligarchic goal (wealth) single-mindedly and without limit, we should explore the idea that, on the contrary, he makes a democracy less of a pure democracy by accepting nondemocratic elements into its constitution (and similarly for oligarchy). Since Aristotle's cast of mind tends to favor moderation (9.21), and since one would in any case think that the way to do a good job in a defective city is to impede the unlimited pursuit of its defective goal, we seem to have found a reasonable alternative to the interpretation we rejected. A good citizen of a democracy is not someone who pushes it ever further towards an extreme; rather, he is someone who opposes such extremism.

Is this reading undermined by Aristotle's statement that a good citizen is someone who preserves his city's constitution (1276b26–9)? So it might seem, if we believe that someone who makes a city less purely democratic weakens it as a democracy. But we must be careful not to make this assumption unthinkingly. Perhaps, on the contrary, moderating a city's democratic tendencies will make it more stable and enduring. Fortunately, we do not have to speculate about Aristotle's view about this matter. In *Politics* V.9, he tells us in no uncertain terms that the way to preserve an oligarchic or a democratic constitution is to blend it with its opposite, so that it is not an extreme oligarchy or democracy (1309b18–35). He compares a defective constitution to a hooked or a snub nose: although these shapes deviate from the ideal of straightness, they need not be unattractive, so long as the deviation is not severe. But if they depart too much from the ideal, they lose all their appeal; in extreme cases they will no longer even look like noses. Similarly, extreme democracies and oligarchies are no longer constitutions, because they have lost all order, and a constitution is by its nature something that imposes order on a city.[15] Citizens should therefore try to preserve imperfect cities by keeping them moderate, that is, by restraining any tendency they may have to develop into their extreme forms.

We are therefore on firm ground when we interpret III.4 in the way proposed. Although Aristotle does not tell us in this chapter how a

---

[15] On the connection between constitutions and order, see III.1 1274b38, III.6 1278b8–10, IV.1 1289a15–18, IV.3 1290a7–8. Where there are no general rules, but every issue is resolved by a new vote—as occurs in extreme democracies and oligarchies—there is no constitution; these are tyrannies of the many or the few. See IV.4 1292a23–32, IV.5 1292b7–10, V.10 1312b5–6, b34–8. Aristotle's defense of the rule of law will receive further attention in 12.5.

10.4. MODERATION AND NOSES

defective political system is best preserved, we now see what he is presupposing: a good citizen of a bad regime is someone who helps to make it less bad by moderating its defects. Eventually, Aristotle brings that assumption to the surface.

Let us recall the conclusion of the first argument in III.4: it is possible to be a good citizen without being a good person. We saw in the previous section how Aristotle gives further support to this conclusion by considering the way in which an ideal city is ruled. He assumes that in such a constitution some citizens will be permanent rulers and others will not; the latter will occupy minor offices, but will always be subordinate to those who are better equipped to govern. They do not need practical wisdom to play their smaller civic role, but merely right opinion. They will be good citizens, but not completely virtuous men.

We can now see that Aristotle is thinking along similar lines in his first argument. The good citizens of defective regimes know how to preserve them, but this will involve moving in different directions, depending on which sort of defective city they live in. A good citizen of a democracy is someone who is able to move it towards oligarchy; a good citizen of an oligarchy knows how to move his city in the opposite direction, towards democracy. Aristotle thinks that these are different skills, because their goals are opposed. If one could renounce one's citizenship in an oligarchy and be granted citizenship in a democracy, one would have to unlearn the habits one drew upon and push the regime in the opposite direction.[16] And so the virtues of citizenship are not perfect virtues, because the latter remain the same, whatever the situation.

We are told in III.4 that one need not be practically wise in order to be a good citizen, and to carry out the orders of a ruler whom one recognizes to be better than oneself. These tasks require nothing more than true opinion. Now we have learned that a similar point lies below the surface of III.4: one does not need full virtue and practical wisdom in order to resist those who aim at pure democracy or pure oligarchy, and to promote moderation in the city's constitution. The mental skills of a virtuous person are of a very high order; being a good citizen of a defective regime does not require that one rise to that level. It requires only the habits of moderation that impede the development of pure democracies or oligarchies.

---

[16] For further discussion of the inflexibility of civic virtue, see 12.3.

10.5. Moderation and Revolution

We saw earlier (10.2) that Aristotle's conception of a good citizen—namely, that he is someone who preserves his city's constitution—should not be accepted without challenge. In particular, we wanted to know why a good citizen should not try to *improve* his city's constitution rather than merely preserve it. What we have now discovered is that for Aristotle this is a false contrast. To improve a defective political system requires keeping it as far away from its pure form as possible, for when it becomes an extreme democracy or oligarchy, it is no longer an orderly arrangement, and therefore no longer a constitution. Just as a nose can deviate from its normal shape only so much before it is no longer recognizable as a nose, so a political regime is no longer recognizable as a political order when it loses all moderation and moves to an extreme. A citizen who causes his city to move closer to this point is not helping preserve its constitution. On the contrary, when democracies and oligarchies become extreme, they are hated by internal and external enemies for their lack of order, and are most in danger of being overthrown. The more moderate a political system is, the more enduring it is likely to be. This is one of the major themes of Books IV–VI, and we will return to it in Chapter 12.

Suppose we agree, at least for the sake of argument, that moderate democracies and oligarchies are more stable than their extreme forms. We are still left with a different question about political change: why should a citizen not try to promote an entirely different kind of political system? In particular, why is revolution—replacing an oligarchy with a democracy, or vice versa—incompatible with good citizenship?[17] To this Aristotle might give either of two replies.

First, he could say that if one tries to replace one political order with another, one cannot be a good citizen of the system that has been replaced, although one can be a good citizen of the new regime. A citizen of a democracy who joins a successful revolution against it might be a good citizen of the oligarchy that arises in its place, but

---

[17] After the defeat of Athens and Corinth by Philip in 337, the League of Corinth, which was dominated by Macedon, prohibited changes from one form of government to another in most cities of mainland Greece. (See Ober, *Political Dissent in Democratic Athens*, p. 292.) One might reasonably conjecture that Aristotle's definition of citizenship in terms of the preservation of an existing constitution is influenced by these political realities. But as we shall see, he also has reasons internal to his political thought for adopting this conception of a citizen's proper role.

surely he cannot be a good citizen of the political system that he has destroyed. It is a conceptual point that a good citizen does not try to destroy his city.

So read, Aristotle's notion of good citizenship is purely classificatory and has no normative force. He is not advising his readers to be good citizens of bad regimes, but merely pointing out what a good citizen is. He does not mean to imply that democracies and oligarchies should be preserved. It is only when a political system is perfect—or good, at any rate—that it should be preserved.

We have good reason to reject this interpretation. For as we have seen, Aristotle will eventually go on to say, in Book V, that moderation is what preserves a defective regime. That is a formula for good citizenship: since a good citizen knows how to preserve his city's constitution, he must do what he can to prevent it from moving towards its pure form. Good democrats must not let their democracy become an extreme democracy; so too good oligarchs. That is not a mere description of what can be expected of democrats and oligarchs; surely Aristotle approves of those who pursue these policies of moderation. Good citizens of defective regimes keep what is bad from becoming worse, and that is a considerable achievement.

Furthermore, we can easily understand why Aristotle believes that no citizen should join a revolution against a democracy in order to establish an oligarchy, or vice versa. Both are defective regimes, for neither is devoted to the common good. Why go to war against one's city merely to exchange one bad constitution for another? The right course of action is to make what is defective less defective, not to substitute one kind of defect for another.

10.6. *From Bad Constitutions to Good*

But now a further question should come to mind: why not change imperfect regimes into good ones? Why preserve a bad political system, when it is possible to overthrow it and replace it with a good one?

This is not really one question but several. By distinguishing cases, we can make reasonable conjectures about how Aristotle would respond. First, we can ask why one should not overthrow a tyrant, and replace him with one of the good constitutions. Aristotle's reply is that this is precisely what one *should* do. Because the tyrant is preoccupied with luxury and power, has no regard for the common good, and is bound by no procedures or laws, this form of rule cannot be regarded as a genuine political system.[18] Therefore, in assuming that a citizen should strive to be a good citizen and preserve the constitution of his city, Aristotle is not committed to saying that one should preserve a tyranny. A constitution is the sort of thing that is worth preserving, because the legal framework it establishes sustains at least a modicum of justice.[19] But that is precisely what a tyrant fails to do.

Second, we can ask why one should not try to overthrow an oligarchy or a democracy, and replace these regimes with one of the political systems Aristotle takes to be ideal in Book III: kingship or aristocracy. Aristotle's reply, I suggest, is that kingship (rule by a single virtuous person) and aristocracy (rule by the virtuous few) require very special circumstances. They succeed only when the population is ready for them, and cannot be imposed on unwilling subjects. (The same could be said of the ideal city of Books VII and VIII.) But these materials are not at hand in oligarchies and democracies. For in these regimes few citizens, if any, have a proper understanding of well-being and virtue; and so few are able to recognize a situation in which one eminently qualified person or a small elite deserves unlimited power. Of course, if someone had amazing powers of persuasion and were able to prove to all the citizens of a democracy or an oligarchy that they should give up their way of life and allow themselves to be governed by a small number of excellent people, Aristotle would have no objection. But such a transformation has never occurred and there is no reason to think it ever will. The only way one could make a change from democracy or oligarchy to aristocracy or kingship would be to force the latter regimes onto an unwilling populace; but if these correct political systems arise in this way, they will never succeed.[20] Aristotle is not opposed in principle to the use of violence or force; he has no objection to overthrowing a tyrant. Violence can sometimes lead to improvements, but good regimes cannot be established in this way.

Third, we can ask why we should not transform oligarchies and democracies into the kind of correct regime that Aristotle calls a

---

[18] See *Pol.* V.11 for Aristotle's fullest discussion of tyranny. See 10.n.15 for the passages in which he denies that tyranny is a genuine constitution.

[19] Recall that Aristotle defines justice in the broad sense as lawfulness (4.3), and holds that 'everything lawful is in a way just' (*NE* V.1 1129b12, 4.5).

[20] This, I suggest, is why Aristotle assumes that rule by one person or a few is correct rule only if those who are ruled are willing to accept their subordinate status. See III.13 1284b32–4, III.14 1285a27–8, a31–2, b3–9.

10.6. FROM BAD CONSTITUTIONS TO GOOD

polity (*politeia*)? Here again, Aristotle's answer is that this is precisely what one *should* do. But in this case, he has a complex justification for his answer, for in Books IV–VI he describes a number of different kinds of oligarchy and democracy, and the reasons for transforming them will vary according to the case considered.

Extreme democracies and extreme oligarchies are tyrannies of the many and the few, and so there is no more reason to preserve them than there is to keep alive a tyranny of one. If these rulers can be deposed and a polity can be established, then such a transformation would receive Aristotle's blessing. Citizens who effect this change could not be accused of failing to preserve their constitution—for extreme democracies and oligarchies are not genuine constitutions. But what of less extreme democracies and oligarchies? Aristotle admits that these are genuine political orders, although of course they are defective. Would it be wrong to try to transform them into polities? It looks as though he is committed to opposing such changes, for a good citizen of an oligarchy or a democracy must preserve these constitutions, and to transform them into polities would be a change of constitution.

This way of reading Aristotle would be reasonable, if he had only written Book III and not IV–VI. But those later books give us a more subtle and complex account of the relationships between polity, oligarchy, and democracy. When the latter two regimes are not extreme, they involve some mixture of oligarchic and democratic elements. A moderate oligarchy balances the interests of rich and poor, but is biased in favor of the rich; similarly, a moderate democracy has a mixture of elements, but is biased in favor of the poor. And in Books IV–VI, a polity is described as a regime in which neither class predominates and the mixture is nearly even.[21] Aristotle would not object to a citizen who tries to make his democracy more moderate by weakening its bias against the rich; similarly, he would have no objection to making oligarchies more inclusive of the poor. Democracies and oligarchies that move closer to being polities are moving in the right direction. It would therefore make no sense for

---

[21] Aristotle says that in common parlance a *politeia* is a mixed regime that inclines towards democracy (IV.8 1293b33–6). But at IV.8 1294a22–3 he applies the term to all regimes that achieve some degree of balance between rich and poor, and this is the idea he pursues throughout IV.9. Note especially his point (IV.9 1294b14–16) that a good mixture has been achieved when the constitution can appropriately be called both an oligarchy and a democracy. In IV.11 he proposes that the best kind of mixture is one in which those who are neither rich nor poor outnumber the combined forces of the rich and poor (1295b34–8). We will discuss the constitution of IV.11 in 12.3.

Aristotle to condemn a city that not only moves closer to being a polity, but actually transforms itself from a moderate democracy or a moderate oligarchy into a polity. And for this reason, he cannot criticize a citizen who tries to bring about such a transformation.

The categories used in Book III make it seem as though Aristotle must oppose such a change, for he says that a good citizen preserves his constitution, and a polity is not a democracy or an oligarchy. But we should take the categories of Book III to constitute a simple taxonomy that prepares the way for the more complex system of the later books.[22] The taxonomy of IV–VI treats moderate democracies, polities, and moderate oligarchies as a single kind: they are all mixed regimes, and differ with respect to the perfection or imperfection of the mixture. The thesis of Book III that one should be a good citizen of one's city and preserve its constitution must be interpreted in the light of the more subtle classificatory scheme of IV–VI: a citizen who helps transform a moderate oligarchy or a moderate democracy into a polity is doing exactly what needs to be done in order to preserve his constitution. He is making his mixed constitution a better mixture, because the better the balance between rich and poor, the stronger and more stable the city.

Our conclusion is that democracies and oligarchies should be changed into polities. If they are extreme democracies or oligarchies, they are not constitutions, and so there is no reason to preserve them. On the other hand, if they are mixed constitutions, then they are of the same form as polities, and making them more balanced is not the kind of transformation that Aristotle opposes.

10.7. Civic Virtue and the Continuity of the Politics

To some students of the *Politics*, Aristotle's interests seem to shift markedly in different books. The idealism of VII and VIII seems at odds with the investigation, undertaken in IV–VI, of the ways in which each existing type of political system is destroyed and

---

[22] My thesis is not that Aristotle changes his mind and decides to abandon the sixfold scheme of *Pol.* III, in favor of the more complex taxonomy of *Pol.* IV. Rather, my idea is that the simple scheme of Book III serves as a useful starting point for political analysis, because reflection on it leads to a more complex understanding. (For further discussion, see 11.10.) That is why Aristotle continues to use his usual six categories in *NE* VIII.10–11: for the purposes of that work, he can continue to work with the simpler scheme of *Pol.* III. (Here I rely on the claim made in 1.5 that the *Nicomachean Ethics* is later than the *Politics*.)

10.7. CIVIC VIRTUE AND THE CONTINUITY OF THE *POLITICS*

preserved.[23] What is remarkable about these middle books is that in them Aristotle investigates the question of how *bad* constitutions can be preserved. Here he seems to look at politics through the eyes of an empirical scientist who sets values aside in order to describe how things work. Or at any rate, if these middle books do exhibit some interest in normative issues, they are issues unconnected to the ones Aristotle explores during his utopian phase. He prizes stability, and is willing to forswear amelioration in order to prevent deterioration.[24] His conception of well-being is held in abeyance. At center stage are the mechanisms that enable any regime, no matter how bad, to last longer.

We have already seen enough to know that this portrait of the *Politics* cannot be sustained. The mere fact that Aristotle investigates defective regimes does not show that he has suspended his interest in improving political systems; on the contrary, the reason why he studies non-ideal constitutions is to show how they can be made more moderate and therefore less defective. Furthermore, his interest in the preservation and destruction of defective constitutions is not unrelated to his ethical concerns. On the contrary, we can take him to be carrying out a single ethical project throughout the whole of the *Politics*. In Books VII and VIII, he designs institutions that facilitate the development and expression of virtue adequately supplied with external goods. In IV–VI, his aim is again to design institutions that promote well-being and virtue; but here, the kind of virtue he seeks to develop is not the full virtue studied in the ethical works, but a less exalted set of skills and therefore a more attenuated form of human well-being. These skills are the virtues of a good citizen.

As we are told in III.4, these civic virtues vary from one kind of

---

[23] This theme is announced at IV.1 1288b30, IV.2 1289b22–6 (cf. *NE*. X.9 1181b18). Jaeger is the originator of this way of reading the *Politics* (see above, 5.1). For an opposed view, see Nichols, *Citizens and Statesmen*, pp. 87–8.

[24] Thus Saxonhouse, *Athenian Democracy*, p. 130: 'in Books 4 and 6 . . . he turns to the endurance of regimes, and the assessment of democracy and oligarchy comes to focus not on the question of justice but on that of stability.' Compare the somewhat different suggestion made by Mulgan that Aristotle is interested in the stability of defective constitutions primarily because he wants them to protect the lives of the small number of virtuous men who live in them. 'It is for this reason, perhaps, that Aristotle places so much emphasis on political stability, rather than on justice or political participation, as the overriding objective of institutional design for everyday states. So long as the constitution is stable, order can be guaranteed and the external goods protected, thus enabling virtuous individuals to live the good life' ('Was Aristotle an "Aristotelian Social Democrat"?', p. 99). See too his 'Aristotle and the Value of Political Participation', pp. 210–11. On this reading, Aristotle sees no hope that defective regimes might do some good for all citizens.

political system to another, and possessing them is compatible with lacking virtue in the full sense. The point of making this distinction between perfect and civic virtue is not to condemn the latter as a mere sham. On the contrary, civic virtue is of interest to Aristotle because in many cases this is precisely what political philosophers and politicians should promote. In non-ideal cities, there will be many citizens who cannot become completely virtuous, because they have not been educated in the right way and circumstances do not permit the introduction of institutions that instill perfect virtue. In these cases, statesmen must lower their sights and design institutions that favor the growth and expression of the virtues of a good citizen. They should foster the emergence of the sort of people who preserve constitutions—people who are opposed to the extremism of pure democrats and oligarchs. The good citizen, being a political moderate, is like the fully virtuous person, whose character lies in a mean between unappealing extremes. The reason why Aristotle thinks that it is worth his while to examine the institutions that preserve defective regimes is that, in doing so, he is teaching his students how to produce some approximation to real virtue. So the *Politics* has a single goal throughout: it is a study of how the polis can contribute to human well-being. It is an investigation of the way institutions promote either full virtue or good citizenship, and the way resources must be deployed for these twin purposes.

If Aristotle had decided, at some point in his development, that political institutions should be assessed solely in terms of their stability and endurance, that would have been an inexplicable change in his orientation. Similarly, had he ever come to think that citizens must be molded so as to serve as mere instruments of the polis, that too would have been a radical and incomprehensible change. But nothing in the *Politics* need be taken as evidence of such a transformation. The recommendations Aristotle makes regarding the governance of democracies and oligarchies can all be seen as various ways of promoting the well-being of democratic and oligarchic citizens. What distinguishes a good democracy from a bad one is a difference that makes the members of these communities better or worse citizens, and therefore improves or damages the quality of their lives.

'Perhaps we should be satisfied if, when all the things are present through which we seem to become decent, we get some share of virtue.' This is how Aristotle expresses himself in the final chapter of the *Ethics* (X.9 1179b18–20), where he tells his readers that their study of well-being and virtue must be put into practice through political activity. Most people, he concedes, will be unaffected by the arguments he has given. How are we to reach them? Through law, he replies. But in order to determine which laws are needed, we must first study political systems—and so the reader is sent to Aristotle's examination of constitutions and to his political writings. The sentence just cited shows that in writing the *Politics* Aristotle's eyes are always fixed on the goal of virtue—not necessarily perfect virtue, but at least 'some share of virtue'. And that sentence also shows his awareness of the difficulty of his task. No statesman or law can magically transform a randomly selected individual into a good person. What politics can do is make sure that 'all the things are present through which we seem to become decent'. If politics cannot transform us into fully realized human beings, it can at any rate create circumstances favorable to the development of something akin to excellence of reason, feeling, and sociability. As Aristotle says, if we can do even that much, we must be satisfied.

10.8. Obedience and the Law

When we encounter for the first time Aristotle's distinction between the qualities of a good citizen and those of a fully virtuous person, we are likely to assume that the point of making this distinction is to call attention to the fact that sometimes one's political duties and one's moral integrity pull one in opposite directions. The law may call upon a citizen to do X, and if he is a good citizen, he ought to do X, since a good citizen obeys the law; but a good person is not the same thing as a good citizen, and it may be wrong to do X.

Aristotle may seem to be making this point in III.4, because the conclusion he wants to draw from his arguments is that it is possible to be a good citizen without being a good man. It is tempting to take that to mean that sometimes being a good citizen requires one to do what a good person should never do. And since Aristotle surely ranks being a good person above being a good citizen, we might take him to be saying here that one should sometimes violate the law.

But this is not what Aristotle is trying to accomplish in III.4, as we have seen. He does not make the distinction between good citizenship and perfect virtue because he thinks that these are at times incompatible ideals. Nothing he says in this chapter or elsewhere suggests that one should deviate from the requirements of good citizenship. He is not addressing himself to the reader who is facing a dilemma about whether or not to obey the law. Rather, he is addressing, as he always does in his practical works, those who are in a position to mold their cities by passing new laws or reforming existing institutions. The message of III.4 is that we should foster both kinds of virtue—those of good men and those of good citizens. That it is possible to be a good citizen without being a good man is a conclusion Aristotle draws only because it drives home the point that one of these goals is easier to achieve and less exalted than the other. His aim in Book III is to examine the different kinds of city there are, and the distinction made in III.4 serves this purpose: in some cities, the best one can hope for is that those who rule are for the most part good citizens; in others—namely in kingships and aristocracies—those who hold the highest positions are not only this, but good men as well.

Does this mean that Aristotle has no interest in the question whether one should obey the law? Does he unthinkingly assume that one must always obey? And if so, why does he not recognize a moral difficulty that leaps to our eyes? The problem of legitimate authority seems so natural to us that we cannot believe it escapes Aristotle's notice. We quickly recognize the force of the familiar question: how are the orders of a state different from the commands of a robber? Both demand our money and threaten harm if we do not comply. In addition, the state may use our money for purposes we find troubling, or command us to serve in wars we consider unjust. Perhaps a good citizen would abide by the decisions of the majority, or the orders of those in power. But surely a good *person* must sometimes disobey? If Aristotle does not concern himself with this issue in III.4, does that mean that he simply ignores the problem altogether?[25]

The answer, I suggest, is this: Aristotle believes that there are certain things one must never do, even if one is commanded to do so

---

[25] Remarkably, there is just one ancient text—Plato's *Crito*—that offers a systematic account of why obedience is owed to the polis. This dialogue did not give rise to an ancient tradition of speculation on this theme. In its place, Greek and Roman thinkers asked whether it is worthwhile to lead a political life (Epicureans saying no, Stoics yes). Those who counseled against such a life were not necessarily advocating a stance of disobedience; and those who defended political activity took it for granted (as Aristotle did) that a life of active citizenship and office-holding must have, as one of its components, a willingness to comply with laws and commands even when they fall short of perfect justice.

10.8. OBEDIENCE AND THE LAW

by someone in a position of power. In the *Ethics*, he considers the case of a tyrant who orders someone to perform a shameful act, and threatens to kill his family if he does not comply (III.1 1110a4–8). Doing such a thing might be pardonable in extreme circumstances, he says, but it can never be praiseworthy; and one certainly ought to accept one's own death rather than yield to such threats (1110a23–7). Aristotle's discussion of tyranny in Book V of the *Politics* expresses the same attitude. He conveys his contempt for those who submit to a tyrant's whims, when he says that tyrants try to kill free and dignified men who have minds of their own (V.11 1313a40–1, 1314a5–9). He assumes that justice does not require obedience to a tyrant's outrageous commands. It might sometimes be expedient to humor the tyrant, but one does not owe him obedience. And the same holds true for other tyrannical regimes: extreme democracies and oligarchies (10.n.15).

But what if one lives in constitutions that are not as defective as that—political systems that are biased in favor of the rich or the poor, and fall far short of perfect justice, but do not command (as tyrants may do) the performance of shameful acts? Such moderately bad regimes may operate in accordance with law, but Aristotle points out that their legality does not rebut the charge that they are biased and unfair (III.10 1281a34–9). As he says, if a political system is unjust, it will produce unjust laws (III.11 1282b11–13). But these passages do not show that, in his opinion, citizens of these unjust regimes are relieved of their duty to obey. They must strive to be good citizens, and a good citizen is someone who has the ability not only to rule well but also to be ruled well (III.4 1277a25–7, b13–16). The good citizen of a mixed democracy or oligarchy participates in its political life, holds office, and tries to prevent the constitution from moving in the wrong direction. But being ruled—obeying the law—is also part of his job.

What we want to know is precisely this: *why* is being ruled part of his job? Aristotle's answer is that when citizens are equal in ability, it is a matter of justice that they share not only in ruling but in being ruled. When one has had one's turn holding office, it is time for others to do that job, and just as one expected to be obeyed, so one must obey in turn (III.7 1279a8–13). This is justice as proportionate equality, and Aristotle has already alluded to it in II.2 as a principle that preserves cities (1261a30–1). He often contrasts this form of rule with the rule of a master over a slave by calling it 'political' rule, implying by means of this terminology and contrast that it is the appropriate way to share power in cities.[26] In many existing cities, it is at least dimly recognized that power should be dispersed and shared by different groups. The exceptions are extreme democracies and oligarchies; they are appropriately called tyrannical because those in power use their offices entirely for their own benefit and treat their economic enemies as mere objects of abuse. In such cities, justice is entirely absent. By contrast, moderate regimes accept some form of power-sharing, though their bias favors the dominant faction. A ruling party that shares power with its opponents is not entirely unjust, if in doing so it partly acknowledges their claims.[27]

Even though citizens typically live in cities that are biased in favor of one class or another, and in which the laws are unjust because they reflect this bias, there is nonetheless a reason, based on justice, for them to participate in their city's political life, to obey those in power, and to respect the laws. For although those who are dominant in such cities are morally defective, they are not entirely lacking in justice, since they accept some degree of reciprocity. Each citizen rules to some degree and is ruled to some degree. Although this mixture is improperly balanced, because some rule more than they deserve, the political system is not entirely corrupt. In return for what other citizens do for you—though this falls short of what perfect justice requires—you ought to do your part by being a good citizen. There must be general compliance with the laws if the city is to survive, and the city's survival is a worthwhile goal whenever the constitution is not entirely bad. That is why each citizen must do his part by obeying the law.[28]

This does not mean that one must obey every law and every command, no matter what it requires. Aristotle is careful to say that one must rule and obey *well* (III.4 1277a27) and that one must rule and be ruled as a free man (b15). These phrases imply that one must avoid slavish submission: when one is ruled, one cannot cede to others the power of a tyrant to command whatever he pleases. To be ruled well is to retain the free man's recognition that there are certain things one must refuse to do, because they are shameful. The injustice of a law is not yet a reason to disobey it, because perfect justice is so rare,

---

[26] See I.1 1252a7–9, I.3 1253b18–20. Political rule is exercised over those who are free and equal (I.7 1255b20, I.12 1259b5–6, III.4 1277b7–9) and typically requires the rotation of offices (I.12 1259b4–5, III.6 1279a8–10; cf. II.2 1261a30–b).

[27] See *NE* VIII.9 1159b26–7: 'in every community there seems to be a certain justice . . .' So too VIII.11 1161a10–11. It exists to a small extent in defective regimes and least in the worst (1161a30–2).

[28] The points made here should be supplemented by the ones discussed in 4.3 and 4.5.

10.8. OBEDIENCE AND THE LAW

and the imperfect justice of a deviant city is worth preserving. But if a law or a command requires one to do something that no decent person should do, one can only disobey.

Our conclusion, then, is that although Aristotle does not make the distinction between a good man and a good citizen in order to reach the conclusion that we should avoid complicity with unjust civil power, other passages indicate that he does not counsel compliance with the commands of whomever happens to be in power. Following the lead of Socrates and Plato, he conceives of a just person as someone who is guided by standards of right and wrong that exist independently of the opinions of the majority (*NE* V.7 1134b18–1135a5). Aristotle advocates some degree of accommodation to unjust regimes, but he is distant from those who, like Machiavelli, counsel the use of all necessary means for attaining civic glory; or those who, like Hobbes, find no effective standard of behavior other than the sovereign's command.

One further point should be noted. It is common in the modern period to think of the immense power of the state as its most salient characteristic, and to regard such power principally as a threat to the freedom of the individual, rather than as an opportunity to promote good. It is widely assumed that adult human beings have a natural right to self-governance, and that it is therefore an affront to be subject to civil power. That is why the problem of obedience to the state is so naturally raised by asking whether its coercive power should be regarded as less offensive than any other form of coercion. *All* limits to our freedom are evil when they are backed by force and not self-imposed. Perhaps the state's power is a necessary evil, but in any case the less of it the better, precisely because it is an evil.

Aristotle does not share the assumption that because laws and civil authorities limit a citizen's freedom, they are at best a necessary evil. He does not think of the polis as intrinsically dangerous to human well-being, nor does he think of the freedom to do as one pleases as intrinsically worthwhile, apart from how it is used (*Pol.* V.9 1310a30–6).[29] For him, the most salient feature of the polis is its power to promote the well-being of its citizens. This potential is rarely exploited as fully as it can be, and in some cases civic power becomes malignant. But so long as we are not living under tyrannies—whether tyrannies of the one, the few, or the many— we should look upon civic power not so much as a threat to be

---

[29] We will return to these themes in 12.5 and 13.3.

minimized as an opportunity to be exploited. To focus entirely on the state as a coercive power, a force that demands obedience, and to ask how such obedience can have a moral grounding, is to look at only one aspect, and not the most important aspect, of politics. Citizenship is not simply a matter of being ruled, but of ruling well and being ruled well. The opportunity to rule well—to exercise one's deliberative skills and thereby to do good to others—is the principal attraction of citizenship; but citizenship cannot be separated from the need to obey well. When philosophers of the modern period isolate obedience from active citizenship, they have already taken up a perspective from which the state appears to be an alien and threatening power. The problem of political authority and obedience can dominate the agenda of political philosophy only if we think of ourselves not as engaged members of the political community but as powerless individuals subordinate to an entity—the state—that stands over us with threatening powers and insulting limitations.

11

Politics III: Correct Constitutions and the Common Good

11.1. The Practical Import of Book III

After Aristotle introduces the distinction between good men and good citizens (III.4), and discusses whether craftsmen should be admitted to citizenship (III.5), he turns to the principal tasks of Book III: classifying political systems and comparing their merits and deficiencies. We are already familiar with his taxonomy, which distinguishes between correct and deviant constitutions and lists three types within each of these categories. Now let us look more carefully at some problems that can be raised about his scheme.

The fundamental concept Aristotle uses in his discussion is the common good. This is to be understood by distinguishing it from its opposite: in deviant regimes, the rulers govern solely in order to promote their own good; but in correct constitutions, they aim at the good of all citizens, not merely their own (III.7 1279a25–39).[1] But

---

[1] Some scholars see difficulties here. If a kingship is a political system in which just one person rules, and a citizen is someone who shares in rule, then there is no one besides the king himself who counts as a citizen. To aim at the good of all citizens, he need only think of himself. Furthermore, how can an oligarchy be a deviant constitution, since the few who are wealthy are the only citizens, and therefore the rulers aim at the good of all citizens? To

what is the practical import of this distinction between correct and deviant constitutions? How does Aristotle intend his readers to use it?

We might reply that Book III is intended as a guide for readers who wish to found a new city. In that case, the distinction between correct and incorrect political systems is a useful one because it tells those colonists to avoid the deviant constitutions and to choose the best of the correct ones. They should establish a kingship or an aristocracy, and by all means they should avoid democracy, oligarchy, and tyranny.

But that answer brings Book III into conflict with VII and VIII, and we have been seeking a way to read III that avoids this contradiction (10.1). And in any case, Book III shows no interest in any of the questions that take up so much of Aristotle's attention in VII and VIII: the size of the ideal city's population, the city's location in relation to land and sea, the division of land, the educational system, and so on. It is best, then, not to read the distinction between correct and incorrect constitutions as an aid to the colonist who seeks to make a fresh start.

A different answer might be suggested: Aristotle's distinction between correct and incorrect regimes is meant to be of value to a reader who is deciding whether to become a citizen of this or that already existing city. But this too is unsatisfactory, for most of Aristotle's readers had no such choice. If they did not participate in the founding of a new community, they could be citizens of just one city: the one in which their parents were citizens.

Perhaps then we should say that correct and incorrect constitutions must be distinguished because existing cities can change their constitutions, and so even when citizens have no choice but to remain in the city of their parents, they need to decide what they should do about its political system. If it is deviant, they might favor a revolution that transforms it into a correct constitution. And even if it is a correct constitution, there might be differences among such regimes that make one better than another. So, citizens might try to transform a correct political system into one that is even better.

the first question, I reply: there can be many small offices in a kingship, and therefore many more citizens than the king (11.10). To the second: an oligarchy is deviant precisely because it rests on too narrow a conception of citizenship; it ignores the good of those who deserve citizen status. For other suggestions, see Miller, *NJR*, p. 212; and the introduction to Reeve's translation, pp. lxviii–lxix. For a full treatment, see Morrison, 'Aristotle's Definition of Citizenship: A Problem and Some Solutions'. He argues that the problem is insoluble, because there are unresolvable tensions in Aristotle's theory.

11.1. THE PRACTICAL IMPORT OF BOOK III

Book III can in this way be read as a revolutionary's handbook, a guide for deciding which regimes to overthrow and which to leave standing.

But this cannot be right either, because in a passage we considered at length in the previous chapter (10.2–4) Aristotle claims that a good citizen is someone who *preserves* his constitution (III.4 1276b26–9). This would not be an obstacle to the reading just proposed, if we took him to mean that we should be good *human beings* rather than good *citizens*; but we also saw in the previous chapter that Aristotle takes good citizenship to be an honorable goal even in deviant or inferior political systems (10.7). So he thinks that the citizens of a polity ought to preserve this political system, not overthrow it and establish an aristocracy or a kingship in its place, even though the latter are better constitutions. Similarly, he seems to assume that even democracies and oligarchies should be preserved, not overthrown; for apparently that is what good citizenship requires.

We are at an impasse. If all political systems are to be preserved, then what is the point of making a distinction between correct and deviant regimes, and what is the practical significance of ranking kingship and aristocracy above polity? On the other hand, if all political systems inferior to the very best are to be transformed, then what is the practical import of classifying polity as a correct constitution?

Our questions suggest that Aristotle should adopt, for his own purposes, a less conservative approach to the study of constitutions. He ought to say that there are times when it is quite appropriate to consider the merits of rival political systems, and to make such constitutional changes as are appropriate to one's circumstances. Aristotle's discussion of constitutional change in Book V recognizes that the transformation of one political system into another is a recurring feature of civic life. It would be foolish to withhold judgment about when the transformation of one kind of political system into another is a change for the better or the worse, or to refuse ever to help or hinder such changes. To form these kinds of judgment, one needs to make the distinctions Aristotle draws in Book III between constitutions that are based on a worthwhile aim (the promotion of the common good) and those that are not. One also needs to ask whether rulers should be bound by law, and which qualifications entitle someone to rule and exercise the privileges of citizenship. And one must be prepared, in appropriate circumstances, to act on these judgments—even if this means that one will be destroying an old constitution and replacing it with a new one. Aristotle is right to think that one worthwhile task of politics is to preserve an already existing constitution, because there are times when any attempt to destroy an old order and establish a new one will only make matters worse. But he ought to have recognized that this is only one worthwhile task of politics among many. In fact, the very distinctions he makes in Book III of the *Politics* have practical value only if there are times when the conservatism built into his definition of good citizenship is no longer appropriate, and a deeper transformation of political life is called for.

11.2. Impartiality and Equality

The common good is one of the essential notions that Aristotle uses to distinguish among constitutions, and we should therefore seek a better understanding of it. Suppose the rulers seek the good of all citizens, but aim much more at the well-being of some than others. Would Aristotle say that the constitution of this city aims at the common good? Or does he implicitly build into the notion of the common good some notion of impartiality, so that when some citizens are singled out for better treatment than others, the common good is not served?

Our question is not whether Aristotle thinks that all goods should be equally distributed among all citizens, for we already know that he rejects the equal distribution of external goods such as wealth and office. In II.7 he opposes Phaleas' proposal that land be divided equally (9.20); in his ideal city there will be differences in wealth (6.9). Furthermore, he thinks that in existing cities high offices should be filled only by those who are most qualified to serve their fellow citizens. Even though he advocates an equal sharing of power in the ideal city, this is because in those special circumstances all will be equally qualified. He does not call for equal rule, but for equal rule only among equals.[2]

But although Aristotle rejects these forms of egalitarianism, we can still ask whether he builds a different kind of egalitarianism into

---

[2] See *Pol.* III.9 1280a11–12. This is what Aristotle calls proportionate equality or equality in accordance with merit, as opposed to numerical equality (4.11). See too V.1 1301b29–35; *NE* V.3–4.

his concept of the common good. Suppose a city promoted the well-being of both rich and poor, but gave far more attention to the rich than the poor, for example by providing them with more and better education. Such a city might give the poor some education—but not as good an education as the rich receive. And suppose that its reason for doing this is simply that it favors the rich over the poor: the rulers think it far more desirable that a rich person live well than that a poor person live well. Are these rulers still promoting the common good, as Aristotle understands this concept?

His answer, I suggest, is no; and the evidence for reading him in this way is present everywhere in Books IV–VI. For in this portion of the *Politics*, he advises oligarchies and democracies to achieve a more nearly equal balance between the rich and the poor.[3] The fundamental idea behind his approach is that, even though these regimes are inherently flawed because of their bias, they can come closer to being correct constitutions—and to promoting the *common* good rather than the good of the ruling faction alone—by attenuating the force of that bias. As Aristotle says: 'the city wishes to be composed of those who are equal and alike, so far as it can' (IV.11 1295b25–6). Later in the same chapter, he complains that in existing cities the rich and the poor seek domination over the rival party rather than a 'common and equal' political system (1296a30). His point is not that the rich should take *some* interest, however minimal, in the poor (and vice versa), but that so far as possible the two factions should regard each other as equals. A 'common' political system is simply one that promotes the common good, and Aristotle calls this an 'equal' constitution because it 'wishes to be composed of those who are equal and alike'. The ideal of the common good, in other words, requires that the good of each citizen be treated as no less worthy of support than the good of any other. Neither the rich nor the poor are to be singled out for special treatment. It is unrealistic to expect existing cities to achieve this ideal fully, but this is the direction in which they should move.

But what if there are a small number of citizens in a defective regime who are virtuous in the strict sense and therefore far better people than the others? Would Aristotle say that they ought to receive special treatment? After all, if the city's aim is to promote genuine well-being—not some false conception of it—then should it not allocate a larger share of resources to those who will use them to

---

[3] See esp. IV.9 V.8–9, VI.3–5.

lead good lives? If two citizens appeal to the city for resources, and one of them would use those resources to live well, whereas the other would waste them, surely it is the first who must be favored. So, it might seem that we cannot attribute to Aristotle the thesis that the good of each citizen is as important as the good of any other.

But if we think a bit more, we can see that, however legitimate it may be for an individual benefactor to favor those who will put his aid to good use, it would be foolish for a city to give favorable treatment to a small but virtuous elite as a general policy. If a constitution were to divide the city into two groups—the virtuous few and the mediocre many—and give the former whatever they need for their happiness, and the latter only as much as is left over, the result would be unceasing civil strife. The virtuous few would have to be constantly on guard against revolution; they would be like masters who spend their lives fearfully overseeing the activities of slaves. And so the purpose of this system—to promote the well-being of the virtuous—would be defeated. To live and rule well, the virtuous few need the willing cooperation of other citizens; they cannot achieve this if they live in an atmosphere of hostility. Their goal in ruling well must be to promote not only their own good but the good of all the other citizens. Admittedly, those others cannot live good lives, if we judge them by the strictest standard of well-being. But even if they cannot become fully realized human beings, they can approximate this goal by acquiring the virtues of good citizens, and using these more ordinary skills in their daily activities. In doing so, they live better lives than they otherwise would. So the well-being of the virtuous few who live in a city with the mediocre many is tied to the well-being of the many. The constitution of such a city cannot benefit either group without equally benefiting the other. It is just as important that the many be good citizens as it is that the few be good men, because these are interdependent goals. Even when there are great differences of character among the citizens, the city needs a 'common and equal' constitution.

Aristotle briefly raises the question we have been discussing, and answers it in the way just proposed. In III.13 he asks: should the politician create laws that favor the better people (who are few) or the inferior people (who are many)? And he replies without hesitation or elaboration that the legislator must look to the good of the whole city (1283b36–42). Here and throughout, he takes the ideal of the common good to mean that no group of citizens should receive greater care than any other. Of course, some citizens will lead better lives than others, because some have a true conception of well-being and others do not. In fact, even when all have a true conception, there is nothing a constitution can do to insure that all have equally good fortune. No power on earth can make us equally well off. What a constitution can do is create conditions favorable to the development of good citizens and (when conditions permit) good human beings. It would be pointless for a political system to create such opportunities for some citizens but not others, for if some receive less favorable treatment, this will make everyone else worse off as well. Exercising good citizenship and virtue are inherently cooperative enterprises, for when some are less well equipped to do their jobs, others suffer as well.

11.3. Cities, Commercial Ventures, and Military Alliances

When Aristotle introduces the notion of the common good to mark the distinction between correct and deviant constitutions, he indicates that the particular good that is to be promoted by the rulers is a highly general one: it is living well (III.6 1278b15-24). People are drawn together to form cities not only in order to survive, and not merely because they find it appealing to spend their days with others, but also because, having acquired some leisure and the freedom to choose the kind of life they think best, they see the political community as something essential to their plans. Living well, not mere living, is the good at which the city aims (I.2 1252b29-30), and so this is the common good that is to be served by its rulers. This point serves as the background to Aristotle's discussion of the various kinds of constitutions, even the ones that are deviant. All rulers manage their city's affairs by basing their decisions on some conception of living well. In corrupt regimes, the good they seek is their own, not that of others; but even so, the good at which they aim when they rule is living well.

The notion of the common good remains at this level of generality for several chapters, but in III.9 Aristotle finally confronts the fact that people disagree about what well-being is, and that this makes a difference to the kinds of constitution they create. All political systems rest on the assumption that there should be equality—but only for those who are genuinely equals. What divides them are the incompatible answers they give to the question: equal in what respect? Supporters of oligarchy think that the wealthy deserve more power than others, because they make superior contributions to the city. They spend more on public projects, and so they should be rewarded by having more control over collective decisions. Democrats respond by insisting that the respect in which they should be compared with oligarchs is their status as citizens. They are free men, not slaves; and in this way they and the oligarchs are equal. They think that each free person should have as much power as any other; and so, in effect, the poor should have more power than the rich (since they outnumber them).

Aristotle believes that we can see what is wrong with the positions of both parties to the dispute by asking what the goal of the political community is. The oligarchs give the poor little or no role to play in the polis because they see the political community as an organization devoted to the accumulation or management of wealth. They think the poor know little about these matters, and are therefore poorly qualified to share in the city. To use a metaphor suggested by Aristotle's discussion in III.12: the rich are like flute players who think that they ought to have the better flutes, because they are more skillful players. Their knowledge of how to manage large estates qualifies them to rule—or so they think, because they conceive of a political community as a business venture. But at this point in the argument of III.9, Aristotle proposes that the aim of the city is not commercial; nor is it defense against external enemies. For these are inadequate conceptions of what it is to live well. The city is instead an organization devoted to making the citizens excellent, because excellent activity, not mere wealth or mere life, is what well-being is.

One intriguing feature of III.9 is that Aristotle does not appeal to his ethical writings to support his claim that virtuous activity is what the city should aim at. Instead, he simply asks us to consider what a city *is*. If a city had mere commerce or self-defense as its goal, then we ought to say that all those who trade with each other, or who form protective alliances, constitute a single city— and obviously they do not. What makes a group of people a single city, he proposes, is the interest they take in the sort of people who are included in their community. They do not think it sufficient that other members of their community refrain from injuring each other; rather, each citizen of a city wants the other citizens to be virtuous. If they do not care about each other in this

11.3. CITIES, COMMERCIAL VENTURES, AND MILITARY ALLIANCES

way, then they do not really form a city in the true sense of the word.

Is there anything to this argument? We might doubt that citizens need be as interested in each other as Aristotle supposes. Must they really care about each other's character? Or, more often than not, are they satisfied so long as none of their fellow citizens does them harm? To see how Aristotle would reply, we should take a hint from his point that cities that form commercial relationships do not establish common offices to oversee compliance (III.9 1280a40–b1). Instead, each city has its own officers and monitors its own citizens. Here Aristotle is presupposing that when a citizen is brought to court for the violation of a law, the jurors must assess his character, in order to decide whether he should be convicted, and if so, what punishment he deserves. They will not confine their deliberations to narrow questions of fact, but will ask whether the accused has been a good citizen and is a good man.[4] Similarly, when citizens elect magistrates, they will ask themselves which of their fellow citizens have the kind of character that qualifies them to fill those positions of power.

Aristotle is certainly right to think that on these occasions citizens evaluate each other's character and not merely their overt behavior. He is not claiming that citizens are busybodies constantly preoccupied with each other's virtue. His idea, rather, is that when they participate in political affairs and make judgments about each other, they are concerned with character and not merely behavior. The Athenians do not care what sort of people the Spartans are; they merely want not to be mistreated by them. But when they elect common officers and sit together on juries, they demand far more. In electing officers, they do not simply ask, 'Will he mistreat me?' They want to know whether the candidate is the sort of person who will be devoted to the good of the city. Similarly, when they serve on juries, they do not merely ask, 'Has the accused ever injured me, or will he ever do so?' They ask whether it is good for the city that he be punished, and to answer this question they take into account his character, as revealed by the services he has rendered the city.

Aristotle's point can be put this way: although people may say that the aim of their city should merely be commerce or self-defense, they are in fact interested in far wider goals, as can be seen from the

---

[4] See *Rhet.* II.1 1377b20–1378a19 on the importance of a speaker's character, both in the assembly and the courts. Dover, *Greek Popular Morality in the Time of Plato and Aristotle*, pp. 292–5, provides a helpful discussion.

thinking that underlies their political decisions. When the rich citizens of oligarchies choose officers, they do not merely consider the wealth of the candidates, but also their honesty and trustworthiness. They want to exclude the poor from power not merely because they think they have no commercial competence, but because they think they are bad people. Taking themselves to be superior in one respect, they generalize wildly and consider themselves superior in all respects; they therefore think they are better people than the poor. And similarly, the poor do not rest content with the claim that since they are free men rather than slaves they should share power equally. They infer from this one kind of equality that they are just as *virtuous* as anyone else (III.9 1280a22–5).[5] So both the rich and the poor tacitly assume that they are qualified to hold office—though the rich claim to be better qualified, the poor to be equally qualified.

Aristotle does not wish to conclude that virtue is the only qualification that citizens seek or ought to seek in each other when they participate in politics. He is acutely aware that a city cannot survive if all of its citizens are poor; he assumes that the financial resources of the city must come from the rich, and that the poor are therefore wrong to try to exclude them from politics.[6] The city needs at least some rich citizens, not merely some virtuous citizens. Similarly, Aristotle realizes that the city has quantitative as well as qualitative needs; that is, it requires a *sizable* population of free men who can make a worthwhile contribution to public decision-making. So the poor are in a way right to insist that their status as free men deserves consideration.[7] Since Aristotle claims in Book III that no city can be composed entirely of virtuous people (III.4 1276b37–8), he is forced to include as citizens those who do not excel as individual decision-makers, but who still contribute something—wealth or collective oversight—to public life. Nonetheless, this does not mean that the rich and the poor can benefit the city no matter how deficient they are as human beings. Some minimal level of political competence must always be demanded of citizens, and Aristotle assumes that when people are *too* poor, they cannot contribute usefully to public life.[8] So, although the city needs bulk, the mere fact that someone is

---

[5] Aristotle expands on this point in V.1 1301a28–b1.

[6] See III.12 1283a18–19, III.13 1283a29–33.

[7] See III.13 1283a40–2. Aristotle explores this point more fully in III.11; see 11.6 below for further discussion.

[8] Aristotle therefore favors a minimal property qualification for citizenship (IV.13 1297b1–8); this must be altered periodically (V.6 1306b9–16, V.8 1308a35–b10). See too 10.n.5.

11.3. CITIES, COMMERCIAL VENTURES, AND MILITARY ALLIANCES

free does not by itself qualify him for citizenship. And although considerable wealth may be a necessary qualification for certain offices,[9] it is never by itself sufficient. Free status is a necessary condition for all civic roles and wealth is a necessary qualification for some of them, but neither is ever sufficient. Every citizen must meet minimal standards of character; and this is the most important qualification of all, because the goal of the city is to promote the development of fully realized human beings who have the resources they need to exercise their powers.

Aristotle's approach might puzzle a modern reader, who is unaccustomed to thinking of the state as an association that demands moral qualifications of its members. We are inclined to doubt that mere reflection on what it is for two cities to be separate cities can lead to the remarkable conclusion that a city in the proper sense of the word must care about the virtue of the citizens, and cannot be a mere alliance in which citizens trade and unite for the sake of defense. But the phenomena to which Aristotle appeals are still features of political life. When we decide which candidates to vote for, we ask what kind of people they are. The character of the accused is not irrelevant to the outcome of a trial. In the United States, felons are, in all but a few jurisdictions, deprived of the right to vote. We care about what kind of people our fellow citizens are, at least when we engage in activities that are characteristic of citizenship.

We should also recall that, in the world of the polis, citizenship was a larger job than it usually is today, since it involved attending meetings of the assembly and taking one's turn in office. And such cities were at times arenas of conflict between opposed factions who doubted each other's moral credentials as citizens. In such a world, where the virtues and vices of one's fellow citizens was rarely a remote concern, it would have been inaccurate to define a city as an association designed solely for commercial exchange and self-defense. Such a proposed definition would have applied far more accurately to relationships between separate cities, and would have failed to pick out what is most characteristic of existing cities.

In the Greek city, the question, 'who is qualified to be a ruler?' could not be separated from the question, 'who is qualified to be a citizen?' because the citizens were also rulers. So anyone who cared

---

[9] See IV.15 1300a15–16 and VI.6 1320b22–5 on the high assessment needed for certain offices; but note Aristotle's emphasis on moral qualifications at V.9 1309a33–b8.

about the character of rulers—and how could this be a matter of indifference?—had also to be concerned about the qualifications of his fellow citizens. That is why it was an important task for Aristotle to answer the question with which he opens Book III: what is a citizen? This cannot be treated as a merely linguistic or descriptive question—a problem about how the word is used—because a citizen is necessarily someone who plays a role in a community and makes a contribution to its well-being. At any rate, a *good* citizen must make such a contribution, and one cannot understand what a citizen is without also understanding what a good citizen does. These concepts—citizen, good citizen, and the well-being of the community—must be investigated as a group, and one of the main points Aristotle makes in Book III is that his conception of well-being shows how these notions are related to each other. He takes it to be a commonplace that a good citizen is concerned with the character of his fellow citizens, at least when he engages in political activity. And he also takes it to be a commonplace that a good citizen cares about the well-being of his fellow citizens. Aristotle's conception of human flourishing enables him to explain these two points and reveal their connection: caring about whether one's fellow citizens are good citizens is caring about their well-being, because their well-being consists precisely in exercising the virtues of citizenship.[10]

11.4. The Common Good in Pluralistic Cities

We are now in a position to answer a further question about the common good. When Aristotle says that in correct constitutions the rulers aim at the common good and not merely their own, he presumably means not only that they aim at what *seems* good to them, but that the good at which they aim really is good. After all, correct constitutions are ones that we should try to establish, or at least imitate. But there would be little value in trying to induce one's fellow citizens to pursue a goal that only seems good to them but in fact is not. If the rulers aimed at something bad, and offered it to every member of the community, not only themselves, we might praise them for their impartial interest in the whole city, but our

---

[10] For further discussion of Aristotle's argument in III.9, see Cooper, 'Political Animals and Civic Friendship'.

11.4. THE COMMON GOOD IN PLURALISTIC CITIES

praise would have to be faint, because by hypothesis they would in fact be doing harm to themselves and others. Aristotle cannot take such a political system to be correct.

But now consider a city in which no single conception of the good is universally accepted by the citizens. That, of course, is not the city described in Books VII and VIII, but such diversity is what we find in nearly every political community that has ever existed, including the cities of the ancient world. Aristotle himself tells us that there is no agreement about what happiness is.[11] He never suggests that typically we find agreement within a single city—that there are disagreements *between* cities about what well-being is, but not *within* cities.

The points made in the previous two paragraphs lead to an apparent difficulty: when a city contains no consensus about what the common good is, how can it be well governed? Suppose those who hold the highest offices have one conception of the good, and those who are ordinary citizens have a different conception: will there not be hostility and mistrust between the two groups? Are ordinary citizens to renounce or ignore their conception of well-being, simply because it is not accepted by those who have more power than they do? It would be hopelessly naive to expect this to happen. But if it does not, how can such citizens willingly obey those in power? The commands of the powerful will express a conception of well-being that the less powerful do not share. Accordingly, the less powerful will think that their rulers are not serving their interests. They want the rulers to promote the common good—not merely what appears to the rulers to be the common good. Can there be a stable and just political community in such a city?

The situation would not be any better if the most powerful leaders disagreed among themselves about the good. Nor would it be better if there were no ruling elite, but all citizens shared power on an equal basis yet disagreed about the good. For some of the legislation adopted by such cities will express the conception of the good held only by a majority, and in these cases the minority cannot agree that the majority are servants of the common good. Surely Aristotle cannot regard such cities, which are torn by fundamental disagreement, as well governed. When he defines a correct constitution as one in which the rulers promote the good of all, he must be presupposing

---

[11] See *NE* I.4 1095a20–2; *EE* I.1 1214a30–b6; *Pol.* VII.1 1323a34–8.

that such a constitution exists only when the citizens have achieved a consensus about where their good lies.

This seems to be a great embarrassment for Aristotle's whole political outlook. Apparently, it is only in an ideal world—the world imagined in Books VII and VIII—that a city can be governed by a correct constitution. Uniformity of opinion about the good cannot occur unless a number of like-minded people establish a new city governed by their vision of human well-being. Perhaps their educational, cultural, and political institutions can perpetuate such uniformity; but in all other circumstances, diverse opinions about human well-being will continue to exist within a single city, and will create political strife. Aristotle realizes that real cities contain this kind of diversity and he is familiar with the hostility it causes. But apparently he does not reckon with the implications this has for his theory of correct constitutions. He must admit—or so it seems—that no city that has already been established can have a correct constitution. For where there is disagreement about the good, rulers cannot achieve the common good.

The solution to this problem consists in rejecting its assumption that citizens can agree that their city is pursuing the common good only if they achieve a consensus about what well-being is. Suppose they have no such consensus, but nonetheless agree that their city ought to promote the conditions that encourage each citizen to be a certain kind of person, namely a good citizen. That, according to Aristotle, would be a way of promoting the common good, and not merely what seems good. For as we have seen (10.3, 10.7), he takes the virtue of a good citizen to be an approximation to the virtue of a good man. A city organized around this conception of the common good would be an approximation of the ideal city of Books VII and VIII. Although it would not promote perfect virtue, it would foster something similar to it.

Furthermore, it was not unrealistic for Aristotle to hope that in existing cities there might be a consensus among the citizens that this should be their common aim. For as we have just seen (11.3), he thinks that the citizens of Greek cities already take a great interest in the character of their fellow citizens. When they select their rulers or serve as members of a jury, they are mindful of the character of their fellow citizens. The hostility between rich and poor would not be so great if neither party had any objection to associating and cooperating with those whose character they despise. So it is not unrealistic to propose good citizenship as the common goal of a community, and to seek consensus about what should be expected of good citizens. The citizens who live in such a city do not have to agree about what well-being is. They can take the good pursued through collective decisions to be one thing, and the good pursued individually to be another. So long as their allegiance to the outcome of collective decisions is strong enough, their city will be stable and will accomplish something of considerable value: they will bring all citizens closer to the goal of living good lives.[12]

11.5. *The Common Good in the Best Constitutions*

We have seen how there can be consensus about the common good in a city even though the citizens have different conceptions of wellbeing. But of course the kind of consensus we have described is, from Aristotle's perspective, not the best that can be imagined or hoped for. The ideal community, from his point of view, is a city in which all citizens accept the conception of the good that he takes to be correct. In both their collective and their individual decisions, they are guided by their recognition that the human good consists in virtuous activity sufficiently equipped with external equipment. That is the ideal Aristotle describes in Books VII and VIII. But what about Book III? Does Aristotle take any of the three correct constitutions discussed in that book to be a regime in which the citizens universally accept his conception of well-being?

I believe he does, for the following reason. The kind of kingship proposed in Book III is one in which a single person is recognized by the other citizens as so far superior to them in character and intellect as to deserve permanent authority over them.[13] No one can deserve such immense power unless he has practical wisdom and understands what human happiness consists in. And since the other citizens voluntarily accept his rule and recognize his wisdom, they too must share that same conception of happiness. They take the king to be aiming at their good, because they agree with him about where their good lies. Even if few citizens governed by the king possess

---

[12] We will return to Aristotle's conception of consensus when we discuss political friendship in 12.9.

[13] Note Aristotle's statement that the other citizens should 'gladly' obey the person of outstanding virtue (III.13 1284b32–4). The context clearly indicates that the other citizens recognize his superiority, for the general problem Aristotle raises here—when does superiority justify ostracism?—presupposes such recognition. Aristotle again builds recognition of superiority into his conception of aristocracy at VII.14 1332b16–23.

POLITICS III: CORRECT CONSTITUTIONS

practical wisdom, each of them has at least a correct notion of where his well-being lies.[14] And presumably the same situation obtains in the kind of aristocracy Aristotle proposes at the end of Book III. For he mentions no significant difference between kingship and aristocracy, except that in the former one extraordinary person governs, and in the latter a small number of such people rule.[15] We should therefore conclude that in both of these constitutions rulers and ruled are guided by the correct conception of well-being.

But what of polity, the political system in which the many rule for the good of all? Does Aristotle assume that here too all citizens will recognize what happiness is? When he first mentions this kind of constitution, he describes it as one in which the citizens are inferior in virtue. As he puts it: 'it is difficult for many to meet an exacting standard in every virtue' (III.7 1279a40–b1). He admits that they can be excellent soldiers (b1–2), but in saying this he implies that they have individual deficiencies in other respects. Precisely where do they go wrong? Aristotle does not say, but it is reasonable to conjecture that they do not recognize that well-being consists in virtuous activity. For this would explain why these citizens are not fully virtuous, and why this constitution, though correct, is not as good as kingship or aristocracy.[16]

But how can a polity be a correct constitution if some or many of its citizens fail to recognize what well-being is? How can all aim at and achieve the common good if there is no consensus about what the good is? We have already seen how to answer these questions (11.4). Even though many members of a polity fail to measure up to the most exacting standards of good character, they can all of them be good citizens. They can take the promotion of civic virtue—an approximation to real virtue—to be their collective goal, even though they do not share the same conception of happiness. Since

---

[14] Recall the distinction made at III.4 1277b26–9. See 10.3 above for discussion.

[15] See III.17 1288a15–19, III.18 1288a41. At III.15 1286b2–7 it is said that aristocracy is better than kingship, but it is likely that at this point Aristotle is merely rehearsing an argument against kingship rather than endorsing the superiority of aristocracy. He takes III.15–16 to be an examination of competing arguments (1287b35–6) and only comes to his conclusions in III.17–18. At *NE* VIII.10 1160a35–6, he holds that kingship is the best political system (for reasons we will discuss in 11.15), and there is no good reason to take this to contradict anything he says in *Pol.* III. See too 11.n.46.

[16] More will be said to confirm this conjecture in 12.3. I believe that the 'military virtue' of the ordinary person that Aristotle refers to at *Pol.* III.7 1279b1–2 is the lesser form of courage that he describes as 'civic' (*politikē*) courage at *NE* III.8 1116a16–29. In calling it *politikē*, he means that it is the sort of courage that typifies those who are citizens of a polity (the regime correctly ruled by the many).

11.5. THE COMMON GOOD IN THE BEST CONSTITUTIONS

they agree about their common goal, and are impartial in their governance of the city, they are not divided into warring factions. Though they are not all perfectly virtuous, and disagree about the good, they still accomplish something worthwhile: they have enough justice to cooperate with each other as equals, and they promote something akin to perfect virtue.

These hypotheses about kingship, aristocracy, and polity help explain why Aristotle elevates the first two above the third in the final two chapters of Book III. Obviously, kingship and aristocracy cannot be superior merely because they are rule by one or few. It is not the number of rulers that matters but their quality; and the quality of rule depends on the conception of the good that guides ruler and ruled. So kingship and aristocracy are superior constitutions because they are guided by the correct conception of well-being.[17]

It might seem puzzling that Aristotle should come to this conclusion. Why should he suppose that when the many rule, the correct conception of well-being cannot be widely accepted, but that when those who rule are a small number, all can recognize where their good lies? But there should be no mystery here. Aristotle's assumption is that the correct understanding of the human good is presently shared by only a few, and that this situation can be changed only through the influence of a small number of people who hold positions of extraordinary power and win the admiration and trust of others. They might make a fresh start in a new land, and establish educational institutions that insure that their ideas about well-being will be widely accepted among future generations. Or they might earn the esteem of ordinary people in existing cities—so much so that they are given kingly power, and their conception of well-being

---

[17] Aristotle sometimes characterizes the differences between political systems by attributing to them different ends: oligarchy is for the sake of wealth, democracy freedom, and aristocracy virtue (10.n.12). So we should not be surprised that the superiority of kingship and aristocracy rests on their relation to perfect virtue, in contrast with the lesser virtue associated with polity. Aristotle calls attention to this aspect of polity in his defense of kingship and aristocracy (III.17 1288a12–15), if we follow manuscripts that have *polemikon* ('military') rather than *politikon* at 1288a13. On that reading, Aristotle says here: 'a multitude is suitable for polity when nature gives rise to a military multitude that is capable of being ruled and ruling in accordance with a law that distributes offices to those who have resources, in accordance with their merit.' Here 'military' refers back to the point, made at III.7 1279b1–2, that although most people lack virtue in the full sense, they can have the lesser kind of virtue that one learns when one is trained to be a good soldier. (See the previous note.) When Aristotle says here that the citizens of a polity have 'resources', I take him to be implying that the constitutional form he calls polity gives the preponderance of power to the middle class (12.3).

comes to be widely shared by others. But when ordinary people who lack an understanding of well-being have great political influence (as they do in a polity), nothing will make them change their minds about the highest ends of human life. They might rule well, despite their deficiencies. But if they rule, no forces will be set in motion to lead them to a better understanding of their well-being.

11.6. The Feast to which All Contribute

We turn now to Aristotle's discussion, in III.11, of the thesis that the many should be the authoritative element in a city, rather than the few who are best.[18] He begins with the remark that this thesis involves a puzzle, but perhaps also contains some truth (1281a40–2). Since the rest of the chapter rehearses arguments both for and against including the many in political life, we are faced with the difficulty of deciding how much merit he sees in these opposed considerations. The mere fact that he records arguments for popular participation does not mean that he fully or even partially endorses them. We have to look at this chapter as a whole, and also outside it, to see where he stands.

The group of citizens Aristotle is talking about in III.11 is one that contains no one who is practically wise or fully virtuous.[19] And the question he pursues throughout the chapter is this: can they compensate for their individual deficiencies by gathering together and combining their meager skills? Just as 1,000 poor people who pool their savings might exercise greater purchasing power than a single wealthy person, so a group of individuals might share their moral or intellectual resources and do a better job of ruling the city than one person who has practical wisdom. Or, to use Aristotle's analogy, a feast prepared by many hands might be better than one provided by a single person. Similarly, an assembly of ordinary people might make better decisions than a few wise people.

Aristotle's response to this suggestion is that it all depends on who the many are and who the few are (1281b15–21). That seems eminently reasonable. After all, whether the pooled financial resources

---

[18] For a perspective on *Pol.* III.11 that differs in some ways from the one I adopt here, see Waldron, 'The Wisdom of the Multitude'.

[19] His assumption throughout Book III is that when rulers are genuinely virtuous, they are at most a few, and that rule by many always involves a lesser degree of virtue (III.7 1279a39–b4, III.13 1284a3–8, III.17 1288a8–19).

11.6. THE FEAST TO WHICH ALL CONTRIBUTE

of the many exceed those of the few depends on exactly which sums of money we are comparing. Similarly, if the few are truly outstanding in their moral skills, their decisions might be better than the decisions made by a large body of highly defective people. But if the many are not *very* deficient, it might be difficult or impossible to find one person who can do a better job than they. Everything depends on who is being compared with whom.

When Aristotle ends Book III with the conclusion that kingship and aristocracy are the best political systems, he is saying that if one or a few individuals can be found who are sufficiently outstanding, then they should permanently hold high office in the city. He takes this to be too obvious to require argument, and we can easily see why. To say that the few are 'sufficiently outstanding' simply means that the pooled resources of the many do not match that of the king. They will not do as good a job as he. And since it has been assumed throughout Book III that political power should be given to those who will best use it to serve the city, Aristotle takes his conclusion to be obvious and inevitable. A king should rule—if there is a king whose merits outweigh the combined merits of all the others.[20] These are demanding conditions, and few can satisfy them; but Aristotle does not think they are impossible to meet.

Suppose, however, that no such person can be found. Suppose that there are a small number of people who have practical wisdom, and a large number who lack it; but that the skills of the few do not outweigh those of the many. In that case, Aristotle holds that the many should collectively possess authoritative power (*kyrion*: 1281a40). The fact that each member of this group is morally deficient does not show that each should be excluded from playing a major civic role, because the important question is whether each has something worthwhile to contribute to collective decisions. Someone's individual limitations can make him an imperfect deliberator, but the issue Aristotle is discussing is not whether he should be assigned some magistracy or other office in which he has to make political decisions on his own, but whether an important role can be played by a group of such people, when they pool their intellectual and moral resources. And he answers affirmatively because he thinks such resources can be combined. The reason why he favors kingship in Book III is not because he denies that such aggregation can occur,

---

[20] In fact, I believe that Aristotle is making a stronger commitment to kingship than that. I turn to this point in 11.12.

but because he imagines a king to be someone so outstanding that the combined powers of the many are no match for his. Because he agrees that the many can pool their skills, Aristotle can defend his claim that a polity—a city in which the many rule for the common good—is a *correct* political system, while leaving room for his thesis that, in certain circumstances, namely, when a man of kingly abilities is available, a polity is not the *best* political system. The common good can be served even when the vast majority of citizens are individually defective, because when they come together to make collective decisions, they can compensate for their individual deficiencies.

11.7. *The Quality of Collective Decisions*

Why is Aristotle so optimistic about the ability of limited people to overcome their limitations? Why should it not happen that when such people come together to form a group, their *deficiencies* are amplified, and their collective decisions are even worse than their individual choices? At one point in III.11, Aristotle takes note of the suggestion that the many are better at judging music and poetry than the few, because they can practice a division of labor: some judge one part, some another, and in this way the whole group judges all (1281b7–10). This general idea can easily be applied to group decisions in which different people are assigned to gather different kinds of information. The total amount of information gathered by the many might be greater than the information gathered by a few. But this point does not take us very far, for in politics we must make wise decisions and not merely pool facts. If the many have a combination of good moral features and bad, then might not their bad features become even worse, as they come into contact with each other? Or, at any rate, why is the total amount of good and bad in the whole group not simply the sum of the good and bad in each of its members?

We might imagine that Aristotle is expressing his faith in the value of discussion. Perhaps he thinks that when people come together to talk things over, each points out the errors that others are making—errors they would not have discovered on their own. If I can see your deficiencies but not my own, and you have the same combination of blindness and insight, then by joining together we can remove each other's defects. But it would be naive for Aristotle

11.7. THE QUALITY OF COLLECTIVE DECISIONS

to suppose that this is the way discussion inevitably or even typically proceeds. People often cling to the same views they had before they entered into discussion. The collective deliberative process sometimes produces intransigence and increases distrust. There is no reason to assume that Aristotle had no experience of this. Anyone familiar with Greek tragic theater and oratory would have been familiar with the point that we often talk past each other, and magnify distrust with hollow rhetoric.

I suggest that we should not take Aristotle to be saying that *whenever* defective individuals come together as a group, they make good collective decisions. He is making a far more cautious claim: when certain kinds of person come together—namely those whose deficiencies are not great—they can make decisions that promote their common good. Certain kinds of person can enter into a discussion and learn from what others are saying. They recognize that they sometimes make mistakes when they are on their own, and that they need to expose their ideas to public criticism. They are not slavishly submissive to authority, and so they demand reasons; but at the same time, they do not see politics as an arena in which the goal is to get others to submit to their will. People of this sort can learn both from each other and from those who are practically wise. When *these* sorts of person get together, they make good collective decisions, despite their lack of perfect virtue.

What evidence is there for reading Aristotle in this way? He tells us that he is not defending the view that any group of individuals, no matter how debased, will overcome their deficiencies when they meet together (1281b15–21). Furthermore, he talks in terms of people coming together or meeting together (1281b5, 1282a17); and the purpose of coming together surely must be public discussion and not a mere recording of votes that have already been decided upon by each individual. He says that people who are not too deficient should be allowed to share in deliberation and judgment (1281b31), indicating that he is thinking of the familiar legal apparatus of assemblies (where the people deliberate) and courts (where they adjudicate). In the assemblies and courts of the ancient Greek world, voting was preceded by public discussion, and decisions were made only after differences were aired.[21] So we have solid evidence that Aristotle is

---

[21] Athenian courts differed from modern juries in that the jurors (often 501 in number, sometimes more) did not hold a discussion after they had heard opposing arguments, but merely cast their votes. Even so, their duty was to listen to and evaluate competing points of view. In the Athenian assembly, any citizen was allowed to speak.

not talking about a mere aggregation of opinions, but about a process of discussion and debate that is carried out before a final decision is made. His point must be that when deficient people participate in this process, then, so long as they are not too deficient, they are capable of reaching a sound conclusion. And the sorts of deficiency he has in mind must be ones that prevent people from listening to such arguments. The citizens of a polity do not come to court in order to promote their own selfish agenda—to injure an enemy or to reward a friend—but to do what is just and beneficial for the whole city.[22]

11.8. Euthyna *and its Critics*

Some of Aristotle's discussion of rule by the many is guided by his familiarity with the legal institution of *euthyna*, which required public officials to be scrutinized and allowed them to be prosecuted after their term of office was over.[23] In Athens during the fourth century, various kinds of official had to submit their accounts to examination before a court of 501 citizens and show that they had committed no crimes. Any citizen who had an accusation to make against these officials could appear before the court and plead his case.[24] Aristotle's idea that the many can pool information and in this way know as much as or more than a few is meant to apply precisely to this situation. He agrees that when the right sort of people participate, this can be a healthy institution. If the people are themselves corrupt, they will misuse the *euthyna*, bring false accusations, and lie in court. But if they are decent enough, they will address their task in the proper manner, and the court procedure will generally lead to the truth.

Aristotle also considers an argument against the value of this process. It holds that just as in each special field of knowledge it is the experts who should make decisions, so too in the political realm (1281b38–1282a14). To determine whether someone is a good

---

[22] If Aristotle were to subscribe to the thesis that individual deficiencies can always be offset by the size of a group, he would have to grant the right of political participation to slaves. To bar them from citizen status, he must affirm the principle that when deficiencies fall below a certain threshold, they cannot be overcome by a process of mutual correction. Of course, the wish to exclude slaves from political life is not Aristotle's only reason for accepting this principle.

[23] See III.11 1281b33–4, 1282a14, 1282a26–7.

[24] See Hansen, *The Athenian Democracy in the Age of Demosthenes*, pp. 222–4.

doctor, let him be examined by those who are doctors, or at any rate those who have made some special effort to understand medicine. According to opponents of *euthyna*, this argument applies to politics as well: the institution is misguided because it allows ordinary citizens, who have made no study of laws, constitutions, or justice, to sit in judgment of those who have investigated such matters.

Aristotle responds in two ways to this elitist analogy (1282a14–23). First, he simply repeats the point that even if the non-expert is a worse judge than the expert, there is an advantage in combining the judgments of the many. Second, he claims that in some cases the non-expert will be no worse than the expert, and might even be better. For example, someone who lives in a house is better suited to assess its merits and deficiencies than the expert who designed it.

Aristotle's point is simply that it requires no sophisticated study of the law or of political theory to determine whether an official has taken a bribe, or has embezzled funds, or has engaged in some other kind of misconduct. Some things are plainly wrong and can be seen to be wrong by the ordinary person. It is therefore best to allow all citizens to come forward with accusations, so long as they are not so debased as to misuse the legal process. More eyes are better able to watch over the officials than a few.

The same arguments are also applied to *archairesia*, the process of selecting officials.[25] When people get together to decide who should fill various high offices, they pool information about the character and conduct of the people they know best. It does not require political expertise to know that someone is too dishonest to be fit for high public office. And it is better for citizens to hold a discussion of such matters before they vote, because even if each does not know everyone, as a group they know all.

11.9. Hierarchies of Power

Aristotle's argument for popular participation in political deliberation recognizes that people are not equally qualified to hold office and to exercise power. Of course, in the ideal city of Books VII and VIII, all citizens are equally competent and therefore share office in turn. But in III.11 he is considering people as he finds them, not as they might be under ideal conditions. He insists that the ordinary

---

[25] See III.11 1281b33, 1282a26–7.

citizen is not qualified for the highest positions of power (1281b25–8), and his argument indicates why this should be so. He assumes that the ordinary citizen lacks practical wisdom. Therefore, if such a person has to make decisions on his own, and not as a member of a large body, he will go wrong. This is precisely the assumption that sets the problem with which Aristotle is struggling in III.11: how can a citizen who is defective in this way nonetheless play an important role in the city by sharing in collective decisions? The very arguments that support giving the ordinary citizen some role to play in the city's life presuppose that he should not play a larger role than that.

Aristotle also assumes that ordinary citizens will be guided in their deliberations by those who are their superiors. He says at one point that the city benefits when the many are combined with better people, just as food tastes better when it combines pure and rough elements (1281b35–8). *Euthyna*, for example, is a process guided by officials chosen to play this role. In the courtroom and the assembly, there are few speakers; most people simply listen. The few who excel in political matters guide public deliberation, but those who are not experts participate in making the final decision.

It should also be noticed that at one point Aristotle points to a different sort of argument in favor of allowing the many to play a civic role: if many inhabitants think they deserve to participate in the city's life, but are not allowed to do so, there is a danger of revolution (1281b28–30). If citizens want the city to continue to exist, and do not wish to live in perpetual fear, then it will be best to admit ordinary people to citizenship and to give them a role to play in selecting and examining public officials. But this point occupies little space in III.11. The main idea developed throughout the chapter is not that democratizing the city will promote stability, but that it will contribute to the excellence of civic life. The many are given a role to play not merely in order to keep them satisfied, but because this serves as a check on the conduct of powerful officials.

Nonetheless, Aristotle's point about the danger of excluding too many inhabitants from political life will come to play an important role when he discusses imperfect regimes in IV and VI. He frequently makes the point that a city must insure that those who want the constitution to be preserved must outnumber those who favor change.[26] Since non-citizens receive few of the advantages of civic

---

[26] See 10.n.5, 11.n.8.

life, they might join forces with disgruntled citizens and try to overthrow the existing political system. A city can protect itself against this danger by relaxing its standards of citizenship. It might not need those additional citizens, were it not for their revolutionary potential; for the city might already have as many citizens as it requires to punish official misconduct and to pool information about the character and behavior of candidates for office. So, in certain situations, the point Aristotle makes about the danger of a revolution can become the decisive consideration in favor of granting citizenship. He is opposed to giving citizen status to those who would simply use the legal system for their own ends and thus undermine the polis from within. But so long as potential citizens would not have this destructive effect, it may be best for the city to give them a share in civic life.

Aristotle's discussion in III.11 leaves a great deal unsaid about the sort of power that should be granted to the many. He cites with approval the Solonian innovation that allowed them to participate in the selection of officials and in the investigation held at the end of their term of office (1281b32–4). He says that the people should be allowed to be members of the assembly and the courts, but does not say what powers those institutions should have, aside from selecting officials and trying them for misconduct. Should ordinary people make collective decisions about the major issues that face the city? Or should this be left to the officials who are chosen by the many? Aristotle does not answer these questions, and it is easy to see why. He is guided by his general principle that offices—including the office of citizenship—should be filled only by those who are qualified for them. Precisely what the role of the ordinary citizen ought to be will vary from one city to another, for, as he will point out in his discussion of democracy in Books IV and VI, the many do not have the same character in all cities.[27] Sometimes they are good at ruling and being ruled, and are not distant from being good people. In that case, Aristotle has no objection to giving them the power to deliberate about major issues, to make law, and to hold minor offices. But in other circumstances, they are far worse, and should merely choose and oversee their leaders, but do nothing more. All of this is consistent with the position he takes in III.11. This chapter merely argues that so long as someone is not too defective in character, he can play a useful role in a city by choosing and watching over the rulers.

---

[27] See IV.6 1292b25–1293a10, IV.12 1296b28–31, VI.1 1317a24–6, VI.4.

11.10. Kingship and Aristocracy Defined

The leading idea of III.11 is that the many might collectively have qualifications for office that match or even outweigh the qualifications of one person or a few. But as we have just seen, although Aristotle accepts this point, he takes it to be compatible with creating powerful offices and filling them with exceptionally well-qualified individuals. The many can pool their talents by choosing their leaders and evaluating them after their terms of office are over. But the populace may not be well equipped to do more than that.

In later chapters of Book III, Aristotle points out that in some cases the many, even with their pooled information, might be collectively less good at ruling than one extremely skillful individual. Such a superb person should be made the supreme ruler of the city. This idea is first presented in III.13 (1283b21-3, 1284a3-15), and it becomes the central theme of Chapters 17 and 18. But Aristotle's presentation of these issues is hard to follow. He considers a number of plausible arguments against giving extraordinary power to any one person, but then appears in a number of difficult passages to brush these arguments aside and to insist dogmatically that kingship and aristocracy are the best political systems.

Despite the weaknesses of this part of Book III, there should be little doubt about the conclusion Aristotle wishes to draw. Of the three correct political systems—kingship, aristocracy, and polity—he holds that the first two are superior to the third.[28] (He concedes of course that polity is sometimes best—namely, when the city has no one whose extraordinary talents surpass the combined skills of the many.) But when there is someone who has the right qualifications,

---

[28] Chs. 15 and 16 canvass arguments for and against kingship, and the central idea of III.11—that many can do better than one—is revived (III.15 1286a24-1286b1, III.16 1287b11-35). Aristotle also stages a debate about whether law should rule rather than a king (III.15 1286a7-21, III.16 1287a8-b6); we will return to this issue in 12.5. It is important not to lose sight of the last line of III.16: 'What those who dispute about kingship say are mainly these things' (1287b35-6). This makes it clear that Chs. 15 and 16 are an inventory of arguments on both sides, and so we must look to III.17 and III.18 for the conclusion Aristotle draws. And there is no doubt that in these chapters kingship and aristocracy are regarded as superior to rule by the many (III.17 1288a15-29, III.18 1288a39-b2). My reading should be contrasted with one that holds that Book III comes to no decision about the best regime. See e.g. Saxonhouse, *Athenian Democracy*: 'As we proceed through the *Politics*, Aristotle begins to leave behind the concern with the insoluble puzzle of the justice of the various claims to rule. He realizes that the problem [is] incapable of resolution' (p. 130). But note that after Aristotle canvasses all of the arguments against kingship, the position he takes at the end of III.13 (1284b22-34)—that it would be unjust to ostracize a kingly person—is reaffirmed (III.17 1288a24-9).

11.10. KINGSHIP AND ARISTOCRACY DEFINED

others ought gladly allow him to have complete control over the city's affairs. Such a city will be better ruled than any other—unless there are several such extraordinary individuals, in which case they should share power. These two systems—kingship and aristocracy—are the best regimes.[29]

Aristotle should not be taken to mean that in a kingship or an aristocracy the many play no active political role at all. The king is likely to need assistants, and so there will be other offices besides his. That is a point made near the end of III.16 (1287b29–30), where Aristotle is rehearsing some of the arguments against kingship. When he comes to the conclusion, in III.17–18, that this is nonetheless the best constitution, he need not be taken to be rejecting the point, made earlier, that there will be lower offices than that of the king. And we should recall (10.3) that in III.4, Aristotle assumes that in the best constitution some will rule permanently, and others will rotate into and out of lower offices. So the sort of kingship he is presumably talking about in the closing chapters of Book III is one in which a king rules over politically active citizens.

Nonetheless, those holders of lower offices are merely assistants to the king, and do not serve as a check on his power. That is why Aristotle speaks of this sort of monarch as someone who 'does everything in accordance with his own wish' (III.16 1287a1–2). In such a political system, there is no court or assembly that meets to scrutinize the behavior of the king. Nor does he need to secure the agreement of anyone else before he acts. (In an aristocracy, there will be several people who are equally extraordinary in political ability. Ruling as a council, they might need each other's agreement, but their decisions would not be reviewed by the many.)

The kind of monarchy that constitutes the best constitution is the fifth form of kingship discussed in III.14: it places unrestricted power in the hands of a king who is 'sovereign in all matters' (1285b29–30). In III.16, it is called a 'total kingship' (*pambasileia*, 1287a8–9).[30] Aristotle discusses a number of other kinds of kingship

---

[29] In what follows I will occasionally, for the sake of brevity, speak as though kingship is the one best regime. One of the arguments canvassed in III.15 holds that aristocracy is better than kingship (1286b2–7), but since III.17–18 do not sustain this point, it is not an argument Aristotle can endorse. His final conclusion in Book III is that when there is one kingly person, he should rule; when several, they should share rule; and there is no reason to wish for one of these situations rather than the other. In the *Nicomachean Ethics* he holds that rule by one person is best (VIII.10 1160a35–6); we will discuss his reason for this preference in 11.15.

[30] Less literally, 'absolute kingship'.

in III.14, but only in order to set them aside as irrelevant to his purpose. The role of king is always one of considerable power, but where he does not have *complete* control over decision-making, his rule does not constitute a distinctive kind of regime. What is essential to kingship, in Aristotle's taxonomy of constitutions, is precisely the total control possessed by one person. (What is distinctive of aristocracy is that, although power is distributed equally among a few, those few have total control over all others.)

By contrast, when the many rule, power is more widely distributed: although there may be a few positions of great power, the assembly chooses these leaders for limited terms and reviews their conduct in the courts. Philosophically and politically, the interesting contrast is not threefold but twofold: between rule by the many on the one hand and rule by one or a few on the other. For in the kind of aristocracy Aristotle describes in Book III, power is not divided among the few in order to guard against its abuse; it is divided only because there are several extraordinary individuals who share it. The real issue Aristotle raises is not whether to have an aristocracy or a kingship, but whether anyone should have as much power as is possessed by the rulers of either of these two constitutions. By linking kingship and aristocracy in the final chapters of Book III and considering them as a group, Aristotle shows that he understands that they raise the same issue, and that their similarities are far more important than their differences.[31] He recognizes and overcomes the limited value of classifying constitutions in terms of rule of one, few, and many. Similarly, in Books IV–VI he holds that there are no significant differences between the three worst regimes—tyranny of the one, of the few, or of the many (10.n.15). The sixfold classificatory system of Book III (three correct regimes, three incorrect) eventually leads to a more complex and illuminating taxonomy: (A) kingship–aristocracy, (B) mixtures (polity, moderate oligarchy, moderate democracy), (C) and tyrannies (of one, many, and few). And finally a fourth type is added: the ideal city of VII and VIII, which, as in kingships and aristocracy, is ruled by the correct conception of the good, but as in the mixtures, is ruled by many.

At several points in his discussion Aristotle speaks in terms of a family of kingly people. He says, for example, that kingship is appropriate for a population that naturally produces a family that is

---

[31] This does not mean that there is no reason at all to choose one over the other. Recall that at *NE* VIII.10 1160a35–6, Aristotle affirms the superiority of kingship to aristocracy (and see 11.15 for discussion).

outstanding in virtue (III.17 1288a8–9).³² What he seems to mean is that the condition most favorable to kingship is one in which a city contains a family that produces generation after generation of outstanding leaders. Each new king rules because he has the qualifications to do so, and not merely because he is the son of the former king. The best situation one could hope for (among traditional regimes) is a kingship that is transmitted from one generation to another and thus endures for a very long time. Aristotle assumes that if this extraordinary situation exists, it will come about because conditions produce a family that far surpasses all others in its ability to produce outstanding offspring. But he does not go so far as to say that there should be a king only if the person who is exceptional enough to qualify comes from such a family.³³ What makes someone suitable to be king is simply his qualifications as an individual, and so whenever a populace recognizes that it has such a person in its midst, it should give him the extraordinary powers of a king.³⁴

11.11. Kingship and Trust

Aristotle rehearses a number of arguments against kingship. A single human being is liable to make poor decisions when he is overcome by anger, whereas a large group making a collective decision is less vulnerable to such irrationality (III.15 1286a31–5). Even if someone is qualified to be king, he will be unable to resist the temptation to transfer power to his son, who may be poorly qualified (1286b22–7). And even if someone is not vulnerable to these weaknesses, he cannot make decisions as well as a large group, just as a meal prepared by a single hand is inferior to a feast to which many contribute (III.15 1286a26–31, III.16 1287b25–36). Evidently, Aristotle is not swayed by these arguments, because in III.17 and III.18 he concludes that kingship and aristocracy are superior to any other form of government. As we have seen, the type of kingship he has in mind gives absolute power to one person. Though there will be inferior officials who aid the king, no institutions or legal safeguards

---

³² See too III.18 1288a35. In III.17 (1288a6–12) the distinction he attempts to draw between kingship and aristocracy is perplexing. For discussion, see 11.n.43.

³³ At III.17 1288a15–19 he seems to be implying that kingship can be justified even when there is no such family.

³⁴ At III.13 1284a3–17 and 1284b25–34 Aristotle speaks only of individual qualifications, not of membership in an extraordinary family.

restrain or dilute his authority. Why does Aristotle come to the astonishing conclusion that this is the best among traditional forms of government?

Part of the answer must be that he transforms the objections to kingship into conditions that must be met by the king. Individuals are susceptible to anger and favoritism; granted, but that means that in order to qualify as a king one must not have such susceptibilities. Groups may make better decisions than individuals; true, but that means that if we ever give someone kingly power, he must have abilities that outstrip those of groups. Aristotle concedes that it is human to have weaknesses, but he infers not that absolute power is ill advised but that a king must be a god among men (III.13 1284b28–34). It is not impossible for such an extraordinary individual to exist; and if he does, it would be unjust to treat him as a mere equal (III.17 1288a24–9).

We should not think that if citizens accept a kingship, they renounce their powers of critical judgment and promise to obey the king no matter what he commands. That would be slavish, and Aristotle could never approve of such a transformation: a good citizen must know both how to rule and be ruled *as a free man* (III.4 1277b13–16). (See 10.3 and 10.8 for discussion.) In establishing or accepting a kingship, the citizens decide that they have so much trust and confidence in the king's moral and intellectual skills that they do not need a constitution that limits his power and provides a method to oversee his conduct. They do not give him a limited term, or establish a procedure by which he may be prosecuted, or appoint officials who will restrict his authority. The reason why they forego these legal safeguards is because, in view of the king's character and ability, they would be inappropriate. Such a legal system would express distrust, but the sort of person Aristotle thinks ought to be king is precisely the sort who can be trusted completely.

Although citizens may reasonably express their trust in this way, in doing so they do not surrender their intelligence. When they obey the king, they do so as free men who are capable of understanding on their own what should and should not be done. The king's commands are not subject to any legal control, but they must still prove themselves in the minds of the citizens. It is not impossible that they were mistaken in giving so much power to one person, and if they discover that they were, they can try to change the political system they established. Of course, it would have been better had they not made this mistake; but if they discover that it was a mistake, there is no reason why they should compound it by continuing to obey someone who is not fit to have so much power over them. Aristotle never speaks of a promise to obey the king; the only justification for his rule is his merit, and so if he does not have the merit they supposed he had, nothing binds them to obedience.

We might object to Aristotle's defense of kingship by saying that placing legal limits on the power of any official is a reasonable way for ordinary citizens to protect themselves. Even when we have great confidence in someone's abilities, it would be foolish to grant him unlimited powers and to forego institutions that investigate and punish his abuse of power. For, as we just noted, it is always possible to misjudge someone's character and skills; however much confidence we have in him, we may be wrong. And it is also possible that over time his character will change for the worse. Since no harm is done in establishing courts or other devices to review his conduct, and much harm might occur if we forego such protection, giving someone unrestricted power would be foolhardy.

But Aristotle does not agree that no harm is done by subjecting the king to such oversight and threatening him with punishment if he misbehaves. To see his point of view, consider this analogy: suppose a husband and a wife hire private detectives to assure themselves of each other's fidelity. If neither has reason to suspect the other, such precautions would be not only foolish but unjust. In personal relations, safeguards against misbehavior express distrust, and such distrust may be undeserved and destroy our relationships. Aristotle believes that the same holds true of political life. Normally, it is appropriate to have less than complete confidence in public officials, but Aristotle claims that a leader might be so extraordinary that expressing distrust by establishing legal safeguards against misbehavior would be an injustice.

We may respond by saying that politics and personal relations are separate realms, and therefore different practices are appropriate to each. But if that is all we can say against kingship, are we not begging the question against Aristotle? Different circumstances call for different political systems. Why not acknowledge that how many legal safeguards we need depends on how much distrust is appropriate, and that this varies from one situation to another?

11.12. Kingship versus Polity

Suppose we concede, for the sake of argument, that in certain circumstances it would be appropriate to give one person kingly powers. That still does not show that a kingship is a better system of government than rule by the many. Kingship may be just when there is a kingly person; aristocracy when there are several such persons; and when there are none, a polity is the best form of government. But why say that one of these political systems is better than the others? Or, to reformulate our question (since Aristotle does not claim in *Pol.* III that kingship is superior to aristocracy): why are kingship and aristocracy better than polity?

We might be tempted to reply: if someone exists who deserves to be a king, then, by virtue of the very fact that he merits this position, he is better at ruling than any existing combination of people. And so, in these circumstances, a kingship is obviously better than a polity. This is perfectly true, but it does not answer our question. For it is equally true that in different circumstances—namely, when no one has kingly abilities—the collective wisdom of a group of people is better than the individual wisdom of any one of them; and in this case polity is better than kingship. What we want to know is why Aristotle thinks that the circumstances that call for kingship or aristocracy are the best circumstances that we can hope for. Admittedly, when there are no kingly persons, polity is best. But Aristotle thinks that, even in their absence, we should wish we had such extraordinary individuals in our midst, for their rule would constitute the best political system. Our question is: *why* should we wish for this? After all, both kingship and polity aim at the common good. Why then should one be better than the other?

If we think that the only relevant difference between these regimes is that the former is rule by one and the latter rule by many, we cannot answer our question. For why should mere numerical difference constitute a difference in quality? And even if we suppose that the king is superior in quality to each individual included among the many, we still cannot answer our question, because Aristotle has himself pointed out that collective skill can outstrip a single individual's skill. To solve our problem, we must return to an idea proposed earlier in this chapter (11.4): Aristotle assumes that in a polity many citizens lack a full understanding of the good. Competing conceptions of well-being exist in such a city, and so, although the citizens look to a single common good when they make collective decisions, this common good is not the full realization of human powers, but the actualization of less exalted skills, the kinds of skill that Aristotle has in mind when he refers to the virtue of a good citizen.

It would be far better for civic matters to be under the control of someone who fully understands human well-being, and who is acknowledged by all other members of the community to possess that kind of wisdom. That is why Aristotle thinks that we should wish for the existence of someone who has such kingly abilities. A polity can avoid civic strife and instill a second-best kind of virtue in the citizens, but it can do no better than this. However well the many rule, they will never be able to produce anything better than civic virtue. The strength of their numbers can never compensate for this deficiency. They can exercise power for the common good, and by pooling information, they can protect the city against corrupt officials. But Aristotle is convinced that a city can accomplish far more than this, if it is guided by a single fully realized person, someone whose skill in making decisions is informed by deep insight into human well-being, and whose emotional life meets the exacting standards spelled out in the *Ethics*.

11.13. *Utopia Transformed?*

Our discussion in this chapter of kingship, aristocracy, and polity has confirmed the point (made in 10.1) that there is a great difference between the ideal city of Books VII and VIII and the three correct political systems of Book III. In the city of VII and VIII, all citizens are fully virtuous and understand the good. All share equally in ruling and being ruled, and there is no king or ruling elite. By contrast, in Book III Aristotle describes two types of good regime, and neither corresponds to the ideal found in VII and VIII. One type is a polity, a city ruled by citizens many of whom lack a proper understanding of the good. A better regime is an aristocracy or a kingship, for in these constitutions political power is not shared equally among all citizens but is concentrated without restriction in the hands of a few. In kingships and aristocracies, the many who are ruled accept the conception of well-being held by their rulers, but do not have a full understanding of it; they have true beliefs about happiness, but lack practical wisdom (III.4 1277b25–9). The assumption of Book III is that if a city is to be ruled by those who are fully virtuous, their numbers must be small, and power must be unequally distributed. In Books VII and VIII, this assumption is absent. How can we explain this difference? I proposed an answer to that question in 10.1, but now that we have become more familiar with the contents of Book III, let us raise it once again. For we are now in a better position to weigh the merits of alternative answers.

It might be suggested that when Aristotle wrote Book III, he was assuming the existence of someone who had the extraordinary powers of a king—perhaps Philip of Macedon or his son Alexander (1.2).[35] And, to continue with this hypothesis, we might say that when he wrote Books VII and VIII he was not so impressed with Philip, or Philip was no longer alive. But this proposal has little to recommend it. Book III says *both* (A) that if there is a kingly person, he should be given absolute power, *and* (B) that if there is none, the many should rule. If the mere mention of (A) were a hint that there is such a person, then by parity of reasoning the mention of (B) would hint that there is none. And in any case, appealing to Aristotle's relationship with Philip, whatever it was, offers no help in answering the question we have raised: why does Aristotle think in Book III but not in Books VII and VIII that only a small number of people can understand what happiness is?

A second sort of explanation would simply be that Aristotle changed his mind and moved to a more optimistic position (if VII and VIII were conceived after III) or a more pessimistic position (if they were conceived in the reverse order). For VII and VIII are certainly more optimistic. In Book III Aristotle holds that in the best city either the rulers will lack full understanding of the common good, or those who are ruled will have true opinion but not practical wisdom. By contrast, in VII and VIII, all citizens have practical wisdom—and that, of course, is a better situation than either of the alternatives discussed in III. So perhaps Aristotle simply allowed himself to express a more hopeful wish, as he grew older (assuming that VII and VIII are later); or perhaps (if III is later) he lowered his sights as he aged.

But this conjecture contains little of substance: in suggesting that Aristotle became more pessimistic or optimistic, it merely redescribes the differences between III and VII and VIII, without providing a real explanation for them. To say that Aristotle became

---

[35] Or perhaps he wanted to let the Macedonian kings suppose that he had them in mind. For this reading, see Kelsen, 'Aristotle and Hellenic-Macedonian Policy', pp. 177–8.

11.13. UTOPIA TRANSFORMED?

increasingly optimistic or pessimistic is simply another way of saying that his description of the ideal constitution changed, and that one of his portraits paints a happier picture than the other. But what we want to know is why this change occurred, and the reply that he became more optimistic or pessimistic does not provide a satisfying answer to this question.

Here is a third possibility. It would be difficult to contemplate Aristotle's two alternatives in Book III—rule by a few, who are wise, or rule by the many, who lack full understanding—without bringing Plato to mind. For the *Republic* describes a city ruled by a wise minority, whereas the *Laws* portrays a city ruled by a multitude who lack full understanding. Although Aristotle never shows sympathy for the thesis, advocated by Plato in the *Republic*, that a training in mathematics and philosophical dialectic is a necessary prelude to the acquisition of political wisdom, he nonetheless expresses in Book III of the *Politics* a highly aristocratic and elitist point of view: he assumes without argument that there cannot be enough of the wise to fill a whole city; insight into the good can be achieved by only a few. Plato proposes a philosophical explanation for this restriction: only a small number of people will ever have the moral and intellectual skills needed to learn as much mathematics, science, and dialectic as are needed to understand the good. In Book III, Aristotle simply assumes that Plato is right about the numbers—wisdom is always the possession of a few—even though he lacks Plato's epistemological grounding for this numerical bias. In other words, Book III seems to be guided by an unthinking elitism on Aristotle's part: wisdom and virtue are necessarily restricted to a small number. We might conjecture that in Books VII and VIII he realizes that this is mere prejudice on his part. In order to correct his error, he returns to the project of depicting utopia, and drops his earlier assumption that if a city is to be ruled by the virtuous, their number must be small.

But this proposal, like the others we have considered, provides no real explanation for the differences we find between Book III and Books VII and VIII. If Book III reveals a Platonic bias that has no grounding in Aristotle's epistemology, then what process of philosophical growth led him to discover that error? What prevented him from recognizing his bias at an early stage of his thinking, and how was he able to uncover it at a later point in his life? The hypothesis under consideration provides no answers to these questions, and none is possible. In effect, then, it merely calls the views of Book III a form of Platonism, and notes the absence of that Platonism in Books VII and VIII.

The unsatisfactory nature of the three hypotheses we have considered should lead us back to our original conjecture with renewed confidence. We should not think of Book III and Books VII and VIII as opposed conceptions of the best constitution, but as different practical enterprises. Book III is an examination of the merits of traditional political systems, and is not a proposal for the transformation of civic life. That is why Aristotle assumes in Book III that, in one way or another, one will have to accept serious imperfections even in well-governed cities. The correct conception of well-being is not widely accepted, and so if the many rule, we will have to make do with their lack of practical wisdom. The best we can hope for is rule by those who have fully realized their capacities for intellectual and emotional development. Even in that case, most of our fellow citizens will be people who merely have correct beliefs, but lack wisdom, about the highest ends of human life. In the absence of institutions that morally educate the whole citizenry, we will have to settle for kingship, aristocracy, or polity. All of them are fine political systems, but only when they are compared with their corrupt counterparts. It is only in Books VII and VIII that Aristotle allows himself free rein to go beyond the limitations of traditional constitutions, and to design a colony in which all citizens, not just a few, have a full understanding of human well-being, and have all of the resources needed to make that conception of happiness a reality.[36]

11.14. Beyond Utopia

Remarkably, Aristotle leaves room in his taxonomy of constitutions for a kind of political system that would be even better than the one

---

[36] The interpretation I have defended should be contrasted with that of Schütrumpf on the one hand and Keyt on the other. Schütrumpf holds that Aristotle's constitutional preferences in Book III conflict with those of Books VII and VIII, and infers that these portions of the *Politics* were written at different times. See *Aristoteles Politik, Buch I*, pp. 39–67, esp. p. 50. Keyt holds that, according to Aristotle, kingship and the city of Books VII and VIII are equally good, each being appropriate to different circumstances. See 'Aristotle's Theory of Distributive Justice', esp. p. 257. Keyt does not discuss *NE* VIII.10 1160a35–6, where kingship is declared the best of the 6 standard constitutions. (We will turn to that passage in 11.15.) Since he regards the ideal regime of *Politics* VII and VIII as the constitution that Aristotle calls an aristocracy in *Politics* III, Keyt ought to take 1160a35–6 to mean that the city of VII and VIII is not the best possible regime—even though Aristotle declares it to be such in these books.

he describes in Books VII and VIII. The only objection that can be made to this better-than-best regime is a formidable one: it would require the existence of a race of godlike beings, individuals blessed with virtues far beyond what is possible for mere human beings. By definition, they would not be human, for if such models of perfection existed, they would have qualities of mind none of us can have. For all practical purposes, such a regime cannot be realized; it is beyond our highest hopes. Nonetheless, it is imaginable, and, as we will see, imagining it—that is, leaving a place for it in our categories of thought—has some practical value.[37]

Such a political system would be a kingship (if one of these godlike beings ruled) or an aristocracy (if several did), but it would be a special kind of kingship or aristocracy that goes beyond the regimes Aristotle has in mind in Book III. As we have seen, he assumes there that in a kingship or aristocracy many of the citizens are good citizens but not fully virtuous human beings, since they lack practical wisdom. But now let us imagine a kingship that lacks this defect: suppose all the citizens of a city have practical wisdom, but one of them has superhuman ethical virtues that entirely set him apart from all others. That, according to Aristotle, would be the best imaginable political system. But since it is not a practical possibility, and since VII and VIII is an exploration of the best *possible* constitution,[38] he gives this extraordinary sort of regime scant consideration. It is briefly mentioned at the beginning of VII.14, where we are told that if there were some who are like gods and heroes, surpassing all others in both body and soul, so that their superiority would manifest itself in every way, then they alone should rule (1332b16–23). His point is that when all the citizens have practical wisdom, they would tolerate permanent subordination to others only if those others were a race apart, so that their physical appearance by itself served as a reliable mark of their psychological eminence. They would not simply be extraordinarily virtuous and talented in the art of ruling; in body and soul, they would be a different species altogether.

Why would such a constitution be better than the more realistic system Aristotle describes at length in VII and VIII? Two compatible answers suggest themselves. First, he is committed to the notion that in principle rule should be awarded to any single individual or

---

[37] See 6.10 and 6.11 for discussion of this superhuman ideal.
[38] See II.6 1265a17–18, VII.1 1323a18–19, VII.4 1325b39.

group of individuals whose skill at ruling surpasses that of all others combined. So even if a city contains several thousand men who possess practical wisdom, it is still theoretically possible that they can be surpassed by some smaller group. Second, as we saw in our examination of the ideal city (6.3), Aristotle thinks that ruling is not a wholly welcome activity, because it is unleisurely and burdensome. It creates a need for rest, and is not what we would choose to do with our leisure. We need to put something in our lives besides the endless cycle of rest and work. This cannot be political activity, which is a virtuous form of work, but work nonetheless. In fact, it would be an improvement in our lot if we could somehow entirely escape from politics, and spend all of our time in the leisurely enjoyment of music, science, and philosophy. Were we ruled by a race of superhumans, we would be entirely free to live a philosophical or quasi-philosophical life.[39]

In this way, Aristotle retains, even in Books VII and VIII, the notion that rule by one or a few is the best political system—so long as that one or those few are truly extraordinary. But in VII and VIII, the demands made on those extraordinary few have been raised: not only must they be superior in soul, but they must have a corresponding superiority in body, so that their distinctness from the human race is manifest to all.[40] By insisting upon this new requirement, Aristotle makes it clear that the possibility of such a situation is not worth taking seriously. All of his intellectual energy is focused on a more feasible ideal—a city full of practically wise citizens who govern themselves. By contrast, in Book III he is not yet considering the possibility that there could be such a city. There, where he restricts

---

[39] The citizens who live in this super-ideal city can still be called political animals, but only in the sense that they have an impulse to live in a large community. See 7.2.

[40] In Book III, Aristotle requires that those who rule in a kingship or aristocracy have a kind of virtue that is beyond what is human, so that it is fitting to call them gods (III.13 1284a10–11, b31). But this simply means that they are extraordinarily virtuous human beings (cf. NE VII.1 1245a25–30). He does not require that they also have different bodies, so that they are an entirely different race. Nothing he says in Book III rules out the possibility that, in his opinion, some human beings have or have had the godlike qualities needed to be genuine kings. To deserve kingship is to be sufficiently superior to one's contemporaries, so it is possible that in earlier and simpler times there were men who were proper monarchs but who would not be so now. See III.15 1286b8–10. To deserve kingship in fourth-century Greece, where, in Aristotle's opinion, there are a few individuals who have practical wisdom, would be extraordinary but not impossible. But to deserve kingship in the community posited in VII and VIII, where *all* citizens have practical wisdom, would be a situation beyond any realistic expectation. Aristotle takes it to be obvious that there have never been individuals who have both the physical and psychological superiority spoken of in VII.14. That is why kingship is taken to be a real though remote possibility in III, whereas VII and VIII merely imagine the possibility of a city ruled by superhuman beings.

himself to traditional regimes, he pins his highest hopes on kingship and aristocracy, and does not insist that the extraordinary few who rule such cities be a race apart, different from us not only in soul but in body.

It should be noted that in his ethical works Aristotle retains as a category of thought the concept of a being whose ethical virtue goes beyond what mere humans can do. In *Ethics* VII.1, he talks of a 'virtue that is beyond us, something heroic and divine' (1145a19–20), but gives no details about how a being possessing such virtue would differ from those who have the virtues described at such length throughout his work. Yet a reader of the *Ethics* might well be puzzled by the category of superhuman virtue. If someone has practical wisdom, justice, temperance, courage, and all the other excellent qualities Aristotle discusses in this work, is he not already perfect? How can anyone be better than that?

The best way to answer this question is to remind ourselves of the legal safeguards Aristotle recommends for the city of Books VII and VIII. Its citizens are ethically virtuous, but even so, their judgment can sometimes be distorted by extraneous factors. Each owns two lots of land, one near the periphery and the other near the center, because without this arrangement exposure to risk would be unevenly distributed, and agreement more difficult to achieve (VII.10 1330a9–23). Furthermore, even in this ideal city, punishments are prescribed for certain crimes, because it is assumed that virtuous people will at times be tempted to act in ways that conflict with the common good.[41] Aristotle's assumption is that even the best of us is better able to lead a virtuous life if the institutions of our community restrict us and aid us in ways that supplement our individual efforts. A fully virtuous person can generally be relied upon to do the right thing for the right reason, for his mind and his emotions have been properly educated; but we would not stop calling someone a good person simply because he occasionally goes astray and needs to be regulated by laws.[42] Someone who needs no external

---

[41] See *Pol.* VII.8 1328b7–9, VII.16 1335b38–1336a2, VII.17 1336b8–12.

[42] According to one of the arguments given in favor of the rule of law, even virtuous human beings can be led astray by passion and appetite (III.15 1286a17–20, III.16 1287a28–32). Aristotle's conclusion in III.17–18 that kingship and aristocracy are the best constitutions, and that rulers in these regimes do not need to be restricted by laws (III.13 1284a13–14), shows that he allows a small number of exceptions. But he can agree that for the most part human beings—even those who have the ethical virtues—need to be restricted by law. Only someone whose virtue is more than human is without this need. For further discussion of the rule of law, see 12.5.

inducement to be virtuous, who can be relied upon never to go astray regardless of the circumstances, is a theoretical possibility, but were such a person to exist, he would have a nature higher than human. Recognizing the ideality of kingship has at least this much practical value: by seeing what someone would have to be like in order to merit such a position, we at the same time come to appreciate the limits of ordinary human nature.

11.15. *The Superiority of Kingship to Aristocracy*

As we have seen, in Book III of the *Politics* Aristotle does not come to the conclusion that kingship is superior to aristocracy or that aristocracy is superior to kingship. In III.17–18 they are treated as equally good alternatives. The only significant difference between them is the one that he affirms throughout Book III: kingship is rule by one, aristocracy rule by few (III.7 1279a25–31).[43] The impression we are left with, when Book III comes to an end, is that this numerical difference is insignificant. Furthermore, nothing in VII.14 hints that one of these systems would be better than the other. He merely says that if there were a superhuman race, it should rule (1332b16–23), leaving open the question of how many such individuals there might be. Presumably he thinks that their number does not matter.

---

[43] Aristotle affirms again in III.13 that the sole difference between these two regimes is the number of rulers (1284a3–5). Unfortunately, he expresses himself in a confusing way when he makes a further distinction between them at III.17 1288a6–12. Here he says that (a) a multitude (*plēthos*) fit to be ruled by a king is one that produces a *family* (*genos*) that is superior in virtue, whereas (b) a multitude fit to be ruled aristocratically is one that produces a multitude 'capable of being ruled in a way that suits free people' by those who are superior leaders. Here Aristotle assumes that ideally a kingship will endure over many generations, and that this is most likely to occur when one outstanding family continues to produce outstanding leaders. By contrast, he does not characterize aristocracy in terms of a single outstanding family: what it needs is superior leaders (not necessarily related by blood). Unfortunately, he muddies the contrast by referring in (b) to the ordinary citizens who are subordinate to the ruling aristocrats: they are a multitude of free men generated by a larger multitude of free men and women. The point he is trying to bring out is that even though the rulers of an aristocracy need not come from a single family, inherited capacities nonetheless play an important role in such a regime—namely, the inherited capacities of those ruled. (Further confusion is created by the fact that some editors of the text substitute *genos* (family, stock) for the second occurrence of *plēthos* (multitude) in (b).) In any case, at III.18 1288a32–6, he indicates that the superiority of kingship does not depend on its being transmitted across the generations. He says that the best among the three correct constitutions is the one in which the best rule—whether that best is one person, a whole family, or a multitude. If it is a multitude—a plurality of unrelated people—it is an aristocracy; if a whole family, it is a hereditary kingship; and if just one person, a kingship that lasts only for the lifetime of the king. The most significant feature of these two passages is that he does not opt for kingship or aristocracy, but treats them as equals.

11.15. THE SUPERIORITY OF KINGSHIP TO ARISTOCRACY

But in the *Ethics*, Aristotle holds that the rule of one person is superior to the rule of a few (VIII.10 1160a35–6). The classificatory scheme he invokes in VIII.10–11 is the simple division used in Book III of the *Politics*: there are three acceptable constitutions—kingship, aristocracy, and timocracy;[44] and three deviations—tyranny, oligarchy, and democracy (VIII.10 1160a31–b21). The acceptable constitutions differ from each other numerically, as do the deviations. Of these, kingship is best, but unfortunately Aristotle does not explicitly say why, here or elsewhere. Nonetheless, he gives us one important indication in this chapter of why he makes this assumption: he says that democracy is the least bad of the corrupt constitutions (1160b19–21). Although he does not here explain why this is so, he says several times in Books IV–VI of the *Politics* that democracy is a better form of government than oligarchy because it is less susceptible to faction.[45] Those who accept the ideology of democracy treat each other as equals and direct their animosity against the rich, whereas oligarchs fight not only with democrats but among themselves. So there is less injustice in a democracy than in an oligarchy, and far less than in a tyranny.

Let us now bring this point to bear on the question we raised. We want to know why kingship is better than aristocracy. These are regimes in which those who rule—the solitary king or the few aristocrats—are equally good men. Aristotle cannot be implying that kingship is better than aristocracy because rule by a few is always rule by those who are inferior to a king. Nonetheless, there is an obvious advantage that rule by one has over rule by a few, even when all the individuals involved in the comparison are equally virtuous. When a few share power, ruling is more difficult, because they must coordinate their plans and make joint decisions. Once a king makes a decision, the matter is settled, and there is no possibility of division within the sovereign power. But when several share power, no one ruler can assume that his way of thinking is exactly like another's; there is always the possibility of disagreement and a need to resolve differences.[46] Rule by one is therefore easier than rule by a

---

[44] This is the term Aristotle uses at *NE* VIII.10 1160a34 in place of 'polity' for correct rule of the many. It derives from his assumption that this regime imposes a property qualification (*timēma*) on citizens.

[45] See 12.4 for textual references and discussion.

[46] This argument in favor of kingship is rehearsed at III.15 1286b1–2. Aristotle presents a counter-argument in the next few lines (b2–7), and the issue is left unresolved (III.16 1287b35–6). If, as I have assumed, *NE* postdates the *Politics* (1.5), then *NE* VIII.10 shows that he eventually decided the issue in favor of kingship.

few—and for the very same reason that democracy is better than oligarchy. Democrats are more likely to arrive at a consensus than oligarchs. And what can be more productive of consensus than rule by one?[47]

---

[47] If this explanation for the superiority of kingship is correct, we have further reason to suppose that even the ideal city of Books VII and VIII will need the principle of majority rule. See 6.11.

12

Politics IV–VI: Non-Ideal Constitutions

12.1. The Four Branches of Politics

We turn now to Books IV–VI of the *Politics*. Here Aristotle turns away from the study of ideal constitutions and focuses instead on the limitations and conflicts of ordinary political life. But it is important not to make the mistake of isolating these books from the others—as though their realistic study of corrupt regimes had nothing to do with the rest of Aristotle's political philosophy. It is clear that IV–VI take III as their starting point and are intended to complete the project begun there. The earlier book leads to the conclusion that kingship and aristocracy are the best regimes, and the later books therefore move on to the other political systems that have not yet been discussed: polity, democracy, oligarchy, and tyranny.[1] Although Aristotle takes the study of ideal and defective

---

[1] See IV.2 1289a26–31, where Aristotle refers back to the sixfold taxonomy of constitutions introduced in III.7. Similarly, in IV.10 (1295a4–5, a7–8) he alludes to his treatment of kingship and tyranny in III.14 (1285a14–b3). I find no passages in IV–VI that are best interpreted as referring to VII and VIII. (The proper order of the books of the *Politics* is an issue we considered in 5.2.) The sentence of IV.2 in which Aristotle refers to his sixfold taxonomy goes on to point out that aristocracy and kingship have already been discussed (1289a30–1). This can easily be read as a reference to III.17–18, and is less plausibly construed as a reference to VII and VIII. (It should be kept in mind that in VII and VIII Aristotle does not call the city he constructs an aristocracy. He shows no interest in the question of how it fits into his classificatory scheme.) At IV.3 1290a1–3, he says that in his treatment of aristocracy he has enumerated the necessary parts of every polis. The context suggests that he

regimes to be distinct components of political science, he never suggests that these are subjects that can or should be studied in isolation from each other. When we examine Books IV–VI more closely, we will see how much light ideal and non-ideal studies shed on each other.[2]

Aristotle begins Book IV with the announcement of a program: just as a physical trainer must not restrict himself to examining the ideal condition of the human body, so too a student of politics must survey many other types of constitution besides the one that is best. In addition to discussing (A) the ideal regime, political science must also study:

B which constitution is 'suitable for which' cities (1288b24);

C the 'assumed constitution' (b28);

D the constitution that is 'most suitable for all cities' (b34–5).

These are not perspicuous descriptions, but if we examine IV.1 carefully, and also consider the way these phrases are used in the remainder of Book IV, we can grasp his meaning easily enough.

Let us begin with (D). This part of political science corresponds to that component of physical training that studies 'for all bodies, which single training suits most of them' (b15). Barring extraordinary circumstances, the ideal physical regimen is beyond the reach of most human beings, and so for practical purposes the trainer must lower his sights. He considers the types of body human beings

---

is thinking of necessary parts that make competing claims to power—rich, poor, craftsmen, prominent people, virtuous people, and so on—and these parts of the city have been discussed in III.12–13. (An alternative interpretation is to take IV.3 1290a1–3 to be an allusion to VII.8 1328b2–23, but the latter passage is not about rival claimants to office.) It is understandable that Aristotle should designate Book III as his discussion of aristocracy, since the conclusion to which the whole book leads is that aristocracy (construed generically to include kingship as well) is the best constitution. For this broad use of 'aristocracy', see V.10 1310b2–3, b31–2. There is one other passage in Book IV that refers back to a previous discussion of aristocracy: IV.7 1293b1–7; here Aristotle leans heavily on the argument of III.4–5, so he is best taken to mean that Book III was a treatment of aristocracy. For a contrasting interpretation, see the introduction to Lord's translation of the *Politics*, p. 16 and pp. 245–6, n. 43; and the footnotes to Simpson's translation of the passages discussed here. See too 10.n.9 on the awkwardness of inserting VII and VIII between III and IV–VI.

[2] The fact that in IV.1 Aristotle instructs his readers to view ideal and non-ideal politics as components of a single study is evidence against Jaeger's thesis (5.1) that they conflict. He claims that in IV.1 'Aristotle felt a certain difficulty in combining Plato's Utopian speculations with this purely empirical treatment... He tried to escape by pointing to the analogy of a double form of medicine and gymnastics... Throughout the introduction to the empirical part one can scarcely help feeling that there is an undertone of polemic against the mere construction of ideals...' See *Aristotle*, p. 269. The fact that Jaeger must appeal to an 'undertone' that he detects in Aristotle's words, and not the words themselves, reflects the weakness of his case.

12.1. THE FOUR BRANCHES OF POLITICS

actually have, and tries to find a single form of discipline and diet that would improve the condition of the largest number of them. Analogously, in the study of politics, we must recognize the limited degree to which most of the people who constitute the citizenry of existing cities can be improved; and we must discover, within these limits, a single constitution that would be suitable for a large number of them. This is the project to which Aristotle turns in IV.11, where he describes a city consisting of a large middle class. We will turn to this aspect of his project in 12.3.

What does Aristotle mean by (B): the part of political science that asks which constitution is 'suitable for which' cities? We can most easily answer this question if we skip ahead to the beginning of IV.12, for he tells us there that this is the topic he is about to consider (1296b13). He then goes on to say that every city can be analyzed as a combination of quality and quantity. The categories into which he places the qualities of citizens are: freedom (that is, the status of a free man), wealth, education, and good birth (b18). Each of these is a claim, grounded in some form of personal merit, to deserve the status of citizen: some people claim to be qualified because they are free, others because they are wealthy, and so on. And among those who claim to be qualified simply because they are free, there are further divisions that Aristotle takes to be significant. He says, for example, that farmers are of a better quality than are the banausoi (b28–9). The legislator must pay attention not only to the different qualities of the people who live in a city, but also to how many there are of each type; and he must weigh these two factors—quality and quantity—in relation to each other (b23–4).

What Aristotle seems to have in mind here is that political leaders sometimes have the opportunity to choose between different regimes. They can use their influence to make their cities highly democratic, moderately democratic, highly oligarchic, moderately oligarchic, or some mixture of moderate democracy and moderate oligarchy. Which option they choose should reflect both how qualified the citizens are and how many have these qualifications. It matters not only that there are wealthy people, educated people, farmers, and craftsmen, but how many there are of each sort, how qualified they are to rule, and how their numbers compare with those in other categories. A constitution suitable for one mix of people is unsuitable for another. This branch of political science does not ask which single way of life is best for a great many citizens; rather, it studies cities in which different citizens have different ways of life, and it seeks the best possible mixture of the available ingredients. It recommends different arrangements for different types of city, and within each type it balances different elements rather than prescribing a single way of life for all.

Now that we have seen how (B) and (D) differ, it might be wondered why Aristotle bothers to list (D) as a separate branch of politics. After all, it looks as though (D) is just a special case of (B): the division of politics that asks which constitution is 'suitable for which' cities ought to consider not only cities that contain various quantities and qualities of rich and poor, but also cities in which the middle class is dominant. My conjecture is that Aristotle singles out (D) as a separate study because among non-ideal constitutions the rule of the middle class is the regime that he favors above all others. The objects studied by the four branches of politics are not equally good regimes. (A) is a study of the best, and it is singled out as a separate division precisely because the regime it prescribes is superior to all others. What I am suggesting, then, is that Aristotle has the same sort of reason for wanting to keep the remaining divisions of politics distinct from each other. That is why the rule of the middle class, discussed at length in IV.11, is studied by a distinct branch of politics, and is not absorbed into a more general category: it is kept separate because it is a cut above many other kinds of regime. We find confirmation for this interpretation in IV.2, where Aristotle assigns to political science the study of the constitution that is 'most choiceworthy, after the best' and 'aristocratic ... yet at the same time suitable for most cities' (1289b15–17). So, (D) is kept distinct from other branches of politics because it has a special task—the examination of the second-best regime.

It should now be clear what Aristotle has in mind when he mentions the remaining branch of politics: (C) the part that studies the 'assumed constitution' (1288b28). Whereas in (B) the political scientist has the opportunity to create a mixed regime—one that is not democratic or oligarchic, but rather some combination of forms—in division (C) he has less flexibility. He simply assumes that the city he is studying has a certain constitution—either a democracy or an oligarchy—and he does the best he can within this limitation. The study of different varieties of democratic and oligarchic constitutions is one to which Aristotle devotes considerable attention, and as we will see, it is one of the most important components of his political philosophy.

Just as we wondered why the regime studied under (D)—the rule of

12.1. THE FOUR BRANCHES OF POLITICS

the middle class—is listed separately and not subsumed under (B), so too we should ask this same question about (C). For it might seem that the general question raised by (B)—which constitutions are suitable for which citizens?—could be interpreted to cover more specific questions about which constitutional arrangements best suit the various groups that predominate in democracies (farmers, shepherds, craftsmen) and oligarchies. Again, we can reply that Aristotle makes (C) a separate category because the regimes it studies are not on a par with others. As he tells us (1288b33), these are the worst constitutions, and he compares this branch of politics to that part of physical training that makes no attempt to shape bodies that can compete successfully against others (b16–18).

It emerges, then, that the objects studied by the four branches of politics can be arranged in decreasing order of value:

A the ideal city,
D the rule of the middle class,
B regimes that cannot be called democracies or oligarchies because they are mixtures of both,[3]
C the various forms of democracy and oligarchy.[4]

Aristotle later tells us that the regimes that fall under (B) should be called 'polities' if they mix together the two factors of free birth and wealth, and 'aristocracies' if in addition to these two factors they also assign a role to the virtuous (IV.8 1294a19–25). Here he is using 'aristocracy' loosely to designate a deviant regime, just as he acknowledges that 'polity' is often used to name a different kind of deviation—one that is mixed but inclines in the direction of democracy (IV.8 1293b34–6). By implication, then, if the term 'polity' is to be used in its strict sense to name a correct regime—one that aims at the common good—then it should be reserved for the constitution ruled by the middle class. Although Aristotle does not say so explicitly, the constitution that is called a 'polity' in Book III is the middle-class regime studied in IV.11. This is the one correct regime investigated in Books IV–VI. The least deviant political systems are

---

[3] Or, to put the same point differently, they can be called both oligarchies and democracies because they are so well mixed (IV.9 1294b14–16).
[4] The study of tyranny also falls under (C), even though strictly speaking it is not a constitution. Where laws are not sovereign there is no order, and where there is no order there is no constitution (see IV.4 1292a24–32 and 10.n.15). Nonetheless tyranny forms one part of Aristotle's sixfold classification and he feels obliged to study it (IV.10). In fact, it emerges that there are ways of moderating tyrannies (V.11), just as there are ways of preventing democracies and oligarchies from taking their most extreme forms.

those that are mixed to such a degree that they cannot appropriately be classified as democracies or oligarchies, but should instead be called 'polities' and 'aristocracies' (using these terms loosely to designate deviant regimes).

It is natural to wonder whether Aristotle's division of politics into four components is needlessly complex. Would it not have been more perspicuous to present a long list of political systems, in order of diminishing merit? Equipped with a complete ranking of constitutions, a political leader could take any existing city, determine what its current constitution is, and then ask how it can be transformed into something better. In favorable circumstances, he might be able to move a given city forward several notches.

With a little thought, however, we can understand why this alternative way of organizing Aristotle's material would be cumbersome. As we shall soon see (12.4), he ranks democracy above oligarchy, because it is less susceptible to faction. But he cannot mean by this that every kind of democracy is superior to every kind of oligarchy. Surely the worst democracies—those that are mere tyrannies of the many—are inferior to many kinds of oligarchy. As a result, if we had to rank all regimes in descending order, we would be faced with such questions as these: is the second-best democracy better than the best oligarchy? is it inferior? or are they equally bad? Such questions—if they can be answered at all—seem impractical. After all, what is the likelihood that a legislator will need to decide whether to establish a second-best democracy or a third-best oligarchy? It is far more useful to partition the legislator's options into two groups: first, situations that leave room for the creation of a democracy, an oligarchy, or some mixture; second, situations in which one must work with a defective regime, whether democratic or oligarchic, and can hope only to prevent it from becoming worse. In effect, this is how Aristotle partitions his subject. If the legislator is not restricted to working within a democracy or an oligarchy, then he should try to build a strong middle class, or, failing that, he should mix various elements so as to create a so-called polity or a so-called aristocracy. However, if he is confined to working within democratic or oligarchic forms, then he should make these regimes as moderate as possible.

These points explain why Aristotle is so concerned in Books IV–VI with the question of how to preserve existing regimes. This is a theme he announces in IV.1 when he says that one component of politics studies 'the assumed constitution' (1288b28), and then adds: 'for one must also be able to study the constitution one has been given, how it can develop from its beginning, and once developed, how it can be preserved for the longest time' (b28–30). Here we might ask why the political theorist should investigate ways to make 'the assumed constitution'—democracies or oligarchies—endure. Why not instead study ways to undermine them and turn them into something better? Why should bad political systems be made more enduring rather than less?

Aristotle's answer, I suggest, is twofold. First, it is unrealistic to assume that democracies and oligarchies can always be transformed into some better constitutional form. In many situations, the most one can hope for is the best possible democracy or oligarchy. Second, an understanding of how to preserve these types of political system is essential for anyone who wants to promote the best kind of democracy or oligarchy. Such regimes are unlikely to endure for long if they are inherently unstable—if, for example, the level of distrust among factions is so high that small disputes can easily turn into a civil war and a change in constitutional forms. Therefore, studying the durability of these political systems necessarily involves understanding how to make them less vulnerable to factional strife and more moderate. And if they are more moderate, they are better regimes. Constitutions that are inherently long-lasting are by their nature better constitutions, not because longevity is by itself a good thing, but because longevity is the by-product of something that is intrinsically worthwhile in bad regimes, namely, moderation. To be moderately bad is to be not so bad—in fact, in many circumstances it is the best one can reasonably expect.[5]

These points will receive further discussion when we turn our attention to the various forms of democracy and oligarchy (12.4). But before we move on, we should raise a question about the practical value of studying defective regimes.[6]

12.2. *Character and Constitutions*

A political community must aim at the well-being of its members, and Books VII and VIII describe in considerable detail how this can be achieved, when circumstances are ideal. But it is far less clear how well-being can be promoted in defective regimes. Most of the

[5] See the discussion of related topics in 10.4–7.
[6] For further discussion of IV.1, see Nichols, *Citizens and Statesmen*, pp. 86–8; Swanson, *The Public and the Private in Aristotle's Political Philosophy*, pp. 224–6; Miller, *NJR*, pp. 183–90; Smith and Mayhew, 'Aristotle on What the Political Scientist Needs to Know'.

citizens of existing cities do not understand where their good lies. Many of them pursue wealth or other external goods in excess, and fail to recognize the centrality of the ethical virtues in a well-lived life. Those who have to work for a living—farmers, craftsmen, laborers, and any others who, in Aristotle's words, have not been 'released from the necessary tasks'—are so deficient that they not only fail to be good men, but fail as well at being good citizens (III.5 1278a9–11).[7] When they participate in civic life, they have too little justice to aim at the common good of all members of the community. They are preoccupied with their own good, or that of their household, or of the political faction to which they belong. When a political leader has to work with such poor material, how can he do the citizens any real good? And if there is no possibility of promoting well-being in these defective regimes, what is the point of studying them?

A certain kind of political theorist could reply that it is one thing to design civic institutions and quite another to promote the virtue or well-being of citizens. Even if all of the citizens have a false conception of happiness and are seriously deficient in character, the political institutions of a city need not reflect the inadequacies of its citizens. The threat of punishment and other devices can keep civil strife and criminal behavior within bounds, so that even though the citizens lack the virtues and misunderstand where their good lies, there is nonetheless civic peace, order, and stability. In fact, civic institutions might be just, or very nearly so, even if the character of most citizens is extremely poor. In such a situation the citizens might be leading very bad lives, but their constitution might be rather good and their city well run.[8]

---

[7] It was argued in 10.4 that a good citizen of a democracy or an oligarchy will know how to preserve it by making it more moderate. Even so, it would be unrealistic to expect that all (or even most) of the citizens of such regimes will be good citizens. These would not be bad constitutions, if all of the citizens were good citizens. So the question arises: how can these defective regimes benefit those among their citizens who are bad citizens?

[8] This is the idea proposed by Bernard Mandeville in *The Fable of the Bees*, and endorsed to some degree by Adam Smith and Immanuel Kant. In 'Perpetual Peace', Kant writes that a republican constitution, 'the only one which does complete justice to the rights of man', can be established even among 'a nation of devils', provided that the state uses the self-seeking energies of citizens to compel each other to obey the law. See his *Political Writings*, pp. 112–13. For the claim that something akin to this idea is also present in the work of Rawls, see Cohen, *If You're an Egalitarian, How Come You're So Rich?*, p. 122. Cohen writes against Rawls's thesis that principles of justice apply only to the basic structure of society, and that the justice of individuals lies in their adherence to that structure. Cohen's thesis that 'justice in personal choice is necessary for a society to qualify as just' (p. 6) is entirely congenial to Aristotle (and to ancient ethics in general). Aristotle defines justice as a characteristic of *human beings*, and analyzes the justice or injustice of *cities* as the outcome of the day-by-day choices and habits of citizens.

12.2. CHARACTER AND CONSTITUTIONS

It should be clear, however, that this outlook is alien to Aristotle. One of his fundamental assumptions is that if citizens have a false conception of justice and happiness, then their city's constitution must be equally defective. The constitution, we must recall, is not just a set of laws that distribute offices, but the way of life of a city (IV.11 1295a40–b1); and a *city* cannot live in one way and its *citizens* another. If they live badly because of their preoccupation with the necessities of life, their emotional deficiencies and false values, then their political system will necessarily reflect those failings. What makes a regime defective is the fact that those in control—democrats in democracies, oligarchs in oligarchies—do not aim at the common good; it is precisely their failing as individuals, not some flaw in the design of institutions, that accounts for the injustice of their political system.

What progress can be made, within these limitations? How can a student of politics achieve anything of real significance, if the city he tries to improve is a democracy or an oligarchy, and the defects inherent in these forms cannot be removed? Had Aristotle replied that in these circumstances a statesman or legislator can promote stability, order, and peace without paying attention to the character of the citizens, and that these social conditions are in themselves worthwhile, he would have radically altered his political philosophy. What he must say instead (and what we will find him saying) is that there are ways to govern democracies and oligarchies so that the character of their citizens is *somewhat* improved—though not so much that they become good citizens and their cities acquire good constitutions.[9]

Aristotle would not be able to answer our question in this way were he to insist that ethical virtue is an all-or-nothing affair—that one either has a virtue or lacks it, there being no possibility of an intermediate state between these conditions. Such a position was proposed by Socrates in the *Phaedo*, and was later adopted by the Stoics.[10] The thought that lies behind this doctrine is that genuine

---

[9] Mulgan suggests, by contrast, that defective regimes must be stabilized solely for the sake of the few virtuous people who reside in them (10.n.24). But if Aristotle cares nothing about the well-being of most citizens in these cities, because they fall far short of perfect virtue, why should he care about the good of most of the citizens who live in a polity? They too fall short of perfect virtue (11.12, 12.3). For that matter, why should he care about the well-being of those who accept the rule of a king? They are not fully realized human beings either (10.3).

[10] See *Phaedo* 68d-69c: only philosophers have genuine virtue, and ordinary people have at most a mere façade. Plato insists that if otherworldly motivation does not underlie virtuous acts, the agent is not really virtuous. He perhaps gives up this extreme view in the

virtue (as opposed to what merely seems virtuous) cannot be a mere matter of proper habits, but requires instead a full understanding of the human good. Someone who can normally be relied upon to do the right thing because he has learnt good habits is a moral sham, unless he has come to understand *why* he should act as he should. If he does not grasp this, he is merely imitating those who have shaped him; he is not an active being who uses his own mind, but a shallow and conventional person who happens to have acquired respectable habits. By chance, he conforms to moral norms, but had he been brought up differently, he might have been a monster. What he possesses is the outer shell of virtue, not the real thing.

Aristotle accepts part of this philosophy: he agrees that *perfect* virtue is not a mere matter of habit, but requires as well an understanding of the human good. But he rejects the idea there is no moral distinction to be made among those who fall short of this ideal. Instead, he holds that the better one's habits—even if they are the habits of an unreflective person—the closer one comes to full virtue, and therefore the better off one is. It is this acceptance of a broad middle ground between virtue and vice that allows Aristotle to answer the question we have raised about defective regimes. Even though the citizens of democracies and oligarchies fall far short of perfect virtue and live inadequate lives, there are important distinctions to be made among them. In the least defective of these regimes, the citizens develop habits that are far superior to the habits of those who exercise power in the worst democracies and oligarchies. Even within democratic and oligarchic regimes, bad as they are, there are ways to improve the character and the quality of life of the citizens.

As we proceed, we will see that this is Aristotle's view. But it is important to emphasize this aspect of Books IV–VI right from the start, because there is a strong temptation, when one first reads them, to think that they are exclusively concerned with questions of institutional design (modes of filling offices, methods of preserving regimes, and so on), and that here the *Politics* is not concerned with character and well-being. One might mistakenly suppose that, according to Aristotle, it is only one branch of politics (ideal political theory) that studies the well-being and virtue of individuals, and that the other branches of politics focus instead on the preservation of institutions. But nothing we have seen in IV.1 signals such an

Republic, since his picture of the decline of the soul in Books VIII and IX suggests that there are degrees of virtue. For expressions of the Stoic thesis that there is no state intermediate between virtue and vice, see Long and Sedley, *The Hellenistic Philosophers*, i. 382–3.

12.2. CHARACTER AND CONSTITUTIONS

abrupt change in orientation, and we will find clear evidence against such an interpretation.

One small but telling piece of evidence can be cited immediately: Aristotle holds that even though tyranny is the worst form of rule (it cannot even be called a 'constitution', since it is not a genuine system of government[11]), it admits of two different forms, one far more severe than the other. If a tyrant decides to preserve his rule by imitating the benevolent measures of a king, he will not only improve his chances of staying in power, but will also turn himself into a better person. 'In character, he will be well disposed towards virtue, or semi-good; not corrupt, but semi-corrupt' (V.11 1315b8–10). If those who live under a tyrant can count on him to place significant limitations on the harm he does, and if he actually does some good for his city, then he is not utterly to be despised, even though his motive is to stay in power and his claim to rule has no justification. He is not a thoroughly evil person, because he imposes significant limitations on the evil he does. His motives are base, because above all he wants power for himself; but because the means he regularly adopts to achieve this end produce some good results for his subjects, he is only half-bad.

In describing the less severe form of tyranny in this way, Aristotle is presupposing that one's character is not constituted solely by one's highest ends, but also consists in the means one adopts and the acts one undertakes to bring about those goals. Someone who builds into his ethical orientation a barrier that prevents him from doing evil has kept his character from being thoroughly contemptible. Conversely, someone whose ends are all that they should be, but who regularly goes badly astray in the way he carries out his projects, has a character that is far from praiseworthy.

What Aristotle says of the tyrant applies as well to those who hold power in democratic and oligarchic cities: though their bias in favor of their own class prevents them from being completely just, they can approximate, to some degree, the lesser ideal of good citizenship. If institutional safeguards in democracies and oligarchies prevent their class bias from becoming extreme, then those regimes will produce citizens whose habits make them, like the less severe tyrant, 'semi-good' and 'semi-corrupt'.[12]

---

[11] See 10.n.15.

[12] Here my interpretation differs markedly from that of Schütrumpf. He writes: 'Der beste Staat ist auch nicht die Norm nach der Aristoteles seine Empfehlungen für die Verbesserung der akuten politischen Probleme gibt. Die tatsächlichen Staaten sind nicht mehr

12.3. Rule by the Middle Class

In Book III, Aristotle holds that in addition to kingship and aristocracy, there is a third kind of regime, called a polity, in which the rulers aim at the common good. This is the one type of correct constitution that receives no extended discussion in that book; he merely says that since a polity is ruled by many, the kind of virtue one can expect of its citizens is not of the highest sort (III.7 1279a40–b2). Where in Book IV can we find his discussion of this political system? In IV.8 he starts to talk about constitutions that are *called* 'polities', but he says that they are not correct regimes but rather mixtures that give more weight to democracy than oligarchy (1293b22–36). What of the polity that *is* a correct regime: where is that discussed?

Evidently this is the political system described in IV.11. It is the regime dominated by the middle class. Aristotle does not explicitly say that the constitution of IV.11 is a polity or even that it is a correct political system. Instead, he introduces it as the regime that answers the questions he had raised in IV.1 and IV.2. In IV.1, he asked which constitution is 'most suitable for all cities' (1288b34–5); in IV.2, which is 'most choiceworthy, after the best' and 'aristocratic ... yet at the same time suitable for most cities' (1289b15–17). And then, in IV.11, he tells us that he is about to describe the regime and way of life that is best for most cities and most human beings (1295a25–6). Since he goes on to contrast the rule of the middle class with biased rule (1296a27–36), he is evidently assuming that these middling men govern with a view to the common good. So this must be the polity Aristotle had in mind in Book III.[13] It is not an aristocracy in the

---

oder weniger verwässerte Formen des besten Staates' (*Aristoteles Politik, Buch I*, pp. 49–50). This reading cannot easily be reconciled with Aristotle's description of the constitution described in *Pol.* IV.11, as we are about to see (12.3). Since democracies and oligarchies can approximate the balance achieved by the regime dominated by the middle class, and that regime is similar in important ways to the ideal city of VII and VIII, it turns out that ordinary regimes *are* more or less watered-down versions of the best state. We should also bear in mind the key Aristotle gives us in the final chapter of the *Ethics* for the interpretation of the *Politics*: 'Perhaps we should be satisfied if, when all the things are present through which we seem to become decent, we get some share of virtue' (X.9 1179b18–20). See 10.7.

[13] An alternative view, distinguishing polity from the middling regime, is proposed by Johnson, *Aristotle's Theory of the State*, pp. 143–54. For criticism, see Miller, *NJR*, pp. 262–3, n. 26. For the view that 'polity is the best regime simply', see Nichols, *Citizens and Statesmen*, p. 74. Here she relies on her thesis that Aristotle is being ironic in Book VII and her claim that the goal of his treatment of kingship in Book III is to show that such rule 'in effect destroys the city' (p. 74). For the view that the middling regime of IV.11 corresponds to the ideal city of VII and VIII, see Johnson, *Aristotle's Theory of the State*, pp. 155–69.

strict sense, since its rulers do not fully possess the virtues. But its constitution is, loosely speaking, aristocratic, in that the citizens are the best (*aristoi*) that most people can be.[14]

Aristotle does not use the term 'middle class'. Instead he says: 'in all cities there are three parts of the city: the very rich, the very poor, and third, those in the middle of these' (IV.11 1295b1–3). The terms that are translated 'rich' (*euporoi*) and 'poor' (*aporoi*) literally mean 'well provided with resources' and 'deficient in resources'. The sorts of resource he has in mind are not restricted to the usual indexes of wealth, but include status, influence, or anything else that affects one's position in social hierarchies. Anyone who has impressive looks, influential connections, a noble lineage, or wealth is at the high end of the social scale; those who are utterly deficient in all of these respects are at the low end; so, to be in the middle is simply to have an intermediate score in all these dimensions (1295b3–11). These are ordinary people who have not been favored or cursed by fortune. Aristotle does not describe their economic situation in any detail, but he must be assuming that they have slaves and do not have to spend their days engaged in hard physical labor. They own and oversee a small plot of land, which is not large or productive enough to allow them to purchase luxuries or to rise to a position of prominence in their community. They are not farm workers or craftsmen or wage-earners—for these are the groups that are dominant in democracies. At the same time, they have too few social or financial advantages to be categorized as 'prominent people' (*gnorimoi*) or 'refined people' ('*charientes*')—the elite groups that hold sway in oligarchies. It is precisely because they are not members of the demos or the elite that they make excellent citizens.[15]

Aristotle's principal thesis in IV.11 is that when one is brought up in an environment of deprivation or surfeit, one develops habits of servility or arrogance. Children who are severely deficient in social resources never learn how to use those resources properly; all they know about wealth is to want more of it and to envy those who have it. Conversely, those who experience no restrictions as children and become conscious of their exalted social status develop contempt for their social inferiors and take pleasure in humiliating them. The

---

[14] See 10.n.6 on the various meanings of 'aristocracy'.

[15] Here and elsewhere I use 'demos' as it is sometimes used in Greek to designate the lower class. For the presence of elites in Greek political life, see Ober, *Mass and Elite in Democratic Athens*, pp. 11–17; and by the same author, 'Aristotle's Political Sociology: Class, Status, and Order in the *Politics*'.

middle people have the good fortune to have escaped the evils that often come with excessive or deficient resources. They are (speaking loosely) virtuous, because nothing in their moral education has led them badly astray. They accept the usual conventions about virtue and limit the demands they make on others. They return good for good and evil for evil, but do not try to get the upper hand over their neighbors. Since they do not suffer severe deprivation, they are not likely to engage in petty criminal behavior; conversely, since they do not have the resources needed to dominate and humiliate others, they are not tempted to show their contempt by flouting the ordinary norms of social behavior.[16] Their limited form of virtue is not the full-fledged excellence that is integrated with practical wisdom about the proper ends of human life. Members of the middle class do not make a study of character and constitutions, as do the students of Aristotle's practical works, and do not organize their lives around a conception of the human good. They are decent but limited people, creatures of good habits who have not been perfected through reflection.

Can they be relied on to act well if their circumstances are greatly altered, and they unexpectedly suffer great poverty or fabulous wealth? A fully virtuous person knows how to cope with any such situation, because his decisions express his deepest thoughts and feelings about the centrality of virtue in human life.[17] A person of middle standing who no longer finds himself in the middle has fewer internal resources to guide him. He has not thought much about virtue and its place among other goods, and so, when his virtue is put to the test, his response is determined more by the force of habit than anything else. If he is now presented for the first time with a sophistic argument for the conclusion that justice is a mere sham, his new situation, whether it is great poverty or wealth, might

---

[16] This is why Aristotle invokes his doctrine of the mean at IV.11 1295a35-40. His point is that just as full-fledged virtues can be located between two vices that involve an excess or a deficiency, so the second-best virtue of the middle-class man can also be located between the extremes of arrogance and servility.

[17] On the virtuous person's ability to make the best of bad circumstances, see NE I.10 1100b35-1101a6. We can infer from Aristotle's description of magnificence (NE IV.2) that a virtuous person can cope equally well with great resources. Throughout my discussion of the middling men of Politics IV.11, I assume that although they are good citizens—they know how to rule and be ruled—they lack practical wisdom and are therefore not good men in the strict sense. See Pol. III.4 on the good citizen's ability to rule and be ruled (1277a25-7, b13-16) despite his lack of practical wisdom (1277a14-16, b25-9). If the middling men had practical wisdom, Aristotle could not describe the constitution of IV.11 as one within the reach of people who have only an ordinary moral education (1295a25-31).

12.3. RULE BY THE MIDDLE CLASS

incline him to accept that conclusion.[18] Someone who has had a complete moral education, who has worked out his ideas about human nature and the human good, and whose emotions are informed by these reflections, is better equipped to deal with whatever comes his way. He can bring his emotional and intellectual skills to bear on a wider range of situations than can those whose habits enable them to cope well with life only so long as their resources remain in the middle range. Habits without reason have a limited scope of application. That is why someone who has developed the habits needed to be a good citizen in one type of constitution would not make a good citizen in a different regime (III.4 1276b31–4).[19]

Although I have been emphasizing the difference between the man of middling resources and a fully realized human being, Aristotle is far more interested in contrasting the decency of the middle class with the deficiencies of the masses and traditional elites. The middle-class person, as Aristotle describes him, does not aggressively assert any claim to power, as do democrats and oligarchs. Such a person does not think (as do democrats) that, because he has the status of a free man rather than a slave, he deserves to hold office; or (like oligarchs) that, because of his wealth or elite status, he is entitled to dominate others. When Book III considers the rival claims to power of various components of the city, it does not discuss the party that says that it should rule because it has middling resources—for there is no such party. The man of the middle does not have an ideology that purports to justify his status; he is a modest, competent, and fair-minded person who is willing to do his share when called upon.[20] That is exactly what Aristotle likes about him, and that is why he thinks that such a person is trusted by others, both rich and poor.

The middling man does not hanker after power or wealth, and so he can be relied upon to rule for the good of others. This is what is missing in cities that have middle classes too small to affect the balance of power. The masses and traditional elites have conflicting

---

[18] Aristotle points out at VII.13 1332b6–8 that the force of nature and habit can be overcome when reason points in the opposite direction. For discussion, see Kraut, 'Aristotle on Method and Moral Education'.

[19] See 10.2 and 10.4 for a discussion of Aristotle's contrast between good citizenship and perfect virtue.

[20] Note Aristotle's criticism at II.9 1271a9–12 of political systems in which citizens seek office. He says that offices should instead be conferred on those who merit them, whether they want to rule or not.

ideologies: the many are disinclined to give the few the special powers to which the latter feel entitled; and the elites are reluctant to acknowledge that the masses can play a useful role in the polis. Furthermore, the extreme disparity in their economic circumstances creates a visceral distrust between them. It is not the middle class that the poor envy, but the rich; not the middle class that the rich despise, but the poor. This is why the poor and the rich cannot cooperate in a system of ruling by turns (IV.12 1297a4–6). If the rich had full control of the city for a limited period, they would use their power to crush the poor; and vice versa. But neither party fears the rule of the middle class. They are trusted because they have no animosity towards any rival group or towards members of their own class. This is why Aristotle says that there is friendship in cities dominated by the middle class (IV.11 1295b23–1296a7). He cannot mean that the citizens are intimately acquainted with each other— that they have the same kinds of relationship as family members and close comrades.[21] Rather, his idea must be that in such a city there is the kind of political friendship that he calls 'like-mindedness' (*homonoia*): because the members of the middle class are trusted, everyone accepts their rule. Disagreements in the assembly are not burdened by distrust and animosity, and it is therefore not difficult to work out compromises acceptable to all.[22]

One of the striking features of the middle regime is its similarity to the constitution Aristotle proposes in Books VII and VIII. That ideal city is not run by any of the traditional elites of Greek politics. Great wealth, a powerful family, and a noble lineage count for nothing in the ideal community; what counts instead is excellence of character and intellect, and all citizens are equal in those respects. Aristotle never mentions the 'prominent people' (*gnorimoi*) or the 'refined people' (*charientes*) in VII and VIII, because these traditional elites have been eliminated, just as the banausoi who hold sway in democracies have been eliminated. In middle regimes, notables and workers are among the citizens, but their numbers are too small to matter. The ideal city creates trust and unity through a common moral education, but the middling regime also exhibits a high degree of civic friendship, because of the dominance of those who have not been raised in luxury or poverty and have therefore developed decent habits. The city described in IV.11 is free of some

---

[21] See 9.6, esp. 9.nn.9 and 14, on intimate friendship.
[22] We will return to this form of political friendship in 12.9.

12.3. RULE BY THE MIDDLE CLASS

of the worst evils of ordinary politics—distrust, entrenched elites, craven masses—but the civic friendship that results is precarious. It depends not on unshakable character and rational moral insight, but on favorable economic circumstances. The middling constitution is not all that it should be, because its citizens have nothing better than conventional decency. They do not understand what well-being and virtue are, and so we cannot fully congratulate them for living well. Even so, Aristotle holds that they achieve something quite rare in politics: they are fair-minded citizens who earn each other's trust and establish civic harmony. Their middling virtue gives them a moderate level of well-being.

A further point should be emphasized before we move on. Aristotle's discussion of the middling constitution teaches us a valuable lesson about his attitude towards the role of political elites. As we will soon see, he thinks that the prominent and the refined have an important part to play in oligarchies and even in democracies. What IV.11 tells us is that even though he is willing to grant considerable power to these traditional elites in certain circumstances, he nonetheless has contempt for them and would prefer to do without them.[23] When the only major elements in a city are the demos and the elite, then we must of course resign ourselves to allowing each to play an important civic role. But Aristotle is not happy with these compromises and searches for a better arrangement. He wishes Greek cities had something better to work with than their two most powerful groups: those who think they are superior because of their elite status, and those who think they are just as good as anyone else simply because they are free men. Best of all would be a city ruled by those who are genuinely good men, but even in the absence of such people there is a way to improve on what most cities have. Ordinary decent people can do a better job of ruling than can the arrogant members of traditional elites. To do an adequate job of running a city, one needs neither the specialized scientific training of a Platonic philosopher nor the connections and wealth of powerful families; one need only be a decent person uncorrupted by excess or deficiency. Sadly, Aristotle thinks, all too few meet even that undemanding standard. Middling regimes are rare (IV.11 1296a22–b2). It is impossible to eliminate the animosity between the very rich and the very poor, and difficult to create a sufficiently large

---

[23] See too *Rhet.* II. 15 1390b24 (the well-born are for the most part worthless) and II.16 1390b32–3 (the rich are insolent bullies).

group in the middle. When this moderate regime cannot be created, one must make the best of a bad situation by lessening the tensions between the masses and the elite.

Aristotle has learnt a lesson from Plato: one must beware of those who seek power only because they have nothing better to do with themselves.[24] Affluence encourages the growth of a passion for domination; but even the lowly enjoy flexing their muscles, when they become part of a crowd and breathe the spirit of democratic ideology. The solution proposed by Plato in the *Republic* is to steer honor-loving and aggressive people into a military life, and to make members of the working class content with their livelihood and families. The ruling class of Plato's ideal city can be trusted to rule well because they are deprived of riches and family connections—two powerful sources of corruption and bias. Furthermore, true philosophers do not enjoy giving orders and exercising power; they would rather contemplate eternity, and accept power only because they see that justice requires them to repay their city for the benefits they have received. Aristotle agrees with Plato that hunger for power is one of the poisons of political life, but he sees no merit in Plato's proposed remedies. If citizens learn how to use their leisure well—by listening properly to music, drama, and poetry—they will recognize its superiority to the unleisurely pursuit of political goals. They will not want to rule all the time, but will instead be happy to share offices with others.[25] Furthermore, it does not require a specialized knowledge of mathematics and other abstruse subjects to be a cooperative and trustworthy person who forswears domination and shares power with others on an equal basis. It does not even require a perfect understanding of virtue and the human good. All it takes is the sort of ordinary moral education received by those whose habits are formed by moderate resources.

12.4. Democracy and its Varieties

We turn now to Aristotle's discussion of democracy and its varieties. We already know from Book III that he defines democracy as rule by the poor. Typically they are the largest component of the citizenry, and so rule by the poor is usually rule by the many (III.8).

---

[24] This theme is introduced at *Republic* 346e–347d and Plato returns to it at 519c–520e.
[25] See 6.3 for the place of music in the ideal city.

12.4. DEMOCRACY AND ITS VARIETIES

Furthermore, Aristotle assumes in Book III that democracy is inherently a corrupt form of government. It is rule by the demos for the sake of the demos, not for the sake of all citizens (III.7 1279b8–9); it is a regime that gives unfair treatment to the wealthy. When we read Books IV–VI, we learn more fully what Aristotle's case against democracy is, and that will be the focus of our discussion. As we have already seen in our examination of the middle regime of IV.11, he thinks that the very rich and very poor are locked in a cycle of distrust, envy, and contempt. Democracy is inherently corrupt because, when there are extreme differences in wealth, and some have superfluities while others struggle with necessities, the deprivation suffered by the poor makes it impossible for them to be fair to the wealthy. But although this point lies at the heart of Aristotle's complaint about democracy, we must deepen our understanding of his argument, by studying his taxonomy of democracies and his rejection of the two ideals he associates with this form of government: numerical equality and freedom.

We should also note that the pathology that Aristotle associates with severe economic deprivation in IV.11 is not the same pathology that plays a large role in his discussion of democracy throughout most of Books IV–VI. In IV.11 he says that those who are extremely poor are utterly passive: they know nothing of how to rule, only how to obey (1295b18–22). But when he develops his taxonomy of democracies, he insists that in the worst kind of democracy the poor play a very active role indeed: they hold frequent meetings and issue tyrannical commands (IV.4 1292a4–38, IV.6 1292b41–1293a10). In its most extreme form, poverty produces a slavish passivity; citizens reduced to this state will always be dominated by the rich. But, as he indicates in other parts of IV–VI, poverty that is not so severe can produce a very different kind of personality.

Before moving on, we should take note of Aristotle's thesis that democracy, bad as it is, is not quite so bad as oligarchy. It is, he says, more moderate (IV.2 1289b4–5). Why so? He gives two reasons. First, democracies have larger populations than do oligarchies, and therefore tend to have a larger middle class. Even when those in the middle are not dominant (as they are in polities), they can still have a moderating effect (IV.11 1296a9–21). This reason for the superiority of democracy does not imply that the demos is any less offensive than are the elite. But when Aristotle states a second reason for the superiority of democracy, he does give the demos some credit. He says that the many are less given to faction than are the few.

Oligarchs do not cohere as a group, but fight with each other as well as with the demos. The many, by contrast, do form a cohesive political unit; they have no animus against each other, but only against the wealthy (V.1 1302a8–15). What underlies this difference between oligarchs and democrats is the ideology and character of the demos. Their ruling idea is that all free men are equal; therefore, when each citizen has exactly as much power as any other, they are satisfied, and seek no further change. They are the sort of people who hate to have superiors but are willing to rule and be ruled as equals. By contrast, the oligarchs do not have an ideology that unites them as a group. Each thinks himself superior to all others; however much power he has, he yearns for more, and looks for ways of humiliating both his rivals and those inferior to him (V.7 1307a15–20). This is why Aristotle says that the acquisitiveness (*pleonexia*) of the rich is more destructive of their constitution than is that of the poor (IV.12 1297a11–13). Although the worst democracies and oligarchies are equally objectionable—they are both tyrannical[26]—the demos is apparently not quite as inclined to transgress social norms as are the elites. Wealthy and aristocratic families are apt to produce a Thrasymachus or a Callicles or an Alcibiades:[27] arrogant, shameless, power-hungry, enamored of luxury, they regard talk of virtue as a sham and flaunt their superiority. Cities dominated by such people as these are unstable and short-lived, though of course it is not their short duration that disturbs Aristotle but rather the shameless behavior they allow. The many, by contrast, do not descend to quite this level of cynicism, because at least they treat each other well. Nonetheless, as we will see, Aristotle thinks that at their worst they are capable of great collective crimes.

When Aristotle describes the varieties of democracy and oligarchy, we should not take him to be engaged in a purely descriptive and empirical project. He is not merely observing cities and reporting, from a stance of ethical neutrality, the way they distribute power and shape the lives of their citizens. (Even the empirical constitutional studies composed by his school contain normative elements, if we may generalize from the one example that has been recovered: the *Constitution of Athens*.[28]) What he gives us in Books

---

[26] See 10.n.15.

[27] Socrates' principal adversaries in Plato's *Republic* Book I, *Gorgias*, and *Symposium*, respectively.

[28] Its historical account of Athenian political institutions is peppered with evaluative remarks (23.1–2: the Areopagus governed well; 28.1: Athens declined after Pericles died).

12.4. DEMOCRACY AND ITS VARIETIES

IV–VI of the *Politics* is a normative taxonomy: it tells us which type of democracy is the best we can strive for, which is most to be avoided, and which political systems lie between these extremes. Many of the features of democracies that he mentions (pay for attendance at meetings, property qualifications, majority rule) are institutions used by existing cities, but Aristotle's project leaves him free to mix them together in ways that do not exactly replicate reality, or to invent new institutions no city has ever tried.[29] His goal is not to rank existing democracies and oligarchies but to guide practice by proposing an ordered series of decreasingly desirable regimes. His readers are expected not merely to understand the world but to change it, by bringing existing democracies and oligarchies closer to ideal democracies and oligarchies. All of this should be evident from the analogy he uses in IV.1, when he presents the four tasks of political theory (12.1). The physical trainer does not have the task of describing the various types of body people actually have, but of discovering how they can be improved—even if the improvements that can be made are quite restricted (1288b10–19). The worst possible body imagined by the trainer must be recognizable as a body, but its purpose is to serve as an example to be avoided, not as a picture of some actual body.

The basic idea behind Aristotle's normative taxonomy of democracies and oligarchies is to accept the existence of distrust between rich and poor as a given, and to put it to good use. In such cities, neither the masses nor the elite have an equal regard for the good of all. Each faction is biased in its own favor, because this is the inevitable result of the wide gap between those who have too little and those who have too much. Since no one aims at the common good, Aristotle assumes it cannot be achieved; there is no mechanism by which one faction's bias can be so evenly counterpoised by the other's that the result is equally good for all. Nonetheless, there are ways of making the two factions nearly equal in strength, so that each group can protect itself against the worst excesses of the other. Because the poor distrust the rich, they can be called upon to perform a public service by keeping the elite from becoming too powerful and corrupt; and so long as the elite is kept within limits,

---

[29] Nonetheless the worst kind of democracy bears a strong resemblance to Athenian democracy as Aristotle describes it in *Ath. Pol.* (see e.g. 28.1, 4; 41.2, 3); and the decline of democracy treated in *Pol.* VI.4 parallels the historical account of *Ath. Pol.* Even so, there are some discrepancies: contrast *Pol.* VI.4 1319b9–10 and *Ath. Pol.* 42.1. For a helpful discussion, see Strauss, 'On Aristotle's Critique of Athenian Democracy'.

they too can perform a public service by using their wealth, education, and connections to achieve civic goals. It would be unrealistic to expect either party to perform its job to perfection. In democracies, the masses abuse their power to bring the elite to court on charges of corruption (VI.5 1320a4–17); and conversely, in oligarchies the elite gives the demos too small a supervisory role. But even if there is never a perfect balance in these regimes, the best of them achieve a level of justice that is worth striving for.[30]

It should be noticed that this division of labor between rich and poor makes partial use of some of the ideas Aristotle discusses in Book III. The rich think that their resources entitle them to have greater power than the poor; they have more to contribute to the well-being of the city, and therefore they deserve high office. Aristotle agrees that there is something to this argument (III.13 1283a30–3), and so in the best democratic and oligarchic regimes of IV–VI he awards the most honored positions to members of the elite. Having grown up with great private resources, they are better equipped to make decisions about the use of public resources. (Recall, however, one of the lessons of IV.11: Aristotle would prefer to reduce their power and give more authority to the middle class.) Similarly, he thinks that although the members of the demos are poorly equipped as individuals to hold high office, they can still achieve a rough kind of justice when they meet together in the assembly and exercise some degree of control over the elite (III.11). The poor can confine the rich to their role as public servants and restrain their tendency to revel in power and humiliate their inferiors, while the rich can see to it that the assembly does not become all-powerful and unrestrained in its decisions. When each faction employs its distrust in this way, democracies and oligarchies are at their best. But when each becomes intoxicated with power, civic life is destroyed.

Let us now discuss in greater detail Aristotle's taxonomy of democracies, leaving aside the intermediate forms and concentrating on the best and worst.[31] In the best democracy, rich and poor are equals, or nearly so. All citizens have some property. Most are farmers and,

---

[30] On the limited justice that can be achieved in defective constitutions, see 4.5 and 10.8. It should be kept in mind that Aristotle acknowledges some merit in each of the claims to power made by rival factions (III.9 1280a9–11, a21–2, III.13 1283a23–42, V.1 1301a25–b4), so it should not be surprising that when each faction is granted some power an imperfect sort of justice emerges. At V.9 1309b31–2 he concedes that democracies and oligarchies can be tolerable (*hikanōs*), though the tone of IV.2 1289b9–11 is much harsher.

[31] The chapters in which Aristotle discusses the varieties of democracy are IV.4, IV.6, and VI.1–5. The forms intermediate between best and worst will receive our attention in 12.8.

12.4. DEMOCRACY AND ITS VARIETIES

because they have little leisure to visit the urban center, meetings of the assembly are infrequent. High offices are filled by election rather than lot, and those who are well qualified (among members of the elite) are selected to serve. The latter are subject to legal scrutiny, and corruption is therefore kept in check. The city is ruled by law. By contrast, in the worst democracy, the participation of the elite in governance is at a minimum. Citizenship standards are lax: for the most part citizens are urban workers who can easily attend meetings of the assembly, and they are paid to do so. Laws lose their importance. Decrees issued at each new meeting of the assembly become the major instrument of governance. The assembly of all citizens is the only important source of power. All other offices become insignificant.

Someone who read only those portions of the *Politics* in which Aristotle draws these contrasts might mistakenly infer that his real goal in designing democracies is to come as close as he can to eliminating the power of the demos entirely. One would be justified in thinking that for Aristotle the masses are useless or worse, and that they are present in his account of democracies merely because by definition a democracy is a political system in which they play a major role. According to this interpretation, Aristotle's real wish is to keep the poor out of politics altogether and to restrict political influence to the wealthy.

But anyone who reads him more carefully can easily see that such an interpretation is mistaken. To begin with, we should recall the point, discussed earlier in this section, that Aristotle ranks democracy above oligarchy. Furthermore, when we read his advice to oligarchies, we find him insisting that the elite should distribute public funds to the poor so that they can buy land, and should pay them to attend necessary meetings of the assembly (VI.5 1320a29-b4). Evidently, he is not in principle opposed to such pay; when he objects to this aspect of radical democracy, his target is the abuse of this device. He thinks that poor people should participate in meetings and should be paid to do so—but not too often.[32] If they are legally free to meet whenever they like, receive pay on each occasion, and are not deterred from holding frequent meetings by

---

[32] An analogous proposal in modern democracies would call for the state to pay poor people to cast their ballots in elections. No doubt those candidates least likely to receive their votes would piously protest that people should vote from a sense of civic duty, not in order to make money. For further discussion of paying the poor to attend the assembly, see 12.6.

any inconveniences or obstacles, then a powerful incentive has been created for them constantly to reconsider actions taken at previous meetings. Why be bound by a previous decision if one can make a decent living by changing one's mind and passing a new decree? Why toil away at a job when one can make enough by flexing one's political muscle in the assembly? When conditions are right, the masses learn to enjoy the exercise of power for its own sake—thus mirroring the arrogance of an unchecked elite.

Such excesses are given further encouragement by the ideology of democracy. 'There are two things by which democracy is thought to be defined: the authority of the majority and freedom. For equality is thought to be just, and equality consists in making authoritative whatever is thought to be the case by the majority, and freedom and equality are doing whatever one likes' (V.9 1310a28–32). What Aristotle means here is that the radical democrat has no other standard of justice than whatever the majority of free men decide. As he says in a parallel passage, 'Democratic justice is having what is equal arithmetically but not in proportion to merit, but if this is justice the majority must be authoritative, and whatever is thought by the majority, that is final and that is justice' (VI.2 1317b3–7). To the Socratic question, 'What is justice?' the radical democrat replies: 'Whatever we (the demos) think.' Just as elitists like Callicles and Thrasymachus mock conventional morality and admire the effrontery of the transgressor, so too there lurks in the heart of the radical democrat a cynicism about conventional moral constraints. That is why the democrat likes to think of freedom as the absence of constraint. It is not only *individual* liberty that he cherishes, but the freedom of his class to define the standards of morality for itself. Conventional standards of decency embodied in widely acknowledged unwritten laws receive no respect when elitists or radical democrats break free of all restraining influences.

Those who design democracies and oligarchies must prevent matters from coming to this point, and they can do so by setting up each faction as a watchdog over the other. That is why in the best democracies the rich and the poor must have roughly equal power: the only way to keep democracy from degenerating into its extreme form is to give the rich more power than they would have if they were merely a handful among the members of the assembly. They are the ones whose economic position makes them distrustful of the demos—a distrust that is entirely justified (as is the distrust felt by the masses towards the elite). When the meetings of the assembly are limited in number and wealthy patricians fill high office, a rough parity among factions is achieved and the excesses of both are avoided. Elitists and the masses exercise a low form of virtue by restraining each other's injustices. Even in cities where virtue is not the acknowledged goal of political life, there is a way of nurturing it to some small degree.

12.5. Freedom and the Law

Freedom is (along with equality) one of the principal goals of democracy, but, Aristotle says, its advocates define it badly: they equate it with doing whatever one likes (V.9 1310a28–32) or living as one chooses (VI.2 1317b10–12). They would like to avoid being ruled—- 'best of all, not by anyone, but if not this, then by turns . . . ' (VI.2 1317b15–16). The democrat wishes there were no infringements on his freedom at all, but realizing that a complete absence of governance would be intolerable, he settles for a minimal degree of regulation. The kind of government that democratic ideology settles for involves ruling and being ruled in accordance with numerical equality: offices are filled not through elections (since elections make sense only if some are better qualified than others) but by lot. Little authority is given to those who hold these offices, because the assembly of all citizens meets frequently and concerns itself with the details of governance. In an extreme democracy, the power of the assembly is so great that Aristotle likens it to that of a tyrant (IV.4 1292a15–32). There is no power over the assembly that restricts it; as a body, it can do whatever it pleases. But Aristotle also implies that in an extreme democracy each individual citizen (in fact, each inhabitant) can, to a large extent, do as he pleases (VI.4 1319b27–32). The assembly does not use its power to impose a large number of restrictions on how individuals may live their lives. One of the ways in which it uses its great freedom as a collective body is to grant each individual citizen a large zone of freedom in which he is allowed to do as he pleases.[33]

Although Aristotle associates democracy with the desire not to be regulated by others, he recognizes that people in general bridle at restraints on their behavior. Members of the elite, for example, would prefer to fill high office without being subject to the scrutiny

---

[33] See further Mulgan, 'Aristotle and the Democratic Conception of Freedom'.

of the assembly. Aristotle advises them to accept such regulation: 'To be subject to restraint, and not to be at liberty to do everything one thinks of doing, is beneficial. For to have the liberty to do whatever one wishes is to be unable to guard against what is base in every human being' (VI.5 1318b38–1319a1). And in the *Ethics*, he notes that it is a general characteristic of people to take offense when others oppose their impulses, even when such opposition is justified (X.9 1180a22–3).[34] Members of the elite are not accustomed by their upbringing to scrutiny, criticism, or opposition by others (IV.11 1295b13–18). Since they take it for granted that they will always be able to live as they please, a life of unfettered freedom never needs to become one of their goals. The poor, by contrast, are raised by parents who give them far less latitude (b18–19), and it is understandable that as adults they should become attracted to a political ideology that promises to leave them alone. Poverty and excess produce people who are either sick of restrictions or unused to them. Both conditions encourage a distorted conception of what it is to be a free man: excessive restriction makes people wish not to be ruled at all, while excessive laxity makes them unused to anything but ruling.

Properly understood, being free—conducting oneself in a way that befits a free man—involves maintaining a proper balance between ruling and being ruled.[35] Always to be ruled by another (unless that other is a godlike being to whom one voluntarily submits[36]) is the condition of a slave; but on the other hand, as Aristotle insists in the passage just cited, if one is a normal human being, even one who is virtuous, it is dangerous to be completely unrestricted (VI.5 1318b38–1319a1). None of us is entirely free of the appetites and passions that lead human nature astray, and so we all profit from

---

[34] 'They cannot bear those people who oppose their impulses, even if they are right to do so.' Aristotle might be making either of two points: (a) People are offended by interference even when it is, unbeknownst to them, in their interest. (b) People are offended by interference even when they realize that interference is in their interest. (a) is the less interesting point, because it hardly needs saying that when X rightly interferes with Y, the fact (unrecognized by Y) that X is justified will not stop Y from feeling aggrieved. (b) is far more perceptive: even when Y admits that he should not have acted on his impulse, he still thinks that X had no business trying to stop him from doing what he felt like doing.

[35] Since Aristotle criticizes democrats for having a false conception of freedom (V.9 1310a28), he implies that, properly understood, it is to be welcomed. At VI.2 1317b2–3 he indicates that the formula they use to define freedom—being ruled in turns—is acceptable, provided it is understood in the right way. He would approve of Locke's statement: 'that ill deserves the name of confinement which hedges us in only from bogs and precipices' (*Second Treatise of Government*, s. 57).

[36] Recall our discussion of kingship in 11.10 and 11.11.

12.5. FREEDOM AND THE LAW

being subject to scrutiny and regulation (11.14). This goes against the grain of human nature, as anyone who has observed a small child can see. But if we are properly educated and develop good habits, we recognize that we benefit from lacking the power to do whatever we please. So the democratic equation of freedom with ruling and being ruled is acceptable, if it is understood in the right way. Democrats mistakenly believe that we should be ruled as little as possible, and they make this mistake because they fail to recognize how an individual benefits from being restricted. They agree that the *city* benefits from the rule of law, but they fail to see that each individual benefits as well.[37]

Let us return to Aristotle's idea that people hate being opposed by other people. When he makes this point in the *Ethics*, he immediately adds: 'but the law is not burdensome when it commands what is equitable' (X.9 1180a23–4).[38] The law, as Aristotle knows, is a human construct.[39] And yet he thinks that our reaction to being subjected to an equitable law is quite different from our reaction to an extralegal command, even when we realize that the person who gives that command is doing so for our own good. He assumes that by its nature law is general in scope: it applies to a wide variety of situations and endures for a considerable period of time. Unlike a decree, it is not a stopgap measure devised to address a particular problem of short duration.[40] Even when a law is created by human beings, its generality makes it easier to bear (assuming it is a good law) than an extralegal command (even when it is a reasonable command). A law is not addressed to particular people at a particular time, but to all members of an ongoing community; and since they have a significant role to play in governing that community, they can view each law as part of a larger order to which they belong. By contrast, when a single individual approaches us and simply tells us

---

[37] Aristotle's treatment of this theme owes much to Plato's formulation of the problem of justice in Book II of the *Republic*. Democrats accept a limited restriction on their freedom only because they recognize the bad consequences of anarchy, just as ordinary people regard justice as a compromise to be welcomed only because of its results. They see why it would be bad if everyone were unrestricted, but not why it is good for each to be restricted.

[38] Here 'equitable' (*epieikes*) simply means 'fair' or 'decent'. As we saw earlier (4.4), Aristotle sometimes uses the same Greek term to designate the sort of justice that corrects the defects inherent in universal rules.

[39] This does not mean that *justice* is the creation of human beings. For the close connection between law and what is believed and practiced, see 4.3. The distinction between natural and legal justice is discussed at 4.7.

[40] See 4.3 for the distinction between laws and decrees. Aristotle contrasts the generality of law with the specificity of court decisions at *Rhet.* I.1 1354a31–b8, and with the specificity of decrees at *NE* V.10 1137b27–32; cf. VI.8 1141b27–8.

what to do, we bridle at his imperiousness, even if we see that we should heed his command. His command is not part of a larger system in which we share.[41]

Aristotle is not saying that the decrees of an assembly—the orders it gives in order to solve a specific and temporary problem—lack justification and are to be disregarded. At times, such orders are entirely appropriate. What he objects to is an assembly that governs largely or entirely through ad hoc rules and short-term commands (IV.4 1292a6–7, a23–37). His assumption is that if an assembly cannot adhere to a fixed and general policy, but addresses each new situation in a way that seems best at the time, it will inevitably give vent to the passion its members feel most strongly at the moment.[42] When an assembly takes on the task of drafting legislation that will endure over a long period of time, and will address a wide variety of situations, it is likely to consider matters about which it does not feel strongly at the moment, and to calculate the long-term consequences of what it is doing. Though it may often go somewhat astray in making law, it is most likely to commit egregious errors if it frequently reacts to matters of great immediacy and disregards the long-term implications of its decisions.

However, it is important to realize that when Aristotle says that in a radical democracy the law no longer rules, and that the assembly acts like a tyrant (IV.4 1292a4–18), he is not merely criticizing it for failing to make decisions of sufficient generality, and for being vulnerable to the distorting effects of emotion. He is also saying that such an assembly will do terrible things, just as a tyrant does terrible things. It will fail to abide by the longstanding customs that decent human beings everywhere recognize as legitimate. A tyrant stops at nothing to get his way: he engages in murder, theft, and every sort of abuse, in order to humiliate others and assert his power. He violates the unwritten laws of every human community, because he is drunk with power.[43] When Aristotle says that the demos of a radical democracy is not ruled by law, he means that outrageous acts can be

---

[41] The idea that freedom involves participation in legislation and is incompatible with servile acceptance of someone else's commands is particularly associated in the modern era with Rousseau and Kant, but it should be apparent that it has a far longer history.

[42] For the connection between passion and the immediacy of an issue, see *Rhet.* I.1 1354a31–b8. For discussion of the Platonic background to this chapter of the *Rhetoric*, and its connection with Aristotle's *Politics*, see Schütrumpf, 'Some Observations on the Introduction to Aristotle's *Rhetoric*'.

[43] The ruthlessness of tyrants is a recurring theme of V.10–11; see e.g. V.10 1311a25–8, V.11 1313a34–1314a29.

12.5. FREEDOM AND THE LAW

committed by crowds and not just by single individuals. To govern and be governed by law is not merely to devise and submit to rules of considerable generality; it is also to live within the limits of widely accepted prohibitions. But a radical democrat thinks that justice is whatever is decided upon by the demos.[44] When this ideology is accepted by people whose sense of justice has been distorted by severe deprivation, who resent restrictions, are full of envy, and have all the time in the world to vent their passions in the assembly, the results will not be pretty.

Books IV–VI make it clear that Aristotle accepts in large part the argument rehearsed in Book III for the rule of law. That argument rested on the premise that even the best of men are vulnerable to passion, whereas the law is not.[45] He does not say in Book III how much stock he puts in that premise,[46] but merely announces that if there is one person or a small number whose virtue is superior to the collective skills of all others, he or they should rule, and the best forms of government are therefore kingships and aristocracies (III.17–18).[47] In these extraordinary circumstances, the law should not be supreme. 'For such people as these there is no law; for they themselves are law' (III.13 1284a13–14). Since these extraordinary human beings never give way to passion, they can be relied upon always to see what must be done in each situation. Of course, there are certain laws of natural justice that they will never disobey: they will never murder or steal from their subjects, for example. But they are not in need of further legal regulation; there are no terms of office for them, or procedures by which their conduct of office is scrutinized. One does not need a punitive legal code to keep genuine kings in line (11.11).

By contrast, the highly defective citizens of democracies and oligarchies are very much in need of legal regulation, and steps must be taken to prevent them from making political decisions in emotionally charged situations. Part of what makes the better democracies and oligarchies tolerable is the willingness of their citizens to restrain themselves by adopting highly general, long-lasting rules and adhering to the customs and unwritten laws acknowledged in all

---

[44] See V.9 1310a28–32 (discussed above in 12.4).
[45] See III.15 1286a17–20, III.16 1287a28–32.
[46] This point is rightly emphasized by Yack, *The Problems of a Political Animal*, p. 183. My reading nonetheless differs from his because I take Aristotle to be assuming that there are unwritten laws of natural justice, and that where law has authority, these unwritten rules are observed. Cf. his view on p. 183, and see 4.n.36.
[47] See 11.10–12 for discussion.

communities. We see how valuable the rule of law is when ruthless men think themselves entitled to govern without restraint. But the rule of law should not only prevail in democracies and oligarchies. Wherever there is rotation of office—as there is in the middling regime of IV.11 as well as the ideal city of VII and VIII—the law rules, for in these regimes it is law that stands over and restricts the power of each citizen (III.16 1287a16–18). Even the virtuous citizens of VII and VIII are vulnerable to the distorting effects of passion. Their perception of the common good may be biased by their individual perspectives, and that is why they are required to have one plot of land near the outskirts of the city and one near the center (VII.10 1330a9–23). Of course, to say that in all of these cities the law should rule is not to say that it must be applied even to situations it was not intended to cover. Because of its universality, law is an imperfect guide, and must be supplemented by equitable judgment (4.4).

Laws adopted by cities governed by defective constitutions can be expected to be defective laws. This is a claim that is made in the closing lines of III.10 (1281a36–9) and III.11 (1282b8–13), and there is every reason to suppose that Aristotle accepts it. But we can now see what he takes the significance of this point to be. Yes, he realizes that the laws of defective regimes will be biased in one direction or another. But he nonetheless believes that the rule of law is a precious thing even in these cities. Although their laws are biased, there are limits to their injustice, if these regimes are not extreme oligarchies or democracies. Those who live in one of these extreme political systems realize how much is lost when the law no longer rules. Although democracies and oligarchies are inevitably sites of injustice, one can do far worse than live under their moderate forms.[48]

One further point should be kept in mind. Aristotle thinks it will be difficult for the adult citizens of moderate democracies and oligarchies to accept their distinct political responsibilities and to abide by the rule of law unless they have been prepared in childhood for their future role as citizens. If the children of the rich are made soft by luxury and never learn to discipline their desires, or if the children of the poor know nothing but obedience and are never trusted to play a more active role, then democratic and oligarchic constitutions will never succeed. The laws must match the habits of

---

[48] Cf. the praise bestowed on Theramenes at *Ath. Pol.* 28.5 for his respect for law. See too 32.2, 33.2, 34.3.

the people, and childhood is the time when those habits begin to develop (*NE* X.9 1179b23–1180a1). The best way to stabilize constitutions—but one that Aristotle says is universally underestimated—is 'an education in relation to one's constitution' (V.9 1310a14). This general principle, which he uses when he constructs the ideal city of Books VII and VIII, is invoked once again when he constructs imperfect regimes. As he says in VIII.1, education must become a common concern, and should not be left entirely within the control of households. The children who will become future citizens do not belong to their parents alone, but are part of the city, as are their parents. It would be too much to expect that in imperfect regimes all citizens will receive the same education, as do the citizens of an ideal city. But although the children of the rich and the poor will not receive one and the same education, all of them must learn the disciplined habits that will equip them, when they become adults, to keep a watchful eye on their political adversaries.

12.6. Weighted Voting

I said earlier (12.4) that in the best democracy rich and poor are equals, or nearly so. The passage I was alluding to is the one in which Aristotle first lays out his taxonomy of democracies. He says: 'The first kind of democracy is the one that is said to be based most of all on equality. For the law in such a democracy says that neither the poor nor the rich are more powerful, but both are the same. For if freedom exists to the highest degree in a democracy, as some suppose, so too does equality, and this condition would exist to the highest degree when all fully share alike in the constitution. Since the people [*dēmos*] are a majority and the opinion of the majority has authority, this is necessarily a democracy' (IV.4 1291b30–8).

Aristotle does not pause to explain more fully what he has in mind here, but moves immediately to his next topic—the other varieties of democracy. What is perplexing about the passage cited is that it seems to contradict itself: first it says that rich and poor are equal in power, but then it says that the people have more power. Aristotle needs this second point in order to be able to call this regime a democracy, and he needs the first to explain why it is the best kind of democracy. When he more fully describes this sub-type a few pages later (IV.6 1292b21–33), he does not resolve the tension; in fact he does not even comment on the egalitarian nature of this constitution.

Fortunately, he clarifies matters in Book VI. At the end of VI.2, he returns to the idea that democracy is based on arithmetical equality, and once again, as in IV.4, he takes this to mean that neither class should dominate the other (1318a3–8). Then, in VI.3, he spells out more fully what this idea involves: arithmetic equality in the best sort of democracy does not involve giving each citizen an equal vote, for that would allow the poor to dominate the rich. We should recall Aristotle's fundamental assumption that deprivation prevents the poor from being unbiased; their economic circumstances incline them to view issues solely from their own one-sided perspective. Accordingly, if all matters in the assembly are decided by the majority and each member has an equal vote, the poor, being more numerous than the rich, will outvote them every time, and the only point of view expressed by public decisions will be that of the poor. In effect, the rich will be unable to exert any influence on the decisions of the assembly, and those decisions will be systematically biased against them. Accordingly, in VI.3 Aristotle proposes that the balance be restored, at least to some extent, by giving the rich additional voting power.

His idea is this. The votes of the rich and the poor are not to be pooled into one sum, but kept separate. Measures that win a majority of both groups are passed. But if there is disagreement—if the majority of the rich conflict with the majority of the poor—then votes are weighted by wealth. To see how this works, let us take the small numbers Aristotle himself uses in this chapter and assume that the wealth of each rich person is three times that of each poor person. Suppose, with Aristotle, that the rich favor a measure by a vote of 6 to 4, and the poor oppose it by a vote of 15 to 5. The figure of 6 is multiplied by 3; and this is added to the 5 votes of the poor to yield 23. Similarly, the figure of 4 is multiplied by 3 to yield 12; and this is added to the other 15 votes of the poor to yield 27. The preference of a large majority of the poor is victorious, because they have won enough support from some of the rich. More generally, the effect of such a system will be to make both rich and poor evaluate proposals not only from their own perspective but from that of their adversaries as well. They are in this way encouraged to search for policies that are beneficial to both sides. Best of all will be those proposals that are favored by most of the rich and most of the poor, but if these cannot be found, alliances will be sought with members of the rival faction. Citizens are thus forced to move outside their own narrow and biased perspective, and to consider the point of view of those who are differently situated.

Why should this be called a democracy at all, rather than an equal mixture of democracy and oligarchy? Presumably Aristotle is assuming that the disparity of wealth is small enough and the numerical strength of the poor great enough that the preferences of the poor will more often than not enjoy an advantage over those of the rich. If, for example, there are 2,000 poor citizens and 200 rich, the poor will be dominant, provided the total wealth of the rich is not ten times greater than that of the poor. Since Aristotle believes that the poor are less vulnerable to faction than the rich,[49] he assumes that in democracies their collective power will often outweigh that of the rich, even when the latter are given additional voting power. The poor may at times split their votes, but their majorities will often be more one-sided than are those of the rich. At the same time, Aristotle must also be making the assumption that there will be significant disagreements among the poor, at least occasionally, and that some of them will favor proposals supported by the rich. Without this premise, he cannot reach the conclusion that, in this form of democracy, the poor do not dominate the rich. We should also notice that if the disparity in wealth were sufficiently large—if it were 100 times greater rather than ten, as we assumed—then weighted voting would transform this regime into an oligarchy. Aristotle's characterization of the best democratic constitution as a system of weighted voting simply assumes that all of these ratios will be within the right range. Although the poor will have some advantage over the rich, that advantage will not be so great that they can refuse to form alliances with their opponents, and work out compromises that appeal to both factions.

A noteworthy corollary of Aristotle's proposal—one that he himself does not state—is that in oligarchies the poor should receive additional voting power in proportion to their lack of resources. After all, in a democracy the voting power of the rich is to be increased not because, as a class, they contribute more to the city than do the poor, but in order to keep their point of view from being ignored. But precisely the converse situation obtains in oligarchies, where there is a danger that the poor have so little power that their votes can never make a difference. So Aristotle ought to say that in

---

[49] See 12.4 for discussion.

such a situation voting power should be inversely related to wealth. If, for example, someone's resources are one fourth of those of the wealthiest citizen, then his vote should be multiplied by four. There is no reason to think that Aristotle would be opposed to such a measure. As we have seen (12.4), the principle that lies behind his taxonomy of democracies is not that the poor should have as little influence on politics as possible, but rather that neither faction should have so much power that it completely dominates the other. Giving the poor additional voting power in an oligarchy would fit perfectly with Aristotle's whole approach to the conflict between these classes.

Finally, we should keep in mind one other device for preventing the poor from having too little power in oligarchies—a device that Aristotle explicitly endorses: they can be paid to attend necessary meetings of the assembly (VI.5 1320b2–3). His view is not that all citizens, rich and poor alike, should be paid, but that compensation should be made to the poor alone, since in oligarchies the rich are already too powerful, and in any case they can afford whatever losses they incur through political participation.[50] The purpose of this institution is to enable and encourage the poor to protect themselves against becoming totally subordinate to the elite. Just as weighted voting in a democracy is a way to bring the rich closer to a position of equality, so paying the poor to participate in an oligarchy is a method of preventing its imbalance from becoming too extreme. Since Aristotle takes democracy to be a system of government dominated by the poor, he sees no value in encouraging as many of them as possible to attend the assembly. Such a measure only serves to increase the dominance of the poor, and is characteristic of the most extreme form of democracy (IV.6 1292b41–10).

12.7. Democracy, Ancient and Modern

Aristotle defines democracy as the rule of the poor for the sake of the poor alone; and because he holds that rule must be for the common good, he condemns democracy as a deviant political system (III.7 1279b8–10). One way to react to his definition and condemnation is

---

[50] For further discussion of paying citizens to participate in a jury or the assembly, or fining them for non-participation, see IV.6 1293a1–10, IV.9 1294a35–41, and IV.13 1297a17–29.

12.7. DEMOCRACY, ANCIENT AND MODERN

to say that it has nothing to do with us: that is not how *we* define democracy, and so Aristotle is not talking about an issue with which a modern democrat need be concerned. But were we to adopt this attitude, we would miss some important points of contact between his political universe and our own. A better approach, I suggest, is this. Using the word 'democracy' as it is often used today, we should regard Aristotle as a deeply anti-democratic thinker—but at the same time we should recognize that, in a different but equally important respect, he is a radically democratic thinker. What he most definitely is not is a philosopher whose politics have nothing to do with democracy as we now understand that concept.[51]

Let us work with a simple and naive definition: democracy is rule by the people. This is a vague formula, but nonetheless a serviceable one, because it leaves open a number of questions that should not be settled by a mere definition. Working with this equation, we can easily state the sense in which Aristotle is anti-democratic: included among 'the people' are working people, and in particular the banausoi that Aristotle wishes to exclude from citizenship. He is opposed to rule by the people in that he is opposed to giving power to *these* people. But having acknowledged this point, we should not lose sight of another feature of his political thought: he is equally opposed to giving exclusive power to elites—either the proposed scientific elite favored by Plato or the entrenched elites of the real world. He holds that cities dominated by the wealthy, the prominent (*gnorimoi*), the refined (*charientes*), and the well-born should be pushed in a more democratic direction, by giving more power to ordinary people who have no special status or significant resources, but who can nonetheless play a useful political role because they can guard against the abuse of power without themselves becoming abusers of power. In the modern political world, a sensible and widely accepted justification for democratic rule is that elites cannot be trusted to rule on their own. Their power needs to be curbed, and the only way to do so is to create a significant political role for the

---

[51] For useful overviews of democratic theory, see Christiano, *The Rule of the Many*; Dahl, *Democracy and its Critics*; Graham, *The Battle of Democracy*; Katz, *Democracy and Elections*. For contrasts between ancient and modern democracy, see Finley, *Democracy Ancient and Modern*; Ostwald, 'Shares and Rights: "Citizenship" Greek Style and American Style'; Wolin, 'Norm and Form: The Constitutionalizing of Democracy'; Wood, 'Democracy: An Idea of Ambiguous Ancestry'; Wood, 'Demos versus "We, the People": Freedom and Democracy Ancient and Modern'. For analogies between the ideology of ancient democracy and the ethos of the modern democratic workplaces, see Manville, 'Ancient Greek Democracy and the Modern Knowledge-Based Organization: Reflections on the Ideology of Two Revolutions'.

demos—ordinary people with little money, education, or status, whose individual influence is small, but whose collective strength can be made large. This is precisely Aristotle's way of thinking about the danger of elites.

In fact, we can go farther: we can say that in a sense Aristotle is not only a democrat but a radical democrat. He thinks that a city that eliminates elites entirely is far superior to one that merely restricts their power by balancing it against the power of the people. As we have seen, both the ideal community of VII and VIII and the more realistic ideal of IV.11 are societies in which each citizen has equal power and offices are shared in turn. In these communities, no small and exclusive group has extraordinary power. For it is a central feature of Aristotle's political outlook that no special expertise or privileged status is required of those who run a community's affairs: all it takes is normal reasoning ability and a good moral education.[52] And as his discussion of the middle regime in IV.11 makes clear, the moral education that makes someone a good citizen need be nothing extraordinary. When a community has a sufficient number of these people, it can distribute power equally; no citizen need be given powers that are not shared equally and in turn by the others. Our formula for democracy—'rule by the people'—can be taken to mean rule by people of just this sort: those who have ordinary reasoning powers and ordinary moral skills. Aristotle thinks that this egalitarian community is far better than one in which considerable power is held by elites. It is not amiss to call attention to this feature of his thought by saying that he is a democrat of sorts.[53]

In fact, one legitimate objection that can be made to Aristotle's thinking is that he is too democratic. It seems naive to suppose that a political community can do without elites entirely. Or perhaps this objection might best be put by saying that the radical egalitarianism Aristotle proposes might work in a small and simple community, but that it is totally impractical in the large

---

[52] On the amateurism of the ideal city, see 6.10. The egalitarianism of the middling constitution is emphasized at IV.11 1295b25–7.

[53] One should also note a common strand that runs between Aristotle and the sort of liberalism that assigns to liberal education a central role in democratic politics. I have in mind the liberalism of Ryan's *Liberal Anxieties and Liberal Education*. Ryan speaks not at all about the maximization of liberty, or its priority over all other goods; his emphasis, rather, is on the important place in a liberal society of those habits of thought that are inculcated by means of a liberal education. In this respect, his politics are not very distant from those I attribute to Aristotle's ideal city (6.12).

nation-states that make up the modern world. According to this point of view, 'rule by the people' should be taken to mean 'a significant degree of rule by the people', and it must be understood that various elites—politicians, business people, professionals, and the like—must also be allowed considerable power. So long as ordinary people have the ability to scrutinize and restrict the powers of these elites, democracy is in place.

But now notice the results to which we are led by this way of thinking: If 'rule by the people' is taken to mean that ordinary people should have sufficient power to guard against the excessive power of elites, then once again Aristotle must be counted as a philosopher who sees the merits of democracy. In fact, if 'democracy' is used in this way, then both his ideal democracy and ideal oligarchy deserve to be called 'democracies' in our sense of the term. For in both regimes, the power of elites is significantly curbed. In his best democracy, the people have somewhat more power than do the elites; and in his best oligarchy somewhat less; but in either case, a rough parity between the two forces is maintained.

Where do these reflections on the various meanings of 'democracy' lead us? We will revisit this subject (13.2), but for now, two modest conclusions can be drawn. First, we inhabitants of the modern world cannot think seriously about democracy without addressing the question of what role, if any, various kinds of elites should play in the life of a nation. Second, a significant portion of Aristotle's political thought is devoted to precisely this issue: how should elite and ordinary people be combined so that each is encouraged to play the role that it performs best?

12.8. The Invasion of the Banausoi

Our discussion of democracy has focused on the best and worst kinds, because these extremes most fully reveal the underlying principles of his political thought. When we turn our attention to the intermediate forms, the principal lesson we learn is one we might have expected from Aristotle: democracies decline when they lower the standards of citizenship. The best democracies are those dominated by citizens who live in the countryside and have time only for a limited number of meetings of the assembly (IV.6 1292b25–34, VI.4 1318b9–11). In such regimes, care is taken to insure that only those are allowed to enroll as citizens whose parents are married and have citizen status; and the property qualification for citizenship is high enough to keep unskilled workers and at least some banausoi—the vulgar craftsmen Aristotle abhors—off the citizen rolls. When these standards are lowered and the urban-dwelling workers are not only allowed to participate in the assembly, but encouraged to do so by monetary compensation, then democracy enters its worst phase.[54] Aristotle's prejudice against craftsmen thus forms a central feature of his taxonomy of democracy.

But notice that we have at least this much in common with his way of thinking: it is a widely accepted assumption of modern political thought, no less than Aristotle's, that citizens should make significant positive contributions to the well-being of a nation. But in the modern world, those contributions are primarily economic in nature, whereas for Aristotle they are primarily political. We are happy about granting citizenship to immigrants only if they are willing to take jobs, work hard, and pay taxes. Of course, they must also obey the law, but this merely calls for restraint rather than positive contributions; and in any case, we require this of everyone, citizens and non-citizens alike. The most effective way to defend a welcoming stance towards immigrant populations is to argue that there are significant economic benefits in such a policy. For us, no less than for Aristotle, the underlying basis for citizenship is reciprocity: we confer an advantageous political status on people in return for economic goods. Aristotle, by contrast, assumes that the principal role of the citizen is to contribute in some way to a city's governance. And this is a perfectly natural assumption for him to make: after all, to be given the status of a citizen is to receive a *political* benefit, and so it is appropriate to expect *political* benefits from the citizen in return. Why should economic benefits entitle someone to a political reward?

These remarks suggest that we should distinguish two aspects of Aristotle's attitude towards banausoi. First, he assumes that the

---

[54] In the best democracy, citizens must have a moderate amount of property, and must be born of citizen parents. The next best democracy drops the property qualification, and increasingly deviant democratic regimes further dilute restrictions on the status of parents. See IV.4 1291b30–1292a4, IV.6 1292b22–41, VI.4 1318b27–32, 1319b6–11. A property qualification will keep unskilled workers (*thētes*) off the citizen roles but cannot reliably disqualify craftsmen, since many of them become rich (III.5 1278a21–5). In several passages, Aristotle emphasizes the need to increase the property qualification in times of prosperity (V.6 1306b9–16, V.8 1308a35–b10; cf. V.3 1303a21–5, V.7 1307a27–9). The idea that property promotes the independence needed for good citizenship is found in other times and places. For the prevalence of this idea in early America, see Wood, *The Radicalism of the American Revolution*, pp. 178, 269.

career of a manual worker detracts from his ability to be a good citizen. This is an assumption we can easily reject. But his second assumption is not so readily dismissed: that a citizen has an active and political task, namely to take part in the governance of a city and to safeguard it against deterioration. He makes this assumption because of his fear of the destructive power of entrenched elites. The reason why he thinks that ordinary citizens must not be passive observers of the political scene, and must not let the wealthy and well-connected run the affairs of the city, is that the worst tendencies of the elite will emerge when they are not carefully watched by the demos. We must not reject Aristotle's conception of a citizen as someone who plays an active role in governance merely because we are not used to thinking in these terms. If, like him, we are concerned about the great power of elites in our polity, then it is natural to look for ways in which ordinary citizens can participate more fully in governance.[55] If we want to reproduce in our own society the measures he endorses for oligarchies, we should pay the poor to vote, and assign their votes greater weight than those of the wealthy.[56]

12.9. Political Friendship

Now that we have completed our examination of non-ideal regimes, we are in a position to understand some important remarks Aristotle makes in the *Ethics* about the kind of friendship that is present in some cities and absent in others. He begins VIII.11 by saying: 'In each of the constitutions there appears to be friendship to the extent that there is justice as well' (1161a10–11). Justice and friendship are not the same thing, but both admit of degrees, and as justice diminishes so too does friendship. Since correct regimes promote the common good and are without qualification just, they also contain a considerable degree of friendship; deviant regimes have a smaller degree of justice, and therefore less friendship (1161a30–1). But what sort of human relationship does Aristotle have in mind when he ascribes these different degrees of friendship to different

---

[55] For a helpful overview of recent work on citizenship, see Kymlicka and Norman, 'Return of the Citizen: A Survey of Recent Work on Citizenship Theory'. A proposal for more direct democracy can be found in anon., 'Full Democracy'. On the notion of participatory democracy, see Graham, *The Battle of Democracy*, pp. 149–69. Putnam's *Bowling Alone* studies the decline of participatory habits among Americans in recent decades.

[56] Recall the points made in 12.n.32 and 12.6.

constitutional forms? The term he uses for this relationship is 'political friendship', but this by itself tells us nothing. We need to know what political friendship is.[57]

It is important to see that he uses this term in two different ways, although (surprisingly) he fails to point this out. One kind of political friendship is present in a city merely by virtue of the fact that it is a city. A city is by its nature a *koinōnia*, a 'community' or 'association,' and every *koinōnia*, however large or small, is a cooperative enterprise that benefits its members (*Pol.* I.1 1252a1–7). Aristotle calls every such relationship a *philia*, 'friendship'. Sailors who work together on a ship are 'friends' in this sense, since they collaborate in order to make a profit or to promote each other's safety. People who regularly exchange goods in a business relationship are 'friends', since each partner benefits others in the expectation of a return. Cities that form an alliance for the sake of mutual protection are also counted as 'friends' in this sense.[58] All that is meant by applying the word *philia* to such a relationship is that the parties take it to be in their interest to cooperate with each other. When cities form alliances or businessmen form partnerships, their motives are self-interested; they benefit others, but only because they expect to get something for themselves from the relationship.[59]

Citizens, according to Aristotle, are friends in precisely the same way. In every city, whether it is a democracy or an oligarchy, a polity or an aristocracy, the citizens cooperate with each other in economic and legal institutions. They exchange goods in the market place, hear cases in court, fill offices when required to do so, serve in battle for their mutual protection, and join in common religious festivals. They cooperate in sustaining these basic civic institutions not because they love or even like each other, but because these forms of cooperation are in their own interest. A citizen who is a craftsman and sells his wares in the market place benefits his fellow citizens not out of sheer benevolence but because he will be paid. Soldiers who train for war need have no higher motive than their own personal security. Just as sailors on a ship realize that they will be safe

---

[57] For other recent discussions of this concept, see Cooper, 'Political Animals and Civic Friendship'; Yack, *The Problems of a Political Animal*, pp. 109–27; Stern-Gillet, *Aristotle's Philosophy of Friendship*, pp. 147–69; Schollmeier, *Other Selves*, pp. 75–96; Swanson, *The Public and the Private in Aristotle's Political Philosophy*, pp. 165–92.

[58] See 9.22 on *koinōnia*, esp. 9.n.39. On sailors as friends, see *NE* VIII.9 1160a15–16; on alliances, *NE* VIII.4 1157a26–8; *EE* VII.10 1242b22–7.

[59] 'Those who are friends because of the advantage do not like each other for themselves, but because they get some good from each other' (*NE* VIII.3 1156a10–12).

12.9. POLITICAL FRIENDSHIP

only if they work together as a group, so a citizen-soldier learns to fight alongside others because he is more likely to survive when he cooperates with his fellow citizens. The political friendship that exists among citizens is nothing more high-minded than this kind of mutually advantageous cooperation.[60]

When this is the only kind of political friendship that exists among the citizens, there is considerable tension between them, as there is in every relationship based entirely on mutual advantage. If nothing holds people together but self-interest, if they have little or no concern with the well-being of others except when this redounds to their own advantage, then each suspects the others of trying to get as much as possible for themselves and contribute as little as possible to others. Aristotle's discussion in the *Ethics* of friendships based entirely on advantage stresses the quarrelsome nature of this relationship (VIII.13 1162b5–21). And, as we have seen from our study of Books IV–VI, the same problem afflicts those who are political 'friends' in democracies and oligarchies, especially in the most extreme forms of these regimes. (The situation is not quite so bad in the best democracies and oligarchies—a point to which we will soon return.) Each faction distrusts the other and suspects that it is trying to get a greater advantage; even if each grudgingly admits that it needs the rival faction, cooperation is nonetheless blended with suspicion, and relationships are always in danger of deteriorating.

So much, then, for one kind of political friendship. The other variety, which Aristotle calls *homonoia*, 'like-mindedness', is more satisfactory, but rarely found. In the *Ethics*, he introduces this notion by saying: 'Friendship seems to hold cities together, and legislators are more concerned with it than with justice; for like-mindedness seems to be in a way similar to friendship, and they are especially eager for this and seek above all to drive out faction, because it is their enemy' (VIII.1 1155a22–6). The kind of political friendship that is necessarily present in every city is entirely compatible with faction. But *homonoia* is not, and that is why legislators would like to create it.

What precisely is this like-mindedness? Aristotle devotes a full chapter (IX.6) to it, and tells us that it is present when the citizens 'agree about what is advantageous and choose the same things and do the things that seem right to them in common' (1167a26–8). He then

---

[60] This is why Aristotle consistently classifies the friendship citizens have with each other as a friendship based on advantage. See *NE* VIII.9 1160a8–28, IX.1 1163b32–5; *EE* VII.10 1242b21–7.

gives some examples: it exists in a city when all citizens agree that offices should be elective, or that an alliance with another city should be made, or that a certain man who is willing to rule should do so (1167a30–2). Notice that all of these are points of considerable generality: citizens can agree to hold elections, but vote for different candidates; they can favor an alliance, but disagree about its terms; they can choose a leader without knowing beforehand what his commands will be. Evidently, like-mindedness is consensus among citizens about the fundamental terms of their cooperation. Disagree as they may about details and particulars, their relationship is not poisoned by hostility, suspicion, and bitterness. Their disagreements take place against a broader background of trust and consensus.

This makes it easy to see why Aristotle says that there is a considerable degree of friendship in just political systems, and far less of it in deviant regimes (*NE* VIII.11). In a kingship and an aristocracy, the extraordinary virtue of the rulers is acknowledged by their subjects; both ruler and ruled gladly accept their hierarchical relationship (11.10–11). And in a polity (or 'timocracy' as Aristotle calls it here[61]), there is also a fundamental consensus that rule should be shared in turns, because no one seeks an advantage over others.[62] By contrast, in oligarchies and democracies, the rival claims to power made by each party remain unresolved; instead, each group rightly suspects the other of harboring a desire to increase its advantage. If some degree of stability is achieved in these regimes, that is not because there is agreement about the fundamental terms of cooperation, but because an equilibrium of opposed forces takes hold. The best that can be hoped for in this situation is that mutual distrust might play a useful role, as each faction keeps a watchful eye on the other and curbs its excesses. The association among such citizens is like any quarrelsome relationship that is sustained over time because distrust is not so great as to undermine all cooperation, and the advantages of continuing the relationship are seen to outweigh the attractions of breaking it off.

Aristotle's statement that 'in each of the constitutions there appears to be friendship to the extent that there is justice as well' (*NE* VIII.11 1161a10–11) implies that there is even some

---

[61] See *NE* VIII.10 1160a33–5 and above, 11.n.44.
[62] What Aristotle says at *NE* VIII.11 1161a25–30 about the friendship that exists in timocracies accords well with his characterization of the middling regime as a site of friendship (*Pol.* IV.11 1295b25–7).

friendship—though a small amount of it—in deviant regimes. He does not discuss these details in the *Ethics*, but now that we have familiarized ourselves with the taxonomy of *Pol.* IV–VI, we can see how to complete his picture. In moderate democracies and oligarchies there is a small degree of *homonoia*, just as there is a limited form of justice; but these qualities disappear entirely when these constitutions become extreme. In moderately deviant regimes, the citizens in a way agree about who should rule, but deep disagreements nonetheless persist. In the best democracies and oligarchies, rich and poor have accustomed themselves to a compromise in which power is shared in a roughly equal way. Each side thinks the other has more power than it deserves, but neither side thinks it worth its while to press the issue, and so they set aside their fundamental differences in order to reap the benefits of distrustful cooperation. There is a limited degree of political friendship in their relationship, just as there is a limited degree of justice. The glue that binds these factions together is weak precisely because fundamental disagreements still persist. Hostility has been subdued but not eliminated. There is always a danger that it will grow, that more extreme political systems will emerge, and that rival classes will abandon the rule of law. When *homonoia* is so weak, cities are most in need of leaders who know how to make corrosive tendencies correct each other. Books IV–VI are a handbook for students of political science who wish to take up this task.

Homonoia—consensus about general matters—is always one proper goal of politics, regardless of the circumstances. Ideally, one would like there to be consensus among citizens about what the good life is, but Aristotle realizes that this can be achieved only in the most unusual circumstances. Failing that, the most one can reasonably expect is that economic conditions will allow citizens to develop a sense of trust and a willingness to cooperate on fair terms. But when the gap between rich and poor grows too large, as it often does, then one must lower one's sights and try to fashion a partial consensus and a rough balance between opposed factions. In ordinary conditions, those who train with Aristotle to lead the political life can expect only modest results, and are painfully aware of how far reality departs from the ideal or even the second-best. It is nonetheless valuable for them to know how large this gap is. The best protection against bitter disappointment in politics is to realize from the start how poor are the materials at one's disposal, and how difficult it will be to make something tolerable out of them. Those who know what would be ideal and therefore how defective reality is are the ones who are best equipped to make modest improvements in the real world.

13

Final Thoughts

13.1. *Idealism and Realism*

Now that we have completed our examination of Aristotle's political theory and can survey its various components as a whole, we should recognize a striking pattern in his thought. He proposes a number of different ways in which human beings might build and sustain satisfactory political communities, but he believes that the likelihood that any one of them will be realized is extremely low. The ideal community to which he devotes most of his attention—the one described in Books VII and VIII—is comprised entirely of citizens who are unqualifiedly wise and just. Although such a city is not an impossibility, Aristotle knows that it has never existed, and he wastes no effort proposing schemes by which existing cities can be transformed into ideal ones. Books VII and VIII show that there is nothing inherent in human nature or human circumstances that requires cities to be sites of hostility and moral corruption. The ideal city described there serves the purpose of revealing how much we are missing in our actual political communities. We must not complacently accept the world as it is, and one effective way to stimulate our dissatisfaction is to portray a splendid community that human beings could create but—perversely—do not. Aristotle does not depict this ideal in the expectation that it will eventually come to pass, if only we persevere in making small improvements in our present political communities. Dissatisfaction with civic life is likely to be our permanent condition. Our job is to make good use of that dissatisfaction.[1]

There are other ideals proposed in Aristotle's *Politics* besides this one, but they too require individuals and circumstances that can occur only rarely (if they have ever occurred at all). Kingship and aristocracy, as these regimes are conceived in Book III, require the existence of an individual or small group of individuals whose virtue is so extraordinary that they can be trusted with unrestricted power over all others (11.10–11). This is a different ideal from the one proposed in VII and VIII, but it is, in Aristotle's eyes, a remote possibility, for people who deserve and are recognized to deserve unchecked power are few and far between. A more far-fetched idea appears briefly at VII.14 1332b16–23, where we are asked to imagine a race of beings superior to ours in body and soul, a race to which we could relinquish all of our political responsibilities (6.10, 11.14). Such godlike creatures would allow mere humans to escape their political responsibilities once and for all—a pleasant dream, but nothing worth dwelling on.

A far more feasible ideal is proposed in IV.11. It is no mere dream to imagine a city comprising primarily men of middling wealth and fortune who trust each other to promote the common good and to share offices on an equal and rotating basis (12.3). Aristotle thinks that his discussion in IV.11 has great practical value, because efforts can be made in many different types of city to give these middling men an important role to play in governance (IV.12 1296b34–40). But he also says that a city in which such people are the *dominant* force has rarely existed (IV.11 1296a36–8).[2] It is rare to find citizens who are devoted to the common good and willing to serve the public out of a sense of fairness, and still more rare to find a community in which such people form the majority. Cities rent by faction, each biased in its own favor, each relishing or fearing domination, are far more common. So even the most feasible ideal found in the *Politics* is one that Aristotle judges to be a distant possibility.[3]

---

[1] In this respect, my reading of Aristotle is like the one defended by Yack throughout *The Problems of a Political Animal*.

[2] Note that a polity exists when the middle class is larger than both other classes combined or each separately (IV.11 1295b34–9). I take Aristotle to mean that even the weaker condition has rarely existed.

[3] Aristotle therefore provides an exception to the claim that 'Greek and medieval thinkers ... entertained very sanguine prospects about the possibility of reasonable agreement about the good life ... The result was that ... [they] usually assigned to the state the task of protecting and fostering substantial conceptions of the good life' (Larmore, *The*

13.1. IDEALISM AND REALISM

This then is one of the central messages of his practical philosophy: politics is typically a bad business and is likely to remain so. He arrives at this sorry conclusion both because of the assumptions he makes about human nature and because he is guided by a normative thesis about the way cities should be governed. That normative thesis is simple and incontrovertible: political power ought to be used impartially for the good of all members of the community. But his assessment of human nature tells him that people have difficulty inhabiting the impartial perspective that service to the community requires (III.9 1280a15–16). Unless human beings are given a splendid moral education or grow up in unusual circumstances that allow them to get by with something less, they will allow pecuniary interests to play too large a role in their political decisions, or will use power as a tool to assert their dominance and humiliate their enemies. Human nature throws up another obstacle to good governance: we do not like to be constrained or regulated by others, and so making laws and getting people to obey them is by its nature a difficult matter (12.5). When we distrust the motives or wisdom of those who make the laws (as we often should), it becomes all the more difficult to achieve a stable legal order. And when we ourselves are put in positions of power, it is difficult to resist the temptation to do what we think everyone else does with such opportunities: use them for the satisfaction of our own desires or those of our political allies.

Aristotle thinks that satisfactory solutions to this problem can be achieved only if certain kinds of person have power. One must find individuals who are perfectly virtuous, or at any rate modest, fair, and public-spirited. When too few have these qualities, no amount of constitutional design or legislation will set things right. When members of a community have little respect for moral norms and ideals, and recognize that others are equally cynical, each will look for ways to use the legal system to advance his own narrow purposes and get the upper hand over others. Public life will be a competition for spoils.

What is a decent person to do in these all too common situations? Withdrawal from politics is a tempting response, and Aristotle is sympathetic to it. Philosophy is a better vocation than politics, for those who are intellectually inclined and talented. But only a few

---

Morals of Modernity, p. 123). Aristotle was pessimistic about the prospects for such agreement, and his belief that the city should promote the good does not rest on any such premise. The same holds true, I believe, of Plato. Indeed, it is not clear where confirming instances of Larmore's hypothesis can be found.

will follow this path, and in any case the withdrawal of decent people from politics would be a disaster for all. One of Aristotle's simplest but most important insights is that bad cities are not all on a par. There are important moral distinctions to be made among them, and one way to lead a worthwhile life is to devote oneself to the task of preventing partially just cities from losing the small moral value they possess. Although no one should be content with civic life as it is, it would be equally mistaken to think that such institutions as the rule of law and the rough justice that distrustful factions can sustain are insignificant moral achievements. Those who are interested in leading a political life in a corrupt city can do so without compromising their moral integrity, although there is no guarantee that their efforts to make improvements will be successful. Unless one chooses a philosophical life—an option available to few—one must not withdraw in moral disgust from the public world and allow one's city to sink to lower levels of corruption. A well-lived public life is possible even in these reduced circumstances.

13.2. *Critic and Ally of Democracy*

Since we live in an age deeply suspicious of utopianism, and expect modest gains at best in political life, the part of Aristotle's thought just described in the previous section will appeal, perhaps more than any other, to contemporary readers.[4] But there is another component of his thought to which we are likely to respond with more mixed emotions. As we have seen in our examination of Books IV–VI, he warns his readers against the dangers of giving exclusive power to two groups: traditional elites on the one hand and 'the people'—the demos—on the other. We are likely to respond warmly to his warning against the first of these groups, but what should we make of the other half of his message? Who should have power, if not the people? After all, it is the essence of democracy that the people should rule—and who today is so foolish as to condemn democracy?

Aristotle's hostility to manual labor and those who must work for a living is a prejudice our age has rightly rejected, but we must be careful not to miss an important element of truth in his attitude. Voters who work for wages, as we all do, are sorely tempted to base

---

[4] For an eloquent expression of this viewpoint, see Berlin, *The Crooked Timber of Humanity*, pp. 1–48.

their decisions not on a desire for the good of all but on their narrow perceptions of financial self-interest. We are all banausoi now. Those who work with their minds are just as vulgar as anyone else, since it is vulgar to elevate narrow occupational perspectives above a concern for the well-being of all. In a commercial democracy like ours—a democracy in which citizens generally vote from selfish and pecuniary motives—all alike are disqualified from exercising power. Aristotle's condemnation of ancient Greek democracy is no mere antiquarian idea, but extends to modern democracies as well, because it is based on the premise that when democratic citizens make political decisions, pecuniary motives exert a powerful influence, and as a result the common good receives too little attention. He admits that the elites—the well-born, privileged and wealthy—are as bad or worse, but their failures do not excuse those of the demos.

At least this much can be said for Aristotle's point of view: being at the bottom of the social hierarchy does not by itself guarantee impartiality or confer moral insight. If democracy is based on the idea that plain human beings who have ordinary human motives are qualified to rule precisely because of their humanity, then it is a political ideology that is vulnerable to the formidable objection that Aristotle puts forward: unless something is done to curb the worst features of human nature, the collective decisions of plain folks will be no better than the decisions made by traditional elites. Only those human beings who have been shaped into moral beings and in whom the evils of human nature have to some extent been curbed can legitimately claim political power. Only democracies composed of such citizens deserve our full support.

In both the ancient and modern world, democracy is associated with political equality, and in this sense two of Aristotle's ideals (those of VII and VIII and of IV.11) are more democratic than any modern nation-state is likely ever to be (12.7). A polity in which all citizens attend meetings and vote in the assembly, in which offices are rotated among all on an equal basis, and in which a sense of fairness prevents monetary considerations from distorting collective decisions: this has now become an impossibility. And as we have seen, Aristotle takes this to be a remote ideal even in his own age. But although we cannot embody this kind and degree of equality in our political institutions, there is another feature of his thinking that can more easily be adapted to modern circumstances. The nations we now call democracies are in fact mixed regimes, in which the rule of the people is heavily diluted and many different sorts of elite—judicial, professional, corporate, moneyed—play a powerful role. In fact, we can legitimately ask how much value there is in calling them democracies at all, rather than oligarchies that have a small democratic component. This is in large part an empirical question, and we are in no position to answer it here. What we can say is that distrust of elites is one of the central features of Aristotle's political thought, and that in this respect he sees considerable merit in democratic politics. The people are rightly suspicious of those who claim higher social standing or greater political insight, and a well-designed constitution will make good use of their distrust. One thing the people can do well—so long as they have not become utterly servile—is to keep a watchful eye on those above them. When cities have to rely on some mixture of elites and ordinary people, as they almost always do, their constitutions must strike a balance between giving too much power to either group. There are times when giving more power to the people and encouraging wider participation in public life is the Aristotelian thing to do.[5]

13.3. Freedom and the Good

As we have seen (12.4–5), Aristotle criticizes democrats for their false conception of freedom, according to which a free person should be allowed to live as he pleases. This aspect of ancient democratic ideology is likely to strike a chord with us modern readers, or in any case with those of us who have been shaped by the liberal tradition, with its emphasis on the importance of allowing people to speak and think freely, to worship and work as they choose, and in general to lead their lives according to their own lights.[6]

But we should be careful not to assume without reflection that the

---

[5] For accounts of Aristotle that place greater emphasis on his hostility to democracy than I have in this work, see Wood and Wood, *Class Ideology and Ancient Political Theory*, pp. 1–5, 209–65; Farrar, *The Origins of Democratic Thinking*, pp. 266–74.

[6] For the view that 'Athenian democratic *eleutheria* [freedom] in several important respects was strikingly similar to the concept of freedom in modern liberal democracies', see Hansen, 'The Ancient Athenian and the Modern Liberal View of Liberty as a Democratic Ideal', p. 99. For some contrasts, see Wallace, 'Law, Freedom, and the Concept of Citizens' Rights in Democratic Athens'. Hansen notes (p. 96) that when Constant made his famous contrast between ancient and modern liberty, he set classical Athens aside as an exception. See 'The Liberty of the Ancients Compared with that of the Moderns'.

13.3. FREEDOM AND THE GOOD

democratic conception of freedom that Aristotle attacks is really something we wish to defend. He says that democrats wrongly equate freedom with doing whatever one likes (V.9 1310a32), and implies that their goal is to have as little regulation as possible (VI.2 1317b14–17). They think that laws should be few in number and that the community should restrain individuals only in ways that are strictly necessary. Although the idea is inherently vague—for how do we decide how much government is necessary?—it has nonetheless attracted many modern thinkers and citizens.[7] One of the many difficulties for this way of thinking is that it threatens to leave the state with too few resources to protect the values often identified with liberalism. If no one will hire me because of my political opinions or my religious beliefs, then my freedom to speak my mind or worship as I choose is worth little. To protect the way of life chosen by individuals who lack economic power, a complex set of legal institutions and intrusions into the marketplace is often necessary.[8]

Since Aristotle lived at a time and place far more uniform in religious practices and beliefs than ours, it is understandable that he should accept without a moment's thought the idea that the city should regulate the religious lives of citizens. Civic support of religious festivals was the common custom in the ancient Greek world, to which no one registered any objections.[9] We have seen in Chapter 6 how Aristotle manages to have philosophy, science, and traditional religion live in peace with each other. But times have changed, religious ideas and customs are more diverse, and a smaller degree of civic involvement in religious life is suitable to the circumstances of the modern world. Rights—for example, the right to practice one religion rather than another, or none at all—have

---

[7] For recent philosophical defenses of a minimal role for the state, see Lomasky, *Persons, Rights and the Moral Community*; Nozick, *Anarchy, State and Utopia*; and Rasmussen and Den Uyl, *Liberty and Nature*. The high standing of Thomas Jefferson in American political life has a great deal to do with his conviction that the best state is the one that governs least. For a brief overview and critique of 'libertarianism', as it is sometimes called, see Kymlicka, *Contemporary Political Philosophy*, pp. 95–159.

[8] Note too that if the state must not encourage or discourage one way of life rather than another, leaving the citizen free to arrive at his own conception of what is worth doing, then no incentives can be created for taking a strong interest in public affairs, and no penalties can be attached to non-participation. There is all the more danger that politics will be controlled by small factions and elites.

[9] There was of course disagreement about the nature of the gods in the ancient Greek world, but no one claimed that religion should be a purely private matter and that the city's support of religious festivals was bad social policy.

become an essential part of our political equipment.[10] Just as Aristotle searched for mechanisms to lower the degree of mistrust between hostile factions, so we citizens of the modern world need modern devices to deal with new dangers. When we affirm the citizen's right to worship as he chooses (or not to worship at all), we are not contradicting Aristotle but merely bypassing him. We are addressing an issue with which he need have had no concern.[11]

But it may be protested that nonetheless an oppressive idea is fundamental to Aristotle's whole outlook on politics: he thinks it appropriate for the polity to make its decisions by appealing to a substantive conception of human well-being. His ideal city is one in which adult citizens collectively impose on a younger generation a single notion of how life should be lived. And even in imperfect cities, where citizens have different conceptions of happiness, Aristotle still makes use of his own theory of well-being and virtue when he makes recommendations about how they should be governed. Just as it never occurs to him that religion and politics should be separate spheres, so too he assumes without a moment's thought that politics and ultimate ends must not be kept apart. On the contrary, he finds it entirely obvious that politics must be guided by a conception of the good. When he designs institutions, he finds it natural to ask how well they promote human flourishing. He assumes that a political leader must ask what is ultimately good for

---

[10] Here I take sides in a lively controversy: was the concept of natural rights unknown to the ancient world? For an overview of the debate, see Miller, *NJR*, pp. 87–93. He argues that the rights to citizenship and property play a central role in Aristotle's political thought (pp. 93–139, 309–31). For criticism, see Kraut, 'Are There Natural Rights in Aristotle?' In acknowledging that we now need conceptual tools and institutions (such as rights) not needed in the world of the polis, I am in partial agreement with Holmes, 'Aristippus in and out of Athens'. But the main theme of his article—that Greek political philosophy has become useless to us because of the greater social differentiation of the modern world—must be recognized as an exaggeration, if the argument of this book is correct. The fact that we must add to what we learn from Aristotle does not mean that we can learn nothing from him.

[11] Though I have in this paragraph contrasted modern religious diversity with the greater uniformity of religious practices of the fourth-century polis, we must be careful not to exaggerate the fragmentation of the modern world or to underestimate the difficulties that would be created by excessive diversity. What would happen, for example, if ancient religions—involving taboos, sacrifices, and social hierarchies deeply at odds with modern sensibilities—were fully active in our midst? The right to worship as one pleases would then become a far more questionable notion. The pride we take in our toleration for diversity tacitly rests on a background of moral and empirical consensus. The separation of religion and politics presupposes that churches, temples, mosques, and the like are fundamentally moral and non-coercive institutions. When they are not, the case for state supervision is strengthened.

13.3. FREEDOM AND THE GOOD

people—and this means not what some people *think* is worthwhile, but what really is such.

Is there anything wrong with this fundamental feature of his political philosophy? We should distinguish three different ways of opposing his idea. First, we might be skeptical about the whole project of inquiring into ultimate ends. That is, we might think that in this area there is no rational way to decide whether one conception of a good life is more defensible or persuasive than another.[12] Second, we might on the contrary believe that this is a matter that can be resolved by reason, and that in fact Aristotle's own conception of human well-being is seriously mistaken. Third, we might think that politics should have nothing to do with ultimate ends—even if Aristotle's view or some other conception of ultimate ends is rationally defensible. Final ends, we might say, are matters to be thought about by each of us individually and privately, but are not to be talked about collectively when we address each other as fellow citizens. In discussing rival candidates, judicial appointments, pending legislation, or any of the major issues of the day, we should censor ourselves whenever we are about to propose or rely on thoughts about which kinds of life are worthwhile and which kinds of good are intrinsically valuable. The only kinds of good we should discuss, when we fulfill one of the responsibilities of citizenship and talk about politics to each other, are those that merely have instrumental value.[13]

Of these three ways of criticizing Aristotle, surely the least promising is the third. For it says that even if some conceptions of the

---

[12] Something close to this view is defended by Barry, *Justice as Impartiality*, pp. 168–73. He argues for the 'inherent uncertainty of all conceptions of the good' (p. 169). See too Putnam, cited in 2.n.12.

[13] No one defends this position in the terms I have used here, but it is sometimes said that the *government* must always act on principles that are neutral between competing conceptions of the good. See e.g. Rawls, *Political Liberalism*, pp. 179–80 ('the government can no more act . . . to advance human excellence . . . than it can to advance Catholicism or Protestantism . . .'); Dworkin, *A Matter of Principle*, p. 191; Waldron, 'Legislation and Moral Neutrality', p. 154. (Rawls, pp. xxiii–iv, 134–5, emphasizes the distance between his version of liberalism and the political practices and thought of the ancient world.) If governments must be neutral in the way proposed by these authors, then political debate about what the government should do must be similarly constrained. Candidates for office must not put forward a vision of the good, if such ideas ought not to inform the principles on which they will act, should they be elected. Furthermore, when citizens become agents of the state—e.g. in referenda—then they too must set aside their conceptions of the good. The more porous the wall between citizens and their government (and in a democracy it ought to be porous), the greater is the silencing effect of the principle that states must be neutral regarding the good. For further discussion, see Galston, *Liberal Purposes*; Kraut, 'Politics, Neutrality, and the Good'; and Sher, *Beyond Neutrality*.

good are more defensible than others, that should make no difference to us when we speak to each other as fellow citizens. Yet how can this be so? If some ways of life can be shown to be better than others, why should the state not use its resources to educate citizens to recognize this fact, and make the better alternatives more easily available to them? And why should we not vote for candidates who will do this?

The best way to defend the idea that in politics we should be silent about substantive conceptions of well-being is to adopt a skeptical stance towards this dimension of normative discourse, and to urge such skepticism on others. After all, if there is no rational way to show that some lives or goods are better than others, then it is a waste of a citizen's time to discuss this issue with other citizens, and any legislative proposals that are based on premises about ultimate ends are without foundation. But notice that the skeptic is forced to make an important concession: he cannot expect others to accept his skepticism without argument. When some of us address civic issues by appealing to a conception of human well-being, the skeptic cannot expect us to censor ourselves simply because *he* thinks that our ideas are incapable of a rational defense. He must enter the fray of argument and convince us of his skepticism. And this means that he must try to understand Aristotle's conception of the good, along with others, and show why they are mistaken, or why we should suspend judgment about them.

The same point applies to those who pursue the second line of attack mentioned above, according to which Aristotle's conception of the good should be set aside because a better one is available to us. Perhaps so; but the only way to decide the issue is to subject his theory to criticism. We must therefore consider the merits of his thesis that human well-being consists in a lifetime of excellence in thought, feeling, and social behaviour, adequately supplied with external resources. To put that thesis to the test, we must spell out in rich detail what it would be like to lead such a life. And since Aristotle is surely right that we are beings who live in large groups (7.2), we must imagine not just one person living such a life, but a whole community. So the question we must put to Aristotle is this: what kind of community would we have, if we all adhered to his ideas about how it is best to live our lives?

That is a question he answers most fully in Books VII and VIII of the *Politics*. Recall what we have found there. In a community organized around Aristotle's conception of well-being, the arts and

13.3. FREEDOM AND THE GOOD

sciences would flourish. All citizens would be well educated. None would live in isolation. All would enjoy their families, friends, and households, but each would also be an active citizen impartially dedicated to the common good. Issues facing the whole community would be discussed openly and thoughtfully, and disagreements would be free of rancor. A sense of justice and friendship would pervade the community. All would have the material resources needed to live well, and inequalities would be too small to excite envy. Citizens would value themselves and each other for their qualities as human beings, not for their wealth or power. They would be strong-minded enough to think clearly on their own, without subservience to others, but each would recognize the need for debate and would welcome advice. None would need to affirm his worth by seeking domination over others.

The attraction of such a community is undeniable. But does it give us all that we should want? Are there better lives than this, or others that are equally good? Or are some ways of life beyond rational comparison? It would be absurd to claim that Aristotle or anyone else has had the final word on these matters. What we can reasonably say, now that we have considered the broad sweep of his political thought, is that he provides us with an excellent starting place for our own reflections.

References

Editions, Translations, Commentaries

Barnes, Jonathan. *The Complete Works of Aristotle: The Revised Oxford Translation.* 2 vols. Princeton, NJ: Princeton University Press.
Irwin, Terence. *Aristotle: Nicomachean Ethics.* With introduction, notes, and glossary, 2nd edn. Indianapolis: Hackett, 1999.
Joachim, H. H. *Aristotle: The Nicomachean Ethics.* Commentary. Oxford: Clarendon Press, 1951.
Kennedy, George A. *Aristotle: on Rhetoric: A Theory of Civic Discourse.* Newly translated with introduction, notes, and appendixes. New York: Oxford University Press, 1991.
Keyt, David. *Aristotle: Politics Books V and VI.* Oxford: Clarendon Press, 1999.
Kraut, Richard. *Aristotle: Politics Books VII and VIII.* Oxford: Clarendon Press, 1997.
Lord, Carnes. *Aristotle: The Politics.* Translated and with an introduction, notes, and glossary. Chicago: University of Chicago Press, 1984.
Newman, W. L. *The Politics of Aristotle.* 4 vols. Salem, NH: Ayer. Repr. 1985.
Pakaluk, Michael. *Aristotle: Nicomachean Ethics Books VIII and IX.* Oxford: Clarendon Press, 1998.
Pellegrin, Pierre. *Aristote: Les Politiques,* 2nd edn. Paris: GF-Flammarion, 1993.
Reeve, C. D. C. *Aristotle: The Politics.* With introduction and notes. Indianapolis: Hackett, 1998.
Rhodes, P. J. *A Commentary on the Aristotelian Athenaion Politeia.* Oxford: Clarendon Press, 1981.
—— *Aristotle: The Athenian Constitution.* Translated with introduction and notes. London: Penguin, 1984.
Ross, W. D. *Aristotle:'s Metaphysics.* A revised text with introduction and commentary, vol. i. Oxford: Clarendon Press, 1924.
—— *Aristotle: The Nicomachean Ethics.* Translated with an introduction. Rev. by J. L. Ackrill and J. O. Urmson. Oxford: Oxford University Press, 1980.
—— *Aristotle: The Nicomachean Ethics.* Translated with an introduction. Rev. by J. L. Ackrill and J. O. Urmson. In Jonathan Barnes (ed.), *The Complete Works of Aristotle,* the revised Oxford translation, vol. ii. Princeton, NJ: Princeton University Press, 1984.
Saunders, Trevor J. *Aristotle: Politics Books I and II.* Translated with a commentary. Oxford: Clarendon Press, 1995.
Schütrumpf, Eckart. *Aristoteles Politik. Buch I.* Translation and commentary. Berlin: Akademie, 1991.

Simpson, Peter L. Phillips. *The Politics of Aristotle*. Translated, with introduction, analysis, and notes. Chapel Hill: University of North Carolina Press, 1997.
—— *A Philosophical Commentary on the Politics of Aristotle*. Chapel Hill: University of North Carolina Press, 1998.
Susemihl, Franz, and Hicks, R. D. *The Politics of Aristotle*. Text, introduction, analysis and commentary to Books I–V (= I–III, VII–VIII). London: Macmillan, 1894; repr. 1976.

Other Works

Anon. 'Full Democracy', *Economist*, 21 Dec. 1996.
Ackrill, J. L. 'Aristotle on *Eudaimonia*'. In Rorty (1980), pp. 15–33.
Adams, Robert Merrihew. *Finite and Infinite Goods*. New York: Oxford University Press, 1999.
Annas, Julia. *The Morality of Happiness*. New York: Oxford University Press, 1993.
Antony, Louise M. 'Natures and Norms'. *Ethics* 111 (2000), 8–36.
Arneson, Richard J. 'Human Flourishing versus Desire Satisfaction'. *Social Philosophy and Policy* 16 (1999), 113–42.
Austin, M. M., and P. Vidal-Naquet. *Economic and Social History of Greece*. Berkeley: University of California Press, 1977.
Avineri, Schlomo, and Avner de-Shalit (eds.). *Communitarianism and Individualism*. London: Oxford University Press, 1992.
Balme, D. M. 'Aristotle's Use of Division and Differentiae'. In Allan Gotthelf and James G. Lennox (eds.), *Philosophical Issues in Aristotle's Biology*. Cambridge: Cambridge University Press, 1987, pp. 69–89.
Barber, Benjamin R. *An Aristocracy of Everyone*. New York: Ballantine, 1992.
Barker, Ernest. *The Political Thought of Plato and Aristotle*. New York: Russell & Russell, 1959.
Barnes, Jonathan. 'Aristotle and the Methods of Ethics'. *Revue internationale de la philosophie* 34 (1981), pp. 490–511.
—— 'Aristotle and Political Liberty'. In Patzig, pp. 250–63.
—— (ed.). *The Cambridge Companion to Aristotle*. Cambridge: Cambridge University Press, 1995.
—— 'Metaphysics'. In Barnes (1995), pp. 66–108.
—— Malcolm Schofield, and Richard Sorabji (eds.). *Articles on Aristotle, ii: Ethics and Politics*. London: Duckworth, 1977.
Barry, Brian. *Justice as Impartiality*. Oxford: Oxford University Press, 1995.
Bell, Daniel. *Communitarianism and its Critics*. Oxford: Clarendon Press, 1993.
Berlin, Isaiah, *The Crooked Timber of Humanity*. New York: Knopf, 1991.
Blundell, Mary Whitlock. *Helping Friends and Harming Enemies*. New York: Cambridge University Press, 1989.

REFERENCES

Bodéüs Richard. *The Political Dimensions of Aristotle's Ethics*. Trans. Jan Edward Garrett. Albany, NY: State University of New York Press, 1993.
—— *Aristotle and the Theology of the Living Immortals*. Trans. Jan Edward Garrett. Albany, NY: State University of New York Press, 2000.
Boegehold, Alan. 'Resistance to Change in the Law at Athens'. In Ober and Hedrick, pp. 203-14.
Brandom, Robert B. *Making It Explicit*. Cambridge, Mass.: Harvard University Press, 1994.
Brandt, Richard. *A Theory of the Good and the Right*. Oxford: Clarendon Press, 1979.
Broadie, Sarah. *Ethics with Aristotle*. Oxford: Oxford University Press, 1991.
Brunschwig, Jacques. 'The Aristotelian Theory of Equity'. In Michael Frede and Gisela Striker (eds.), *Rationality in Greek Thought*. Oxford: Clarendon Press, 1996, pp. 115-55.
Brunt, P. A. 'Plato's Academy and Politics'. In *Studies in Greek History and Thought*. Oxford: Clarendon Press, 1993, pp. 282-342.
—— 'Aristotle and Slavery'. In *Studies in Greek History and Thought*. Oxford: Clarendon Press, 1993, pp. 343-88.
Burnyeat, Myles. 'Aristotle on Learning to be Good'. In Rorty (1980), pp. 69-92.
—— *A Map of Metaphysics Zeta*. Pittsburgh: Mathesis, forthcoming.
Cambiano, Giuseppe. 'Aristotle and the Anonymous Opponents of Slavery'. In M. I. Finley (ed.), *Classical Slavery*. London: Frank Cass, 1987, pp. 21-41.
Campbell, Mavis. 'Aristotle and Black Slavery: A Study in Race Prejudice'. *Race* 15 (1974), 283-302.
Charles, David. 'Comments on M. Nussbaum'. In Patzig, pp. 187-201.
—— *Aristotle on Meaning and Essence*. Oxford: Clarendon Press, 2000.
Christiano, Thomas. *The Rule of the Many*. Boulder, Colo.: Westview Press, 1996.
Chroust, Anton-Hermann. *Aristotle*, vol. i, London: Routledge & Kegan Paul, 1973.
Code, Alan. 'Owen on the Development of Aristotle's Metaphysics'. In Wians, pp. 303-25.
Cohen, David. *Law, Sexuality, and Society*. Cambridge: Cambridge University Press, 1991.
—— *Law, Violence, and Community in Classical Athens*. Cambridge: Cambridge University Press, 1995.
Cohen, G. A. *Self-Ownership, Freedom, and Equality*. Cambridge: Cambridge University Press, 1995.
—— *If You're an Egalitarian, How Come You're So Rich?* Cambridge, Mass.: Harvard University Press, 2000.
Constant, Benjamin. 'The Liberty of the Ancients Compared with that of the Moderns'. In *Benjamin Constant: Political Writings*, trans. and ed. Biancamaria Fontana. Cambridge: Cambridge University Press, 1988.

Cook, Kathleen C. 'Sexual Inequality in Aristotle's Theories of Reproduction and Inheritance'. In Ward (ed.), pp. 51–67.
Cooper, John M. *Reason and Emotion*. Princeton, NJ: Princeton University Press, 1999.
—— 'An Aristotelian Theory of the Emotions'. In Cooper (1999), pp. 406–23.
—— 'Aristotle on the Forms of Friendship'. In Cooper (1999), pp. 312–35.
—— 'Friendship and Good in Aristotle'. In Cooper (1999), pp. 336–55.
—— 'Greek Philosophers on Euthanasia and Suicide'. In Cooper (1999), pp. 515–42.
—— 'Political Animals and Civic Friendship'. In Cooper (1999), pp. 356–77.
Curren, Randall R. *Aristotle on the Necessity of Public Education*. Lanham, Md.: Rowman & Littlefield, 2000.
Curzer, Howard. 'Aristotle's Account of the Virtue of Justice'. *Apeiron* 28 (1995), pp. 207–38.
Dahl, Robert A. *Democracy and its Critics*. New Haven, Conn.: Yale University Press, 1989.
Davidson, Donald. 'Rational Animals'. In Ernest Lepore and Brian P. McLaughlin (eds.), *Actions and Events: Perspectives on the Philosophy of Donald Davidson*. Oxford: Blackwell, 1985, pp. 473–80.
Davies, J. K. *Wealth and the Power of Wealth in Classical Athens*. New York: Arno Press, 1981.
Davis, David Brion. *The Problem of Slavery in Western Culture*. Ithaca, NY: Cornell University Press, 1966.
DePew, David J. 'Politics, Music, and Contemplation in Aristotle's Ideal State'. In Keyt and Miller, pp. 346–80.
—— 'Humans and Other Political Animals in Aristotle's *Historia Animalium*'. *Phronesis* 40 (1995), 156–76.
Diamond, Jared. *Guns, Germs, and Steel: The Fates of Human Societies*. New York: Norton, 1997.
Dougherty, Carol. *The Poetics of Colonization*. New York: Oxford University Press, 1993.
Dover, K. J. *Greek Popular Morality in the Time of Plato and Aristotle*. Oxford: Basil Blackwell, 1974.
Düring, Ingemar. *Aristotle in the Ancient Biographical Tradition*. Gothenburg: University of Gothenburg, 1957.
Dworkin, Ronald. *A Matter of Principle*. Cambridge, Mass.: Harvard University Press, 1985.
—— *Sovereign Virtue*. Cambridge, Mass.: Harvard University Press, 2000.
Eberly, Don. E. (ed.). *The Essential Civil Society Reader*. Lanham, Md.: Rowman & Littlefield, 2000.
Erskine, Andrew. *The Hellenistic Stoa*. Ithaca, NY: Cornell University Press, 1990.
Euben, J. Peter, John R. Wallach, and Josiah Ober (eds.). *Ancient Political Theory and the Reconstruction of American Democracy*. Ithaca, NY: Cornell University Press, 1994.
Everson, Stephen. 'Psychology'. In Barnes (1995), pp. 168–94.

REFERENCES

Farrar, Cynthia. *The Origins of Democratic Thinking.* Cambridge: Cambridge University Press, 1988.
Finley, M. I. *Democracy Ancient and Modern*, Rev. edn. New Brunswick, NY: Rutgers University Press, 1988.
Fisher, N. R. E. *Slavery in Classical Greece.* London: Bristol Classical Press, 1993.
Fortenbaugh, W. W. 'Aristotle on Slaves and Women'. In Barnes et al., pp. 135–9.
Frankfurt, Harry. 'Equality as a Moral Ideal'. *Ethics* 98 (1987), 21–43.
Frede, Dorothea. 'Mixed Feelings in Aristotle's *Rhetoric*'. In Rorty (1996), pp. 258–85.
Galston, William A. *Liberal Purposes.* Cambridge: Cambridge University Press, 1991.
Garlan, Yvon. *Slavery in Ancient Greece*, rev. and expanded edn. Ithaca, NY: Cornell University Press, 1988.
Garnsey, Peter. *Ideas of Slavery from Aristotle to Augustine.* Cambridge: Cambridge University Press, 1996. Cited as *IS*.
Gauthier, David. *Morals by Agreement.* Oxford: Clarendon Press, 1986.
Georgiadis, Constantine. 'Equitable and Equity in Aristotle'. In Spiro Panagiotou (ed.), *Justice, Law and Method in Plato and Aristotle.* Edmonton: Academic Printing & Publishing, 1987, pp. 159–72.
Gerson, L. P. *God and Greek Philosophy.* London: Routledge, 1990.
Gewirth, Alan. *Self-Fulfillment.* Princeton, NJ: Princeton University Press, 1998.
Gomez-Lobo, Alfonso. 'The *Ergon* Inference'. *Phronesis* 34 (1989), 170–84.
Gosling, J. C. B., and C. C. W. Taylor. *The Greeks on Pleasure.* Oxford: Clarendon Press, 1982.
Graham, A. J. *Colony and Mother City in Ancient Greece.* Manchester: Manchester University Press, 1964.
Graham, Keith. *The Battle of Democracy.* Totowa, NJ: Barnes & Noble, 1986.
Gray, John. *Isaiah Berlin.* Princeton, NJ: Princeton University Press, 1996.
Griffin, James. *Well-Being.* Oxford: Clarendon Press, 1986.
—— *Value Judgement.* Oxford: Clarendon Press, 1996.
Griffin, Miriam T. *Seneca: A Philosopher in Politics.* Oxford: Clarendon Press, 1992.
Guthrie, W. K. C. *The Sophists.* Cambridge: Cambridge University Press, 1971.
Halliwell, Stephen. *Aristotle's Poetics.* Chapel Hill: University of North Carolina Press, 1986.
—— 'The Challenge of Rhetoric to Political and Ethical Theory in Aristotle'. In Rorty (1996), pp. 175–90.
Hansen, Mogens Herman. *The Athenian Democracy in the Age of Demosthenes.* Oxford: Basil Blackwell, 1989.
—— 'The Ancient Athenian and the Modern Liberal View of Liberty as a Democratic Ideal'. In Ober and Hedrick, pp. 91–104.

Hardie, W. F. R. *Aristotle's Ethical Theory*, 2nd edn. Oxford: Clarendon Press, 1980.
Harris, J. W. *Property and Justice*. Oxford: Clarendon Press, 1996.
Harris, William V. *Ancient Literacy*. Cambridge, Mass.: Harvard University Press, 1989.
Harrison, A. R. W. *The Law of Athens*, vol. ii, 2nd edn. Indianapolis: Hackett, 1998.
Hauser, Marc D. *Wild Minds*. New York: Henry Holt, 2000.
Holmes, Stephen. 'Aristippus in and out of Athens'. *American Political Science Review* 73 (1979), 113–28.
Hornblower, Simon. *The Greek World 479–323 BC*. London: Methuen, 1983.
—— and Antony Spawforth (eds.). *The Oxford Classical Dictionary*, 3rd edn. Oxford: Oxford University Press, 1996.
Hurka, Thomas. *Perfectionism*. New York: Oxford University Press, 1993.
Hursthouse, Rosalind. 'A False Doctrine of the Mean'. In Sherman (1999), pp. 105–20.
Irwin, T. H. 'The Metaphysical and Psychological Basis of Aristotle's Ethics'. In Rorty (1980), pp. 35–53.
—— 'Aristotle's Method of Ethics'. In Dominic J. O'Meara (ed.), *Studies in Aristotle*. Washington, DC: Catholic University of America Press, 1981, pp. 193–223.
—— 'Homonymy in Aristotle'. *Review of Metaphysics* 34 (1981), 523–44.
—— *Aristotle's First Principles*. Oxford: Clarendon Press, 1988.
—— 'Disunity in the Aristotelian Virtues'. *Oxford Studies in Ancient Philosophy* 1988, supplementary vol., pp. 61–78.
—— 'Aristotle's Defense of Private Property'. In Keyt and Miller, pp. 200–25.
—— 'Aristotle's Philosophy of Mind'. In Stephen Everson (ed.), *Companions to Ancient Thought*, vol. ii: *Psychology*. Cambridge: Cambridge University Press, 1991.
—— 'Ethics as an Inexact Science: Aristotle's Ambitions for Moral Theory'. In Brad Hooker and Margaret Little (eds.), *Moral Particularism*. Oxford: Clarendon Press, 2000, pp. 100–29.
IS: see Garnsey.
Jacoby, Russell. *The End of Utopia*. New York: Basic Books, 1999.
Jaeger, Werner. *Aristotle: Fundamentals of the History of his Development*, 2nd edn. London: Oxford University Press, 1948.
Johnson, Curtis N. *Aristotle's Theory of the State*. New York: Macmillan, 1990.
Joint Association of Classical Teachers. *The World of Athens: An Introduction to Classical Athenian Culture*. Cambridge: Cambridge University Press, 1984.
Jolly, Alison. *Lucy's Legacy*. Cambridge, Mass.: Harvard University Press, 1999.
Kahn, Charles H. 'The Normative Structure of Aristotle's *Politics*'. In Patzig, pp. 369–84.

Kant, Immanuel. *Political Writings*. ed. Hans Reiss, trans. H. B. Nisbet. Cambridge: Cambridge University Press, 1970.

Kateb, George. *Utopia and its Enemies*. New York: Free Press of Glencoe, 1963.

Katz, Richard S. *Democracy and Elections*. New York: Oxford University Press, 1997.

Kelsen, Hans. 'Aristotle and the Hellenic-Macedonian Policy'. In Barnes et al., pp. 170–94.

Kenny, Anthony. *The Aristotelian Ethics*. Oxford: Clarendon Press, 1978.

—— *Aristotle on the Perfect Life*. Oxford: Clarendon Press, 1992.

Kerferd, G. B. *The Sophistic Movement*. Cambridge University Press, 1981.

Keyt, David. 'Aristotle's Theory of Distributive Justice'. In Keyt and Miller, pp. 238–78.

—— 'Three Basic Theorems in Aristotle's *Politics*'. In Keyt and Miller, pp. 118–41.

—— 'Aristotle and Anarchism'. *Reason Papers* 18 (1993), 133–52.

—— and Fred D. Miller, Jr. (eds.). *A Companion to Aristotle's Politics*. Oxford: Basil Blackwell, 1991.

Kitcher, Philip. 'Essence and Perfection'. *Ethics* 110 (1999), 59–83.

Kolnai, Aurel. *The Utopian Mind and other papers*. London: Athlone Press, 1995.

Kraut, Richard. 'Two Conceptions of Happiness'. *Philosophical Review* 88 (1979), 167–97.

—— *Aristotle on the Human Good*. Princeton, NJ: Princeton University Press, 1989.

—— 'Plato's Defense of Justice'. In Richard Kraut (ed.), *The Cambridge Companion to Plato*. Cambridge: Cambridge University Press, 1992, pp. 311–37.

—— 'Desire and the Human Good'. *Proceedings and Addresses of the American Philosophical Association* 68 (1994), pp. 39–54.

—— 'Are There Natural Rights in Aristotle?' *Review of Metaphysics* 49 (1996), 755–74.

—— 'Aristotle on Method and Moral Education'. In Jyl Gentzler (ed.), *Method in Ancient Philosophy*. Oxford: Oxford University Press, 1998, pp. 271–90.

—— 'Aristotle on the Human Good: An Overview'. In Sherman (1999), pp. 79–104.

—— 'Politics, Neutrality, and the Good'. *Social Philosophy and Policy* 16 (1999), 315–32.

—— 'Return to the Cave: *Republic* 519–521'. In Gail Fine (ed.), *Oxford Readings in Philosophy: Plato: Ethics, Politics, Religion, and the Soul*. Oxford: Oxford University Press, 1999, pp. 235–54.

—— 'Aristotle's Critique of False Utopias'. In Otfried Höffe (ed.), *Aristoteles Politik*. Berlin: Akademie, 2001, pp. 59–73.

Kullmann, Wolfgang. 'Man as a Political Animal in Aristotle'. In Keyt and Miller, pp. 94–117.

Kymlicka, Will. *Contemporary Political Philosophy: An Introduction.* Oxford: Oxford University Press, 1990.

—— and Wayne Norman. 'Return of the Citizen: A Survey of Recent Work on Citizenship Theory'. *Ethics* 104 (1994), 352–81.

Labarrière. Jean-Louis. 'De la phronèsis animale'. In Daniel Devereux and Pierre Pellegrin (eds.), *Biologie, logique, et métaphysique chez Aristote.* Paris: Centre National de la Recherche Scientifique, 1990, pp. 405–28.

Larmore, Charles. *The Morals of Modernity.* Cambridge: Cambridge University Press, 1996.

Lawrence, Gavin. 'The Function of the Function Argument'. *Ancient Philosophy* (forthcoming).

Leighton, Stephen. 'Aristotle and the Emotions'. In Rorty (1996), pp. 206–37.

Locke, John. *Two Treatises of Government*, ed. Peter Laslett. 2nd edn. Cambridge: Cambridge University Press, 1967.

Lomasky, Loren J. *Persons, Rights and the Moral Community.* Oxford: Oxford University Press, 1988.

Long, A. A., and D. N. Sedley. *The Hellenistic Philosophers*, vol. i. Cambridge: Cambridge University Press, 1987.

Lord, Carnes. *Education and Culture in the Political Thought of Aristotle.* Ithaca, NY: Cornell University Press, 1982.

—— and David K. O'Connor (eds.). *Essays on the Foundations of Aristotelian Political Science.* Berkeley: University of California Press, 1991.

Lynch, John Patrick. *Aristotle's School.* Berkeley: University of California Press, 1972.

MacDowell, Douglas M. *The Law in Classical Athens.* London: Thames & Hudson, 1978.

McDowell, John. 'Deliberation and Moral Development in Aristotle's Ethics'. In Stephen Engstrom and Jennifer Whiting (eds.), *Aristotle, Kant, and the Stoics.* Cambridge: Cambridge University Press, 1996, pp. 19–35.

—— *Mind, Value, and Reality.* Cambridge, Mass.: Harvard University Press, 1998.

—— 'Some Issues in Aristotle's Moral Psychology'. In McDowell (1998), pp. 23–49.

—— 'Two Sorts of Naturalism'. In McDowell (1998), pp. 167–97.

—— 'Virtue and Reason'. In McDowell (1998), pp. 50–73.

MacIntyre, Alasdair. *After Virtue.* Notre Dame, Ind.: University of Notre Dame Press, 1981.

—— *Dependent Rational Animals.* Chicago: Open Court, 1999.

Malkin, Irad. *Religion and Colonization in Ancient Greece.* Leiden: Brill, 1987.

Manville, Philip Brook. 'Ancient Greek Democracy and the Modern Knowledge-Based Organization: Reflections on the Ideology of Two Revolutions'. In Ober and Hedrick, pp. 377–99.

Matthews, Gareth. 'Gender and Essence in Aristotle'. *Australasian Journal of Philosophy* 64 (1986), supplement, 251–63.

Mayhew, Robert. 'Aristotle on Property'. *Review of Metaphysics* 46 (1993), pp. 803–31.
—— 'Aristotle on the Extent of Communism in Plato's *Republic*'. *Ancient Philosophy* 13 (1993), 313–21.
—— *Aristotle:'s Criticism of Plato's* Republic. Lanham, Md.: Rowman & Littlefield, 1997.
Mill, J. S. *Considerations on Representative Government*. Indianapolis: Bobbs-Merrill, 1958.
—— *On Liberty with The Subjection of Women and Chapters on Socialism*, ed. Stefan Collini. Cambridge: Cambridge University Press, 1989.
Miller, Fred D., Jr. *Nature, Justice, and Rights in Aristotle's Politics*. Oxford: Clarendon Press, 1995. Cited as *NJR*.
Modrak, Deborah. 'Aristotle: Women, Deliberation, and Nature'. In Bat-Ami Bar On (ed.), *Engendering Origins: Critical Feminist Readings in Plato and Aristotle*. Albany, NY: State University of New York Press, 1994, pp. 207–22.
Montesquieu, *The Spirit of the Laws*, trans. and ed. Anne M. Cohler, Basia Carolyn Miller, and Harold Samuel Stone. Cambridge: Cambridge University Press, 1989.
Morrison, Donald. 'Xenophon's Socrates on the Just and the Lawful'. *Ancient Philosophy* 15 (1995), 329–47.
—— 'Aristotle's Definition of Citizenship: A Problem and Some Solutions'. *History of Philosophy Quarterly* 16 (1999), 143–65.
Mulgan, R. G. 'Aristotle and the Democratic Conception of Freedom'. In B. F. Harris (ed.), *Auckland Classical Essays presented to E. M. Blaikluck*. Auckland: Auckland University Press, 1970, pp. 95–111.
—— *Aristotle's Political Theory*. Oxford: Clarendon Press, 1977.
—— 'Aristotle and the Value of Political Participation'. *Political Theory* 18 (1990), 195–215.
—— 'Aristotle and the Political Role of Women'. *History of Political Thought* 15 (1994), 179–202.
—— 'Was Aristotle an "Aristotelian Social Democrat"?' *Ethics* 111 (2000), 79–101.
Nichols, Mary P. *Citizens and Statesmen*. Lanham, Md.: Rowman & Littlefield, 1992.
NJR: see Miller.
Nozick, Robert. *Anarchy, State and Utopia*. New York: Basic Books, 1974.
Nussbaum, Martha C. *The Fragility of Goodness*. Cambridge: Cambridge University Press, 1986.
—— 'Nature, Function, and Capability: Aristotle on Political Distribution'. In Patzig, pp. 153–87.
—— 'Aristotelian Social Democracy'. In R. Bruce Douglas, Gerald M. Mara, and Henry S. Richardson (eds.), *Liberalism and the Good*. London: Routledge, 1990, pp. 203–52.
—— 'The Discernment of Perception: An Aristotelian Conception of

Private and Public Rationality'. In *Love's Knowledge*. New York: Oxford University Press, 1990, pp. 54–105.
—— 'Aristotle on Emotions and Rational Persuasion'. In Rorty (1996), pp. 303–23.
—— *For Love of Country*. ed. Joshua Cohen, with respondents. Boston: Beacon Press, 1996.
—— 'Aristotle, Politics, and Human Capabilities'. *Ethics* 111 (2000), 102–40.
—— *Women and Human Development*. Cambridge: Cambridge University Press, 2000.
—— and Amélie Oksenberg Rorty. *Essays on Aristotle's De Anima*. Oxford: Clarendon Press, 1992.
Oakeshott, Michael. 'On Being Conservative'. In *Rationalism in Politics and other essays*. Indianapolis: Liberty Press, 1962, pp. 407–37.
Ober, Josiah. *Mass and Elite in Democratic Athens*. Princeton, NJ: Princeton University Press, 1989.
—— 'Aristotle's Political Sociology: Class, Status, and Order in the *Politics*'. In Lord and O'Connor, pp. 112–135.
—— *Political Dissent in Democratic Athens*. Princeton, NJ: Princeton University Press, 1998.
—— and Charles Hedrick. *Dēmokratia*. Princeton, NJ: Princeton University Press, 1996.
Osborne, Robin. 'The Economics and Politics of Slavery at Athens'. In Anton Powell (ed.), *The Greek World*. London: Routledge, 1995, pp. 27–43.
Ostwald, Martin. *Nomos and the Beginnings of Athenian Democracy*. Oxford: Clarendon Press, 1969.
—— 'Shares and Rights: "Citizenship" Greek Style and American Style'. In Ober and Hedrick, pp. 49–62.
Pagden, Anthony. *The Fall of Natural Man*. Cambridge: Cambridge University Press, 1982.
Parfit, Derek. *Reasons and Persons*. Oxford: Clarendon Press, 1984.
Patzig, Gunther (ed.). *Aristoteles' 'Politik': Akten des XI. Symposium Aristotelicum*. Göttingen: Vandenhoeck & Ruprect, 1990.
Pellegrin, Pierre. 'On the "Platonic" Part of Aristotle's *Politics*'. In Wians, pp. 347–59.
Price, A.W. *Love and Friendship in Plato and Aristotle*. Oxford: Clarendon Press, 1989.
Putnam, Hilary. *The Many Faces of Realism*. Lasalle, Ill.: Open Court, 1987.
—— *Renewing Philosophy*. Cambridge, Mass.: Harvard University Press, 1992.
Putnam, Robert D. *Bowling Alone*. New York: Simon & Schuster, 2000.
Rasmussen, Douglas B., and Douglas J. Den Uyl. *Liberty and Nature*. La Salle, Ill.: Open Court, 1991.
Rawls, John. *Political Liberalism*. New York: Columbia University Press, 1996.

—— 'Kantian Constructivism in Moral Theory'. In Samuel Freeman (ed.), *John Rawls: Collected Papers*. Cambridge, Mass.: Harvard University Press, 1999.

—— *A Theory of Justice*, rev. edn. Cambridge, Mass.: Belknap Press, 1999.

—— *Lectures on the History of Moral Philosophy*, ed. Barbara Herman. Cambridge, Mass.: Harvard University Press, 2000.

Raz, Joseph. *The Morality of Freedom*. Oxford: Clarendon Press, 1986.

Reeve, C. D. C. *Practices of Reason*. Oxford: Clarendon Press, 1995.

—— 'Philosophy, Politics, and Rhetoric in Aristotle'. In Rorty (1996), pp. 191–205.

—— *Substantial Knowledge*. Indianapolis: Hackett, 2000.

Rist, J. M. *The Mind of Aristotle: A Study in Philosophical Growth*. Toronto: University of Toronto Press, 1989.

Rorty, Amélie Oksenberg (ed.). *Essays on Aristotle's Ethics*. Berkeley: University of California Press, 1980.

—— *Essays on Aristotle's Rhetoric*. Berkeley: University of California Press, 1996.

Rorty, Richard. 'Universality and Truth'. In Robert B. Brandom (ed.), *Rorty and his Critics*. Malden, Mass.: Blackwell, 2000, pp. 1–30.

Rosati, Connie S. 'Brandt's Notion of Therapeutic Agency'. *Ethics* 110 (2000), 780–811.

Ross, W. D. *Aristotle*. London: Methuen, 1923.

Rowe, Christopher. 'Aims and Methods in Aristotle's *Politics*'. In Keyt and Miller, pp. 57–74.

Ryan, Alan. *Liberal Anxieties and Liberal Education*. New York: Hill & Wang, 1998.

Salkever, Stephen G. *Finding the Mean*. Princeton, NJ: Princeton University Press, 1990.

Sandel, Michael J. *Liberalism and the Limits of Justice*. Cambridge: Cambridge University Press, 1982.

Saunders, Trevor J. 'Plato's Later Political Thought'. In Richard Kraut (ed.), *The Cambridge Companion to Plato*. Cambridge: Cambridge University Press, 1992, pp. 464–92.

Saxonhouse, Arlene W. 'Family, Polity, and Unity: Aristotle on Socrates' Community of Wives'. *Polity* 15 (1982), 202–19.

—— *Women in the History of Political Thought*. New York: Praeger, 1985.

—— *Fear of Diversity*. Chicago: University of Chicago Press, 1992.

—— *Athenian Democracy*. Notre Dame, Ind.: University of Notre Dame Press, 1996.

Scaltsas, Theodore. 'Reciprocal Justice in Aristotle's *Nicomachean Ethics*'. *Archiv für Geschichte der Philosophie* 77 (1995), 248–62.

Scanlon, T. M. *What We Owe to Each Other*. Cambridge, Mass.: Belknap Press, 1998.

Schneewind, J. B. (ed.). *Moral Philosophy from Montaigne to Kant*, vol. i. Cambridge: Cambridge University Press, 1990.

Schofield, Malcolm. 'Ideology and Philosophy in Aristotle's Theory of Slavery'. In Patzig, pp. 1–27.

Schollmeier, Paul. *Other Selves*. Albany, NY: State University of New York Press, 1994.

Schütrumpf, Eckart. 'Some Observations on the Introduction to Aristotle's *Rhetoric*'. In David J. Furley and Alexander Nehamas (eds.), *Aristotle's Rhetoric*. Princeton, NJ: Princeton University Press, 1994, pp. 99–116.

Scruton, Roger (ed.). *Conservative Texts*. New York: St. Martin's Press, 1991.

Sealey, Raphael. *Demosthenes and his Time*. New York: Oxford University Press, 1993.

Sen, Amartya. *On Ethics and Economics*. Oxford: Basil Blackwell, 1987.

Sher, George. *Beyond Neutrality*. Cambridge: Cambridge University Press, 1997.

Sherman, Nancy. *The Fabric of Character*. Oxford: Clarendon Press, 1989.

—— (ed.) *Aristotle's Ethics: Critical Essays*. Lanham, Md: Rowman & Littlefield, 1999.

Shields, Christopher. *Order in Multiplicity*. Oxford: Clarendon Press, 1999.

Shiner, Roger. 'Aristotle's Theory of Equity'. In Spiro Panagiotou (ed.), *Justice, Law and Method in Plato and Aristotle*. Edmonton: Academic Printing & Publishing, 1987, pp. 173–91.

Sober, Elliott, and David Sloan Wilson. *Unto Others*. Cambridge, Mass.: Harvard University Press, 1998.

Smith, Nicholas D. 'Plato and Aristotle on the Nature of Women'. *Journal of the History of Philosophy* 21 (1983), 467–78.

—— 'Aristotle's Theory of Natural Slavery'. In Keyt and Miller, pp. 142–55.

—— and Robert Mayhew. 'Aristotle on What the Political Scientist Needs to Know'. In K. I. Boudouris (ed.), *Aristotelian Political Philosophy*, vol. i. Athens: International Center for Greek Philosophy and Culture, 1995, pp. 189–98.

Sorabji, Richard. *Animal Minds and Human Morals*. Ithaca, NY: Cornell University Press, 1993.

Sterelny, Kim, and Paul E. Griffiths. *Sex and Death*. Chicago: University of Chicago Press, 1999.

Stern-Gillet, Suzanne. *Aristotle's Philosophy of Friendship*. Albany, NY: State University of New York Press, 1995.

Stich, Stephen P. 'Do Animals Have Beliefs?' *Australasian Journal of Philosophy* 57 (1979), 15–28.

Strauss, Barry S. 'On Aristotle's Critique of Athenian Democracy'. In Lord and O'Connor, pp. 212–33.

Striker, Gisela. 'Emotions in Context: Aristotle's Treatment of the Passions in the *Rhetoric* and in his Moral Psychology'. In Rorty (1996), pp. 286–302.

Sumner, L. W. *Welfare, Happiness, and Ethics*. Oxford: Clarendon Press, 1996.

Sunstein, Cass R. *The Partial Constitution*. Cambridge, Mass.: Harvard University Press, 1993.

Swanson, Judith A. *The Public and the Private in Aristotle's Political Philosophy*. Ithaca, NY: Cornell University Press, 1992.
Taylor, Charles. *Philosophy and the Human Sciences*. Cambridge: Cambridge University Press, 1985.
Tise, Larry E. *Proslavery: A History of the Defense of Slavery in America, 1701–1840*. Athens: University of Georgia Press, 1987.
Urmson, J. O. 'Aristotle's Doctrine of the Mean'. In Rorty (1980), pp. 157–70.
Vander Waerdt, P. A. 'Kingship and Philosophy in Aristotle's Best Regime'. *Phronesis* 30 (1985), 249–73.
Velleman, J. David. 'Brandt's Definition of Good'. *Philosophical Review* 97 (1988), 353–71.
Waldron, Jeremy. *The Right to Private Property*. Oxford: Clarendon Press, 1988.
—— 'Legislation and Moral Neutrality'. In *Liberal Rights*. Cambridge: Cambridge University Press, 1993, pp. 143–67.
—— 'The Wisdom of the Multitude'. *Political Theory* 23 (1995), 563–84.
Wallace, Robert W. 'Law, Freedom, and the Concept of Citizens' Rights in Democratic Athens'. In Ober and Hedrick, pp. 105–19.
Walzer, Michael. *Spheres of Justice*. New York: Basic Books, 1983.
Ward, Julie K. (ed.). *Feminism and Ancient Philosophy*. New York: Routledge, 1996.
Whiting, Jennifer. 'Aristotle's Function Argument: A Defense'. *Ancient Philosophy* 8 (1988), 33–48.
Wians, William (ed.). *Aristotle's Philosophical Development*. Lanham, Md.: Rowman & Littlefield, 1996.
Williams, Bernard. 'Justice as a Virtue'. In Rorty (1980), pp. 189–99.
—— *Shame and Necessity*. Berkeley: University of California Press, 1993.
Wolin, Sheldon S. 'Norm and Form: The Constitutionalizing of Democracy'. In Euben et al., pp. 29–58.
Wood, Ellen Meiksins. 'Democracy: An Idea of Ambiguous Ancestry'. In Euben et al., 59–80.
—— 'Demos versus "We, the People": Freedom and Democracy Ancient and Modern'. In Ober and Hedrick, pp. 121–38.
—— *Peasant-Citizen and Slave*. London: Verso, 1988.
—— and Neal Wood. *Class Ideology and Ancient Political Theory*. New York: Oxford University Press, 1978.
Wood, Gordon S. *The Radicalism of the American Revolution*. New York: Vintage Books, 1991.
Yack, Bernard. *The Problems of a Political Animal*. Berkeley: University of California Press, 1993.
Young, Charles. 'Aristotle on Temperance'. *Philosophical Review* 97 (1988), 521–42.

Index Locorum

Aristotle
Categories
5 2b31–3: 258

12 14a26–9: 256
12 14a29–35: 256
12 14b4–8: 265,
  266n.26

Topics
II.6 112a36–8: 53n.4

Physics
II.1 192b8–15: 243

History of Animals
487b34–488a7: 249
488a7–10: 250

Parts of Animals
IV.10 687a7–23: 84

Metaphysics
I.1 980a21: 237

V.11 1018b9–29: 256
V.11 1019a1–4: 256

VII.1 1028a16–17: 258
VII.1 1028a32–6: 257

VII.10 1035b4–7: 257

X.8 1074a38–b14: 204

XII.7 1072b13–30: 79

Nicomachean Ethics
I.1 1094a1–2: 51
I.1 1094a9: 227

I.2 1094a18–26: 3
I.2 1094a18–22: 52
I.2 1094a22–6: 52
I.2 1094a26–b7: 3
I.2 1094a26–8: 16n., 92
I.2 1094a27–8: 3

I.2 1094b7–10: 95, 95n.38

I.3 1094b14–16: 246
I.3 1095a2–3: 4n.3
I.3 1095a4–8: 58–9

I.4 1095a14–20: 53
I.4 1095a20–5: 53
I.4 1095a25–6: 57
I.4 1095b4: 59

I.5 1095b23–6: 66
I.5 1095b31–1096a2: 66
I.5 1095b33: 67
I.5 1096a1–2: 58
I.5 1096a4–5: 77
I.5 1096a5–7: 216

I.7 1097b2–4: 59
I.7 1097b8–11: 252
I.7 1097b9–11: 95, 123
I.7 1097b28–33: 82
I.7 1097b33–1098a3: 86
I.7 1098a3–17: 54
I.7 1098a4–5: 69
I.7 1098a16–17: 67
I.7 1098a17–18: 77n.
I.7 1098a20–1: 54, 64, 70
I.7 1098b3–4: 56, 57

I.8 1099a7–21: 74
I.8 1099a32–3: 75

I.10 1101a15: 349

I.13 1102a21–3: 287
I.13 1102b13–29: 283

II.2 1103b26–9: 91, 99, 176,
  193
II.2 1103b28: 60

II.4 1105a22–6: 287
II.4 1105a22–3: 287
II.4 1105a31–2: 287

II.6 1106a15–24: 121

II.7 1108b3–6: 140
II.7 1108b7–9: 157n.

III.1 1109b30–2: 344
III.1 1109b35–1110b9: 345
III.1 1110a4–8: 381
III.1 1110a5–7: 345
III.1 1110a23–7: 381

III.3 1112a34–b11: 230, 232, 239
III.3 1112b2–9: 289

III.5 1113b6–7: 96

IV.1 1120a34–b3: 119n.30
IV.1 1120b2–3: 161
IV.1 1121a12–13: 161

IV.2 1122b19–23: 135

IV.3 1124b24–6: 135
IV.3 1125a3: 168
IV.3 1125a19–27: 161

V.1 1129a4–5: 156
V.1 1129a26–b11: 111
V.1 1129a32–3: 136, 145
V.1 1129b2–3: 136
V.1 1129b6–10: 137
V.1 1129b11–12: 111
V.1 1129b12–14: 111
V.1 1129b12: 135
V.1 1129b14–17: 113, 117
V.1 1129b14–15: 113n.23, 120
V.1 1129b15–16: 134
V.1 1129b16: 113n.24
V.1 1129b17–19: 113, 115, 116, 117, 119
V.1 1129b19–25: 113n.23, 346
V.1 1129b19–23: 115
V.1 1129b24–5: 115
V.1 1129b25–1130a10: 107
V.1 1129b25–6: 118
V.1 1129b25: 111, 134
V.1 1129b26–7: 118–19
V.1 1129b26: 122
V.1 1130a10: 119–20n.31

V.2 1130a24–8: 136

V.2 1130b2: 136
V.2 1130b4: 136, 138
V.2 1130b10–14: 103
V.2 1131a1–9: 154

V.3 1131a10–11: 156–7
V.3 1131a27–9: 146, 147
V.3 1131a29–32: 146

V.4 1132a1–2: 146
V.4 1132a5: 148
V.4 1132a9–14: 149
V.4 1132a24–7: 148–9

V.5 1132b21–2: 152
V.5 1132b27: 152
V.5 1132b28–30: 153
V.5 1132b29–30: 153
V.5 1133a7–24: 154
V.5 1133a25–9: 153–4
V.5 1133b23–6: 154
V.5 1133b32–1134a13: 158
V.5 1134a8–9: 158, 159

V.6 1134a26–8: 125–6
V.6 1134b8–15: 126
V.6 1134b9–12: 126–7
V.6 1134b15–17: 126

V.7 1134b18–1135a5: 383
V.7 1134b18–19: 125, 127
V.7 1134b19–20: 127
V.7 1134b19: 132
V.7 1134b20–1: 127, 128
V.7 1134b20: 129, 130, 131
V.7 1134b24–7: 246
V.7 1134b25–6: 129
V.7 1134b29–30: 129
V.7 1134b33–5: 130
V.7 1134b35: 127
V.7 1135a1–3: 127
V.7 1135a5: 130, 131–2, 133

V.8 1135b26–1136a1: 168

V.9 1136a10–b14: 163
V.9 1136a27–8: 163
V.9 1136a31–b9: 161
V.9 1136b4–5: 164

V.9 1136b6: 161
V.9 1136b7–8: 163
V.9 1136b9–13: 161
V.9 1136b20–1: 164
V.9 1136b22: 165
V.9 1136b32–4: 143
V.9 1136b34–1137a4: 143
V.9 1137a4–17: 107

V.10 1137b21–2: 109n.19

V.11 1138a4–26: 161
V.11 1138a4–14: 162
V.11 1138a6–7: 162n.
V.11 1138a14–20: 163
V.11 1138a23–4: 161
V.11 1138a28–b5: 170n.58
V.11 1138b5–13: 169–70, 171
V.11 1138b7–8: 170
V.11 1138b8–9: 170n.58

VI.4 1140a3005: 288

VI.7 1141a20–2: 77
VI.7 1141a26–8: 68

VI.9 1142b29: 286
VI.9 1142b30–1: 286

VI.13 1144b14–21: 367
VI.13 1144b30–2: 107
VI.13 1144b32–1145a2: 119n.31

VII.1 1145a19–20: 423

VII.4 1148a30–1: 142

VII.6 1149a9–11: 264n.

VII.10 1152a25–7: 76
VII.10 1330a9–23: 423

VIII.1 1155a22–6: 467
VIII.1 1155a22–4: 356n.41
VIII.1 1155b1–10: 265

VIII.9 1159b31–5: 355

VIII.10 1160a31–b21: 425
VIII.10 1160a35–6: 425
VIII.10 1160b19–21: 425

VIII.10 1160b32–5: 126

VIII.11 1161a10–11: 356n.41, 465, 468
VIII.11 1161a30–1: 465
VIII.11 1161b5–6: 299n.42

VIII.12 1162a17–19: 248

VIII.13 1162b5–21: 467

IX.4 1166a6–8: 355

IX.6 1167a26–8: 467
IX.6 1167a30–2: 468

IX.9 1169b17–19: 248

X.3 1174a1–2: 65
X.3 1174a9: 74

X.5 1175a21–b1: 74
X.5 1175a29–1175b1: 74
X.5 1175b24–6: 74

X.7 1177b4–15: 95
X.7 1177b12–15: 200–1

X.8 1178b8–22: 141
X.8 1179a20–2: 58

X.9 1179b4–20: 176
X.9 1179b18–20: 96, 378–9
X.9 1179b23–1180a1: 457
X.9 1179b31–1180a24: 176
X.9 1180a22–3: 452
X.9 1180a23–4: 453
X.9 1181b12–23: 181
X.9 1181b15–22: 187
X.9 1181b15: 19, 181
X.9 1181b17–18: 183n.

Eudemian Ethics
I.4 1215a25–37: 216

VII.10 1242a22–3: 248

Politics
I.1 1252a1–7: 355, 466

I.2 1252a2–3: 247

INDEX LOCORUM

I.2 1252a17–23: 253
I.2 1252a24–6: 242
I.2 1252a29: 242
I.2 1252a32: 296
I.2 1252b5–9: 290
I.2 1252b12–14: 241
I.2 1252b17: 242
I.2 1252b29–30: 240, 391
I.2 1252b30: 242, 245
I.2 1252b32–4: 244
I.2 1253a2–4: 263
I.2 1253a2–3: 242, 257
I.2 1253a2: 247
I.2 1253a7–8: 250
I.2 1253a9–18: 251
I.2 1253a10–14: 251
I.2 1253a19–20: 242
I.2 1253a19: 253, 258, 259, 354, 357
I.2 1253a20–5: 213n.40
I.2 1253a23: 257
I.2 1253a25–6: 255
I.2 1253a26–9: 255
I.2 1253a27–9: 262, 263
I.2 1253a29–30: 241, 247
I.2 1253a30–1: 243, 256
I.2 1253a32–3: 253
I.2 1253b30–1: 245

I.3 1253b20–3: 278

I.4 1254a8: 281n.13

I.5 1254b2–16: 296
I.5 1254b4–6: 170n.58
I.5 1254b22–3: 282, 283, 285
I.5 1254b32–4: 294n.31
I.5 1255a31–b2: 290

I.6 1255a3–7: 285, 304
I.6 1255a4–5: 278
I.6 1255b12–15: 299n.42

I.13 1260a12: 214, 285, 286, 289
I.13 1260a13: 214, 286n.
I.13 1260a35–6: 297
I.13 1260b13–20: 199n.13

II.1 1261a13–22: 254

II.2 1261a15–b15: 309

II.2 1261a15–22: 339
II.2 1261a18: 307, 360
II.2 1261a22–3: 307
II.2 1261a30–1: 381

II.3 1261a15–22: 310, 312
II.3 1261a15–16: 314
II.3 1261a18–20: 313
II.3 1261a18: 310
II.3 1261a20–1: 311
II.3 1261a21–2: 313
II.3 1261a22–4: 311, 314
II.3 1261a30–b6: 314
II.3 1261b16–32: 309
II.3 1261b20–30: 315
II.3 1261b30–2: 314
II.3 1261b30–1: 315
II.3 1261b31–2: 316
II.3 1261b31: 312
II.3 1261b32–40: 309, 316
II.3 1261b33–8: 330
II.3 1262a14–24: 309–10

II.4 1262a25–40: 310
II.4 1262b15: 309, 316
II.4 1262b24–9: 309–10

II.5 1263a2–3: 327
II.5 1263a3–8: 327–8
II.5 1263a3–4: 339
II.5 1263a4–5: 329
II.5 1263a8–21: 330
II.5 1263a8–10: 331
II.5 1263a10–15: 332
II.5 1263a25–6: 337
II.5 1263a27–9: 336
II.5 1263a28–9: 330
II.5 1263a29–30: 321
II.5 1263a30–40: 329
II.5 1263a30–3: 329, 338
II.5 1263a33–9: 338
II.5 1263a37–b6: 333
II.5 1263a37–9: 336
II.5 1263a38–9: 328, 337
II.5 1263a39–40: 342, 344, 345
II.5 1263a40–b5: 330
II.5 1263a40–1: 334
II.5 1263b5–14: 339
II.5 1263b5–7: 330
II.5 1263b7–14: 330
II.5 1263b7–9: 339–40

INDEX LOCORUM

II.5 1263b8: 341
II.5 1263b9–11: 310
II.5 1263b15–16: 330
II.5 1263b23–5: 346
II.5 1263b29–37: 331, 339–40
II.5 1263b32–4: 310–11
II.5 1263b36–1264a1: 333
II.5 1263b36–7: 307, 312
II.5 1264a1–5: 352
II.5 1264a6–7: 322n.
II.5 1264b17–22: 213
II.5 1263b2–3: 333

II.6 1265a38–b16: 350
II.6 1265b10–12: 96
II.6 1265b33–5: 308

II.7 1266b8–24: 350
II.7 1266b24–35: 348
II.7 1267a37–41: 351
II.7 1267b9–10: 348

II.8 1268b38–1269a3: 104
II.8 1269a3–4: 308, 354

II.9 1271a26–39: 223
II.9 1271a26–37: 329
II.9 1271b10–17: 343

II.10 1272a12–26: 223

II.11 1273b26: 307

II.12 1274a25: 4n.3

III.1 1274b41: 13
III.1 1275b18–20: 362

III.2 1275b22–34: 362
III.2 1275b37–9: 362

III.4 1276b26–9: 370
III.4 1276b16–34: 368
III.4 1276b21–9: 363
III.4 1276b26–9: 387
III.4 1276b30–4: 363
III.4 1276b31–4: 441
III.4 1276b35–7: 364
III.4 1276b37–8: 364–5, 365n., 394
III.4 1277a1–3: 364
III.4 1277a5–12: 366

III.4 1277a14–15: 367
III.4 1277a25–7: 367, 381
III.4 1277a27–9: 367
III.4 1277a27: 382
III.4 1277b7–13: 367
III.4 1277b13–16: 381, 414
III.4 1277b14–17: 367
III.4 1277b15: 382
III.4 1277b25–9: 369, 417
III.4 1277b28–9: 367

III.5 1278a8–11: 369
III.5 1278a9–11: 434

III.6 1278b15–24: 391
III.6 1278b17–21: 248
III.6 1279a8–13: 381
III.6 1279a17–21: 266

III.7 1279a25–39: 385
III.7 1279a25–31: 424
III.7 1279a28–30: 212
III.7 1279a40–b2: 438
III.7 1279a40–b1: 400
III.7 1279b1–2: 400
III.7 1279b8–10: 460
III.7 1279b8–9: 445

III.9 1280a15–16: 473
III.9 1280a22–5: 394
III.9 1280a25–b36: 356
III.9 1280a40–b1: 393

III.10 1281a11: 359
III.10 1281a34–9: 381
III.10 1281a36–9: 456

III.11 1281a40–2: 402
III.11 1281a40: 403
III.11 1281b5: 405
III.11 1281b7–10: 404
III.11 1281b15–21: 402, 405
III.11 1281b25–8: 408
III.11 1281b28–30: 408
III.11 1281b31: 405
III.11 1281b32–4: 409
III.11 1281b35–8: 408
III.11 1281b38–1282a14: 406
III.11 1282a3–4: 287
III.11 1282a14–23: 407
III.11 1282a17: 405

INDEX LOCORUM

III.11 1282a41–b13: 104
III.11 1282b8–13: 456
III.11 1282b11–13: 381

III.12 1282b31–1283a3: 350

III.13 1283a30–3: 448
III.13 1283b21–3: 410
III.13 1283b36–42: 390
III.13 1284a3–15: 410
III.13 1284a13–14: 455
III.13 1284b4–5: 272
III.13 1284b17–19: 272
III.13 1284b19–20: 272
III.13 1284b28–34: 414
III.13 1284b32–4: 399n.13

III.14 1285a19–22: 291, 292
III.14 1285b29–30: 411

III.15 1286a26–31: 413
III.15 1286a31–5: 413
III.15 1286b8–10: 292
III.15 1286b22–7: 413

III.16 1287a1–2: 411
III.16 1287a8–9: 411
III.16 1287a16–18: 456
III.16 1287b25–36: 413
III.16 1287b29–30: 411

III.17 1288a6–12: 424n.
III.17 1288a8–9: 412–13
III.17 1288a12–15: 401n.
III.17 1288a24–9: 414

III.18 1288b2–6: 187

IV.1 1288b10–19: 447
IV.1 1288b15: 428
IV.1 1288b24: 428
IV.1 1288b28–30: 432–3
IV.1 1288b28: 428, 432
IV.1 1288b34–5: 428, 438

IV.2 1288b16–18: 431
IV.2 1288b28: 430
IV.2 1288b33: 431
IV.2 1289b4–5: 445
IV.2 1289b15–17: 430, 438

IV.4 1290a30–1: 231
IV.4 1291b30–8: 457
IV.4 1292a4–38: 445
IV.4 1292a4–18: 454
IV.4 1292a6–7: 454
IV.4 1292a15–32: 451
IV.4 1292a23–37: 454

IV.6 1292b21–33: 457–8
IV.6 1292b25–34: 463
IV.6 1292b41–1293a10: 445, 460

IV.7 1293b7–21: 232

IV.8 1293b22–36: 438
IV.8 1293b34–6: 431
IV.8 1294a10–11: 231
IV.8 1294a11–14: 231
IV.8 1294a19–25: 431

IV.11 1295a25–6: 438
IV.11 1295a40–b1: 15, 435
IV.11 1295b1–3: 439
IV.11 1295b3–11: 439
IV.11 1295b13–18: 452
IV.11 1295b18–22: 445
IV.11 1295b18–19: 452
IV.11 1295b23–1296a7: 442
IV.11 1295b24–5: 355n.
IV.11 1295b25–6: 389
IV.11 1295b34–9: 472n.2
IV.11 1296a9–21: 445
IV.11 1296a22–b2: 443
IV.11 1296a27–36: 438
IV.11 1296a30: 389
IV.11 1296a36–8: 472
IV.11 1296a38–40: 8

IV.12 1296b13: 429
IV.12 1296b18: 429
IV.12 1296b23–4: 429
IV.12 1296b28–9: 429
IV.12 1296b34–40: 472
IV.12 1297a4–6: 442
IV.12 1297a11–13: 446

V.1 1302a8–15: 446

V.7 1307a15–20: 446

V.9 1309b18–35: 370

V.9 1310a14: 457
V.9 1310a28–32: 450, 451
V.9 1310a30–6: 383
V.9 1310a32: 477

V.10 1311b1–2: 8

V.11 1313a40–1: 381
V.11 1313a41–b6: 223
V.11 1314a5–9: 381
V.11 1315b8–10: 437

VI.2 1317b3–7: 450
VI.2 1317b10–12: 451
VI.2 1317b14–17: 477
VI.2 1317b15–16: 451
VI.2 1318a3–8: 458

VI.4 1318b9–11: 463
VI.4 1318b38–1319a1: 452
VI.4 1319b27–32: 451

VI.5 1320a4–17: 448
VI.5 1320a29–b4: 449
VI.5 1320b2–3: 460

VII.4 1325b39: 192
VII.4 1326b2–24: 8
VII.4 1326b5–7: 226

VII.7 1327b23–36: 291
VII.7 1327b24–5: 291
VII.7 1327b26–7: 291
VII.7 1327b26: 291
VII.7 1327b27–8: 292
VII.7 1327b28: 292
VII.7 1327b29–33: 8, 300

VII.8 1328b5: 325
VII.8 1328b7–10: 326
VII.8 1328b10: 325
VII.8 1328b11: 326

VII.9 1329a2–4: 227, 230
VII.9 1329a6–17: 226
VII.9 1329a27–34: 203, 228

VII.10 1329b34–5: 352
VII.10 1329b41–1330a2: 328, 329
VII.10 1330a2: 222
VII.10 1330a3–13: 322

VII.10 1330a3–5: 222
VII.10 1330a5–8: 326
VII.10 1330a5–7: 223
VII.10 1330a9–25: 220
VII.10 1330a9–23: 229, 456
VII.10 1330a9–13: 223, 335
VII.10 1330a15–23: 341
VII.10 1330a32–3: 297

VII.12 1331b6: 203
VII.12 1331b15: 225
VII.12 1331b21–2: 192–3

VII.13 1332a30–1: 192–3

VII.14 1332b16–27: 233
VII.14 1332b16–23: 421, 424, 472
VII.14 1332b23: 225–6n.64
VII.14 1332b26–9: 226
VII.14 1332b26–7: 227

VII.16 1335b16–18: 199n.13

VII.17 1336b9–10: 222

VIII.1 1337a21–30: 207, 327
VIII.1 1337a27–9: 213, 272–3

VIII.3 1338a39–40: 199
VIII.3 1338b2–4: 199

Rhetoric
I.1 1354b7–11: 142

I.2 1356a26–7: 16n.

I.5 1361a21–4: 323n.

I.8 1366a21–2: 16n.

I.12 1373a4–5: 139

I.13 1374a28–33: 108n.
I.13 1374a35–6: 109
I.13 1374b18: 167–8

Plato
Apology
23b: 174

31c–e: 174
36e–d: 148

Gorgias
483a–d: 245–6
521e: 174

Laws
720a: 288
720b–c: 288
863e: 170n.58
873c–d: 162n.

Phaedo
118a: 175

Republic
416d–17b: 322
443c–d: 121, 170
444a–b: 170n.58
462a–b: 312n.3
488a–489e: 172
500c: 171
VI 496b–d: 133
VI 496d–e: 133
VI 592b: 133

Symposium
210a–12a: 319
216a–b: 175–6

General Index

Ackrill, J. L. 53n.5, 56n.7, 181n., 252n.
activity (*energeia*) 67
Adams, Robert Merrihew 23n.
adultery:
  and law 116, 117, 346
  and *pleonexia* 137, 150
  and sensual pleasure 125, 138, 139, 150
  and well-being 117
  as involuntary suffering 148, 154
  presupposes traditional family 310
  varying motives for 136, 142–3
akrasia ('incontinence', 'weakness of will'):
  defined 75–6
  not unjust 161–3
akroatēs ('listener', 'pupil') 4n.3
Alcibiades 175–6, 446
Alcidamas 278n.3
Alexander the Great 7, 418
amusement:
  and slavery 297
  component of well-being 200
Amyntas III 7
anger:
  and mean 71, 123
  and verbal abuse 115, 125
  and well-being 333–4
  arises more slowly in a group 413
  at self 162
  contrasted with *pleonexia* 150
animals, *see* good: of non-human animals
Annas, Julia 242n.4
Antiphon 278n.3
Antony, Louise M. 85n.34
Archytas 152n.45
Arendt, Hannah 14n.
aristocracy:
  accepted by willing subjects 374, 468
  aims at virtue 147, 368
  and elitism 419
  and majority rule 231–2
  equal to kingship 399–400, 412, 416
  guided by correct understanding of well-being 400–1
  includes defective constitutions 431–2
  includes rule by the middle class 430–1, 438–9
  inferior to city of Books VII–VIII 187, 361
  inferior to kingship 424–6
  not subject to the scrutiny of the demos 411, 412, 455, 472
  of elite social status 445–6
  of super-humans 421, 422, 472
  ruled by excellence 380
  several meanings of 9n.10, 231n.72, 232, 360, 360n.6, 431, 427–8n.1
  subject to the rule of law 455
  superior to polity 186, 360–1, 366, 400, 404, 410, 416–17, 419
  thought superior to kingship 400n.15
Arneson, Richard J. 23n.
Asia 194, 291–3
assembly:
  and taxation 343
  deliberates about justice 175, 230
  ineffective in expressing generosity 342
  in Athens 221–2, 226
  of ideal city 226–7, 236–7, 325, 353, 359
  see also majority rule
Athens:
  assembly and council of 221–2, 226
  Aristotle's relationship to 7–8, 9, 10, 11–12
  common meals in 221–2
  education in 206–7
  euthyna in 406
  homosexuality in 216
  liturgies in 326
  ostracism in 272
  population of 12–13
  slavery in 279–80
  Solonian 308
  see also Constitution of Athens
athletics:
  and ethical dramatization 81
  as locus of public honors 147
  critique of training of 202n.23
  financed by liturgies 326
Austin, M. M. & P. Vidal-Naquet 215n.45, 326n.19
autonomy:
  as the absence of moral facts 36–7
  diminished in slaves 285–90
  of Greek cities 8
  Putnam on 39n.
  see also education: for autonomy; freedom; self-sufficiency
Avineri, Schlomo & de-Shalit, Avner 354n.
Balme, D. M. 250n.
banausoi ('vulgar'):
  broad and narrow uses of the term 215n.45
  defense of Aristotle's prejudice against 464–5

GENERAL INDEX

deficiencies of 215–17, 234
farmers superior to 429
now we are all 475
see also crafts
barbaroi, see foreigners
Barber, Benjamin R. 360n.7
Barker, Ernest 369n.13
Barnes, Jonathan 52n., 67n., 85n.34, 252n., 276n.31
Barry, Brian 479n.12
bees as political animals 22n., 250–1
Bell, Daniel 354n.
Berlin, Isaiah 239n.73, 474n.
bias:
    absent in middle class 438
    caused by friendship 142
    devices for diminishing 230, 318–22, 340, 456
    of Plato 419
    of rich and poor 375, 381–2, 389, 437, 448, 458–9
    Plato's device for eradicating 444
    proper form of 334
    see also common good; impartiality
Blundell, Mary Whitlock 320n.12
Bodéüs, Richard 203n.24
Boegehold, Alan 352n.36
Brandom, Robert B. 89n.
Brandt, Richard 23n., 46n.15
Broadie, Sarah 71n., 74n.23, 76n.26, 85n.34
Brunschwig, Jacques 167n.
Brunt, P. A. 9n.11, 278n.3
Burnyeat, Myles 4n.3, 52n., 192n.1
Bywater, I. 113n.24

Callicles 139n., 245–6, 446, 450
Campbell, Mavis 277n.2
Cambiano, Giuseppe 278n.3
Carthage 222, 222n.57, 232, 306–8
Chaeronea 7
charientes ('refined people') 439, 442, 461
    see also elites; *gnorimoi*
Charles, David 85n.33, 215n.46
children:
    as parts of their parents 126–7
    education of in ideal city 198, 226
    follow their feelings 58–9, 64
    need parental nurture 74n.24, 315–18
    proper development of 29–30, 41, 64–5, 70, 78, 85
Christiano, Thomas 461n.
Chroust, Anton-Hermann 6n.8
citizens:
    defined 362
    'belong to the city' 207–8, 213, 272–3
    components of city 12–13
    governing role of 126, 217, 354, 395
    must outnumber non-citizens 359–60n.5
    proper role of 362–76, 376, 379, 381, 396
    see also property: as qualification for citizenship
city:
    compared to an organism 213, 243–3, 254–76
    composite by nature 253–4, 307
    constantly re-invented 241
    contrasted with state 13, 14, 382–3
    developed from household and village 240–2
    distinguished from commercial and military alliances 391–6
    exists by nature 241–6
    exists for the sake of living well 240, 242, 275, 391
    number of inhabitants and citizens 12–13
    priority of 94, 207, 210–14, 253–76, 354
    proper size of 8
    requires a kind of unity 274, 307, 309–14, 331, 333, 339–40, 353, 442
civic friendship, *see* friendship: civic
civic virtue, *see* citizens: proper role of
class, *see* middle class; poor; wealthy
Code, Alan 182n.3
Cohen, David 209n.35, 216n.48
Cohen, G. A. 221n.54, 434n.8
colonies:
    and ideal constitution 9, 196–7, 361, 420
    and Macedonian conquests 9–10, 194
    equal division of land in 221
collective wisdom, *see* wisdom (collective)
commerce:
    and *koinōnia* 354–5
    not the goal of civic life 392–5
    undermines good citizenship 215–16, 475
    see also justice: reciprocal
common good:
    and commercial reciprocity 155–6
    and constitutional change 373–4
    and corrective justice 148–9
    and merit 147
    and priority of the city 267, 271, 275
    Aristotle's contribution to 177
    as equal and impartial treatment 388–92
    can be promoted in ordinary cities 134
    can be served even in pluralistic cities 396–404, 417
    contrasted with utilitarian aggregation 210–14
    distinguishing mark of correct constitutions 385
    involves proper distribution 118
    laws aim at 113

GENERAL INDEX

mandatory goal for all citizens 207, 342–6
not served by egalitarian transfers 350–1
served by conventional rules 134
served by ostracism 272
served by private possessions 326–7, 336–7, 347
see also bias; impartiality
common meals:
  as egalitarian device 349
  as unifying institution 220–4, 237, 307, 321, 325
  poor citizens excused from supporting 222, 326, 329
  supported by collectively owned land 335–6, 344
communitarianism 353–6
community 12n.
  see also friendship: civic; *koinōnia*
conflict:
  cannot be eliminated by prohibiting private property 346–8
  caused by communal ownership 333
  caused by emotional disorders 143
  caused by scarce resources 96
  diminished by consensus about final ends 195, 196, 224, 236
  diminished by dual lots 230, 341, 423
  diminished by rule of the middle class 442
  distinguished from diversity 44–5
  major subject for political theory 5
  not presupposed by civic priority 270–1
  often irresolvable 195–6, 443
  resolved by majority rule 229–34
consensus about final ends:
  absent in polity 400
  how to cope without 397–8
  in ideal city 195–7
  in kingship and aristocracy 399–400, 425–6
  see also conflict
conservatism:
  as moderation 111, 352–3, 369–70, 387–8
  in method 54–6
Constant, Benjamin 476n.6
constitution:
  always to be preserved 372–6
  as allocation of power 13–14, 15, 359
  as way of life 15, 195, 231, 368, 429–30, 435, 438
  correct and deviant distinguished 183, 186, 252, 358–9, 368, 385–8, 391, 396–8, 399–400, 410, 412, 465
  of Athens 11, 11n.16, 446
  of ideal city 8, 9, 130–1, 134, 173–4, 185–6, 189–90, 192–246, 306–8
  stability of 308, 370, 372, 376–7, 377n.24, 378, 408, 432–3, 446, 468

see also aristocracy; democracy; kingship; oligarchy; polity; tyranny
Constitution of Athens 11, 446
contemplation:
  no protection against misfortune 58
  relation to science and religion 77, 78–9
  the supreme activity 94–5
  undertaken by few ideal citizens 198
  unfamiliar to Aristotle's students 55–6
continence, *see akrasia*
Cook, Kathleen C. 215n.44
Cook Wilson, John 162n.
Cooper, John M. 69n.20, 73n., 163n., 247n.11, 355n., 396n., 466n.57
Corinth 7, 372n.
courage:
  and rule-following 125
  as a mean state 159–60
  commanded by law 117
  essentially tied to fear 137
  fully exercised only in battle 135, 270
  relation to justice 119–20
crafts:
  and deliberation 286–90
  and equal exchange 154
  and function 82
  and instrumental relations 466
  and justice 151–2, 169
  do not produce cities 244–5
  each aims at a different good 51, 87
  hierarchically organized 82
  in Asia 291–3
  ordinary practitioners distinguished from experts 287–8
  prejudice against 215–16, 369, 464
  require political oversight 93
  see also banausoi
Crete:
  common meals in 222, 223, 321n.15
  dependence on farm labor 218n.
  mixed constitution of 307–8
  reputation of 306
Curren, Randall R. 207n.31
Curzer, Howard 160n.

Dahl, Robert A. 461n.
Davidson, Donald 68n.18
Davies, J. K. 217n.50, 280n.7
Davis, David Brion 277n.1, 277n.2, 278n.4
decency, *see* justice: and equity
decrees, *see* law
deliberation:
  can excel in large groups 404–9
  capacity of craftsmen for 215
  component of well-being 251–2
  either practical or productive 286–7

GENERAL INDEX

habits of craftsmen degrade 219
impaired in women 214, 286n.
incapacity of slaves for 289–304
of assemblies requires majority rule 232
presupposes objective solutions 27–8
presupposes uncertainty and variability 230, 232
uniquely human 69, 86

democracy:
and common meals 222–3
and equality 445, 448, 450, 458, 475
and standards of citizenship 440, 449, 464
Aristotle's commitment to 460–3, 475
as class bias of the poor 144, 444–5, 447, 460, 474–5
as rule by non-elites 24n., 461–3, 475
best among corrupt constitutions 425, 431–2, 445
defines justice as majority rule 450, 455
extreme form not a city or constitution 253, 370, 372, 375
gradual development of 293
ideal city is a 236
in Athens 11
little understanding of well-being in 374
majority rule not unique to 231
minimizes regulation 208, 368, 450–3, 476–7
moderated by weighted voting 458–60
must be moderated 369–70, 372–3, 375, 389, 447–8, 450–1
political friendship in 465–9
proposes free status as criterion of merit 147, 368, 392
requires widespread acceptance 44–5
rule of law in 455–7
stabilized by education 457
superior to tyranny 115n.
takes different forms 409, 436, 444–51, 463–4
tyrannical form of 106, 375, 382, 432, 445, 451, 454, 456
use of lot in 449, 451
worth improving 173, 436, 437, 446
see also demos; equality; freedom; poor (class)

demos:
and democracy 445
as curb on the power of elites 461, 465
contrasted with middle class 439
meaning of 24n., 439n.15
not given to faction 445–6
plays a small role in modern nation-states 228
unqualified for high office 448
see also banausoi; democracy; poor (class)

Demosthenes 7–8
DePew, David J. 80n., 251n.
Diamond, Jared 294n.32
disagreement, *see* conflict
distrust, *see* trust
diversity:
of conceptions of well-being 38, 43
of constitutions 8
of cultures 21
of goods 37
of interests and talents 43–6
Dougherty, Carol 194m.4
Dover, K. J. 103n., 298n.40, 393n.
drama, *see* music
Düring, Ingemar 6n.8, 9n.11
Dworkin, Ronald 23n., 349n.32, 352n.35, 479n.13

Eberly, Don E. 354n.
education:
as claim to citizen status 429
as method of civic unification 307, 333, 442
cannot eliminate disagreement 230
cannot remedy natural deficiencies 282
contrasted with specialized expertise 287–8
for autonomy 353
in Athens 206–7
in drawing 199
in ethics 60, 199, 229, 233, 441, 462
in music and poetry 80, 199, 203, 206
in philosophy 198
in reading and writing 198, 199
in science and mathematics 78, 199, 205–6, 237
in Sparta 10n.13, 206, 307
in well-being 87–8, 195, 441
military 198, 199
must be public and equal 198, 202, 207, 224, 228, 236, 272–3, 307, 325, 326, 327, 344, 348, 349, 356, 361
must be relative to the constitution 457
non-ideal 378
not provided beyond childhood 204
of emotions 334, 337
of kings 366
of reason 90, 353
of the middle class 440
religious 204
required for good citizenship 217
egoism 21n.
elites:
absent from ideal city 236, 361, 462
and slavery 280n.7
contrasted with demos 24n.
contrasted with middle class 439, 441–3

508

in Greek democracies and oligarchies
    447–51
  in modern democracies 228–9, 463, 476
  in Plato's *Republic* 325
  in well-regarded cities 307
  inferior to demos 445–6
  justified by craft analogy 406–7
  merit honor 448
  require oversight 451–2, 461, 463, 465, 476
  resist oversight 452
elitism:
  Aristotle's alleged 6, 449–50
  Aristotle's brand of 419
  Aristotle's opposition to 406–7, 450–1
emotions:
  and self-mastery 75
  and virtue 120, 122–3, 144
  as threat to sound judgment 33–4, 59
  central to well-being 65, 123
  require education 65
  responsive to reason 69
  see also anger; envy; greed; pleasure; *pleonexia*; spite
Empedocles 105n.11
energeia, *see* activity
envy:
  absent from ideal city 224, 481
  as a vice 140
  felt by the poor 144, 347, 439, 442, 445, 455
  tied by Hume to justice 165–6
Epictetus 296n.
Epicureans:
  counsel against the political life 380n.
  practical orientation of 20n.
  reject Aristotle's conception of the soul 84
equality:
  achieved by a polity 400, 444, 462, 473
  and democratic ideology 425, 445, 446, 450, 451, 458, 462–3, 475
  and the common good 388–92
  and political rule 381
  approximated by defective cities 448, 451, 457–8, 461, 469
  demanded by the poor 394
  fostered by common meals 222–4
  in exposure to risk 229–30
  in external resources 221, 307, 346–51, 481
  in land distribution 221, 236, 326, 349–50
  in political power 8, 224, 227, 236, 359, 31, 417, 462
  of education 224, 236
  of moral skills 226–7, 360, 381, 407, 417, 442
  presupposed by corrective justice 148–50
  two kinds of 125–6, 450
  unjust to kings 414

  see also impartiality; justice: as equality; justice: corrective; justice: distributive
equity, *see* justice: and equity
ergon, *see* function
Erskine, Andrew 305n.53
essence:
  of human beings 85n.34, 91–2
  philosophy as the study of 197–8
  possessed by all living things vii
ethics:
  distinguished from politics 16–17, 94n.
  inexact discipline 124n.
  not to be studied apart from politics 4n.4, 176
  practical discipline 91–2, 99, 176, 193
Ethics, *see Nicomachean Ethics*
eudaimonia ('happiness') 53n.4
  see also good: of human beings; happiness
Eudemian Ethics:
  organization of 186–7
  relation to other works 17–19, 18n.26, 19n., 99n., 181, 183n.
Euripides 265
euthyna ('correction,' 'examination of accounts') 406–8
Everson, Stephen 68n.17
examined life, *see* Socrates
'experiments of living' 45
excellence, *see* virtue

faction, *see* conflict
fairness, *see* justice: and equity; justice: as equality
family:
  and household justice 126–7, 170
  component of well-being 237–8, 252, 316, 330–1, 339
  locus of tension 318
  moral influence of 96
  must not be our sole community 211
  natural phenomenon 246, 247–8
  source of bias 142, 307–10, 319–22, 375
  uniquely qualified to meet needs 208–9, 318–20, 331, 340
  see also children; marriage
Farrar, Cynthia 476n.5
feast to which all contribute, *see* wisdom (collective)
Finley, M. I. 461n.
Fisher, N. R. E. 279n.6, 280n.7, 280n.9, 281n.11
flourishing, *see eudaimonia*; good: of human beings; happiness
foreigners:
  dependency of nation-states on 219

GENERAL INDEX

some fit for slavery 280, 284n.19, 290–5, 290–1n., 302–3, 302n.
some human in shape only 264n.
subject peoples in ideal city 218n.
Fortenbaugh, W. W. 215n.44, 287n.22, 297n.36
fortune (good):
  ideal city impossible without 193
  possessed by middle class 439–40
  to live in the age of the polis 240–1
  unequally distributed 221, 236, 391
  see also misfortune
Frankfurt, Harry 349n.32
Frede, Dorothea 69n.20
freedom:
  as a virtue 199, 216, 281, 304, 382, 414, 452
  as the absence of constraint 37, 208, 211, 322–3, 326–7, 345–6, 367, 382–3, 449–53, 476
  as the absence of moral facts 37, 39–42
  as social (non-slave) status 114, 125–6, 135, 147, 228, 234, 249–50, 288, 291, 392, 394, 429, 431, 441, 443, 446
  from irrationality 46, 76
  from necessity 216–17, 297–8, 332, 391
  see also liberalism
friendship:
  and choice 318–19
  and community 465–6
  and generosity 339–42
  and non-instrumental beneficence 75
  as external resource 75
  as source of bias 142–3, 318–19
  civic (political) 5n., 222, 230, 237, 314, 321–2, 328, 329–30, 333, 337, 338, 342–4, 355
  cosmic 265
  heterogeneity of 73
  intrinsic goodness of 32, 35–6, 62
  need for intimate 209, 237, 252, 316, 331, 340
  need for non-intimate 211, 251–2, 319–22, 330, 355
  philosophical puzzles about 51
  sustained by virtue 73
  superiority of civic 271, 274–5
function (human):
  as indicator of well-being 63–7
  and metaphysics 82–6
  and reason 67–9
  and virtue 69–71
  superior to that of other species 86–90

Galston, William A. 479n.13
Garlan, Yvon 280n.9, 280n.10, 284n.20, 291n.27
Garnsey, Peter 277n.2, 278n.3, 278n.4, 278n.5, 280n.8, 281n.11, 296n., 298n.40, 304n.50, 304n.51, 305n.52
Gauthier, David 23n.
Georgiadis, Constantine 167n.
generosity, see liberality
Gerson, L. P. 203n.24
Gewirth, Alan 23n.
gnorimoi ('prominent people') 439, 442, 461
  see also charientes; elites
god, see religion
Gomez-Lobo, Alfonso 67n.
good (the):
  method for investigating 31–2, 47–9, 51–63
  need for improving Aristotle's theory of 21–2, 51, 81
  of human beings 3–5, 20–49, 63–4, 76–81, 86–90, 146
  of non-human animals 48–9, 83–4, 86–90, 86n.
  often misunderstood 195–6
  political role of 478–81
  skepticism regarding 21–2, 479–80
  see also children: proper development of; common good; goods; subjectivism
goods:
  and evils in human life 31–3, 43, 47–9, 50
  distinguished from the good 52
  incompleteness of Aristotle's list of 30–2, 38, 42–3, 45–6, 91
  multiplicity of 35–6, 51
  require organization 49, 50–4, 81
Gosling, J. C. B. and C. C. W. Taylor 74n.23
government 14–15
Graham, A. J. 194n.4, 221n.55
Graham, Keith 461n., 465n.55
Gray, John 239n.
greed:
  and pleonexia 136, 137, 138, 141
  as emotional handicap 73
  human tendency towards 209
  see also wealth
Gregory of Nyssa 278n.4
Griffin, James 23n.
Griffin, Miriam T. 305n.52, 305n.53
Grotius, Hugo 16on.
Guthrie, W. K. C. 246n.
gymnastics:
  component of ideal curriculum 199, 352
  public support for 202n.23

habituation:
  and civic virtue 371, 436, 440–2, 456–7
  can be overturned by reflection 308, 354
  can overturn natural tendencies 130
  can produce servility or arrogance 439, 442

510

ethical principles learned through 56n.9
impediment to insight 30, 127–8, 215–16
preparation for understanding 57–8, 60–2
produces an approximation to virtue 97, 435–6, 440–2
requires completion through reflection 59, 436
Halliwell, Stephen 202n.22
Hansen, Mogens Herman 11n.15, 13n.18, 13n.20, 209n.35, 226n.65, 279n.6, 326n.19, 406n.24, 476n.6
happiness 53
see also eudaimonia; good (the): of human beings
Hardie, W. F. R. 71n., 74n.23, 76n.26, 102n.3
Harris, J. W. 324n.
Harris, William V. 207n.29
Harrison, A. R. W. 151n.43
Hauser, Marc D. 68n.18
hedonism 21n.
Hegel, G. W. F. 6, 354n.
Hellenistic schools 20n.
Heraclitus 265
herald 226
hierarchy:
in natural world 170–1, 366
of ends 52, 63, 82–3
of social groups 149, 170–1, 281, 366, 407–9, 439, 461, 475
see also elites; elitism; equality; family; kingship; slavery
Hippocratic corpus 291n.29
Hippodamus 306
Hobbes, Thomas 6, 39n., 104, 104n.8, 383
Holmes, Stephen 14n., 478n.10
homonoia ('likemindedness') 44–5, 442, 467–70
see also consensus; friendship: civic
homonymy 254–5, 267–9
honor:
and common good 147–8
and military life 444
and suicide 163
as a resource 81
chosen for itself 59–60
deficient desire for 161
excessive desire for 122, 132–3, 136–9, 140, 143, 157–8
given to the elite 448
given to the gods 203–5
given to the old 237
justice requires distributing 107, 126, 175
not the good 63, 66–7
Hornblower, Simon 6n.6
Hornblower, Simon and Antony Spawforth 223n.59, 291n.26

household, *see* children; family; slavery; women
human nature:
and common use of private property 338
expressed through rationality 283
expressed through self-love 333, 334, 337
expressed through sociability 247–8
ideal city compatible with 193, 209–10, 230, 353, 471
pathologies of 132, 139, 209–10, 452, 473, 475
places limits on love 315–16
surpassed by kings 424
unchanging 91
see also nature
Hume, David 23n., 39n., 165–6, 165n.
see also neo-Humean naturalism
Hurka, Thomas 23n., 85n.34
Hursthouse, Rosalind 71n.
husbands, see family

ideal polis, *see* constitution: ideal
impartiality 21, 309, 388–91, 399, 473, 481
see also bias; common good; equality
incontinence, *see akrasia*
individualism 353
inequality, *see* equality; justice: as equality
inexactness, *see* ethics: an inexact discipline
injustice, *see* justice
Irwin, T. H. 4n.3, 52n., 67n., 68n.17, 84n.30, 101n., 107n.15, 109n.18, 112n.21, 113n.23, 113n.24, 124n., 129n., 162n., 255n., 341n.27, 349n.33

Jacoby, Russell 239n.
Jaeger, Werner 182–3, 182n.2, 182n.3, 183n., 188n.13, 377n.23, 428n.2
Jefferson, Thomas 477n.7
Joachim, H. H. 162n.
Johnson, Curtis N. 438n.13
Joint Association of Classical Teachers 279n.6, 326n.19
Jolly, Alison 68n.18
juror:
can be moved by *pleonexia* 142–3, 158
guided by arithmetical equality 148–9
justice requires service as a 175
must aim at common good 117–18
must assess character 393, 398
needs equity 109–10, 166–9
willing to apply defective laws 112, 124–5
justice:
admits of degrees 97, 101, 116, 130, 134, 172–3, 253

an uncharacteristic mean 158–60, 164–5
and bias towards friends 270–1, 320
and equity 108–11, 166–9
and motivation 122, 136–45
as equality 98, 102–3, 107, 114, 120, 123–4, 136–41, 142, 162, 165–8
as lawfulness 98, 102–8, 109, 111–18, 120, 122, 124–5, 137, 138–9, 142, 161–2, 167, 168
component of well-being 123
conforms to the mean 98, 101, 102, 156–60
corrective 107, 148–50, 152–3, 158
distributive 107, 143–4, 154–7, 148, 157
natural and legal 104, 125–32, 133–4, 169
political and household 125–7, 151
political philosopher as paradigm of 101, 176
reciprocal 150–6, 157–8, 169
requires active citizenship 75, 100–1, 107, 114, 132–6, 169, 171, 175
requires flexibility 101, 108–11, 163–5, 166–9, 456
the major ethical virtue 4–5, 98, 119–25
the other-directed virtue 119–25, 161–2, 169, 170–1
see also common good; envy; equality; *pleonexia*; spite

Kahn, Charles H. 9n.11
Kant, Immanuel 23n., 39n., 434n.8, 454n.41
Kateb, George 239n.
Katz, Richard S. 461n.
Kelsen, Hans 9n.11, 418n.
Kennedy, George A. 109n.18
Kenny, Anthony 18n.
Kerferd, G. B. 246n.
Keyt, David 11n.14, 214n.43, 244n.8, 247n.11, 256n.19, 256n.20, 420n.
kingship:
  accepted by willing subjects 374, 399, 401, 468
  arguments against 413–14
  compared to rule over desire 170n.59
  depends on trust 414–15
  equal to aristocracy 399–401, 412, 417
  hereditary 412–13
  inferior to city of Books VII–VIII 10, 187
  less common over time 292
  not promised obedience 414
  not subject to scrutiny of the demos 411, 413, 455, 472
  of Macedon 7
  requires godliness 414
  requires lower offices 411
  ruled by excellence 380, 414
  subject to the rule of law 455

super-human 421, 422, 472
superior to aristocracy 424–6
superior to polity 186, 360–1, 400, 403–4, 410, 416–17, 419
to be imitated by tyranny 437
varieties of 411
Kitcher, Philip 85n.34
koinōnia ('community') 12n., 354–6, 466
Kolnai, Aurel 239n.
Kraut, Richard 53n.4, 53n.5, 56n.7, 58n.12, 59n., 77n., 128n., 172n., 196n., 200n.17, 200n.19, 201n.21, 202n.22, 218n., 241n.2, 272n.30, 298n.39, 334n.24, 441n.18, 478n.10, 479n.13
Kullmann, Wolfgang 247n.11
Kymlicka, Will 477n.7
Kymlicka, Will and Wayne Norman 465n.55

Labarrière, Jean-Louis 68n.18
land:
  equal division proposed by Phaleas of Chalcedon 348
  how divided in ideal city 220–1, 228, 229–30, 236, 322, 349–50, 423, 456
  not to be sold 322–3, 344
  of middle class 439
  some should be owned privately 222, 328, 335–6
  some should be owned communally 335–6
  to be purchased for the poor 449
  see also property
Larmore, Charles 472–3n.3
Las Casas, Bartolomé de 277n.1
Lawrence, Gavin 67n.
law:
  addresses all matters 114–15, 116, 120
  can be unjust 103–4, 115–16
  component of ethical life 101, 124
  contrasted with decrees 105–6, 276, 449–50, 453
  exists only when recognized 105
  importance of studying 4
  includes unwritten norms 105
  inevitably overgeneral 108–11
  promotes well-being to some degree 116–18
  rule of 111, 113, 115n., 423n.42, 449, 453, 454, 455–6, 469, 474
  to be obeyed even when unjust 110, 117, 379–83
  see also freedom: as the absence of constraint; justice: and equity
League of Corinth 372n.
legislative science (*nomthetikē*) 111–12, 114
Leighton, Stephen 69n.20
leisure:
  childhood preparation for 361

GENERAL INDEX

component of well-being 200–1
devoted to music 201–2
impossible outside the polis 241
not a private matter 210
political activity incompatible with 422, 444
size of class that can live at 217n.50
supported by slavery 281–2
wealth required for 222
Leuctra 10, 10n.13
liberalism 36, 40–1, 208, 476–7
liberality (generosity):
  and choice 342–6
  can never be excessive 72
  creates vulnerability to unjust treatment 168n.
  requires care of self 119n.30, 161
  undermined by excessive taxation 339
  undermined by the abolition of property 330, 339–42
like-mindedness, see consensus; friendship; homonoia
liturgies:
  defined 325–7
  as an advantage of wealth 349
  fund musical performances 224n.62
  mitigate dangers of private property 321
  not a device for achieving equality 352
  performed in many cities 353
  subject to collective control 339
  see also taxes
Locke, John 6, 452n.35
Lomasky, Loren J. 477n.7
Long A. A. and D. N. Sedley 305n.53, 436n.
lot, see democracy: use of lot in
love, see friendship
Lord, Carnes 6n.8, 80n., 188n.12, 365n., 428n.1
Lyceum 7
Lynch, John Patrick 7n.

MacDowell, Douglas M. 106n.13, 153n., 216n.48, 226n.66, 280n.9, 280n.10, 326n.19
McDowell, John 32n., 63n., 124n.
Macedon 6–11, 194, 372n., 418
Machiavelli, Niccolò 6, 383
MacIntyre, Alasdair 68n.18, 85n.34, 354n.
magnificence 135, 349n.33, 440n.17
magnanimity 72, 135, 161, 168
majority rule:
  generosity and 341–2
  must be skewed by democracies towards the rich 458
  reflects limited deliberative skills 232–4
  used in ideal city 232

used in many constitutions 231
see also voting
Malkin, Irad 194n.4
manual labor, see banausoi
Mandeville, Bernard 434n.8
Manville, Philip Brook 461n.
marriage:
  creates social unity 322
  not permitted for slaves 280
  regulated by the city 208, 318
  transformed in Plato's Republic 309–10
  see also family
mass, see demos
Matthews, Gareth 215n.44
Mayhew, Robert 256n.20, 323n., 332n., 343n.28
mean:
  applied to friendship 142
  applied to justice 150, 156–60
  as a structure of virtues and vices 71
  desire for equality not a 160, 164–5
Menn, Stephen 188n.14
merit, see justice: distributive
metaphysics:
  and essence vii, 85n.34, 91–2
  and modern science vii, 83–4
  and parts of bodies 274–5
  and senses of 'prior' 256, 259–60
  and soul 83–4
  and traditional religion 203–4
  rejection of Plato's 171–3
  see also homonymy
Metaphysics (Aristotle) 186, 197–8, 306
middle class:
  and four branches of politics 430–2
  and Philip 8
  limited virtue of 438–46, 462
  rarely dominant 472
  see also polity
military:
  defense and dual plots 229–30
  effectiveness and civic priority 269–70
  expertise subordinate to politics 82, 92
  friendship 466
  in Plato's Republic 444
  liturgies 325–6, 344
  obligatory service in 208, 226, 271, 353–4
  protection as goal of civic life 393
  training 198, 199
  virtue in a polity 400
Mill, J. S. 46n.14, 211n.
Miller, Fred D., Jr. 214n.42, 244n.5, 247n.11, 256n.20, 257n.22, 259n., 263n., 323n., 359–60n.5, 362n., 386n., 433n.6, 438n.13, 478n.10
misfortune:
  alleviated in ideal city 222–3, 236

513

delight in others' 139–41
deprives good people of happiness 74n.24
diminishes significant choice 39–40
knowledge of does not require experience 58
not a subjective matter 31
not always unjust when undeserved 141
of rational impairment 68–9
mistrust, *see* trust
Modrak, Deborah 215n.44
Montesquieu, Charles Louis de Secondat 291n.29
Moore, G. E. 39n.
Morrison, Donald 103n., 386n.
Mulgan, R. G. 95n.38, 215n.44, 215n.46, 369n.13, 377n.24, 435n.9, 451n.
music:
  akin to philosophical contemplation 201–2
  as relaxation 210
  as the unfolding of cognitive powers 81
  available only to human beings 48, 79–80
  component of adult leisure 201–2
  component of childhood education 198, 199, 237
  component of well-being 38, 207
  differences in quality of 304
  elite activity in Athens 206–7
  enriched by variety 43–4
  ever changing 238
  fosters a sense of community 237, 321
  funded by ideal city 224, 237
  performed at *symposia* 222–3
  presupposes common ends 44
  requires resources and leisure 241
  superior to politics 444
  well judged by ordinary people 404

nature:
  as basis for slavery 278, 282–95, 301–3, 305
  as grounding for ethics 63n., 85n.34
  as origin and goal 242, 242n.4, 246
  contrasted with convention 127–32, 133–4, 178
  every city exists by 242–6
  makes city prior to individual 253–4, 259–61, 264–7; *see also* city: priority of
  makes us political 247–53, 263
  see also human nature
nemesis ('righteous indignation') 139–40
neo-Humean naturalism 63n.
Nero 145n.
Newman, W. L. 9n.11, 188n.12, 369n.13
Nietzsche, Friedrich 23n.
Nichols, Mary P. 215n.44, 377n.23, 433n.6, 438n.13

Nicomachean Ethics:
  intended audience of 4n.3
  organization of 186–7
  relation to Aristotle's other works 3–5, 16–19, 99n.
Nicomachus 7, 17
nomimos, *see* justice as lawfulness
nomos, *see* law
Nozick, Robert 239n., 477n.7
Nussbaum, Martha C. 23n., 56n.7, 69n.20, 85n.34, 124n., 213n.39, 215n.46, 324n.
Nussbaum, Martha C. and Amélie Oksenberg Rorty 84n.31

Oakeshott, Michael 352n.35
Ober, Josiah 10n.12, 11n.15, 182n.3, 194n.5, 224n.61, 226n.66, 290n., 298n.40, 326n.19, 372n., 439n.15
objective list theory 50n.
oligarchy:
  akin to modern democracies 463, 476
  dominated by the prominent (*gnorimoi*) and refined (*charientes*) 439, 442, 461
  equates merit with wealth 392, 394, 441
  extreme form not a city or constitution 253, 370, 372, 374
  gradual development of 292
  in Athens 11
  inevitable bias in 447
  inferior to democracy 425, 432, 445
  little understanding of well-being in 374
  majority rules in 231
  must be moderated 369–70, 372–3, 375–6, 389, 447, 450
  not united by an ideology 446
  partial correctness of 448
  political friendship in 466–9
  restricts power to the wealthy 15, 144, 147, 368, 392, 394, 448
  rule of law in 455–7
  should give aid and power to the poor 449, 459–60, 465
  stabilized by education 457
  superior to tyranny 115n.
  takes different forms 436, 446–7
  tyrannical form of 106, 375, 381–2, 432, 446, 456
  worth improving 173, 436, 437, 447
Osborne, Robin 280n.7
ostracism 272, 399n.13, 410n.
Ostwald, Martin 105n.11, 461n.

Pagden, Anthony 277n.1
pain, *see* pleasure
Pakaluk, Michael 73n., 355n.
Parfit, Derek 23n., 50n.

GENERAL INDEX

Pellegrin, Pierre 182n.3, 184n.9, 365n.
Peloponnesian War 11
perception of ethical properties 124n.
Persia 8
Phaleas of Chalcedon 221, 306, 307, 348, 351, 388
Philemon 278n.
Philip II of Macedon 7, 8, 418
philosophical life:
  an unfamiliar conception of the good 55–6
  as the unfolding of our cognitive powers 81
  defended against criticism 205–6
  in strict and loose senses 197–202
  provides no guarantee against misfortune 58
  superior to political life 94–5, 473–4
  unites science and religion 78
Plato:
  against factionalism 309, 319
  alleged rational intuitionism of 39n.
  Aristotle's opposition to 9n.11, 63n., 99, 100–1, 102, 103, 121–3, 132–6, 151, 169–74, 182–3
  death of 7
  mixes ethics and politics with other subjects 16
  on childhood education 202
  on forms 171–2, 256
  on reason and emotion 69
  on the good 55, 63–4
  practical orientation of 20n.
  teacher of Aristotle 7
  works discussed:
    Apology 174, 176
    Crito 155n., 175, 380n.
    Euthyphro 175
    Gorgias 6, 139n., 170, 174, 175, 245–6, 446n.27
    Laws 162n., 194, 225, 227n.69, 288, 308, 419
    Phaedo 175, 435
    Republic 6, 69, 99, 100, 102, 118n., 121–2, 133, 151, 170, 171–2, 174, 176, 194, 214, 228, 237, 254, 274, 307–9, 310–25, 331–2, 339, 347, 419, 444, 461
    Symposium 175–6, 319, 446n.27
pleasure:
  and spite 139–40
  component of virtuous life 74
  component of well-being 197
  consensus about value of 38
  good in all contexts? 34–5
  in misfortune 34–6
  multiplicity of 74
  not the sole good 35–6
  pleonexia and 138
  provides evidence against subjectivism 36
  provides no evidence for subjectivism 36
  varies in value 35, 74
pleonexia:
  defined 136–41
  in broad and narrow senses 142–3
  in commerce 156
  more destructive in rich than poor 446
  not the sole cause of unjust acts 142–3
  threat to the legal order 150
  to be eliminated rather than moderated 160, 164
  see also justice: as equality
Plutarch 222n.57
poetry, see music
polis, see city
politeia, see constitution; polity
political animals 21–2n., 95, 123, 247–53, 258–9, 263
political friendship, see friendship: civic
political rule:
  defined 382n.26
  compared to rule over desire 170n.59
  contrasted with rule over a slave 381–2
political system, see constitution
politics:
  as a way of life 92–7, 101, 176, 205–6, 422, 444, 473–4
  as master discipline 3, 92–3
  distinguished from ethics 16, 94n.
  not to be studied apart from ethics 4n.4
  not to be studied by the young 4n.3
  studies and promotes human good 3, 16, 92–3, 96–7
  studies constitutions 93–4, 176, 193–4, 427–33
Politics of Aristotle
  outline of contents of 183–7
  proper order of Books 183–9
  relation to ethical treatises 16–19, 182–3
  unity or disunity of 181–7, 357–63, 376–9, 385–6, 417–20, 436
polity (as one kind of constitution):
  achieves civic virtue 400
  as deviant regime 431–2
  as mixed government 412
  explanation of correctness of 404, 406
  Greek word for 358n.2
  inferior to other correct constitutions 401, 404, 410, 416–17
  little understanding of well-being in 400
  political friendship in 468
  rule by middle class and 438–44
  to be approximated by democracy and oligarchy 374–7
  see also middle class

515

poor (class):
  definition of 224n.61, 439
  cannot perform liturgies 349
  civic responsibility for 146, 343-4
  claim to be as qualified for office as rich 394
  class solidarity among Athenian 290-1n.
  danger of lawlessness among 96, 440
  democracy as biased rule by the 444-5
  have no claim to equal resources 351
  hostile towards rich 347, 389, 398, 442, 443, 469
  in Sparta 329
  justice requires concern for 117-18
  less transgressive than the wealthy 446
  mistreated in oligarchies 144, 392, 394
  politically passive and active 445, 456
  should receive aid and power in oligarchies 449-50, 465
  sick of restrictions 452
  sometimes properly denied citizenship 394-5
  supported by ideal city 222-4, 236, 329
  to be balanced against the rich 375-6, 447-8, 450-1, 457-60, 465, 469
  trust the middle class 441-2
  see also democracy; demos
Popper, Karl 14n.
power:
  allocated by constitution 13-14, 195, 225, 362
  and ostracism 272
  and respect for law 382
  and rotation of office 311
  as basis of law 114, 117
  as threat to freedom 383-4, 452
  disconnected from justice 129-30
  excessive desire for 61, 145, 175, 209, 374, 437, 444, 446, 448, 456, 473
  ideally should be equal 226, 227-8, 236, 325, 388, 407
  in Hobbes 104
  inferior to philosophical understanding 94
  limitations sometimes unnecessary 399, 410-11, 413, 415, 472
  must sometimes be resisted 117, 276, 374, 380-1, 382-4
  needed for well-being 75
  of assembly 226, 325, 359, 449
  of city over all matters 93
  of experts 228-9, 309, 325, 406-7
  of juror 158
  of Macedon 7-11
  of office-holder 227
  of parents 327
  of slaveowner 295, 298

of taxation 343
rival claims to 392, 394, 402-4, 416-17, 424-6, 441-2, 443, 446, 447-8
should be proportionate to merit 126, 175, 227-8, 366-7, 388, 393, 407-8, 475
to be justly allocated 107, 146, 159, 175
to be shared by masses and elites 234, 306-7, 381-2, 407-9, 444, 447, 451, 458-63, 465, 469, 474, 475
to serve the common good 21, 266-7, 276, 383-4, 403, 473
Price, A. W. 73n., 355n.
priority of the city, see city: priority of
privacy, see liberalism
property:
  arguments for collectivizing some 335-7
  arguments against collectivizing all 237, 254, 274, 280, 295-6, 316, 323-46
  arguments against equalization of 348-51
  as bundle of legal rights 324n.
  as natural right 478n.11
  as qualification for citizenship 359-60n.5, 394n.8, 425n.44, 464, 464n.54
  taxes on 326n.19
  see also land; slavery
punishment:
  by imprisonment 153n.
  falls under corrective rather than reciprocal justice 152-3
  for suicide 162
  mitigated by equitable jurors 108-10
  prescribed in ideal city 423
  sensitive to character 393
  severity of 150n.
  unnecessary to threaten kings with 455
  virtue not undermined by threat of 345-6
  see also justice: corrective
Putnam, Hilary 39n., 68n.18, 479n.12
Putnam, Robert D. 465n.55
Pythagoreans 63-4, 152-3, 152n.45

Rasmussen, Douglas B. and Douglas J. Den Uyl 477n.7
Rawls, John 20n., 23n., 30n., 39n., 44n., 46n.15, 165n., 434n.8, 479n.13
Raz, Joseph 23n.
reason:
  can judge highest ends 59
  distinguished from intelligence 68
  part of human essence 91
  properly controls emotions 76
  untrustworthy when divorced from experience 58
  well-being consists in activities of 54, 64, 65, 68-70, 86, 89, 91
reciprocity, see justice: reciprocal

GENERAL INDEX

Reeve, C. D. C. 52n., 67n., 203n.24, 218n., 253n.17, 294n.31, 343n.28, 365n., 386n.
regime, *see* constitution
religion:
  as culmination of the *Metaphysics* 186
  as the unfolding of cognitive powers 81
  can be reconciled with philosophy and science 78
  continuous with practical philosophy 79
  creates social unity 321, 466
  financed by liturgies 326
  in ideal city 78, 203–5, 228, 237, 321, 326, 344
  in modernity 205
  limitations in Aristotle's thoughts about 235, 477–8
  supported by common land 322, 335, 344
  to provide no solace in misfortune 141
republic, *see* polity
responsibility:
  compatible with creativity 41–2
  for character 96
  for starvation and poverty 146
  small communities provide no escape from political 208–9, 210, 219
  subjectivism promises escape from 40–1
revenge 24–5, 32–4
revolution:
  against the virtuous 390
  equalizing resources useless as device for avoiding 351
  good citizenship and 372–3, 386–8
  to be avoided by enlarging role of citizens 408–9
  see also constitution: stability of
Rhodes, P. J. 11n.16
relaxation:
  at common meals 307
  at *symposia* 222–3
  enhanced by opposition 44
  need for 200
  provided by music 210
Rist, J. M. 182n.3
Rorty, Richard 219n.
Rosati, Connie S. 46n.15
Ross, W. D. 4n.3, 39n., 101n., 107n.15, 113n.24, 162n., 167n., 188n.13, 203n.24, 252n.
rotation of office:
  as check against corruption 325
  as just method for sharing honor 146
  component of the rule of law 456
  creates rulers and ruled 311
  in ideal city 200, 226, 227
  in kingship and aristocracy 366, 411
  in polity 472
  no longer attainable by all citizens 475
Rousseau, Jean-Jacques 248, 354n., 454n.41
Rowe, Christopher 182n.3
rules, *see* law
Ryan, Alan 462n.53

Salkever, Stephen G. 85n.34, 215n.44
Sandel, Michael J. 165n., 354n.
Sartre, Jean-Paul 23n.
Saunders, Trevor J. 227n.69, 247n.11, 259n.
Saxonhouse, Arlene W. 215n.44, 287n.22, 377n.24, 410n.
Scaltsas, Theodore 152n.46
Scanlon, T. M. 23n., 31n.8
Schneewind, J. B. 160n.
Schofield, Malcolm 283n.18, 284n.19
Schollmeier, Paul 466n.57
Schütrumpf, Eckart 420n., 437–8n.12, 454n.42
science:
  as a non-normative enterprise 84–5, 89–90
  as the study of soul 83–4
  as the unfolding of human powers 81
  can be harmonized with philosophy and religion 778
  intrinsic value of 78
Scruton, Roger 352n.35
Sealey, Raphael 6n.6
self-harm 161
self-love 127
self-sufficiency:
  achieved by civic life 125–6, 242
  compatible with our political nature 251–2
  impossible for individual human beings 255, 262–3
  of highest good 251
Sen, Amartya 31n.9
Seneca 145n., 304n.51, 305n.52, 305n.53, 334n.23
Sepúlveda, Juan Ginés de 277n.1
Sher, George 23n., 479n.13
Sherman, Nancy 124n.
Shields, Christopher 255n.
Shiner, Roger 109n.19
Sidgwick, Henry 39n.
Simpson, Peter L. Phillips 13n.21, 188n.12, 369n.13, 428n.1
Skeptics 20n.
slavery:
  accepted by Stoics 278n.4, 304
  Aristotle's conception of 277–305
  attempts to justify rest on intellectual errors 145
  in Christian thought 278n.4, 304n.50
  in Greece 279–81

517

in Hebrew and Christian Bibles 278n.4
see also slaves
slaves:
   as parts of their masters 126–7, 170
   as political animals 249–51, 252
   compassion for compatible with acceptance of 145
   owned by middle class 439
   ruled by masters as body by soul 170n.59
   see also slavery
Smith, Adam 434n.8
Smith, Nicholas D. 215n.44, 279n.5, 295n., 298n.37
Smith, Nicholas D. and Robert Mayhew 433n.6
Sober, Elliott and David Sloan Wilson., 21n.
Socrates:
   advocates withdrawal from ordinary politics 133
   as counter-example to Aristotle's conception of justice 174–7
   champion of examined life 32n.
   proponent of objective ethical standards 383
   regards ordinary virtue as a sham 435
   see also Plato
Solon 308, 409
Sorabji, Richard 68n.18
soul:
   as cause 77
   as organization of the body 67–8
   as potential for life processes 83
   cities grow without nutritive 244
   related to body as master to slave 170n.59
   uniqueness of human 86
Sparta:
   as a mixed constitution 307
   as an aristocracy 232
   common meals in 222, 222n.57, 321n.15, 329
   communal use of property in 329, 338–9. 353
   criticized for militarism 104, 206
   decline of 10
   dependence on farm labor in 207n.31, 218n.51
   emphasizes education 10n.13
   reputed to be well-governed 306
   underfunding of public treasury in 343
   see also education: in Sparta
species 86–90
Speusippus 63–4
spite 139–40, 144
state, *see* city
status, *see* demos; elite
Sterelny, Kim and Paul E. Griffiths 84n.32
Stern-Gillet, Suzanne 466n.57

Stich, Stephen P. 68n.18
Stoics:
   accept slavery 278n.4, 304–5, 304n.50, 305n.52
   condemn anger 334n.23
   endorse the political life 380n.
   practical orientation of 20n.
   reasonably regard freedom as a preferred indifferent 305n.53
   reject Aristotle's conception of the soul 84
   reject degrees of virtue 435
Strauss, Barry S. 447n.
Strauss, Leo 14n.
Striker, Gisela 69n.20
subjectivism:
   defined 22–4, 26–7
   allure of 23, 36–46
   critique of 26–49, 56n.8
   varieties of 24–6, 46–7
suicide 162–3
Sumner, L. W. 23n., 32n.
Sunstein, Cass R. 31n.9
super-human beings 225, 233, 421–5, 472
Susemihl, Franz and Hicks, R. D. 188n.12
Swanson, Judith A. 215n.44, 433n.6, 466n.57
symposia ('drinking parties') 222–3
syssitia ('common meals'), *see* common meals

taxes:
   justified because citizens 'belong to the city' 207
   must not undermine generosity 339, 342–6
   on property in Athens 326n.19
   one among few civic obligations imposed by nation-states 353–4, 464
   see also liturgies
Taylor, Charles 354n.
temperance:
   law commands acts of 115
   needed by slaves 297
   presupposes the existence of the family 331
   relationship to justice 119, 125, 137
Theages 133
theater, *see* music
theōria, *see* contemplation
Thrasymacus 446, 450
Thucydides 10, 198n.12, 209n.35
timocracy 468
Tise, Larry E. 277n.2
toleration 41
tradition 354
trust:
   and *homonoia* 469
   as basis for kingship 413–15, 472
   component of friendship 73

flourishes in ideal city 325, 442
fostered by common meals 223
in absence of a common conception of well-being 397–9
in democracy and oligarchy 433, 441, 445, 447, 450, 461, 467, 468, 473–4, 476
in Plato's rulers 444
of middle class 441–3, 469, 472
of public officials 394, 401, 473
sometimes diminished by discussion 405
undermined by excessive anger 123
undermined by *pleonexia* 156
tyranny:
and justification of punishment 149
exemplified by extreme democracy and oligarchy 106, 375, 381–2, 432, 445, 451, 454, 456
forbids common meals 223
incompatible with meaningful freedom 39–40
not a genuine constitution 276, 373–4, 437
not owed obedience 381, 382
prevails in Asia but not Greece 293
rule by edict rather than law 106, 276
severe and moderate forms of 437
should be overthrown 373–4
unlawfulness of 117

ultimate end, *see* happiness
unity, *see* city: requires a kind of unity; education: as method of civic unification; friendship: civic
Urmson, J. O. 71n., 252n.
utilitarianism 210–14
utopia, *see* constitution: of ideal city

Vander Waerdt, P. A. 225n.63
Velleman, J. David 46n.15
virtue:
admits of degrees 436
as a mean state 71
as the skillful application of general norms 125
cannot be excessive 72
cannot be used without resources 74–5
civic contrasted with perfect 363–4
component of well-being 54, 70–6
not yet fully possessed by Aristotle's students 60
of slaves 297
regulates affection 142
required for sound judgment 73
requires service to the community 271
students of ethics need experience of 60–1
superior to continence 75–6
sustains friendship 73

the central value of human life 72, 81
tied to pleasure rightly felt 74
to be chosen for itself 59–60, 63
see also anger; citizens: proper role of; courage; justice; liberality; magnanimity; magnificence; mean; temperance

voting:
and bias 143, 474–5
and character 395
and generosity 341–2
and impartiality 320, 353
and pooling information 407
as a civic responsibility 151, 168
as a juror 109
in accordance with a conception of well-being 480
mandatory 208
not available to foreign workers 218–19
weighted 458–60, 465
see also majority rule

Waldron, Jeremy 324n., 402n.18, 479n.13
Wallace, Robert W. 209n.35, 476n.6
Walzer, Michael 213n.39, 354n.
wealth:
and liberality 72, 73, 161
Aristotle's 6
as a system of rights 323n., 324n.
equal citizenship indifferent to 150
equalization of 348–9, 350
moral problem of unearned 217–18
necessary resource for civic life 394
necessary resource for individual well-being 81
not the highest good 61, 63
not to be maximized 72
pathologies of too little or too much 439–42, 443–4, 445, 447
produced by slavery 281
proper attitude towards 224
the goal of oligarchies 231, 368, 392
to be used for the common good 325–7
unequal in ideal city 221
used by oligarchs as the criterion of merit 147, 392, 394
votes in democracies to be weighted by 458–60
see also wealthy (class)
wealthy (class):
better off than the poor 349
claims exclusive right to power 392, 441, 443, 448
hostile towards poor 6, 346–8, 389, 392, 394, 398, 442, 444, 447, 469

internal conflict among 446
justice requires attention to 117–18, 389
mistreated in democracies 144, 445
must perform liturgies 224n.62, 325–6, 339, 349, 351, 353, 393
number in Athens 217n.50
oligarchy as biased rule by the 11, 15, 106, 186
owns silver mines in Laureion 280
to be balanced against the poor 376, 447, 450, 457–60, 462, 465, 469
to receive weighted votes in democracies 457–60
transgressive tendencies of 446
trust the middle class 441
slaves owned primarily by? 300
subject to taxation 326n.19, 339, 343, 464
uniquely qualified for high office 394
unused to restrictions 452, 456–7
see also oligarchy; poor; wealth
well-being, see happiness; good (the): of human beings; goods
Wians, William 182n.3
Whiting, Jennifer 67n.
Williams, Bernard 142n., 279n.5, 290n., 298n.38
wisdom (collective) 402–9
wisdom (practical: *phronēsis*):
 distinguished from productive skill 287
 expressed in traditional stories 201–2, 210
 human and super-human varieties of 233, 422–3
 impossible for slaves 301
 may be exhibited collectively 342, 403

necessary condition of every ethical virtue 107, 367
 necessary condition of excellent rule 367, 399
 not needed by excellent citizens 367, 369, 371, 417
 not possessed by middle class of *Politics* IV.11: 440
 possessed by all citizens of the ideal city 418
wisdom (theoretical: *sophia*):
 acquired by few even in ideal city 198
 approximated through music and religion 206
 as understanding of non-human things 77
 not needed for ethical activity 172, 228, 419
 requires metaphysical training 198
wives, see family
Wolin, Sheldon S. 461n.
women:
 as political animals 249–50, 252
 excluded from politics 214, 234
 have impaired deliberative faculty 214, 286–7n.
Wood, Ellen Meiksins 279n.6, 280n.7, 461n.
Wood, Ellen Meiksins and Neal Wood 6n.7, 352n.35, 476n.5
Wood, Gordon S. 464n.
work, see leisure
workers, see banausoi

Xenophon 103n., 176, 222n.58, 338n.

Yack, Bernard 132n., 244n.5, 354n., 455n.46, 466n.57, 472n.1
Young, Charles 60n.
youth, see children